Superbrands

10th Anniversary Edition

AN INSIGHT INTO SOME OF BRITAIN'S STRONGEST BRANDS 2005

Argentina • Australia • Brazil • Canada • China • Czech Republic • Denmark • Egypt • Finland • France Germany • Greece • Hong Kong • Hungary • India • Indonesia • Ireland • Italy • Japan • Kuwait • Lebanon Malaysia • Mexico • Morocco • The Netherlands • Norway • Pakistan • Philippines • Poland • Portugal Russia • Saudi Arabia • Singapore • Slovakia • South Africa • South Korea • Spain • Sweden • Switzerland Taiwan • Thailand • Turkey • United Arab Emirates • United Kingdom • United States of America

www.superbrands.org/uk

MANAGING EDITOR
Angela Pumphrey

EDITOR & AUTHOR
Jennifer Small

AUTHOR
James Curtis

PICTURE EDITOR
Emma Selwyn

BRAND LIAISON DIRECTORS
Simon Muldowney
Claire Pollock

DESIGNERS
Chris Harris
Adrian Morris

Special thanks goes to **Mintel** for providing a considerable
amount of market research material.

Other publications from Superbrands in the UK:
Business Superbrands Volume IV ISBN: 0-9547510-6-X
Cool BrandLeaders Volume III ISBN: 0-9547510-1-9
Sport BrandLeaders Volume I ISBN: 0-9547510-4-3

For more information, or to order these books directly
from the publisher, email brands@superbrands.org or
call 01825 723398.

For Superbrands international publications email:
brands@superbrands or telephone 0207 379 8884.

© 2005 Superbrands Ltd

Published by Superbrands Ltd
19 Garrick Street
London
WC2E 9AX

www.superbrands.org/uk

Printed in Spain

ISBN: 0-9547510-8-6

Contents

JOHN NOBLE

Director
British Brands Group

The British Brands Group is delighted to support Superbrands 2005. This year's qualifying brands may be diverse – from different sectors, different sizes and of different ages – but all have performed outstandingly and have distinctive personalities. They have succeeded in striking a deep chord with their consumers, establishing powerful relationships within a highly competitive, noisy marketplace. They deliver consistently and create trust, reassurance, loyalty and ultimately competitive edge.

These brands recognise that superior performance must be delivered not only in what they do but how they do it, and they are prepared to invest in the long term to achieve it. Consumer insight and innovation have been key to a success that all brands aspire to achieve.

PAUL GOSTICK

International Chairman
The Chartered Institute of Marketing (CIM)

The Chartered Institute of Marketing

Competition in the marketplace is fierce and brands play a central role in influencing customer choice. Strong brands are clear about what they are and understand their unique promise of value. They connect and engage with their customers, evoking strong emotional responses. Brands provide a clear competitive edge and create a powerful relationship with the consumer, delivering what they promise time after time.

The Chartered Institute of Marketing exists to promote the value of brands and marketing as a whole and is proud to endorse Superbrands as a key resource, which independently identifies many of the UK's most successful brands. These brands command recognition and respect for their achievements in a highly competitive market. The case studies in this publication give an insight into the evolution of these exceptional brands, looking deep under the covers to determine exactly what marks them out from the rest.

TESSA GOODING

Director of Communications
Institute of Practitioners in Advertising (IPA)

IPA

All the brands in this seventh volume of Superbrands show a demonstrable link in the communications triangle that is client, agency and customer in delivering a successful marketing strategy. The list is wide ranging and covers both established brands, and newer brands. Each one tells its own fascinating story and gives us an insight into the business strategies used, and their outcomes. This fact alone makes this book worth having on your bookshelf. Between them they have won some of today's most coveted creative and effectiveness awards. However, the ultimate accolade of their success must be that they deliver on their individual brand promises. And it is the customer that decides this, not the advertising industry.

Angela Pumphrey

**Managing Editor
Superbrands**

It is a pleasure to introduce the seventh edition of Superbrands. This is a particularly significant year for the Superbrands organisation as it marks our 10th Anniversary.

The organisation exists to celebrate achievements and exceptional practice in branding. It is therefore wonderful to see brands such as American Express®, DHL, Duracell®, KLEENEX® and Seven Seas® which featured in our first publication, launched in 1995, appearing in this edition. These, along with the other exceptional brands that you will find in the pages that follow, have been highly rated by the independent and voluntary Superbrands Council, which is made up of eminent figures from the world of branding. All its members have a deep understanding of what makes an exceptional brand. Using a shortlist of just over 1,000 brands the Council was tasked with identifying the strongest based on their personal perceptions of the brands strength and quality in the market. When scoring, they keep the following definition in mind; "A Superbrand has established the finest reputation in its field and offers consumers emotional and tangible advantages over other brands, which (consciously or sub-consciously) customers want and recognise." We have found that the aggregate perceptions of experienced marketing professionals is as valuable a guide to brand excellence as any other apparently more scientific processes. It enables the brands to be judged against their peers across a diverse range of sector.

For this publication, we asked the Superbrands Council to comment on what they think branding will be like in 2010 and hope that you find their thoughts insightful.

In addition, we have commissioned a report into the subject of brand valuation to aid marketers' understanding of how to measure the financial value of their brands. This can be found on page 192.

We hope that the following best practice examples from some of Britain's strongest brands help to further understanding of branding and the work and investment needed to become, let alone remain, one of the UK's finest.

Dr Kevin Hawkins OBE

**Director General
British Retail Consortium
(BRC)**

It has often been said that a brand is a 'badge of reassurance'. At a time of sliding consumer confidence, stagnant or falling retail sales and fierce competition in all consumer-facing markets, brand strength is a fundamental condition for commercial survival. As consumers husband their resources, repay debate and rebuild their savings, whatever they do decide to spend, particularly on non-essential items, will be strongly influenced by their perception of the brand name on the product.

For many consumers, value for money is and will remain the deciding factor, but value is about more than price. Product functionality, performance, safety, reliability and after-sales service are all critical influences. In the case of a retail brand, the end-to-end experience of shopping in the store also weighs with most consumers. But whether we are talking of Superbrands or brands with less pulling power, the operative word is 'trust'. A high level of trust does not insulate any brand from the slings and arrows of the market place, but we all know how goodwill, which has taken years to accumulate, can be lost in a tiny fraction of that time.

The BRC has a membership which includes retailers with brands which are strong and growing stronger, those which were once strong, then declined and are now turning themselves round, and those which are struggling. Many, however, aspire to reach the top echelon and are working hard to achieve their goal. Superbrands are and will remain an inspiration to all brand owners.

I am therefore very happy on behalf of the BRC to introduce the seventh edition of Superbrands.

The Superbrands Recipe

What will a Superbrand be like in 2010?

STEPHEN CHELIOTIS

Chairman
Superbrands Council

DRAYTON BIRD

Chairman
Drayton Bird Associates

Few people have influenced how we think about brands and how you build them more greatly than Rosser Reeves, who coined the idea of the USP, and David Ogilvy.

One day over dinner they discussed who had influenced them most. They agreed on one name. It was that of John Caples, a quiet, brilliant copywriter devoted to testing what sold and what didn't – a subject dear to any intelligent marketer.

The Wall Street Journal interviewed Caples when he was quite old. One question was: do you think the principles you discovered still apply? He replied, "Times change; people don't."

Tomorrow's Superbrands will not be unlike today's.

They may offer little more than their competitors physically. They may even cost a little more. But people will prefer them because of something that has little to do with what they are, but everything to do with how people *feel* about them.

VANESSA EKE

Managing Director UK, Ireland & AdEx International
Nielsen Media Research

The top advertising Superbrands are not so different as they were five or 10 years ago, so why will that change in the next five years?

A Superbrand, whether it's prestige, niche or mass market transcends class, generation and fashion. In the bathroom Colgate toothpaste, in whatever shape or form, will continue to sidle up to Gillette razors even if they shave at Mach 17 with ten blades. The 1.4 kids will be eating their Kellogg's downstairs while the teenager will be hogging the Vodafone or the Nokia sensory mobile, while Mum and Dad rev up the Mercedes, BMW, Toyota or good old Ford still dreaming of the Aston Martin. DB12 fuelled by Shell/BP super enviro-friendly fuel.

It's not a case of who the brands will be in five years time but how many new ways they will find to contact you, touch you, get under your skin and make you want more.

Brands dead? Not a chance. Talk to your average nine year old.

DAVID HAIGH

Chief Executive
Brand Finance

Superbrands are not simply heavily promoted names. They may start as names or trademarks but they acquire unique personalities, which identify and differentiate them from the increasingly crowed marketplace. In order for these brands to maintain their 'super' status in the future, they will need to continue developing innovative personalities, which make them stand out from the crowd.

Through careful management and targeted promotion, the Superbrands of 2010 will still be at the forefront of consumer's minds. They will still encourage customers to embrace a particular set of values and attributes, which will ensure differentiation from the competition and continue to attract consumer recognition and loyalty.

Consistent yet flexible, the Superbrands of 2010 will continue to meet the demands of the ever-changing environment. Being a Superbrand of tomorrow is no longer about shouting louder; it's about shining brighter.

DAVID MERCER

Head of Design
BT

It is said a day is a long time in politics, a point that could be true of many things, including brands or even Superbrands. There have certainly been a number of well-known brand calamities resulting from a slip of the tongue or an unguarded moment. However a differentiating factor of Superbrands is their propensity for longevity and resilience to suchlike slips or turbulence in the wider world around them.

Accepting that five years is not such a long timeframe to consider, I would confidently speculate that in 2010 Superbrands will be rather similar to how we know them now. Brands will continue to extend across international borders to become globally ever more ubiquitous. One point of difference will be that well-known and successful companies and brands based in the developing world will gain increasing acceptance and status in western economies. Branding is seen as vital by these companies who are hungry to succeed and to attain the lucrative benefits of becoming truly global. By 2010 we shall be as familiar with these new Superbrands in the UK, as we are with the Superbrands that are with us today.

CHRIS POWELL

Director
DDB London

It is more likely to be a service brand, and, in particular, an internet service brand.

Big brands appearing in just a few years, like Google or Friends Reunited have, is a phenomenon of the internet. We can expect many more by 2010. The question will be if they have the staying power or whether they are just temporary symptoms of a fast changing technology to be gone as quickly as they arrived.

As service industries increasingly dominate the economy the challenge will be for them (especially financial service companies) to put down the strong roots that which can only come from convincingly personalizing their services to a mass market. They have failed so far.

MARK CRIDGE

Managing Director
glue London

In the next five years the whole world shall go digital. The analogue TV and Radio signal will be switched off from 2008, Sky+ shall be in most satellite homes, digital Poster sites shall be just about everywhere and every internet connection will be broadband. I think few agencies and fewer clients have truly thought through the implications of this for their businesses.

When all content is digital, it can all be shared. Opinions spread quickly and consumers translate this word of mouth into real actions. Increasingly any brand shall be nothing more

than the collective opinion of the consumers of your product.

A Superbrand in 2010 will therefore be any brand that has learned how to participate with those consumers in an interactive world. A Superbrand will actively seek out and embrace these opinions and remain central to those consumers' lives.

LUCY DAVISON

Director, Marketing & Communication
Research International

Sensory excellence, superb design, authentic ingredients and the right communications will be the platforms for the brand leaders of the future. The key strategy for survival will be to create a truly differentiated product experience and high intensity, continuously evolving relationships with consumers. Our global qualitative studies reveal that consumers are increasingly seeking an intense experience from brands – and this applies as much to washing powder as to luxury fashion brands. The growing backlash against the homogenised identity of many global brands

means that in the future brands will need to find the right balance between global reach and local feel and between individualised identity and membership of a global tribe.

STEPHEN FACTOR

Managing Director
TNS, UK

So many of the Superbrands featured in this book measure their lifespan in decades, if not centuries. Five years seems just a moment in a Superbrand's on-going relationship with the consumer. Yet western society has cranked up the speed dial. The increasing ease of communication and speed of information has pushed evolution closer to revolution. So it is for Marketing, so it must be for Superbrands.

One trendwatcher has heralded the rise of Masters of the YOUniverse; consumers increasingly empowered, better informed and

more switched on. Others ring the death knoll on the primacy of the 30 second TV slot. The internet, digital TV, PVR's and the myriad of other communication channels have all put paid to mass communication.

The classic imperatives remain of staying true to the brand and delivering genuine value to the consumer. Yet the Superbrand of 2010 will build an even more intimate and personal relationship with its consumers.

WINSTON FLETCHER

Chairman
Advertising Standards Board of Finance

Despite the innumerable, well-publicised threats to the future of brands and branding, the reality is that brands grow more important daily – and this trend is set to continue as far ahead as the eye can see. In a world of ever increasing competition, and of increasing choices and purchase decisions, consumers increasingly need strong brands to help them select what they want, from the vast cornucopia of products and services available.

This increasing competition will fragment markets still further. Inevitably there will be more

specialist, minority brands, appealing to specific consumer segments. And to meet this competition Superbrands will build a plethora of line extensions, the totality of which will meet the increasingly sophisticated demand for a wide range of similar (but associated) products in similar (but associated) markets. So Superbrands will continue to provide consumers with very real tangible and emotional benefits – across an ever widening spectrum of product specifications.

JACQUI HILL

Market Development Director – Personal Care
Lever Fabergé

In many respects a Superbrand in the future will be defined in much the same way as now i.e. it will need to stand tall and clear in people's minds, be relevant and aspirational to a wide group of consumers and be sufficiently three dimensional to have a sense of robust personality.

What *will* however be different is *how* you get to be a Superbrand. As consumers become increasingly inundated with branded messages and the speed of innovation in many categories gallops away, it will become more challenging for any brand to achieve this status. In the past

Superbrands could be built by shear spending power, already today that is not always sufficient and certainly by 2010 marketers trying to build a Superbrand will need to be far more wily to out think not only their direct category competitors but all other brands competing for consumers mind space.

But what a wonderful challenge to face our industry.

ELEN LEWIS

Editor
Brand Strategy

Brands are becoming a little softer around the edges. The savvy ones know it's no longer about telling people what to do and what to think, but about involving and interacting with consumers more. Consumers don't just want the visual spectacle of a show, they also want to be taken back stage.

So Nike publishes the addresses of its factories all over the world. innocent Drinks invites its consumers to pop into 'Fruit Towers' for a chat. Cobra Beer uses its fans' short films in advertising. IKEA has known for a long time about

the importance of getting its customers to build their own furniture.

By 2010, this trend will be even more prolific. Brands will realise that openness, transparency and genuine involvement and interaction with their consumers is the only way to garner genuine loyalty and value.

JONATHAN MILDENHALL

Post Graduate
Harvard Business School

For companies that are lucky enough to be responsible for Superbrands, success in 2010 will be dependent on them embracing an organisational mindset of creative Disruption. Superbrands must be prepared to constantly do, undo and redo. Superbrands can no longer ride the crest of a consumer wave. Like Apple has done with the launch of the ipod and PlayStation will do this year with the launch of PSP, Superbrands must become the driving force that creates the consumer wave.

Superbrands must constantly Disrupt from the conventional business thinking that limits real long-term development and value. In addition, Superbrands will need to develop compelling consumer-facing visions. The successful visions will be defined not by category but by genuine leadership of thought and action. That action must embrace the modern media landscape and, where possible, create opportunities for authentic brand engagement.

MICHAEL PETERS OBE

Founder & Chairman
The Identica Partnership

The main challenge for Superbrands over the next five years will be to survive the onslaught of public and media cynicism. This together with the much heralded demise of the 30 second TV commercial will mean *seriously good ideas* will be needed in brand communication departments everywhere.

As ever, those brands that succeed will be those that continue to surprise, to innovate and to deliver on their promise.

I believe that designers will play a key role in keeping the best of the Superbrands at the top of their game, in terms of innovative communications, imaginative new products and thrilling brand

experiences. I am also sure that those brands which adopt new and dynamic technologies will inspire consumers and are certain to reap the rewards.

After all, a Superbrand in 2010, as in 2005, should never disappoint.

NICOLA WATTS

Global Portfolio Strategy & Research Director
Cadbury Schweppes

Superbrands consistently deliver the desired consumer experience. They have clear positionings and values achieved through message consistency across all consumer touch points. They have evolved to keep ahead of competition and changing consumer tastes.

This won't change.

At the heart of managing any Superbrand is the need to change consumer behaviour in its favour through precise consumer understanding that is practical and actionable.

This won't change.

What *will* change is the speed and need for evolution as consumers peel away from the homogenous groups that they once were, removing the need for mass demand and mass media.

What *will* change is how Superbrands are marketed, as all Marketing tools were developed to meet the needs that mass demand and mass media require.

With the demise of mass marketing, you can argue that Marketing itself has failed as a discipline, by neglecting the most basic principle of adapting to remain relevant.

Market

In 2003, the UK directory enquiries market was de-regulated. The process consisted of inviting companies to enter a lottery run by a Government body Oftel (now Ofcom) to get one of the new directory numbers, all of which would be a six figure number and start with the prefix 118.

The overhaul, intended to bring improved value for the £300 million callers spend on some 700 million calls to the directory enquiries service every year, saw the closure of 192 on August 24th 2003.

The Number acquired the rights to use 118118 and 118811. While the volume of calls to 118 numbers has shrunk compared to 192, The Number continues to grow, taking many hundreds of thousands of calls each day.

Achievements

According to Ofcom's latest directory call statistics, The Number accounted for more than 50% of the total number of calls to all 118 numbers on the BT network on the sample day of February 16th 2004. Independent research based on 400 calls over the period October 27th to November 21st 2003 found that more than 90% of 118118 callers got the number they wanted first time.

In fact, The Number's 118118 and 118811 services are 96% accurate across the board according to research by Ofcom, the Government's telecoms watchdog.

The brand has consistently been recognised by the marketing industry for its creativity and effectiveness. Among the many awards in 2004 it came first in the Financial Times Creative Business 50 Awards, won the Marketing Society Award for 'Best Marketing Communications Campaign', and also carried off a Gold Award at the IPA Effectiveness Awards.

History

The Number is a subsidiary of the US directory assistance specialist INFONXX, which was founded in 1991 in Bethlehem, Pennsylvania.

In the Oftel lottery it got 118811 – better than BT's 118 500, but the best number was self-evidently 118 118. A small telecoms company in Reading won this. Robert Pines, chief executive at INFONXX asked the marketing team if they thought it was worth reducing the marketing budget by £2 million in order to buy the 118118 number. It took them all of 20 seconds to say yes. Robert left the room to do the deal on his mobile phone. INFONXX now had the easiest new number for people to remember: 118118.

The Number's core belief was that in the battle to dominate the £300 million directory enquiries market (as it then was) was that first in the mind would be first in the market.

Switch off of 192 occurred on August 26th 2003. And from December 10th 2002 any of the new Directory Enquiry numbers were allowed to operate alongside 192. The major rival was set to be BT, which with 80% of the 192 market would be the natural brand leader in the new 118 market. The major rival for the number two spot would be Conduit, the aggressive Irish-originated directory service that had drawn 118 888 in the Oftel lottery.

Once it became clear to The Number that Oftel had no plans to run marketing campaigns telling the public that 192 was going, The Number realised that this was a major opportunity. While 118118 may be a simple number, why should consumers bother to remember it? There are already lots of numbers – phone numbers, computer passwords, PIN numbers – that people have to remember.

Its goal was to advertise heavily in order to be the first new number that the majority of people would recall. The marketing campaigns meant that the

118118 number was so embedded into people's memories that by the time Ofcom reported MORI's research on recall in May 2004, 118118 scored 73%, with BT's 118500 at less than half with 32%. Today, The Number employs 2,000 people at its Cardiff and Plymouth directory assistance centres.

Product

The Number offers two services: 118811 and 118118. The first, 118811 is a simple replacement for 192 at the same price of 40p from most fixed phones (mobile charges vary) with no additional charges or services.

The more well-known of the two, 118118, costs 14p a minute and 49p to call from most fixed phones (mobile charges vary) and offers a full range of services with no hidden charges.

Recent Developments

In September 2004, 118118 became the first directory service to give callers instant access to the national train timetable over the phone.

National Rail Enquiries is by far the nation's most commonly requested directory number, and with 170,000 calls a day to the service, providing train times on 118118 could save millions of callers having to redial.

The service is provided in partnership with a third party provider of train and ticketing services. Chris Moss, chief executive of The Number, said: "We got the idea from a caller who asked us if we could look up a train time to save being put through to National Rail Enquiries."

As well as providing train times, The Number is able to transfer callers who would like to purchase tickets to thetrainline's call centre to complete their booking.

The new service is part of The Number's aim to make its 118118 service much more useful than 192 ever was. Other 118118 services that 192 never used to offer include cinema programme and performance times, searching for hotels by type and location, finding nearby trades and services, giving driving directions and connecting callers direct. 118118 The Number now also offers a free service on the web at www.118118.com. 118118 is now striving to lead the way in the market and go from being just directory enquiries to providing directory assistance.

Promotion

The Number launched its UK directory assistance service on December 10th 2002. Though the 118118 brand goes well beyond advertising, it shouldn't be forgotten that advertising – about £17 million worth in 2003 (of which £11 million was on TV) – played a crucial role in spreading the brand. It made its TV advertising debut on March 9th 2003, with the first in a series of award-winning commercials featuring the 118 pair of numbers as hirsute 1970s runners and the slogan 'Got your number!'

The 118 Runners, played by Colin Carmichael and Darren McFerran, quickly became a hit with the UK public. Their trademark vest, as worn in the campaign created and written by advertising agency WCRS, was the must-have garment in Summer 2003, with tens of thousands sold to raise £200,000 for Cancer Research UK.

Prompted by advertising and accelerated by ambient media placement, the 118118 runners soon took on a life of their own. Ambient

media can almost be regarded as 'artificial PR' and agency Naked extended the reach of the 118118 campaign in everything from barber shops to street traders in Oxford Street to dumper trucks. The brand planted two Runners in the Centre Court crowd at Wimbledon, where BBC cameras picked them up. In addition, it sent the Runners running all over Britain in every high street in every shopping centre so that hundreds of thousands of people actually saw a real Runner.

The launch strategy for The Number was purely about number memorability. The goal was to get 118118 into people's heads and replace 192 by being the first to market and therefore the first in mind.

Moving a campaign on at the height of its success is a brave thing to do but necessary to keep the brand fresh. In 2004 the 118 boys transformed into 1970s detectives in a campaign to promote the brand's range of services and begin to build the brand into being more than just a number and about directory assistance. The charades and song campaigns of summer 2004 went further to support these product messages as it was felt that consumers were now at a point of understanding around directory services where they were ready to find out what more was on offer – 'got your train times', 'got your cinema and film info' and 'got your hotel info'.

In 2005 The Number is now at a point of national leadership for quality and range of services. 118118 is the UK's most called number and easily the most popular service according to the 2005 Ofcom report which awarded the brand 96% general accuracy. This achievement has been marked by a shift from the '118 twins' campaigns used since 2003. The new treatment shows everyday people being touched by the effect of 118118 to allow

them to do extraordinary things as 118118 is now faster, smarter and more helpful than before.

As well as giving out numbers, names, addresses and other useful information, 118118 operators regularly find themselves dealing with challenging, amusing and often downright bizarre requests among the millions of calls each week. One caller was looking for an exorcist because he had a ghost in his house, while a girl called to sing her Pop Idol audition down the phone.

Inspired by these bizarre requests, The Number has compiled Quirk, a charity book that observes the unusual, extraordinary and down-right funny traditions, hobbies, and places that make the UK uniquely quirky. All proceeds from sales of Quirk will go to three organisations: the Plain English Campaign, Surfers Against Sewage and Pets as Therapy.

Brand Values

The Number's cheeky and irreverent brand personality developed to cut through in what some would describe as a dull but highly competitive market. This was demonstrated when The Number issued its own version of BT's 'public notice' advertisement on the adjacent page of the national press.

Everything The Number does is based on its core principle of 'Go Further'. The idea is that it always makes the effort to 'Go Further' for its customers and challenges itself to exceed their expectations.

'Go Further' is about the importance of innovation and imagination. For example, it means that 118118 operators will be able to tell callers opening times of shops or services such as chemists, they will make an effort to understand regional accents and will always try to use their initiative when answering a call.

www.118118.com

118118

❯ 118118 donated 20,000 runners' vests to be sold at Cancer Research Shops for the charity, raising more than £200,000.

❯ A single was released by The Young Punx in honour of 118118.

❯ The 118 runners' vest soon became 'the outfit' for fancy dress parties and stag nights, with more than 5,000 requests made for vests each week.

❯ 118118 'runners' have been seen kitted out in Thailand, Australia and The Gambia.

❯ 118118 operators have responded to requests for a vet for the pet Iguana who'd eaten his owner's cannabis at 3am and a caller asking if he needed a passport to go to Manchester. He was calling from Northampton.

PUBLIC NOTICE

BT Directory Enquiries is being updated.
The old 192 number is being replaced by a radical new directory enquiries concept. Being helpful.
The new number is:

118 118

ADDITIONAL SERVICES WE OFFER YOU
THAT BT 192 NEVER BOTHERED TO OFFER INCLUDE:
Putting your call straight through
Classified searching; local plumbers, florists etc.
Numbers texted to your mobile for free
Listings information, eg: cinema times and
film listings nationwide

To minimise any confusion caused by the disappearance
of 192 and to make things more convenient
for you we advise making a note of this number
or storing it in your mobile phone.

Not BT
(thank goodness)

Market

To millions all over the world, American Express is the gold standard for plastic money and Travellers Cheques – as the Company that first introduced the Travellers Cheque and lead the way in terms of plastic payment, American Express continues to occupy a place as one of the market leaders in travel and financial services. Its Brand, some 155 years old this year, is recognised the world over by individuals and corporations that use its products and services to help them manage their lives, whether that is through booking the dream holiday, or managing a portfolio of shares.

Today, American Express has more than 65 million cards in circulation worldwide, and in 2004 alone US$416.1 billion was spent using American Express plastic.

In 2004, the Company reported an income of US$3.4 billion, created through its offering of travel and financial services including credit and charge cards, currency operations, travel insurance, personal loans, online brokerage and international banking.

In the UK, the card market continues to grow and become ever more crowded as new players from online banks to football clubs offer credit cards and financial products to their customers. American Express, however, has always been well placed to differentiate itself in this highly competitive sector with its wealth of experience and its broad portfolio of products.

Achievements

American Express has truly achieved the status of a global brand, one that continues to redefine the experience of international travel for both the business and leisure traveller. The Brand's products and services are available in more than 200 countries and the Company employs over 78,000 staff around the world. American Express is committed to driving the Brand forward to ensure it maintains its position as the world's leading provider of travel and financial services.

History

The Company's origins date from the opening of America's 'Wild West' frontier in 1850 and are linked with two legendary names, Henry G Wells and William G Fargo. Originally the duo, with the help of John Butterfield, launched an express freight company at a time when business was driven by the need for the safe and speedy transportation of gold bullion and bank notes. During the 1860s as the US edged towards civil war, the Company transported vital supplies to Union army depots and undertook the risky task of delivering election ballot forms to troops in the field. In 1882 American Express introduced the Money Order as a safer alternative to shipping large amounts of cash. By 1886 American Express had established links with banks across Europe enabling US immigrants to transfer money to their families overseas. The Company also started to pay money by telegraph and sell small drafts or money orders which could be cashed at more than 15,000 outlets. Five years later the world was introduced to the American Express Travellers Cheque. The revolutionary idea not only guaranteed that dollar cheques could be converted into a variety of currencies but also guaranteed that they were refundable if lost or stolen. In addition, American Express offices in England, France and Germany took their first steps into the travel business by selling tickets for transatlantic ships. In the early 1920s American Express expanded its travel

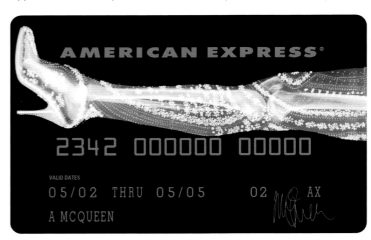

and international financial operations to Latin America and the Far East. The business continued to grow after World War II and in 1958 launched the iconic green American Express Card. The Card not only provided holders with a flexible means of payment in outlets throughout the world, but conferred an immediate status on the holder, a mark of exclusivity that continues today.

In 1963, American Express launched its first Green Charge Card in the UK, which proved to be an immediate success.

In 1970 in response to growing demand from business executives it launched the Corporate Card to facilitate on-the-spot payment of business expenses and in 1972 the Company was behind the first mass roll-out of magnetic stripe cards.

In 1996 the Brand further broadened its base by introducing its first credit card in the UK and three years later delivered the payment industry's first nationwide roll-out of smart cards in the US with Blue. To coincide with the Company's 150th anniversary in 2000, the Green Card was given a fresh contemporary look with new added benefits which reflected the holder's changing aspirations and lifestyle. Today American Express provides expense management tools to more than 70% of Fortune Magazine's top 100 companies.

In 2000 American Express launched an innovative scheme to donate funds to the Arts with its Culture Card. Created in conjunction with Arts and Business, the card offers staff discounts at cultural venues in the areas where American Express employees are based. It also provides financial support to participating venues, through the American Express Foundation.

Product

American Express operates in three core areas, travel, finance and consultancy and its main businesses are American Express Travel Related Services, American Express Financial Advisors and American

NO. 7 ON THE LIST OF TABLES FOR TWO

Number 9 is
in the dining carriage of the
Orient Express.
Number 8 is in Monte Carlo in front of a croupier.
Number 7 however, you practically levitate above.
A white mud treatment washes away any traces of tension
and with Membership Rewards® picking up the bill, there's
no stress on your wallet either. In fact the points Members
earn on everyday purchases can be redeemed for almost any
indulgence – from mud packs to Margaux.

For more ideas visit americanexpress.co.uk/dreams

FOR WHATEVER DREAMS ARE ON YOUR LIST

Express Bank. The banking division comprises three divisions: correspondent, consumer financial services and commercial and private banking. However American Express Travel Related Services is the largest of the three divisions and generates around half of the Company's profits. In August 2004, American Express announced the global re-launch of its corporate travel organisation newly named, American Express Business Travel. The organisation has created a new, redefined American Express ready to serve the business travel needs of any customer, of any size, anywhere in the world, with a focus on savings, service and control for the business travel buyer.

As well as travel, it operates American Express Card products. American Express is perhaps most famous for its charge card which has no pre-set spending limit and is available in Green, Gold, Platinum and Black, which is named Centurion, and is available by invitation only. Centurion offers the ultimate in personal service with a benefits package that is unmatched by any other card. With Centurion, American Express took personal service to a new level giving its Cardmembers access to dedicated teams of round-the-clock experts in travel, entertainment and finance, seven days a week, 365 days a year.

Charge card and credit Cardmembers all benefit from the award winning American Express Membership Rewards Programme which gives users a point for virtually every pound spent on the card and that allows Cardmembers to redeem these points for a wide range of rewards from free flights to wines to luxury retail goods.

Recent Developments

American Express strives to be at the forefront of innovative development via providing exceptional treatment and services for its Cardmembers and employees. In 2004 American Express was recognised by Fortune Magazine as one of the Top 10 Companies to Work For in Europe along with the Financial Times nominating it as one of the Top 50 Companies to Work For. As part of these awards the Company was evaluated on several criteria. American Express ranked highly on elements such as perks, most loyal and charitable staff, pensions and equal opportunities. American Express, has at the heart of its definition – a place where employees "enjoy the people they work with, have pride in what they do and trust the people they work for." Employees at American Express benefit from comprehensive training, extensive reward and recognition policies, open communication, unrivalled advancement opportunities and the chance to work internationally. This is allied to their commitment to 'Blue Box Values' guaranteeing employees are treated as individuals, with extensive benefits packages and a commitment to philanthropy and employee well-being.

In 2004 American Express announced the launch of its first prepaid, reloadable travel money card in the UK – the American Express Travellers Cheque Card. The Travellers Cheque Card is a new and flexible way to carry money abroad – it combines the convenience of a payment

card with the safety benefits of American Express Travellers Cheques.

American Express extended the launch of the world's most exclusive Card – Centurion in five European markets including Italy, Spain, France, Netherlands and Sweden. Centurion customers in these markets range from captains of industry and entrepreneurs to stars of sport, stage and film. Centurion offers Cardmembers literally hundreds of benefits and services ranging from acquiring tickets for a sold out sporting event to organising for a celebrity chef to cook a special meal for a private dinner party.

Promotion

Celebrating five years of Centurion in the UK, fashion designer Alexander McQueen and American Express co-hosted one of the most talked about parties of summer 2004, entitled 'Black'. The event featured a legendary catwalk show, a cutting edge Black art auction of items donated by A-list celebrities including Madonna,

David Bailey and Kate Moss. For the occasion McQueen designed a special limited edition Black Card which was a great success. The relationship with fashion duo Boudicaa continued with American Express assisting them with the presentation of their Fall/Winter 2005 collection at New York Fashion Week. Boudicca's desire to elevate the awareness of their Brand and build a larger international business was made possible by their unique partnership with American Express.

In the sporting arena, American Express is in its second year of its association with Wimbledon, expanding the Company's worldwide commitment to tennis. The agreement sees American Express as the Official Card of Wimbledon in the UK. The first marketing initiative was entitled 'Wimbledon on the Water' which saw Monica Seles and John McEnroe playing tennis on a floating court on the Thames, a charity tennis game, free live concert by RnB sensation Alicia Keys and classic Wimbledon fare of strawberries and cream with glasses of champagne and Pimms to bring a real taste of summer to the City, all free for members of the public to enjoy.

As one of the leading advertisers in the financial services sector the Company's 'Lists' campaign was designed to educate and demonstrate how American Express provides products and services that are essential to an aspirational lifestyle. Things on the dream list, included swimming with elephants, getting exclusive spa treatments in far away lands and dining in complete luxury on the Orient Express. The most recent global campaign launched in 2004 introduced the tagline 'My life. My card.' It featured extraordinary individuals including actor Robert DeNiro, professional golfer Tiger Woods, comedian and television show host Ellen DeGeneres and professional surfer Laird Hamilton. In the UK, Chelsea football coach Jose Mourinho was the celebrity whose 'My Life My Card' ad aired at the beginning of April 2005. The common theme for 'My Life, My Card' campaign was that, achievers of all types choose American Express.

Brand Values

American Express continues to enjoy an international reputation for prestige and excellence as a result of its commitment to constant innovation to drive the Brand forward. This innovative spirit which pioneered the original Charge Card in 1963 has witnessed American Express consistently develop ground breaking products to suit consumer spending needs. Despite many imitators, American Express distinguishes itself in a competitive market place by combining first class products with superior customer service.

www.americanexpress.com

Market

As a household essential, toilet tissue is already one of the UK's largest grocery product categories – and it is increasingly growing in terms of diversity and competition.

British consumers spend an amazing £845 million buying two billion rolls of toilet tissue every year, but this is not all used for the purpose for which it was intended (Source: Kimberly-Clark). Indeed, since UK toilet tissue is generally recognised as the softest in Europe, it is often used for functions such as make-up removal and nose-blowing.

Some 99% of the UK market favours soft toilet tissue, with 43% preferring coloured toilet tissue, as consumers endeavour to match the colour of their toilet tissue with the décor of their bathroom (Source: ACNielsen 2005).

In 2005, there has been an increase in sales of premium toilet tissue variants, led by Andrex®, as it responds to changing consumer needs. Nevertheless 80% of the category is dominated by mainstream products (Source: ACNielsen 2005).

Achievements

Andrex® has been the leading brand in the toilet tissue market since 1961. The brand has grown by more than £20 million in the past year, achieving a 32.8% value share and 28% volume share of the dry toilet roll market.

Sales of the brand are driven by high-quality products supported by insight-led, high-profile PR, advertising, promotion and point-of-sale programmes. In any year, more than half of the UK will have bought a pack of Andrex®.

Promotion, packaging, advertising and PR awards achieved by the brand over the past 20 years recognise how Andrex® continues to bring the puppy to life.

History

Although the Andrex® brand takes its name from the St Andrew's Mill, Walthamstow, where it was first produced in 1942, Andrex® was originally developed from a design for a gentleman's disposable handkerchief, which were sold exclusively in Harrods department store, London. Prior to this softer tissue, consumers used harsher products referred to as 'shinies', which were sold mainly through chemists – the most famous brands being Bronco and Izal.

Andrex® was endorsed by Hollywood films stars of the day, who demanded that studios stock softer toilet tissue rather than the ubiquitous 'shinies'. By 1961 the brand achieved market leadership – a position it has retained ever since.

The Andrex® toilet tissue range has been greatly extended in recent years. It can be purchased in a range of colours and pack sizes, which have been continuously developed since 1957 when the brand launched its first colour variant; Magnolia. In 1966 a full range of coloured variants were introduced.

1972 saw the first UK screening of the original Andrex® puppy commercial. The original concept was blocked by television regulators as it was thought that the image of a little girl running through her house trailing a roll of Andrex® would encourage wastefulness. So, the little girl was replaced by a playful Labrador puppy and the campaign went on to become one of the best-known commercials in the country.

Andrex® is manufactured by Kimberly-Clark alongside its other well-known global brands that are household essentials for people in more than 150 countries. Every day, 1.3 billion people – nearly a quarter of the world's population – use Kimberly-Clark's brands to enhance their health, hygiene and general well-being. With brands such as KLEENEX®, Andrex®, Huggies®, Pull-Ups®, Kotex® and Poise®, Kimberly-Clark holds the number one or number two share position in more than 80 countries worldwide.

Product

Consumer-led product development and innovation is a consistent focus for the Andrex® brand.

Having been first to market with moist toilet tissue in 1992, Andrex® updated its product in April 2005 with a premium-feel tub and an easy-dispensing sheet. The product is lightly moistened for an extra clean and fresh sensation. This segment of this category is now worth £11.2 million (Source: ACNielsen 2005).

In 2001, Andrex® launched an Aloe Vera variant of its brand and thereby established an entirely new segment in the toilet tissue market, appealing to those who seek extra comfort through the natural kindness of Aloe Vera. In early 2005, Andrex® re-launched the variant with a new packaging design, a new TV advertising campaign and new point-of-purchase materials supported by an investment of £1.3 million.

Consumer response to Andrex® enriched with Aloe Vera has been outstanding. Indeed, since its launch in 2001, it has almost doubled in size year-on-year, now making it a £31 million UK variant.

Recent Developments

May 2005 saw Andrex® launch its newest variant to date: Andrex® Quilts. The new product resulted from consumer insight, which showed that some consumers were looking for opportunities to trade up to thicker, more luxurious toilet tissue products that were still affordable. Andrex® Quilts represents a 'little softer, a little thicker, a little luxury' for the consumer.

In December 2004, Andrex® launched a limited edition Andrex® winter pack. The new pack, which featured two Labrador Retriever Puppies playing in a winter scene, was all about celebrating the winter period in a visually engaging way. The launch was supported through the sponsorship of an ice rink at Bluewater, Europe's largest retail and leisure destination. All of the winter imagery was transferred onto the ice rink, offering a perfect opportunity to strengthen the visual cue of the packaging.

In July 2004, Andrex® refreshed its packaging strapline on its mainstream product from 'soft strong and long' to 'tuggable huggable softness'. In 1972 when 'soft strong and long' was first used, it was unique to Andrex® but over the years other brands began to use combinations of 'soft', 'strong' and 'long'. It became a generic statement, no longer unique to Andrex® even though it was still true. As a result, 'tuggable huggable softness' was established.

Early in 2004, Andrex® launched its 'Puppies on a roll' variant. For the first time, the energetic and playful Andrex® Puppy was embossed onto white toilet tissue, creating a new and fun product to strengthen consumers' bond with the brand. The launch was supported by an intense through-the-line campaign, which coincided with the Andrex® Puppy being voted into Madame Tussauds as the nation's favourite fictional TV character. When the Andrex® Puppy moved into the world-renowned London attraction, photos of the Puppy appeared in the press in more than eight countries around the world, making the Puppy an international icon.

The campaign was supported by free mobile phone icons, downloadable from the Andrex® website, alongside a radio campaign across 18 radio stations in the UK and the Republic of Ireland. After just eight months on the market, one in ten UK homes had tried the product.

Promotion

Andrex®'s renowned Puppy advertising has been running for more than 30 years and ensures the brand is instantly recognisable. The Puppy has become the embodiment of the brand, symbolising the qualities of softness and strength that are at the heart of the Andrex® brand.

The Puppy has featured in around 120 commercials to date, generally appearing in the family home, but also with various other animals including an elephant and a giraffe.

It took until as recently as 1991 for the product to be shown in the bathroom. The 'Little Boy' execution was one of the most successful in the history of Andrex® advertising and was voted the favourite commercial of 1991 by viewers. It is still recalled by consumers, despite not being televised for almost 15 years.

As a brand icon, the Puppy is also used in a variety of other marketing and promotional devices. This has included calendars as well as a joint activity with Disney's 101 Dalmatians, along with regular soft-toy promotions.

In 1999, the Andrex® Puppy Appeal raised £110,000 for the National Canine Defence League, now known as the Dogs Trust, which helped the charity care for more than 11,000 dogs.

To celebrate the 30th year of Puppy advertising in 2002, significant investment was made in sales promotion activity, with a national on-pack 'Finders Keepers' promotion that rewarded customers with the opportunity to win one of 30,000 special prizes that had supposedly been 'buried' by the puppy.

Today, Andrex®'s promotions continually evolve to keep pace with ever-changing consumers' needs. Innovation and creativity are crucial to ensuring the brand is always driving the category forward.

Brand Values

Having achieved a remarkable position as one of the UK's leading non-food brands, Andrex® listens to its consumers continuously to ensure that its product range is relevant and appealing.

The Andrex® Puppy stands for many of the quality cues of Andrex® toilet tissue, such as softness and strength, yet also strives to tap into the emotional positioning of family and friendship values, encompassing charm, trust, vulnerability, caring and mischievousness.

www.andrexpuppy.co.uk

® Registered Trademark of Kimberly-Clark Worldwide Inc. or its affiliates.

Andrex®

> One in ten homes has an Andrex® Puppy toy.

> Andrex® sells 29 rolls of toilet tissue every second – enough rolls to go twice around the earth every day.

> When rolled out, a roll of Andrex® is the same length as a blue whale, the largest creature on earth.

> www.andrexpuppy.co.uk gets more than 1,000 hits a day.

> When Andrex® offered free puppy mobile phone downloads, 25,000 people downloaded them in less than 12 weeks.

Ann Summers

Market

It's difficult to define the market in which Ann Summers trades, as it's one very much created by the retailer itself. No other company does it like Ann Summers. Others sell lingerie, but nobody sells sexy lingerie with which you'll have more fun, than Ann Summers. Some companies sell sex toys but nobody has championed them, challenged those who've tried to ban them or marketed them with such a flourish, as Ann Summers. And if you're looking to accessorise your girls' night out or hen party with fun gifts, games and outfits, nobody does it better than Ann Summers. Ann Summers sells lingerie, sex toys and lots of fun or put another way, as it says on the front door of its head office, it is a 'business doing pleasure'.

As well as innovating in the scope of its product range, Ann Summers has also been at the forefront of multi-sales channel retailing, as it successfully combines a mature but extremely buoyant direct selling Party Plan operation with its burgeoning retail and online businesses. Over the last few years, all three channels have enjoyed unprecedented growth, as the market created, driven and dominated by Ann Summers has gone from strength to strength.

In terms of customers, Ann Summers is very much a company run by women for women. Ann Summers' Parties are a women only affair, whilst 70% of retail customers and 60% online are women.

Achievements

Ann Summers' Parties are the heart and soul of the Ann Summers business. It was Jacqueline Gold who convinced her father that women wanted to buy these type of products and that they would enjoy the shopping experience all the more if they could do it with friends, at home and at a time that suited them. And so the Ann Summers Party was born. Today it has 7,500 Party Organisers who hold 4,000 Parties every week. Each Organiser is part salesperson, part entertainer, part entrepreneur and part sexpert. The fact that the Party Plan business continues to grow year-on-year, making it the most successful direct selling company in Europe, is a testament to the passion and enthusiasm of the Party Plan team and the enduring appeal of the Ann Summers Party.

With more than 120 stores and further rapid expansion planned, Ann Summers retail is now the largest part of the Ann Summers business and one of the fastest growing companies on the high street. With the recent opening of its Valencia store, Ann Summers is now set to take Spain by storm. Its web site www.annsummers.com is one of the top 10 most visited online fashion retailers in the UK.

At the head of Ann Summers and the heart of its success, Jacqueline Gold's personal achievements have mirrored those of the company. Jacqueline was voted the second 'Most Powerful Woman in Retail' by Retail Week, one of 'Britain's top 10 most powerful women' by Cosmopolitan, top 12 UK women by Good Housekeeping, one of 'Britian's 100 Most Influential Women' by the Daily Mail, 'Business Communicator of the Year' and is listed in Debrett's 'People of Today' for her contribution to British Society.

History

The Gold brothers, David and Ralph, acquired Ann Summers in 1972. Jacqueline Gold, daughter of David, joined the company in 1979, working her way through the ranks of the company to reach the Chief Executive post in 1987.

After presenting the Party Plan concept to the board in 1981, Jacqueline convinced them that it could be a winner. The concept quickly took off and became the most successful Party Plan network in Europe, a position it maintains today.

Product

As the UK's leading pleasure retailer, Ann Summers is most famous for its sexy lingerie and its world famous and best selling Rampant Rabbit vibrator. Ann Summers sells a complete range of sex

toys, lingerie, oils, lubes and massage oils, books and DVDs and hen night novelties.

Its best selling products include the Platinum Rampant Rabbit vibrator, French Tease and Pin-up lingerie, the Love Bug sex toy, Sister of Mercy nurses outfit and Fly Me air hostess outfit, Chocolate Body Drizzle and Slide & Ride lubricant.

Recent Developments

Ann Summers has embarked on an ambitious expansion plan that will ultimately see 200 stores on high streets throughout the UK. To date, expansion has included stores in Spain, Ireland and the Channel Islands.

In addition, Ann Summers has recently unveiled a new store design to rave reviews and record sales. The new concept store at the Trafford Centre, Manchester is the first of a multi-million pound roll out, that will extend to 35 stores over the next 12 months, with Nottingham, Leeds, Glasgow and London scheduled to get the new look. Each of the new stores will also include a Knickerbox concession.

The new store has been designed to better reflect the brand's core values: feminine, sexy and witty. The walls are draped with white voile curtains and flooded with soft light. Intricate wallpaper is used to highlight key lingerie sections and bespoke crystal chandeliers adorn the ceiling. The store layout is much more open with perimeter fixtures and freestanding units – a reflection of the changing attitudes to shopping at Ann Summers – but is still designed to have an intimate boudoir feel.

Humour is dotted throughout the store, from signage and ticketing to the changing-room doors that have a spy hole window that opens on the inside, proclaiming a 'peep show' on the outside, for customers who want to parade for their waiting partners.

The store is also designed to be much sexier, with texture being an important focus. Rubber, plush carpet, padded leather, satin and smooth lit-edge acrylic, have been used throughout to departmentalise the store and reflect the change of pace as customers move from Ann Summers and Knickerbox lingerie at the front to bondage at

the back. Modern new mannequins – many provocatively posed – also help to raise the store temperature.

Jacqueline Gold says: "Our team of designers have been creating an incredibly sexy lingerie collection of the highest quality – and our new store design is just as beautiful. It will feel like you're stepping into an exciting and intimate boudoir: it's very feminine and very sexy."

Promotion

Ann Summers is arguably one of the best companies at self promotion and PR, in part because it had to overcome so much prejudice and so many obstacles to achieve its success. Most famously, Jacqueline Gold fought and won a High Court case against the Job Centre which refused to advertise vacancies in Ann Summers' stores.

On a lighter note, Ann Summers has secured impressive press coverage for its high profile and witty marketing campaigns that have included the 'A Rabbit Is For Life, Not Just For Christmas' campaign designed to promote its famous Rampant Rabbit; 'Carpet Burns Night' – a typical Ann Summers twist on the traditional Scottish celebration and 'National Orgasm Week', its annual promotion to encourage the nation to enjoy more orgasms.

With stores in just about every major shopping centre including the new Bull Ring in Birmingham, Trafford Centre Manchester, Covent Garden, Oxford Street and Edinburgh's Princess St, people's perceptions of Ann Summers is changing. Gone are the days when landlords were reluctant to have Ann Summers as a tenant, for fear that this might some how signal a decline in the moral fabric of the local community. Just as the TV programme Sex & The City heralded a cultural change in the way that women talk about sex and relationships, so Ann Summers has liberalised the nation's attitude to buying sexy lingerie and sex toys.

Brand Values

Ann Summers has become the by-word for having sexy fun. Whether that is getting your girlfriends round and having an Ann Summers Party, taking them shopping for sex toys or taking your partner and trying on some lingerie in an Ann Summers shop – you'll experience a mixture of emotions – from laughter to excitement, that few other brands could generate.

Jacqueline Gold says: "Ann Summers offers a range of products designed for total pleasure. From sensual lingerie to playwear, edible body paints and massage oils to toys and novelties, there is something for everyone. It's all about attitude – our products are fun and sexy. There is no stereotypical Ann Summers customer, they are confident outgoing people with a tremendous sense of fun."

www.annsummers.com

THINGS YOU DIDN'T KNOW ABOUT

Ann Summers

› Ann Summers sells two million sex toys each year.

› When the Rampant Rabbit made its TV debut in Sex & The City it sold out in Ann Summers the very next day.

› One in three women in the UK have been to an Ann Summers Party.

› 4,000 Ann Summers' Parties, attended by more than 35,000 women, are held every week in the UK & Ireland.

› Ann Summers was voted one of the '100 Best Companies To Work For' in 2005. In the Sunday Times/Department of Trade & Industry's survey, 88% of Ann Summers' staff said they 'laugh a lot with colleagues' while 85% said their 'team is fun to work with'.

› During Ann Summers' National Orgasm Week 2004, more than one million people pledged to have their best-ever orgasm.

› The Ann Summers website attracts in excess of 500,000 unique visitors per month.

Market

Over the past few years, the UK internet market has been dynamic and competitive, as the landscape has shifted from a rather narrow focus on dial-up services to a much wider vision of a broadband future, where internet services enable people to really make the most out of their time online and beyond.

By the end of 2004, the number of broadband connections in the UK passed the six million milestone, approximately 38% of all internet connections (Source: Ofcom).

With the substantial uptake of broadband, 2004 was a good year for most Internet Service Providers (ISPs). Broadband is key to the continuing growth of the internet, particularly for AOL, as it enables the delivery of exciting content, such as music, film and advanced communications.

Achievements

This year marks the 10th anniversary of AOL's presence in the UK. During that time the company has built a strong reputation on the basis of its wide-ranging appeal, from families looking for a safer, more secure online experience, to experienced internet users who want to take advantage of the benefits of high-speed broadband services.

AOL currently has more than 2.3 million members in the UK, including more than one million on AOL Broadband. Worldwide, AOL enjoys a membership of more than 28 million.

Building on its established presence in the UK internet market, AOL is continually evolving to meet the needs of increasingly sophisticated internet users, with advanced features and increased personalisation making it possible for AOL members to customise their online experience.

In an intensely competitive broadband marketplace, AOL is focused on providing a compelling mix of high-speed access, content and services, without limiting the time people spend online, or the amount they download or upload. With more exciting services in the pipeline, and internet users continuing to discover new online experiences, AOL's unlimited stance is a compelling message to the market.

AOL has always placed great emphasis on its social inclusion policy and the Community Investment programme at AOL UK seeks to extend the benefits of the online

medium to those who would most benefit from it, but who are often the least likely to obtain access through traditional means. The priority areas are young people, particularly those outside of mainstream education, and people with disabilities.

In 2003, AOL teamed up with the national charity Citizens Online to launch the AOL Innovation in the Community Awards, designed to help charities and community groups make the most of the internet. 60 organisations across the UK have already benefited from the awards scheme.

History

AOL UK was formed in late 1995 as a joint venture between America Online Inc and Bertelsmann AG as a division of AOL Europe, and the service first launched in the UK in January 1996.

November 1998 saw the first UK television advertising campaign hit the screens. Featuring 'Connie', its aim was to promote AOL as a family-oriented internet option. A large part of AOL's appeal for families is its commitment to making the online experience safer and more secure, and Connie quickly became an instantly recognisable icon for this aspect of the service, and for AOL UK as a whole.

In 2000, AOL successfully campaigned for the introduction of flat-rate internet call charges, to replace outmoded minute-by-minute metered access, putting the UK as a whole at the forefront of the global internet revolution. At that time, AOL UK became one of the first providers in the UK to deliver consumer-friendly flat rate internet access with the launch of its AOL Flat Rate price plan, which was a new way of packaging internet services for consumers.

2002 was a pivotal year for AOL, as it launched AOL Broadband to UK consumers. At that time, 1.7 million UK members were already enjoying the company's flat-rate pricing plan on narrowband, and AOL was in a good position to deliver on the promise of Broadband Britain, which was high on the public agenda.

Launching in July 2002, AOL Broadband combined the benefits

of high-speed internet access with the AOL brand trademarks such as ease of use, convenience, security, exclusive content, community and customer care.

Since the initial launch in 2002, the AOL Broadband offering has evolved and developed in response to a more demanding customer base. As broadband uptake has increased, AOL has continued to add additional content and services, as well as a complete framework for protecting people online, with the AOL Safety & Security Centre.

The company began a substantial promotional partnership with Dixons Group in February 2004 when AOL became the preferred online service provider across Dixons Group stores nationwide, encompassing PC World, Dixons, Currys and The Link outlets. AOL's retail partnerships see a presence in over 4,200 stores in the UK, including successful relationships with ASDA, Comet, Boots and Blockbuster to target a range of consumer segments and provide an unrivalled high street presence. In addition, AOL is loaded on the majority of branded consumer PCs in the UK including HP, Dell, Packard Bell and Sony.

AOL also works closely with other media owners such as News International and Associated Newspapers to deliver themed promotions across multiple marketing channels.

AOL provides a comprehensive broadband portfolio, which aims to offer

choice, value and clarity in what is a very competitive market. In May 2004, AOL introduced an entry-level broadband product to encourage even more people to experience the benefits of high-speed internet access, and the portfolio now includes speeds of up to 2Mbps, catering for internet users who want to make the most of downloading music files and watching streamed video clips online.

AOL plans to build on its success so far, allowing it to enter new markets such as voice services with equally compelling consumer offers and customer service. AOL's goal is to become the undisputed broadband leader in the UK.

Product

Unlike many other ISPs, AOL does not limit customers' time online or the amount they can upload or download. AOL's broadband portfolio offers a range of speeds, appealing to individual needs, while the unlimited aspect means that AOL customers can make the most of the web's content and services.

All AOL members have access to market leading customer support, an advanced Search tool, powered by Google, and up to seven email addresses per AOL account. In addition, AOL Broadband members receive McAfee Firewall Personal Plus and Home Networking support as part of their monthly AOL subscription.

On average, AOL members spend more than one hour a day online, with access to more than 20 channels of AOL online content, from Entertainment and News to Parenting, Shopping and Money, as well as email and access to the internet.

As the internet and the needs of online consumers evolve, AOL is always looking at new ways of developing its content offering to ensure the medium becomes a greater part of people's daily lives. For example, AOL's News, Sport and Entertainment channels are integral to the service, and provide exciting content for both dial-up and broadband customers.

Key to AOL's appeal in these areas are its strong sense of online community, which encourages members to interact with the service and with each other; and its exclusive content deals that enable AOL to offer unique benefits to its members.

Exclusive audio and video music content, and video sports content are two examples of AOL's strategy in this area. AOL's Music channel regularly attracts more than one million unique visitors per month (Source: comScore Media Metrix), and offers a raft of exclusive programming and content designed to appeal to music lovers. This includes radio@AOL Broadband, with more than 100 channels of commercial-free digital radio stations.

Other offerings include Sessions@AOL, which are AOL-produced live performances and in-depth interviews, only available to AOL members. Recent Sessions@AOL have included Keane, Scissor Sisters and Morrissey.

Recent Developments

As broadband connectivity has changed the face of the 'established' internet connectivity business, the market as a whole has moved onto its second phase of significant growth. Changes in technology and the possibilities that these provide in terms of offering new types of services mean that AOL is looking wider than the internet services market for the future.

Just as internet connectivity has changed the way many businesses work and operate, the internet consumer market is beginning to see a change in the way that services are delivered, via different channels and by different providers.

Voice telephony, interactive television services, video on demand, software provision and many other services are beginning to emerge from a range of non-traditional providers, including AOL.

Where millions of members have already trusted AOL to provide them with their access to the internet and a world of content, the next phase of development for the AOL brand is about ensuring that it offers the services and support that customers need to unlock the potential of broadband services.

The first stage in this evolution was the recent launch of AOL Talk, a home telephone service based on Carrier Pre-Select, which offers potential savings to millions

of phone users. Initially available to existing and new AOL internet subscribers, it will be launched as a standalone product during 2005. AOL Talk extends AOL's 'unlimited' philosophy to the home phone market, with unlimited UK local and national calls, without the usage limits common to many phone providers. With AOL Talk, AOL is making clear its commitment to the home phone market, with a focus on competitive, easy to use services.

Promotion

AOL aims to continue to present its products and services in user friendly, simple-to-understand ways so that the benefit is clear to the consumer.

The company also endeavours to differentiate itself from its competitors by delivering propositions that offer clarity and transparency in terms of what consumers pay, what they get and their commitments.

In a market characterised by consumer confusion around pricing and tariffs, AOL strives to continue to champion the cause of the simplicity that its research suggests is so important to consumers.

As the breadth of AOL's product and service offering increases, there will be a requirement for AOL to promote its offerings through channels and in ways that let consumers experience AOL before they choose to join. While the free-trial mechanism has provided this experience of the product to date, future marketing and promotions will be developed that ensure that the more complex and involved products AOL is beginning to offer can be experienced in simple ways – online, in-store and beyond.

Brand Values

The AOL brand is centred on the idea of helping its members unlock the potential of the internet – not simply being a provider of technology, but a provider of user-friendly benefits that make a difference in people's lives.

The AOL brand will be supported and delivered by providing members with the most comprehensive, easy-to-use package of interactive information, entertainment and services.

The values that have taken AOL to its position of success – user friendly, straightforward, approachable and reliable – are as valid today as when it launched. The company aims to make sure these values are appropriate to the needs that its members and potential members have of a service provider in this rapidly-developing market, both today and tomorrow.

www.aol.co.uk

THINGS YOU DIDN'T KNOW ABOUT

AOL

> AOL members in the UK spent a combined total of more than one billion hours online in 2004.

> AOL blocks more than one billion junk emails globally each day before they even reach members' in-boxes.

> Nearly 100 million users are on the AOL Instant Messenger service globally, sending 2.5 billion messages every day.

Market

It is 40 years since a couple of Yorkshire brothers opened a small supermarket in the town of Castleford when such stores were in their infancy. Today, supermarkets have come of age and grown out of all recognition from their early days in terms of size and range of products. The Big Five alone, which includes ASDA, account for combined sales of £62 billion (Source: Mintel).

The 21st century shopper is more affluent, sophisticated and food conscious with higher expectations and needs than his/her predecessor and willing to experiment with a range of foods and lines which, 40 years ago, were considered not only 'exotic' but also prohibitively expensive, except to the fortunate few.

Food accounts for 16% of the average household's weekly outgoings (which is £385) with the majority of the population (50.3%) doing their shopping once a week. A smaller group (14.6%) shop two or three times weekly (Source: Mintel). The rise in the number of homes with fridges, freezers and microwaves, coupled with the growth of car ownership has revolutionised how, when and where we shop. Additionally, in this time-conscious age, the supermarket's one-stop shop ethos is lost on few consumers. Out-of-town developments have helped remove the headache

of congested city-centre shopping for those favouring a more leisurely, family oriented approach to buying everything from their weekly groceries to clothes for the children.

ASDA has found that even in a climate of greater economic prosperity, consumers now perceive getting good value for money as a sensible and acceptable thing to do. A cultural shift towards rising aspirations and higher expectations of material well-being is also taking place. This has led to the majority of people aiming towards making their disposable income go further. British shoppers value supermarkets. It is hardly surprising that ASDA and its Every Day Low Pricing (EDLP) policy is a firm favourite with shoppers, making it the UK's second-largest supermarket group.

Achievements

ASDA is one of the UK's top value food and clothing superstores. Average prices at ASDA, which carries out more than 13 million transactions a week offering a mix of fresh food, grocery, clothing, home, leisure and entertainment goods, are almost 10% lower than competitors. ASDA has received countless accolades. In 2004, for the seventh consecutive year, it was voted 'Britain's best value supermarket' by The Grocer magazine and the UK's favourite store for range, price, service and reliability in a survey by ACNielsen. Over the years, ASDA has raised millions for charities as well as being involved with local communities. Last year 'colleagues', which is how ASDA refers to all its employees, raised more than £4 million for local good causes. A crowning achievement for such efforts has been the Nestlé Social Commitment Award.

As well as looking after its customers and the local community, ASDA cares equally for its colleagues and suppliers. It has been consistently named as one of Britain's Top 100 Companies to Work For – an amazing accolade as it employs as many people as the other 99

companies combined. Such prizes have been underlined by The Castle Award, recognising ASDA's commitment to providing equal pay and opportunities for women through innovative working practices ranging from introducing the first supermarket store manager job share scheme at Barnsley in 1999 to the 'School Starter' programme, which allows parents to take a half day holiday on their child's first day at school. ASDA has also been named top employer by Personnel Today magazine and won awards for its innovative share schemes (11,000 employees pocketed £14.5 million worth of shares in 2002). ASDA places great importance on using local suppliers, working with more than 2,600 and buying £1.1 billion of produce from them annually. Its own Code of Trade Practice goes further than the industry standard, with special provisions for small and developing suppliers.

History

ASDA came into being in 1965, although its roots are firmly embedded in the Yorkshire dairy business of the 1920s, when the Stockdale family operated its own milk wholesaling business.

The Stockdales joined forces with other local farmers and through a process of acquisition and diversification became a public company. Associated Dairies & Farm Stores Ltd was formed in 1949. Enterprising brothers Peter and Fred Asquith joined the company in the 1950s and began developing a supermarket concept. Their first supermarket, aptly named 'Queen's', opened at the former Queen's Theatre in Castleford, Yorkshire, offering 'permanent reductions', an early forerunner to EDLP. Two years later, the Asquiths opened the third store under the ASDA name. The 1970s and 1980s witnessed a period of further growth, with the purchase of furniture retailer MFI, Allied Carpets and the Gateway stores chain.

Amid much attention from the press, the US food retailing giant, Wal-Mart,

Welcome to hassle free shopping

It's as easy as 1, 2, 3, and ASDA will deliver to your door.

Shop online at
www.asda.com
skyactive

bought ASDA for £7 billion in 1999. As part of the Wal-Mart family, ASDA has retained its identity and remained true to its principles of better value and always backing British farmers and growers. The union has been very successful and ASDA has since gained millions of new customers. Six thousand price cuts were made in 2000 and the following Spring ASDA cut shoppers combined grocery bills by a further £52 million. Since 1999 it has invested more than £1 billion in lowering prices.

Product

ASDA today has 278 stores throughout the UK, including eight standalone George stores and two ASDA Living general merchandise stores. It has a flexible approach to store sizes, which vary from between 10,000 and 100,000 sq ft, aiming to place the right development in the right catchment. The largest units or 'Supercentres' offer food, general merchandise, clothing and white/brown goods. The superstore is a mini-equivalent of its big brother. Small stores do not come any smaller than Billingham's 8,000 sq ft, but are designed to suit the urban commuter, who might need a sandwich for lunch or last minute ingredients for that evening's meal.

ASDA's own-label brands – Smart Price, ASDA Brand, Good For You!, Organic and Extra Special, are bestselling brands in their own right and have been developed to meet specific customer needs. In response to consumer demand, ASDA implemented a three-year pledge to ensure its own-label products were healthier, reducing fat, sugar and salt levels by 10% and in the process taking out 900 tonnes of salt without compromising on price, quality or shelf-life. The initiative includes removing allergenic ingredients such as gluten and milk and lowering

levels of additives linked to hypersensitivity in children. ASDA has been at the forefront of developing in-store 'food-to-go' counters, introducing Curry Pot in 1996. This success prompted the superstore to launch Tex-Mex, Chinese, fish and chips and rotisserie chicken ranges.

In striving to serve all customers, ASDA has been truly innovative. Schemes for the disabled range from using Braille guns to label tinned goods, electric shopping scooters and 'trolley-vators' that lift shoppers to the higher shelves. The UK's first multilingual superstore in Bradford featured customer signage in Urdu, Punjabi and English. In 2004 it opened a store in Peterhead, north-east Scotland with signage in Doric, the local dialect.

The brand's online home shopping service, www.asda.com, launched in 1998 and is operational in more than 30 stores throughout the UK with coverage constantly growing. The service offers a range of more than 20,000 products delivered to customers in temperature-controlled vans. From its website, ASDA also offers competitively priced life, travel and pet insurance products.

Recent Developments

ASDA works constantly to improve products and services while delivering its promise of EDLP. It recently embarked on a multimillion pound review of its own-label business, which accounts for just over half of its total sales. In true ASDA style, the review resulted in reducing prices while increasing volume.

ASDA also continues to drive down non-food prices. In May 2001, the superstore was victorious in its six-year campaign to abolish retail price maintenance for over-the-counter medicines. The campaign ended a practice that meant consumers were paying in excess of £300 million on over-the-counter branded products annually. ASDA celebrated by cutting prices by 50% on 36 healthcare items. In endeavouring to maintain lower prices while retaining quality, ASDA broke the Net Book agreement and bought better value books and reduced the price of comics.

ASDA has re-launched its general merchandise departments with 5,000 new lines, delivering previously unheard of prices in the UK with toasters, kettles and irons under £8 and microwaves for less than £30. In parallel, it expanded into new speciality areas such as opticians, pharmacies, jewellery and photo departments – the latter offering prices 30% lower than the high street. By the end of 2002, ASDA was the UK's sixth-largest chain of opticians and is accelerating its pharmacy development, after a partial victory in its battle to relax the UK pharmacy opening controls.

The George clothing range, which now encompasses everything from baby clothes to beachwear, launched in only five stores in 1990, has now grown to a £1 billion business and is the UK's second-biggest fashion retailer. George Essentials launched in 2001, with prices averaging 30% lower than standard ranges with no compromise on quality. George Fast Fashion appeared the following April. It captures the latest styles and trends as they come off the catwalk with a brief to produce clothes from design to store in only seven weeks. The ranges are refreshed every four weeks, reflecting the growing desire of shoppers to be inspired by new and fresh fashion items every time they shop.

Promotion

ASDA has invested heavily in promotional and advertising activity, spending £24 million annually on television alone. Commercials that underscore ASDA's good value use the 'pocket the difference' tagline while featuring ordinary shoppers and staff in everyday situations.

A variety of in-store publications – What's New at ASDA, George Magalogues and ASDA Magazine – keep customers informed of new products, while broadening their understanding of the non-food range. ASDA Magazine, with a readership of five million, is the UK's most popular women's monthly. ASDA has also made clever use of below-the-line advertising, using rickshaws to publicise the launch of its Dewsbury store.

As part of its promotional strategy, the superstore has run a variety of entertainments or 'retailments' for customers. These have included drive-in movies, fireworks parties and skating nights. ASDA was a key sponsor of the 2001 Commonwealth Games and part of its commitment to the regeneration of Manchester was the opening of a superstore.

Brand Values

ASDA is a people-focused company with a caring nature. Central to the brand's personality is its aim to maintain a genuine interest in what customers think and feel so it can be prepared to do the best for them. ASDA hopes to be perceived as consistent and trustworthy and to present customers with an offer where they can expect low prices whenever they shop and whatever they shop for, whilst ensuring quality is not sacrificed.

www.asda.co.uk

25% off

THINGS YOU DIDN'T KNOW ABOUT

ASDA

> ASDA sells 750,000 cans of Smart Price baked beans a week.

> The combined volume of apple and pears sold annually in ASDA stores are enough to fill 342 football pitches.

> ASDA sells 28.6 million sandwiches annually, enough to stretch from London to New York.

> ASDA is the UK's biggest take-away, selling 500,000 curry portions a week.

> ASDA sells six million pairs of men's underpants annually.

Market

Approximately 45% (25,576,253) of the UK's population actively used the internet in January 2005, with 83% of these internet users using a search engine to find the web address they were looking for (Source: NOP World).

Search engine traffic was strong in January 2005, with around 230 million visits to all search sites, 15% more than during the same month in 2004 (Source: NOP World).

In terms of user numbers, Ask Jeeves is the fourth-largest search site in the UK behind Google, MSN Search and Yahoo Search. Google remains the clear market leader but the other three search sites are constantly battling for position with similar user numbers (Source: Nielsen Netratings).

Achievements

Ask Jeeves' revenues for the year to December 31st, 2004 reached US$261.3 million. These 2004 revenues represent 144% growth over revenues of US$107.3 million for 2003.

Ask Jeeves recognises the fact that 60% of its users are female and March 2005 saw Prima Magazine, the UK's fifth-highest selling women's magazine, award Ask Jeeves its Make Life Simple Award for the Top Time-Saving Website.

The search engine was a finalist in the 2005 ISPA award for the Best Search facility and a finalist in the 2005 Imperatives award for Best Use of Search and Best Advertising Campaign.

Furthermore, Ask Jeeves was recently recognised as 'one of the most relevant and accurate search engines' by BBC Online in independent trials.

Ask Jeeves explored new partnership opportunities by joining forces with Virgin Radio to create a new Toolbar product to deepen listeners' relationships with the station by driving customer loyalty. The on-going partnership also provides additional revenue streams and further joint branding opportunities.

Ask Jeeves created a bespoke Virgin Radio branded toolbar which can be downloaded exclusively from the nation's rock and pop radio station website, virginradio.co.uk.

History

Ask Jeeves was founded in 1996, in Berkeley, California, by David Warthen, chief technology officer and veteran software developer and Garrett Gruener, venture capitalist at Alta Partners and founder of Virtual Microsystems.

It officially launched in April 1997, while Ask Jeeves for Kids (AJKids.com) launched in February of 1998.

Later that year, Ask Jeeves reached 300,000 searches per day and signed its first syndication deal with Alta Vista. At the start of the following year, Ask Jeeves began answering 700,000 searches a day and was up to one million searches by May and two million by October of the same year.

At the time, the search engine's initial public offering in July 1999 marked the third most successful first-day performance in history.

In December 1999, the company launched Ask Jeeves International before establishing Ask Jeeves UK. The UK site officially launched in February 2000.

In September 2001, Ask Jeeves made the decision to acquire Teoma Technologies and then refocused its operations on the user experience. When the Teoma technology was integrated into Ask.com in December of that year, the company saw an immediate 25% increase in user satisfaction.

In October 2002, Ask Jeeves lead the search industry when it discontinued all pop-up and pop-unders from Ask.com. The company soon after removed all banners from Ask.com and added Spell Check technology.

In January 2003, Ask Jeeves announced its first profitable quarter, which was for Q4 of 2002. The company's stock performance during 2003 spoke volumes: it was the 51st best-performing stock out of 3,229 companies on NASDAQ. The price of Ask Jeeves stock soared more than 500% throughout the course of the year.

In May 2004, Ask Jeeves completed the acquisition of Interactive Search Holding, adding a diverse portfolio of websites, portals and desktop applications, all with search as their foundation.

As a result of this acquisition, Ask Jeeves became a top-ranked website, according to Nielsen Net Ratings, and the fastest-growing search property on the internet, according to Forrester Research.

Today, Ask Jeeves is a publicly traded company on the Nasdaq Index and is headquartered in Oakland, California, with offices throughout the US, as well as in London, Dublin, and Tokyo.

Product

As one of the fastest-growing web properties on the internet, Ask Jeeves provides consumers and advertisers with information-retrieval products across a diverse portfolio of websites, portals and desktop search applications.

Ask Jeeves' search and search-based portal brands include: Ask Jeeves (Ask.com and Ask.co.uk); Ask Jeeves Japan (Ask.jp, a joint venture); Ask Jeeves España (Beta site es.ask.com); Ask Jeeves for Kids (AJKids.com); Bloglines (Bloglines.com); Excite (excite.com); iWon (iwon.com); Fun Web Products (www.funwebproducts.com); My Way (myway.com); and Teoma (teoma.com).

The company owns the search technology Teoma, a proprietary natural language processing technology, as well as portal and ad serving technologies.

In addition to powering several of the Ask Jeeves brands, the company syndicates its technologies.

Ask Jeeves' strategy is to offer users more than just 'ten blue links' by taking users directly to the most relevant results. The company is constantly innovating as it strives to provide the best search experience for users. All of Ask Jeeves' recent product developments have been user-centric, developed with feedback and research into user behaviours and desires in mind.

Ask Jeeves' Teoma technology means it can answer natural-language questions and key-word searches to allow the user freedom in the way they search. Ask Jeeves has put a lot of energy into how to display search results based on analysing the query being asked and subsequently the results that experience shows they will be looking for.

2004 was a key year for Ask Jeeves in terms of product innovation and new product launches. Through extensive quantitative and qualitative market research over the past five years, Ask Jeeves identified three types of query: 'browsing', 'specific detail' and 'transactional', and in 2004 was able to apply the findings and adapt its product to deliver the most relevant results.

In a 'browsing' search, the user is looking for information around a topic without something specific in mind, for example searching for 'history of Bath'. To help this user, Ask Jeeves offers Related Search topics to the right of the page and editorially selected Recommended Results to help narrow down and define the actual search required.

Increased broadband use means people are using search as a tool to dip in and out of to help find quick facts and details. In a 'specific detail' search, Ask Jeeves' proprietary Smart Search tool uses intuitive technology to recognise when users are asking a direct question and provide direct answers straight to the results page, for example searching for 'weather in London'. This means users can conduct effective searches faster.

In a 'transactional' search, the user is looking to research a product or service they would like to buy, or actually make that transaction. Ask Jeeves' partner Kelkoo provides online price comparisons to compare prices direct from the results page.

Recent Developments

In November 2004 Ask Jeeves began offering its Binoculars service, which is designed to make the process of wading through search results easier. The tool allows users to achieve the desired result of their web search more quickly, by being able to see a mini preview pane of any site before choosing whether to click through and open the link up fully.

Users hover their cursor over the Binoculars tool icon that sits above each link on their search results page and the tool instantly presents a thumbnail size sneak preview of the web page. Being able to view the site before physically clicking through to it helps users to save time and make a more informed decision about whether it is a relevant result for them or not.

The following month, MyAskJeeves, the personal search system for ask.co.uk, was launched. The service enables users to create their own personal web index and save searches, organise them into personal folders, email to friends and also crucially search within their own saved results.

The service is free, simple to use and does not require registration. Not only a method of saving search information, MyAskJeeves also provides users with additional storage for their personal search index ensuring once a website is found, users never loose a link.

In February 2005, Ask Jeeves acquired Bloglines, www.bloglines.com, a free online service for searching, subscribing, publishing and sharing blogs and rich web content. Bloglines will continue to operate as an independent brand in the Ask Jeeves portfolio and retains its name.

Promotion

2004 was an evolutionary year for Ask Jeeves. The brand implemented a repositioning that brought the site, product, logo and character into line with a market that is fast-paced, constantly innovating and technologically advanced.

The first half of 2004 saw the birth of 'the Find Engine' as a communication proposition that positioned the brand against the real benefit of searching and took the high ground first from its competition.

An outdoor, radio and online campaign promoted this positioning through creative material depicting Ask Jeeves as the solution when users are looking for difficult-to-find things.

Executions included a chameleon on a green background being picked out by an arrow from the Ask Jeeves logo as well as the arrow from the logo pointing directly through a winding maze.

Copy clarified the message with 'Find the Chameleon' and 'Find the Quickest Way' respectively.

Online advertising allowed the user to try and find the things for themselves before Ask Jeeves popping up with the arrow pointing it out. The online advertising campaign, produced by Profero, won the IAB's Creative Showcase.

Meanwhile, the Jeeves character was made slimmer, more confident, smart and sophisticated and, therefore, more relevant to a younger, more savvy internet audience. The logo was updated accordingly along with a cleaner, easy-to-use site design, informed by extensive user research and usability testing.

The overhaul led to advertising that built on the Find Engine proposition and brought the new Jeeves to life in two TV spots that displayed Jeeves participating in a number of different situations from snowboarding, to listening to an MP3 player, to skydiving and 'zorbing'.

The ads raised brand awareness and, again, online advertising was invested in to provide the final connection and access point.

Brand Values

Ask Jeeves has fought back and built share in one of the world's toughest markets, helped by a uniquely identifiable brand and a differentiated and easy to use site design.

The Ask Jeeves brand stands for the key values of trust, reliability, speed, comprehensiveness and authority.

www.ask.co.uk

THINGS YOU DIDN'T KNOW ABOUT

Ask Jeeves

> Ask Jeeves is the seventh most popular online property in the UK, with 10.2 million users in February 2005 (Source: ComScore networks).

> The most-used measurement conversion on the Ask Jeeves site is miles into kilometres, while the most-used currency conversion is dollars into euros. 'Jennifer Aniston hairstyles' is still the top celebrity hair search.

> The most popular destination for flight queries is Tenerife.

> Paris Hilton has overtaken Jordan to take second place behind Britney in the searched-for pin-up stakes.

> The most searched for king and queen are King Arthur and Queen Victoria.

> The most searched for dog breed is the Staffordshire Bull Terrier.

> The top search beginning with 'z' is Zelda.

Market

In the UK there is continuing heavy demand for prestige cars, largely because of the relative buoyancy of the economy, high levels of employment, high expenditure on consumer durables and low interest finance.

New car registrations in the UK reached 2,567,271 million in 2004, maintaining the previous year's record of 2,579,050 in 2003 and 2,563,631 in 2002 (Source: Society of Motor Manufacturers and Traders). The 2005 market is expected to reach 2.45 million units.

Achievements

2005 sees Audi celebrate 25 years of 'quattro', its pioneering four-wheel drive technology. Indeed, Audi is a company committed to technological innovation and its list of achievements includes being the first company to run systematic crash testing for passenger cars and the first car manufacturer to introduce catalytic converters as standard in the UK.

Its innovation and design have won Audi many awards, including What Car? Coupe of the Year in 2000, 2001, 2002 and 2003 for the Audi TT and What Car? Compact Executive of the Year in 2001, 2002 and 2003 for the A4.

Striped to just 1500kg of Vorsprung durch Technik. 0-62 in 5.9 seconds. The new 237bhp TT quattro Sport.

The new Audi A3 Sportback.

Following the upheaval of World War II, the company needed a new name and Audi was resurrected in 1965, along with the company's first post-war vehicle with a four-stroke engine. In the 1980s, Audi's core brand statement 'Vorsprung durch Technik' entered the English language. It is a phrase that sums up not only Audi's technical excellence but also its emotional attitude to design.

1980 also saw Audi engineers set a milestone in drive technology with 'quattro' permanent four-wheel drive. As the pioneer of four-wheel-drive technology, Audi set a benchmark as early as 25 years ago with the presentation of the quattro coupe.

The numerous successes that ensued on rally courses and circuits around the world testify to the efficiency of this superior drive concept. Audi drivers are ensured that they can rely on the additional driving pleasure, mobility and safety that quattro offers in all driving situations.

The principle is simple: in the same way that four brakes ensure better deceleration, four driven wheels enable better acceleration and higher cornering stability. Audi quattro four-wheel drive is the systematic application of this basic physical principle: power distribution for improved and safer driving.

As testament to its engineering performance, 2004 saw Audi achieve its 50th race victory in five years with the Audi Le Mans R8 sports car, now the most successful modern-day prototype ever. The R8 has set new standards, not only for performance, but also for reliability: there has not been a single engine failure in a race to this day. Audi engineers have also demonstrated the brand famous ethos, 'Vorsprung durch Technik' in other areas: the R8 was the first Le Mans prototype with a pneumatic gear shift and remains unique in this respect, helping it to achieve success.

History

In 1899 August Horch, a pioneering engineer with a reputation as a problem-solver, set up his own business. By 1901 he had created his first automobile and the following year became convinced of the need to use light-weight alloys to reduce mass. This was the start of Audi, which even today uses this same principle in its A8 model, that is around 50% lighter than if it were made of steel.

In 1932, four previously independent motor vehicle manufacturers: Audi, DKW, Horch and Wanderer merged to create Auto Union AG, which then became the second-largest motor vehicle manufacturer in Germany.

THE NEW AUDI A3 SPORTBACK. VORSPRUNG DURCH TECHNIK.

In addition, depending on the driving situation and road surface, quattro technology also distributes drive power continuously between the front and rear axles. Especially on slippery surfaces, this means better traction, even in conditions in which vehicles with two driven wheels are no longer able to grip.

Today, Audi is an international developer and manufacturer of high-quality cars. The company produces cars in Germany, Hungary and China, sells more than 650,000 cars annually and employs more than 50,000 people.

Product

Audi has long recognised that consumers don't buy cars for purely rational reasons. It therefore wanted to appeal to their emotional side so, in 1999, the unmistakable Audi TT was launched to great acclaim. It has since become a design classic and has been hailed as one of the few cars that has changed little from concept stage to final production.

Audi also appeals to the emotions with its other marques, for example the Audi A8 luxury saloon, the sporty A3 and the new Audi Q7, due for launch in 2006.

Across its product range, Audi's innovations have been numerous and include FSI direct injection petrol engines for road and racing, giving the performance of petrol with the economy of a diesel, multimedia interfaces for in-car entertainment and information, new generation piezo injection TDI engines for state-of-the-art refinement, heightened performance, improved fuel consumption and low emissions.

Strides have been made in the area of gearboxes; multitronic® provides a seamless automatic transmission, with the economy of a manual. In addition DSG (Dynamic Shift Gearbox) is available on TT and A3 3.2 models, paddles on the steering wheel and a two-clutch system means the vehicle doesn't lose power or momentum between gear changes.

Recent Developments

The lightest and quickest Audi TT quattro yet was launched in May 2005, combining increased power with reduced weight. Limited to 1,000 right-hand-drive cars, the weight of the Audi TT Coupé quattro Sport has been reduced by 49kg to 1,416kg, meaning it can achieve 0-62mph in 5.9 seconds and can reach a maximum speed of 155mph. The car also features 18-inch alloy wheels as well as Recaro bucket seats.

Another debut for 2005 is the four-door version of the Audi RS 4 quattro saloon, which launched at the Geneva Motor Show in March and becomes available in autumn 2005. The first B-segment Audi RS saloon epitomises 'Vorsprung durch Technik' through numerous advances, including the combination of eight-cylinder power, FSI direct petrol injection and a new generation of four-wheel drive technology. It is capable of achieving 0-62mph in 4.8 seconds and features 19-inch alloy wheels, a tapered sports steering wheel, RS bucket seats and an engine starter button. The idea is to invoke the feel of a racing car along with the comfort, quality and attention to detail traditionally associated with Audi.

The new Audi Q7 makes its market debut in 2006. This luxury seven-seater features Audi's latest quattro four-wheel-drive technology, now in its sixth generation. The new car has been described as the 'ultimate expression' of quattro, which celebrates its 25th anniversary this year.

The prototype of a new SUV generation, the Audi Q7 is the culmination of the long-awaited 'Pikes Peak quattro' study. High-performance petrol and TDI engines ensure

outstanding road performance, while quattro permanent four-wheel drive and cutting-edge suspension make for optimum grip and driving pleasure on any terrain.

Before the Audi Q7 makes its international exhibition debut at the 2005 Frankfurt Motor Show in September, it will undergo intensive tests in tough conditions, including Arctic regions and burning deserts.

Promotion

The philosophy behind the latest Audi UK brand offensive is that Audi cars are 'not just made from the same materials as other cars. They have an ingredient that makes them absolutely unique. Audi cars are made from 'Vorsprung durch Technik.'

This concept is being used consistently through all marketing activity in the UK in a series of campaigns that aim to position Audi as the most desirable car brand in Britain.

The first part of the integrated campaign – the television commercial for the new A8 – was launched in September 2004. The message then continued with the launch of the A3 Sportback later the same month, but with awareness generated via print, poster, direct marketing and a viral email film.

Audi believes that 'Vorsprung durch Technik' is far more than an advertising slogan. Over the coming years, it is expected to play a major role as Audi strives to reach the position of number-one prestige car brand in the UK.

Brand Values

Built upon the cornerstones of design and technology, Audi has become a byword for intelligent, sophisticated German innovation. Today, the brand stands for advanced technology, sophistication and head-turning elegance, tempered by pure emotion.

www.audi.co.uk

AVIS

Market

Avis is synonymous with vehicle rental. Alongside other major players such as Hertz, Europcar and easyCar, it dominates the sector. Indeed, Avis is the car rental market leader in the European, African and Middle Eastern markets, with around eight million customers annually within these regions (Source: Mintel). In addition, Avis has the largest fleet and widest choice of vehicles. As a whole, the car hire industry has had to battle with a series of problems in recent years, including the fuel crisis, car-pricing realignment affecting supply chains and the downturn in global travel since 9/11. However, over a five year time frame, growth has still been seen in this market.

Achievements

From humble beginnings at Detroit Airport, Avis has built itself into a world-leading brand and is an instantly recognisable name to consumers and business users all over the world. Avis now have 20 million annual customers in over 161 countries and 4,850 locations. Avis has successfully pioneered car rental in several international markets, including Central and Eastern Europe, where it subsequently expanded its operations. It was the first car rental company to open an office in East Germany after the fall of the Berlin Wall – a move that helped it springboard into neighbouring former eastern

service excellence. Recent awards include: being named 58th Best UK Company to work for in 2005 (The Times Top 100 Companies); Business Travel World award for best Business Car Rental Company 2005; Best Business Car Rental Company and Best Leisure Car Rental Company across Europe; Business Traveller publication voted Avis the Best Car Rental Company in Europe and Best Car Rental Company Worldwide in 2004; Renault; Fleet Support Group and being awarded Accreditation Status for its Car Club product.

History

Warren Avis opened the first Avis office at Willow Run airport, Detroit, in 1946. At that time, he had a grand total of three cars, but it was the world's first ever car rental operation at an airport. By 1953, Avis was the second largest car rental company in the US and was already expanding overseas, opening franchised operations in Mexico, Canada and Europe. By 1963 it was struggling with a 10% US market share, compared to 75% for Hertz. It launched an advertising campaign that proved crucial in turning its fortunes around. The slogan, 'We're only No.2. We try harder' emphasised its commitment to customer service and remains at the core of its brand today. The slogan has subsequently been recognised as one of the ten best of all time.

speed of use with a simple four step booking process that allows the user to get a quote in just 30 seconds and make a booking in 90 seconds. Avis also pioneered the development of 'direct connect' with its partners' web activity. Direct connect works in conjunction with a partners', website, for example Flybe, and pulls the car rental information to correspond with the customers' flight information. It provides an automatic quote and allows the customer to book in one-click by accepting the quote, direct connect does the rest.

In 1997 Avis Europe re-floated on the London Stock Exchange to fund expansion of the business.

In March 2000, an all-new central reservations centre, based at Salford Quays in Manchester, went live. Staffed by 250 agents, the centre takes over one and a half million calls and makes over 150,000 outbound calls every year. Avis agents are multi-lingual.

In 2003, Avis acquired Budget, bringing together two global car rental

bloc territories, like the Czech Republic and Romania. It has achieved a similar goal in the former Soviet Union and, when it opened an office in the Ukraine in 1997, it became the first and only car rental company to have an office in every European country. This gives it an unrivalled European network – including a presence at 75 major European airports.

The brand has been similarly pioneering in Africa, where it now has representation in over 85% of the region. Again, this has given it greater coverage than any of its competitors. In the Middle East, it is represented in 90% of the region and in Asia, and is licensed to operate in 27 territories. In 2003, Avis and Shanghai Automotive Industry Sales Corporation (SAISC) announced the first equity joint venture Chinese car rental company, with plans to open 70 rental stations in 26 cities within five years.

Avis has been pioneering in its commitment to customer service levels since the mid 1960s, including the introduction of the first computerised reservation system 'Wizard' in 1972. A track record of external accreditation underlines Avis' commitment to delivering on its 'We try harder.' promise to its customers every day through

In 1965, Avis officially launched Avis Europe to look after its growing operations in Europe, Africa and the Middle East. By 1973, it was market leader in these areas – a position it still holds today.

Avis entered a worldwide advertising and marketing agreement with General Motors in 1979 to feature GM cars in its fleet worldwide. The strength of this relationship led to the signing of Europe's largest fleet partnership agreement in 2003.

In 1986, Avis Europe legally separated from its owner, Avis Inc, and became the first ever car company to float on the London Stock Exchange. In three years, it tripled its market value, before reverting to private ownership again in 1989. In 1987, Avis Inc became employee-owned, with a £1.2 billion Employee Stock Ownership Plan – this made it the largest employee owned company in the US and a role model for other companies to follow.

The brand's impressive technological track record continued and in 1996 it became the first car rental company to launch a website – www.avis.com, allowing customers to make or modify a booking online. The www.avis.co.uk website is recognised for its ease and

companies. Both brands benefit from increased network strength and customer base, taking advantage of global commercial opportunities through their relationships within the Cendant car rental group, providing one of the largest fleets and rental networks in the world.

Product

Worldwide, Avis has 4,850 rental locations and globally buys more than 500,000 vehicles annually in over 160 countries. Annually, it completes around 20 million rental transactions, generating annual gross revenue of approximately £1.7 billion. Avis has 120 offices throughout the UK. Its network of outlets is split between those wholly owned by the company and licensees.

Warren Avis got the idea for airport-based car rental during World War II when he was a bomber pilot. He used to carry his motorbike in the bomber so that he could always have transport wherever he landed.

Today, the company maintains relationships with more than 50 of the world's airlines and offers streamlined services at airports. For instance, with British Airways at Heathrow, customers can return their car and check-in for an onward BA flight at the same desk. Avis recognises that time is now our most precious commodity and has developed products and services to help speed up the car rental process and save the customer time. With services like Avis Preferred, customers can enjoy some of the quickest service in the industry. Having completed a personal profile just once, customers can call ahead and then arrive at an Avis Preferred desk to find a car pre-assigned with all the paperwork completed and the keys ready. There is no requirement to complete any further rental agreements.

Returning a car is just as quick – the Rapid Return service allows the vehicle details to be entered into a revolutionary hand held device. The device, which operates at 15 of Avis' busiest locations in the UK, and at major airports across Europe, enables staff to complete check-in at the car, calculating the bill and issuing a receipt. This means that the whole process can take as little as 60 seconds from start to finish, providing improved service and visibility to customers.

Prestige Cars offers a wide range of luxury vehicles chosen for their reputation and status including a full range of Mercedes, BMW, Jaguar and Porsche models. Its Chauffeur Drive service offers limousines with uniformed drivers.

Avis also provides services tailored for business users, like Avis Advance, and MaxiRent – a flexible programme for long term rentals designed to facilitate fleet management.

Avis was an early leader in technical support systems, with the introduction of its Wizard computerised reservation system in 1972. This is still in operation today and is the most extensive online, real time reservation, rental and management information system in the industry. Wizard controls the fleet, knowing where every car can be found, who they are rented to and when they will be returned. Wizard is also invaluable when it comes to managing company fleet costs and travel policy. Reports can be customised for corporate customers so they can optimise the management of their rental costs.

As part of its 'Caring for our Climate' environmental initiative, Avis has planted in excess of 200,000 trees to offset carbon dioxide emissions made by cars. All vehicles on the Avis fleet use the latest low emission technology by operating a six-month rule – no vehicle is, on average, more than six months old – while a 40-point check between each rental ensures vehicles operate to maximum efficiency during their rental life.

Recent Developments
Avis continues to promote responsible car usage with the support of Future Forests, the international climate change

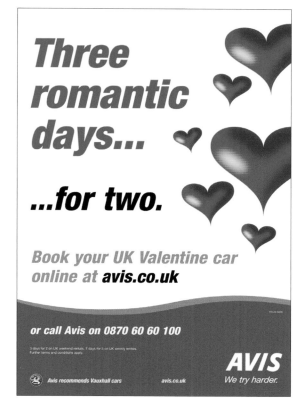

business, and the Edinburgh Centre for Carbon Management, by implementing a market-leading three-point plan to reduce and offset carbon emissions. Over the last 12 months Avis' staff and customers, in conjunction with Future Forests, offset approximately 18,500t CO_2 through a combination of clean-energy technology projects and public-access, long-term native forestry schemes across Europe. Since the start of its partnership with Future Forests in 1999, Avis has planted a total of some 200,000 saplings over a period of four years to offset greenhouse gas emissions.

Avis has also expanded its Car Club product, Urbigo. This allows members, who pay a small monthly membership fee, to rent on an hourly basis, and pick up cars from specially allocated points as and when they need them. It is designed to be a cost-effective alternative to car ownership or long-term rental. The scheme started in Oxford, but has now been developed in several locations in the London area.

Avis is a member of the exclusive FTSE4 Good Index, which independently evaluates the corporate social responsibility of a company to the interest of ethical and environmental stakeholders. In addition, the company is A rated by the Safety and Environmental Risk Management Rating Agency.

In 2002 Avis was awarded Investors in People status and received the highest possible ranking for an organisation being assessed for the first time. Avis provides a four year development programme, in partnership with the Nottingham Business School, for all new rental agents.

Since launching the first car rental website in 1996, Avis has continuously developed its online service to customers, introducing the new look www.avis.co.uk in 2003, which enabled customers to book online in under 90 seconds in only four steps, and with just four hours notice. The website now also offers pre-paid rental discounts and regular offers.

Avis is the market leader in the development of profitable, revenue generating partnerships. Typically it creates partnership contracts with key airlines, hotel groups, credit card and rail companies, with the key focus on the development of preferential products and services for customers. In total Avis is in partnership with over 200 organisations and reaches an audience of over seven million. The brand looks upon its working relationships with its partners not as a supplier-based relationship but as two organisations working together to achieve a common set of objectives.

Promotion
Avis is one of the most promotionally active of the major car rental brands, making extensive use of media including press, outdoor, POS, radio and the internet. Campaigns are run on a national, regional or local level, with additional promotional activity with key partners and on the web. Recent national campaigns have included a Valentine's 'Three romantic days for two' offer and 'Keep your lolly!' discounted online leisure rentals.

Avis believes that one of the critical success factors for strong travel partnerships is the marketing activity that the partners undertake together. With partners such as bmi, direct mail, joint advertising, and email activity has taken place. Other bespoke promotions have included: Home page buttons and banner advertising; Joint press and PR activities, such as national and regional competitions; Point of sale materials in Avis rental stations and partner locations; Local PR activities to support new routes, hotel openings etc and staff incentive schemes.

As well as national activity Avis also carry out targeted local plans on a tactical level to support key parts of its network. These included bespoke direct mail campaigns, advertising activity, events and promotions.

Brand Values
The company is driven by a singular vision which was established in 1965 – 'to be the best and fastest growing company with the highest profit margins in the car rental business'. These values are encapsulated in the 'We try harder.' slogan. From the 1960s, when Avis made a virtue of being second biggest but the best in terms of service, it has put the customer at the centre of the business. Empathy (understanding customer needs), Honesty (value for money and integrity) and Humanity (putting the customer first) underpin the 'We try harder.' philosophy. These values have contributed to Avis having one of the strongest and most consistent corporate cultures in the world.

www.avis.co.uk

AVON

Market

The UK mass market for cosmetics, fragrances and toiletries, in which Avon operates, was worth around £3.3 billion in 2004 (Source: TNS).

Avon is the world's largest direct seller and sixth-largest global beauty company. In 2004, through its unique network of 4.9 million independent Representatives, Avon handled over a billion customer transactions.

The UK is the fourth-largest market for Avon, with sales exceeding £280 million. Avon is the second-largest mass beauty company in the UK, and its share in the beauty market has increased year-on-year in recent years. In 2004, Avon sold more skincare items, lipsticks, bottles of fragrance, eye make-up and nail enamels than any other manufacturer in the UK (Source: TNS).

In the UK, in value terms, Avon is number one in the mass fragrance market, number two in the mass cosmetics market and in the top five in the mass skincare market (Source: TNS).

Achievements

For more than 117 years, Avon has provided women with the opportunity for financial independence, often at times and in places where few other options exist. It provided one of the first opportunities for women to be financially independent at a time when their place was traditionally in the home. Today, almost five million independent sales Representatives worldwide enjoy the flexible earnings opportunity that Avon provides. In the UK there are eight million customers buying from 160,000 independent Avon Representatives.

As a business of women serving women, Avon established the Avon Breast Cancer Crusade in 1992. Since then, Avon has raised more than £10 million to support breast cancer charities. Long term charity partner, Breakthrough Breast Cancer, has received almost £9 million, which has contributed significantly to the establishment of the Toby Robins Research Centre and the ongoing work that is being done there. More recently, Avon has committed funds to support the Breakthrough Generations Study, which aims to understand the lifestyle factors that may influence the risks of contracting breast cancer. By sponsoring Breakthrough

Breast cancer's Fashion Targets Breast Cancer campaign in 1998, 2000, 2002 and 2003, Avon had a dramatic effect in bringing the subject of breast cancer to the attention of the public and the media. The campaign unites the fashion industry to raise awareness and funds for research into breast cancer. Today, there are 16 more Macmillan Breast Care Nurses, funded by Avon, working with women to help deal with the day-to-day practicalities of breast cancer. In 2002, Avon celebrated its ten-year anniversary of supporting the fight against breast cancer. £1.6 million was raised for Breakthrough Breast Cancer, exceeding Avon's target of £1 million and representing a third of the charity's annual running costs.

In 1989, Avon was the first major beauty company to stop testing products and ingredients on animals and

does not request others to do so on its behalf. As the first major company to stop animal testing, Avon took a proactive role by opening an in-house cell culture facility, dedicated to the development of vitro alternatives to testing on animals. Today, Avon actively supports FRAME (Fund for the replacement of Animals in Medical Experiments), the foundation working to find viable alternatives to animal testing.

History

Avon began life as the California Perfume Company in America in 1886, giving women the opportunity to earn by selling fragrance and cosmetics door-to-door.

Mrs P.F.E. Albee was the very first agent taken on by the company's founder, David H McConnell, who started out as a door-to-door book salesman, giving away small bottles of perfume that proved to be more popular than the books themselves. In these early days, Mrs Albee sold her goods to her customers in much the same way as today's Avon Representatives.

In 1939, the company name was changed to Avon. Company legend has it that this happened after McConnell visited a friend in Stratford-upon-Avon and was so impressed with the area's beauty that he renamed the company and 20 years later in 1959 began trading in the UK.

From these small beginnings, Avon has established itself as a global leader in the beauty industry. Today, Avon sells in 143 countries through 4.9 million independent sales Representatives.

Product

The Avon product portfolio, covering make-up, skincare, fragrance, toiletries and hair care, is split into a wide range of brands, designed to address the needs of women across the globe.

Avon Colour is the flagship cosmetics brand, offering a spectrum of shades and products that offer value for money, market-leading technology and of-the-moment shades. Award winning Avon Colour consists of a wide range of makeup essentials as well as three targeted franchises: Perfectwear, Arabian Glow and Sheer Botanicals. The first offers long-lasting transfer-resistant make-up. The second consists of a collection of bronzing beauty

products offering a sun-kissed shimmer. The third infuses lightweight colour with botanical ingredients for fresh modern glamour.

Within the Skincare business, Anew is the number one brand, which again is segmented into three core franchises. Anew Retroactive targets the early signs of ageing, Anew Ultimate is formulated using 'gold mesh' technology to uplift sagging skin, while Anew Clinical is a selection of highly targeted products designed to provide a cost-effective and painless alternative to cosmetic surgery.

Leading the Toiletries business is Planet Spa, which combines ingredients from around the globe in collections such as African Shea Butter, Mediterranean Olive Oil and Dead Sea Minerals.

Advance Techniques is one of the fastest-growing haircare collections in the UK, designed to offer salon-professional formulas at mass market prices. Since 2003 the range has been endorsed by Lino Carbosiero, who has worked with celebrities such as Madonna and TV presenter Cat Deeley.

Avon also offers a comprehensive range of beauty supportive products tailored to meet the needs of today's women. The Fashions – which include accessories, lingerie, and jewellery collections – and Lifestyle ranges perfectly complement the core beauty product offering.

Recent Developments

2004 saw the launch of the first in a trilogy of premium fragrances. Endorsed by actress Salma Hayek, 'Today' was

designed to take Avon's fragrance business to a more luxurious level, with prestige packaging and rare ingredients. The second two fragrances, 'Tomorrow' and 'Always', launched in 2005, complete the trilogy.

In 2005, Cellu-Sculpt Anti-Cellulite Body Sculpting Treatment was re-launched with new 'Fat Burning Technology' that promises to both increase the rate of fat burning, while also preventing fat molecules from forming. Cellu-Sculpt is the bestselling product within Avon's Solutions brand and has a loyal following of women who are brand advocates.

In 2005 a new franchise was added to the Anew brand: Anew Alternative is designed to combine the wisdom of the East with the technology of the West. The product range is based on research in pharmaceutical science, combining the healing power of exclusively harvested eastern herbs with advanced western technology to stimulate the skin's natural ability to fight the signs of ageing.

In 2005, as part of its ongoing commitment to supporting the breast cancer cause through the Breast Cancer Crusade, Avon announced an association with Breast Cancer Care through the commitment of funds to their Peer Supporter Network.

PERFECT WEAR

introducing
shine supreme

PROFESSIONAL LASER RESULTS WITHOUT THE SURGERY

Promotion

Avon's primary channel for promotion is its brochure, which currently reaches one in three women in the UK every three weeks. The brochure allows Avon a unique opportunity to talk to the customer, providing detailed tips and advice at the point of sale.

The Avon Representatives and Sales Leaders also ensure the message is shared with women, with 160,000 Representatives visiting UK homes with Avon products every three weeks.

However, for customers who prefer to shop direct, Avon's online shop offers one of the widest ranges of health and beauty products in the UK.

Providing a public face for the brand is Tamzin Outhwaite, who specifically promotes Avon Colour and represents the idea of accessible glamour.

Avon's advertising is focused on its Colour and Skincare businesses, and creative executions are developed globally to address the needs of women worldwide. The 'ding dong' campaign first ran in the 1960s and has endured the past 40 years, but now a new wave of TV and press advertising is intended to give the brand a revived identity in the minds of UK women.

For Avon, maximising its advertising spend meant ensuring that slots and spaces were bought in titles and programmes where maximum impact could be created and where messages would have the greatest resonance with the intended audience. Celebrity press and TV profiling around shows such as 'Sex & the City', which provides a good fit with the target consumer group ensured the target audience would get the optimum number of opportunities to see the Avon message.

Committed to the Avon Breast Cancer Crusade, Avon has been a partner with the charity Breakthrough Breast Cancer for more than ten years. The fundraising continues with annual campaigns.

Brand Values

The Avon company vision is 'to be the company that best understands and satisfies the product service and self-fulfilment needs of women globally.'

Avon strives to offer accessible, high-quality beauty and fashion at outstanding value for money. The relationships shared between Avon Representative and Avon customer are often based on friendship rather than simply financial transactions.

www.avon.uk.com

Let's talk
about cellulite and how we hate it

Cellu-Sculpt

Stop dreaming, start believing.
You'll see tighter arms, a flatter tummy and a great deal less of your thighs*.

AVON

THINGS YOU DIDN'T KNOW ABOUT

Avon

> Avon was first to mass-market AHAs, gentle 'fruit acids' for clearer, more vibrant skin.

> Avon was the first beauty company to deliver stable vitamin C for youthful skin tone in Avon Solutions Source C.

> In the UK alone, 160,000 Representatives sell to six million customers every three weeks with the Avon brochure.

> Mick Jagger's mum was an Avon lady, while his ex-wife Jerry Hall modelled extensively for Avon in the 1970s. Other famous faces to model for Avon in the early stages of their career include Sophie Anderton, Leslie Ash, Sadie Frost and Marie Helvin.

> It is estimated that since 1959, more than four million women in the UK have been Avon Representatives in their lifetime.

> Across the world, in a year, Avon produces 600 million brochures in more than 25 languages.

Market

Born out of an idea from two housewives for a product that would guarantee perfect gravy every time, Bisto, the powder that 'Browns, Seasons and Thickens in One' was created in 1908. Nearly 100 years later, the Bisto brand is still the strongest in the gravy market.

In 2005, the gravy market was worth just under £100 million (Source: IRI). Bisto's share of this valuable market is 63.2% (Source: IRI). The nearest branded competitor, Oxo, has 9.2% market share (Source: IRI).

Bisto also operates within the dry sauces market, which is worth more than £80 million. The dry pour-over sauces market is worth almost £30 million and Bisto has a 12.2% share of it (Source: IRI).

Achievements

Despite changing lifestyles and diets, gravy – and particularly Bisto – still really matters to people.

Regardless of shifting tastes, gravy remains a firm favourite for UK households with UK gravy penetration at 77.3% (Source: TNS Superpanel).

With its broad product range, the Bisto brand caters for people with a range of tastes as well as those with different cooking skills. The Bisto brand has 100% distribution, meaning that every grocery outlet in the UK is likely to have Bisto on its shelves (Source: IRI).

Consistently high investment behind Bisto has enabled it to achieve long-term brand-leader status in its market.

Following a regional test, Bisto Rich Gravy Granules were launched nationally in 1979, in response to consumers' desire to be able to make the gravy they loved easily.

Five years later the range was extended to include chicken flavour and onion flavour granules, as well as two sauces: cheese sauce and parsley sauce. Turkey granules have since been added to the range.

In 1991, Bisto launched a new fuller flavour beef granule. Packaged in a glass jar it offered a fuller flavour than the standard granule, again in response to those consumers who weren't used to adding, or able to add, their own special touches to gravy. Fuller-flavour chicken and onion variants were added in 1993 and the whole range was re-launched as Bisto Best.

Bisto alone accounts for almost 1.3 billion meals (1.296 billion servings) a year (Source: TNS); that's why its makers are always looking at ways to improve Bisto gravy granules. In 1999 Bisto re-launched with a new improved finer granule that is easier to mix and gives smoother gravy.

Gravy Granules were voted number 16 by consumers in The Grocer magazine's 'Greatest Grocery Ideas of The Century' (January 29th 2005).

The Bisto brand is available in many countries around the world – Canada and Europe being the most significant in terms of turnover.

History

In 1908 Mrs Roberts and Mrs Patterson were cooking together and could not get their gravy just right. Their husbands both worked at the Cerebos salt works and were charged by their wives to create a product that would guarantee perfect gravy every time.

Experiments began and, later that same year, Bisto was launched. Bisto's name was derived from the unique benefit it offered: 'Browns, Seasons and Thickens in One.'

Bisto was built as a brand on its functional benefits all the way through the two wars. The Bisto Kids, introduced in 1919, were created by the famous cartoonist Wilf Owen. Their cast-off, cut down clothes and endearing mischievousness were an instant hit and by the 1920s and 1930s the kids were almost cult figures. All of this went towards securing Bisto's place at the very heart of the nation.

In fact it was only the advent of the National Health Service and the promise of a better and more prosperous Britain at the end of World War II that meant the ragamuffin kids began to seem out of place. As a result their appearance in advertising was significantly reduced.

Nevertheless, The Bisto Kids played a key role in early Bisto advertising by firmly establishing Bisto in British culture and bringing the famous phrase 'aah, Bisto!' into everyday use.

One of Britain's best-loved brands, Bisto's heritage and expertise has grown since the birth of Bisto Powder in 1908. Since then, Bisto has grown through a clear understanding of consumer needs.

It is apparent that Bisto really does matter to UK consumers – they still care whether they have gravy or not, whether it's light or dark, thick or thin, lumpy or smooth.

Product

Bisto offers products in three different sub-segments of the gravy market; powder, granules and sauces.

Bisto Powder is a gravy base, which was first launched in 1908 and was the only Bisto gravy product until 1979. This product has been found to appeal to cooks who enjoy making their gravy from scratch. Almost 10% of people that make gravy use Bisto Powder and Bisto is the brand leader with 90.1% value share (Source: IRI).

Bisto Granules were launched in 1979 as a more convenient and easier way of making gravy. With consumer concerns in mind, Reduced Salt Granules were launched in August 2003, to aid in the reduction of salt in consumers' diets. Drum Granules account for a 67.0% value share of the gravy-makers market. Here, too, Bisto is the brand leader with 67.0% value share (Source: IRI).

Bisto Best was launched in 1991 and appeals to people who like the traditional 'meat juice flavour' of gravy but prefer to prepare gravy instantly rather than from scratch. The Jar Granules segment is growing in size and importance and accounts for 15.6% value share of the

gravy-makers market. Bisto Best is the brand leader in this segment, with 61.8% value share (Source: IRI).

Bisto Gravy Sauces were launched in May 2004 and target two-person households and mid-week meal occasions. The One-Shot Gravy Sachet segment is worth more than £8 million, 8.3% of the gravy-makers market and is growing at 24.6% year-on-year (Source: IRI).

However, Bisto doesn't just make gravy. The brand offers a range of dry pour-over sauces that were first launched in 1984. In 2003, the range was re-launched with new packaging and above-the-line support. Bisto ranks second in the market in terms of volume, with a 27.1% share and is showing strong growth with volume sales up 41.0% year-on-year (Source: IRI).

Bisto also offers chilled and frozen products: Bisto Roast Potatoes, Bisto Crispies, Bisto Yorkshire Puddings and Bisto Frozen Mashed Topped Pies.

Recent Developments

It's not just rival products that Bisto strives to beat, the brand also has to remain healthy and contemporary.

Over the past century there have been enormous changes to how and what we eat, most notably in the past 25 years. The family is far less likely to sit down to a traditional 'meat and two veg dinner' every evening and far more likely to eat separately – wanting something convenient and quick. Bisto has had to adapt.

However, luckily for Bisto there has been a revival of the 'great British dinner' over the past few years. Dishes such as sausages & mash and cottage pie are becoming fashionable again. All of the products have different demographics: from the gravy powder that appeals to 'start-from-scratch' cooks, to the instant pour-on sauces for people in a hurry. So as the way people eat changes so do Bisto's products.

Recent product developments include Bisto gravy sauces, which were launched in May 2004 to increase consumption of Bisto in the mid-week meal occasion with two people. Three flavours are currently available: Roasted Onion & Ale, Rosemary & Red Wine and Black Peppercorn & Roasted Garlic.

Other recent launches aimed at getting Bisto involved around the plate are two frozen potato products: Bisto Roasts and Bisto Crispies. Both Bisto potato products have the added appeal of being infused with Bisto flavour. Further to this, a range of Bisto Yorkshire Puddings were launched in September 2004 and Bisto Frozen Mash Topped Pies in March 2005.

Bisto's packaging too has moved on to keep up to date, most recently in July 2005. This new design makes the most of Bisto's brand properties (Bisto logo; aah! and Vapour Trail) in a single impactful badge.

Promotion

The Bisto brand has been built on powerful and motivating communication. Advertising has been key to Bisto's brand awareness since way back in 1919 when 'The Bisto Kids' were introduced.

In addition, there are other very strong ciphers attached to the Bisto brand; such as the aroma trail and the words 'aah! Bisto'. Over the years, all these elements have been consistently evolved in Bisto advertising campaigns – to reflect changing needs of consumers and their culinary tastes. However, the powerful aroma trail and 'aah! Bisto' still feature in all Bisto advertising today.

Recent advertising contemporises the brand through the creative concept 'Bisto brings it together', centred around the thought of Bisto bringing people and food together. The most recent TV commercial, featuring Bisto cheese sauce rather than gravy, ran in winter 2003 and 2004 and was called 'Bisto Photos'. Posters were used in conjunction with TV advertising.

The advertising spend on Bisto products has increased over time reflecting the importance of the brand to its owner, RHM, which acquired Bisto in 1968. Advertising generally runs in key winter eating periods such as Christmas – when roasting is more prevalent.

Brand Values

Bisto aims to help consumers enhance well-balanced meals into delicious family favourites. Bisto stands for real, wholesome food and is seen as a down-to-earth brand. For consumers, the key message is 'Bisto brings the meal and people all together'.

Compliments a juicy conversation.

Bisto brings it together.

BlackBerry™

Market

The global market for mobile email is growing rapidly, with business technology research firm Strategy Analytics recently putting the value of the mobile email market at US$11 billion by 2007.

This growth is being brought about not only by businesses wanting their staff to be more productive by staying in touch while travelling, but also by a recognition from individual consumers that mobile email can make their lives easier by allowing them to stay in touch with friends and family as well as work.

Businesses are increasingly opting to invest in mobile email. A recent pan-European study by O₂ and Quocirca found that investment in mobile technology is expected to outstrip growth in traditional IT spend as businesses look for new efficiencies and opportunities. Corporate mobile spend is set to grow eight times faster than conventional IT investment in 2005, the survey revealed.

The Meta Group predicts that three quarters of UK businesses will be using wireless email within three to four years.

Achievements

The international award-winning BlackBerry® was developed and manufactured by Research In Motion® (RIM). Launched in North America in January 1999 and first introduced to Europe in September 2001, it comprises software, services and advanced BlackBerry wireless devices, integrating email, phone, SMS, browser and an organiser.

In less than five years, three million people worldwide have become BlackBerry users.

Leading consumer technology magazine, T3, wrote: "If you need to stay in touch with email while on the road, BlackBerry is currently the slickest, most convenient way of doing it – bar none." The Sunday Times Style section wrote that BlackBerry was "becoming the ultimate fashion statement and communication tool", while BBC News described BlackBerry as "a must-have accessory among senior executives and celebrities."

Indeed, this rise in profile has seen BlackBerry feature in pop videos and fashion photo shoots as well as cartoons and the device can count a host of celebrities among its fans.

BlackBerry users include everyone from employees in multinational law firms, global banks and Government organisations to Hollywood film stars, musicians and international athletes.

The recently launched BlackBerry 7100 series has won numerous awards, including What to Buy for Business, Best Buy 2005 Award, What Cellphone, Award of Excellence 2004, and Stuff, Hot Buy Award for January 2005.

Currently more than 80 leading network operators worldwide are working closely with RIM to introduce BlackBerry to corporate customers and individual users. The Java-enabled version of BlackBerry for GPRS/GSM networks is currently available in Austria, Belgium, France, Germany, Hungary, Ireland, Italy, the Netherlands, Ireland, Poland, Portugal, Spain, Sweden, Switzerland, Turkey and the UK. Further European growth is planned.

History

Research in Motion (RIM), is a market and technology leader in wireless communications. It was founded in Waterloo, Ontario, Canada, in 1984 by Mike Lazaridis, inventor, entrepreneur and philanthropist and who is still RIM's co-CEO and President.

In 1999, Lazaridis came up with the idea of 'pushing' email to a device that could fit into a pocket and the BlackBerry wireless email solution was born. In 2001, BlackBerry first became available in the UK but it was not until 2003 that the device really took off, with the launch of the BlackBerry 7230™ with a colour screen for business customers as well as individual consumers.

Celebrating its 20th anniversary in 2004, RIM reached a corporate milestone of more than one million subscribers worldwide. BlackBerry 7100 series was launched in the second half of 2004 and 14 months after reaching the one million mark, RIM tripled its subscriber numbers to three million.

In 2005, RIM has more than 2,000 employees and offices in North America, Europe and Asia-Pacific.

Product

BlackBerry is about the freedom of being in control. The idea is that someone with a BlackBerry device can be in touch when out and about, at all times. Whether a busy executive managing their work and social life, or a parent juggling a job and a family, with a BlackBerry device the individual is in control of their daily life, business and information, all through one device. With a BlackBerry device, users are always able to take a call, read or respond to an email, plan their diary or read a presentation.

Indeed, once someone has tried BlackBerry, they often find it very difficult to live without. Indeed, in a recent survey, more than 40% of business travellers said they wouldn't be parted from their BlackBerry device.

Essentially, BlackBerry is a wireless communications solution designed for mobile professionals and enterprises that want to be able to manage their business and personal communications while on the move.

When combined with a network operator's wireless data network, BlackBerry comprises advanced, lightweight devices, software and services to provide users with a wireless extension of all their communications needs.

Wireless services include email, voice, SMS, personal applications and browsing and for business users these extend to calendar, internet and intranet browsing, plus the ability to access other corporate data stored behind the company firewall. With its 'Always On, Always Connected®' functionality, the BlackBerry device remains connected at all times. Email is pushed directly to the device and the inbox simultaneously.

European carrier partners for BlackBerry include BT Mobile, KPN, mmO₂, Mobistar, O₂ Ireland, Orange, SFR, Swisscom, Telefonica Moviles, Telfort, TIM, T-Mobile International, TMO Czech, TMO Hungary, Turkcell and Vodafone.

The BlackBerry experience is now available on other handsets. Partners include Nokia, Sony Ericsson, Motorola, PalmOne, Samsung, HTC and Siemens and software platforms Palmsource, Windows Mobile, Symbian and other Java devices.

Recent Developments

BlackBerry launched the BlackBerry 7100 series in Europe toward the close of 2004. The new handset is slimmer than traditional BlackBerry devices, incorporating RIM's breakthrough SureType keyboard technology that combines a phone keypad and a QWERTY keyboard to fit elegantly within the size constraints of a traditional 'candy bar' phone design.

BlackBerry 7100v™ launched on September 16th 2004, available exclusively from Vodafone, while BlackBerry 7100t™ and BlackBerry 7100x™ were both announced in early 2005, and are available from T-Mobile and O₂ respectively.

Meanwhile, RIM has continued to develop its range of BlackBerry handhelds, launching BlackBerry 7290™ in November 2004. The handheld includes all the classic features of the BlackBerry 7200 series as well as a quad-band phone, Bluetooth® support, a brighter colour screen and enhanced memory.

The BlackBerry licensing programmes enable mobile device manufacturers to integrate BlackBerry connectivity into their handsets for both enterprises and individual users.

BlackBerry Connect enables manufacturers to integrate BlackBerry communications software and technology into their handsets but to retain their own overlying applications. Agreements have so far been announced with Nokia, HTC, Sony Ericsson, Motorola, Siemens and Samsung. RIM supports Microsoft Windows Mobile, Symbian, PalmOne, PalmSource and Java devices.

The first commercially available device offering BlackBerry Connect was the Nokia 6820 smart phone. Other devices announced by manufacturers to include

BlackBerry connectivity include O₂'s Xda II, T-Mobile's MDA III, the Sony Ericsson P910 smart phone, Motorola MPx and MPx220, and future Nokia Series 80 devices, such as the Nokia 9500 Communicator.

BlackBerry Built-In was launched on August 2nd 2004, allowing other manufacturers to incorporate BlackBerry software applications into their mobile devices in addition to supporting BlackBerry wireless services, so that users can access the full BlackBerry experience. The first handset to incorporate BlackBerry Built-In is the Siemens SK65, which was made commercially available in early 2005.

Promotion

In BlackBerry's early years, promotions targeted top Wall Street executives, for whom the proposition of instant email on the move remains extremely attractive and useful for work. These people could justify the expense of the device because, even if it saved a single deal, BlackBerry paid for itself. Wall Street executives loved it and the buzz created helped to open many doors for RIM as BlackBerry became more popular.

With the launch of the BlackBerry 7100 series in late 2004, the brand took a decisive shift to the mainstream, which was reflected in its promotional strategies. BlackBerry 7100v was launched at an event at London's luxury Sanderson Hotel. Celebrities and media were invited and BlackBerry 7100v's were given to popular personalities, helping to raise BlackBerry's kudos and position it as an aspirational device.

The launch of the BlackBerry 7100x in Dublin in March 2005 continued to reinforce the position of BlackBerry as a must-have device. Irish media and celebrities were invited to a launch event to hear music from popular singing sensation G4. The BlackBerry 7100 series is increasingly being seen as a high-end lifestyle device across Europe.

Through strategies such as these, BlackBerry has achieved high brand recognition in North America and Europe. Customers ask for the product by name and the brand has entered common parlance – with terms such as 'flirtberry' frequently used by the media to capture its popular essence.

Brand Values

The BlackBerry brand is about trust. It is a tool and an ally – a pocket-sized resource that can be depended upon to keep the user in touch with work, as well as family and friends. Quietly and unobtrusively, everything the user needs is there, easy to use, dependable and indispensable. BlackBerry embodies success, energy and immediacy.

The BlackBerry brand represents the concept of instant connectivity, and as a result is the choice of mobile professionals who feel that they gain a competitive advantage by always being in the loop. BlackBerry is trusted to provide this instant connectivity by delivering an uninterrupted wireless communication platform and 'Always On, Always Connected®' technology.

www.blackberry.com

BlackBerry

> More than 90% of people who try a BlackBerry go on to buy the product.

> BlackBerry provides more than just email – it offers games, personal productivity applications and corporate applications.

> Research conducted in 2003 suggests that users gain nearly an hour of personal time each day by being able to manage their email on the move.

> Celebrity BlackBerry users include Beyoncé, Madonna, P Diddy, Sarah Jessica Parker, George Clooney and Tommy Hilfiger.

> Mike Lazaridis, founder of RIM, won a Scientific and Technical Oscar in 1999 for developing a fast way to read time codes on film.

Market

The fashion doll market is a highly competitive arena where Barbie had reigned supreme as the number one bestselling fashion doll for 44 years.

Industry commentators never believed the day would come when Barbie's dominance in the fashion doll market would be seriously challenged, but today Bratz has the clear lead in the fashion doll battle in the UK.

The dolls 'with a passion for fashion' distributed in the UK by Vivid Imaginations, owned more than 56% of the total UK fashion-doll market by February 2005 (Source: NPD Data).

Achievements

In 2003, by the age of three, Bratz had generated US$25 billion in global revenue. In the UK in the same year, Bratz retail sales were up 287% and the fashion-doll market grew by 10%. Bratz – aimed at girls aged 7-12 – held a 21.5% market share within the fashion doll sector. Five Bratz dolls were listed in the Top 10 fashion-doll market and Lil' Bratz – designed to appeal to a younger audience from age 4-6 – reached the number two slot of the Total Mini Doll Market with 9.9% share.

By 2004, Lil' Bratz had gained 22% of the Total Mini Doll Market with a 152% year-on-year increase in sales. Seven out of the Top 20 mini dolls were Lil' Bratz.

By December 2004, Bratz's share of the fashion-doll market had reached just over 45%, making it the number-one bestseller, and it had doubled sales in less than a year to reach more than £70 million (Source: NPD Data). Today, its share is almost two-thirds of the fashion doll market.

In October 2004, Bratz was listed in the British Association of Toy Retailers (BATR) Top 10 toys for Christmas. For the first time, Barbie was not included on the list. Bratz has been named BATR UK Girls Toy Of The Year in 2002, 2003 and 2004.

History

Bratz was introduced by Isaac Larian, an Iranian Jew described in the toy industry as a 'charismatic entrepreneur'. Larian went to America to become a structural engineer in 1971 but instead he founded MGA, now the biggest privately owned toy company in the world.

In 2000 MGA identified a gap in the market for a group of dolls with a focus on friendship, attitude and a 'passion for fashion'. The first drawing of a Bratz doll was shown to Larian's seven year-old daughter Jasmin, (now immortalised as the doll Yasmin) who liked the drawing. Larian commissioned a prototype and Yasmin, Cloe, Sasha and Jade were born in June 2001 when the Bratz pack was introduced by MGA. Since then the brand has become one of the world's premier toy lines and girl's lifestyle brands.

At the end of 2002 the Bratz Boyz and Lil' Bratz were launched to diversify the range and bring the Bratz brand to a wider age group and audience.

A year later Bratz was the number one fashion-doll brand in Spain, with six of the top ten slots in the

Australian Toy Chart and over two million dolls shipped to Scandinavia.

The same year, the UK marketing and distribution rights for Bratz were taken up by Vivid Imaginations, the UK's second-largest toy company. The brand had been on sale since summer 2002 in the UK, and had taken a 21.5% share of the market by the end of 2003. The primary objective for Vivid's 2004 campaign was to double market share, the secondary aim was to build a 'lifestyle' brand for 7-12 year old 'tween' girls with products they could share with friends.

Today Bratz is the number one fashion doll in the UK with UK and Ireland toy sales alone exceeding £90 million at retail.

Product

Designed for 7-12 year olds, Bratz are red-, brown-, blonde- or indigo-haired 'multi-ethnic' dolls. Cloe, Dana, Jade, Sasha, Yasmin, Fianna, Nevra and Meygan stand 11.5in high and if they were human they would be around 5ft 6in tall. There is a black Bratz, an Asian Bratz and a Eurasian Bratz. Isaac Larian says: "Bratz are not all blonde and busty like Barbie. I decided to make Bratz multicultural. A Mexican child thinks her Bratz is Mexican, a Brazilian child thinks her Bratz is Brazilian."

Bratz are produced in Southern China, where careful attention is paid to the makeup – each doll goes through 16 workers just to paint the eyes. The dolls are dressed in miniature versions of clothes that children might see on the high street and each Bratz doll comes with a wide range of accessories.

Professional designers are employed by the brand to replicate the clothing children see on pop stars on TV shows and the clothes the dolls wear are changed three or four times a year, just like the real fashion industry. 2004 saw the introduction of a number of Bratz ranges including: Girls Nite Out, Wild Life, Sun Kissed Summer, Wintertime Wonderland, Tokyo A Go Go, Funk Out and Flashback Fever.

Alongside the core Bratz doll line runs the Bratz Boyz, Cade, Dylan, Eitan, Cameron and Koby.

In addition, there is the Lil' Bratz range – a separate set of characters designed to appeal to a younger audience from age 4-6. The range incorporates playsets and doll assortments.

Recent Developments
As an extension to the range, Bratz Babyz was launched in January 2005 along with lifestyle products introduced including room accessories and consumer electronics.

There are 11 new Bratz themes being launched throughout 2005. For example, the Rock Angelz range was introduced in the summer, supported by movie and music launches. In 2005 a CGI animated Bratz movie entered the shops, while a 26-episode TV series is set to hit TV screens in 2006 and a live action movie is planned for release in autumn the same year.

Bratz is no longer just a range of fashion dolls. It has become a complete lifestyle property for girls, with products such as the Electric Funk range, which includes the Beauty Boom Box that

Bratz licences in the UK, for products as diverse as magazines, posters, perfume, sweets, hats, tissues, underwear, jewellery, games, socks and stickers.

Promotion
Unlike many toy brands, which restrict their marketing activity to key seasonal periods such as Christmas, Bratz is supported by Vivid Imagination's heavy year-round marketing investment. Bratz marketing campaigns tap into the brand slogan 'The only girls with a passion for fashion', with the goal to mark the dolls out as toys for girls with attitude. The objective is to grow sales by 15% year-on-year to create a £90 million brand at retail by keeping the Bratz message front of mind through TV advertising, destination-channel sponsorship and the power of PR.

Throughout 2004 Bratz was advertised on TV every week of the year on key target audience channels. In 2005 Bratz advertising includes a massive above-the-line

Available now at...
WOOLWORTHS | big W

VIVID imaginations

features a reversible CD player that flips over to become a light-up beauty mirror. There's also the Livin' Bratz range, featuring real room furnishings such as the Luscious Lip lounge chair. There are 36

campaign to ensure Bratz is on air every week of the year.

In 2004, TV media budgets were quadrupled to £3 million, with five new ads running through the summer. Created for US TV, they combined live action CGI animation and the dolls themselves. There was a heavy emphasis on the dolls' fashions. The PR campaign concentrated on getting coverage in the key 'tween' girls' magazines, and the national press. A sponsorship deal was struck with girls' destination channel Nickelodeon that centred on a three-month on-air competition inviting girls to design an outfit for Bratz,

encouraging girls to express their 'passion for fashion'. The objective was to engage girls outside of traditional TV spot advertising. There were more than 2,000 entries, with the winner walking the catwalk wearing her design on air. This promotion ran in Easter 2004 and a similar mechanic repeated a year later due to its success.

Vivid focused on increasing the depth of listings at retail aiming for permanent displays and incremental growth of shelf space. Retail presentations were designed to deliver the credible brand values. Installations across retail partners around the country included an in-store Bratz 'shop' in Hamleys in May 2004, a Toys R Us 24ft feature wall across all stores for six months and prominent feature in department stores and the key catalogues.

Brand Values
Bratz – 'The only girls with a passion for fashion' – are designed to be edgy, trendy, aspirational and sociable, with attitude. Innovation is key for this inspirational, trend-setting lifestyle brand spanning girls aged 7-12.

www.bratzpack.com

THINGS YOU DIDN'T KNOW ABOUT

Bratz

> More than 80 million Bratz dolls have been sold in the past four years.

> Bratz is the number one lifestyle brand for girls aged 7-12.

> Bratz has more than 250 licensees worldwide.

> Bratz is distributed in more than 50 countries.

> The Bratz 'pack' of core dolls consists of: Yasmin, Jade, Sasha, Cloe with other characters added depending on the range.

Market

BT is one of the UK's best known companies with more than 20 million business and residential customers. Originally a supplier of telephony services, the company is also a leading provider of internet services and a major force in global networked IT services. This makes it one of Europe's leading providers of telecommunications services.

The UK telecoms market is worth tens of billions of pounds and is characterised by intense competition, whether it be for traditional voice services, mobile telephony or high speed broadband internet. This means that BT has to fight hard to win and maintain business. It is here that a well trusted and successful brand can play a vital role.

BT's transition as a company is reflected in its new identity, launched in April 2003, along with more recent marketing and advertising activities designed to raise awareness of its global IT and networking services business.

Achievements

BT is the driving force behind the successful take-up of broadband internet services across Britain. The company has rolled out services across the UK, spent millions on marketing campaigns and developed a portfolio of consumer and business products.

In April 2005, BT connected its five millionth wholesale broadband customer, beating a target set by the company a year ahead of schedule. Broadband is now one of the country's fastest growing consumer products of all time, boasting a comparatively higher take up rate than television, CD players, video recorders or mobile phones.

99.6% of UK homes and businesses will be connected to broadband-enabled exchanges by summer 2005, putting the UK ahead of any other G7 country in terms of availability.

BT's focus is now targeting ways in which broadband availability can improve people's lives, both at work through greater productivity and at home by delivering a whole range of new services.

The transformation of BT has seen strong growth in BT's global networked IT services' business. This has seen BT win major contracts with companies and organisations including Unilever, Honeywell, the Ministry of Defence, Barclays, Visa and Abbey, in

BT Equinox 1200
- See All Features
- Colour Screen
- SMS Text Messaging
- SIM Card Transfer
- BT Design

Hide Handset   Hide Base   Show Info.

addition to making substantive progress on its contract with the NHS to deliver tangible benefits to doctors and patients alike.

BT's global position has been substantively reinforced by a series of key acquisitions: Infonet and Radianz in the US and Albacom in Italy.

BT continues to make great strides in corporate social responsibility (CSR), and is committed to maximising its positive impact on society through leadership in this field. The company has been named the leading telco in the Dow Jones World Sustainability Index for four consecutive years and is the holder of the prestigious Queen's Award for Enterprise for Sustainable Development.

BT's customers and employees have raised more than £2.5 million for Childline, the cost of 875,000 conversations with children that call for help. On the environment, BT's initiatives to tackle climate change save one million tonnes of CO_2 each year – the equivalent of taking 300,000 cars off the road.

History

BT dates back to the inception of the first telecoms' companies in the UK in the early 19th century. As these companies amalgamated, were taken over or collapsed, the survivors were eventually transferred to state control under the Post Office and ultimately to the privatised British Telecommunications plc.

In its early days, UK telephone services were provided by the General Post Office (GPO). In 1896, the GPO took over the private sector trunk service and, in 1912, it became the monopoly supplier of the telephone service with some local exceptions.

In October 1969 the Post Office transformed from a Government department to become a public corporation. During 1980-1981, a series of further developments saw the responsibility for telecoms' services transferred from the Post Office and British Telecom was created.

The Government announced its intention to privatise British Telecom in July 1982 and, during November 1984, more than 50% of British Telecom shares were sold to the public. Privatisation had enabled British Telecom to become more

responsive to competition in the UK and to expand its operations globally, enter into new joint ventures and manufacture its own apparatus. Further sales of the Government's holdings of British Telecom shares occurred in December 1991 and July 1993.

In April 1991, the company unveiled a new trading name, BT, and a new structure designed to cater for the needs of different customers – the individual, the small business or the multinational corporation.

The next major development, in June 1994, was the launch of Concert Communications Services, a US$1 billion joint venture between BT and MCI Communication Corp to deliver a global end-to-end connectivity network. This alliance progressed further in November 1996 with the announcement of plans to merge the two companies and create a global telco, Concert plc. BT ultimately decided to sell its share in MCI to WorldCom for US$7 billion.

In July 1998, BT announced the formation of a 50:50 global venture with AT&T, launched as Concert in January 2000. Following a downturn in the global telecoms' market, Concert was unwound, returning its assets and customers to the parent companies.

A restructuring and debt reduction programme led to the UK's largest ever rights issue in May 2001, raising £5.9 billion and, in November 2001, BT's mobile business – re-branded as mmO2 – was demerged from BT.

The new BT Group plc is structured so that BT Group provides a holding company for the separately managed businesses which make up the group: BT Retail, BT Wholesale, and BT Global Services. Each focuses on its own markets and customers.

Product

BT supplies an extensive range of products and services to residential and business customers. These include local, national and international voice calls, narrowband and broadband internet services, ICT solutions and services for businesses and many others.

These services are underpinned by BT's core strength and are a vital part of the UK's economic infrastructure – its extensive network, updated constantly to meet the requirements of both today and the future.

In addition to this 'invisible' network, BT is highly visible through its thousands of payphones and internet kiosks. These provide a valuable service to communities across the UK. Although usage has been falling as a result of the increase in mobile

Sustainable development is vital for the success of modern business

let's make a better world

phones, BT is committed to providing a service where there is no alternative.

Broadband is at the heart of BT and the company has made dramatic progress – connecting more than five million wholesale broadband customers and making high speed internet access available to more than 99.6% of UK homes and businesses in Summer 2005. The company has also developed a series of attractive packages for consumers and businesses to ensure further success, in addition to innovative products including Voice over IP.

More than a third of BT's wholesale connections are provided to the end user through BT Retail. This division of the business offers consumers a wide choice of broadband products. These range from Broadband Basic, an introductory product, through to the comprehensive BT Yahoo! broadband service with its parental controls and stimulating content.

Recent Developments

In March 2004, BT announced radical changes to its prices for millions of customers. This revision benefited the overwhelming majority of BT customers, who continue to see the costs of their calls reduced substantially. Central to the change was the abolition of the BT 'standard' rate call, which other companies had used to give misleading price comparisons. From July 2004, BT Together Option 1 became the new 'standard' ensuring that customers could make meaningful price comparisons.

The new prices meant that BT became cheaper for most calls than its major cable rivals and within a few pence of its key competitors and were designed to ensure that BT maintains its market share in the face of competition from more than 200 other companies.

In November 2004, BT took the first step to creating the world's first fully converged fixed-mobile service by launching its Mobile Virtual Network Operator business to the corporate market, in partnership with Vodafone UK.

BT announced a major transformation of its retail broadband service in February 2005, giving the company's 1.4 million retail broadband customers a new super-fast standard. Most consumer and business customers had their speed increased to 2Mb – as much as four times faster than before.

The higher speeds pave the way for new services such as video-over-broadband and also allow customers to get more from multiple connections – ideal for families, enabling them to simultaneously connect a PC, laptop, games console or other internet-enabled devices.

BT is committed to investing more than £10 billion to replace its networks, systems and services with an IP-based '21st Century Network' across the UK by 2009. When complete, it will carry all voice, video and data traffic on a single, state-of-the-art network. Technical trials started in late 2004, with a full-scale trial scheduled to begin in 2006 – the precursor to the mass migration of customers to the new network.

Promotion

BT is renowned for the excellence of its marketing, having won numerous plaudits over the years. The breadth and depth of its marketing across its extensive portfolio makes it one of the largest advertisers in the UK.

For the past two years all BT marketing campaigns have built from a common brand platform, using the end line 'more power to you', with its focus on the customer. BT's aim is to provide services that empower the customer – whether a consumer or a business – to achieve far more through the use of these services than would otherwise be possible.

Marketing campaigns centre on three key themes – customer care, added value and innovation. These themes reflect the changing nature of BT as a company.

BT has evolved from being a simple supplier of telephony services to a provider of complete solutions that match customer needs. These solutions include telephony – both fixed-line and mobile – but they also feature email and far wider ICT services so that the customer can meet all their needs through BT.

To recognise BT's position as a global IT and networking services company, in September 2004 it launched the biggest business-to-business advertising and marketing campaign in its history. Running in multiple languages in international and local media across Europe, the Americas and Asia Pacific, it was also BT's first truly global campaign.

BT invested more than £26 million on this campaign, positioning BT as the ideal partner and guide to help enterprises negotiate an increasingly networked economy driven by digital data and communications. BT called this the digital networked economy.

Brand Values

BT unveiled a new corporate identity to replace the 'piper' logo in April 2003. The new mark was the company's first visual identity change since 1991 and only the second since it became British Telecom in 1980. The piper did an excellent job for BT and became one of the country's most recognisable marks. However, it had become associated with some outdated perceptions of BT as simply a fixed-line telephone company.

BT's business and its culture had changed so it was important to have a brand identity that represented the multi-faceted nature of the business. The new logo was designed to represent BT being in tune with the multimedia age as well as communicating the company's international reach.

www.bt.com

Sometimes just knowing that there's someone there who really cares can make you *feel better.*

feel better **BUPA**

Market

With the advance of scientific progress, overall public health is improving. Yet, with an ageing population, an expanding range of treatments and a more affluent society, the need for healthcare services is rising and consumer demand often goes beyond what the NHS can offer.

Spending on health and care cover products in the UK, including private medical insurance, health cash plans, dental benefit plans and long-term care insurance, reached £4.1 billion in 2003, according to healthcare analysts Laing & Buisson.

The largest portion of health and care 'cover', some £3.27 billion, was spent on private medical expenses cover (private medical insurance and self-insured corporate schemes). The rest consists of £417 million spent on health cash plans, £284 million on dental benefit plans (private capitation and insurance) and £136 million annual spending on long term care 'cover' products (Source: Laing & Buisson).

The number of people with private medical insurance (PMI) policies in the UK or enrolled in medical schemes self-insured by employers, was 4,155,000 at the end of 2003, down 0.2% on the previous year. This follows marginal growth in 2002 (up 1%) but overall growth of 10% in the past five years (Source: Laing & Buisson).

Private healthcare is primarily funded by private medical insurance, the market for which has boomed since the early 1980s. Of this market, some £1.1 billion in revenue, a 40% share is accounted for by BUPA, protecting nearly three million lives.

BUPA is a broadly based health and care organisation. Health insurance is just one of the markets in which BUPA operates, others include care homes, health at work, hospitals in the UK as well as funding and provision markets overseas.

Achievements

BUPA effectively pioneered the concept of private medical insurance in the UK, leading the market right up to the 1980s when rapid expansion drew a number of new groups into it. It has retained a strong lead over its competitors and remains the pre-eminent brand in a now competitive sector.

BUPA has made some highly significant contributions to UK healthcare, such as its decision in 1974 to relieve pressure on the NHS by building its own private hospitals. The first of these opened in 1978. When the market for private medical insurance mushroomed in the 1980s, BUPA's investment in hospitals proved a shrewd move. BUPA now owns a network of hospitals across the country.

Other important achievements include BUPA establishing the first truly comprehensive international private medical insurance scheme in 1982, covering treatment anywhere in the world.

It has also pioneered new relationships with the NHS, opening the first privately run NHS Diagnostic Treatment Centre at Redwood in Surrey in 2002 and carrying out thousands of operations per year on behalf of the NHS at its other hospitals.

BUPA pioneered the development of health screening and specialist occupational health services in the UK, opening the first BUPA Medical Centre in 1970. Now, in 2005, it operates 42 Wellness Centres offering a wide range of services, including health assessments, dental care, private GP consultations, musculoskeletal medicine and stress management.

BUPA is now the biggest provider of screening services, not just in the UK but also in Western Europe, carrying out 80,000 health assessments every year.

In almost 60 years, BUPA has grown to become an international health and care company at the forefront of its industry with bases on three continents and more than seven million members. A provident association without shareholders, BUPA continues to reinvest its surpluses into improved facilities such as medical equipment, the latest technology and buildings.

History

BUPA was formed in 1947 to provide strength and security for the members of seventeen regional provident associations which had existed since the late 19th century. These amalgamated on April 3rd 1947 to form The British United Provident Association which soon became known as BUPA.

BUPA was formed to provide high quality medicine and to preserve freedom of choice in health care believing that, with the National Health Service being introduced a year later, there would still be a need for some form of complementary service to enable people to choose where, when and by whom they were treated.

In the early 1950s, reality was beginning to erode some of the original principles on which the NHS had been formed and many more people started to consider the benefits of private treatment. By 1955, BUPA registrations exceeded 200,000, including 2,000 company group schemes.

By the 1960s, these numbers had doubled to 400,000 and 4,000 respectively and by its 20th anniversary in 1967, BUPA membership totalled 1.5 million people.

BUPA pioneered the concept of health screening and opened its first screening centre in London in 1970. By 1981, BUPA's membership had soared beyond all expectations to cover over three million people and the number of company schemes for employees totalled 40,000.

At that time the organisation entered a new era in its development with the opening of its own purpose-built hospital in Manchester providing patients with some of the most sophisticated facilities in the country.

The late 1980s saw BUPA's international ambitions take a huge leap when it acquired Sanitas, the largest private health care organisation in Spain, with its own medical insurance schemes, hospitals and clinics.

Rapid expansion of all services was the theme of the 1990s and BUPA now also owns and runs over 250 care homes and a network of health screening centres in the UK.

There was also phenomenal growth in its worldwide business operations and today BUPA, with over 40,000 staff across the globe, has a major presence in countries across Europe, Asia and Australia, with a range of insurance, health and care services and more than seven million customers.

Product

While private medical insurance remains the part of the business BUPA is best known for, the brand has expanded into many other areas. For example, BUPA is the UK's largest provider of care homes, has a wide-reaching network of its own private hospitals and provides health assessments and occupational healthcare solutions to companies.

BUPA Membership is the market leader in the UK market for private medical insurance, providing cover to over three million people in the UK. BUPA also provides cover for staff in over half of the FTSE 100 companies. Every year, BUPA spends £780 million on healthcare for its members, including £100 million on cancer treatments. Among the services offered to BUPA members is a personal health plan, BUPA Heartbeat, which is tailored to an individual's needs. Members also have access to information from qualified nurses 24 hours a day, through the BUPA HealthLine.

In addition to private medical insurance, BUPA Membership's range also includes critical illness cover, travel insurance, dental cover and a cash plan for everyday health expenses.

BUPA Hospitals are another important part of the group's product offering, covering a wide range or procedures and attracting a growing number of customers from the NHS.

The BUPA Wellness division offers health assessments and treatment in 42 Wellness Centres across the UK. Equipped with leading-edge technology to assess fitness and detect early signs of disease and illness, BUPA Wellness also offers customers private GP, dental and musculoskeletal services. For BUPA, the biggest growth area for Wellness services is corporate business, including on-site provision.

With the UK's ageing population and growing need for long-term care, BUPA

has also become increasingly involved in the supply of residential and nursing care for the elderly. BUPA Care Services is currently the UK's largest private provider of care home places, with 258 residential and nursing homes providing care to more than 16,000 residents. It is a little known fact that nearly 70% of BUPA care home residents are publicly funded.

BUPA International is a fast-growing part of the group, caring for approximately two million members worldwide, in places as diverse as Hong Kong, Spain, Ireland, India, Australia, Singapore, China, Malaysia, Thailand and Saudi Arabia.

BUPA's first overseas ventures in the 1970s were designed to cover British overseas territories in Gibraltar, Malta and Hong Kong. Subsequent overseas developments include BUPA Thailand, set up in 1996 and BUPA Middle East, formed in Saudi Arabia in 1996. In 2001 businesses in Singapore, Malaysia, Hong Kong and China were consolidated into BUPA Healthcare Asia.

In Spain, BUPA owns Sanitas, one of Spain's leading private medical insurance brands, providing cover to over one million members. Sanitas has now also expanded to provide care homes in addition to its hospitals and clinics.

In Australia, BUPA acquired the country's third-largest private medical insurance group, AXA Healthcare Australia, in February 2003. The group has one million members, representing an 11% share of the market.

Other products in BUPA's wide-ranging portfolio include childcare facilities and services. The group currently operates a chain of 35 'Teddies' day nurseries catering for 2,000 children aged three months to four and a half years.

Recent Developments

The UK health and care market has been changing dramatically in recent months and further developments are likely over the next few years, both due to structural and attitudinal changes within the NHS and the expansion of the private sector, which is seeing new entrants and different types of policy. As a result, new models of private care are burgeoning.

This changing context has led BUPA to the decision to move on from its successful cartoon advertising campaign,

which emphasised the accessibility of BUPA to an audience wider than might traditionally have considered BUPA services. The animation campaign improved overall perceptions of BUPA and the challenge now is to translate positive perceptions into active consideration and purchase of its products and services.

Promotion

The challenge for BUPA's marketing is to continually remind people of the benefits of private health and care in a way that makes BUPA the only and obvious brand to choose, both for rational and emotional reasons.

The advertising strategy now being used by BUPA aims to convey the simple and powerful idea that you will 'Feel Better' with BUPA. The idea is that with BUPA, customers are with the best, have excellent and pleasant facilities and prompt access to the optimum care where and when they want it.

This promise is being used across all BUPA businesses: all are dedicated to making people Feel Better, physically in terms of the standard of treatment and care they receive and, emotionally, because these standards provide reassurance and peace of mind.

The advertising uses a metaphor for the peace of mind and sense of optimism customers get from BUPA: the idea is that they feel better with BUPA in the way that a loved-one's kiss makes everything feel better, hence the 'kiss it and make it better' soundtrack to the TV ads.

This idea likens the relationship customers can have with BUPA to other valuable relationships and indicates that BUPA will look after them in a personalised way.

Brand Values

BUPA is a brand that is heavily guided by its mission statement: 'Taking care of the lives in our hands.'

Beyond this, BUPA is an organisation that has well-defined values that guide its business and brand behaviour. It is a provident association, which means that it has no shareholders and therefore re-invests profits back into its health and care business. This sense of existing for the good of the nation, rather than the City, is reflected in other ways. The organisation is committed to being ethical and accountable and respectful.

From a communications point of view, BUPA is determined to be seen as a leading and expert brand that is equally very open, accessible and empathetic. It is a warm, friendly, welcoming brand that emanates health and vitality.

www.bupa.co.uk

Market

The typical British consumer now takes at least one holiday abroad annually, but complements this with one or two domestic trips, usually the short breaks that have been the saviour of British domestic tourism since the 1980s. In 2003, the British took an estimated 104.8 million domestic holidays, including short breaks of one to three nights (Source: Mintel).

Key providers of accommodation in domestic tourism have been stimulating the demand for short breaks, by responding to changing demands and shifting away from the traditional two weeks annual holiday. Prominent in this respect have been hotel chains and traditional holiday centres, offering weekend or midweek breaks.

Even if volumes of holidays are fairly static, tourism in the UK has benefited from higher spending per trip and per day. The average spend per British holiday is increasing, reaching £173 in 2003 from £156 in 1999 (Source: Mintel).

According to Mintel, this increase is a reflection of higher expectations among consumers brought up with the standards of holidays abroad, and an outcome of domestic tourism now having a more upmarket bias. Indeed, Mintel found that the most affluent and educated (AB) respondents have the highest propensity towards taking domestic holidays or short breaks.

Achievements

Center Parcs introduced a unique, new concept to the holiday market in Holland more than 30 years ago and did the same in the UK when it opened Sherwood Forest, its first village, in July 1987 by offering short-break holidays on a year-round basis, in addition to longer stays during traditional holiday periods.

Center Parcs is now one of the most popular destination choices for holidays in the UK. More than 1.5 million visitors enjoy a Center Parcs Holiday in the UK each year, and its success can be seen by the average occupancy figures of over 90% at all villages and repeat bookings of more than 60%.

Since it arrived in the UK, Center Parcs has regularly been rewarded for its development of domestic tourism, innovation and commitment to sustainable development. In 1987 it received the 'Come to Britain' Trophy from the British Tourist Authority for most outstanding new tourism development.

Most recently, it received the Nottinghamshire Business

of the Year Award, the Prima Baby Readers Best Buy Award for Best UK Holiday and the Tommy's Campaign Parent Friendly Award for Best UK Holiday provider.

Notably, it has also been recognised for its longstanding commitment to sustainable development. Center Parcs is firmly committed to sustainable tourism and was the first in the UK leisure industry to achieve the coveted ISO 14001 standard, setting new standards for environmental awareness and care in UK tourism.

In 2004 it achieved the Forestry Stewardship Council Certification, issued for the sustainable management of its woodlands.

Center Parcs' recycling operation is well-advanced, not only ahead of other companies, but also beyond current Government targets. While local authorities throughout the UK are expected to recycle 12% of their total waste and most businesses recycle around 2%, Center Parcs recycles 18% of its total waste.

History

In 1953 Piet Derksen, who later founded Center Parcs, opened his first Sporthuis Centrum store in Rotterdam. As the first sports department store in Holland, it was an unparalleled success. Sporthuis Centrum expanded into a chain of 17 innovative and spectacular stores within just a few years.

In 1967 the 'Villa in the Forest' idea was born out of Derksen's love of getting away from the hustle and bustle of everyday life and getting back to nature. He bought an area of forest and built 30 villas, equipped with colour TV and central heating and an outdoor pool. Professor Jaap Bakema, an eminent Dutch architect, was asked to design this first all-season holiday village. He formulated a design that used simple, natural materials. There was to be nothing that did not harmonise with the woodland and strong emphasis was given to features such as large windows, which brought nature closer – guidelines that are still followed today.

More than a decade later, the first village with a Subtropical Swimming Paradise was opened. This was the first village with a volume of some 600 villas and a comprehensive village centre, all built in one go.

In 1986, with a view to international expansion, the company changed its name to Center Parcs. A year later, Center Parcs expanded into England, where the first British village was built: Sherwood Forest in Nottinghamshire.

At the beginning of the 1990s, Scottish & Newcastle became the new owner of Center Parcs and the second village in England, Elveden Forest, was opened in Suffolk. Four years later, the third English village, Longleat Forest, was opened on a 400-acre site on Lord Bath's Estate in Wiltshire. Following on from the ambitious renewal programme completed in the villages during the late 1990s, Center Parcs embarked on its millennium concept with new investments and innovations that affected all aspects of the Center Parcs product.

In 2001, Center Parcs UK (encompassing the three villages in the UK) was taken over by DB Capital Partners. A year later, the fourth UK village, Oasis Whinfell Forest, was acquired. The same year saw an £18 million investment programme at the Sherwood Forest village that saw the introduction of the new Aqua Sana World of Spa, a project to double the size of the 'Jardin des Sports', as well as new, higher quality, 'Executive' accommodation, including three- and four-bedroom villas and some luxury apartments.

In 2003, Center Parcs UK completed a multi-million pound rebuilding and development programme at Elveden

Ten Pin Bowling   Pétanque   Tennis   Nature Trails   *CenterParcs*

Short breaks at Center Parcs. Everyone is different.   For a brochure call 08708 408 438 quoting reference 11423 or visit www.centerparcs.co.uk

Forest, that saw the introduction of a new Piazza, an open Village Square area, a Sports Plaza and Sub Tropical Swimming Paradise. Later the same year, MidOcean Partners sold Center Parcs to a consortium of investors and the company was floated on the Alternative Investment Market (AIM).

On March 1st 2005 Center Parcs (UK) Group plc was admitted to the Official List and began trading on the main market of the London Stock Exchange.

Product

Center Parcs strives to offer high-quality accommodation in fully equipped villas, apartments and lodges, which are set amongst the trees and streams of the forest, each with its own private patio.

The villages are set in a forest environment, typically 400 acres in size, offering an extensive range of sports and leisure activities plus numerous restaurants, bars and retail outlets and a superb spa facility. Woodland, water and a natural, healthy environment are the essential elements.

The Subtropical Swimming Paradise is at the heart of each village. The temperature inside is a constant 84 degrees Fahrenheit, with wild water rapids, water slides, spa pool, wave pool, solaria and children's play pools, surrounded by luxuriant tropical plants and trees.

Recent Developments

It is Center Parcs policy to continually invest to enhance and improve the guest experience at its villages. During the past year several improvement projects have been completed.

At Sherwood Forest, 10 new exclusive four bedroom villas, with two-storey luxury accommodation set in private grounds with steam room, sauna and outdoor hot tub, have been created, along with a new family raft ride, 'Grand Cascade', in the Subtropical Swimming Paradise (the first of its kind in the UK), plus a new Nature Centre.

At Oasis Whinfell Forest, developments include an Aqua Sana World of Spa, refurbishment of accommodation and the addition of executive lodges. The past

year has seen the redevelopment of the central Butterfly Centre, with the addition of three new shops – 'Treats', 'Natural Elements' and 'Funtastic', and three new restaurants – 'Luciano's', 'Café Refresh' and the Pool Bar.

Elveden Forest re-opened with brand new facilities in July 2003 and in 2004 10 'exclusive' four bedroom villas were added.

At Longleat Forest, 10 exclusive four bedroom villas have been added, while the Sports Café has been completely redeveloped and offers a relaxing place to enjoy a drink or meal, with the choice of a table inside or

out on a beautiful terrace overlooking the lake. Major refurbishments have also taken place in the Plaza, with the extension of the Italian restaurant Luciano's and the introduction of a new Coffee Shop and Hair & Nails salon. New treatment rooms were also added to the Aqua Sana to enable the village to meet increased guest demand.

Promotion

Center Parcs' target market is primarily ABC1 families with children looking for a high quality break that the whole family can enjoy. In addition, young professionals and empty nesters are also attracted by the quality of the experience, the enormous wealth of activities and, most notably, the Aqua Sana World of Spa.

The Center Parcs marketing department's main aim is to identify and satisfy guests' needs and demands for their short-break holiday. Guest questionnaires are provided in each villa to gather valuable feedback on the total product offering. This allows Center Parcs to assess the success of village operations and consequently plan developments and marketing activities at each village with an integrated approach to enhance the Center Parcs brand.

The Center Parcs experience is marketed via an annual brochure, direct marketing, television advertising, with supporting information on Teletext and, increasingly, the web. The TV campaign is timed to support the annual brochure mailing in September, with a heavy emphasis in January too, a key period for planning holidays. The company has its own in-house reservations department, which deals with both bookings and brochure requests.

Direct marketing is becoming increasingly important to Center Parcs as more and more of its guests are repeat visitors. Communication with guests takes many forms, including booking incentives during off-peak periods; informing guests of village improvements; and encouraging repeat bookings; online and offline.

The Company's database provides a foundation for all strategic mailing activities and by utilising customer profiling tools such as geo-demographics and customer

lifetime values, the marketing process can be executed with precision.

The natural surroundings of the forest environments are pivotal to the Center Parcs experience. To this end, the company has in place national biodiversity plans to protect and restore ecological features native and appropriate to the locality of each of its villages. In addition, Center Parcs supports a number of environmental charities with projects throughout the UK, including The Tree Council, the RSPB, The Woodland Trust and The Young Peoples' Trust for the Environment.

Center Parcs works not only within the communities in which it operates, but also in the wider UK community. Children are a high priority for Center Parcs, which is why it works closely with a number of charities that conduct research into caring and finding cures for children with terminal illnesses. Center Parcs also donates obsolete equipment, including items such as computers, bikes, bedding and electrical goods, to good causes.

Brand Values

In a world of change and pressure 'time squeeze' has resulted in leisure time becoming priceless. Center Parcs seeks to meet the increased need to spend quality time with friends and families, to disconnect from daily routine and pressure and to enjoy hassle-free holidays and leisure.

Center Parcs aims to offer a 'short-cut to quality time' with its high quality short breaks that provide a wide choice of facilities, along with excellent service and value. It believes that the combination of nature, comfortable accommodation, a huge range of relaxing and exhilarating activities, proximity and a car-free environment, make Center Parcs an ideal choice for those seeking space, a safe environment, freedom of choice, relaxation and fulfillment.

www.centerparcs.co.uk

THINGS YOU DIDN'T KNOW ABOUT

Center Parcs

> There are more than 180 indoor and outdoor activities to choose from at each Center Parcs village.

> Each Center Parcs village is set in more than 400 acres of forest, of which less than 10% is developed.

> Oasis Whinfell Forest is home to one of the UK's few surviving colonies of red squirrels. Center Parcs works closely with Red Alert North West to protect them. Visitors can meet the squirrels during a guided Squirrel Session with a ranger.

> Center Parcs in-house reservations department can handle up to 5,000 calls per day.

CLASSIC *f*M

Market

Today, new technology is revolutionising the radio broadcast market. The advent of digital radio is already delivering its promise of up to 210 new services broadcasting via DAB, cable and satellite, while the internet has fuelled a global explosion of some 9,000 online radio services.

Digital is the future for radio in the 21st century and Classic FM is right out there in front – it was the first commercial station to go digital in 1999 and currently uses the very latest in cutting-edge technology.

Digital radio isn't the only new way of tuning in to Classic FM – 300,000 people now log on to classicfm.com every month. The website is not only packed with information about classical music, musicians and composers but also means listeners can get in touch with presenters while they're on air, vote for their favourite pieces of music and generally have their say.

The third innovation in radio listening comes courtesy of digital TV. Classic FM broadcasts on Sky Digital Channel 856. So, if people have difficulty tuning in to FM transmissions, they can still hear Classic FM in digital sound quality via their television.

Achievements

With a weekly audience of 6.2 million adults and a monthly audience of ten million, Classic FM is now the world's largest commercial radio station. Additionally, the station has half a million listeners under the age of 15. The number of 15-44 year old listeners is growing at a rate of 9% a year.

Classic FM's pioneering approach to its programming, advertising and marketing has won the station many accolades, including more than 10 Sony Radio Academy Awards. Classic FM has been voted UK Sony Station of the Year three times, having been nominated for the award on four occasions.

The Classic FM brand has also won much praise across the world of marketing, winning the Marketing Society Brand Development of the Year Award in 2002, along with the prestigious Business Champion of the Year Award from Arts and Business for its work with children. In 2003 Classic FM won Marketing Week's Media Brand of the Year Award and, in 2004, the Hollis Sponsorship Award for Education for its work in schools.

History

Something strange was afoot one summer's day in 1992. As listeners across the UK tuned in between 100 and 102 MHz, they found themselves listening to birdsong. Nothing else – just birdsong.

Then, just after 6am on the morning of September 7th 1992, instead of starlings and sparrows, Handel's Zadok The Priest rang out from radios all over the country. That great choral masterpiece heralded the birth of Britain's first independent national radio station – Classic FM. And, since then, it has become part of the fabric of British life, with 6.2 million people tuning in every week.

From the beginning, the vision was to treat Classic FM not simply as a radio station but as a brand in its own right. This philosophy has driven forward a number of new and successful ventures over the years.

Classic FM's main record label, launched in 1993, has to date sold more than two million CDs. The latest release, Classic FM Music for Babies, was released in the spring of 2005.

The first issue of Classic FM Magazine rolled off the presses in 1995 and is now the biggest-selling classical music title on UK newsstands, with more than a quarter of a million readers a month.

Add to this live concerts and events across the UK, the Classic FM Credit Card and Classic FM TV, the world's first 24/7 classical music video channel and Classic FM has transformed itself into one of the UK's premier lifestyle brands.

Product

Classical music is at the heart of everything Classic FM stands for. With a CD library of more than 150,000 tracks of the world's finest recordings, the station has a mission to make classical music an accessible part of everyone's lives, regardless of their age, which is why the station starts young, with music education in schools playing an important part in its work.

Classic FM Music Teacher of the Year Awards actively supports the inspirational work of classroom music teachers keeping music-making alive in our schools.

Coupled with this, 2004 saw Classic FM and Yamaha inspire a whole new generation of classical music lovers with their biggest ever 'Vision' schools tour. More than 50 schools participated and children got the opportunity, not only to hear a live band perform, made up of students from the Guildhall School of Music and Drama, but also

to play more than 100 musical instruments themselves. Each child was also offered their own, free, introductory music lesson and more than 90% of primary school children who attended the day later signed up.

The school tour was just one of the many highlights of Classic FM Arts & Kids Week. The week-long initiative, in association with the Prince of Wales Arts & Kids Foundation, sought to give children hands-on experience of all aspects of the arts, from poetry to dance to classical music.

Arts & Kids week is part of the commitment that Classic FM has made to encourage the 500,000 children who listen to the station every week to get more involved in music making. Classic FM also partners with Youth Music, Music for Youth and the National Children's Orchestra in developing projects that inspire young lives.

Music education remains at the heart of many of Classic FM's community activities. The radio station also works on specific education projects with its partners – the Royal Liverpool Philharmonic Orchestra, the Royal Scottish National Orchestra, the London Symphony Orchestra, the Philharmonia Orchestra, English National Ballet and Welsh National Opera.

The station is keen for listeners to play an active part in choosing the music that is played on Classic FM through its annual Hall of Fame poll. Since 1996, more than a million votes have been cast, making the chart the biggest regular

survey of classical music tastes anywhere in the world. Everyday, thousands of listeners take part in the daily online chart 'Classic FM Most Wanted' and also choose the music for the Lunchtime Requests programme.

Recent Developments

Classic FM has grown its market share year-on-year despite increased competition from new DAB Digital Radio Services.

Among the highlights of Classic FM's programmes in 2004 was the broadcast of the traditional Christmas concert for the Royal Household from Buckingham Palace. The concert, which has its roots in the late 1800s and featured one of the country's most celebrated choirs, had never previously been broadcast anywhere in the world.

A number of new series were introduced to the Classic FM schedule in 2004. Composers' Notes with John Suchet delved into the financial affairs of classical music's greatest composers. Two new shows underlined Classic FM's commitment to connecting new audiences to classical music: Backstage UK, in which listeners were taken behind-the-scenes at some of the UK's leading arts organisations and The Classic FM Guide to the Orchestra, which introduced listeners to the different sections of the orchestra.

More than three million listeners tune in regularly to Simon Bates' weekday morning show, now by far the most listened-to programme on UK commercial radio.

The station has also been busy off air, launching four new books in 2004 including Stephen Fry's 'Incomplete and Utter History of Classical Music', which has already sold in

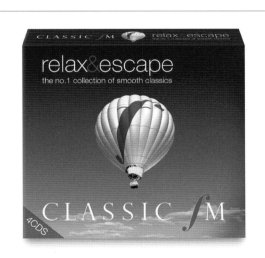

excess of 25,000 copies. The Classic FM record label also launched eight new CDs, including a range designed for first timers to classical music and which has sold in excess of 100,000 albums with releases such as 'Music for Babies' and 'Music for Driving'. An audio book, 'The Story of Classical Music', created for children and narrated by Classic FM presenter Aled Jones, was nominated for a Grammy Award.

Classic FM also took a step closer to its listeners in 2004 with the launch of 'Behind the Music' – an email newsletter that has become so popular that 300,000 listeners now request it every month. This programme-driven initiative allows Classic FM to talk about the month's highlights and allows audiences to interact with the station by making requests and giving their views.

Promotion

Classic FM's promotion has concentrated on two different target markets in order to grow its audience base. Traditional above-the-line brand advertising using outdoor, cinema, TV and broadsheet press has been used to talk to a national audience. Alongside this, strategic partnerships have been set up with music and arts organisations to promote the brand to people at a local level. These partners include festivals such as Mostly Mozart at the Barbican. Other partners include Symphony Hall Birmingham, The Philharmonia Orchestra, The Welsh Proms, Canterbury Festival, The Lowry, The Royal Liverpool Philharmonic Orchestra and many more.

In September 2004, Classic FM launched an initiative to bring the relaxing benefits of listening to the station 'in-car' to a wider audience. This industry first was its own fleet of taxis, each playing Classic FM in the back of the cab to allow new audiences to listen to the radio station.

In December 2004, Classic FM and Roberts Radio signalled their continued commitment to DAB digital radio with the announcement of a major two-year partnership. Together, Classic FM and

Roberts Radio will develop new co-branded products and drive take-up of the new technology.

To launch this initiative, Classic FM ran its biggest ever on-air digital radio promotion. The station gave away a Classic FM branded Roberts digital radio every hour for a week. More than 90,000 listeners entered the competition, making this the most successful digital radio promotion in the history of UK radio.

Brand Values

Classic FM remains committed to presenting classical music to an ever-increasing audience though the values of modernity, relevance, involvement and accessibility.

In a crowded marketplace, Classic FM retains its relevance as the antidote to both the stresses and strains of everyday life. It encourages involvement through interaction and brand extensions and, most importantly, has finally diminished the perception that classical music is elitist.

www.classicfm.com

Registered Trade Mark

Market

The Coca-Cola Company is the world's largest beverage Company and the leading producer and marketer of soft drinks. In the last 10 years, it has doubled the number of products it has in Great Britain to 80. Coca-Cola is the number one selling soft drinks brand worldwide, and in Great Britain, Coca-Cola and sugar free diet Coke are the country's two biggest soft drinks.

A renewed emphasis on health is fuelling consumer demand for choice and increasing desire for diet and light soft drinks. Currently, 34% of Coca-Cola Great Britain's volume for carbonated soft drinks is from light/low-sugar drinks (Source: Inform). By the end of 2006, that figure is expected to reach 50%.

72 Clubs. The 'Coca-Cola' Football League. The Real League.

This continuing trend has significantly strengthened the market position of diet Coke. In fact, sales of sugar free diet Coke at grocery have now overtaken Coca-Cola. Capitalising on this, Coca-Cola Great Britain invested £12 million more in diet Coke in 2005, as well as introducing a new 'Z' range of zero-added-sugar versions of the Company's well-known brands – Fanta, Sprite, Dr Pepper and Lilt.

Achievements

Coca-Cola is the world's most valuable and recognised brand, consistently heading the Business Week/Interbrand Top 100 Brands survey. In 2004, it led this global superleague with a brand value of US$67.4 billion.

The Coca-Cola Company and its bottling partners operate the world's largest distribution system, allowing consumers in more than 200 countries to drink more than one billion servings of Coca-Cola products every day.

The iconic status of Coca-Cola is thanks largely to its legendary marketing. The 1971 'Hilltop' TV commercial, featuring the song 'I'd like to buy the world a Coke', is one of the most famous advertisements of all time and broke new ground in its day for being one of the first global advertising campaigns.

Coca-Cola has had a longstanding relationship with football, lasting over 30 years in Great Britain, and from August 2004 became the new title sponsor of the Football League. Founded in 1888, this is the oldest league of football clubs in the world, and to many, represents the heart and soul of English football. The Football League renamed the divisions for the start of the 04/05 season and Coca-Cola

GB launched a number of initiatives with Powerade and Coca-Cola aiming to bring innovation and renewed excitement to the League competition. One of these celebrated fans' relationships with their local clubs by changing the familiar Coca-Cola brand colours into those of all 72 clubs, ensuring that each club had bespoke Coca-Cola branding at the ground. It also introduced the Coca-Cola £1 Million Goal Chase, challenging clubs to score more goals during the season than ever before. If they did, Coca-Cola would donate £1 million to fund a young, up-and-coming or apprentice player at each of the 72 clubs. In 2005, Coca-Cola launched an innovative on-pack promotion to give fans the unique opportunity to 'Win a Player' for their club, worth up to £250,000.

History

Coca-Cola was invented in 1886 by John Styth Pemberton, a pharmacist in Atlanta, Georgia. Even at this early stage, the power of branding was important, with Pemberton's partner, Frank M Robinson, naming the dark brown liquid 'Coca-Cola' because he thought the two Cs would work well in advertising. Having laid the foundations for the product and the brand, the two sold their interests to the Atlanta businessman, Asa G Candler in 1888.

The famous signature 'flourish' of Coca-Cola was registered as a trademark in 1893. Candler was a marketing genius and ensured that the Coca-Cola trademark appeared on countless products, from clocks to glass chandeliers.

The design for the famous Coca-Cola glass 'Contour' bottle was created in 1915. It was done to protect the brand from a growing army of imitators, determined to cash in on its success. The Company wanted to communicate to consumers that there was only one authentic Coca-Cola. Designers were given the brief to create a bottle that people would recognise as a Coca-Cola bottle, even if they felt it in the dark.

In 1919 the Candler family sold The Coca-Cola Company to Atlanta banker Ernest Woodruff and a group of businessmen. In 1923 Ernest's son Robert Woodruff, elected president of the Company, decreed 'Coca-Cola should always be within an arm's reach of desire', setting down a principle that remains central to the Company's distribution strategy today.

By the outbreak of World War II, the drink was being bottled in over 44 countries. The war helped boost the brand's international distribution and profile, as US soldiers posted abroad demanded and were sent Coca-Cola in vast quantities.

In 1982 diet Coke was launched. This was the first brand extension of the Coca-Cola trademark and an instant success: by 1984, it was the third biggest soft drink in the US and

by 1990 the second biggest soft drink in the UK.

Yet in the meantime, Coca-Cola suffered a setback. In April 1985, after extensive taste testing, the Company unveiled a new taste for Coca-Cola in the US and Canada. Consumer reaction was unprecedented – an outpouring of loyalty for original formula. The Company took heed, and just three months later the original formula was back on the shelves as Coca-Cola Classic in those countries.

Product

The Coca-Cola Company offers a broad range of soft drink brands, including carbonated soft drinks, juices, waters and sports drinks to suit tastes across the globe for all generations.

Always anticipating changes in consumer desires, The Coca-Cola Company is not only known for its world-leading marketing, but also for a new product development strategy driven by local consumer insights.

As well as introducing successful new products elsewhere in its range, the Company has applied its new product development skills to the Coca-Cola and diet Coke family, introducing brand extensions such as Vanilla Coke, diet Coke with Lemon and, most recently, diet Coke with Lime. These complement the core

Coca-Cola and diet Coke flavours, as well as Cherry Coke, caffeine-free diet Coke and Vanilla diet Coke.

Recent Developments

In 2005, diet Coke received a major investment with the introduction of the sugar free descriptor on diet Coke packaging. Also in 2005, sugar free diet Coke with Lime was introduced, with a taste specially formulated for the British public.

In summer 2005, Coca-Cola treated British consumers to a double first, introducing an all-new limited edition variant, Coca-Cola with Lemon. Great Britain was the first country in the world to experience Coca-Cola with Lemon, which itself is the first-ever limited edition variant of the core Coca-Cola brand.

Promotion

The huge value and global appeal of the Coca-Cola brand is thanks to The Company's excellence in marketing.

In January 2004 the 'Real World of Coca-Cola' campaign was introduced to Great Britain. This celebrates what makes Coca-Cola special to British consumers and brings to life what people love about the brand in an inspirational way. It also marks a revival of the brand's iconic communication, using the Coca-Cola core brand values to emotionally engage and inspire consumers.

The first ad to air in this campaign was 'I Wish'. This shows how one person can inspire others and bring people together by sharing bottles of Coca-Cola and expressing her hopes and aspirations in an infectiously optimistic way. This was the first UK-originated Coca-Cola TV advertisement to run in the US.

The long anticipated follow-up to 'I Wish' was launched in summer 2005. Called 'Bring Me Sunshine', the commercial features the song made famous by the 1970s comedy duo Morcambe and Wise, but this time as an up-tempo and infectious version sung by the American singing legend, Willie

Nelson. The ad was shot over four days and features an actor who in the guise of an ordinary man is out and about on a sunny day delivering bottles of ice cold Coca-Cola to random people he meets. The end result captures the reactions of real people to another person who is trying to connect with them through a smile, a hug and an ice cold Coca-Cola. Initially people are suspicious of his motives, but get to understand that his actions are simply a gesture of goodwill which evoke a sense of optimism and brings a smile to their faces.

The campaign also continues the long association between Coca-Cola and music. 'Bring me Sunshine' joins other classic tracks from Coca-Cola ads, such as 'Teach the World to Sing', 'Eat My Goal' and more recently, 'I Wish'.

In early 2005, a major television ad campaign was launched for sugar free diet Coke. Featuring 'Tort', an animatronic tortoise with a mantra of 'Live fast, love life and feel good in your shell', the campaign marks a shift in focus for diet Coke in the UK, from glamour to humour and fun. This reflects an increasingly important way of connecting with British consumers and also shows how the brand is broadening its unisex appeal.

As well as the Tort ad campaign, sugar free diet Coke was also supported by a massive sampling campaign. Over six million cans of sugar free diet Coke were distributed – meaning that approximately one in every eight of the UK adult population received a free can of diet Coke.

Coca-Cola has always been at the forefront of outdoor advertising and for almost 50 years has had an illuminated billboard looking down on London's famous Piccadilly Circus. With the aid of an expert team of British designers and computer programmers, Coca-Cola has harnessed the latest technology to create Britain's biggest permanent LED display on the acclaimed site, and the largest curved sign of its type in the world, bringing dynamic animated advertising to the heart of London.

Coca-Cola in Great Britain uses two major passions – music and football – to connect with and inspire consumers. In music, the successful launch of the legal downloadable music site, www.mycokemusic.com was a major success, backed by the Company's largest-ever on-pack promotion on 200 million packs, giving consumers the chance to instantly win one of 20 million downloads. In the first week, the site received a record number of visitors, with 185,000 hits.

In 2005, Coca-Cola unveiled another major music promotion, teaming up with Shazam Entertainment, a music 'tagging' service that allows people to identify tracks simply by dialling a number and then pointing their mobile phone at the source of the music, be it in a club, shop or on the radio. This taps into a new trend in how consumers access and enjoy music, using a mobile device. Once the consumer has 'tagged' the track, Shazam can then help them buy the music, or download it to their phone as a ringtone or MP3.

The link between Coca-Cola and music is also exemplified by its sponsorship of the UK's first Official Download Chart and music download sales have now reached the point where they are included in the Official UK Singles and Album Charts, which Coca-Cola also sponsors.

For more than 30 years Coca-Cola has been a committed supporter of football at all levels – from grassroots competition to sponsorship of the UEFA European Championships™ and FIFA World Cup™.

The partnership between Coca-Cola and the Football League represents the brand's biggest-ever commitment to domestic football, running for three seasons from the beginning of the 2004/05 season. In 2005, Coca-Cola launched 'Win a Player', the most successful consumer promotion for football to date. This prize draw gave consumers the chance to win £250,000 for their beloved football club to spend on a new player, or players. The promotion, open to fans of teams in the Football League and Scottish Premier League, allowed people to enter online or by text. As well as winning a player for their club, the winner was also given a personal cheque for £10,000. The promotion had over one million entries and showed that Coca-Cola understands the passion of the real football fan.

Coca-Cola not only supports international tournaments, but also grass-roots football, helping to encourage young people to take part in and enjoy the game. Coca-Cola in Great Britain oversees two major grass-roots competitions of this kind, the Coca-Cola 7's in Scotland, and the National Schools Cup in England.

Coca-Cola also has strong links with the world of fashion and design, and uses its iconic Contour bottle to showcase stunning design. In 2003 and 2004 Coca-Cola partnered with leading British designer Matthew Williamson, creating limited edition collections based on his trademark designs.

In 2005, Coca-Cola created more limited edition Contour bottles, called the 'Sunshine Collection.' The Company asked a number of celebrities to describe, through words or symbols, what brings them sunshine, giving them a red pen and a white Coca-Cola bottle to use as their canvas. Four celebrities' designs were chosen, including the shoe designer Manolo Blahnik, designer Jonathan Saunders, the DJ Trevor Nelson and the Brit Award winning band Scissor Sisters. A limited edition range carrying these designs went into production and was made available exclusively at Harvey Nichols.

Brand Values

Consumers continue to be passionate about loving both the Coca-Cola brand and the product – an insight which has led to the use of a new slogan, 'Love Coca-Cola' in its advertising. The core Coca-Cola values are optimism, togetherness, uplifting vitality and authenticity. As a product, Coca-Cola delivers uplifting refreshment.

www.coca-cola.co.uk

for those who love life

sugar free great taste

COSMOPOLITAN

Market

The magazine market has come along way since Cosmopolitan launched in February 1972. Back then, Cosmopolitan was the seminal magazine, cost 20p and sold out in three hours.

Today, it competes with more than 200 titles, all fighting for female attention and all the while fuelling an insatiable appetite to read magazines. The British market place has one of the highest per capita consumption rates of magazines in the world.

Despite the unprecedented level of competition in the women's magazine market, Cosmo has remained a dominant brand in the UK – currently enjoying its highest circulation figure for 24 years. In the second half of 2004 Cosmopolitan was the number one premium-priced women's glossy with a circulation of 478,394 (Source: ABC).

Over the same period its readership, which includes people who may not purchase a copy but may read copies passed on from friends or at the hairdresser, was 1.8 million, putting the magazine 40% ahead of its nearest competitor (Source: NRS).

What's more, Cosmo delivers a uniquely high solus readership with 791,000 Cosmo readers who do not read any competing magazine. The product is as relevant to all young British women, and unlike many other magazines does not suffer from a disproportionate weight in London with a readership split of slightly more northern girls picking up Cosmo, with its national coverage being split 52% in favour of the north and 48% in the south (Source: NRS).

Cosmo has been the Life and Relationship bible since 1972. 33 years on, in a highly competitive, time poor, and overloaded world, relevance counts for more than

from the title. In an overloaded world of products and services, readers trust Cosmo to edit out the noise and help make their consumer choices for them.

Starting with the magazine product, Cosmopolitan enjoys a multi-layered and rich relationship with readers spanning online, research, emails and events. Readers respond in their thousands allowing Cosmo to develop an ongoing meaningful and interactive dialogue.

Achievements

Since 1972, Cosmo attributes its success to the brand DNA, consistent voice and the constant ability to innovate and evolve for its generation. In February 2002 Cosmopolitan celebrated its 30th birthday. The event was reported in The Times Leader, which wrote: "Cosmo is bigger than a magazine; it is a brand, an empire, a state of mind. Brash, engaging, hyperbolic, foolhardy, wilfully witless on occasion in a way that everyone needs. Its greatest compliment has been not only that it has shaped all women's magazines in its image, but that it has transformed a whole genre of men's magazines. The new men and old (enough to know better) lads who disport themselves in Loaded and the like owe their attitude to the indefatigable Amazon that is Cosmopolitan. She could still teach them a few tricks."

In the UK, Cosmopolitan quickly became the voice of a generation with pioneering spirit. In the 1970s it fought for the social and sexual equality of women, while the 1980s and 1990s were about establishing an independent role for women. Then in the 2000s Cosmo has been standing up for balance, choice and 'doing what's right for me'. Today, as always, buying your first copy of Cosmopolitan is a rite of passage for all young women, a gateway to womanhood.

including the FT, and often on the front page, plus broadcast news – setting the news agenda for the day.

Throughout the years, the impact of Cosmo's campaigning has been recognised with prestigious industry awards including BSME Innovation of the Year in 2003 for the magazine's Rapestoppers Campaign. The magazine has also been awarded the BSME Women's Magazine Editor of the Year in 1991, 1993, 1999, 2001, PPA Consumer Magazine of the Year in 1992, and the P&G Beauty Award in 2004 for the magazine that has best supported the Beauty/Grooming Industry.

Cosmopolitan is now the world's biggest magazine with 55 international editions, holding the number one spot in 43 of the markets in which it operates. Every month, 8.2 million copies are sold worldwide and read by 39 million females. All the Cosmopolitan magazines strive to be different, using an intelligent, upfront attitude and a willingness to boldly go where others fear to tread. The magazines are designed to reach out to the millions of young women looking for self-improvement, a rewarding job, a good relationship and better sex.

History

Cosmopolitan had existed in the US since 1886, but was mainly devoted to

heritage. A magazine purchase today, is an act of trust – 'you know something I don't'.

The strengths of Cosmo are drawn from the inherent breadth and depth of content, and now as the only premium priced magazine in its sector, every feature must contribute to a package which enables a reader to both observe life and more importantly, change her life. The USP of Cosmo is to 'inspire women to be the best they can be', as a result readers feel engaged, empowered and able to achieve anything they want to.

A crucial part of the product mix is the 2,000 pages of advertising that appear in Cosmo each year. A vital source of inspiration for the readers, the advertised brands benefit from a powerful implied endorsement

Since its launch Cosmo has consistently campaigned on a variety of issues that affect women from rape to voting. In 2005 the power of the Cosmopolitan brand meant that for a three week stretch leading up to the May General Election, Cosmo was never out of the headlines. The strength of the magazine's 'High Heel Vote' campaign saw editor Sam Baker featured on the cover of The Observer, putting the 6.8 million young women in the UK who were unlikely to vote in the spotlight, which led to a piece in the Daily Telegraph headlined: 'Women's mags set the political agenda'.

Having launched the campaign and interviewed the three main political parties' leaders on issues that matter to young women meant that on some days Cosmo appeared in every tabloid and broadsheet newspaper,

fiction. It was the object of an impressive US re-launch in 1965, orchestrated by Helen Gurley Brown. In 1965 she described prevailing attitudes to relationships and sex as: "If you're single with no engagement ring in sight, then throw yourself off the Grand Canyon. If you're single and having sex, then its time to stick your head in the oven."

Following the success of the US title, based on the concept by Helen Gurley Brown, Cosmo launched in the UK in March 1972 under the editorship of Joyce Hopkirk, former women's editor of The Sun.

The first issue, supported by a 45 second television campaign by Saatchi & Saatchi, said to readers: "You're very much interested in men, naturally, but you think too much of yourself to live your life entirely through them." Its first print run of 350,000 sold out before lunchtime on the first day. The second issue had a print run of 450,000, which sold out within two days.

From the beginning, Cosmo spoke to women in a revolutionary way. For the first time sex – and more importantly sexual confidence and well-being – were discussed frankly and openly. Cosmopolitan is held by many social commentators to have done as much, if not more, to educate women – and their partners – about sex and women's health than any other communication channel.

Today, Cosmo is one of the flagship brands of the National Magazine Company, a wholly owned subsidiary of the Hearst Corporation, a publishing house that strives to recognise the

the launch of Cosmo's little sister CosmoGIRL! aimed at 12-17 year old girls and matching Cosmopolitan in style. CosmoGIRL!, launched as a dual platform with www.cosmogirl.co.uk, is designed to inspire mid-teens to 'get what you want out of life'.

Building on the strengths of its magazines, the Cosmopolitan brand has diversified into other areas, such as licensed merchandise carefully selected to fit with the brand's personality. The Cosmopolitan Collection includes handbags, swimwear, bedding, soft furnishings and beauty accessories, plus a collection of books on relationships, sex, beauty and emotional well-being.

Recent Developments
Cosmo has only had seven editors over its 33 years. The seventh is Sam Baker, who joined the magazine in July 2004 with a brief to evolve the magazine design and content. She immediately embraced the Cosmopolitan heritage and core brand values, with the re-introduction of the monthly Naked Male Centrefold and Sex and the Single Girl column.

Baker is no stranger to the world of glossy women's magazines. Having successfully re-launched the seminal teenage magazine Just Seventeen as J-17, she went on to become the award-winning editor of Company Magazine and founding editor of Shop. Under her editorship, Company Magazine experienced the most successful period in its history, with a 50% upturn in circulation. Baker's reputation as a writer earned her an incredible book-deal and she left Company Magazine to finish her first novel, Fashion Victim. Now completed, the book will be on sale in Summer 2005, also marking Baker's first anniversary as Cosmo editor.

Promotion
Cosmopolitan is a benchmark women's magazine brand. To its readers, it is as relevant now as it was in the 1970s, 1980s and 1990s.

Today, with 33 years of brand saliency, The National Magazine Company is investing in its brand to ensure continued success and ringfence as well as protect the unique position as it has successfully done for the last 33 years. 2005 marks the first of a three year brand communication campaign, the first above-the-line strategy since 1972.

importance of magazines as brands. Its philosophy is to create and nurture brands – not just magazines – and to focus on developing and fostering readers' experience of the brand.

Product
Cosmo's core business is the magazine, which now has an extended family with Cosmopolitan Hair & Beauty and Cosmopolitan Bride, both of which are unique to the UK. In addition, 2001 saw

The campaign unveils a new strap line 'Bring out the Cosmo in You', which is designed to reflect Cosmo's 'be the best you can possibly be' and to reinforce its 'Fun Fearless Female' positioning.

Created by London creative agency Clemmow, Hornby and Inge, the headlines include: 'Conserve energy, light up the room yourself', 'Behind every great man there'll be a queue of them' and 'Give your relationship the kiss of life'.

Brand Values
Cosmopolitan's mission is to celebrate fun, glamour and a passion for life, and to inspire young women to be the best they can possibly be. It achieves this through its eight core editorial pillars: Relationships and sex, men, real life stories, beauty & shopping, careers, emotional health and well-being, issues and campaigns. The essence of the brand is encapsulated in a carefully defined set of core brand values glamorous, sexy, intimate, fun and fearless, with a passion for life.

www.cosmopolitan.co.uk

THINGS YOU DIDN'T KNOW ABOUT

Cosmopolitan

> More than 125 male celebrities have posed naked for Cosmo, including Burt Reynolds, Roger Moore, Vidal Sassoon, Lenny Kravitz and Graham Norton. The first naked centrefold, in April 1972, was Paul de Feu – Germaine Greers' husband at the time.

> Cosmo cost just 20p when it first went on sale in 1972.

> Michael Parkinson, Melvin Bragg, Helen Fielding and Jilly Cooper have all been contributors to Cosmo.

> More than 400 issues of Cosmo have been published.

Market

Outside of the industry, DHL is often still referred to as a courier company – a term that harks back to the days when international packages were accompanied throughout their journey by a single person. To this day, many people still believe that the DHL man who collects a package for their office or front door is the same person who will be delivering it in New York, Tokyo or wherever.

In reality, this image of the company (and the industry) is 20 years out of date. Today, DHL alone handles over 100 million packages a year in the UK and more than one billion worldwide. DHL is no longer a company that just carries urgent documents for those that can afford it – it is an essential partner for thousands of businesses providing fastest possible access to markets and customers around the world. The boom in e-commerce is also widening DHL's traditional customer base to include more and more home consumers who are using the internet to shop around the world. Not surprisingly, the speed and peace of mind that DHL provides is highly valued.

The express and logistics industry is a crucial facilitator of trade, productivity and investment and global revenues are estimated to be over €1.5 trillion. The market is highly competitive and to survive it is no longer enough to just ship goods from point A to point B.

Achievements

DHL invented the international express delivery industry, pioneering the concept of international door-to-door delivery of time-sensitive documentation and later expanded the concept to include parcels and dutiable items.

The secret behind DHL's growth over the last 35 years has been in delivering what its customers want – a factor supported by the fact that many of the companies that started doing business when it started operating remain customers today.

Throughout its history, DHL has made real breakthroughs – political and technological – on behalf of its customers. In the mid 1970s, it was the driving force behind postal reform in the US, championing the vision of tailored value-added services for business that were different to those offered by the postal authorities. The company has also successfully harnessed technology to keep its service levels at the forefront of the market. In 1979 it developed one of the first word-processing computers in the world, the DHL1000, which greatly increased the efficiency of processing orders and documentation. In 1983, it was the first express delivery company to introduce a 'track and trace' system, helping customers to follow the progress of their deliveries.

DHL's unofficial motto has always been 'first in, last out'. This relates to the company's global reputation for operating in virtually every country in the world and, in particular, for maintaining a presence under difficult and often dangerous circumstances. DHL was the first delivery company to re-open in Afghanistan and was the first air operator allowed to fly into Baghdad airport following the removal of Saddam Hussein. Not surprisingly, the company's unrivalled delivery network is also relied upon by governments and aid agencies during times of emergency or crisis – the tsunami disaster in Asia being just one recent example.

History

The name DHL was made up from the initials of the three company founders Adrian Dalsey, Larry Hillblom and Robert Lynn. Together they had an ingenious idea: they personally flew shipping documents from San Francisco to Honolulu in Hawaii allowing ship cargoes to be cleared by Customs before the actual ships had even arrived. This saved shipping operators a fortune by substantially cutting down wasted days in port and gave birth to a new industry – international air express.

After that things took off fast. In 1970 DHL obtained a foothold on the US East Coast, expanded into the Pacific rim in 1971 and, in 1974, established its first European base in London. Since 1977 DHL has also had a presence in the Middle East, and in 1978 DHL leased its first office space in Germany. Realising early on that the transfer of data via fax significantly reduced the business potential of classic document delivery, the year 1980 saw the addition of express shipping of dutiable goods as a new service. In 1983 DHL was the first express services provider brave enough to venture into the Eastern block and the first to enter the People's Republic of China in 1986.

The Deutsche Post World Net group has held a stake in DHL since

1998. The full acquisition of this now worldwide market leader by the German global player in 2003 represents a milestone in the company's history.

Product

DHL has five strong brand areas: DHL Express, DHL Freight, DHL Danzas Air & Ocean, DHL Solutions and DHL Global Mail.

DHL Express provides express and time definite shipping – but much more than traditional international air services. A brand new road express service to mainland Europe and one of the largest same day delivery networks in the UK and Ireland are just two features of the new DHL Express portfolio. It is a service not just for businesses but also for consumers. DHL delivers to retail outlets and to consumers who have purchased from traditional catalogues, online sites or even auction sites like eBay.

DHL Freight handles partial, full and special deliveries for all of Europe, moving goods by road, rail and combined transport.

DHL Danzas Air & Ocean specialise in airfreight and sea transport along with freight forwarding for major industrial projects.

DHL Solutions operates in the realm of storage and procurement logistics and has a specialist division for high street retailers.

DHL Global Mail offers international outbound letter mail to business customers.

What makes DHL unique in 2005 is its ability to offer any type of delivery for any size of shipment to virtually anywhere in the world. With a fleet of 250 aircraft, 75,000 vehicles, 5000 offices in 227 countries and more than 170,000 staff, DHL is a formidable operation.

Recent Developments

2003 marked a 'rebirth' of the DHL brand. The Deutsche Post World Net group concentrated all express and logistics activities under the internationally renowned brand of DHL. The same year DHL substantially strengthened its network inside North America through the acquisition of the US express company Airborne.

The visual integration of DHL into the corporate design of Deutsche Post World Net is part of the Group's strategic branding decision. DHL adopted the major corporate design elements of the group such as the colour yellow and typography. The DHL logo was slightly modified while keeping its most characteristic and familiar elements.

Promotion

DHL is one of the best-known brands in the world, which is partly due to a number of memorable marketing campaigns. (Ten years after the event, many still recall the DHL campaign featuring the Diana Ross song 'Ain't No Mountain High Enough'.)

The global DHL re-launch campaign focused around the statement 'More': DHL can now do even more than before with more speed, more power, more efficiency, more services and more products. The 'More' message was translated into the various individual national languages of Europe, Asia and Africa. The globally run 'Pyramid' television advertisement reflected DHL's comprehensive logistics expertise. The message: The ancient Egyptians would have relied on DHL when they were building the pyramids.

Another important promotional platform for the company – certainly as an internal marketing and team building tool – is the long-standing DHL EuroCup football tournament. Founded in 1982, the competition started life as a small friendly competition between colleagues from the Netherlands, Belgium and the UK. Nowadays, it is an annual tournament with 3,000 employees from over 20 countries competing.

Brand Values

Perhaps the greatest testament to the DHL brand is that 'to DHL' something has become a generic term around the world for sending an item in the fastest possible way.

As a pioneer and continual innovator in the logistics sector, DHL capitalises on the extensive experience of its specialised divisions Express, Freight, Danzas Air & Ocean, Solutions and Global Mail to refine its unique product portfolio. The brand stands for enduring attributes such as speed, reliability, transparency, professionalism, flexibility and most of all closeness to the customer. DHL knows precisely the wishes and needs of its customers by virtue of its local presence throughout the entire world.

www.dhl.co.uk

DIRECT LINE ®

Market

A total of £8 billion is spent in the UK on motor insurance annually by more than 35 million private motorists, all of whom are legally obliged to insure themselves and their cars as well as other people against injury and damage.

The 1990s industry price war helped to push premiums down for many motorists but resulted in a battle for supremacy among the growing number of companies in an overcrowded market.

The introduction of direct selling, which cut out the middleman, helped to change the face of the insurance market. The approach to selling insurance over the telephone was pioneered by Direct Line. The simplicity of its selling methods modernised the world of motor insurance and revolutionised the insurance market across all sectors from motor to home insurance, pet cover to life assurance. It also raised the expectations of millions of customers in terms of value for money and customer service.

Growing use of the internet – by 2004, 52% of UK households had internet access (Source: National Statistics 2004) – added further changes to the market structure. More than 25% of UK internet users purchased a financial services product online in 2003 (Source: Forrester 2003).

Today, Direct Line is the UK's leading direct motor insurer and one of its largest home insurers. Direct Line operates in four geographical territories – the UK, Spain, Italy and Germany – and in the UK alone employs over 10,000 people. In total, there are more than 7.5 million Direct Line policyholders.

Achievements

Direct Line is one of the biggest and best-known general insurance companies in the UK. The red phone has become the icon for a business renowned for having transformed financial services following its arrival onto the UK motor market 20 years ago.

Direct Line used its unique business model across many UK insurance sectors – from motor, home, travel, pet and life insurance to mortgages, loans and savings – quickly establishing itself as a leading player in each, and also internationally in motor.

By dealing direct with customers over the telephone and using sophisticated computer technology to streamline processes, Direct Line has passed the resulting cost and efficiency benefits in the form of cheaper premiums and faster service, delivered at a time to suit customer needs.

Direct Line has over four million UK customers who buy more than five million products annually. 3.1 million UK drivers are insured by Direct Line, as are over one million homeowners. In addition, Direct Line Pet and Travel Insurance are both leading providers in their sector. Home Response 24, Direct Line's newest product launched in 2002, continues to grow.

Announcing a 30% year-on-year increase in the number of policies sold online in 2004, www.directline.com is also a leading UK internet general insurance provider.

Direct Line's international expansion has also enjoyed great success. 1.6 million Direct Line policies are owned outside the UK, and in Spain, it is the largest tele-direct motor insurer with more than one million policies. In 2004, all territories: Spain, Italy and Germany, enjoyed growth rates of more than 15%.

History

Direct Line is a wholly owned subsidiary of the Royal Bank of Scotland. When it launched in 1985, Direct Line was the first insurance company to use the telephone as its only method of selling motor insurance policies direct to customers. Using the advantages afforded by its technological efficiency, it was able to reduce premiums for millions of motorists while offering a faster, more efficient and convenient service than had ever before been available.

Such was its success in the motor insurance sector that in 1988 Direct Line went on to use the same business model to challenge the grip that mortgage lenders exercised on the home insurance market, introducing buildings and contents insurance as its

second core product. During the 1990s, the company added other financial services, including mortgages, loans, pet and travel insurance, to its portfolio of products, quickly establishing itself as a leading player in each new market.

In 1998, Direct Line entered the roadside recovery service, mounting a direct challenge to traditional motor breakdown companies. Its individual approach enabled it to price significantly lower on average than existing companies and as a result Direct Line Breakdown now has more than 850,000 customers.

Building on its reputation for providing a fast and efficient service, Direct Line began operating via the internet in 1999. In typical Direct Line style, the company quickly grew to become a leading UK internet general insurance provider. Key to the success of Direct Line's web operation is its full integration with services offered by telephone, ensuring a seamless customer service.

International expansion has always been one of Direct Line's aims. In 1995, it embarked on its first overseas venture in Spain with Linea Directa. In March 2001, its geographical expansion continued in Europe and resulted in the red phone brand being launched in Germany, and Italy at the start of 2002.

Product

Each of Direct Line's products are designed with the same basic philosophy – to offer customers a clear, straightforward, good value alternative to products that are sold through traditional distribution

Value and expertise

DIRECT LINE ®
CarInsurance

20% introductory discount on your Home Insurance

0845 246 3122
directline.com

DIRECT LINE ®

Direct Line Insurance plc. Calls may be recorded. Conditions apply.

An **EXCLUSIVE** addition to your policy

24 hour vet helpline

Expert advice when you really need it

- Friendly professional advice from a vet or veterinary nurse, 24 hours a day
- For the cost of a local call you could save time and money while keeping your pet in the best of health
- An exclusive service for Direct Line Pet Insurance customers

DIRECT LINE ®
PetInsurance

in association with vetfone

channels. Products are designed to be adapted to the needs of individual customers and customer service is at the heart of the Direct Line proposition. All staff members are trained in customer care and sales processes are reengineered to cut out complicated forms and jargon. One of Direct Line's earliest revolutionary actions in this respect was to remove the need for motor insurance 'cover notes' by arranging for all documents such as policy schedules and insurance certificates to be laser-printed immediately and forwarded by first class post to customers, usually for delivery the following day.

better govern the financial services industry and to protect consumers.

In an industry first, Direct Line announced in late 2004 that its motor policyholders' No Claims Discounts would not be affected if they were involved in an accident with an uninsured driver. Ever the consumer champion, Direct Line has worked hard with industry bodies and the media to reduce the number of uninsured drivers on UK roads.

of public recall, helping to heighten awareness to levels normally associated with high profile consumer brands. The red phone icon became a huge success with UK consumers, representing innovation, value for money and leading customer service. It is now also well on the way to achieving similar recognition overseas.

Today, the famous red phone continues to appear in all of Direct Line's advertising and marketing communications and is a constant 'cheeky but likeable' symbol of Direct Line's brand personality. It evokes feelings of friendliness, fun, innovation and the arrival of a 'rescuer' – emotions rarely associated with the dry world of insurance.

Innovative technology also helps to keep down costs and reduce premiums. For example, most customers use credit cards or Direct Debits to pay for Direct Line products so that payments can be processed electronically, keeping overheads to a minimum.

Automated call handling systems also ensure that the company can quickly and effortlessly re-route its 15-plus million calls each year between its six call centres around the country. As a result, the length of time customers have to wait to speak to an operator is kept to a minimum.

Recent Developments
In January 2005, responsibility for regulation of the financial services industry was shifted to the Financial Services Authority (FSA). Direct Line is fully compliant with the new FSA regulations, which were designed to

Telephone Voice Recording was introduced earlier in 2004 to further protect the interests of Direct Line customers. All conversations are now recorded, enabling Direct Line to ensure that the level of cover offered accurately reflects the information provided by each party and simplifying claims and complaints processes by reducing the number of forms required.

In 2003, Direct Line launched artificial intelligence software onto its website to provide a simple and fast way for customers to ask questions and automatically receive answers at every stage of the internet transaction process. Reflecting Direct Line's ongoing commitment to providing customers with efficient, direct service via multiple channels, this technology now answers thousands of questions every week.

Promotion
When Direct Line launched in 1985, its aim was to sell cheaper car insurance direct to customers using modern technology to speed up and simplify the sales process while keeping costs down.

The company's first television advertisements appeared during the late 1980s but its branding breakthrough came in 1990 when the first television commercial featuring the distinctive Direct Line red phone on wheels appeared on UK screens.

Soon after its introduction, the Direct Line red phone and its associated jingle rapidly established high levels

From January 2004, Direct Line took on the sponsorship of the Channel 4 suite of home and lifestyle programmes, including Location Location Location, Grand Designs and Property Ladder. This sponsorship provides a natural link and a strong opportunity for Direct Line to showcase a range of products, including Home, Home Response 24 and Direct Line Financial Services.

Charitable sponsorship remains an important focus for Direct Line. The company is continuing its partnership with Brake, a non-profit safety organisation that works to stop death and injury on UK roads and care for people traumatised by crashes. It is also continuing its work with Victim Support, the national charity for victims of crime, by funding research into improving the support given to victims of burglary.

Direct Line has also been a keen supporter of Comic Relief. In 2005, more than 300 staff volunteered time and Direct Line its phone lines to raise upwards of one million pounds for charitable causes in the UK and internationally.

Brand Values
Direct Line has set itself a mission to succeed. The company as a whole strives to treat customers in a way that is always people-focused, challenging, passionate, action oriented and straightforward. It is customer-focused, innovative and pioneering. Its level of consumer awareness in the UK is high, reflecting the success of the red phone icon. The culture is non-hierarchical and 'can-do', allowing the business to come up with new ideas and translate them into concrete benefits for customers as quickly as possible.

www.directline.com

THINGS YOU DIDN'T KNOW ABOUT

Direct Line

> In Direct Line's first three months, it gave 9,000 motor insurance quotes over the phone. It now handles this number in one day alone.

> Direct Line's first office opened in 1985 in Croydon with just 63 staff. Direct Line now employs well over 10,000 people.

> The person who sold Direct Line's first policy is still with the company, working in Sales and Customer Service in Croydon.

> Direct Line sells a motor insurance policy every six seconds of every working day.

> 10 million motor policies have been sold in the UK since Direct Line's launch.

> A customer notifies the company of a claim every 30 seconds.

⌖ DOCKERS®

Market

In the UK, 36 million pairs of men's trousers, not including jeans, are sold each year (Source: TNS). This is the market in which the Dockers® brand competes.

Dockers®' primary consumer target within 'casual men's bottoms' (excluding jeans) category is 25-34 year old males who account for approximately 70% of its overall consumption.

Within this age group, average consumption for UK men is 1.3 pairs per year per person, compared to women in the same age group at 3.2 pairs. Roughly 60% of men's bottoms are sold in the retail or mass channels, but since Dockers® is a wholesale brand, it does not compete in these channels, and is chiefly sold through department and multiple chain stores and fashion independents throughout Europe.

In the UK, Marks & Spencer, ASDA/George and Next are the largest retailers within the total 'bottoms' category. But the main competitors to the Dockers® brand include Gap, Topman and Zara within the own-brand retail channel, and Polo Ralph Lauren, Gant, Calvin Klein, Hackett and Tommy Hilfiger in the branded wholesale channel.

Achievements

The Dockers® brand is a registered trademark of Levi Strauss & Co (LS&CO.), which was founded in 1853 by Bavarian immigrant Levi Strauss. The parent company is one of the world's largest brand-name apparel marketers with sales in 2004 of US$4.1 billion across more than 110 countries.

In less than 20 years since its conception, the Dockers® brand has become one of the world's largest casual apparel brands, generating annual worldwide net sales in 2004 of approximately US$0.8 billion, including more than US$25 million in licensee royalties.

Launched in 1986 in the US, the Dockers® brand soon became the leader in casual pants. It remains the leading casual pants brand in the US and has a worldwide presence, with sales in more than 50 countries in North America, Latin America, Asia and Europe. The Dockers® brand was piloted in Europe in 1993 and launched a year later, and is now sold in approximately 20 European countries, offering total casual outfits to its target 25-44 year old male consumer.

In 2004, the Dockers® brand celebrated its 10th anniversary in Europe. Along with a new sub-range called Made In History, which returned the Dockers® brand to Levi Strauss & CO.'s 19th century workwear roots, a European web presence was launched for the first time at www.eu.dockers.com. This provided an

original user experience, holding all the individuality of the Dockers® garments and adopting many of the brand's design elements. Available in five languages – English, Italian, French, German and Spanish – the website not only allows consumers to enter the world of the Dockers® brand, but also to experience the current season's collection from the comfort of their own home.

The online product catalogue is interactive and allows the user to 'Choose a Look' by mixing and matching tops and pants to create personal wish lists, which can be emailed or printed out. The store locator provides information on where to find the range and, by adding these stores to a wish-list, consumers can easily identify where to purchase their favourite Dockers® products.

The www.eu.dockers.com website won 'Best Commerce Site' at the Flash Forward Film Festival 2004 in New York.

History

The first military khakis were developed by a British lieutenant stationed in India during the 1840s. He replaced his troops' stifling uniforms with loose, white, cotton versions, which were dyed with plant extracts to help the soldiers merge into the dusty terrain; the shade became known as British 'khaki', the Hindi word for dust-coloured.

After the US military's experience with stiff, restrictive uniforms prone to shrinking and shredding in the field during World War I, they commissioned the development of a tougher yet breathable, comfortable yet durable fabric. The result was Cramerton® Army Cloth, created by the US fabric mill, Galey & Lord. Dockers® continues to employ this heritage fabric in its K1 pant, a reconstruction of the original World War II

Army-issue, along with other seasonal pants and jacket styles, identifiable by the 'Cut From the Original Cloth™' twill tag inside the garment.

The earliest recorded detail of non-denim trousers in the LS&CO. company archives was in 1906, although the company was known to be producing styles before this date.

Business was good for khakis after the war. Young returning veterans brought khakis back with them, as they had been issued with them as their military uniform. Their younger brothers and friends, who had not been to war, wanted to emulate them and began wearing khakis themselves.

In 1955, Levi's® 'Casual' Line started making twill pants and in 1958, 'Tab Twills' were introduced, made from the Cramerton® cloth. During the 1960s, numerous styles of casual pants were introduced, made of twill, corduroy and Bedford cord although these disappeared in the early 1970s as denim dominated the market.

Jeans became an icon for social change in this era, first through images of civil rights marchers wearing denim, and later anti-war protesters in jeans. Khakis were the pants worn by college students who didn't protest, and who were thus considered part of the 'establishment'.

It wasn't until 1984, when the Levi's® brand in Argentina developed a line of 'nautically-inspired' fashion jeans that the name 'Dockers', reflecting the English term used to describe longshoremen, came about. The Dockers® brand was introduced in the US in 1986 and in Europe in 1994 to bridge the gap between jeans and dress pants.

The Dockers® brand became the key to the 1990s casual code when 'Casual Friday' was an office buzzword. Since then, men's style and employer's attitudes have diversified and the Dockers® brand has expanded from a line of men's casual pants to collections of tops, underwear, outerwear and accessories.

Product

The Dockers® brand specialises in the design and manufacturing of khaki trousers, offered in a variety of fabrics and a wide range of colours across its standardised fits: D1 Extra Slim, D2 Slim, D4 Regular, D5® Classic and the looser Relaxed Fit. To provide a total look and enhance the wearing experience, each season new styles are introduced and existing styles updated across the portfolio, and a complete range of tops and outerwear are made available to further express the Dockers® brand and its presentation at retail.

The latest Dockers® seasonal collection provides clothing designed to keep wearers comfortable while maintaining a contemporary, urban

edge. Fabrics, finishes and colours are geared up for winter – washed-down moleskin, brushed twills, box cotton and over-dyed bleached denim come in authentic faded work-wear blues, oranges and greys highlighted with vintage reds and yellows.

Fall/Winter 2005 also sees the launch of the Dockers® Industrial range, inspired by LS&CO.'s US workwear roots. Vintage pieces have been sourced and archive detail examined and re-interpreted for modern-day wear, keeping many of the original features. The 'Industrial Regular Mark II' pant features over-dyed, bleached denim, double-front closures and triple-stitching for an industrial feel.

The key outerwear piece of the collection is the 'Pacific North Parka', a three-quarter-length, down-filled and hooded parka with a vintage finish to give the garment a truly worn look.

In addition to its clothing lines, Dockers® Europe has exclusive licensing agreements to produce a range of belts, bags, luggage and small leather goods with Brington Industries and bodywear with Schiesser Lifestyle GmbH, all under the Schiesser® brand label.

Recent Developments

In order to ensure greater integration and collaboration with the rest of the European operation, the Dockers® organisation will be located in the Levi Strauss Europe Brussels Headquarters as of summer 2005, thus increasing opportunities for leveraging resources

across the organisation. LS&CO. intends to build on the global strengths of the brand by ensuring that the positioning of the Dockers® brand is aligned across Europe, the US and the rest of the world. This is intended to give the Dockers® brand consistent global positioning so that the brand's attributes are recognised throughout the world. The Dockers® brand will build on its foundation of casualwear by focusing on style and performance.

Promotion

In March 2003 the Dockers® brand launched its biggest marketing campaign to date in support of its innovative liquid-repellent 'Zero-Care' and 'Clean Fabric System' products. Drawing on the principles of Easy Care, and without compromising on comfort or silhouette, the Zero-Care system guaranteed no-iron, non-crease, quick-dry products, offering a further development within the realms of easy living. The fabric technology harnesses a patented INVISTA™ Teflon® finish, creating a product that resists liquid and stains. The fabric treatment acts like an invisible shield, withstanding hot coffee, red wine and even rich cooking sauces, keeping the product cleaner for longer. The line was launched in stores across 22 European cities in Spring 2003, supported by a major integrated communication campaign including TV in Spain. In the UK, outdoor mega-sites were placed in high-traffic areas in London, Manchester, Glasgow and Dublin, supported by local press advertising and

advertorials aimed at targeting commuters and after-work socialisers. The campaign was further strengthened with impactful six-sheet campaigns, including interactive 'Adquarium' executions in London and Manchester which featured a pair of Dockers® pants apparently suspended in a bubbling tank of water.

Since 2003, the Dockers® brand's marketing activity has focused on extending its reach through public relations and impactful retail execution. To amplify the liquid-repellent message, interactive windows enabling consumers to effectively spray water onto khakis via an external touch-pad were installed in major retailers.

For 2004, a brand new retail identity was created and launched, evolving the brand's presentation from the 'pants wall' execution, which had established itself as the retail format of the 1990s.

The launch of the 'Made In History' equity range in Spring 2004 enabled the Dockers® brand to increase its distribution to retailers selling more premium lines of casual wear and capture the interest of the Style press, raising overall brand awareness. Associated product-placement programmes seeded limited-edition pieces with industry and celebrity personalities.

The Mega Window project, involving live art installations in major department stores throughout 2004, grabbed consumer interest in London and Dublin and across France, and is being rolled out further in 2005, for example, in Italy.

LS&CO. believes in giving back to the community. Within Europe, Levi Strauss & Co. and the Levi Strauss Foundation (LSF) fund community projects in 12 communities across 10 European countries. Grants are developed proactively in co-operation with local Levi Strauss Europe (LSE) staff. Each year a philanthropic budget of around US$1 million is spent on community projects in Europe. In one recent two-year period, the Dockers® brand's employees alone donated an additional €33,000 to local projects in Amsterdam, the home of the Dockers® brand at that time. Over the past 10 years, the LSF has donated an additional half a million dollars to support HIV/AIDS, ethnic minority groups and disaster relief in the Netherlands.

Brand Values

LS&CO.'s corporate values – empathy, originality, integrity and courage – are the foundation of the company and also define its brands. These values help to determine how Dockers® competes in the marketplace, how it exists as a business entity in society and how employees work together within the company. The Dockers® brand is a trusted menswear brand that was launched as the original American khaki pants brand for the 'regular guy'. Born in the city of San Francisco, with an attitude that liberated men from existing dress codes, the brand's heritage as a khaki pants leader and specialist has evolved into its current brand character: stylish, optimistic, humorous, genuine and versatile. The Dockers® brand is a statement about a way of life, for men who strive to live life to the fullest.

www.dockers.com

DURACELL®

Market

The battery market is currently worth £319 million (Source: IRI/GfK) in the UK alone and a staggering 90 million batteries were sold between June and August 2004 alone (Source: IRI/GfK), highlighting the success of this multi-million pound market.

There has been a substantial growth in AA and AAA batteries or 'cells' in recent years, which has primarily been fuelled by the sales of high-tech devices such as digital cameras, CD walkmans and MP3 players which require portable power solutions.

Battery manufacturers are now working closely with devices manufacturers to introduce modern, slim line products that better meet the needs of today's consumer. On average, shoppers buy around 25 batteries a year (Source: IRI/GfK) and Duracell®, the UK's market leader, continually leads the category with an extensive product profile to power these trends.

Achievements

Since Duracell®'s arrival in the UK in the 1970s, the popularity of alkaline batteries has risen and zinc batteries have been in decline.

By the late 1980s, Duracell® had achieved the successful elimination of virtually all mercury from its batteries and made dramatic improvements to performance. In the three decades of Duracell history, the life expectancy of an AA cell has increased by nearly 100%, while remaining much the same in terms of size and design.

In 1992, Duracell® gained the British Standards Kitemark for product excellence and 1995 saw the introduction of titanium dioxide to its batteries, which acted as a catalyst to make the other ingredients work harder and give more power.

In 1996 Duracell® introduced its Powercheck™ battery tester on-pack and then on the actual cell to determine how much life the battery had left. Duracell® then went one step further in monitoring the lifespan of a battery by printing 'best before' dates on all packs and batteries.

At the turn of the new millennium, Duracell® earned the prestigious Gold Lion at the Cannes International Advertising Festival in 2002. The award for 'Best Event' was presented to Duracell® for its spectacular use of the London landmark, Battersea Power Station, when it launched its new range of Duracell® Ultra M3 batteries.

The former power station, which overlooks the River Thames, was transformed into four giant replica Duracell® Ultra M3 batteries to celebrate the occasion.

2003 saw the launch of Duracell® Solutions, where each of the five major cells was assigned a colour to help consumers select the correct battery sizes.

The following year saw Duracell® as pioneers in the latest in portable-power technology with the introduction of the first-ever CP1 lithium primary prismatic battery into the UK market. The high-power lithium primary prismatic battery was developed in direct response to the demand for a portable 'always ready' source of power for compact digital cameras. Its design enable manufacturers worldwide to design thinner, sleeker devices and it won an Innovation Award at the PMA Convention and trade show in Las Vegas in 2004.

2005 sees the launch of the equivalent innovation in portable audio power – the Duracell® LP1 alkaline prismatic battery. It is developed in direct response to consumer demand for a slim line audio power source to cater for those on the move and has already been adopted by leading audio device manufacturers.

Duracell® continues to lead and innovate the category with the introduction of its new and improved formula across Duracell® Plus and Duracell® Ultra M3 in April 2005. Duracell®'s new improved formula enhances technological performance across Duracell® Plus and Duracell® Ultra M3, resulting in longer-lasting portable power.

History

The 21st century marked the 200th birthday of the battery, which was invented in 1800 by Alessandro Volta who described it as a 'construction of an apparatus of unfailing charge, of perpetual power'.

The Voltaic Pile battery, based on Volta's design, was constructed in 1813 and covered 889 sq ft – a far cry from the slim line cells being launched today.

The first portable batteries were seen at the turn of the last century where they were used in conjunction with flashlights – so called because the battery power could only sustain an intermittent light. By World War I, batteries were being used extensively in communication equipment and from there technology moved fast, simultaneously reducing the cell size and increasing its capacity.

The story of Duracell® began in the early 1920s with a scientist named Samuel Ruben and a manufacturer of tungsten filament wire named Philip Rogers Mallory. Ruben and Mallory united inventive genius with manufacturing muscle, which was the bedrock of Duracell® International, revolutionising battery technology.

In the 1950s, Samuel Ruben went on to improve the alkaline manganese battery, making it more compact, durable and longer lasting than anything before it. At about the same time, Eastman Kodak introduced cameras with a built-in flash unit that required more power than zinc carbon cells could provide. The cameras needed alkaline manganese cells but in a new size, the AAA – this put alkaline cells on the map – and the Duracell® brand was introduced in 1964. Soon, the consumer market for Duracell® batteries rocketed.

Today, Duracell® continues to lead the way with continuous product innovation, recently reflected in the New Improved formula across its Duracell® Plus and Duracell® Ultra M3 cells, as well as the world's first slim line Prismatics range.

Product

Over the past 40 years, Duracell® has built a reputation for manufacturing and supplying superior batteries that consistently

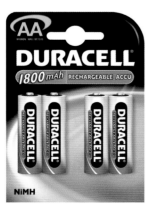

lead the market in performance, quality and innovation. Duracell® recognises that different devices demand different levels of performance and offers a range of products to ensure consumers can select the right battery for the right device.

The two major brands are Duracell® Plus, suitable for everyday devices and Duracell® Ultra M3, specially formulated for today's high-tech devices such as digital cameras and MP3 players.

In addition to its core portfolio, Duracell® offers a range of speciality batteries for watches, electronic, security, photo lithium and photo devices as well as NiMh rechargeable batteries, which boast vibrant packaging introduced in 2004.

Duracell® is also renowned for its collection of Duracell® Torches, suitable for the home, car, outdoors and personal use, with the introduction of Duracell® Kids torches in 2005.

which enable device manufacturers to design thinner, more portable devices that run on convenient, 'always ready' power that does not require recharging.

In August 2005 Duracell® launched Kids Looney Tunes torches – a collection of five torches reflecting the Looney Tunes characters and the Duracell® bunny.

Promotion

Duracell® is known for its long-lasting portable power solutions and clearly reflects its key messaging in advertising and media support.

In 2004, Duracell® once again showed its support for the Government's Fire Safety campaign by running a number of regional editorial competitions across the UK to win a home fire-safety kit – this support will continue in September 2005.

The Duracell® European Toy Survey is now in its sixth year and gains credibility for asking the toughest audience of all – children – to vote for their top 10 toys. A hospital tour around the UK and Ireland takes place in September and the campaign extends to the important lead-up to Christmas with a number of radio live-link interviews.

READY FOR BLAST OFF?
Duracell's New & Improved Formula is our very latest advance in battery technology. Duracell has packed in extra power to make our batteries last even longer and take you further than ever before.

NEW & IMPROVED DURACELL

Recent Developments

The New Improved Formula launch in April 2005 once again reinforced Duracell®'s position as market leader at the forefront of technological innovation. The enhanced performance is reflected on-pack across Duracell® Plus and Duracell® Ultra M3 and meets consumer and trade expectation for consistent superior performance.

Duracell®'s latest innovation in portable power is seen in the Duracell® Prismatics range, a new line of primary prismatic batteries for emerging digital cameras and portable digital audio devices, two of the fastest growing device categories.

The new prismatic batteries are revolutionary in their sleek, flat design,

Duracell® builds an emotional bond with consumers through a shared interest with sport by supporting the FIFA World Cup in 2002 and the preparation of the 2006 World Cup Sponsorship.

In 2005 the Duracell® Powerhouse appeared at some top UK summer music festivals, reinforcing Duracell®'s connections with music and the 16-34 year-old music consumers who are known for their usage of high-tech digital devices.

This activity was supported with a series of advertorials and sponsorships in men's lifestyle and music press as well as editorial competitions to win tickets to the festivals and cutting-edge MP3 players. The activity guarantees a consistent ongoing profile for Duracell® among this consumer audience and creates an opportunity to highlight Duracell®'s key brand messages.

Last but not least, Duracell® is well known for its legendary Duracell® Bunny icon, which remains the face of the brand for consumers worldwide. 2003 saw the anniversary of the iconic Duracell® Bunny as it celebrated its 30th birthday.

Brand Values

Duracell® is the UK's number one battery brand (Source: IRI/GfK) and remains at the forefront of technological innovation within the market. By producing reliable, longer-lasting portable power solutions that meet the demands of the modern day consumer, Duracell® remains the trusted market leader.

www.duracell.com/uk

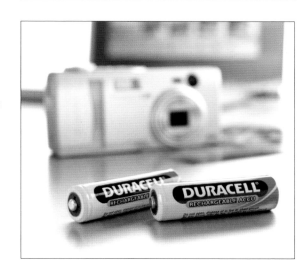

dyson

Market

Dyson launched its first no loss of suction vacuum cleaner, the Dual Cyclone™ DCO1 in 1993 and today, one-in-three UK homes has a Dyson vacuum cleaner.

Dyson vacuum cleaners are now available in 38 countries, with around two thirds of its sales coming from overseas. Indeed, Dyson machines are bestsellers in Europe, Japan and Australia.

Two years ago Dyson launched in the US, the world's largest vacuum-cleaner market. It is already the number one vacuum cleaner in the US, a notoriously difficult market to crack.

Dyson's total profits, which more than doubled to £102.9 million in 2004, are invested into Dyson's lifeblood – research and development.

Achievements

Vacuum cleaners first appeared in 1901, but the technology stood still for almost a century, until 1978. James Dyson – frustrated with his so-called top-of-the-range cleaner clogging and losing suction – ripped apart the bag and began the first of 5,127 prototypes. After 15 years of developing and defending his Dual Cyclone technology, James Dyson finally launched the DCO1 in 1993.

Instead of a bag that clogs with dust, Dyson vacuum cleaners use cyclones and centrifugal force to separate the dirt, dust and debris from the air. The dirt is collected in a clear bin, which in 1993 was seen as rather radical and a possible hindrance by some conservative retailers. However, within two years of going on sale, DCO1 was the UK's bestselling vacuum cleaner, its success fuelled by word-of-mouth recommendations.

Dyson machines are also exhibited in museums around the world including Science Museum in London, the San Francisco Museum of Modern Art and the Danish Design Centre in Copenhagen.

Everyone joining Dyson has the opportunity to build their own machine in their first week. Whether they work in finance, graphics or engineering, each understands how their machine works and what makes it different.

James Dyson passionately believes that more people should appreciate the importance of engineering. The James Dyson Foundation was established to support design and technology-related education and every year Dyson engineers go into schools and universities to hold workshops both in the UK and overseas. More than 700 students are given hands-on experience of design engineering every year.

Dyson also loans its reverse-engineering education boxes to schools. Each box contains a vacuum cleaner for product analysis, a DVD and case studies to help students understand more about industrial design and engineering.

As well as educational endeavours, the James Dyson Foundation also supports scientific and medical research. £1.7 million was raised by the Foundation for Breakthrough Breast Cancer, while supporting Sir Ranulph Fiennes' Antarctica Solo expedition. Nearly £2 million was raised for the Meningitis Research Foundation and between 2003 and 2005, Dyson raised £500,000 for the charity CLIC (Cancer and Leukaemia in Childhood).

In the past ten years, Dyson has received numerous awards including Philanthropist of the Year in 1997; Design Week's Designer of the Decade in 1999 and 2000, Japan Industrial Designer's Association award in 2002, and a Queen's Award for Innovation in 2004.

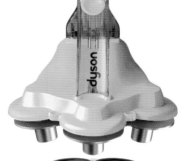

History

James Dyson has always looked for ways to make technology work better. In 1969, whilst studying at the Royal College of Art, he helped design the Rotork Sea Truck, a flat-hulled, high-speed landing craft. Jeremy Fry, Rotork's founder, taught James about experimentation and step-by-step development.

In 1974, James Dyson invented the Ballbarrow. The Ballbarrow used a

ball instead of a wheel, preventing it from sinking into soft ground, it had big feet – giving it stability – and a tough plastic bin that didn't rust.

In 1978, when renovating a new home, James became frustrated with his new vacuum cleaner. It clogged, lost suction, let out a dusty smell and generally made a mess. James turned this frustration into a quest to finally dispose of the dirty bag and develop a vacuum cleaner that did not lose suction.

After five years of frustration, perspiration, obsession and creation, he came up with his patiently-awaited answer – Dual Cyclone™ technology. James met the major vacuum cleaner manufacturers who each dismissed his invention, possibly due to the prospect of lost revenue from replacement vacuum cleaner bags.

It was Japan, the home of consumer electronics, which recognised James' invention for the technological revolution it was. Licensed in 1986 under the name of G-Force, the pink and lavender machine, which was designed by James, sold for £1,200 each.

In 1992, using G-Force royalties, James was finally able to set up his own factory and start manufacturing his own machine under his own name in the UK. The first DC01 rolled off the production line in May 1993 and became an instant success. Six years later, the Dyson Research, Design and Development Centre opened in Wiltshire.

The same year, Dyson was forced into a long court battle with Hoover over patent infringement. Hoover was eventually found to have infringed Dyson's design and was ordered to withdraw the offending product from the market and pay compensation of £4 million.

Product

Based in Malmesbury, Wiltshire, 350 Dyson engineers and scientists constantly strive to develop new and better technology and in 2005 alone, Dyson invested £50 million in research and development.

Dyson's cyclones have evolved into Root Cyclone™ technology, giving greater cyclone efficiency. Dust and air

flow into the main outer cyclone, where the larger particles and fibres are removed. The air then passes through the shroud, which acts as a dust and fluff separator. After the air has passed through the shroud it then passes into the inner chamber.

The inner chamber has multiple exits. The air passes into each inner cyclone where it is spun, creating high G forces that remove very fine dust. The fine dust is expelled into the centre section of the bin. Clean air passes into the top chamber and exits through the pre- and post-motor filters and out through the exhaust.

In addition to vacuum cleaners that don't lose suction, Dyson engineers developed two-drum washing machine technology, which replicates hand-washing and reduces wash times. Two drums rotate in opposite directions, so the clothes dance around the drums, opening up the fabric so that water and detergent can permeate the weave, ensuring a quicker and more thorough wash.

Rigorous testing is fundamental to Dyson. Engineers conduct 30,000 hours of testing every month and use 150 different mechanical test rigs to replicate and exaggerate the usage of vacuum cleaners in the home. An acoustics team spends all day, every day analysing noise and vibration levels in a semi-anechoic chamber. In addition, Dyson uses a replica house in which to test its products in situ.

Dyson also makes machines that are better at preventing and destroying allergens in the home. Its in-house microbiology lab has one of the few pure house dust-mite cultures in the UK.

Recent Developments

Released in Japan in June 2004, the DC12 is Dyson's smallest vacuum cleaner. Designed exclusively for the Japanese market, it is powered by the Dyson Digital Motor, a switched-reluctance motor that spins at more than 100,000rpm – seven times faster than a Formula One car engine. Incorporating aerospace materials, the Dyson Digital Motor took more than six years to develop and unlike conventional vacuum cleaner motors, has no fixed magnets, no carbon-emitting brushes and no commutator.

The Ball™ is Dyson's latest vacuum cleaner and marks the biggest step forward since DC01. While traditional uprights are rigid, cumbersome and tiring to use, with The Ball™, Dyson engineers have placed the body of the machine on top of a ball, which houses the motor – its centre of gravity. This gives the machine great manoeuvrability; cleaning is more efficient as it quickly zig-zags around furniture.

Promotion

Dyson sales originate principally from word of mouth and store staff recommendations. Marketing at Dyson is about exploring technology and showing people why its machines are different.

James Dyson says: "For me, the best designs are the result of someone questioning everything around them – looking at the same things as everyone else, but thinking something different. Good design is about how something works, not just how it looks. You can easily fall out of love with something if it doesn't work properly – but you stay in love with something that performs and works properly."

Brand Values

James Dyson believes that products and technology should simply work properly.

Dyson's visual communication is simple and focuses on the engineering of the machine itself. All communication represents engineering values and functionality rather than style.

www.dyson.co.uk

early learning centre

Market

The UK toy market was worth more than £2.2 billion in 2003 and was growing at 5% per annum (Source: Mintel, September 2004).

The core under-six age-group sector accounts for 16%, or £345 million of the UK toy market, and it is this highly aggressive sector in which Early Learning Centre competes.

Early Learning Centre faces increasingly stiff competition in its marketplace, not only from high street toy retailers such as Argos and Woolworths but also from the rise of internet retailers and the recent expansion of supermarkets into the toy category.

Yet, while the competitive landscape has become more intense, Early Learning Centre continues to be the leading toy retail brand in its sector and has seen its market share rise in recent years.

Achievements

From its humble beginnings as a home-run mail-order business, Early Learning Centre has become one of the most familiar and respected brands on UK high streets. As well as its 213 stores in the UK, it also has over 50 franchised stores in 13 countries around the world.

In addition to its multi-national status, Early Learning Centre is also a truly multi-channel business, with its own dedicated stores, 44 concessions in Debenhams department stores, products supplied to leading stores such as Sainsbury's and Boots, and a successful direct business through both mail order and the internet. The online channel, www.elc.co.uk, was launched in 1999 and proved such a success that it achieved full profitability in its first year and won the New Media Age Best Retail Website award in 2003.

But perhaps Early Learning Centre's greatest achievement, and the secret of its success, is that it has never strayed from its founding purpose – to help children develop and learn through play.

Over the years, Early Learning Centre has received countless awards for its innovative products, which are all designed to stimulate children's development whilst giving them a huge amount of fun. In the Annual Prima Baby Awards 2004, Early Learning Centre won no fewer than five awards for its Baby Activity Pool, the Lavender Lamb Arch & Quilt, Doll's House, Baby Ducks bath toy and Fairy Stories & Nursery Rhymes Audio Tape. In the 2004 Right Start awards, the company won a Bronze Medal in

the Best Toy Category for its Wooden Pirate Ship and was Highly Commended for its Learn to Dress Rosie toy.

Most recently, Early Learning Centre won the Tommy's Parent Friendly Award 2005 for Best Toy Brand.

History

Early Learning Centre was established in 1974 by John Beale. Like many great entrepreneurs, his idea was born out of a personal frustration – he simply couldn't find sufficiently inspiring toys for his own children – rather than an ambition to get rich. So he set about creating a toy business that would inspire and stimulate children to develop as they played.

Initially the business was based on a book-club model, whereby customers were sent a monthly selection of toys to try out with their children, from which they could choose what to keep or return.

This principle of enabling customers to try toys with their children before purchase is still important to Early Learning Centre today. Indeed, Early Learning Centre stores are unique in encouraging customers to take products out of boxes so that their children can experience playing with them before the decision to purchase is made. Early Learning Centre stores still devote every Tuesday morning to 'Playtime', when customers are invited to play with lots of new toys and join in organised activities and competitions.

Back in the mid 1970s, customer demand for Early Learning Centre toys was strong enough for Beale to open the first store, at 67 London Street, Reading, with a second following in Oxford in 1977. By 1980, the business had 10 stores across the country and the main warehouse was moved to Swindon, where it remains.

In 1982, Beale sold 51% of the business to Fine Art Developments. By 1984 the business had rapidly expanded to 90 stores and John Beale sold his remaining shares. John Menzies group bought the business in 1985 and continued the store expansion, reaching 213 stores soon after.

Leveraging the power of the Early Learning Centre brand name, the company began selling its own-branded products to Sainsbury's in 1997 and also began a concessions' business in Debenhams stores in 1999, the same year that the online business began.

In 2003, a range of Baby and Toddler Early Learning Centre branded products was launched in Boots the Chemist, again adding to the reach of the Early Learning Centre brand.

In 2004, the business was bought by Eagle Investments and became part of Chelsea Stores Group (along with the children's emporium, Daisy & Tom). Both the Chairman of Chelsea Stores Group, Tim Waterstone (founder of book retailer Waterstone's) and the CEO, Nigel Robertson, bring a wealth of retail experience to Early Learning Centre.

Product

The heart of the Early Learning Centre brand is the products it sells. The retailer spends more than £1 million a year on new product development and launches more than 750 new toys every year.

As a result of this investment – and a reflection of the power and distinctiveness of the brand – 80% of Early Learning Centre sales are its own-branded products. These are all designed to stimulate children's development in a host of different ways and Early Learning Centre prides itself on working closely with child development experts, from child psychologists to nursery school teachers and with Mums and children, to design and create the products.

The range of products is not only segmented by age group, but also development area. It breaks down into nine categories:

'Baby and Toddler' – these are the first toys to awaken the senses and encourage early exploration; 'Sport and Activity' – these are toys to help children get active, strengthen muscles and help develop co-ordination; 'Learning is Fun' – toys that encourage letter and number recognition and help prepare for school; 'Making Music' – musical toys to help children express themselves and develop self-confidence; 'Bookworm Corner' – introducing children to the world of reading, stories, knowledge and understanding; 'Puzzle it Out' – fun puzzles and games to help children develop reasoning skills; 'Let's Pretend' – imaginative toys that help children explore their identity and develop self-confidence; 'Action and Adventure' –

adventure toys that stretch the imagination and encourage group play and social skills and finally; 'Art and Creativity' – drawing, painting and making toys that develop creativity and self-expression.

Recent Developments

Following the acquisition of Early Learning Centre by Chelsea Stores Group in 2004, the brand is enjoying a renaissance.

A programme of store refurbishments is underway, aimed at creating an inviting, inspiring and interactive retail environment for children and parents to enjoy spending time in, while also making the stores easier to navigate. There are areas where products can be tried out, as well as information and advice points on how Early Learning Centre products help children develop.

The packaging is undergoing change too. Designed by packaging design specialist Parker Williams, it now includes helpful icons to demonstrate how each product helps with child development along with 'Play-tips' on each pack that give parents some helpful ideas on how to get the most out of playing with their children.

At the same time, Early Learning Centre is stepping up its commitment to developing cutting-edge, unique products that are designed around the developmental needs of children. Every month an innovation team, which includes designers and leading experts in child development, creates new product ideas to fill Early Learning Centre's shelves, ensuring that the retailer's in-store offer continues to be unparalleled.

Early Learning Centre is also developing closer and richer relationships with customers. For example, it recently launched the Baby & Toddler Toy Guide, a combined customer magazine and catalogue that gives ideas and inspiration for playing with babies and toddlers and helping them make the most of their critical first years of development.

Promotion

Historically, Early Learning Centre has relied on the power and distinctiveness of its brand offer and has not needed to spend large sums on advertising in order to encourage custom.

Its most powerful promotional tool has always been the catalogue, which has become a well-thumbed reference book in many households with children under the age of six. In fact, four million copies are distributed every year in the UK and Ireland alone. Available in store and also mailed out to customers, the catalogue is not only used for buying products directly but also as a browsing aid for subsequent purchases in store and online.

The shop windows of Early Learning Centre's 213 stores are an excellent promotional tool to drive footfall into stores.

Early Learning Centre also promotes heavily to those buying gifts, who constitute around 40% of its customers. These promotions tend to focus on the idea that giving an Early Learning Centre product is about more than giving just a toy, it is about giving the gift of creativity, learning, confidence, or music, to a child.

In recent years, direct marketing has been the most effective way to communicate with customers, with high levels of segmentation available, working with partners such as the pregnancy and new-parent direct marketing and sampling company, Bounty.

Early Learning Centre also supports those who are involved in child development. It gives childminders, nurseries, playgroups and schools a 10% discount on all products to encourage them to use products that will help children grow.

The company is also a proud supporter of the NSPCC, working with customers to raise more than £500,000 to help children and families in need.

Brand Values

Early Learning Centre is very well understood in the minds of consumers, perhaps because it has grown out of a deep insight that most people would agree with: when children are playing with the right kind of toys, play can be enormously beneficial to their development. Indeed, this insight provides the binding glue for the group of consumers who find that Early Learning Centre provides the best choice of toys for their children.

The Early Learning Centre brand is about child development, but is also about having fun. As far as the Early Learning Centre brand is concerned, each individual child can develop, no matter what level they begin at. Early Learning Centre's brand attitude and product range are designed to help every child explore their own potential in their own way.

The core offer of Early Learning Centre is: a range of products that provide creative, stimulating play to benefit children's development. And the core idea is: Helping children be all they can be.

These two concepts fuel every aspect of the brands expression, from the products in stock, to the participative 'open-box' nature of the stores, to the helpfulness, supportiveness and expertise of the staff, to the added-value advice and information that Early Learning Centre makes available to its customers in its catalogues, on its packaging, and on its website.

www.elc.co.uk

Elastoplast

Market

The First Aid Dressings category, which includes plasters, dressings, bandages and tapes, is notoriously low interest, with consumers generally purchasing to ensure their cupboards are stocked for future use. Nevertheless, in late 2004 the market was worth £62.7 million, with plasters or 'strips' constituting 60% of all category sales (Source: IRI).

Although own-label dominates the category, with 49.9% share, Elastoplast is the number one brand in the market, with 29.4% share of the category (Source: IRI).

The market is seasonal, peaking during the summer months when consumers tend to stock up in order to go on holiday. Although new product development accounts for a small proportion of the category – around 1% of value sales – innovation is key to driving growth in what is already a mature market.

There is a high degree of overlap between First Aid Dressings purchasers and purchasers of antiseptics, foot care and supports (Source: IPSOS Brand Image Monitor Study).

Achievements

Acquired by Beiersdorf from Smith & Nephew in 2000, Elastoplast has consistently been the leading brand in the First Aid Dressings market and as such the brand has become synonymous with plasters.

Elastoplast has built a solid and enviable reputation as the most recognisable and trusted First Aid Dressings brand in the UK, with 97% of people recognising the brand and 81% of people having bought an Elastoplast product (Source: IPSOS Brand Image Monitor).

Known as Elastoplast in the UK and other Commonwealth countries, the brand trades under Hansaplast across Europe and Asia, Curad in the US and Curitas in South America; together forming the world's leading First Aid Dressings brand.

History

It was around 1880 that the ingenious pharmacist Paul Carl Beiersdorf and the young doctor Paul Gerson Unna met. This was the start of a most valuable collaboration that was to last for 10 years and a friendship that was to last until Beiersdorf's death in 1896.

Unna, the doctor, urged Beiersdorf to help him in his quest to find a way of applying exact dosages of medication to treat various skin diseases. Beiersdorf, the pharmaceutical technologist, rose to this new challenge and developed a product – the gutta-percha plaster dressing – to meet the requirements that Unna had identified.

For the first time, here was a product that used the absorption capacity of the epidermis to treat the skin. Here was a completely new type of plaster that was the first to offer an accurate dosage of medication for skin treatments. On March 28th 1882, Beiersdorf took out a patent to protect the manufacture of his medicated plaster.

From then on, Unna provided Beiersdorf and his team with a seemingly endless supply of ideas. The gutta-percha plasters were followed by ointments, pastes in stick form and medicated soaps. By 1890 the product range consisted of 105 types of gutta-percha plasters and 30 kinds of medicated soaps.

Around the same time, Smith & Nephew, founded in Hull in 1856, was expanding into wound dressings. 30 years later, Lohmann AG a company specialising in the development of medical devices, adhesive tape systems and non-woven fabrics, invented Elastoplast (Tensoplast) Fabric – a new innovative kind of cloth spread with adhesive, which could be used on both bandages and dressings of various sizes.

The British patent for the manufacture of novel adhesive bandages and the corresponding rights to the trademarks of Elastoplast were bought by Smith & Nephew in 1927, giving the company the right to manufacture, sell and distribute the product in all countries that were part of the British Empire.

In 1931, Lohmann was forced to sell the Elastoplast manufacturing rights and trademark to Beiersdorf AG. This marked a new agreement between Smith & Nephew and Beiersdorf, whereby the latter could manufacture and sell elastic plasters in the British Empire and Britain, but not under the Elastoplast name. Smith & Nephew could sell elastic plasters outside Britain but not under the name Elastoplast.

Two years later, Smith & Nephew granted Beiersdorf's subsidiary in Britain a non-exclusive licence to manufacture and sell Elastoplast surgical bandages in the UK.

At the turn of the millennium in 2000, Beiersdorf bought back the rights to sell and manufacture Elastoplast products in the UK and Commonwealth countries.

Product

While the traditional adhesive fabric plasters remain the brand's most recognised product, Elastoplast now encompasses an entire portfolio of wound-care solutions, ranging from core plasters to advanced wound care.

The core range of Elastoplast plasters includes everything to meet the needs of an everyday cut and graze: the traditional fabric plasters, water resistant plasters, cushioned plasters for extra padding, and sensitive plasters which are kind to sensitive skin.

With children the most susceptible to cuts and grazes, Elastoplast was the first brand to introduce the character plaster to the market, with the launch of Mickey Mouse plasters in 1989. Over the years a series of character plasters has followed, including characters such as Winnie the Pooh and Disney Princesses, designed to ensure that small misfortunes are quickly forgotten.

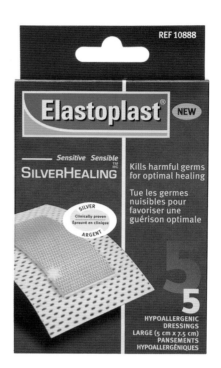

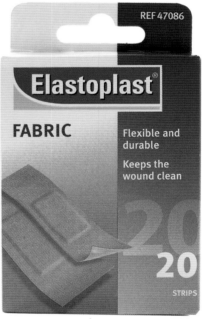

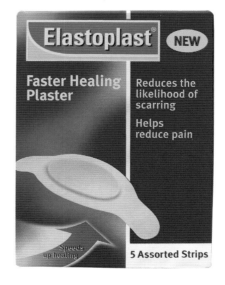

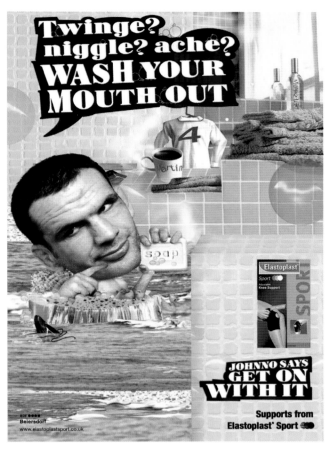

New plasters containing silver.
They kill germs.

Elastoplast SilverHealing Plasters have a fine silver mesh within the plaster that kills germs.

- Silver is clinically proven to kill germs.
- Silver has antiseptic properties for long lasting protection from infection.
- Silver is hypoallergenic and feels like a regular plaster.

Life happens. Elastoplast helps to heal.

destroying process is of high interest to mothers as they can be confident that their children's wounds are unlikely to become infected once the plaster is applied."

Promotion

Elastoplast has a strong promotional heritage with campaigns such as the 'There, there, there' campaign of the 1990s, designed to promote the caring and reliable values of the brand.

While the Elastoplast brand values remain the same today, technological progression has led to the development of the advanced wound care market. This means that education is more important than ever in ensuring that consumers are fully aware of the scope of products available to treat their everyday wounds.

Consumer education is achieved via an integrated marketing strategy incorporating above- and below-the-line advertising, PR, online, ambient media and point of sale.

The Elastoplast Sport range is supported by a similar strategy, where again education is key to connecting with the consumer in a relatively low-interest category. Since 2004, an important part of the Elastoplast Sport promotional strategy has been the sponsorship of Martin Johnson, the former England rugby captain and 2003 Rugby World Cup winner.

The Martin Johnson partnership has enabled Elastoplast Sport to speak to the sports consumer in their language, with a face they recognise. Of the Elastoplast Sport range Martin Johnson says: "It's a reliable brand that brings with it the credibility of top sportspeople using it in the professional game."

Brand Values

Elastoplast strives to be perceived as a caring and reliable brand that knows best how to heal injured skin using plaster technology. Its personality is that of a valued companion, always there when needed. It aims to offer uncomplicated and innovative solutions to everyday problems and pains, which help people get on with enjoying their lives.

www.elastoplast.co.uk

Following the success of other new additions to the Elastoplast range, Beiersdorf has successfully extended the brand into the Sports Supports market, with the launch of Elastoplast Sport in September 2003. Within less than two years of its launch, the Elastoplast Sport sub range has also built a strong reputation as one of the leading brands in the Sports Supports market, with its range of tapes and elasticated and adjustable neoprene supports.

Recent Developments

As brand leader, Elastoplast is also seen as a strong innovator, thanks most recently to its advanced wound-care range of products. The range includes a Burn Relief Spray and Burn Plasters for the treatment of burns and Scar Reduction Patches proven to permanently reduce the appearance of both new and old scars in eight weeks.

At the beginning of 2005, Elastoplast launched SILVERHEALING™, the first range of mass-market plasters and dressings in the UK to harness the natural antiseptic power of metallic silver. Adapted from silver technology used in hospitals, the wound pad contains metallic silver under a polyethylene net. On contact with moisture in the wound, silver ions are released, destroying bacterial cell structures and inhibiting their functions, killing almost all known germs and bacteria.

Within modern hospitals, silver is a widely accepted powerful antiseptic, aiding the successful treatment of serious wounds. This scientifically proven treatment method has now been adapted in the form of SILVERHEALING™ technology to provide this highly protective wound-care treatment in the home.

The range is endorsed by Dr Chris Steele from ITV's 'This Morning', who says: "Technology that is regarded highly by medical professionals is now being used by Elastoplast to help prevent wound contamination. The wound pad contains silver particles that are continually released to attack the bacterial membranes in the wound to destroy the germ's cell structure, thus optimising the natural healing process. This bacterial

Emirates

Market

Against a backdrop of soaring oil prices, the growth of low-cost carriers and in an ever more competitive marketplace, Emirates remains buoyant and successful, providing a high level of service on all its routes, at an affordable cost to its customers.

The rise and challenge of budget airlines has impacted on the traditional airlines, although Emirates' priority is serving those passengers who demand and expect a high level of comfort and convenience and an overall high-quality flying experience on medium and long haul flights.

In the UK, the airline category is dominated by two successful, well-established brands, BA and Virgin. However, with the growth in number of departures from the UK expected to continue, many airlines will take a share in the expanding market. The number of departures from the UK is expected to increase at an annual average rate of 4% to reach 72.8 million by 2008 (Source: Euromonitor).

Rising real incomes have led to people taking more holidays, with short city and weekend breaks also gaining in popularity. The traditional beach holiday, while still the preferred holiday type for the majority of travellers, is losing share in favour of independent holidays containing a variety of cultural and experiential based activities.

Achievements

From a standing start nearly 20 years ago, Dubai-based Emirates has risen to become one of the world's most successful airlines. Emirates receives no subsidies from the Government yet its growth has never fallen below 20% per year and it has doubled in size every three and a half years for its first 11 years, and every four years since.

For the financial year 2004-2005, Emirates Group announced net profits of more than US$708 million, its best-ever 12 month period, representing more than a 49% increase on the same time for the previous year.

Determined never to compromise on the standard of its products or services, Emirates has won more than 250 awards since its inception. These include Airline of the Year in 1994, 1998, 1999 and 2000; Best International Airline 1998 from the Daily Telegraph and Best Airline from The Observer in 1994, 1996, 1997 and 1998. More recently, in 2004, Emirates was voted 'Best Economy Class' and 'Best Airline to the Middle East' by industry commentator Skytrax.

However, achievements are not just about profits and awards. Emirates has always set out to push the boundaries forward in terms of innovation. In 1992 Emirates was the first airline to install personal video systems in all seats in all classes throughout its fleet and all First Class seats had video cassette players. Almost ten years later, Emirates became the first airline in the world to supply passengers with the Airogym, a device enabling passengers to exercise whilst sitting. The airline followed this with another industry first, using revolutionary cabin 'mood lighting' to help passengers adjust their internal body clock to their destination time zone.

Throughout its brief history, Emirates has set far-reaching ambitions for its business, striving to innovate and offer the highest levels of service.

Emirates operates from its home base in Dubai, where it competes with more than 110 carriers. Dubai actively promotes an Open Skies policy, encouraging competition between Emirates and the other carriers that fly there.

History

Launched on October 25th 1985, Emirates is a Dubai-based international airline. Initially flying with two leased aircraft – a Boeing 737 leased from PIA and an Airbus 300 B4 – Emirates' first flight was to Karachi. More services quickly followed, to India, Germany, Sri Lanka and Egypt. Two years later, Emirates began its first UK service between Dubai and Gatwick. In 1996, Boeing 777s were introduced

to the fleet allowing new long haul services from the Emirates hub in Dubai direct to Melbourne.

From 1,000 seats a week in 1987, Emirates now offers almost 25,000 seats a week from five UK gateways via Dubai to a wide variety of destinations in Australasia, Asia, the Indian Ocean, the Indian subcontinent and Africa.

Today, Emirates operates 84 flights per week from five UK airports: London Gatwick, Heathrow, Birmingham, Manchester and Glasgow. In 2004, Emirates carried 12.5 million passengers to more

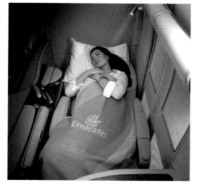

than 75 destinations in 55 countries on five continents.

Product

The Emirates fleet of 76 planes is constantly being upgraded to keep it one of the youngest in the skies.

The Boeing 777-300, the largest member of the Emirates fleet, can carry a total of 434 passengers, with 49 Business Class seats and 385 Economy seats, in a two-class configuration (the aircraft can also be operated in a three-class configuration of 18 First, 42 Business and 320 Economy Class seats).

The Airbus A330-200 provides one of the quietest cabins in the sky, designed to encourage privacy and a feeling of spaciousness.

The new Emirates Airbus A340-500 is the first of a new generation of passenger airliners. It offers more personal space, a quieter cabin and a wider range of in-flight entertainment than ever before. This aircraft boasts a First Class section with private suites, personal wardrobes, massage-enabled seats, mini-bar, dine-on-demand service and mood lighting.

The aircraft's US$8 million ICE (Information, Communication and Entertainment) system offers more than 500 channels of entertainment. The information section includes monitoring of the flight progress, news updates via satellite and information about Dubai and the Emirates Group.

www.emirates.com/uk

Emirates. Official Partner of
2006 FIFA World Cup.
Keep discovering.

The availability of satellite telephone, Wi-Fi and fax machines allows passengers to stay in touch with colleagues and friends during their flight.

On the ground, First and Business Class Lounges in Dubai offer passengers bedrooms to rest, showers, a 24-hour buffet and bar service, televisions, trouser presses, massage chairs, business centres, free internet and Wi-Fi, newspapers and magazines. First and Business Class passengers, along with Gold card or top tier members, of the airline's frequent flyer scheme, Skywards, also have the use of lounges at airports right across the Emirates network.

Recent Developments

Currently flying to 78 destinations in 54 countries, Emirates operates nearly 550 flights per week from the airline's base at Dubai International Airport, UAE.

Having launched services to the Seychelles on January 2nd, Seoul on May 1st and Alexandria on May 15th, Emirates will round off the year with new services to Hamburg.

At the 2004 Farnborough Air Show, Emirates announced firm orders for four Boeing 777-300ER planes, while at the Paris Air Show in June 2003, Emirates announced the largest aircraft order in aviation history, for 71 aircraft worth US$19 billion.

July 2000 saw Emirates become the first airline to commit to purchasing the revolutionary new Airbus A380. Emirates has 45 of the 21st century double-decker aircraft on order, more than any other airline, and around one-third of the aircraft's total order book. Emirates will be one of the first airlines to operate the aircraft, with the first aircraft due to enter service in October 2006. Emirates' fleet of Airbus A380s will operate in three different configurations, with a capacity ranging from 489 to 644 passengers.

Promotion

Since the airline's inception, Emirates has aimed to do things differently, to take an alternative path to that which other airlines have taken. While this is evident in terms of product and service innovation, the airline believes it is equally true in its approach to promotion.

While others may look to showcase what's inside the cabin, Emirates looks to concentrate on redefining and enhancing the travel experience. While others may look to leverage national associations, Emirates looks to be global. While others talk about passengers, Emirates strives to think of its customers as guests.

The Emirates 'Keep discovering' campaign works across all markets and all media and is based on the compelling thought: 'When was the last time you did something for the first time?'

Emirates also recognises the importance of sponsorship in building stature and awareness for a relatively new entrant in a highly competitive market. Sponsorship has enabled the airline to build an ongoing relationship with its passengers. Emirates has invested heavily from Rugby Sevens to Premiership football and from the Melbourne Symphony Orchestra to the Americas Cup.

In 2003 Emirates announced that it was to become the first ever global

airline partner of the FIFA World Cup, taking place in Germany in 2006, while in October 2004 Emirates announced a £100 million sponsorship deal, the biggest ever football sponsorship, with Premiership giant Arsenal. Starting in the 2006/07 season, the partnership includes 'Fly Emirates' shirt sponsorship for eight years and stadium naming rights for the next 15 years. Arsenal will also set up a football academy in UAE as part of the partnership.

Emirates will support Team New Zealand in its challenge for the next America's Cup, the world's premier yacht racing event. Emirates Team New Zealand will mount a campaign to regain the Cup from its current holder, the Geneva-based Swiss team Alinghi, in the 33rd edition of the regatta that will culminate in the waters off the Mediterranean city of Valencia, Spain in 2007.

Brand Values

Emirates strives to present its customers with a warm, human and welcoming face whether they are entering a lounge, boarding a plane, logging on or calling in. Beyond this, the brand is committed to innovation, progression, independence, open-mindedness and dynamism. These are all values that Emirates believes set it apart and above the competition – and values that it hopes inspire customers all over the world.

www.emirates.com/uk

THINGS YOU DIDN'T KNOW ABOUT

Emirates

> In 1993 Emirates became the first airline to equip its entire Airbus fleet with in-flight phones, and a year later became the first airline to equip its fleet with in-flight fax machines.

> Emirates employs cabin staff of more than 100 different nationalities.

> Emirates purchased approximately 70,000 cases of wine in 2003/04. The Emirates Flight Catering Company (which produces meals for all carriers that fly into and out of Dubai) purchases approximately eight million eggs and 1.1 million lbs of tomatoes each year.

> The Emirates Flight Catering Company in Dubai produces around 54,000 meals per day, of which 70% are for Emirates.

> In 2003 Emirates became the first airline in the world to operate the new ultra-long range Airbus A340-500 and offer more than 500 channels of in-flight entertainment, the widest choice in the skies, for every passenger in every class.

FERRERO ROCHER

Market

A box of chocolates has become the gift of choice for many occasions, from a simple thank you to a grand gesture of love. The UK chocolate confectionery market is worth in excess of £3 billion. Within this, the premium gifting boxed chocolate sector is worth £612 million and is growing at 7.5% year-on-year (Source: ACNielsen December 2004).

One of the strongest consumer trends in the segment is towards premium single inlaid boxes, where value is increasing with the introduction of new lines at higher price points. Competition is fierce, with key premium players such as Ferrero Rocher, Lindt and Thorntons, in addition to the traditional manufacturers, Cadbury, Nestlé and Masterfoods, fighting for a larger share of consumer spend in this end of the market.

Not surprisingly, the market for premium gifting boxed chocolate is highly seasonal – boxed chocolates account for almost half of all chocolate sales over the Christmas period, as well as other key gifting periods throughout the year, namely Valentines Day, Mothers Day and Easter. Ferrero Rocher excels during these key trading periods, during which it cements its dominant position in the market place, with the help of consumer-driven, heavyweight investment.

Achievements

Instantly recognisable, Ferrero Rocher has become a unique brand in the boxed chocolate market. It is synonymous with quality and luxury, offering a sophisticated product that is ideal for gifting and entertaining, at an accessible price for the consumer.

In a mature and competitive market, Ferrero Rocher continues to demonstrate why it has become such an iconic brand with impressive and continued growth and sales that are at a 20 year high (Source: ACNielsen 2004).

Gifting is a major growth trend in the boxed chocolates market, and is a strong motivator for purchases. As a result, Ferrero Rocher has produced a variety of new packs both for seasonal and special event purchases. The success of such launches adds incremental sales, as well as enhancing the brand's profile.

Strong seasonal sales have helped Ferrero Rocher to achieve a 12% market share of the boxed chocolate segment, but it also performs strongly throughout the year thanks to powerful presence at point of sale, constant pack innovation and consistent heavyweight consumer support (Source: ACNielsen 2004).

History

Ferrero Rocher was created in Italy in 1983 by the innovative mind of Mr Michele Ferrero, who has created many of the most inventive confectionery creations over the last 30 years including Kinder Surprise, tic tac, Giotto, Kinder Bueno, Happy Hippo and many more. In the same year it was launched in the UK, Germany and France. Since then, it has grown to become one of the largest and best-recognised confectionery brands in the world, and is now sold in more than 40 countries across five continents.

SHARE THE MAGIC
THIS CHRISTMAS

Key to its success has been its positioning as an accessible premium gifting product, which is successfully communicated by distinctive glamorous packaging and its iconic and highly memorable advertising campaigns.

Product

Ferrero Rocher is a praline-filled hazelnut and chocolate shell, wrapped in gold foil packaging that has instant consumer recognition.

Today, the product comes in a number of specifically targeted pack formats, including a seasonal cube and Christmas-tree shaped box; an Easter egg format; and various sizes to meet consumer needs all year round. The bestselling format is the 24-piece pack, which is enjoying 6% growth. A new 'diamond' effect pack has just been introduced to further enhance the premium values of the brand.

Recent Developments

Understanding the consumer is at the heart of Ferrero Rocher's brand-building strategy. While the boxed chocolate audience is maturing, with core consumers being over 50, Ferrero Rocher has been broadening its appeal to the younger, 35 to 50 age group, bringing new consumers and therefore incremental sales to the category.

The growth in premium assortment boxed chocolates has been met by Ferrero with the new Ferrero Prestige

Roses are red,
Violets are posher.
You'll have a good night
if you remember Rocher.

Don't forget Valentine's Day.
February 14th.

FERRERO
ROCHER

range, which marries the instantly recognisable Ferrero Rocher brand with two new products: Ferrero Cappuccino and Ferrero Rond Noir.

The growth of indulgence in the impulse market has also been met by Ferrero Rocher. Here, the brand has identified an opportunity for its four-piece impulse pack

Promotion

Ferrero Rocher is responsible for one of the all-time classic commercials – 'Ambassador's Reception'. The famous ambassador advert made its return to the screens in 2003, but this time with a humorous and contemporary twist, as the ambassador was female. In 2004 the creative moved on further with 'Share the Magic', with the aim to expand the role of Ferrero Rocher beyond that of just a formal gift to one that is also relevant to broader social occasions, while maintaining all of the aspiration and glamour synonymous to the brand.

The objectives of the updated execution were to drive modernity and relevance in a salient way and engage a younger consumer target. This was achieved, with results showing the ad was highly successful, with penetration

of the brand increasing by two percentage points to January 2004 (Source: TNS 2004).

As one of the top advertising spenders in the chocolate confectionery market, Ferrero Rocher invested £3 million over the 2004 Christmas period

alone. The campaign was truly multi media featuring both TV – across all stations – with a heavyweight outdoor campaign. In addition, spontaneous awareness of Ferrero Rocher grew by 21% (Source: TNS 2004).

The brand builds sales on its reputation and image, adding value to the category through innovation and heavyweight marketing and advertising investment.

Brand Values

Ferrero Rocher's heritage lies in the impact it creates when consumers give and receive it. The values of the brand are driven out of the brand appearance and communication and are synonymous with quality, glamour, trust & refinement.

Ferrero Rocher is one of the consumer's number one choices for gifting and entertainment; and will continue to play to this strength.

In order to achieve its objectives, the company is committed to serious investment in premium locally relevant advertising and marketing activities.

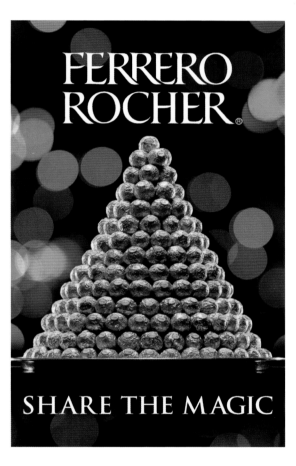

Market

As UK society continues its love affair with beasts of the four-wheeled variety, the number of UK households owning one or more cars increased from 70% in 1997 to 73% in 2003 (Source: Euromonitor).

There were a record 2.6 million new car registrations in the UK in 2004 and the market is expected to register growth of around 8% to reach 2,779 thousand new car registrations by 2008 (Source: Euromonitor). New car sales are made almost exclusively through franchised dealers, accounting for 85% of total sales in 2003 (Source: Euromonitor). Yet it's not all bad news for the environmentalists – diesel registrations have increased since emission-based taxation was introduced by Gordon Brown in 2002.

The biggest market sector continues to be the 'lower medium' family cars or 'super-minis' such as Ford Focus, which represent over one third of all cars sold – a total of 874 thousand units in 2003 (Source: Euromonitor). This sector is bolstered by the popularity of medium 'people-movers'. This sub-sector grew by 50,000 sales in 2004 and 60% of this growth came from the launch of the Focus C-MAX (Source: SMMT). Super-minis are predicted to remain the largest sector until at least 2008, accounting for 38% of all volume sales (Source: Euromonitor).

The UK market for passenger cars is highly concentrated with the three major groups, Ford, Volkswagen and General Motors controlling more than 45.5% of sales in 2004 (Source: Euromonitor).

Achievements

Ford Motor Company has been the leading brand in the UK car market for 28 consecutive years and boasted a 15.6% share of the market in volume terms in 2003 (Source: Euromonitor). Its Focus product has been the UK's bestselling car since its launch in 1999, while the Ford Ka and Mondeo lead the sectors of the market in which they compete. Ford's turnover in 2003 was US$164.3 billion, a 1.2% increase on the previous year.

Ford also competes in the commercial vehicles (CVs) or vans market. More than 50% of the CV market is made up of panel vans, which is dominated by the Ford Transit, the UK market leader since it was launched 40 years ago. The company sold 390,000 Transit's in 2004, an increase of 7.2% on 2003.

However, Ford's achievements in the motor industry run deeper than the manufacture and sale of cars. On October 10th 1901 Henry Ford's brand new race car won its first-ever event. As a result of that win he gained sufficient financial backing to set up the Henry Ford Company and the world-famous marque was founded.

Since that debut victory, in a century of Motorsport, Ford-powered cars have won countless races, rallies and speed record events and numerous National and World Championships. The company has achieved 175 Grand Prix wins – more wins than any other engine maker and 56 Formula One teams have used Ford Cosworth engines.

History

Ford Motor Company entered the business world on June 16th 1903 when Henry Ford and 11 business associates signed the company's articles of

incorporation. With US$28,000 in cash, the pioneering industrialists gave birth to what was to become one of the world's largest corporations.

Perhaps Ford Motor Company's single greatest contribution to automotive manufacturing was the moving assembly line. First implemented at the Highland Park plant in Michigan, US, in 1913, the new technique allowed individual workers to stay in one place and perform the same task repeatedly on multiple vehicles that passed them. The line proved tremendously efficient, helping the company surpass the production levels of its competitors – and make its vehicles more affordable.

Henry Ford insisted that the company's future lay in the production of affordable cars for a mass market. Beginning in 1903, the company began using the first 19 letters of the alphabet to name new cars. In 1908, the Model T was born. 19 years and 15 million Model T's later, Ford Motor Company was a giant industrial complex that spanned the globe.

In 1911 Ford established its first UK manufacturing plant in Trafford Park, Manchester. 20 years later the first vehicle was built at the new Dagenham manufacturing plant. Car production at the Dagenham plants finally came to an end in February 2002. The plant's transition to a global centre of excellence for Ford diesel engine design and manufacture heralded the start of a new era in Ford's manufacturing quality.

In 1925, Ford Motor Company acquired the Lincoln Motor Company, thus branching out into luxury cars and, in the 1930s, the Mercury division was created to establish a division centred on mid-priced cars.

In the 1950s came the Thunderbird and the chance to own a part of Ford Motor Company. The company went public and, on February 24th 1956, had about 350,000 new stockholders. Henry Ford II's keen perception of political and economic trends in the 1950s led to the global expansion of Ford in the 1960s and the establishment of Ford of Europe in 1967, 20 years ahead of the European Economic Community's arrival.

1967 saw the Ford Escort launch across Europe. It proved to be the UK's bestselling car ever with 4.6 million sold before being finally discontinued in July 2000. In 1976 the Fiesta was launched, revolutionising the small-car hatch sector.

It was followed by the Sierra in 1982, with two million produced in Dagenham by 1998 before it was replaced by the Mondeo, which was the first 'world car' from Ford. It was sold in more than 60 countries and was named 1994 European Car of the Year. Three million have been sold worldwide to date.

Ford Motor Company began the 20th century with a single man envisioning products that would meet the needs of people in a world on the verge of high-gear industrialisation. Today, in the 21st century, Ford Motor Company is a global family of automotive brands consisting of: Ford, Lincoln, Mercury, Mazda, Jaguar Cars, Land Rover, Aston Martin and Volvo.

Product

Ford is beginning its second century of existence with a worldwide organisation that retains and expands Henry Ford's heritage by developing products that are designed to serve the ever-changing needs of people in the global community. Ford offers a full range of cars and commercial vehicles. Its offering in the small cars segment starts with the Ka, StreetKa and SportKa range, through the well-established Fiesta, up to the taller and tougher Fusion.

With its launch in 1998, the now-iconic Ford Focus kick-started the so-called 'C' segment. Rapidly becoming Britain's bestselling car, the Focus now has more than 65 international awards. Based on the platform of the all new Focus, launched in January 2005, there is also the Focus C-MAX, Ford's compact MPV.

Ford is also a leader in large-cars. The 2005 Mondeo offers a distinctive design along with high performance and fuel efficiency, alongside low CO_2 emissions. And with its Intelligent Protection System, it offers exceptional safety levels. For those seeking a more luxurious family car, Ford offers the Galaxy. Finally, there is the Ford Ranger, built on a rugged ladder-frame chassis, with a choice of two- or four-wheel drive.

The Ford commercial vehicles (CVs) range has been specifically designed to become an essential tool in the everyday tasks of its drivers. Ford CVs range from the Fiesta Van, through the well-known

Transit range, to the Tourneo Connect, designed so that drivers using the vehicle for work purposes can fold down or remove the rear seats to make a spacious van. And come the weekend, it's a family vehicle with room for five people plus luggage.

Recent Developments

The arrival of the all-new Ford Focus in January 2005 was the biggest event in Ford's 2005 calendar. The new Ford Focus family includes three-door, five-door and estate models and draws upon the Focus C-MAX multi-activity vehicle introduced in 2003. It is designed to make use of cutting-edge premium technologies, such as Bluetooth® wireless technologies and Voice Control.

Ford's best-known commercial vehicle, the Transit range, celebrated its 40th anniversary in 2005 with the launch of a range of special edition Transit and Transit Connect models. For 40 years Ford has built a range of more than 500 Transit models to help millions of Britons to build their businesses.

February 2005 saw the launch of the Fiesta ST and its appearance at the Geneva Motor Show in March.

Capitalising on Ford's extensive motor-sports' heritage, the Focus ST boasts a 2.5 litre turbocharged engine that delivers power and refinement and a tuned chassis for a confident ride.

Ford is currently looking to regain its sporting credentials. Its current participation in the World Rally Championship offers the ultimate proving ground for development of new technologies and processes that enable the company to deliver a better product to its customers. Ford has a long tradition in rallying, formerly with the Escort, and now with its best selling Focus product. World Rallying is arguably the toughest form of motor-sport and thus provides an ideal product development platform.

Promotion

Ford needs to promote many different sub-brands across a wide spread of market sectors. Indeed, Ford was the top advertiser in the car market in 2004, with a spend of more than £66 million.

In its advertising Ford needs to find a balance between consistency across its brands, while still tailoring communications to the key customers for each one.

In recent years this has been addressed at a strategic level by promoting each 'nameplate' on the basis of an attribute that, in some way, also supports the central idea that Ford makes dependable cars. The three key models that receive the greatest investment are Fiesta, Focus and Mondeo.

The Fiesta has been promoted as 'Rock Solid' through a series of 'Fiesta fantasies' such as being a pinball or an ice hockey puck. This approach is deemed appropriate to

younger customers who are very important to the small car market.

The Focus is promoted on a platform of 'Premium Product Quality', reflecting the aspirations of a more mature target group to enjoy the highest standards of engineering and finish, without paying over the odds.

The Mondeo has been promoted on a safety theme since the launch of the current model in 2001. The key target audience is families with children, for whom the car's ability to protect its occupants is a very high priority.

In terms of corporate social responsibility, Ford is focusing on renewable energy. 100% of the electricity for the new Dagenham diesel centre comes from wind turbines at London's first wind farm. The UK's largest solar panels are also providing energy for Ford's new Centre of Engineering and Manufacturing Excellence.

Over the past five years, Ford has raised £1.25 million for the charity Breakthrough Breast Cancer and is also supporting youth through several grass-roots projects including Football de Salao, Thames Gateway Youth Football Project and Lords Taverners under-14 Cricket.

Brand Values

Henry Ford was arguably the greatest industrial pioneer of the 20th century, driven by his vision of making the benefits of car ownership accessible to 'the great multitude'. These democratic values are still at the core of the company. It takes an egalitarian, non-judgemental attitude and is continually looking for ways to enable ordinary people to get more out of automotive ownership.

The company's culture is allied to an optimistic, 'can-do' spirit and a strong sense of social responsibility. Bill Ford, Henry's great-grandson, is CEO of the company, which makes it an organisation for which 'family values' is much more than a catchphrase.

www.ford.co.uk

Ford

❯ Ford has been Britain's top-selling car manufacturer since 1976.

❯ Ford Focus C-MAX is the first car to receive a seal of approval from the British Allergy Foundation. It's also the first car ever to receive a four star rating for child protection from Euro NCAP.

❯ Every year Ford spends £300 million on research and development, making it the biggest spender in the automotive sector.

❯ New Ford vehicles are 85% recyclable.

❯ The famous Ford script logo has remained largely unchanged since it was first registered in 1909.

❯ Ford directly employs more than 55,000 people, making it the UK's leading employer.

GEⓈRGE

Market

When it comes to buying clothes and shoes, supermarkets are today, becoming the place to go. More than half – 56% – of the UK population have bought clothing or footwear in supermarkets in the past year (Source: Fashiontrak). Of those, 33% have bought from George, making it a key player in terms of increasing penetration in the supermarket sector.

The total UK clothing and footwear market, worth £29.9 billion in the year to March 2005 and growing by 1%, has extended its reach to supermarkets in the past few years (Source: Fashiontrak). Indeed, supermarkets now account for 18% of volume sales, of which George accounts for almost half (Source: Fashiontrak). George's value share increased from 1.2% in 1997 to 3.3% in 2005, while its volume share increased from 2.6% in 1997 to 8.8% in 2005 (Source: Fashiontrak).

Competing with high street fashion retailers, value fashion retailers and other supermarket fashion retailers, the price of clothes has decreased in George over the past five years.

Achievements

Established in 1990, George has steadily risen in popularity over the past 15 years. Today it is the UK's biggest fashion retailer by volume and fourth by value (Source: Fashiontrak).

It has consistently achieved awards voted for by the press and for shoppers. It won Prima magazine's High Street Fashion Awards for Value for Money Retailer of the Year three times and Childrenswear Retailer of the Year twice as well as winning the One to Watch award.

Most recently at the Tommy's Parent Friendly Awards, George carried off the prize for Best Children's Clothing 2005.

George at ASDA is recognised as an exemplary employer. It won the overall prize in the inaugural National Council for Work Experience Awards, the first initiative specifically set up to recognise, encourage and reward the provision of quality work placements for students. In addition to winning the overall prize, George at ASDA won the category for organisations with more than 250 employees.

red hot value

men's & ladies' jeans*

were £4 now £3

ASDA
www.george.com
For details of specific store opening times, call our customer service line on
0500100055

GEⓈRGE

History

Until the 1980s, shopping for clothes in Britain could often be a dull activity. Most clothing stores were traditional and old-fashioned, selling fairly uninspired products. All this changed in 1982, when the Next chain of fashion stores launched its then unique and innovative shopping concept. The man behind this revolution was George Davies – regarded by many as a fashion retailing genius.

While Next was making its mark, the ASDA supermarket chain was starting to struggle and by 1990, was almost bankrupt. However, the appointment of Archie Norman as new chief executive signalled a change to ASDA's position in the market.

Part of Archie's strategy was to create a mix of products that would be unrivalled. He hired George Davies to set up ASDA's own private-label clothing brand – George. In 1990 George Davies launched the George label in 100 ASDA supermarkets and achieved sales of £130 million in the first year. By 1992 sales had increased by 40%, and in 1995, ASDA acquired the George business. During the same year George broke the £500 million sales barrier.

In 1999, ASDA's new parent Wal-Mart declared that George was "the jewel in the crown".

Within less than 10 years, George's second fashion retailing revolution was well underway. Until this time, buying clothing in a supermarket had meant only the basics, a T-shirt or perhaps a pair of socks.

In 2000, George Davies left the company and Andy Bond took over as Managing Director, leading a phase of exceptional growth. A year later George was sold for the first time in Germany, launching in five Wal-Mart stores. Also in the same year, George went on sale in the US.

In April 2002, Fast Fashion for womenswear was launched in 251 stores. The range captures the latest styles and trends as they come off the catwalk – from design to store in eight weeks, and is refreshed every four weeks.

In September 2003, George Collection, a premium range of clothing for womenswear and menswear launched in the UK.

By the end of 2003 George had achieved sales of £1 billion. In 2004, George was sold in 253 of ASDA's 271 stores and in six stand-alone stores. Today it employs 6,300 staff worldwide.

In 2004 George launched its website, www.george.com which showcases the brand.

Product

Fashion is about inspiration, creativity and excitement. George customers want the brand to help them develop their own look. Its designers stay close to all the trends as they come through from catwalks, celebrities and the media. But it believes it should also give customers what they want, not what George thinks they should have. Therefore, when designers are developing George ranges, they listen to customers all

fast fashion▸ at GEⓈRGE

the time to make sure they are giving them trends translated into wearable, affordable clothing.

The George brand produces Menswear, Womenswear, Childrenswear and Footwear. In Menswear it offers basic essentials, footwear, 'George Collection', skiwear, 'Admiral' and Levis. In Womenswear it offers lingerie, footwear, nightwear, accessories, 'G21', 'Fast Fashion', 'George Collection', maternity wear, 'Petites', skiwear and 'Michelle for George' lingerie. In Childrenswear it offers 'George Collection jnr', 'Mary-Kate and Ashley', 'Barbie', skiwear, schoolwear, 'Dressing-up' and footwear.

Recent Developments

In Spring 2004, following on from the success of George Collection for womenswear and menswear, George extended the range into childrenswear. The launch of George Collection jnr in April 2004 was supported with press advertising in key monthly titles aimed at mums, a PR campaign and in-store POS.

G21, aimed at the 16-24 age group, was launched in 60 stores in May 2004. Within this fashion-conscious range, the latest looks were arriving in stores every two weeks.

There are now eight standalone George stores in UK high streets and in 2004, George launched in Canadian and Mexican supercentres and was trialled in Japan. George is now sold in eight countries worldwide.

Promotion

As George expands globally it becomes increasingly important that the brand is marketed consistently.

Through its marketing the George brand values of style, quality and value are communicated. These brand values are key to differentiating George in a competitive marketplace.

George invests £8 million per annum in advertising and promotional activity, which includes TV advertising, press advertising, in-store point-of-sale material, ASDA Magazine fashion editorial pages, George Mini-Mag, PR, customer research and its website. In-store, the point of sale strategy 'Good, Better, Best' is designed to communicate value, quality and style. 'Good' communicates the value proposition with black and white price-led point of sale material. 'Better' uses photographic point-of-sale material, while 'Best' communicates style and includes the George Collection; G21; Fast Fashion and Michelle for George.

The first George TV ad campaign 'So you think supermarket clothing is boring?' went on air in February 1997. Since that time, George has produced TV ad campaigns to support seasonal launches, back to school and promotional events.

In Spring 2004, George focused on promoting the style and fashionability of the brand through its TV advertising with the 'Make an Entrance' campaign. The 'Make an Entrance' campaign continued into Summer 2005, as an integrated campaign, which followed through into in-store POS, the George brochure and website.

The ASDA Magazine, featuring 15-18 pages of George fashion editorial each month, is Britain's most widely read women's monthly magazine with a circulation of three million (Source: ABC). In addition the George 'mini-mag' is published five times a year with a circulation of two million. In 2004 a schoolwear 'mini-mag' was inserted into Prima magazine.

The ASDA and George at ASDA purpose is 'To make goods and services more affordable for

everyone'. Its stores all strive to play a positive part in all aspects of life in their local community, from establishing a new local supplier to working with the emergency services in the area.

George is committed to cause related marketing: George and ASDA combined is the biggest fund-raiser for breast cancer in the UK. Through the Tickled Pink charity it creates awareness of breast cancer in the UK and sells a range of clothing, lingerie, nightwear and accessories from which all profits go to the charity. Liz Hurley, Naomi Campbell, Kate Moss, Jennifer Anniston and Scarlett Johannsen are among the many celebrities who have been photographed wearing a George Tickled Pink T-shirt to raise money for breast cancer.

Brand Values

George has established itself as a stylish, quality brand that has revolutionised the value fashion market in the UK over the past 15 years. It is now set to become a global fashion brand.

In the past, it was generally assumed that customers had to compromise — if the price was low, the quality was bound to suffer and style would be sacrificed or there would be low expectations. The retail market was divided between discount stores offering low-price basics and upscale stores with well-designed, good quality garments at much higher prices.

George was designed to be different. Right from the start, the brand offered customers style, quality and value. These three words are at the heart of the brand — they define it and are the three pillars upon which George is built and the reason for its success.

www.george.com

Gillette®

Market

As a market that is currently worth £268.4 million in the UK alone (Source: TNS 52 w/e March 19th 2005), the male blades and razors category continues to grow, primarily driven by new product development and market innovation. In recent years there has been a significant consumer shift within this category from disposable razors to the new generation of premium system razors, with over 61% of men who wet shave now opting for a system razor (Source: NCS 2004).

Several other factors have contributed to the continuous growth of the male blades and razors category – the most high profile of which has been the emergence of product endorsement from sporting icons, which has heightened interest in the male grooming category.

The Gillette brand remains the acknowledged leader in shaving with a value share of 72.9% and continues to drive the majority of this market growth (Source: TNS 52 w/e March 19th 2005). In the UK alone, 13.6 million individuals used a Gillette male blade and razor product in 2004 (Source: TNS 52 w/e January 4th 2005).

Female grooming is also maturing into a very important part of the health and beauty category as women increasingly view the process of hair removal as an important step in their beauty routine. The £70 million female blades and razors market accounts for 20% of value sales of the total category and in 2004 the category grew by more than 15% (Source: IRI Infoscan 52 w/e December 25th 2004). Growth has been driven by consistent new product innovation. The increase in female products arriving on the market has drawn increasing numbers of female consumers into this new and developing category.

The fastest-growing sector is system razors, which accounts for 28% of the category value sales and is key to driving future sales of systems blades (Source: IRI Infoscan 52 w/e December 25th 2004).

Achievements

Gillette regularly develops its extensive product range to better meet consumers' needs and continues to be the market leader with a more than 72.9% value share of the blade and razor category (Source: IRI Infoscan 52 w/e March 19th 2005 for the razors & blades category as a whole).

Gillette's success is predominantly driven by regular product innovation, which has earned the brand a loyal

consumer base on a global scale. With the introduction of cutting-edge design combined with advanced shaving technology, the Gillette brand is one that is trusted and strives to meet the demands of modern consumers.

This strong focus on innovation has led to the development of technological enhancements within the female category from 'lubrastrips' and 'intensive

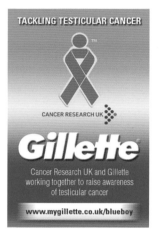

moisture'™ strips to three 'comfort-coated'™ blades and soft cushions, providing a comfortable glide.

History

The Gillette Company was founded in Boston in 1901 by travelling salesman King C Gillette. Frustrated with traditional cut-throat shaving, he started work on a razor that was to revolutionise the shaving market – the Safety Razor.

It was at this time that Gillette's strong technological foundations were established. The 1903 launch of the Safety Razor was groundbreaking, as new processes for tempering and hardening mass-produced steel were discovered. This resulted in the 'wafer thin' metal needed to create the razor, something that had previously been dubbed a 'technical impossibility' by Thomas Edison.

The success of the Safety Razor made Gillette a household name and was deemed to have changed the face of a nation. In order to keep up with the rapid growth, a factory was established in South Boston in 1905 under the new name of the Gillette Safety Razor Company.

Strong domestic growth prompted international expansion. Overseas operations commenced in 1905, with a manufacturing plant just outside Paris and a sales office in London. Annual blade sales had risen to more than 40 million units before the outbreak of World War I.

The next true innovation was the Techmatic razor, launched in 1967. This was the first system razor with a 'continuous band' meaning consumers would no longer have to touch the blade. The pace of innovation increased from 1971 onwards and a series of world firsts were achieved, including the release of GII, the first twin-bladed razor in 1971. This was followed soon after in 1976 by the first twin-bladed disposable razor and in 1977 the revolutionary pivot-headed razor, Contour, was released.

While developments in the 1960s and 1970s focused mainly on blades, the 1980s and 1990s saw improved features for a smoother, more comfortable shave. Contour Plus, in 1985, heralded the first 'lubrastrip' and 1990 saw the company's first ever Pan-Atlantic launch, with the introduction of Sensor in 16 countries. Sensor featured the first spring mounted blades and shell-bearing pivot. Three years later, SensorExcel was launched with soft, flexible 'microfins' designed to sweep hair up, allowing the blade to cut closer.

Product innovation was a clear priority in 1998, with the launch of MACH3®. This revolutionary triple-bladed shaving system was followed in January 2003 by MACH3Turbo®, which presented a whole host of advancements to the MACH3 design, primarily, improved blade technology.

Gillette also has a strong history of innovation in the female market, introducing the first-ever razor for women 'Milady Decollete' in 1915 and the first disposable for women, Gillette Daisy, 60 years later in 1975.

The 1990s heralded a period of huge change in female shaving with Gillette releasing Sensor for women in 1992, which was then surpassed by the new and very much improved SensorExcel for women. In 2000 Gillette unveiled Venus® – a unique triple-bladed razor, designed specifically for women. In 2002 Venus® Passion was introduced, broadening the appeal of the product even further by offering Venus in a vibrant pink colour.

Today, thanks to continuous new product development, Gillette continues to be the number one brand within the male and female shaving markets both in value and volume share (Source: TNS 52 w/e March 19th 2005).

Product

Gillette's portfolio has expanded significantly since the release of the original Safety Razor. Today the company's diverse grooming range has a product to meet the needs of all consumers, at all price points.

Gillette provides a fully integrated grooming solution for men with the shaving range extending from entry level disposables such as Blue II the basic twin-blade razor, right through to the superior

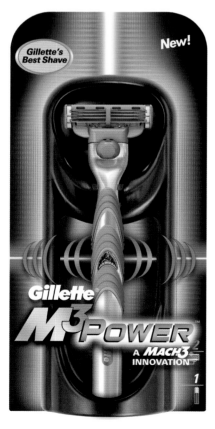

battery-powered M3Power Nitro, launched in 2005.

MACH3Turbo® Gel is specially formulated to partner with the technology of the MACH3 and M3Power range of products. The new Anti-Friction™ formula delivers Gillette's best razor glide and provides continuous protection, perfectly complementing the Gillette male blades and razors range. Additional Gillette products also include aftershave cooling gel, aftershave balm and splash, antiperspirants, deodorants and shower gels.

Gillette's female shaving products range from Sensor and SensorExcel system razors through to the premium Venus Divine system and disposable range. Venus Divine combines pioneering innovation and proven technology to offer a superior shave for the modern-day woman. SatinCare® Skin Soothing gel contributes to Gillette's market share of the shaving preps category and successfully completes the female shaving portfolio.

Recent Developments

Building on the heritage of Mach3Turbo, 2004 saw the launch of Gillette's first battery powered razor – the Gillette® M3Power™. It comes equipped with micro-pulses, delivered to the shaving cartridge and patented PowerGlide™ blades. Its micro-pulses were designed to provide a boost to shaving performance by raising the hairs for a closer shave.

In 2005 the M3Power Nitro was launched, combining the technology and energy of M3Power, enhanced with a premium black handle and neon green glow for a striking visual effect. The M3Power Nitro razor is expected to broaden appeal to the younger market and build category value by increasing razor and premium blade consumption.

Gillette boosted the Venus portfolio with the launch of Venus Divine® in 2004, its added features included intensive moisture strips, three comfort-coated blades and soft cushions for an even closer shave.

2005 saw the range develop even further with the Venus Divine® Paradise, offering female consumers a new coral colour alternative. Comfort coated blades and a two-coating layer ensure a more comfortable glide and the 'lubrastrips' positioned before and after the blades prepare the skin and soften the hair. It is designed to capture the eye of the female consumer and enhances the brand's 'Reveal the Goddess in You®' messaging.

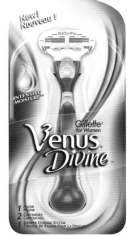

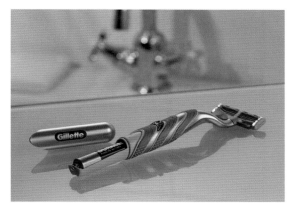

At the same time, Gillette introduced Venus Divine® Disposable razors to offer consumers a disposable option whilst still retaining all the benefits they have come to expect from a Venus Divine product – there's no need to change the blades, simply throw away the razor and replace. Venus Divine Disposables contain all of the benefits of the Gillette Venus Divine system razor in a disposable format, providing a 'divinely' close shave for 'divinely' smooth skin.

Gillette also introduced Girl2Goddess™ – these starter kits supported by MTV were marketed as being ideal for girls who are exploring shaving for the first time.

Promotion

The Gillette brand has a high recognition rate, in no small part due to its strong investment in advertising. The hugely successful and long-running 'Best A Man Can Get' campaign, which began in the 1980s, had a massive influence, with today's consumers still recalling the catchy song.

Since the launch of MACH3 Gillette has focused heavily on brand values and cutting-edge technology. Yet the launch of M3Power reinforced a far more emotional connection between the consumer and the Gillette brand, which continues to be supported with high-profile advertising featuring David Beckham. The campaign includes TV, outdoor, online and press media and reinforces the brand's credibility, targeting its core range of male consumers.

August 2005 saw the start of a heavyweight media campaign surrounding the launch of the M3Power Nitro. New advertising, focusing on Nitro's exhilarating performance and energy, hits TV at the beginning of August, combined with extensive support in the press, outdoors and on the internet.

Historically, Gillette has used sport and sporting icons such as David Beckham, as a major promotional vehicle and embarked on its first sponsorship deal with a radio broadcast of the US World Series back in 1939. Today this association remains strong, with sponsorship continuing to play a large part in Gillette's integrated communications strategy.

In 2004 the brand's sponsorship of premiership football on Sky Sport's 'Gillette Soccer Saturday' continued with the build-up towards the FIFA World Cup 2006, making Gillette the longest-running sponsor of the event.

Gillette is also building brand awareness through the sponsorship of various rugby events throughout 2005-2006 – the Six Nations and The Rugby League Tri Nations. Recently, Gillette became the official male grooming partner of Premier Rugby, the England team and the Welsh Rugby Union and it is building a portfolio of Gillette rugby ambassadors with Brian O'Driscoll, Jason Robinson, Paul Sculthorpe and Gavin Henson. The objective of associating the brand with sport is that after building an emotional bond with consumers through a shared interest, Gillette's credible position is enhanced by successful product performance, which has sustained the brand's sales performance over the decades.

In terms of marketing to female consumers, Gillette linked up with MTV in April 2005 to support the launch of the limited edition Gillette Venus Divine 'Girl2Goddess' starter kit.

The Girl2Goddess campaign offered teens the opportunity to live like a goddess and the competition was promoted on air and hosted online at www.mtvenus.com. It was also highlighted on packs across the UK, building the brand's association with such a popular channel and reaching a new wave of female consumers.

Brand Values

Gillette is dedicated to driving innovative technology that will develop and produce hair-removal products that deliver a superior shave performance, both in terms of closeness and comfort. Its male image is masculine, confident and well-groomed, while the female image is fun, youthful and energetic. Gillette is positioned at the premium end of the market, offering superior quality products that set the grooming industry standard.

In essence, the Gillette Company celebrates world-class products, world-class brands and world-class people. It is committed to growth through innovation to maintain its position as a world leader in the consumer products marketplace.

www.gillette.com

OFFICIAL SPONSOR
FIFA WORLD CUP GERMANY 2006
Gillette®
The Best a Man Can Get

THINGS YOU DIDN'T KNOW ABOUT

Gillette®

> By the end of 1904 – Gillette's second year of trading – more than 90,000 Americans possessed a Gillette Safety Razor.

> Today, more than 90 million men worldwide use a razor from the MACH3 family.

> On average, men shave five times per week (shaving frequency increases with age).

> Venus razors are now used by more than 40 million women worldwide.

> The pink Venus Passion equated to nearly 60% of all Venus Razor sales in 2002, its first year (Source: IRI Infoscan 52 w/e December 2002/03).

Good Housekeeping

Market

In 2004 the women's lifestyle/fashion magazine market saw a year-on-year copy sales increase of 4.5% to a total of 6.3 million copies a month, with a value of £185 million in cover-price revenue each year (Source: ABC July-December 2004).

The flourishing sales of many established titles, such as Good Housekeeping, along with the launch of new titles (32 women's interest titles since 2002), have all contributed to a growth in this market and indicate the continued demand for quality lifestyle magazines that respond to the changing needs and interests of women.

The increasing affluence of society, with an ever growing number of AB women in older age bands, offers a lucrative prospect for the women's magazine market. Increasing life-expectancy coupled with decreasing fertility rates has produced a gradual but sustained increase in the ratio of older to younger people, the result being an ageing population. Between 2004 and 2009, the number of over-60s is projected to grow at over five times the rate of the general population. These figures represent a tremendous resource, which many publishers are looking to capitalise upon (Source: Mintel British Lifestyle report March 2005).

Good Housekeeping operates in a mature market, where the age of its readers is typically 40+. As such, it is ideally placed to absorb the demands of the ageing population.

The key to understanding the over 40s is to appreciate that they do not feel old – on the contrary, they're feeling young again. This baby boom generation has been at the forefront of social, economic and political change at every stage of their lives and now sees the over 40s embracing age-defying treatments and refusing to 'grow old gracefully'. They seek adventure, they're after excitement, they have renewed energy and they're drawn to new adventures. With more time at their disposal, they're more creative and have the feeling that if they don't realise their dreams now, they never will. It is Good Housekeeping's ability to champion this market and

consistently and quickly adapt to the needs of its readers, since it was launched in 1922, that has made it one of the most successful magazines of all time.

Achievements

No gimmicks, no gadgets and not a cover-mount in sight, yet for the seventh consecutive ABC period, Good Housekeeping has shown a year-on-year circulation increase. The latest ABC figures for January-June 2005 will take the circulation well over 450,000. NRS reports an adult readership in excess of 1,400,000 and that Good Housekeeping has more ABC1 women readers aged 25-54 than any other women's monthly magazine in the UK (Source: NRS July-December 2004).

Good Housekeeping boasts the largest subscription base of a women's magazine in the market, with 43% of its readers currently subscribing to the title on a monthly basis. Recent orders have seen subscriptions break the 200,000 barrier and Good Housekeeping is predicting further record subscription levels in the next ABC period (Source: NRS July-December 2004).

Good Housekeeping is a global brand, published in four languages and in 16 editions, with 71 million copies sold worldwide each year.

As leader in its market, Good Housekeeping enjoys incredibly high recognition levels in the UK. Over 50% of Good Housekeeping female readers do not read any

other magazine within the core competitive set, 72% do not read any women's weekly magazine, either, and 47% do not read newspaper colour supplements (Source: NRS July-December 2004).

The magazine's consistent circulation growth is simply a result of top-quality editorial combined with a month-in, month-out commitment to meeting the readers' needs.

History

Good Housekeeping is part of The National Magazine Company ('Natmags'), a wholly owned subsidiary of the Hearst Corporation. The National Magazine Company was established in the UK in 1910 by William Randolph Hearst, founder of the US communications giant, Hearst Corporation.

In the years after the end of World War I, British women found themselves living in a world unimaginable a decade earlier. Most women did not yet have the vote but the tragic mass slaughter of young men on the battlefields had forced them out into the workplace and made many of them rethink whether marriage – the ultimate destiny of young women until then – was a realistic option.

In 1922 the new magazine Good Housekeeping was launched to help women find a way of coping with the

changes being thrust upon society. In 1924, the GHI (Good Housekeeping Institute) was also launched to provide unbiased advice on the best consumer products available which were then featured in the pages of the magazine. Partly a manual for living, Good Housekeeping was also a forum for women to explore bigger themes.

Throughout the 83 years since then, Good Housekeeping has remained one of the most enduringly successful magazines in the world, never ceasing publication, not even during the paper shortages of World War II, when it was deemed vital for the war effort, so was printed in a smaller handbag-style size.

Today Good Housekeeping's mission remains unchanged. The challenges that faced women in the 1920s may be very different from the challenges they face today. However, Good Housekeeping still tackles the most important issues, while also informing women on everything from balancing work and home life, through cooking healthy recipes on a budget, to trimming your finances and how to look good and dress well. As women's expectations have evolved and grown, so Good Housekeeping has grown, too.

Product

There is more to Good Housekeeping than just 'good housekeeping'. It's a lively, inspirational and essential part of women's lives in the 21st century. It aims to be the one magazine the reader can always trust – expertise and tireless attention to detail delivered in a positive and accessible way, giving readers direct access to the 'best of everything'. Good Housekeeping brings a wealth of information and advice to its readers, keeping them up to date and balancing practical solutions with achievable inspiration in a no-nonsense format. Championing women and enriching their lives, it's intelligent, progressive and always a uniquely rewarding magazine.

Whether it's a profile of a high-powered celebrity or an interview with an unknown woman with a remarkable story to tell, Good Housekeeping digs that bit deeper and goes that bit further to bring the highest level of journalism to women's magazines.

Good Housekeeping also contains strong fashion content and inspiring beauty, helping the reader to choose what will work for her.

Some of the most authoritative and trusted health pages are also part of the magazine. Regularly praised by doctors and other health professionals, as well as the readers, for offering clear and helpful advice.

Good Housekeeping covers a wide range of topics surrounding the home. Styles from minimalist to shabby chic, ethnic to traditional country are discussed.

For the cookery department of Good Housekeeping it's about easy, achievable, delicious food using quality ingredients, with an emphasis on time saving and healthier eating. The goal is to prove that fast cooking doesn't mean compromising on flavour and to include sumptuous menus for special occasions or the more experienced cook. The skilled cookery team produces food pages that will appeal to women with busy lives and all the recipes are triple tested in the Good Housekeeping Institute kitchens for guaranteed results.

Good Housekeeping is the only consumer lifestyle magazine with an independent consumer research centre, the Good Housekeeping Institute (GHI), established in 1924. The GHI was set up to provide readers with unbiased, independent research findings on consumer products.

More recently, in 2000, the Good Housekeeping Institute launched an accreditation scheme. The scheme allows manufacturers and retailers of food and non-food products to apply for access to the 'GHI-accreditation' logo. The logo reflects the benchmarks for quality that the GHI has been setting since 1924. Only after a consumer product has passed a series of rigorous consumer quality tests can the GHI-accreditation logo be used for marketing, PR and advertising purposes during a 12-month period. The GHI currently has 36 accredited products, bringing the trust and authority of the Good Housekeeping brand to a wide-reaching consumer audience outside the pages of the magazine.

Good Housekeeping is also personally in touch with more than 10,000 readers every year. More than 55 reader events are organised each year, ranging from gardening evenings to cookery demonstrations and from beauty workshops to fashion shows. Readers have the opportunity to meet the people who work on the magazine and have practical observation of their expertise.

Recent Developments
Championing its understanding of women, Good Housekeeping sponsors 'Women of the Year', an award that was founded 50 years ago to celebrate the achievements of women from every field.

In addition, the Good Housekeeping Inspirational Women Awards give readers the opportunity to nominate women whom they admire and respect, whose special qualities bring out the best in others and whose efforts deserve real recognition. This year's winner will be announced in September 2005 and will receive £2,000 towards their chosen charity or cause.

The Innovation Awards attract hundreds of entries from manufacturers and Good Housekeeping readers. Offering media publicity, the awards have been covered on TV and radio and in national newspapers.

Good Housekeeping has also organised fashion awards. Its fashion team works with top high street and designer brands to bring the glossy fashion pages of the magazine to life with an exclusive catwalk show for over 400 readers, held at London's Savoy Hotel.

The Good Housekeeping Food Awards were launched in 2004. Readers were invited to vote for their favourite food, ingredients, restaurants and supermarkets. Among the 2004 category winners were Green & Black's chocolate for that 'moment of indulgence', Waitrose was the favourite supermarket, Jamie Oliver took first place among the celebrity chefs and the Manoir Aux Quat' Saisons in Oxfordshire cornered the vote for 'best restaurant'.

In 2003 Good Housekeeping launched its own range of branded products, the Good Housekeeping Essentials range. Set up to add value to everyday life, tested and approved by the Good Housekeeping institute, every item has been selected for its innovative and user-friendly design. To complement the bakeware and utensil ranges already available, a woodware range was launched in June 2005 and a cookware range is expected to launch later in the year.

Promotion
Core to Good Housekeeping's promotional strategy is to work closely with its editorial teams to reinforce the values of the product and ensure that what it is offering readers will meet their needs.

The team at Good Housekeeping continually evaluates the editorial position and, as part of ongoing research, assesses readers' perception of the magazine through focus groups and reader panels. These give the editorial team up-to-date information on trends in appeal of the articles and the likes and dislikes within the editorial sections of the magazine.

The magazine also endeavours to work closely with third parties to enhance the magazine's position both at the newsstand and with its loyal subscriber base.

As part of the National Magazines portfolio, there is also scope for the title to work in-house with sister titles to make the most of joint ventures and direct-mail opportunities.

Brand Values
Good Housekeeping brand values are summed up as trusted, expert, progressive, full of integrity and it is a consumer champion.

Good Housekeeping believes that it is the benchmark against which all other women's magazines are judged. It combines unrivalled authority with consistent quality, value and entertainment. With an unsurpassed level of reader loyalty and trust, it has unique experience of 'grown-up women' and their lives. Its ongoing success and widespread appeal is due to the breadth, depth and excellence of the editorial content and the contribution of the Good Housekeeping Institute, its unique consumer research centre.

www.goodhousekeeping.co.uk

Gossard™

Market

Women have never been so independent and aware of what they want. From finance to fashion, the UK is fast becoming a nation of women who want – and can have – it all.

These consumers are increasingly demanding fashion-led lingerie. This has resulted in a number of new brands and retailers entering the market: a fiercely competitive arena that is set to grow. Indeed, in 2005 alone there are more than 200 brands in the UK market.

The UK lingerie market is valued at £1.25 billion; this is an increase of 15% over the past five years (Source: TNS January 2005). Bras account for almost 60% of this market (Source: TNS January 2005).

Achievements

In Gossard's long history, the company has earned an exemplary reputation for quality, comfort and fit, with fashion-led ranges to suit every woman.

From its beginnings in Chicago at the turn of the 20th century, through to the launch in London in 1922 and the first UK factory in Leighton Buzzard, Bedfordshire in 1926, Gossard has become a truly international company with proven commitment to introducing Gossard lingerie around the globe and is now sold in over 30 countries.

In recognition of the company's high manufacturing standards, Gossard was the first UK lingerie manufacturer to be awarded the BS5750 Quality Award. Gossard was also awarded The Queen's Award for Export achievement (1995 and 1996) as well as the UK Fashion Export Award (1991, 1994 and 1995).

Little has changed regarding Gossard's commitment to quality and fit, but the company is now firmly positioned as a modern, innovative, feminine brand for the woman of today.

Can you face a full length mirror?

The Gossard Line of Beauty

Gossard has always been a pioneer in the lingerie field – the first to introduce innovative new shapes and concepts. From front fastening corsets to the Wonderbra, from the sheer Glossies range to diamante G-Strings to the revolutionary SuperSmooth – Gossard has long been at the forefront of lingerie development.

History

While visiting Paris, Henry Williamson Gossard, an American representative for a wholesale dressmaking company, was inspired by the actress Sarah Bernhardt, whose figure he saw transformed by a specially designed corset when she played the unusual role of Napoleon II, a 20-year-old boy dying of consumption. Henry immediately knew the corset would be a hit with fashionable women around the world.

In 1901 he founded the H.W.Gossard Company in Chicago and set about producing corsets and 'top quality merchandise'. He travelled from Chicago to Paris twice a year to purchase exquisite fabrics including silks, brocades and lace for his 'foundation wear' and soon built up a strong business that would go on to revolutionise the fashionable lingerie market around the world.

comfort with support

inches away the easy way

Almost ten years later, the company began exporting to the UK, opening an office in London and producing its first sales catalogue for the UK market, featuring corsets and brassieres for a variety of figures including the short, stout and elderly. Fabrics included silks, satins, brocades, cotton, surgical and hand-knitted elastic and suede.

In 1926 the first UK factory opened in Leighton Buzzard, where the company is still based today. Until around this time bras – as we know them today – didn't really exist. Although brassieres had appeared in various basic formats, from shapeless garments that resembled camisoles in the early 1900s to bust bodices that flattened the bust of the 'Flappers' in the 1920s – it wasn't until the 1930s that bras started to take on the form and function of what we now recognise as a bra.

In the 1950s Gossard became part of the Courtaulds Textiles Group and introduced its first lightweight girdles with Silkskin – a lightweight, pre-shrunk girdle featuring an innovative wonder fibre, Nylon from DuPont.

The turn of the millennium saw Sara Lee Corporation buy Courtaulds Textiles, making Sara Lee the owner of the Gossard brand. Today, after 80 years in the lingerie business, Gossard remains one of the most widely recognised and well-loved lingerie brands in the UK.

Product

Over eight decades in the lingerie business, Gossard's products have evolved in line with both fashion and social acceptance.

The 1960s saw Gossard pioneer the pantie-girdle and bra-slip in the UK, both thought to be very daring at the time. Later the same decade, the company diversified and focused on producing fashionable bras, including the now world-famous Wonderbra.

As women turned to burning their bras as a sign of liberation and freedom in the 1970s, Gossard responded by developing its Glossies range of sheer, shimmering underwear, providing a very natural look under clinging clothes.

Around the same time, it was noted that women's figures were starting to change. They were becoming taller and fuller in the bust and, as a result, the demand for larger cup sizes was increasing. Women that fell into this category required the same level of fashion and style that their smaller-busted friends were wearing, so Gossard developed ranges up to DD. Today Gossard offers bras up to an F-cup.

'Co-ordination' was the by-word of the 1980s and with it Gossard introduced its popular Ritz collection of co-ordinates from A-E cup and a basque style.

In the 1990s, Playtex acquired the Wonderbra brand when Gossard's licence to produce it expired. To counteract the loss, Gossard launched the Ultrabra – the first time a cleavage bra was available for larger cup sizes. Ultrabra Super Boost hit the market a few years later with the claim: 'Biggest Cleavage ever... or your money back!'

With a little support I can have a lot of fun!

Gossard
It fits my body and my feelings

THE LOOK

THE FEEL

THE ONLY THING YOU'LL FEEL IS FANTASTIC **Gossard** Super Smooth

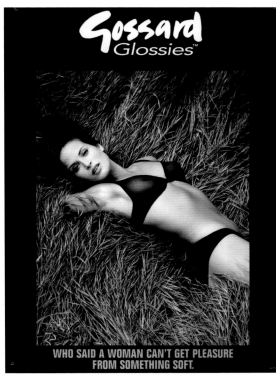

WHO SAID A WOMAN CAN'T GET PLEASURE FROM SOMETHING SOFT.

In 2002 the trend for low-rise trousers and hipsters emerged, and women became more and more concerned about visible panty-lines. In response to this need, Gossard launched G-Strings – a collection of decorative G-strings that could be worn everyday or on special occasions. The G-Strings were heavily embellished featuring diamante shapes on the back and capturing the trend of lingerie that was worn to be seen. The response to the innovative launch was fantastic and within two months of launch the diamante T-bar sold out across the whole of the UK.

Also launched in 2002 was a designer collection created especially for Gossard by British womenswear designer Elspeth Gibson. This first captured the interest of designer associations on the high street.

The Gossard range today consists of three sub-brands: Gossard SuperSmooth, 'the invisible bra with the visible effect'; Gossard Superboost, 'for the ultimate cleavage'; and Gossard Collection, a range of fashion inspired co-ordinates from A-F cup sizes.

Recent Developments

In January 2005 Gossard launched its most innovative product yet – Gossard SuperSmooth. Following extensive consumer research, the SuperSmooth range was designed to meet every lingerie expectation simultaneously.

The SuperSmooth bra uses revolutionary no-stitching and no-seam technology to provide invisible support and

a comfortable second-skin sensation. Moulded cups are designed to give an enhanced silhouette and the look is ultra-modern with signature Gossard styling.

Promotion

Gossard strives to respond to ever-changing consumer needs and communicates this via its advertising and PR strategies.

Campaigns over the past few decades have included: 'Wonderbra: Say Goodbye to your feet', 'Superboost: Boob Job for £19' and the 'Girl in the grass' campaign for the Glossies range, which featured Sophie Anderton, shot by Herb Ritz, with the strapline: 'Who said a woman couldn't get pleasure from something soft?'

In 2002, Gossard ran a national TV campaign created by TBWA for its 'Altogether' range, showing that women never want to be caught out wearing underwear that doesn't match. The ad featured a woman who has been hit by the 34B bus. She is seen hurtling down a hospital corridor, and into the 'Bus Incident Room'. She is extremely distressed and becomes hysterical as the nurses begin to remove her clothes – she is wearing uncoordinated underwear and has just been found out.

The G-Strings: G4ME national TV, press and poster campaign was based around the concept of wearing attractive underwear for oneself rather than for men. It also featured an SMS campaign offering money off vouchers. PR activity has always supported Gossard advertising campaigns and in 2002, Gossard ran a competition to give away a diamond encrusted G-String worth £25,000.

Over the past few decades Gossard has launched the career of models such as Kate Groombridge, Emma Griffiths and Sophie Anderton by signing them as the 'face' of the brand. They have all gone on to have successful careers in modelling and television.

In 2005, Gossard has signed model Maria Gregerson as the new face of the brand. Maria fronts the new SuperSmooth press and poster campaign created by TBWA, 'SuperSmooth: The only thing you'll feel is fantastic', as well as gracing the pages of many magazines and newspapers as the new Gossard Girl.

Mary McCartney Donald, breast cancer awareness campaigner, and daughter of Sir Paul McCartney, shot the ad, which is designed to create a real connection with women. Bucking the trend for lingerie ads that focus on the way the product looks, the SuperSmooth campaign focuses on how the bra makes the wearer feel.

Brand Values

Gossard is positioned as the brand with the expertise to combine alluring feminine style with no compromise on comfort, for women who want to feel special: 'Sexiness and comfort without the compromise'.

Gossard's commitment to understanding the consumer through research, and the fact that this knowledge directly influences UK-based design and marketing teams, ensures that Gossard understands and delivers what today's woman wants.

Gossard offers women lingerie that is sophisticated, glamorous and alluring so that she looks as sexy as she feels.

www.gossard.com

BOOB JOB £19   superboost Gossard

THINGS YOU DIDN'T KNOW ABOUT

Gossard

> The average bra uses up to 100m of thread, has up to 50 components (including hooks and eyes, wings, cradle, centre gore and wire casing) and can take up to 28 sewing operations to complete.

> During World War II the Gossard factory was turned over to assist with Britain's war effort. During that time its workforce produced everything from brassieres for the Wrens to sails, single-seat fighter dinghies and almost 700,000 parachutes.

> 70% of women wear the wrong bra size. This stresses the importance of getting properly fitted for each bra to ensure the correct support and the perfect shape.

> In the 1960s, Gossard first launched the Wonderbra within an advertisement for a new girdle, for decency. But it was the lacy, low-cut bra that stole the heart of the female population.

Horlicks

Market

Adults today sleep on average seven and a half hours a night, compared to nine hours at the turn of the 20th century. Two-thirds of Brits get less than eight hours sleep and one-third get less than six hours a night. In fact, one in three people will suffer from insomnia at some stage in their life.

Bring on Hot Milky Drinks (HMDs) – a market that's worth £113.1 million and is growing at a rate of 8.7% annually, compared to the overall Hot Beverages market, which is valued at £1.3 billion and is in decline at a rate of 0.1% per year. Hot Beverages is also made up of coffee (£640 million, growth of 1.3%), tea (£545 million, decline of 2.7%), fruit & herbal tea (£33 million, growth of 10%).

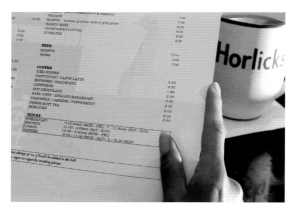

Horlicks is the leading brand in the HMD category (Source: Nielsen, Scantrack, Sterling Value of Hot Milky Drinks, Total Trade, MAT Feb 2005). Other key brands within the HMD category are Cadbury Hot Chocolate, Cadbury Highlights, Options and Ovaltine.

The primary reason that people use HMDs is to drink before bedtime to help them sleep. This is backed up by studies that show that a hot milky drink such as Horlicks can promote a good night's sleep (Source: Southwell P R, Evans C R and Hunt J N. Effects of a Hot Milk Drink on Movements During Sleep. British Medical Journal 1972, 2, 429-431).

Achievements

Sleep has become a national obsession and increasingly talked about by consumers. Are we getting enough 'restful' sleep? How many hours do we need to function? And as if to prove the point that the nation has become enthralled in the 'sleep-fixation' debate, sales of Horlicks have increased significantly.

With a record brand investment programme of more than £3 million, 2004 was a good year for Horlicks, with sales up 13% since 2003. In fact, sales have now reached

the highest ever point in the brand's history. This acceleration of brand sales has helped drive overall HMD category growth recently. Indeed, ACNielsen reported this to be 6.7% (for the 12 weeks ending November 27th 2004).

It would seem that households across the nation are learning the importance of a good wind-down routine before bedtime in order to get a restful night's sleep – and Horlicks is playing an important part in this.

In recent months, celebrities and media-types have been quaffing Horlicks in celebrated haunts such as The Embassy Club and The Groucho Club before heading off for an early night. This looks set to continue, with Horlicks being included in Elle magazine's list of 'Top 25 Things for 2005'.

History

Established 132 years ago, Horlicks Malt Milk was the first dried milk food successfully marketed throughout the world. The founders, James and William Horlicks, were

born in 1844 and 1846 respectively at Ruardean in Gloucestershire. When they reached their late teens both men went to London, where James joined a homeopathic chemist in Bond Street and William a saddler in Lisle Street, where he became a fully-fledged mechanic.

In 1869, William left for the US and worked for a year or two with a distant cousin in the quarrying business at Racine, Wisconsin. Meanwhile, James qualified as a pharmacist (also in 1869). Before leaving England in 1873, he was working on a dried infant food prepared from malt and bran to mix with milk and water. James could not raise the necessary capital to market and produce a new drink himself in London and so left to join his brother in America.

Later in 1873, a partnership was formed under the name of J&W Horlicks in Chicago to manufacture James' artificial infant food and a patent was granted by the US Patent Office. The product enjoyed success from the start, with James taking responsibility for selling to the medical profession and to the

pharmaceutical trade, while William looked after the production and financial matters.

Two years later they moved to larger premises at Racine, where wheat and barley were in abundant supply, together with a good source of spring water. Helped by advertising at medical conferences sponsored by the company, sales soon began to boom.

As Horlicks Food required the addition of sterile milk, an obvious product innovation was the addition of milk to the process. Since James was concerned with selling, it was left up to William to produce the first 'malted milk', which was patented on June 5th 1883.

Around 1890, James returned to England to set up a London office, where the company stayed until the establishment of the factory at Slough in 1906. The business went from strength to strength until World War I. James died in 1921 and it was then decided that William should keep the American business covering America, Canada, the Caribbean and South America, while Sir James' son would take ownership of the English company covering the rest of the world. Each would run independently but preserving liaison and exchange of information. William died in 1936, aged 90.

In 1931-1933, the product was re-styled as 'Horlicks', dropping the 'Malted Milk' from the advertised description. This paved the way for the highly successful 'Night Starvation' story, which dramatised the benefits of sound, refreshing sleep resulting from the regular bedtime consumption of Horlicks.

At the end of 1968, two large British companies (Beecham Group and Boots Ltd) made substantial offers to the shareholders of Horlicks. Early in 1969, the offer from the Beecham Group – worth approximately £20 million – was accepted and Horlicks Limited became part of the Beecham Empire. Under the guidance of the Beecham group, sales of Horlicks from the Slough factory had more than doubled to over 19.3 million kilograms a year by 1995.

Today, Horlicks is a registered trademark of the GlaxoSmithKline group of companies.

Product

The association between Horlicks and sleep is deep-rooted – people have drunk Horlicks as part of their bedtime ritual for many years, seeing it as an excellent way to help relax and unwind and one of the most enjoyable ways of helping restful sleep. Scientific research showed that Horlicks had a positive effect on sleep quantity and quality.

Horlicks is a nourishing malted drink with a unique combination of wholesome ingredients, combining malted barley, wheat and dairy ingredients.

Horlicks is available in two formats, Original Malt to which milk is added and Instant, to which water is added. Instant Horlicks comes in three flavours: Malt, Malted Chocolate and Hot Chocolate.

Recent Developments

There are some classic British brands that you could accuse of living in the past but Horlicks is not one of them. 2004 saw Horlicks redesign its packaging as it seeks to own the area of restful sleep.

The new packaging has taken a 'do not disturb' sign as an analogy for restful sleep. The new look also communicates what is described as 'the great new taste' of the brand, now with a more creamy flavour and includes 'Tips for Relaxation' on each pack.

Horlicks has enhanced its new identity by creating a number of partnerships with some of the coolest venues in London. As a nation, we are reappraising the value of sleep. Our longer working hours and hectic lifestyles mean that increasingly we are burning the candle at both ends. The makers of Horlicks thought it only natural to be available in venues where the ambience is all about enjoying one's self and then getting a good night's sleep.

At the Embassy London, Horlicks has been added to the bar menu in the Private Members' bar. Horlicks is also on the bar menu of the infamous Soho private members' club and The Groucho Club, as well as from room service in their 19 bedrooms.

The Zetter, the new restaurant and rooms in London's Clerkenwell, has already been voted among the top 50 hip hotels by Condé Nast Traveller this year, after only opening in March, and guests can also enjoy Horlicks on room service and the bar menu.

At The Rivington, the smart modern British bar and grill in the middle of trendy Shoreditch, Horlicks was offered as a digestive and as an alternative to caffeine stimulants such as tea and coffee which can keep people awake ahead of bed.

As well as trendy urbanites, the makers of Horlicks identified another new market to tap into: children. In 2004 a new children's bedtime drink, Snoozoo,

was launched. It was designed for children to have as part of their bedtime routine, while also delivering vitamins and minerals in child-friendly chocolate, strawberry and banana flavours. So Horlicks continues to establish itself as a key player in the promotion of healthy sleep habits.

Promotion

Restful sleep has been at the core of Horlicks promotional strategy since 1929 when the slogan was, 'The bedtime drink that ensures a night of sound sleep.'

From the 1930s to late 1970s, advertisements for Horlicks focused on delivering a good night's sleep, thus allowing the consumer to keep going throughout the day. The advertising campaigns aimed to educate the consumer on the seven phases of sleep: sound sleep, deep sleep, hypnotic trance like qualities, shallow sleep, fatigue and depression as well as night starvation.

By the 1990s, the line 'Horlicks' sleep leaves you feeling renewed & refreshed' was used and sleep had become a widespread consumer concern.

In an omnibus survey carried out in September 1996 for Horlicks, 94% of participants agreed that they felt more able to cope with the day after a refreshing night's sleep and 60% believed that hot milky drinks could help them relax and sleep better.

The marketing focused on the end benefit of a good sleep, which offered consumers a new and relevant point of entry into Horlicks. The advertising began to address the consumer need for better sleep, building on Horlicks brand equity and the new brand values of optimism and energy.

In 2003, the brand began using the 'How Do They Sleep at Night?' concept. The advertising illustrates that Horlicks can help you get to sleep, no matter what's on your mind. Horlicks chose familiar 'hate' characters such as baggage handlers, bus drivers and traffic wardens and showed them acting in ways that should leave them feeling guilty and unable to sleep at night because of the way they live their lives and treat others.

What viewers see, however, is that they actually have no trouble sleeping restfully because they drink Horlicks before bed. Thus the new strapline: 'Horlicks can help anyone get a restful night's sleep'.

The TV executions were supported by radio and sampling campaigns, with over one million samples given away across the winter 2004-2005 period.

Brand Values

Horlicks can play an important part in evening wind-down routines. The brand believes that to prepare and settle down to enjoy a warm cup of comforting Horlicks, makes the drinker naturally stop, relax and unwind – it helps the drinker feel relaxed and ready for bed.

Horlicks offers the reassurance that you can go to bed, confident you'll drift off, rather than tossing and turning until the early hours.

Horlicks believes that everyone deserves a good night's sleep. That's why Horlicks has made its mission to help Britain sleep better.

www.horlicks.co.uk

Horlicks and Snoozoo are registered trademarks of the GlaxoSmithKline group of companies.

Market

Bread has been a staple food item for many since 1000BC, when the first truly modern bread was made in Ancient Egypt.

Today, with more than 200 varieties available in the UK, bread is probably the one food eaten by people of every race, culture and religion. It is naturally packed with more essential vitamins and nutrients than any other single source. Bread is an excellent source of protein, complex carbohydrates, calcium, iron magnesium, potassium and zinc, as well as the B vitamins.

The UK bread and morning goods market is worth more than £3 billion and is one of the largest sectors in the food industry (Source: IRI). Hovis commands the number-one position within the wrapped bread market and is bought by more households than any other bread brand (Source: IRI). Although white bread has traditionally been the UK's firm favourite, brown bread has been gaining popularity over the last few years. Hovis is the clear leader in the brown bread market with over 30% value share and continues to grow by 17% year-on-year (Source: IRI).

Achievements

The Hovis brand has an illustrious history as one of the UK's oldest bread brands. Throughout its existence, Hovis has been synonymous with high quality and has developed many different products in line with a changing society.

Keeping abreast of changing consumer demands, Hovis has continued to lead the way in innovation, not only producing bread for most sectors of the market but creating new segments. In 1999

the brand introduced Hovis Crusty bread (which maintains its crusty outside and soft inside for up to four days) and in 2001 it launched Best of Both, a white loaf with the amount of wheatgerm found in wholemeal bread. In less than four years, Best of Both has become a £52 million brand, driving the Healthy White segment and making itself the clear market leader.

In addition to new product development, Hovis, as the leading bread brand, has challenged the category norms. Against a background of long-term volume decline in the bread category and with low retail bread pricing, Hovis knew that a step-change was necessary for the new millennium in order to grow the value of the bread category.

It is essential that consumers value bread, both financially and for its healthy qualities. In summer 2001 Hovis introduced a radically new packaging design across its core lines that disrupted the fixture and made consumers take note and so the now-iconic Hovis 'beans' and 'tomatoes' packaging was born.

The re-launch, plus the new product development of Best of Both, drove category value growth and double-digit growth for the brand.

Following the major re-launch of summer 2001, Hovis was awarded the IPA Effectiveness Award (silver) and the Brand Design Gold Award for packaging and advertising.

Further endorsements were received in the form of the FAB Awards for packaging and advertising in 2002.

History

Hovis bread began life in 1886 with the cumbersome name of 'Smith's Patent Germ Bread'. It was the brainchild of Richard 'Stoney' Smith who had long considered discarding the wheatgerm in wheatgrains because of its instability as a wanton waste of the most nutritive properties of wheat. He experimented and perfected a method of steam cooking which preserved the wheatgerm without destroying its nutrients.

Fitton & Sons, Millers of Macclesfield, was charged with marketing Smith's invention. The company held a national competition to find a new name for the product. It was won by a London student named Herbert Grime, who took the Latin 'hominis vis' ('strength of man') and shortened it to Hovis.

Much of the early success of Hovis can be attributed to John Figgins Morton who set about devising advertising campaigns that firmly established Hovis as a household name. The earliest Hovis advertisements were aimed at the trade in an effort to attract bakers to become Hovis agents.

Three years of trading gained widespread acceptance of wheatgerm bread and by 1890 the name Hovis had been established and elaborate plans to promote the name to the fullest extent had been introduced. By 1895 Hovis was claiming that sales of Hovis bread had exceeded 1,000,000 loaves per week.

In 1916 the earliest reference to 'Don't say Brown – say Hovis' first appeared. Hovis advertising in World War I was not prolific and mostly reflected the economy. During World War II, slogans such as 'Make Hovis Your Ration for The Duration' were introduced, while a booklet entitled 'Sandwich Suggestions for the Shelter' was produced. After the war, Hovis advertising became more co-ordinated and a consistent theme and slogan were produced and adhered to.

Commercial television began in the UK in 1955 and Hovis made a tremendous impact by revisiting the slogan that became famous: 'Don't Say Brown – Say Hovis'. A highly successful series of short sharp commercials followed featuring George Benson. This slogan was in use until 1960 when it was changed to 'The Golden Heart Of Hovis' and 'Home Is All The Better For Hovis'.

Today, the great success story for Hovis is truly reflected in its value sales, which have grown from £20 million in 1980 to more than £293 million in 2005 (Source: IRI).

Product

Hovis has come a long way since the days of Richard 'Stoney' Smith's original wheatgerm flour. Although renowned for its wheatgerm bread (renamed Hovis Brown in 1997), Hovis also makes white, wholemeal and Granary loaves, along with a whole range of other products.

Never afraid of innovation and always ready to respond to the needs of its consumers, Hovis introduced its innovative square rolls, the Hovis Cobble, in 1994 and the Half Loaf in 1995. The following year saw the launch of the Hovis Luxury Fruited range, including a Fruit Loaf, Toasting Buns and Scones. Hovis also produces Hovis Farmhouse, a loaf with all the flavour of a traditionally baked farmhouse loaf but the convenience of modern wrapped, sliced bread.

Following the ground-breaking success of Hovis Crusty White in 1999, a Crusty Golden Brown version was introduced the following year. At the same time, in July 2001, Hovis Best of Both was launched, spearheading the drive into creating the new healthy white bread segment.

Recent Developments

Moving into the 21st century saw Hovis boldly entering a brave new world with the introduction of its revolutionary and much prized 'big food' packaging – featuring baked beans, tomatoes, cucumbers and melted cheese imagery covering the whole pack.

Supported by a completely new £7 million advertising campaign, which featured cartoons that reflected the rather hectic nature of modern family life, a far cry from the sepia 'tinted' imagery of yesteryear, the re-launch clearly established Hovis as the nation's favourite bread brand. Since the launch, Hovis White Square Cut, proudly displayed in the iconic 'beans' packaging, has become the bestselling loaf.

The following year, in April 2002, Hovis focused its attention to the Rolls category, developing and launching a unique range of Square Rolls suitable for the lunchbox occasion and packed to prevent damage in transit.

Based on the brand truths of 'family values' and 'good for you', Hovis has continued to highlight and drive the healthy qualities and nutritional benefits

of bread to an increasingly more 'health-conscious' consumer, introducing appropriate new products to meet consumer needs, across the various bread sectors. These include Hovis Best of Health in 2003, two versions of Hovis Lower Salt, in the ever-popular Square bread format – in White and Wholemeal varieties and also a Hovis Lower Carbs, a white bread that contains 25% less carbohydrate than standard, all in 2004.

In between, Hovis continued to build on the health message by ensuring that all products with the entire bread range were 'free from artificial preservatives and flavourings'; becoming the only brand to do so.

Promotion

The 1970s signalled Hovis' commitment to modern advertising. The brand changed its advertising agency and within two years had introduced the nostalgic theme by Dvorak that became such a prominent feature of the 1970s and 1980s. Together with the famous film director, Ridley Scott, the agency produced a series of commercials that won their way into the hearts of the general public. The now famous 'Bike Ride' commercial made in 1973 won five awards and became part of national television history. The nostalgic Hovis commercials produced during the decade 1972-1982 won more than 30 international awards.

By 1994, the slogan on the TV adverts was changed to 'Raised The Hovis Way', reinforcing Hovis' emphasis on tradition and the family. In 1997 the adverts continued under the 'Raised The Hovis Way' banner but focused on people and their partiality for different Hovis loaves.

Hovis has ensured that it remains the number one bread brand into the 21st century.

New advertising with heavyweight media spend featured a cartoon family depicting real-life situations and the role that Hovis played in providing everyday goodness for busy, modern families. This re-launch had a dramatic effect, with share growing – particularly in white bread – to increase Hovis' brand leadership.

In 2003, Hovis became the only major brand to remove artificial preservatives and flavourings from its bread. This was supported with TV advertising until 2005. The Best of Both product has also been consistently advertised from launch in 2001 and is now worth £52 million in terms of value sales.

2005 has seen further improvements to the goodness delivered by Hovis products. All Hovis white bread is now the 'Healthiest Ever' with extra wholewheat goodness, lower salt and no artificial preservatives. This has been supported with new advertising and packaging, ensuring that Hovis remains at the forefront of consumer expectations.

Brand Values

For more than 119 years, since Richard Stoney Smith found a way of retaining the wheatgerm goodness in flour, Hovis has been a bread brand synonymous with goodness.

Providing 'everyday goodness' is at the heart of the brand and, through consistent marketing support and innovation, consumers still believe Hovis provides the most goodness of any bread brand. It is also the most trusted bread brand, with 78% of the consumer vote in the Reader's Digest Most Trusted Brands survey and perceived to be the highest quality (78%), demonstrating it's enduring appeal and the virtues of a long heritage.

www.hovisbakery.co.uk

THINGS YOU DIDN'T KNOW ABOUT

Hovis

❯ The first Hovis advert appeared in 1888, in the form of an analyst's report on the nutritional value of bread baked from germ flour. Professor William Jago said: "The prepared germ meal and flour yield a bread far superior in nutritive value, flavour and texture."

❯ The founder, Richard Smith, died in 1890 and is now buried in Highgate Cemetery. His grave is marked by a special headstone in remembrance of his particular contribution to the British diet.

❯ During World War II, Hovis donated a spitfire to the RAF. It was named 'Hominis Vis', latin for 'the strength of man', which in its shortened form became the brand name Hovis.

❯ In 2000 Hovis 'Boy on a Bike' was voted as one of the nation's favourite advertisements in a poll carried out by The Sunday Times and Channel 4.

❯ 110 years after Hovis flour was first introduced, Hovis is the number-one bread brand in the UK.

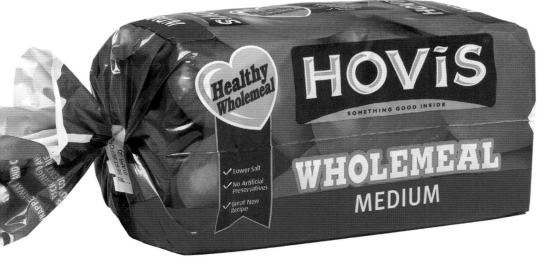

Market

This isn't news to parents, but to those who have not had the pleasure of a baby it is difficult to imagine just how many nappies one little tiny person can go through. On average a baby will be changed seven times a day.

Multiply this by the number of babies in the UK and this adds up to a lot of nappies.

Indeed, a total of 2.5 billion nappies are bought in the UK each year in a market worth approximately £415 million (Source: ACNielsen).

This highly competitive marketplace is dominated by two major players – Kimberly-Clark's HUGGIES® and Pampers from Proctor & Gamble.

Category originator Pampers is the market leader with 66% value market share, yet in a market that enjoys strong consumer loyalty, HUGGIES® has a 19% market share (Source: ACNielsen).

Achievements

HUGGIES® are designed and produced using the very latest nappy technology. The research and development team at Kimberly-Clark has spent years studying the technical aspects of nappies and their impact on dryness, comfort and skin health. This has resulted in the current HUGGIES® range being the best-performing HUGGIES® to date.

Best-selling HUGGIES® Super-Flex nappies have been awarded five prestigious awards in 2004 – Platinum, Best Buy & Best Value, Silver and Editor's Choice proving that Super-Flex is setting the standard for fit and absorbency.

According to the Prima Baby editor, HUGGIES® Super-Flex nappies are the best nappy for fit and leakage protection and so were awarded the magazine's coveted Best Buy rosette.

Furthermore in the nappy Oscars, HUGGIES® Super-Flex was honoured with the Platinum Award in leading magazine Baby & Toddler Gear Summer Edition 2004. The brand has also been awarded the Silver prize in the Best Nappy Category of The Mother & Baby Awards for Newborn and Super-Flex.

Not being content as a shining light in the parenting press, HUGGIES® Super-Flex was short listed in the prestigious Media and Marketing Europe Awards. It may be a new sub-brand on the block, but when it comes to creative marketing campaigns, Super-Flex showed other household names including Apple how it's done by winning the Best Launch Award.

The winning campaign, Super-Flex Baby Shapes/Baby Thoughts was one of the most successful UK product launches for HUGGIES® and has resulted in turning the business around and establishing a strong base to regain market share. Overall brand awareness has also improved as result of a sampling campaign in summer 2004.

History

HUGGIES® was launched in the UK in 1993 and quickly began to take market share from Pampers. It has maintained a competitive edge with innovative developments such as the addition of adhesive stretch ears in 1995 and the introduction of a breathable outer cover in 1998 – a market first.

Further product innovations over the following three years included improved fastening, increased absorbency and an even more breathable outer cover have helped to build the HUGGIES® brand.

With breathable technology, HUGGIES® was the first nappy clinically proven to protect against nappy rash. Furthermore, its research into keeping babies skin naturally healthy is supported by the British Skin Foundation.

A big development on the HUGGIES® brand occurred in 2001 when the 'Challenger Brand' strategy was adopted in order to revitalise the brand. This led to the positioning 'HUGGIES® gives your child the freedom to develop and thrive' and a brand architecture that segmented the range into three sub-brands, namely Beginnings, Freedom and Adventurers, each with different product specifications to reflect the needs of babies at different stages of their development.

The trade response to this category innovation was considerable. The re-launch was hailed as the single biggest event in the nappy category since HUGGIES® was first launched in the UK. Its success was also reflected in the strong launch support it received from leading grocery retailers.

HUGGIES® continues to innovate and is a highly successful global brand, occupying the number one or two positions in most markets in which it operates.

Product

At the centre of the HUGGIES® brand is its understanding of the varying needs of babies at different stages of their

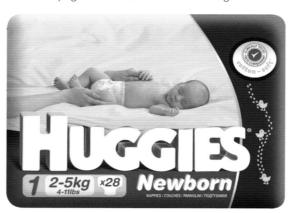

development. The HUGGIES® portfolio consists of a range of products that help babies get from wet to dry.

Skin health is a key concern for parents with newborn babies. HUGGIES® Newborn has a Baby Soft inner liner, a super soft outer cover and unique flap material for the gentlest touch on the baby's skin. HUGGIES® claims there is no softer 'Newborn' nappy with the leakage protection of HUGGIES® Newborn. HUGGIES® Newborn nappies have been specially designed to protect the baby's delicate skin from nappy rash and soreness and keep them comfortable right from the start.

Nappies that fit better are proven to work better. HUGGIES® Super-Flex is designed to enable babies to get on with their everyday baby business leak-free. With their baby shape and super-stretchy waistband, the product fits snugly on the baby. And because it fits better, it's less likely to leak, keeping the baby dry and comfy whatever position he gets into.

Knowing that extra care has gone into the details provides mums with confidence. With a specially designed cover, snug elasticised waist and curved leg elastic, HUGGIES® Supremes are shaped to match the toddler's need for growing independence and action. The nappy width is narrower and has a cutaway, tailored shape to give an improved fit for active babies. The slimmer fit gives the baby extra freedom of movement so that when he wear HUGGIES® Supremes he can do whatever he wants.

Babies need a specific product to have fun in the water but still provide dryness from little accidents for them – and everyone else. HUGGIES® Little Swimmers have a unique absorbent material that won't swell in water like nappies and stretchy sides for a comfortable fit. They also feature tear away sides for easy removal.

Recent Developments

HUGGIES® has recently launched its first two-in-one nappy, designed to have all the convenience of a pant with the absorbency of a HUGGIES® nappy. New HUGGIES® Convertibles 2-in-1 nappies offer two ways to change, because once a baby starts to find his feet, parents may find he's reluctant to give them up again, especially at nappy-changing time. Other times however, the toddler is happy to lie down. HUGGIES® Convertibles 2-in-1 come pre-fastened to pull on like a pant, and the adjustable stretchy fasteners makes it fit for the baby's movements. In addition, HUGGIES® Convertibles 2-in-1 easy-open sides enables it to be used like a normal nappy.

Because delicate skin needs pure delicate care, HUGGIES® have launched HUGGIES® Pure, a wipe that offers gentle

cleaning like cotton wool and water with the convenience of a wipe. Fragrance free, alcohol free, it has been clinically tested and is suitable for sensitive skin.

With Aloe and Vitamin E, HUGGIES® +ALOE wipes help to keep the skin healthy. Softly quilted to clean gently and effectively, they have a light fresh fragrance that leaves the skin smelling fresh and clean.

The new HUGGIES® 3-in-1 Wipes kit is designed to make life easier for parents once they have decided to start taking their new baby out and about. With dispensing tub, refill pack of wipes and handy travel case, it contains everything parents need to ensure their baby is clean and comfortable, no matter where they are.

Promotion

HUGGIES® is promoted as a modern, innovative brand that is focused on babies' needs. The HUGGIES® marketing campaigns focus on delivering a synergistic message and building upon its positioning and personality. The brand identity, packaging design and exploitation of the visual equities have been at the core of this.

HUGGIES® packaging has been designed to communicate the notion that HUGGIES® allows one's child the freedom to develop and thrive. The packs are produced in vibrant colours and have a distinct look and feel that aims to capture the image of a child engrossed in their own world.

This ethos is reflected throughout the HUGGIES® range, so that parents will make the connection between their own

baby and the babies featured on-pack through the photography that captures a real baby doing real things. Whilst a mother's presence is not overt in the design, it aims to clearly reflect that she is there.

For the launch of the award-winning HUGGIES® Super-Flex, eye-catching and emphatic creative was built on consumer insight, using a baby-centric view of the world and developed by ad agency Ogilvy & Mather.

An innovative communications strategy maximised the media investment by focusing on key peak airtime programmes at launch to maximise coverage and then moving to daytime TV to maximise frequency and sustain the campaign over a longer period of time. TV was supported by a full 360 degree communications programme including bus, poster and press advertising.

Campaign momentum was maintained by innovative use of sponsorship on TV and radio. In-store, promotions and packaging were aligned with above-the-line work, delivering a consistent and compelling proposition. This campaign won the Best Launch award at the 2004 Media and Marketing Europe Awards.

Building on the successful media model of the HUGGIES® Super-Flex launch, HUGGIES® Convertibles 2-in-1 was

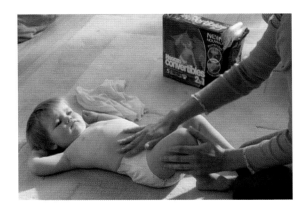

supported with a full 360 degree campaign that carried the key message 'two ways to change' through-the-line. The TV advertising has been received positively by consumers and helped establish Convertibles as a truly innovative product in the market.

Brand Values

HUGGIES® brand values have been based on consumer insights. Research found that mothers are intuitively aware of how babies discover, explore, experiment and learn to deal with the world. The majority of mothers also believe that babies should be 'free' to pursue life's adventures.

HUGGIES® look to share parents' sense of amazement at how their child develops and encourages this. It understands that babies can be messy, noisy, bewildering and a little disruptive at times – as well as being truly amazing.

In recognising this, HUGGIES® products aim to facilitate babies' individuality at each stage of its development. They hope to allow babies to 'forget' that they are wearing nappies – helping give them the freedom to explore.

www.huggiesclub.com

THINGS YOU DIDN'T KNOW ABOUT

HUGGIES®

> The HUGGIES® family includes HUGGIES® Pull-Ups training pants and Dry Nites night time absorbent pants.

> HUGGIES® invented the potty training pant category with the launch of HUGGIES® Pull-Ups.

> Kimberly-Clark is among Fortune magazine's 'Most Admired' companies and was recently named on the Sunday Times list of '100 Best Companies to Work For'.

> In 2003, HUGGIES® celebrated the 10th anniversary of its UK launch, having already achieved Superbrand status.

Hush Puppies

Market

For some an obsession, but for most a necessity, shoes are part of the fabric of life. The UK market for footwear has grown by 1.9% since 2003 to reach a value of £5.1 billion (Source: Euromonitor). Women's footwear is the largest sector of the UK market, with 47.7% of the market, representing a value of £2.4 billion in 2003 (Source: Euromonitor).

Hush Puppies is a leading brand in the casual footwear market, competing against other high-profile brands such as Clarks, Kickers, Diesel and Camper.

In the future, the UK footwear market is forecast to grow by nearly 7.6% to reach a value of £5.5 billion in 2008. The women's sector is set to continue dominating the market with a value share of 46.3% by 2008 (Source: Euromonitor).

Achievements

Established since 1958, Hush Puppies has become a global brand, which over the past few years has succeeded in re-positioning itself to a prominent position within the fashion sector of the footwear market.

Hush Puppies' latest achievement is the Good Housekeeping Institute accreditation for its Wolverine Worry Free Suede fabric, which has undergone rigorous testing to prove that the fabric repels water, red wine, mud and dirt and stays new and natural looking longer.

During the tanning process Teflon® is added to the suede, therefore the properties are within the fabric and cannot wear off. Water forms beads instead of sinking in, keeping the shoes dry whatever the season. A simple brushing restores the suede to like-new conditions. The suede also allows air to freely circulate, keeping the wearer's feet cool and dry. This 'breathability' is designed to give feet all-day comfort that is synonymous with the Hush Puppies brand.

History

In 1958 cult American shoe brand Hush Puppies was creatively conceived. Famed for radically revolutionising contemporary casual footwear, the brand entered the market when US tannery company Wolverine crafted a classic suede Oxford shoe, fashioned from Native American pigskin leather.

Hush Puppies owes its name to a colloquialism used after a Wolverine employee observed that his friends' barking dogs were instantly silenced when fried cornmeal balls (also known as hush puppies) were thrown at them. At the same time, sore feet were also commonly known as 'barking dogs' thus 'Hush Puppies' was the new name given to the Wolverine shoe.

Launched in the UK by high street footwear giant Saxone, in 1959, just a year after going on sale in America, they became a sell-out. Offering both comfort and style, the brown suede shoes fast became a firm fashion favourite throughout the late 1950s and the staple uniform for Mods everywhere in the swinging 1960s.

By 1965, Hush Puppies shoes had ensured that Wolverine successfully dominated the American casual footwear market. In the 1990s Hush Puppies became hot property once again as loafers and lace-ups were once again the shoes to be seen in on the streets of New York. Fashion editors and stylists were spotted scouring second-hand shops and street markets for authentic, vintage Hush Puppies.

The craze continued onto the catwalk as Hush Puppies made their way into John Bartlett's Spring/Summer 1995 Menswear collection. Bartlett hailed them as: "The quintessential American shoe....an American icon." Displaying a range of Hush Puppies in a myriad of rainbow hues from lavender to lime he sparked a massive resurgence in the demand for Hush Puppies Originals.

Hush Puppies Originals were soon the toast of the New York shopping scene, stocked by exclusive stores such as Charivari, Pleasure Swell and Barneys. American designers Anna Sui and Gene Myer also followed in the footsteps of John Bartlett by showcasing Hush Puppies in their fashion collections. English designer Paul Smith was the first to stock the new colourful Hush Puppies in the UK.

Product

The Hush Puppies Autumn/Winter 2005 range sees a new younger styling in the men's range, but with all the additional benefits consumers have come to expect from Hush Puppies.

In the men's shoes, wearers can expect comfort from the BOUNCE range, flexibility from WAVE REFLEX, the wider fitting option of DUAL FIT and a unique contoured foot-bed from the exclusive BODYMOC range.

In the ladies' shoes, wearers can expect stylish, ageless footwear available in vibrant colours, rich suede and unusual character leathers. Heels, flats, stitching detail, ties and fur trims all add to the array of boots and shoes on offer for Autumn/Winter 2005.

The core product benefits still feature, including hand stitched units for extra comfort, HP02, which cushions feet on a bed of air and Zero G 'the shoe that is almost weightless'.

Hush Puppies does not just produce shoes for adults, but is also well-known for its children's range. This season, its adult ranges have influenced the children's styling, with fur-trim boots and detailed fashion shoes for girls and a sportier Velcro styling for boys.

Of course, the main consideration when it comes to children's shoes is not style but comfort and fit, so Hush Puppies has developed a unique three-way fitting system.

A third of children require a different fitting between the left and right feet. Hush Puppies unique three-way fitting system allows it to tailor the fit of each individual shoe, giving a different fitting for each foot if necessary.

Each pair of Hush Puppies comes with three unique sets of precisely calibrated footbeds, E, F and G. The footbed construction incorporates an arch support to assist the child to develop correctly and all the footbeds are covered in twill fabric to keep the foot cool and can be removed for cleaning in warm soapy water.

Hush Puppies has incorporated this unique system into some fashion-conscious styles along with the essential year-round basics, which offer full- and half-sizes, Velcro fastenings, buckle adjustment, lace fastenings and padded collars. Heart and flower detailing with patent leathers and metallic trims ensure the girls' school styles are attractive as well as functional.

Hush Puppies Children's range offers a varied selection of infants, juniors and seniors styles across size ranges of infants' size three up to seniors' size eight at good value for money.

Recent Developments
Having re-positioned the brand globally to a more fashionable position, Hush Puppies has expanded its business into Eastern Europe in 2004.

2004 also saw the introduction of the 'BODYMOC' range. This is a range of men's shoes that have a deep contoured removable footbed to ensure maximum comfort. 2005 has seen the footbed further developed to

provide an anti bacterial protection – HYGENILAC®, which is designed to help prevent fungal infections such as Athletes Foot. This footbed allows the foot to breathe and stay cool, resisting the build up that causes odours and infections. This hygienic protection is guaranteed for the lifetime of the footwear. HYGENILAC® is proven in a number of environments and materials, but is exclusive in the footwear market to Hush Puppies.

The children's range of fitted footwear will also have the benefit of HYGENILAC® used on the covering of the calibrated footbeds.

Promotion
In recent years, the Hush Puppies brand has shifted its image from 'the old brown suede shoe worn by Dad' to feature up-to-date product styling and tongue-in-cheek marketing campaigns.

The brand strives to be seen as ageless and all about style and fun. Hush Puppies regularly invest in press advertising in titles such as Elle, Eve, Glamour, Instyle, New Woman GQ, Arena and Men's Health.

In winter 2004, Hush Puppies embarked upon a more interactive kind of promotion, testing its new Wolverine Worry Free Suede fabric among real wearers. Despite the extensive testing it carries out in its laboratories, Hush Puppies know that its shoes must be fit for the purpose for which they are designed. It decided that the best place to test the Worry Free range was on the streets themselves – and the wetter the better.

So, in September 2004, a press release was sent out announcing that shoes were to be given away to 50 residents of Hawick, situated in the Scottish Borders and officially the wettest place in Britain. Hundreds applied, and the first 50 people to come forward were given a free pair of Hush Puppies shoes from the new Wolverine Worry Free Suede range. The recipients of the shoes were then asked to try them out throughout the winter in wet and varied climate conditions to see if the footwear lived up to the claim of being the first suede shoe to be truly weather resistant.

After almost six months of wear, the testers were sent a questionnaire to assess how well the shoes had withstood the wear and tear of everyday use, coupled with whatever the unpredictable winter weather could throw at them.

The respondents had all worn the shoes at least several times in the previous six months, with more

than 80% stating that they had worn the shoes regularly or very regularly since receiving them in September. Despite enduring the most challenging of weather conditions in the UK, including rain, ice and snow, most of the testers felt that their footwear had maintained its good looks, with many expressing surprise at how easy the shoes were to keep clean and care for.

All of the testers said that they would be happy to recommend the shoes to a friend – many had either bought an additional pair of Hush Puppies as a result of their free pair, or had relatives or friends who had bought a pair on their recommendation.

Brand Values
As the Hush Puppies brand moves forward, it strives to retain all the core qualities synonymous with its name, never compromising on the comfort and quality expected from Hush Puppies – a heritage brand but not old-fashioned. The brand is about an attitude, not an age, with style and fun.

www.hushpuppies.co.uk

THINGS YOU DIDN'T KNOW ABOUT

Hush Puppies

> Hush Puppies have been spotted on a plethora of style-conscious celebrities such as Mick Jagger, David Bowie and Liam and Noel Gallagher.

> Hush Puppies have recently featured the infamous Neil and Christine Hamilton photographed in cult-film style poses in its press advertising.

> In the words of Jefferson Hack, editor of style bible Dazed and Confused: "Hush Puppies are cool – definitely."

> Hush Puppies three-way fitting system allows it to assess a child's foot on all three dimensions – length, width and depth – of each foot separately to give an accurate fit.

Market

2004 saw the UK drinking over 21 million litres of smoothies. Whilst it is still a fairly young market, the smoothie sector is growing rapidly at a rate of 28% each year, far faster than chilled juices. It is now worth an estimated £94 million.

innocent is the leading brand in this UK smoothie market and second largest brand in the chilled juice category after Tropicana. It has a market share of 44% (Source: ACNielsen Scantrack MAT to w/e April 16th 2005) and has grown by 60% each year since it was founded in 1999.

Achievements

innocent has grown over six years from start up to become the UK's biggest smoothie brand. innocent is the third fastest growing company in the UK (Source: Sunday Times Fast Track Survey 2004) and has won numerous awards.

Great successes from 2004/5 include winning the Best Soft Drink in the UK award for the third year running at the Quality Food & Drink awards (a bit like the food industry Oscars); Best Employer of the Year at the National Business Awards; Guardian Top Employer of the Year 2005; as well as Best Live Event for Fruitstock, innocent's free music festival as voted by The Event Awards.

Each year innocent has been in business, it has grown by 60%. Turnover in 2003 was £10.6 million, rising to £16.7 million in 2004 and is forecast to be £27 million in 2005.

History

innocent has been making little tasty drinks since 1999. Founders Rich, Jon and Adam had talked about starting a company ever since they met at university. After a couple of false starts, they struck upon the idea of crushing up lots of healthy fruit and sticking it into bottles. They surmised that there were people out there just like them, looking for an instant, natural shot of good health. And, most importantly, one that actually tasted nice too.

To test out this idea, they bought £500 worth of fruit, turned it into smoothies and sold them from a stall at a little music festival in London in summer 1998. Above their stall was a sign that read 'Do you think we should give up our day jobs?', beneath which was a bin saying 'YES' and a bin saying 'NO'. At the end of the weekend the 'YES' bin was full, so they went to work the next day and resigned.

After selling the first ever 'proper' innocent smoothies in April 1999, the company has grown by 60% each year. And nothing much has really changed. Each innocent smoothie still contains your recommended daily intake of fruit. Fruit Towers has grown to accommodate 70 people who are passionate about what they do, whilst having a bit of fun along the way. And Rich, Jon and Adam are still friends.

Product

From day one, the drinks they set out to make were innovative through their absolute insistence on naturalness. innocent was the first company in the UK to make smoothies with just pure crushed fruit and fresh (not concentrated) juices, and absolutely nothing else.

And since that day, whilst always sticking to the core principles of making natural, nice tasting drinks innocent has expanded its range and continued to innovate.

There are now six smoothie recipes, including an ever-changing seasonal recipe. And innocent also makes other drinks, such as thickies (bio yoghurt and fruit blends), super smoothies (smoothies designed with a specific healthy purpose), juicy water (spring water and fresh juice) and new for 2005 kids smoothies (just like the grown up ones but in child-friendly packaging and without the bits).

The company has continued to break ground through innovations in ingredients, packaging formats and product categories.

innocent is the only company to offer smoothies in one litre take home cartons; to have launched the only totally natural, not from concentrate, smoothie for kids — an easy way for parents to add an extra portion of fruit to their children's lunchboxes; to have developed a smoothie that contains carrots (innocent fruit & veg smoothie); to have offered adults a truly natural thirst quenching drink with the juicy water range; and to have used beetroot as an ingredient in a smoothie (beetroot, apples, pear & ginger detox smoothie for January).

All of this has led to sales of over 600,000 bottles each week and an unbeaten track record in winning taste tests and awards.

Recent Developments

Each year innocent brings in a new product range that challenges the norm of the chilled juice market. Last year, that innovation was putting smoothies into one litre Tetra cartons. This move was born from the insight that over 80% of juices are consumed in large pack formats, whilst smoothies were traditionally only available in little bottles

for consumption on the go. innocent's launch of one litre smoothie cartons has opened up the smoothie category to a whole new range of consumers and now people can have smoothies in their fridge and share them with all the family. The impact of this innovation on the growth of the overall smoothie category has been significant and take home smoothies now account for over 40% of innocent's overall volume.

2005 has seen the introduction of smoothies that have been created especially for children. It is notoriously hard to encourage kids to eat healthily, and after looking into the kids drinks markets, innocent realised there was an opportunity for them to offer something unique for children. The kids smoothies have been developed to appeal to younger palates, using fruits they like and without bits. Each wedge contains nothing but fruit, providing

one daily fruit portion and 100% RDA of vitamin C, so parents can rest assured the drinks are doing some good. In a climate of increasing concern about what the nation's children are consuming, the drinks have already been a huge hit with children, parents, outlets and the media alike.

And the plan to become Europe's favourite little juice company is on track. This year has seen launches of innocent smoothies in both the Netherlands and France. The company has already been the number one smoothie brand in Ireland for three years.

Promotion

One of the founding principles of innocent is that it is the reality of what companies do, and not the image, that matters. The first and foremost marketing tool is therefore the contents of the little bottles themselves, and extensive sampling activity has always been central to the company's marketing strategy.

The details are very important to innocent. The copy on its labels changes constantly, which enables innocent to have an ever-changing conversation with its drinkers. innocent answer at least 200 consumer calls and emails every week with individual responses. The bottle caps say 'enjoy by' instead of the standard 'best before'. And innocent has done some imaginative things to its vehicle fleet, covering ice-cream vans in turf and sticking horns and udders onto its cow vans (which also moo).

In 2003, innocent decided that it would be a nice idea to say thanks to everyone who'd bought its drinks and helped it since the company began. So innocent organised Fruitstock, the first ever free music festival to be held in London's Regent's Park. The success of the

sampling roadshow in 16 cities throughout the UK and Ireland. 2005 sees innocent extending its above-the-line activity to support its vision of further driving growth of the smoothie category by introducing smoothies to wider audiences of consumers. 2005's campaign will include a combination of national press, 'foodie' magazines and innocent's first ever TV commercial. True to the principle of concentrating on the product, the commercial shows the entire fruit contents of a one litre smoothie carton popping into the carton one by one and ends with the line 'innocent smoothies – loads of fruit, and that's it'. Creative development and production was handled in-house by innocent.

innocent has been a responsible business from the outset. This is reflected in everything from its choice of energy

Brand Values

Everything innocent does is made by nature. And that means only using nature's finest ingredients in its drinks, with nothing added whatsoever.

This principal applies to more than just the drinks. Being natural informs every aspect of the company and brand – from the choice of stationery to the fact that whenever you call the 'banana phone', you'll always speak to a real person. All of innocent's communication is simple and honest and every single person at innocent does their daily business in a way they can feel proud of. The innocent brand is an extension of the love and nature that goes into each drink. And the principles of sustainability and responsibility run through every part of the business, from the way the fruit is procured to the use of recycled plastic in the bottles to looking after the team at innocent through profit share schemes, access to equity and other perks like monthly massages, free yoga and travel scholarships.

www.innocentdrinks.co.uk

Hello. Can we tell you something?

We're innocent and we make smoothies. You might have seen our drinks in the shops before; if not, the picture above might help you to recognise them next time. Anyway, it's all pretty simple. We just get hold of loads of fruit and squash it into our bottles and cartons. For example, the carton in the picture contains 27 strawberries, 10 apples, 2½ bananas and a dash of fresh orange juice. That means there are 8 portions of fruit in every carton, and no rubbish like concentrates, preservatives or additives. Nothing that your body doesn't need. Just the purest, freshest fruit. And that's it.

 innocent
your daily fruit

they grow on trees

(well, sort of)

weekend outstripped all expectation, with 40,000 people attending. 2004 saw over 80,000 people attend to enjoy more sunshine, music, a farmers market and even some yoga lessons. This year will see the third Fruitstock festival.

During winter 2004, teams of grannies and innocent consumers worked very hard to create 24,000 mini bobble hats. These were put on innocent smoothie bottles on sale in EAT cafes across the UK. For each smoothie sold wearing a little hat, 50p was donated to Age Concern and Extra Care to help keep people warm in the winter. The campaign was a great success that proved it is possible to run promotions that benefit everyone involved, and teach them how to knit at the same time.

innocent ran its first national above-the-line activity in 2004, using outdoor advertising to support a national

supply (green), to giving excess stock to Crisis to be distributed to the homeless and deprived urban areas across the UK.

2004 also saw the birth of the innocent foundation, a separate registered charity devoted to finding good things to do with innocent's money, both in the countries where it sells its drinks and in those where it sources its ingredients. Projects range from protecting rainforests in Brazil to helping HIV sufferers in Uganda to setting up beehives and achieve some economic self-sufficiency.

Market

Intel has been one of the main drivers of a revolution that has fundamentally changed our society. The company is the world's largest manufacturer of computer chips, and paradoxically also one of the best-known consumer brands. Today, chips can be found all around us – in products as wide ranging as cars, toys, mobile phones and even alarm clocks. In fact we now have access on a daily basis to computer technology more powerful than NASA had when it first sent man to the moon.

Due to an increase in consumers' knowledge of technology teamed with a successful marketing strategy, many purchasers of computer equipment now demand to know what brand of processor is in the computer they are considering purchasing. The 'Intel Inside®' campaign started this trend. According to Mercury Research, Intel commands an 82.2% market segment share of the PC processor market.

But Intel is not just a component maker – it is providing the means to create ever more powerful communication tools, whether these are desktop PCs or wireless devices. Its stated goal is to be the pre-eminent supplier to the internet economy.

To do this, Intel has to stay ahead in a market where the technological bar is constantly being raised. The latest revolution to rock the online world is the rise of the mobile internet. 'Wi-Fi' is opening up the power of online connectivity and networking to people on the move, using either their laptops or personal digital assistants. Intel has been at the forefront of this development with Intel® Centrino™ mobile technology, designed specifically for mobile internet users. To cater for this new and exciting opportunity, 'wireless hotspots' are springing up all over the country. Wireless living is being so enthusiastically embraced across the world that there are now 56.3 million Wi-Fi hotspot subscribers (Source: Instat).

Achievements

When Intel was founded in 1968, it had 12 employees, operated out of a leased building in a quiet corner of California, and recorded year one revenues of US$2,672.

Nowadays, the company has 80,000 employees and is worth nearly US$175 billion. In the first quarter of 2005, Intel reported profits of US$2.2 billion – a 25% increase on the same period in 2003.

Intel's market leadership can be ascribed to a series of scientific breakthroughs and well-timed alliances. It came up with the first microprocessor, the 4004, in 1971, after being approached by a Japanese calculator manufacturer. Ten years later, IBM chose the company's 8088 processor for use in the first ever PC.

By 1993, Intel had introduced its first Pentium® processor. Since then, the company has continued to render its own products obsolete almost every year – a strategy unheard of in any other business. As founder Gordon Moore comments; 'If the auto industry advanced as rapidly as the semiconductor industry, a Rolls-Royce would get half a million miles per gallon, and it would be cheaper to throw it away than to park it.'

Intel's introduction of Intel® Centrino™ mobile technology has been another major achievement, bringing wireless internet technology to the mass market. Intel is now one of the companies very much at the forefront of the Wi-Fi revolution.

History

In 1968, computer boffins Robert Noyce and Gordon Moore created Intel. At the time, Moore stated; 'We are

The secret of working wirelessly? It's in there.

the true revolutionaries.' But it was to be another 30 years before his words rang true. In the meantime, Moore and Noyce had set out to create a more efficient computer memory, based on semiconductor technology. They came up with the 1103 in 1970, and it became the world's biggest-selling semiconductor device.

However, their most significant breakthrough came when a Japanese company called Busicom asked them to design 12 chips for a range of calculators. At the time, each electronic product required its own individually tailored chip. But Intel engineer Ted Hoff felt that it might be possible to create a single chip capable of carrying out a wide range of different functions – an advanced computer 'brain'. The invention worked, and Intel realised that it had created a product with almost limitless applications. Yet there was a problem: under the terms of the original contract, Busicom held the rights to the product. However, the Japanese company was in some financial difficulties at this point, so Moore and Noyce negotiated the purchase of the rights to the chip for just US$60,000.

Originally known as a 'microcomputer', Intel's first microprocessor – the 4004 – went on the market in 1971. By the time the company introduced the 8008, a few years later, its early predictions had begun to materialise: the chip revolutionised supermarket cash registers, traffic lights, petrol pumps, airline reservation systems and arcade games to name but a few applications. As fast as its chips were installed, Intel created smaller and more powerful versions.

In the early 1980s, IBM began tentative talks with Intel over the possibility of using its 8088 processor for an undisclosed new product.

Since IBM had never before used an outside supplier, the details were shrouded in secrecy. Only when the deal was finally struck did Intel realise it was providing the brain of the first PC – although at the time, neither of the two companies realised how big the home computing market would become.

Intel continued to develop ever more efficient microprocessors, including the Pentium® processor in 1993, which became its most famous brand name. The company

now has the Pentium Processor Extreme Edition 840, the world-first desktop dual-core processor. Dual- and multi-core processors are designed by including two or more full execution cores within a single processor enabling simultaneous management of activities. When combined with Intel's Hyper-Threading Technology, this platform empowers computer users to take advantage of high-definition video, high-quality sound and 3-D visualisation for their audio, video, digital design and gaming tasks.

Product

Intel produces the chips, boards, systems, software and communication equipment that make up the architecture of the high-tech world.

Your mobile entertainment theatre? It's in there.

According to research carried out by Intel in 1991, only 24% of European PC buyers were familiar with its logo. One year later that figure had risen to 80%, and by 1995 it had reached 94%.

Now more than 2,500 computer manufacturers are licensed to use the Intel logo. It is expanding its advertising onto the web and is continuing to run its own TV campaigns alongside co-branded spots. But this success has a price – Intel says that since 1991, it has spent more than US$7 billion convincing consumers that the best technology carries the 'Intel Inside®' logo.

Intel also uses public relations to raise awareness of its brand and technology. The Intel Centrino Mobile Technology balloon was built in the summer of 2003 to mark Intel's attendance at the Bristol Balloon festival, where it made its inaugural flight from the main arena and symbolised wireless freedom by cutting loose on its first ascent.

Since then, as well as being used for charity prizes and competition prize flights, the balloon has flown many times at events over the UK and abroad, including the Newbury Show, Bristol 2004 and Alberque in the US, which is the world's biggest balloon festival with more than 2,000 entries. Overall, around 500 people have flown in the balloon in the past two years, including members of the public, industry and press.

Microprocessors are the tiny brains that control the central processing of data in personal computers, servers, workstations and a myriad of other electronic devices. Intel designs processors for a number of different markets and applications, from the high-end Pentium 4 processor to the Intel® Celeron® processor for 'value' PC and mobile systems.

Intel is one of the companies leading the booming new wireless mobile communications market. Intel® Centrino™ mobile technology delivers cutting-edge notebook performance – even in the lightest, easy-to-carry notebook PC designs.

Recent Developments

Intel invested more than US$4.8 billion in research and development in 2004, and many of Intel's recent activities have centred on promoting the use of mobile internet solutions.

It recently unveiled a new family of processors based on Intel XScale® technology, designed to bring wireless broadband connectivity and performance to advanced mobile phones and PDAs.

The processors are designed to meet the multimedia, low power and security requirements of handheld mobile devices, but have enough computing power to provide full motion video-conferencing capabilities and DVD-quality video playback.

Intel recently announced the availability of its first WiMAX product, providing equipment manufacturers and carriers with the ability to deliver next-generation wireless broadband networks around the world.

WiMAX, short for Worldwide Interoperability for Microwave Access, is a standards-based wireless technology for providing high-speed, last-mile broadband connectivity to homes and

businesses and for mobile wireless networks. Intel's WiMAX silicon delivers the features needed to provide cost-effective, high-speed wireless modems for homes and businesses.

Initial deployments of WiMAX will enable delivery of broadband internet access to remote areas not currently served by DSL or cable, and will make it possible to wirelessly connect buildings up to several miles apart. Because it is standards-based, WiMAX technology is expected to make it easier and more cost-effective for new and existing broadband users to enjoy wireless internet access.

Intel has recently been working on UK trials of the emerging WiMAX technology with the Science Museum at its Wroughton site, where many of the Museum's large-object collections are housed in 11 old aeroplane hangers across a 545 acre site. WiMAX is allowing the curators at the various sites to communicate electronically with each other and also keep updated records of the various artefacts within the remote buildings.

Promotion

The awareness of the Intel brand has grown alongside awareness of chips themselves, and Intel has become associated with technological leadership, quality and reliability.

This situation has come about thanks to the Intel Inside® programme. Launched in 1991, it was the first attempt by a component manufacturer to directly target consumers, rather than the computer industry.

The main challenge was the fact that Intel was not a standalone product – it was a component, buried deep inside another device. As part of its research, the company studied successful consumer marketing techniques used by other companies supplying an ingredient of a finished product, such as NutraSweet, Teflon and Dolby. Its advertising agency Dahlin, Smith & White came up with part of the solution – the slogan 'Intel. The computer inside.' This was later contracted into the famous 'Intel Inside®'.

At the same time, Intel began approaching computer manufacturers with the idea of a co-operative marketing programme whereby Intel would share the cost of any ads that showed its logo. In the first year, 300 companies took it up on the offer. Meanwhile, in 1995, Intel embarked on TV ads promoting its product. These included an animated logo and the now familiar five-note signature melody.

Brand Values

Intel's external brand values are evident from its advertising, which emphasises groundbreaking technology, quality and reliability. Intel also aims to be open, egalitarian and disciplined.

When Robert Noyce and Gordon Moore were building Intel, they were keen to banish hierarchies, preferring a company with no executive suites, no pinstripe suits and no reserved parking spaces. Among its six guiding principles, which include customer orientation, quality, risk-taking and results, Intel also sets itself the goal of being 'a great place to work'. In this way, it aims to keep the spirit of its founders alive.

www.intel.com

JAEGER

Market

Jaeger is a classic British womenswear, menswear and accessories brand that is embedded with heritage and success. Its history, which spans over 100 years, can neither be replicated nor copied but is envied by many of its competitors. It is Jaeger's past success that provides it with such an exciting and solid platform for future growth into the 21st century.

Jaeger's key unique selling point (USP) is the brand's in-house design team and emphasis on product development and luxury fabrics which are used across the entire range.

Achievements

Jaeger currently has 46 free standing shops in the UK and Europe, having recently opened five new shops in the UK. Its flagship store was set up after World War II and is still the company's top performing store. It is located on Regent Street in Central London and trades on 16,000 sq ft spread over four floors.

In addition to the free standing shops the Jaeger brand is sold through 36 'shop in shops' with recent high profile additions including Harrods. Jaeger was the first British brand to operate on a concession basis when it opened as a shop in shop in Selfridges in the 1930s. Jaeger will re-open in Selfridges in Autumn 2005.

The international arena has been targeted by Jaeger since the 1970s when it opened shops in Paris and the US. Jaeger is a world class brand with international recognition, currently trading in Zurich, Belgium, Copenhagen, Dubai, Tokyo and Chile and this provides a solid backdrop for further expansion overseas. Indeed, Japan has been identified as a major growth

market for Jaeger, it already has a flagship store in Tokyo, two shop in shops, and has a further 10 shops scheduled to open during 2005. In addition, Hong Kong, China, and the North American arena are being assessed as potential new and exciting markets.

Jaeger has an aggressive expansion programme to increase accessibility of the brand. This is central to Jaeger's growth strategy and targets both the domestic and international markets. The new store opening programme will result in at least 100 retail outlets in the UK and Europe by the end of 2005 and further increase its global store network by 50% over the next three years.

History

Jaeger has an enviable and fascinating track record. Dr Gustav Jaeger, a German professor, developed a theory that people would be healthier and live longer lives if they dressed in clothes derived from animal products, such as wool, rather than vegetable fibres. His theory was developed into a commercial exercise and in 1884 Lewis Tomalin, a British Accountant, set up the first store known as Dr Jaeger's Sanitary Woollen System.

Jaeger's woollen ranges were enthusiastically received by a prominent list of people including Oscar Wilde, George Bernard Shaw, and explorers such as Sir Earnest Shackleton and Captain Scott, who tested the claim of 'warm in winter and cool in summer'. Jaeger's clothing proved to be so successful that by the turn of the century Jaeger was able to introduce camel hair, alpaca, angora and cashmere to its ranges. During World War I demand for woollen items escalated, this opportunity was grasped by Jaeger who expanded its ranges to include items such as sleeping bags and horse blankets.

Jaeger's ability to exploit new opportunities and trends continued. The 1920s marked the beginning of a more carefree culture and this was reflected in the company's strategy; the emphasis moved from health to style. New ranges were introduced including knitted sportswear as well as ready-to-wear suits. Jaeger's undeniable success soon resulted in the opening of its first factory, new shops as well as a new shop in shop within Selfridges. The outbreak of World War II presented Jaeger with further opportunities and production shifted back to utility wear for the troops. This was soon reversed after the war and new ranges, that included fresh colours and styles for the leisure and sportswear market, were unveiled.

Jaeger's strategy continued to evolve, reflecting customer needs with innovative introductions such as washable synthetic fabrics to compliment the woollen ranges. The brand was now well established and known to be at the forefront of fabric development and for the production of top quality stylish clothing. The strength of the brand allowed it to expand into international markets and by the 1970s it was represented in both Europe and the US.

However, the latter decades of the 20th century proved more difficult. The company was taken over and subsequently became part of Coats Viyella. The brand suffered and failed to keep pace with increasing competition and the demands of a new generation of consumers. In March 2003, entrepreneur Harold Tillman identified Jaeger's past successes and future potential and acquired the brand. He has subsequently attracted Belinda Earl, who previously headed up the department store Debenhams to join Jaeger as Chief Executive. Belinda Earl has pulled together a dynamic and experienced management team whose focus is now to restore Jaeger as a premium world-class brand.

Product

The cornerstones of Jaeger's womenswear collection are its coats, tailoring and knitwear. The majority of these products are made from luxurious yarns and fibres such as wool, cashmere, camel-hair, silk and angora. True to its British heritage the range also includes timeless fabrics such as pinstripes, herringbones, tweeds and plaids.

The collections modern classic styling and high quality fabric and make, ensure that each style becomes an investment piece that will endure many seasons of wear and become a vintage piece of the future.

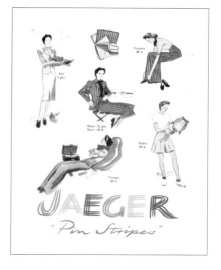

The touch and feel of a Jaeger product is superior and luxurious. The trims are of the highest specification and the attention to detail, even the inside of the garment, gives pleasure to the wearer.

The handwriting is clean and graphic and often uses contrast borders and bindings. The prints too are graphic stripes, zig-zags and spots – every collection will include an animal print and graphic floral. Key signature colours are black, navy and ivory with strong highlights enhancing the monochrome classics.

Although the collections are built on modern classics they will always have a relevance to the moment, with seasonal trends and key items being an essential part of each range. The collection is designed to suit different lifestyles from a strong businesswear offer through to luxurious separates and casualwear.

From the manufacture of 'greatcoats' for the aristocracy, to the knitting of 'plaid socks' to wear with 'plus fours', Jaeger menswear has, since the turn of the 20th century, been at the forefront of Gentleman's dressing.

Through support of its own specialised UK manufacturing, company policy required that the product should be of high quality manufacture utilising the best available fabrics to uphold the long standing tradition of elegance, value and longevity in all of Jaeger men's products. Today the manufacturing landscape has changed and like many of its premier contemporaries Jaeger has moved its production 'offshore', to enable the brand to compete successfully in a complex marketplace. Whilst doing so, none of the old values have been ignored and together with its suppliers, the Jaeger team strive to produce quality products which offer the same values as a century before.

Tailoring historically was always at the forefront of a gentleman's wardrobe. Even with today's attitude to dress, Jaeger menswear still retains its position in the market place, where it is known for well cut tailoring. Suits are made from some of the finest Italian fabrics, styled in a modern Savile Row cut and finished by hand at one of the most up to date factories in the world. Equally, coats, shirts and ties are produced from some of the finest

fabrics available to complement the wardrobe of the modern day professional.

The future offers new challenges and a new exiting direction for the menswear business. In a changing world of dress code, life style and climate change, casual wear is seen as the new growth area for the menswear business. Smart casual dress is seen as the primary thrust to complement the already successful formal wear business. In years to come, this sector will doubtlessly be the foundation for the next period of growth for Jaeger menswear. Adhering to the old values the company will maintain its drive to produce functional quality products with some of the most modern production methods in order to keep pace with the trends and to carry the mens business forward throughout the 21st century.

The Jaeger accessories collection is the fastest growing product area and attracts new customers to the brand. New developments in the last year include the expansion of handbags and jewellery and the launch of the Jaeger beach collection. Jewellery has proved to be a huge success – sales have more than doubled in the last year with beautiful pieces, being sourced from all over the world. The exquisite leather collection is sourced and made in Italy using the finest quality materials. Christmas sees the launch of an extensive gift collection including scented candles, stationery, small leathers and limited edition jewelled evening bags.

Recent Developments

Jaeger London, a new collection of womenswear launches in September 2005 in 16 Jaeger stores across the UK and Europe, with supermodel Erin O'Connor as its face.

The iconic pieces, many of which have been influenced by the extensive Jaeger archive, are sure to be classics of the future.

The collection continues to broaden the appeal of the Jaeger brand and has successfully created clothing, which is relevant to women's lives.

The range is aimed at 25+ women who have been searching for beautiful quality ready to wear, which is sharp and directional to add to their wardrobe.

Jaeger's strategy has recently been developed by the newly appointed management team. It is designed to maximise the potential of the Jaeger brand and drive profitability. It is based around four key values: ensuring the customer is central to decision making; delivering consistency; strengthening and widening the appeal of the brand and aggressively entering new markets. This strategy has been developed to maximise the

strengths of Jaeger's past and the future opportunities that the retail sector presents.

Promotion

Key to Jaeger's strategy is to really deliver what it promises, offering relevant merchandise and consistent standards to all its customers throughout the year in all its outlets.

Jaeger is positioned as a classic British brand with a strong quality and stylish image. Its strategy now focuses very closely on these brand characteristics but also moves them forward into the 21st century by introducing a more modern element. This modern streak strengthens its appeal as an elegant desirable brand and is reflected in its more contemporary advertising campaigns. Jaeger's brand values are communicated though its advertising in strategic media at times to reflect arrival of product in store and all marketing activity.

In addition to this work, Jaeger's website – www.jaeger.co.uk – is being constantly updated to reflect brand values and act as a showcase for the season's collection. Furthermore, the site is scheduled to become transactional during 2006.

The Jaeger account card is another powerful tool to the business and Customer Related Marketing (CRM) is increasingly used to communicate to customers in a timely and relevant manner.

Brand Values

The Jaeger brand is known for delivering stylish, quality clothing at affordable prices.

Jaeger's brand values are Premium, British, Affordable, Elegant, Innovative, Original, Modern Classic and Quality. These distinctive brand values are embedded in all that Jaeger does from merchandise design to store layout. The brand essence of Jaeger is Accessible Luxury.

www.jaeger.co.uk

THINGS YOU DIDN'T KNOW ABOUT

Jaeger

❯ Norman Parkinson shot some of the early Jaeger fashion photography.

❯ Jaeger was worn by Kirsten Scott Thomas in The English Patient.

❯ Jaeger was the official mens stylist for the 2005 Baftas.

❯ In 1984, for Jaeger's centenary celebrations, models rode camels and were walked up and down Regent Street.

❯ Sir Earnest Shackleton wore Jaeger on his many arctic expeditions.

Market

Over the past few years the consumer food-service business has been exposed to beatings at the hands of the downturn in the global economy, the slowdown of gross domestic product and reduction in the number of international visitors coming into Britain. What's more, fat-fearing UK consumers are turning to healthier and safer food and expect new food business propositions to match up to their demands. Despite these factors negatively impacting sales, the British food-service industry proved to be more resilient than analysts and experts expected.

The industry posted positive growth, increasing by 25% since 1999 and reaching value sales of £26.5 billion in 2004 (Source: Mintel). The number of consumer foodservice units stood at 177.6 thousand in 2003, representing a rise of 6.8% on 1999. A total of 5,224 million transactions were achieved in 2003, representing an increase of 15.6% on 1999 (Source: Euromonitor).

Fast food continued its positive performance during the review period, representing the single most important area in 2003 in terms of transactions. It stood at a 53.6% transaction volume share of overall consumer foodservice in 2003, up from its 52.2% share in 1999 (Source: Euromonitor).

Achievements

Over the course of 2004 and 2005, KFC has successfully launched a new 'singing soul' campaign. This follows the success of the 'Soul Food' campaign in 2003 and 2004 and takes the brand essence throughout the business, communicating it at all consumer touch-points. Through its 'soul food' strategy, it effectively changed public perception of its brand and built an emotional relationship with its consumers, without compromising the immediate sales requirements of retail marketing. The launch of the 'singing soul' campaign with the new endline 'Servin up Soul' has now moved the brand to another level. Everyone who features in the new campaign appears to be a soul singer taking part in

normal, everyday discussions that are sung in a classic soul style with emotion and dramatic vocal acrobatics.

KFC Corporation, based in Louisville, Kentucky, is the world's most popular chicken restaurant chain. In the UK, KFC sells its famous fried chicken through its 680 UK stores. Globally, KFC is owned by Yum! Brands Inc (formerly Tricon Global Restaurants), which operates more than 33,000 restaurants in more than 100 countries and territories. Four of the company's brands – KFC, Pizza Hut, Taco Bell and Long John Silver's – are global leaders in their categories. Internationally, Yum! Brands opens about three new restaurants each day, ranking it among the restaurant industry's fastest growing international retailers.

History

In 1939, Colonel Harland Sanders first gave the world a taste of his most famous creation, Original Recipe Kentucky Fried Chicken. Since that time, millions of people the world over have come to love his home-style side dishes and hot and fresh biscuits.

Colonel Harland Sanders, born September 9th 1890, actively began franchising his chicken business at the age of 65. Now, the KFC business he started has grown to be one of the largest quick-service food service systems in the world. And Colonel Sanders, a quick service restaurant (QSR) pioneer, has become a symbol of entrepreneurial spirit.

The Colonel's father died when he was six, so his mother was forced to go to work, leaving him to take care of his three-year-old brother and baby sister. This meant doing much of the family cooking. By the age of seven, he was a master of several regional dishes.

At age ten, he got his first job working on a nearby farm for US$2 a month. When he was 12, his mother remarried and he left his home, for a job on a farm. He held a series of jobs over the next few years, first as a streetcar conductor and then as a 16-year-old private, soldiering for six months in Cuba.

After that he was a railroad fireman, studied law by correspondence, practiced in justice of the peace courts, sold insurance, operated an Ohio River steamboat ferry, sold tires, and operated service stations.

When he was 40, the Colonel began cooking for hungry travellers who stopped at his service station in Corbin, Kentucky. He didn't have a restaurant then, but served food on his own dining table in the living quarters of his service station.

As more people started coming just for food, he moved across the street to a motel and restaurant that seated 142 people. Over the next nine years, he perfected his original recipe and the basic cooking technique that is still used today.

Sanders' fame grew. Governor Ruby Laffoon made him a Kentucky Colonel in 1935 in recognition of his contributions to the state's cuisine. And in 1939, his establishment was first listed in Duncan Hines' Adventures in Good Eating.

In the early 1950s a new interstate highway was planned to bypass the town of Corbin. Seeing an end to his business, Sanders auctioned off his operations. After paying his bills, he was reduced to living on his US$105 Social Security checks.

Confident of the quality of his fried chicken, Sanders devoted himself to the chicken franchising business that he started in 1952. He travelled across the country by car from restaurant to restaurant, cooking batches of chicken for restaurant owners and their employees. If the reaction was favourable, he entered into a handshake agreement on a deal that stipulated a payment to him of a nickel for each chicken the restaurant sold. By 1964, Sanders had more than 600 franchised outlets for his chicken in the US and Canada. That year, he sold his interest in the US company for US$2 million to a group of investors including John Y Brown Jr, who later was governor of Kentucky from 1980 to 1984. Sanders remained a public spokesman for the company.

Under the new owners, Kentucky Fried Chicken Corporation grew rapidly. It went public on March 17th 1966 and was listed on the New York Stock Exchange on January 16th 1969. More than 3,500 franchised and company-owned restaurants were in worldwide operation when Heublein Inc acquired KFC Corporation on July 8th 1971 for US$285 million.

Kentucky Fried Chicken became a subsidiary of R J Reynolds Industries (now RJR Nabisco), when Heublein was acquired by Reynolds in 1982. KFC was acquired from RJR Nabisco in October 1986 by PepsiCo for approximately US$840 million.

In January 1997, PepsiCo Inc announced the splitting of its brand – KFC, Taco Bell and Pizza Hut – into an independent restaurant company, Tricon Global Restaurants.

In May 2002, the company announced it received shareholders' approval to change its corporation name to Yum! Brands. The company, which owns A&W All-American Food Restaurants, KFC, Long John Silvers, Pizza Hut and Taco Bell restaurants, is the world's largest restaurant company in terms of outlets with nearly 32,500 in more than 100 countries and territories.

Product

To ensure that the 'Soul Food' strategy introduced in 2003 was a truly centralised brand idea, it was important to take it to the very heart of KFC's business – the product.

Its core products are Buckets, Burgers and Twisters and Colonel's Crispy Strips chicken with home-style side dishes. But little had occurred in terms of new product development within KFC since 2001. 'Soul Food' gave new focus to the new product strategy. The first 'Soul Food' product to hit the stores was 'Warm Chicken Salad'. The success of salad has led to a new variant being developed, and more 'Soul Food' products will feature on KFC's menu over the next 18 months. Concept testing has demonstrated that these products have a positive effect on perceptions of KFC, both in terms of variety, product quality and consumer perceptions of the brand.

The new positioning also impacted on the pricing strategy. This was an offering for real people and as a result, it needed to sell proper, wholesome food at a reasonable price. Prior to repositioning the brand, the lowest priced item on KFC's menu was £2.99, which was a barrier to purchase for many consumers. 'Soul Food' meant that pricing was looked at in a different way and the case for a value product, at less than £1 was put forward. The Mini Fillet Burger launched in 2004 and it is having a hugely positive impact upon sales and perceptions of the KFC brand.

Recent Developments

The 'Soul Food' philosophy has also made a real impact upon KFC's retail estate. Stores have been designed along the key elements of the philosophy. The first phase of roll out was completed in February 2004.

'Soul Food' has manifested itself in all aspects of communication, from window posters to the menu boards and staff uniforms. Stores have been refitted and the bright reds, blues and yellows, which are generic and expected within QSRs have been replaced with more natural colours and materials to make the atmosphere less plastic and more real.

Promotion

At the beginning of 2003, KFC's business was in a challenging situation. The QSR market was in decline, struggling in the face of increasing competition from pizza, ethnic takeaways, supermarket ready meals and a raft of sandwich retailers. Moreover, the media focus on the evils of fast food had demonised the category and fuelled concerns over healthy eating. Consequently, the major players in the QSR sector were all experiencing significant declines.

In order to rise to the challenge, KFC needed to overhaul not only its product and high street presence, but also its image.

At the heart of this was the 'Soul Food' concept, which was most visibly and dramatically brought to life by advertising, created with advertising agency BBH. In fact, 'Soul Food' proved to be an effective creative springboard and led to TV executions that amplified the holistic soul food experience. Each execution was able to communicate individual product messages, to different targets, on different occasions. In striking contrast to the conventions of the category, products were shown being consumed in the midst of the action. Gone are the generic cutaways to flying drumsticks, raining lettuce and bouncing buns. Soul music has been an important component of the advertising, providing KFC with a specific media property that has helped to make KFC ads famous.

This strategy has been successful at building consumers' relationship with the brand and against more rational measures. In fact, the advertising has scored exceptionally well on measures such as branding, recognition and cut through. Indeed, 'Soul Food' executions led to the highest levels of cut through since KFC launched Popcorn Chicken in early 2000. These executions also delivered branding scores that are at an all time high. Spontaneous brand awareness is also rising as a result of the 'Soul Food' campaign now at the highest for over three years.

The ads have also succeeded in engaging and connecting with consumers. A large number of viewers agreed that they felt that the 'Soul Food' campaign was for 'people like me'.

Brand Values

The aim of the KFC overhaul was to give the brand meaning to its consumers. KFC's vision is to create bright and fun interiors, with people of all ages, races and backgrounds mixing together. Research has shown that KFC is now perceived as a fun and inclusive brand with all the main values of 'Soul Food' being understood and adopted.

www.kfc.co.uk

Kinder®

Market
The UK chocolate market is one of the most competitive and crowded in the world, with more than 1,000 brands and countless more products. The total chocolate market in the UK is worth £6.1 billion, subdivided into a number of chocolate confectionary categories from boxed chocolate to single products (Source: ACNielsen).

For any brand, trying to achieve standout in such a landscape is a difficult task. For Kinder, this was a particular challenge, as the brand made its first entry to the UK once the market was already dominated by the three chocolate giants Cadbury, Nestlé and Mars.

Today Kinder strives to provide an alternative to the traditional brands and has established itself as a strong player in the children's chocolate confectionery market.

Achievements
In the UK, Kinder is a leading confectionery brand going from strength to strength. Its success comes as no surprise to its parent company, Ferrero, as Kinder is the leading chocolate brand in the European market as a whole, with total sales in excess of US$1 billion across the world (Source: ACNielsen).

Ferrero's focus now is on developing the Kinder brand in the UK, where Kinder's share of the children's confectionery market currently is 16%, but growing rapidly. However, as the manufacturer of a wide portfolio of children's products, the brand can boast a unique selling point.

As the children's specialist in confectionery, Kinder strives to target children responsibly. Intrinsic to its products is a regard for what parents need when it comes to treating their children without overindulging them. The fact that Kinder is enjoying year-on-year growth of more than 35% shows that it is building trust and authority amongst parents (Source: ACNielsen).

Indeed, having recently launched adult-targeted Bueno growing at 12% year-on-year in a stable market, now a top-10 selling chocolate bar (Source: ACNielsen) Kinder has proven that although it was born as a children's chocolate brand, adults cannot resist the underlying Kinder values. Kinder believes that what is

good for children cannot be bad for adults, and women have discovered this product as one of their favourites. The fact that it is light tasting and comes in controllable portions means that it is also relevant to them.

History
The opportunity to develop a chocolate brand specifically suitable for children was identified in the late 1960s during the 'Baby Boom' era. Ferrero, an Italian family company, recognised that there was a gap in the market: lots of children who would grow up wanting chocolate, but no chocolate was designed specifically for children.

The challenge Kinder faced was how to move into a very crowded chocolate market and ensure that it was unique, different and relevant. To achieve this, it approached new product development from the two-pronged perspective of creative thinking and technological expertise. This has enabled the brand to continually innovate and create a range of products that provide a real point of difference from anything else available in the shops.

The first Kinder product to launch was Kinder Chocolate in 1968, followed by the iconic Kinder Surprise in 1974.

In the UK Kinder Surprise was launched in the late 1970s, but it is only in recent years that Kinder has accelerated its marketing efforts in the UK market. Kinder Bueno was launched in 2002, Kinder Chocolate in 2003, Happy Hippo in 2004 and Kinder Country in 2005. This has given the brand momentum, providing frequent news to captivate consumers' imaginations and helping establish Kinder as a brand that is continually offering something new and different.

Today, Kinder is more than simply a chocolate brand. Having expanded into new product categories, either by

creating them through Kinder Surprise, or by innovating into the children's biscuit category with Happy Hippo, Kinder has been able to expand its footprint into other areas where its brand values are appreciated and create a true option for consumers through its point of difference. Its growth shows that Kinder is conceptually a modern interpretation of a parent's wish to treat her child.

Product
The Kinder product range is driven by the desire to be different: each product created has to meet the requirements of children and the parents who feed them.

All Kinder products are free from artificial colourings and preservatives, are 'full of milky goodness' and come in small child-sized portion controlled packs to avoid over-indulgence. As a responsible manufacturer Kinder believes in helping parents treat their children responsibly.

Kinder Chocolate was designed as the first chocolate where consumers could actually see the milk content inside the chocolate. While all other brands were either milk chocolate or white, being able to see the milky inside became a reality and a unique selling point across the entire Kinder product range.

Kinder Surprise was designed to appeal to three key needs: 'the thrill of a surprise; a toy to play with; and finally, the pleasure of eating chocolate'. The three elements have been the recipe for its success over the past 30 years, and the brand is still viewed unique by consumers today. Kinder prides itself on knowing how to produce chocolate and toys that are in line with the latest children's trends.

Kinder Bueno and Happy Hippo employed the groundbreaking technique of moulding wafer. This

opened up possibilities to be more creative with the shape used to enclose the creamy filling, giving rise to the 3D hippo-shaped children's biscuit.

Kinder's forthcoming products will share this sense of innovation, being highly visual products that are involving and appealing for both parents and children.

Kinder products are quality controlled right into the store with a dedicated team of auditors randomly spot-checking the product to assess its freshness and quality. This is designed to ensure that Kinder products reach the hands of consumers at the quality and standard the brand intended.

In addition, Ferrero is committed to investment in Kinder product development, investing 3% of global sales back into new product development, with the aim always to be unique and innovative.

Recent Developments

In recent years, Ferrero has been focused on building the presence of the Kinder brands in the UK and studying the nation's consumer trends to develop the most compelling and relevant mix of products for UK parents and children. It has also focused on developing UK compelling positionings and communications to truly connect with consumers.

This led to the launches of three new products in as many years, including the phenomenal successes of Kinder Bueno, Happy Hippo and Kinder Country. Through this activity Kinder has been able to build a strong, unified and impressive portfolio presence in the market.

Kinder has also developed an umbrella brand strategy for all current and future products supporting it with a leading share of voice within the children's confectionery market.

Promotion

In the past, Kinder's fame has been driven by the success of Kinder Surprise, which still retains the number one novelty chocolate position (Source: ACNielsen). Yet with Kinder's ambitions in this country, there was a need to communicate a broader product range than Kinder Surprise.

To achieve presence and increase top of mind awareness, and in order that it can compete with the three chocolate competitors of Cadbury, Nestlé and Mars, Kinder has committed to investing in advertising;

with an annual spend giving Kinder a 49% Share of Voice in children's confectionary. Each new product launch over the past three years has been supported in the same way.

Kinder's target audience has consistently been parents. The brand reassures them that Kinder is a good choice for treating their children. This has lead to TV campaigns that talk to parents by extolling the virtues of the new product launches of Bueno, Happy Hippo and Kinder Chocolate – the contradictions of Bueno 'smooth and pleasurable yet light and crispy', the 3D fun inventiveness of Happy Hippo, and the milky portion-controlled design of the Kinder Chocolate.

However, while talking to parents, Kinder tries not to ignore the child inside everyone. It believes that parents trust the Kinder brand as it understands the world of their children. Kinder tries to occupy the shared space between parents and children – the fun place where adults forget their grown-up pressures and momentarily enter the captivating world of childhood again.

This strategy has led to promotional activity which engages both children and parents. Recently the brand ran a Looney Tunes on-pack promotion across the Kinder Kids portfolio and was supported by Looney Tunes advertising, prizes and Looney Tunes characters inside Kinder Surprise. Kinder's recent sponsorship of the 'Lemony Snicket' movie afforded the brand an opportunity to create

brand presence at the moment of entertainment enjoyed by both parents and children.

All consumer promotion for the Kinder brand is selected on the criteria that it fits with the brand values and will help to grow equity.

Brand Values

As a confectionery brand offering a wide range of products including chocolates, toys and biscuits, Kinder is designed especially for children. The Kinder brand values – aimed to capture the essence of childhood and parenthood – are driven by the inventiveness that lies at the core of all the Kinder products. The brand is imaginative and adventurous, capturing the spirit of childhood, but is also reassuring and comforting, just like a cuddle from mum. Kinder is invented and designed for children's pleasure, but with parents' happiness in mind as well.

www.magic-kinder.com

Kinder

❯ More than four million Kinder Surprise eggs are eaten every day around the world.

❯ Kinder is a global US$1 billion brand operating in 28 countries worldwide (Source: ACNielsen).

❯ The Happy Hippo product was originally inspired by one of the Kinder Surprise toys.

❯ Kinder uses children's fiction authors to write stories that then provide them with the inspiration for their products and toys.

Market

Operating in one of the most hotly contested youth markets in the country, Kiss 100 FM is a leading commercial radio station for young London and a thriving national radio brand, reaching 90% of the UK (Source: Ofcom).

It is the market-leading commercial radio station for London audiences under the age of 35, attracting an average of 1.5 million listeners in the capital every week (Source: RAJAR).

Kiss has been at the forefront of the digital radio revolution and is now an award-winning multi-platform brand, available on FM as Kiss 100 in London as well as nationwide via DAB digital, satellite, Freeview, cable, and online. In total, Kiss has more than two million listeners nationwide and can also boast the highest spontaneous recall for any digital radio station (Source: GfK/DRDB).

Achievements

Winning its initial licence in 1989 was an achievement in itself for Kiss, as the team that had launched it in 1985 as a pirate station took the brave step of closing down to apply for a licence.

Since inception and through to the present day, Kiss has stood for innovation and a desire to break new ground, striving to keep one step ahead of the crowd in delivering dance music in all its genres.

Kiss was the first commercial station to launch a 'listen again' feature on its website, www.kiss100.com. It has proved popular with Kiss' listeners, who can download, rewind and repeat their favorite shows when they want them. This feature is designed to bring radio to the new time-starved, technologically driven generation. The Kiss 100 website is visited by almost half a million unique users every month.

Indeed, throughout its 20 years, the desire to continually innovate and develop has seen Kiss remain a decorated station, both for its on-air sound and for its talented behind-the-scenes team. Over the years, Kiss has received more than 15 Sony Radio Awards

and numerous other accolades at ceremonies including the British Radio Awards, Media Week Awards, Ethnic Music Awards, EMMA Awards, NTL Awards, UK Garage Awards, Hip Hop Awards, DJ Magazines Awards, MOBO awards as well as several awards at the New York Radio Festival Awards including the prestigious award for Best International Programming. Most recently, it won the 2005 Sony Award for Best Station Sound.

Kiss prides itself on being a breeding ground for talent in the UK radio industry. Alongside the current talented line-up, many internationally renowned DJ's, including Judge Jules, Danny Rampling, Tim Westwood, Trevor Nelson, Roger Sanchez, Spoony and the Dreamteam and Fabio & Grooverider first played their music on Kiss.

History

Kiss was originally created because there was nothing like it in the market. Led by Gordon Mac, a group of people who were passionate about the new exploding dance-music scene in London, but couldn't find an existing home for their music, decided to create one.

Operated as a pirate station for its first five years, Kiss became legal in 1990 as the radio authority recognised the gap in the market for a station with the profile of Kiss and awarded it a licence. The station has always been home to cutting-edge DJs and today its line-up remains one of its key strengths. Whether it is hip hop or R'n'B, garage or drum'n'bass, breaks or reggae, Kiss 100 DJ's will be playing it.

Celebrating its 20th anniversary in 2005, Kiss has been part of the fabric of the dance music scene since its very early days, with a range of DJ's and music providing a platform for the music that London's young people were listening to. Kiss has constantly strived to further the cause of dance and urban music by discovering new music and new talent. Today its market-leading position is testament to its constant innovation and evolution.

Product

Over the course of its two decades on air, Kiss has become more than just a radio station. Having attracted millions of listeners across the country, Kiss is now at the centre of a multi-platform brand that spans radio, TV, events, club nights and branded CDs. Kiss is a CD to listen to, it's a club night to rave at on a Saturday night and it's a holiday to go on with mates. Kiss prides itself on offering its audience a myriad of possibilities to get involved with and 'touch' the brand. The Kiss community is ever expanding.

Under the Kiss programming banner there are many highly successful brand extensions, such as 'Kisstory' and 'Smooth Grooves', which are not only on-air appointments to listen, but are also extended into bestselling compilation albums and club nights.

Kiss is positioned to represent a way of life that is about being young and having fun. With its tagline: 'Kiss, the

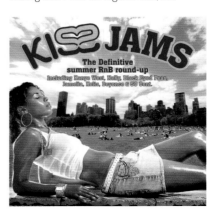

Pirate Soundclash is just one of Kiss' many innovative promotions and programming initiatives which ensures Kiss continues to be famous for finding and developing new talent.

Promotion

Every Kiss communication, both above- and below-the-line, represents the idea that Kiss is 'the station for young, fun London'. Kiss listeners are urban and ambitious as well as sociable and the promotion of Kiss has reflected this.

Kiss has become synonymous with creative, edgy, award-winning communications from its 'Live Sexy' campaign through to 2004's 'Kiss on the Green' working with top-class advertising agencies such as Mother, Naked and HHCL/Red Cell.

Kiss is all about offering its listeners an unforgettable experience. It has long been synonymous with big events in London, having been involved in some way with almost every big dance and urban music event to arrive in London in the past 20 years, from the beginnings of Notting Hill Carnival to the launch in 2004 of The Urban Music Festival with The Princes Trust.

Whether holding summer parties in Ibiza or 'Kiss in the Snow' in Austria, the idea is that the Kiss party is open to all who want to come along and join in.

station for fun young London', it is a lifestyle brand that strives to act as an enabler to ensure that people get the most out of their lives and the most out of their city. Through its programming, promotions and partnerships, it is about offering choice to its listeners by showing them all the different ways they can experience their city.

Kiss is driven by ratings by day and reputation by night.

All its radio programming is done in the unique Kiss style. It attracts some of the best DJ's in the world and broadcasts more than 40 hours a week of specialist programming, for example John Digweed's house show, Tayo's breakbeat show or Shortee Blitz's urban and Hip Hop show.

Just about every type of music the London club scene has to offer is represented on air, creating really strong appointments to listen. The station plays white labels, bootlegs and remixes and some Kiss DJ's have found their true home at Kiss, often after

being sacked from rival commercial radio stations whose formats restricted their creativity. These DJs have found a niche for their edgy presenting styles on Kiss.

Recent Developments

Like its listeners, who are ever-young and live their lives ever-faster, Kiss continually aspires to change, develop and grow. With constant innovation and change, Kiss strives to lead the way and remain London's point of reference for dance and urban music.

Kiss 100 began 2005 with some new talent to join its dance and urban line-up. Young London funk outfit The Loose Cannons, (a.k.a Kaiser Saucy and Lord Fader) now get Friday nights moving with a weekly late-night Friday show.

The Loose Cannons have been joined by former pirate radio star DJ Wec, one of the standout finalists on Kiss 100's 'Pirate Soundclash' contest in 2004. The pirate Soundclash was originally launched in 2003 to celebrate the station's pirate heritage. Seeking out the very best underground talent, the Kiss listeners chose who should be awarded the coveted slot on the Kiss schedule. The

Brand values

The essence of Kiss – a curator of British youth culture – is about being young and having fun. It has strived to stay ahead of the pack by allowing its listeners to step inside the brand and become part of the fabric of the station. The ubiquitous nature of its distribution on new mobile and digital platforms means that Kiss is future-proofed for the 21st century.

www.kiss100.com

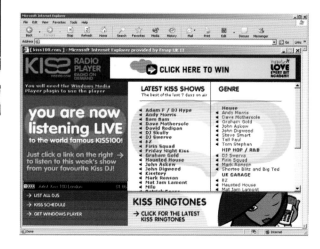

THINGS YOU DIDN'T KNOW ABOUT

Kiss 100

> Kiss was named after the successful youth radio brand of the same name in the US.

> Every summer and winter, Kiss listeners can holiday with Kiss DJs on all-inclusive package holidays that not only offer them activities during the day but also VIP nights out.

> June Sarpong, now a Channel 4 TV presenter, started her career answering the phones at Kiss on Saturday afternoons.

> Every weekend Kiss clubs play host to thousands of party-goers at a variety of nights borne out of the station's programming strands such as 'Kisstory' and 'Smooth Grooves'.

> Kiss have sold 5.4 million albums to date, including 30 which have been in the Top 10.

escape with bam bam breakfast

livesexy

Market

Facial tissues are commonly recognised as essential allies in the war against colds, flu and hayfever but they were originally positioned as cold cream and make-up removers.

The facial tissue market is now worth £171 million (Source: ACNielsen) and has grown by 22% in the 10 years since 1995, driven by product innovations that have brought new consumers into the category.

The launch of KLEENEX® Ultra Soft in 1994 created the premium sector of the tissue market, which now accounts for almost a quarter of the total category value (Source: ACNielsen). Similarly, the launch of KLEENEX® Balsam in 1996 created a new segment of the market, the medicinal segment, which now accounts for 17% of the category and which has continued to grow each year since its launch.

In recent years, the 'Pocket Pack' format has been growing in popularity, with a 16% growth in the number of Pocket Packs sold in 2004. More than two individual pocket packs are now sold in the UK every second. KLEENEX® remains the indisputable segment leader with 50% Pocket Pack market share in 2004 (Source: ACNielsen).

In total, 67% of UK households buy facial tissue at least once a year and KLEENEX® is the only major branded player in the market, with 49% market share (Source: ACNielsen).

Achievements

KLEENEX® is the world's most famous tissue brand and largely pioneered the disposable tissue market. The brand has remained the market leader in the UK since production began in 1924. KLEENEX® has constantly stayed ahead of the market and has sustained a reputation for quality and reliability as well as having a warm image.

KLEENEX® is the number five brand within Non-Grocery brands (excluding laundry detergents) (Source: ACNielsen) and its sales have doubled in volume in the past ten years. In 2003 KLEENEX® achieved record market share of 51.1% MAT, peaking at 53.9% in February 2003 (Source ACNielsen).

KLEENEX® Balsam has been a successful addition to the KLEENEX® range and is now the fastest growing KLEENEX® variant. In January 2005 it achieved a record monthly value share of 16%, with more than one box being sold every two seconds in the UK (Source: ACNielsen).

History

Kimberly-Clark was founded in 1872 but it was wartime ingenuity that led to the development of the company's first consumer product. The cellulose wadding tissue, trademarked Cellucotton by Kimberly-Clark, was first developed in 1914 and became an essential medical item during World War I.

It was used in wartime hospitals and first aid stations, where it often stood as an ideal substitute for surgical dressing when cotton was scarce. Army nurses adapted this wadding for menstrual uses and soon after, in 1920, Kimberly-Clark began producing Kotex® feminine pads for the public. This then led to the company developing the KLEENEX® facial tissue.

KLEENEX® tissue was first presented in response to the array of cosmetics and cold creams then launched in the market as a cold cream remover. KLEENEX® tissue was positioned as a disposable substitute for facial towels.

In 1929, KLEENEX® introduced the 'pop-up' format to its range, making it easier for consumers to dispense tissues as and when they needed them. At the same time, coloured tissues were introduced. Through extending choice to the consumer, KLEENEX® tissue steadily gained users. However, it was still regarded somewhat as a luxury item.

Its primary usage was revealed through a consumer test in 1930, which clearly demonstrated that more than 60% of KLEENEX® tissue consumers used the tissues as a disposable handkerchief, as opposed to its original intended use as a cold cream remover. As a consequence, Kimberly-Clark swung the positioning of its product towards this section of the market, and pioneered its usage as a handy disposable tissue suited for use on the move. Advertising enforced this usage and sales promptly soared.

KLEENEX® tissue was unavailable for civilian use during World War II. However, production of the base product – the wadding – continued but was diverted once again to the war effort and adapted for industrial uses; such as insulation. Once the war was over, tissue production resumed and production facilities increased to meet growing demand.

In 1956, KLEENEX® For Men was launched as 'the' big, strong mansize tissue, later advertised as being 'A full foot square for a mansize blow'. Its size, strength and distinctive packaging appealed to both men and women and it quickly became the market leader, where it has remained for almost 50 years. It is not, therefore, surprising that KLEENEX® for Men drives the image of KLEENEX® in the UK as being warm, generous and reliable. In fact, Kimberly-Clark research has found that when consumers are asked about the KLEENEX® brand, the first connection they make is with this product.

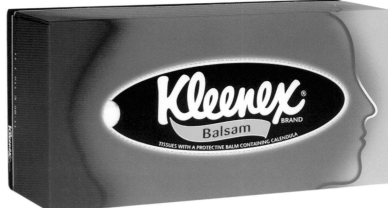

In 1967, Kimberly-Clark introduced KLEENEX® Boutique tissues in attractive upright packaging and a new sub-brand was born.

KLEENEX® Travel tissues were launched in a flexible pack for out-of-home use. The next major innovation saw the introduction of the first, dry-to-the-touch, lotion treated tissues in 1994 – KLEENEX® Ultra (later re-branded in 1996 as KLEENEX® Ultra Soft). At launch, more than 20% of buyers of KLEENEX® Ultra Soft were new buyers to the facial tissue category (Source: ACNielsen).

In 1996, KLEENEX® UltraBalm tissues were launched. These were the first tissues to leave behind a unique and clinically proven protective balm, containing calendula, to help prevent the nose from becoming red and sore. The launch of KLEENEX® UltraBalm tissues resulted in KLEENEX® facial tissues being named as the fastest-growing brand in the UK (Source: ACNielsen 1996). KLEENEX® UltraBalm was re-branded as KLEENEX® Balsam in 1998 and continues its rapid growth due to its Cold & Flu positioning.

In 2000 the KLEENEX® brand celebrated its 75th anniversary.

Product

The basic ingredient of KLEENEX® tissue is high quality cellulose fibre, which is obtained principally from wood pulp that is processed into creped wadding. Kimberly-Clark only purchases fibres from those suppliers who follow sustainable forestry practices and their environmental practices are also regularly reviewed. The ideal KLEENEX® tissue fibre is derived from selected tree species to ensure that they contribute to the desirable characteristics of softness, absorbency and strength in the KLEENEX® tissue.

Throughout the manufacturing process, Kimberly-Clark looks for ways to reduce the amount of energy used and has embarked on an ambitious energy-reduction programme which, in the past five years, has achieved a significant improvement in energy efficiency. The company now uses recycled materials in about half of its total European production.

KLEENEX® tissues are subjected to a series of quality and performance checks including tests for softness, absorbency, strength, size and colour. The KLEENEX® brand has a strong heritage and consumers trust KLEENEX® tissues to offer them the best quality and most reliable product on the market and, therefore, such checks are important to retain consumer loyalty.

KLEENEX® facial tissue products are re-launched on a regular basis and always feature really tangible product improvements, such as increased softness, thickness and strength. The KLEENEX® name will only be applied to products that are demonstrably the best in their category.

Recent Developments

KLEENEX® has driven many innovations in the facial tissue market recently: KLEENEX® Travellers – specifically designed for use in a car, KLEENEX® Christmas Cube – to inspire and excite consumers during the festive season, KLEENEX® Cosmetic Cube – to use with a cleanser for make-up removal and KLEENEX® Wipes – the first moist KLEENEX® product targeted at young adults on the go.

In September 2004, KLEENEX® For Men, the UK's number one facial tissue, was re-launched. With its distinctive packaging and reputation for tissue strength it had been the number one-selling tissue for almost 50 years and had a large base of loyal consumers. The brand rejuvenation was immediately evident to consumers in the new pack design, which was updated to give a sense of modernity and dynamism in order to attract new, younger users to the brand whilst still drawing on recognisable cues of historical designs to retain the strong base of KLEENEX® For Men brand loyalists.

Promotion

KLEENEX® tissue has always been promoted through magazine, newspaper and TV advertising.

Over the past three decades, KLEENEX® facial tissue has enjoyed a continuous advertising presence and, in most of these years, has enjoyed 100% share of voice as the only brand advertising facial tissues.

The re-launch of KLEENEX® For Men was supported by the brand's first TV advertisement for more than five years in January 2005. With a simple storyline of a father crying over the birth of his child in a hospital maternity ward, the advert took one of the most poignant and recognisable moments in adult life in order to illustrate the emotional and functional support that KLEENEX® For Men tissues offer to consumers.

The re-launch was also supported with a high profile PR campaign designed to establish a link between KLEENEX® For Men and male emotion. A report entitled 'The KLEENEX® For Men Crying Game Report' was commissioned in conjunction with the Social Issues Research Centre in Oxford to understand why, where, when and how often men cry. The research found a growing acceptance of men displaying emotion, with almost a third of men questioned admitting to shedding a tear in the previous month.

The PR campaign also included a five-week sponsorship of the James Whale show on Talksport Radio and the TV sponsorship of '100 Greatest Tearjerkers' on Channel 4 in February 2005. This TV sponsorship was the first ever undertaken by KLEENEX® For Men and a creative animated graphics approach provided examples of situations in which men might find themselves shedding a tear or two.

For more than ten years, KLEENEX® has run on-pack consumer promotions during two key seasons – Cold & Flu (Winter) and Hay Fever (Spring-Summer). Consumers have been offered the opportunity to collect the ovals from KLEENEX® boxes to send off for specially-developed premium products or kits.

The hay fever promotion was launched in 1991 and has collected nine Institute of Sales Promotion Awards, including the Grand Prix Award for the best UK and European promotions of 1991.

Developing promotions around real consumer insights has ensured their success and popularity with shoppers. The 2004 KLEENEX® Winter promotion was inspired by 'Sofa Sanctuary' Insight, that when you feel under the weather, all you want to do is curl up on the sofa wrapped in a fluffy blanket, with all essentials within easy reach – box of tissues, hot drink, TV remote, hot water bottle and a phone for 24/7 sympathy. This was supported by special research done for The KLEENEX® Winter Warmer Report, according to which 58% of Brits spend up to seven hours a week snuggling on the sofa.

Inspired by this insight KLEENEX® developed the ultimate snuggling accessory – the KLEENEX® Sofa Snuggler. Made from cosy fleece, with handy pockets for a hot water bottle, tissues and the TV remote, it was a perfect antidote to cold winter evenings and helped to reinforce the KLEENEX® values of warmth, care and a personal touch.

The promotion created a lot of interest among consumers as well as the media, where it received support from various regional and national radio stations and newspapers.

Brand Values

Throughout the world, the KLEENEX® brand name stands for quality, softness and reliability, as well as warmth and affection. The brand targets people at their most human – when they are experiencing life's ups and downs and aims to make people feel better, helping to lift their spirits. This is communicated in KLEENEX® advertising via the strapline 'Thank Goodness for KLEENEX® tissues!'

www.kleenex.com/uk

KwikFit>

Market

The automotive aftermarket in the UK is worth more than £8 billion a year, the value of which is driven by an ageing car parc, changing product lifecycles, legislation and the non-discretionary nature of the products and services that Kwik-Fit provides.

In a market consisting of more than 10,000 fast fit, independent garages and franchised dealers, the Kwik-Fit brand guarantees consistency and provides an easy choice, in a world in which there is more choice for motorists with less time than ever before.

Employing more than 9,000 people, the Kwik-Fit Group now provides an expanded range of products and services that includes; tyres, emissions, brakes, batteries, suspension, lubrication, servicing, vehicle glass repair and replacement, air conditioning and financial services.

Kwik-Fit's continued growth will be driven by increasing its sales of its core products to cash and fleet customers supported by brand investment, supply chain improvements, the roll-out of new products and services and an ongoing focus on Kwik-Fit's scale advantages.

There are 22 million licensed cars on UK roads that are more than three years old which means that Kwik-Fit, as the UK market leader, is well placed to continue increasing its share of this substantial car parc.

Achievements

Established in 1971, Kwik-Fit has been trading for 34 years and is Europe's leading automotive parts repair and replacement specialist. The famous 'you can't get better than a Kwik-Fit fitter' campaign, launched in 1984, helped Kwik-Fit become a household name and through continuous brand investment now enjoys spontaneous brand awareness of 81%. As market leader, the Kwik-Fit brand is distinctive, well known, trusted and respected.

The brand's achievements have also been recognised by a number of prestigious awards. Kwik-Fit Fleet has won over 49 fleet industry awards in its 18-year history, more than any other fleet operator. Underlining its reputation for innovation and service Kwik-Fit Fleet was awarded 'Best Fast Fit Company' in March 2005 by Fleet News, the UK's leading fleet industry publication. Most recently, Kwik-Fit Insurance Services was listed in The Sunday Times 100 Best Companies to work for – rising to 15th position.

Alongside its success in business, Kwik-Fit has contributed much to the local community in which it operates. In the last 10 years almost £3 million has been donated to initiatives that have supported youth development and business enterprise.

History

In 1971 the first Kwik-Fit centre was opened in Edinburgh. Rapid growth

followed and this attracted the attention of a small listed conglomerate, G A Robinson. Kwik-Fit was amalgamated into the Group but the advent of the three day week caused major problems for most of G A Robinson's constituent companies. The businesses were sold with the exception of the tyre centres and the company name was changed to Kwik-Fit. As a newly created stock exchange listed company, one of Britain's most exciting specialist retail success stories had begun.

In 1979, with 52 centres, Kwik-Fit acquired Euro Exhaust centres giving Kwik-Fit a total of 136 centres (and its first centres in Holland). This was followed in 1980 by the purchase of Firestone's 180 centres for £3.2 million. With more than 200 centres nationally, Kwik-Fit entered the 1980s as a successful business that had developed and dominated its own niche market.

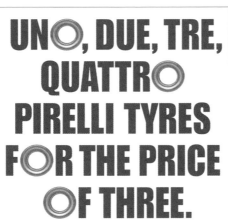

Kwik-Fit Fleet was formed in 1986 to serve the specialist needs of the company car driver. This service has been enhanced further and now provides; Kwik-Fit Mobile (the UK's largest mobile tyre fitting company); a Business Drive Card for fleets of less than 25 vehicles; the Kwik-Fit Tyre Management Programme; enabling fleet customers to outsource their vehicle tyre maintenance for a negotiated fee per vehicle. Kwik-Fit Fleet now retains a 70% share of the large corporate customer vehicle leasing market.

The Group's activities were expanded in 1995 to include Kwik-Fit Insurance Services. Offering branded motor insurance on behalf of a panel of leading insurance companies, Kwik-Fit Insurance Services' unique 'outbound customer contact' model has helped the business grow and become one of the UK's leading insurance brokers.

In 1999, Kwik-Fit completed the acquisition of 400 Speedy centres and 160 Pit Stop Centres. Covering France, Belgium, Spain, Switzerland and Germany it gave the Kwik-Fit Group one of the most extensive European networks in the automotive repair business.

A rapid change in ownership followed when, in 1999, Kwik-Fit was acquired by The Ford Motor Company and then, in 2002, Kwik-Fit was sold to CVC Capital Partners, a leading private equity company.

Kwik-Fit's most recent acquisition was announced in 2004 when a further 43 fast fit centres were acquired from Axto in France. The Kwik-Fit Group now operates 1,913 motorist centres and mobile tyre fitting vehicles.

Product

Operating on a 'drive-in-while-you-wait' basis, Kwik-Fit has developed a product range and expertise in areas that cover motorists' essential needs. Tyres, brakes and emission systems are Kwik-Fit's core products and account for over 25% of the automotive aftermarket. A culture of continuous improvement has enabled Kwik-Fit to create a fast, efficient, friendly experience backed by quality, choice and value for money.

Convenient, accessible and well-presented centres are located close to where people live, work or shop. Quality parts are supplied by leading manufacturers, direct to centres, based on a 'just-in-time' stock replenishment system. Together with an improved supply chain where a 'hub and spoke' system is being rolled-out to improve further short notice product availability, Kwik-Fit is well placed to meet the demands of almost every motorist immediately.

Kwik-Fit people also help to make the difference. Supported and trained to be the best in the industry, through four training centres in the UK, including a purpose built training academy, Kwik-Fit people can work towards nationally recognised qualifications. This complements Kwik-Fit's bespoke training programmes. Kwik-Fit invests more than £3 million in training programmes annually and the Government's Adult Learning Inspectorate recently recognised Kwik-Fit as one of the top businesses for staff training in the UK engineering, technology and manufacturing sectors.

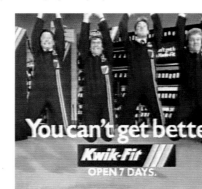

Measuring performance is critical. Through regular tracking studies and market research Kwik-Fit gathers customer feedback. It also encourages all customers to comment on the standards of service they receive. A telephone helpline and a reply paid questionnaire are available to every customer and, from its Customer Survey Unit, thousands of customers are contacted every day, within 72 hours of their visit to a Kwik-Fit centre. With this information Kwik-Fit are able to identify ways in which they can further improve their service. Contacting more than one million customers a year, this survey is the largest continuous research programme in the industry.

Recent Developments

With thousands of different makes and models of vehicles on the road today and hundreds of different tyre sizes, finding the right tyre for a car online can be a real chore. In fact, 78% of Britain's motorists don't know the exact size specification of their vehicles' tyres. For this reason, Kwik-Fit's website allows motorists to find the tyres quickly and easily by identifying their make and model of car. This is the UK's first online tyre search facility that doesn't require motorists to always know their tyre size.

The new website also helps motorists locate their nearest Kwik-Fit centre or, alternatively, arrange to have their tyres replaced by one of Kwik-Fit's 200 mobile tyre fitting vehicles. Motorists can also book their MoT online and request an e-mail or SMS text reminder when their insurance, vehicle service, MoT or road tax renewals are due.

To help ease the burden of these non-discretionary purchases, in January 2005, Kwik-Fit launched a new payment card for the motorist. Called 'The Car.d' it offers a range of motoring related benefits that recognise we all spend money on motoring but rarely get anything back for doing so. Motoring related discounts and cash back on

petrol purchases are available together with extended interest free payment terms to help relieve the surprise, burden and stress of motoring expenditure.

In 2004, Kwik-Fit started to trial a centre refurbishment and modernisation programme. It encompassed a review of Kwik-Fit's image and identity in-centre and at the kerbside and is aimed at improving the customer experience from arrival to departure. Initial research confirms that visitors consider the refurbished centres even more distinctive, welcoming and customer focused.

Promotion

You don't have to be an industry insider to know there's a lot of mistrust of garages out there. People don't want to worry about tyres, brakes and exhausts. When there's a problem they need it sorted, quickly and painlessly – which is why thousands of these people choose Kwik-Fit to sort them out and get them back on the road, every day.

In a departure from its previous product based and price led TV advertising, Kwik-Fit's latest campaign acknowledges the very real and genuine concerns that motorists so often express about the industry as a whole. By using animation techniques, the latest advertisements play to this stereotype that motorists so often spontaneously describe. By simply acknowledging these concerns rather than ignoring them, lets motorists know that Kwik-Fit cares how they feel.

Kwik-Fit takes its standards of customer service very seriously and regularly contacts customers to check they were happy with the service they received. Spontaneously, hundreds of customers write to Kwik-Fit every year to compliment them on their service.

It was this contact that was further inspiration for the new advertising idea.

Through the new advertising, Kwik-Fit illustrate customers' real and actual experiences of visiting Kwik-Fit centres. These insights are taken directly from the hundreds of customer letters that they receive and are a genuine reflection of the way their customers feel towards Kwik-Fit.

The TV campaign featuring 'talking heads in an animated world' lets these peoples' stories speak for themselves at the same time as recognising their concerns about the industry.

This new work has enabled Kwik-Fit to reach a wider audience and, through the mix of live action and animation, has created work that is motivating, relevant and distinctive. The style of the new advertising is also seen to build on the brand image established by the original Kwik-Fit fitter campaign.

The role that value plays in determining customer preference is greater than ever before and, to compete, that preference must be justified on a daily basis. For this reason, Kwik-Fit continually works the relationship between price, quality and service across all its communication. This includes delivering price promotions in press and third party and supplier offers at point-of-sale.

Brand Values

Kwik-Fit's purpose is to keep people moving and to keep people safe through outstanding customer service. Kwik-Fit repairs or replaces the most frequently required automotive parts and its vision is to be 'the first choice for every motorist'. Beyond the now famous proposition 'you can't get better than a Kwik-Fit fitter', Kwik-Fit now aim to offer 'more expertise for your money'. Its brand values include being dependable, accessible, helpful, efficient, proud and professional.

www.kwik-fit.com

THINGS YOU DIDN'T KNOW ABOUT

Kwik-Fit

> Kwik-Fit sells one in five exhausts in the UK.

> The first centre was opened 34 years ago in Edinburgh.

> If all the tyres sold by Kwik-Fit in a year were stacked on top of each other, they would be 100 times bigger than Mount Everest.

> Kwik-Fit solves a motorist's problem every eight seconds.

lastminute.com

Market

Over the course of the past decade, technology has changed the way consumers live. With the advent and proliferation of mobile phones, multi-channel TV, round-the-clock banking, digital photography, eBay, Google, Apple, Amazon and Sky+, life has become on-demand. Consumers have become used to getting what they want, when they want it, and spontaneity rules.

tell me why I don't like Mondays.

cultural R&R from **£89**

Because you could be here instead.

3* Paris 2nts **£89**
3* Budapest 2nts **£129**
5* Warsaw 2nts **£165**

Our best ever city-break deals.

lastminute.com
holidays • hotels • flights • car hire

Prices include flights (Eurostar for Paris) and are based on 2 people sharing. Paris: room only, available Sat-Mon 2-4 April '05. Budapest and Warsaw: room only, available Sat-Mon 23-25 April '05. Prices are correct at time of going to press and are subject to availability and conditions. lastminute.com acts as an agent for ATOL protected operators. Booking fees may apply.

The UK now boasts mobile phone penetration of more than 80%, email and internet usage among 75% of the population and online or direct travel purchases among 50% of the population (Source: Mintel).

There is a huge choice of travel and leisure products currently available to consumers, and with many suppliers, a high speed of change and great price sensitivity, the market is perfectly suited to the online sales channel.

Achievements

lastminute.com provides a marketplace for travel and leisure products and services, and since launching in 1998, it has experienced growth on a huge scale. The brand has now established itself as one of the most visited and most recognised of all ecommerce companies.

Even with the very high level of competition for online travel and leisure sales, lastminute.com has consistently remained top of the tree in terms of brand awareness and market share.

It is the number one online travel and leisure site in the UK. In the key summer months of July and August in 2004 lastminute.com came top in terms of visitor share, with 10.7% and 10.13% market share respectively and outperformed all other travel players in the market, including easyJet and Expedia (Source: Hitwise).

To help support its continuous growth, lastminute.com has tailored and developed its offering to take advantage of emergent social trends including significant growth in time-poor cash-rich customers, a desire to travel and go out more as well as later parenting.

Purchase patterns in the travel sector are also changing rapidly with more short-break holidays, more independent travel, a demand for greater flexibility and importantly for lastminute.com, a trend towards bookings being made late.

As lastminute.com's customer base has grown, so have the number of suppliers who provide products and services for the site. lastminute.com now has individual relationships with thousands of key suppliers including international airlines, hotels, tour operators, theatre, sports and entertainment promoters, restaurants and gifts suppliers, both in the UK and internationally.

The company has mirrored the success of its UK site with site launches in major European markets and through a programme of acquisition of complementary businesses and brands. Over the past five years it has acquired 13 businesses, including Degriftour, Travelselect, holiday autos, Medhotels and Online Travel Company. The increased scale delivered by these acquisitions combined with rapid organic growth has seen the business's turnover grow to more than £1 billion in 2004.

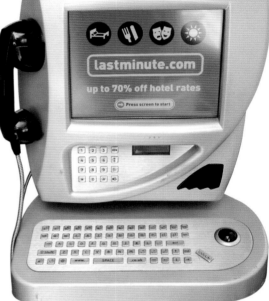

lastminute.com
up to 70% off hotel rates
Press screen to start

History

lastminute.com was founded by Brent Hoberman and Martha Lane Fox in 1998, based on the idea of matching last-minute supply and demand using the power of the internet.

The pair began with a kitchen table business plan, moved on to two desks in London's Portobello area and, as the number of staff grew, several further moves followed until the website was launched in October that year.

By the end of March 1999, more than 90,000 people had registered with the site and in excess of 200 suppliers were offering their products and services through the site. The brand was known as a leader of the dot com revolution.

The company undertook an Initial Public Offering in March 2000 and is listed on the London Stock Exchange. Its initial business concept was to help suppliers efficiently sell unused products or 'distressed inventory', which in the travel and leisure industry can be

put some colour in your cheeks

more beaches. hotter deals.
enjoy every **lastminute.com**

hot beaches for swingers

more beaches. hotter deals.
lastminute.com

significant. The lastminute.com value proposition has been built on price, convenience and inspirational ideas. An early aim of the company was to 'encourage spontaneous, romantic and occassionally adventurous behaviour'.

As lastminute.com was able to show its value to both customers and suppliers, it increasingly incorporated non-distressed inventory, and now sells a full range of products across each of its categories. The business vision has not changed, the aim remains to provide inspiration and solutions for its customers.

A key strategic area for lastminute.com is its differentiation through lifestyle products which include theatre tickets, unique and unusual gifts, restaurant bookings, and a host of other products from ipods to U2 tickets. These products provide real reasons to come back to the website on a regular basis and help build strong, ongoing relationships with the customer.

Product

lastminute.com offers its customers everything to do with going away, going out and staying in. That includes package holidays, short breaks, hotels, flights, trains, theatre tickets, restaurants, sports events, rock and pop DVDs, gifts, experiences, dating and auctions.

It aims to be the only place consumers need to go for inspiring leisure time solutions, offering cool places to stay, eat and spend their leisure time and holidays that consumers can't get anywhere else.

Shopping and browsing on lastminute.com is designed to be different from exploring other e-commerce sites. Indeed, more than 40% of visitors to the site visit at least twice a week. By providing a content-rich environment and developing a host of personalisation and community-based features to attract and retain customers, lastminute.com strives to remain a unique destination in the e-commerce arena.

Recent Developments

lastminute.com was a pioneer in the development of the dynamically packaged holiday, where customers build their own holiday online, as opposed to choosing a pre-packaged holiday. The growth of this sector has been driven by the growth in consumer demand for independent and flexible travel.

lastminute.com has also put a big focus on the development of a comprehensive hotel product both in the UK and internationally. Using intitiatives such as 'top secret hotels', where the customer does not know the exact hotel at the time they book, but ends up staying at top quality four and five star hotels at the fraction of the price, lastminute.com has become a signifcant force in the rapidly expanding online hotel market.

lastminute.com has also pioneered the use of new forms of technology in its distribution strategy and today enjoys partnerships with Sky, Vodaphone, O2 and Orange by providing content on these companies' platforms. lastminute.com aims to provide a service that every customer can access every day and is committed to delivering its products via the most convienient method for the customer. Recent innovations include location-based services, which provide tailored offers relevant to the customer's location.

Promotion

lastminute.com has consistently been promoted with an integrated combination of online and offline marketing. A series of media firsts and innovative creative have continued to stamp the innovative side of the brand throughout its marketing activity.

Central to the promotion of the website and to customer retention is the lastminute.com weekly email newsletter. The newsletter alerts subscribers to the best of the offers on site as well as special promotions, competitions and deals. But it is much more than just a series of offers, it reflects the character of the brand and the site and is a unique marketing tool. Today, the lastminute.com newsletter is sent to ten million people globally each week.

Online marketing includes a host of distribution channels from affiliate schemes to larger partnerships with big name brands such as AOL and Tesco.com. Online advertising via search engines such as Google

and Overture combined with viral marketing provide a powerful integrated approach. lastminute.com's offline marketing is multi-facted, using a variety of media including outdoor, press, radio, ambient activity and promotional partnerships with brands including Fanta and McDonald's.

lastminute.com is also a regualar user of emerging media, recently being the first company to use 'adwalkers' to promote a limited tactical offer. PR has always been central to the company's marketing strategy and has been fundamental in achieving and maintaining the high levels of awareness that the brand enjoys. Contextual and event-based marketing have been used to great success in the past with executions focused on events such as the royal wedding and general election.

A strong visual indentity using the famous lastminute.com pink combined with copy-based advertising was used effectively in the company's early days, with memorable executions including 'surprise your girlfriend, take her sister to Paris'. Several different creative styles have been used, but the latest campaigns have returned to the brand's hertitage developing a highly recognisable, consistent visual and tonal style, always with an interesting twist.

Brand Values

lastminute.com strives to be seen as simple, smart, inspirational and providing unique value. It aims to give consumers the inside track on how to find smarter travel and leisure solutions without paying more for them.

The brand has always strived to achieve a mischevious, spontaneous and 'non-corporate' tone of voice designed to give it a clear point of difference from its competitors. It encourages its marketers to be brave and push boundaries that just wouldn't be possible with other brands.

www.lastminute.com

THINGS YOU DIDN'T KNOW ABOUT

lastminute.com

> In 2004 people booking through lastminute.com would have filled the equivalent of 3,000 jumbo jets.

> If lastminute.com put all of the tickets it sells annually together side by side they would reach from John O'Groats to Land's End.

> lastminute.com is the biggest independent retailer of theatre tickets in the UK.

> lastminute.com sells everything from holidays in the Maldives to candy g-strings.

> Nearly two million customers book a hotel through lastminute.com each year.

> When it first started in 1998, the lastminute.com brand was blue.

L'ORÉAL
PARIS

Market

In today's beauty and youth-oriented society, consumers will go to ever-greater lengths to keep themselves looking fit and young. The combined health and beauty market in the UK was worth a massive £5.5 billion in 2004, growing by 4% over 2003 (Source: IRI, TNS, FBA, Salon Syndicate). Haircare and skincare combined make up 47% of this, with both categories growing by over 5% per year.

When it comes to the quest for eternal youth, the market for facial skincare products is intensely active, with 70% of women using them. In the 1990s, facial skincare was mostly categorised into moisturisers, cleansers and toners, but, the market is now fragmented into specialist targeted solutions for all types of skin and lifestage.

In 2004, Mintel found that UK consumers spent £531 million on facial skincare products – a 37% increase since 1999. By 2009, Mintel says that spend will reach £666 million.

The world's steadily ageing population is fuelling demand. The UK is no exception to this inexorable demographic shift, with the proportion of 55-64 year-olds expected to grow from 10.2% to 12.1% between 1999 and 2008. So-called 'age management' products are growing particularly fast, with data from IRI showing 22% growth between 2003 and 2004, compared to 7.4% for facial beauty products. Nearly a third of all facial skincare products sold now have an age management function.

Increasing numbers of working women, with more money to spend on their appearance, are also driving demand for skincare products. People are more prepared to undergo cosmetic procedures, with minor plastic surgery, botox and collagen injections far more widespread now than they used to be. According to the American Society for Aesthetic Plastic Surgery, there has been a 471% increase in non-surgical cosmetic procedures, such as chemical peel, micro-dermabrasion or botox, since 1997.

In response to this, skincare products are becoming more and more hi-tech, positioned as alternatives to invasive treatments, or even cosmetic surgery.

And it's not just women fuelling growth in the market. Men are taking better care of themselves too, spending £95 million on male skincare and shaving products in 2004. Male Toiletries, including deodorants and shower products, account for an additional £402 million.

As consumers turn to more hi-tech and innovative products, the 'salon' market for health and beauty products is growing fast, by over 10% year-on-year. However, some 60% of health and beauty products remain targeted at mass-market consumers.

L'Oréal Paris enjoys a strong position in all of its key markets. It is the global leader in hair colourants, and, in the UK, jointly leads the facial skincare sector with a 16% market share (Source: Mintel).

Achievements

L'Oréal UK has been present in the UK for over 70 years, during which time it has become the fourth largest subsidiary of L'Oréal in Europe and the fifth worldwide. Globally, the L'Oreal Group is the world's leading cosmetics company, with an impressive portfolio of 17 international brands, sold in 130 countries.

The L'Oréal brand has evolved enormously in recent years, leading the way with research and development. R&D is key to the brand's growth

and, with a record of registering 500 patents a year, L'Oréal is doing more than any company in the industry to drive innovation and product performance. The L'Oréal Group employs nearly 2,980 people in its research laboratories worldwide and spends over 3% of its entire turnover on research – a figure which has reached €507 million in 2004. The development process for each product takes a team of 30 researchers anything from two to 10 years.

Some of the highly innovative products patented by L'Oréal include Ceramide R, which strengthens capillary fibres in the hair, Mexoryl SX and XL, which protect the skin against the sun, and Boswelox™, an advanced complex to fight the ageing effects of skin contractions.

As part of its research programme, The L'Oréal Group combines the skills of chemists, physicists, biologists, doctors and mathematicians. L'Oréal also invests in dermatological research.

The group's research centres are spread across three continents: Europe, North America and Asia. These ensure products are adapted and fine-tuned to best suit the needs of their local market. In 2003 L'Oréal opened the L'Oréal Institute for Ethnic Hair and Skin Research. This is the world's only research centre dedicated to furthering the knowledge of skin and hair of African origin.

L'Oréal's strong performance comes from the very top. The group's Welsh-born Chairman and Chief Executive Officer, Lindsay Owen-Jones, has been ranked number 16 in a global survey conducted by the FT, which rated the world's most respected leaders. The survey also ranked the organisation, L'Oréal, in the top 20 most respected companies.

History

In 1907 Eugène Schueller, a young French chemist, developed the first synthetic hair dye, and he named his brand of hair colourants Auréole. He continued to develop further dyes, formulating and manufacturing his own products, which he then sold to Parisian hair salons.

In 1909 Schueller registered his company as the Société Française de Teintures Inoffensives pour Cheveux – which was later renamed L'Oréal. From this early stage, research and innovation were key factors in the development of Schueller's business. By 1920 he was employing three chemists and by 1984 L'Oréal had 1,000 chemists worldwide.

The distribution of L'Oréal products was also carefully considered and grew rapidly. By 1912 L'Oréal products were available in Holland, Austria and Italy, closely followed by expansion into the US, South America, Russia and the Far East. In 1936 sunscreen was introduced to the L'Oréal Group's range.

Product

L'Oréal Paris is the signature brand of the L'Oréal Group. The group in the UK also consists of well known beauty brands such as Lancôme, Biotherm, Shu Uemura, Garnier-Maybelline and Vichy. Professional products include L'Oréal Professionnel, Kerastase, Redken, and Matrix and fragrance brands such as Armani, Cacharel and Ralph Lauren. Over a third of L'Oréal Group's turnover in the UK is generated by L'Oréal Paris.

L'Oréal Paris is the only beauty brand whose products cater for women 'from top to toe'. In cosmetics, star products in the range include Glam Shine, True Match foundation, Lash Architect and Volume Shocking Mascara.

In skincare, L'Oréal Paris Dermo-Expertise continues to grow, strengthening its profile as a luxury product. It caters for all ages, with Pure Zone aimed at the younger market, Hydrafresh for women in their 20s, Visible Results for the 30s, Revitalift for

40s and Age Perfect for 50s. Wrinkle De-Crease is a recent innovation containing Boswelox that targets first expression lines and wrinkles.

L'Oréal Paris is also a leader in bodycare, with its Body-Expertise range and leaders in the anti-cellulite market with their Perfect Slim range. In suncare, the L'Oréal Paris Solar Expertise range includes Milk Spray mist, which provides the protection of a lotion in a mist. The Sublime Bronze self tanning range includes new Instant Tan and Self Tan wipes.

In haircare, leading brands include the Elvive Shampoo and conditioner range and Elnett Hairspray and Mousse. Studio Line Hot range is advertised by the global pop star, Beyonce. As a world leader in hair colourants and the UK number one with 32% of the market, L'Oréal Paris' key brands include Excellence, Recital Preference, Couleur Experte, Feria and Color Pulse.

Innvoation – Couleur Experte is the first at home base colour and highlights kit. L'Oréal Paris has the widest range of colours, with over 124 shades of hair colour.

Recent Developments

L'Oréal Paris is regularly adding advanced new products to its wide portfolio.

Among its newest products is Refinish – a new generation of home-use

skincare that renovates the skin with spectacular and immediate results. Devised as two formulae – a micro-dermabrasion kit and a post-treatment optimising moisturiser – Refinish smooths away skin texture irregularities, boosts complexion radiance, fades fine lines and leaves the skin feeling ultra soft.

As well as Refinish, L'Oréal Paris has introduced another hi-tech weapon for women fighting the effects of ageing, called Renoviste. This is its first-ever anti-ageing 'glycolic peel kit', providing a home solution for what is formerly a professional 'chemical peel' procedure.

A recent addition to L'Oréal Paris Body Expertise range is the new Perfect Slim Patch. This is an anti-cellulite patch and is L'Oréal Paris' first targeted treatment patch to reduce the appearance of cellulite in stubborn areas. The patented formula's main ingredient, Caffeine Cx, promotes micro-circulation in the skin. Tests show that 79% of women found that Perfect Slim Patch had a visible effect on the appearance of their skin. Perfect Slim also comes as a gel or cream, and recently topped an independent consumer study conducted on 200 women in France. Judged the best Anti-Cellulite product, Perfect Slim was proven by the study to reduce the circumference of women's thighs who tested the product by up to 2cm. The effectiveness of Perfect Slim has helped L'Oréal's Body Expertise range increase its sales by 116% in units to date.

New Men Expert is the first skincare line from L'Oréal Paris, exclusively for men. In the range, expert solutions for every skincare type include moisturisers, eye creams, cleansers and shaving products.

Recently, L'Oréal Paris launched its first 'Beauty Boutique' in Boots flagship store in Sedley Place off Oxford Street in London.

Promotion

The L'Oréal Group has had a strong history in its promotional activity. It commissioned promotional posters from graphic artists such as Coupot and Savignac, when advertising was still in its infancy. In 1933, Schueller created and launched a magazine called Votre Beauté, which was devoted to women and their well-being.

In 1937, Schueller took part in a popular French radio programme which launched the 'Clean Children' campaign. In 1947 L'Oréal produced their first television advert and during the 1950s L'Oréal not only continued this activity but was one of the first brands to be advertised in cinemas with a commercial for Ambre Solaire. In 1953 L'Oréal won an advertising Oscar for its work.

In recent years, The L'Oréal Paris brand has established a recognised advertising image using the strapline 'Because you're Worth It'. This reflects the brand's commitment to beauty research, and its mission to enable women to feel as good about themselves as possible.

L'Oréal Paris is unrivalled in the endorsement it receives from some of the World's most glamorous women, including Natalie Imbruglia, Charlize Theron, Andie McDowell, Beyonce Knowles, and Claudia Schiffer. These women are chosen not simply because of their beauty but their aspirational view on life. The most recent addition to this 'Dream Team' is actress Eva Longoria, best known from the TV hit show 'Desperate Housewives', where she portrays Latin beauty Gabrielle Solis.

As well as its high profile advertising, L'Oréal also promotes its brand through targeted sponsorship, such as teaming up with La Cité des Sciences in Paris to stage 'Hair', a major exhibition at the Natural History Museum in London. The exhibition examined everything to do with hair – its biology, the science behind hair products, hair fashion through time and its influence on culture around the world.

Since 1998, L'Oréal Paris has also been a major sponsor in film, being the Official Partner of the International Film Festival held in Cannes. This sponsorship reinforces the connection made in the mind of the consumer between L'Oréal and the glamorous film industry.

Public relations plays a crucial part, with fashion and beauty magazines regularly highlighting L'Oréal Paris products in their editorials. There was a major PR frenzy about L'Oréal's Perfect Slim anti-cellulite range for example, attracting coverage on Sky News, GMTV and Good Morning, as well as extensive articles in national

papers The Guardian, The Daily Express, The Daily Mail and The Independent. In one week, newspaper coverage of Perfect Slim reached an audience of five million people.

L'Oréal Paris also has a very successful loyalty programme, which runs online and offline. It has more than doubled its membership since launch in December 2003 with over 200,000 women signed up to receive exclusive updates, previews, samples and money off coupons. Research into the programme shows that these women spent up to 91% more on L'Oréal Paris products than test groups exposed to traditional media only.

L'Oréal Paris makes sophisticated use of the internet to promote its brand. In the UK, this includes a detailed website comprising brand information, celebrity information and five interactive tools allowing users to find their perfect skincare regime or hair colour, make-up tips or even a tool that allows them to upload their own photo and then try the latest make-up and hair colour on their own image.

L'Oréal Paris also recently launched a brand boutique on Boots.com – the first time Boots has given such a presence to a mass-market brand outside its own No7 brand.

L'Oréal Paris sponsored Julien Macdonald's show at London Fashion week in 2005. The look for the show was created by James Kaliardos, International Make Up Artist for L'Oréal Paris. The new limited edition Elnett hairspray can, designed exclusively by Julien Macdonald for L'Oréal Paris, was also unveiled at the show.

Brand Values

L'Oréal Paris is a premium mass-market brand, offering consumers accessible luxury through leading edge products that outperform the competition.

L'Oréal Paris' core values are also driven and substantiated by massive investment in scientific research and technology.

L'Oréal Paris talks to women and men of all ages who believe in technology for beauty products, are stylish and fashionable – and are happy and confident to purchase beauty products for themselves without a sales advisor. The brand's philosophy encompasses a passion for innovation, performance and style.

www.lorealparis.co.uk

THINGS YOU DIDN'T KNOW ABOUT

L'Oréal Paris

> L'Oréal Paris does not test any of its products on animals.

> Research isn't just confined to cosmetics. The advanced research labs look at innovations in other fields, such as Episkin – a method of 'growing' skin in the lab that has a valuable contribution in areas such as skin grafts.

> The L'Oréal Group is present in more than 130 countries worldwide and employs 50,000 people.

> 135 L'Oréal products are sold per second throughout the world.

> L'Oréal registers 500 patents per year and over 3% of Group turnover is invested in R&D each year.

Market

The UK total cold drinks market is a large and competitive arena in which many famous powerful brands wield large marketing budgets.

The market is an ever-evolving test for brands that wish to continue to grow in a category that is currently worth more than £5 billion (Source: ACNielsen).

Within the cold drinks market, increases in the soft drink category have been slowing. However, growth has been driven considerably by the energy drink sector, which was worth more than £392 million in 2004 (Source: ACNielsen).

The Energy drink category continues to grow at pace with brand extensions and new entrants to the market emerging every year. This represents both a challenge and an opportunity for the category's leading brands.

Since its launch, Lucozade has been the market leader in the Energy drink category with just under 60% value share of the category. Key competitors include Red Bull and Powerade, whilst recent years have witnessed the introduction of several private label sport and energy drink launches from the major grocers.

The rest of the market is made up of a plethora of smaller brands, predominantly operating in the stimulant drinks sector, and distributed via the impulse channel and the on-trade environment.

Achievements

Launched in 1927 as a provider of energy during recovery from illness, Lucozade is the original energy drink and has been the category driver ever since. Lucozade Energy is currently the category leader with sales worth £250 million in 2004 (Source: RSP).

In 1982 Lucozade was repositioned from a drink that aided recovery to a drink that replaced lost energy. As a result of this, together with high-profile advertising and

Fuel supplement. Increases endurance in top athletes.

new product development, the brand has consistently enjoyed over 10% year-on-year growth, cementing its position as the clear category leader.

Launched in 1990 to phenomenal success, Lucozade Sport was the UK's first mainstream sports drink. The brand now has a 15% value share of the Energy category and is the UK's leading sports drink (Source: ACNielsen). The range has also been extended to include a nutrition bar and carbohydrate gel.

Further innovation followed in 2003 with the launch of Lucozade Sport Hydro Active, a fitness water specially designed for exercisers and gym-goers.

History

In 1927 a pharmacist in Newcastle formulated Lucozade after a fruitless search for something to help his children during times when they might be suffering from a cold or the flu. He formulated a palatable, easily digestible glucose drink that could help recovery from sickness by providing energy when the children did not feel like eating food.

Just over a decade later, the brand was bought by Beecham and was distributed nationwide, soon becoming renowned across the country as a trusted symbol of recovery.

The 1950s and 1960s saw Lucozade begin heavyweight national advertising support. The result was classic advertising of the age depicting sick children enjoying Lucozade.

However, by the 1970s there was a decreasing role for Lucozade in peoples' lives as the general population began to grow healthier and the incidence of illness became less frequent. The days of the heavy annual cold and the epidemics of flu were in significant decline. As a result, sales of Lucozade began to drop.

An initial brand repositioning, which remained rooted in health and recovery, sought to position Lucozade as a healthy provider of energy to help people recover from the natural daily lulls in energy they might suffer during the day. This was not a great success and the brand's future looked to be in jeopardy.

It was in 1982, however, that the most significant and successful re-positioning took place. 'Aids recovery' was removed from the bottle and was replaced with 'Replaces lost energy'.

Lucozade became a brand that could provide energetic, busy and successful people with the energy they needed to perform to their full potential.

Using the Olympic Decathlete Daley Thompson as a brand icon, Lucozade went from strength to strength. With a succession of new flavour launches and innovations in packaging, the brand became one of the 1980s famous success stories.

In 1990 the Lucozade brand diversified further with the launch of Lucozade Sport, a range of isotonic sports drinks. In balance with natural body fluids, the brand promised to 'get to your thirst, fast'.

Lucozade Sport was the first brand to launch with a sports sponsorship deal, namely British Athletics and the FA Carling Premiership and continues to be endorsed by some of Britain's leading athletes including footballer Michael Owen.

Lucozade Sport Hydro Active, launched in 2003, is positioned as a fitness water for people who exercise or go to the gym. This carries on a tradition for Lucozade Sport in creating a new sector that is in tune with changes in lifestyles and reflects the development of sport & physical activity.

Product

Since its launch, Lucozade has remained at the cutting edge of energy provision with improved formulations, new products, scientific development and, for Lucozade Sport, research in the Lucozade Sport Science Academy (LSSA).

Lucozade provides a number of different products in its range to cater for all energy and hydration needs: Lucozade Energy, Lucozade Sport and Lucozade Sport Hydro Active.

Lucozade Energy, the original energy product, is a carbonated glucose drink that is a fast and effective provider of energy to the body and brain. It is available in its classic Original flavour as well as in Tropical, Lemon, Orange, Citrus Clear and new Wild Berry, available since April 2004.

Lucozade Energy is also available in tablet form to make energy provision convenient wherever the consumer may be. The tablets are available in Original, Orange and Lemon varieties.

Lucozade Sport is an isotonic sports drink that helps boost performance when consumed before, during and after sport. As a crucial part of sporting preparation, Lucozade Sport comes in a number of flavours: Orange, Lemon, Mixed Citrus and Berry.

Lucozade Sport Hydro Active is a low-carbohydrate fitness water containing electrolytes, vitamins and calcium. It is designed to provide better hydration than water during exercise.

Recent Developments

Lucozade Energy continues to drive category growth by offering consumers exciting ways of engaging with the brand, resulting in developments such as Lucozade Energy, proving that it is an effective provider of energy for the brain as well as the body with proven effects to benefit concentration, focus and alertness.

In addition, 2004 saw Lucozade Energy announce that it would be the official sponsor of the World Rally Championship, which races in 16 countries across four continents.

Lucozade Sport's role as essential preparation for sport has created new opportunities for the brand. Of particular note was England's victory at the Rugby World Cup 2003. The England rugby team use Lucozade Sport: Matt Dawson and Jonny Wilkinson are both sponsored by the brand.

The launch of Lucozade Sport Hydro Active has created a new sub-brand and market sector of fitness water. Launched in May 2003, Lucozade Sport Hydro Active has had an immensely successful first year.

Promotion

The Lucozade brand has a long history of bold advertising.

Heavyweight advertising started in the 1950s and 1960s, communicating the benefits Lucozade offered during recovery from cold and flu. Typically, poorly children were depicted being given Lucozade at times when they were suffering with colds and Lucozade became known as 'the nice part of being ill'. With several flu epidemics during the two decades Lucozade established itself as a trusted household name.

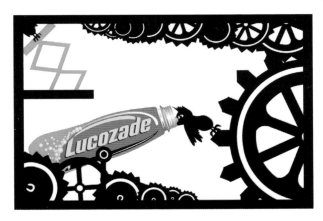

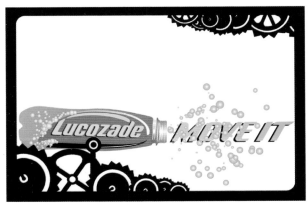

It was in the 1980s, however, that Lucozade advertising really came into its own with the famous and groundbreaking Daley Thompson campaign. As the Olympic gold medal winning decathlete, Daley was an ideal embodiment of someone who needed seemingly limitless amounts of energy in order to perform and the campaign, along with its stirring Iron Maiden soundtrack, is still remembered today.

Since then Lucozade Energy has used a number of iconic figures in advertising, including Olympic 100m Sprint gold medal winner Linford Christie and, most recently, 'Tomb Raider' heroine Lara Croft. The result has been a significant acceleration in the increase in sales following the introduction of each new icon with the brand doubling in size since 1988.

In 2004 Lucozade Energy launched its latest communications campaign with a distinctive animation style that continues the brand's history of iconic advertising. Based on the idea that Lucozade Energy drinkers have the energy to make things happen, the advertising celebrates the way someone with infectious energy can kick-start a chain reaction of events, transforming mundane and boring environments into energetic scenes of fun and spontaneity.

In addition, Lucozade's sponsorship of the World Rally Championship (WRC) includes the use of the WRC in a Lucozade Energy consumer promotion: after competing in two rally heats, the winner is trained up as a licensed rally driver and flown to Australia where they can take part in the real Australian WRC event, competing against the professionals.

Lucozade Sport's advertising has featured some of Britain's leading sporting icons. The brand was launched using the England and Liverpool footballer John Barnes and, since then, advertising has featured the then England football captain Alan Shearer during the late 1990s when Lucozade Sport first advertised the fact that it could 'keep top athletes going for 33% longer'.

The 2005 campaign continues this tradition, with the new TV execution featuring Liverpool and England midfielder Steven Gerrard. This campaign builds on the 2004 communications platform – and sporting truth – of the importance of preparation, demonstrating how Gerrard drinks Lucozade Sport to fuel his performance on the pitch. It continues to reinforce the importance of fuelling up with Lucozade Sport through the retention of the 'Are you ready?' endline.

The Lucozade Sport Hydro Active advertising campaign for 2005 builds on the positioning established since the brand launched in 2003. It communicates the message that Hydro Active has been specifically designed for exercise and can hydrate more effectively than water alone.

Brand Values

Whilst Lucozade's image may have changed since 1927, Lucozade has remained a trusted brand that people have relied on for times when they want an edge in whatever they are doing. Constantly testing

and developing new ways to give people that small but meaningful edge, Lucozade is an innovator within its field and aims to continue to be so.

Lucozade is a bold and dynamic brand, with an independence of spirit, a 'can-do' attitude and a 'never-say-die' approach to life which is coupled with its rich heritage in health, and convalescence. As a result, consumers have a warmth of feeling for the brand not typically associated with the energy drink category. Ultimately, consumers talk about the Lucozade 'magic': an indefinable quality that sums up Lucozade's taste and thickness and its ability to deliver energy when you need it.

For Lucozade Sport, the values are closer to those of a real sportsman. The brand is gutsy and committed and truly savvy, offering real performance benefits. Magic doesn't work with sports participants: they want to know what Lucozade Sport will actually do for their performance on the field.

Lucozade Sport Hydro Active takes a slant on the Lucozade Sport values but with more focus on exercise benefits rather than sporting performance. Exercisers or those with active lifestyles want a brand that is spirited and alive and in line with their perspective on exercise – that it is a means to feeling and looking great and a key part of an active lifestyle.

www.lucozade.co.uk

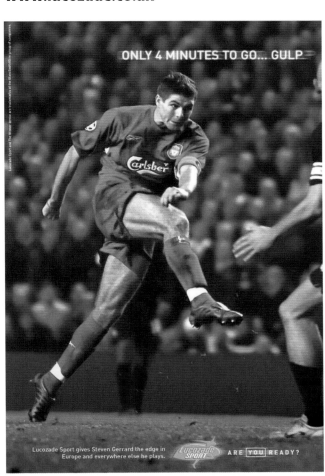

THINGS YOU DIDN'T KNOW ABOUT

Lucozade

> More than seven bottles of Lucozade Energy are sold every second.

> Lucozade was once advertised as a solution to car sickness.

> The market research for the famous Daley Thompson campaign consisted of asking a waiter in a Chinese restaurant what he thought of the idea.

> The team behind the blockbuster film 'The Matrix' created the innovative Hydro Active advertising.

> Lucozade can be found around the world as far afield as Nigeria, Poland, the Caribbean, South Africa and New Zealand.

Market

LYCRA® is a brand that since its invention 40 years ago has become an integral part of the fashion industry. Invented by DuPont, the LYCRA® fibre gives fabric added comfort and flexibility in a wide range of clothes across all garment categories. Although LYCRA® has been around for over four decades, demand for the product from clothing manufacturers continues to grow. Leading designers claim fibre technology to be their most fundamental inspiration as they strive to make garments with the flexibility and high performance values needed to match the lifestyle of the 21st century consumer. People today expect more from their clothes than style alone; market research highlights that comfort, ease of care, durability, breathability and lightness are all extremely important. Today LYCRA® is the leading brand within the portfolio of INVISTA brands, including STAINMASTER®, ANTRON®, COOLMAX®, THERMOLITE®, CORDURA®, SUPPLEX®, TACTEL®, Polarguard®, ESP® and Avora® FR.

In September 2003 INVISTA became the new name of DuPont Textiles & Interiors (DTI). The name change represented a step towards separating from the parent company DuPont. This was completed in April 2004 with the purchase of INVISTA by Koch Industries Incorporated.

Achievements

A fabric ingredient and not a fabric itself, the fact that LYCRA® is such a well-known name all over the world, bears testament to INVISTA's marketing efforts. LYCRA® boasts a global awareness of over 90% and, according to Interbrand, is among the top ten clothing and textile brands in the world, sitting alongside names like Levi's and Armani.

And it is not just a famous name – it is also an invention of great significance, being cited by the Council of Fashion Designers of America as one of the 20th century's most important fashion innovations.

Over the years, INVISTA has constantly kept abreast of developments in fashion and fibre technology, launching products that have maintained the fame and market-leading position of LYCRA®. Where some brands die when fashions change, INVISTA has consistently reinvigorated and reinterpreted LYCRA® to answer changing consumer needs especially in the ever changing world of fashion.

History

LYCRA® was invented in 1959 by a team of scientists at DuPont, originally as a replacement for rubber in corsetry. Before LYCRA® was invented, consumers endured saggy, baggy, stretched and bunched clothes. But when the DuPont scientist Joe Shiver perfected a revolutionary new fibre – code named K – that all changed.

In the 1960s LYCRA® revolutionised the way in which fabrics could be used. In beachwear it replaced thick and heavy swimsuits with light, quick-drying garments like the bikini. In 1968, the medal-winning French Olympic ski team became the first high-profile sports personalities to wear ski suits with LYCRA® – a trend that soon spread to other sports. By 1972 Olympic swimmers swore by the sleek, lightweight suits contoured with LYCRA®. The fibre soon became an integral part of performance wear for millions of amateur and professional athletes.

In the 1970s, the brand started to make an impact on the fashion scene, as disco fever and interest in fitness made leggings and figure-hugging leotards the look of the moment. Leggings and stretch jeans with LYCRA® are among the defining looks of the decade. By the mid 1980s, over half of all women's hosiery and underwear relied on LYCRA® for a close, comfortable fit.

During the 1990s, LYCRA®'s position in the sports market strengthened through the development of hi-tech fibres such as LYCRA® POWER in compression shorts, which helped reduce athletes' muscle fatigue. This decade also saw the rising popularity of the fibre not just in women's fashion but in men's too. President Clinton gave the brand an important endorsement by sporting a suit made with LYCRA®, not to mention the interest sparked by the England football team's decision to don business suits made with LYCRA®.

Product

LYCRA® is a man-made elastane fibre. Never used alone, but always blended with other fibres, it has unique stretch and recovery properties. LYCRA® adds comfort, fit, shape retention, durability and freedom of movement. This is achieved thanks to the unique properties of the fibre, which can be stretched up to seven times its initial length before springing back once tension is released.

Any natural or man-made clothing fibres can be mixed with LYCRA®. Very small amounts of LYCRA® can transform the performance of a fabric – the amount

of LYCRA® in a material can be as little as 2%. There are various ways of integrating LYCRA® with other fibres to provide fabrics for all needs.

INVISTA carries out continual research and development in fibre technology. This is supported by an understanding of the market and ever changing fashion trends coupled with an awareness of developing consumers wants and needs.

An example of this brand development was the launch in 2001 of the campaign Jeans with LYCRA®. This garment marketing concept brought enhanced fit and freedom to denim and was welcomed by designers and manufacturers who were looking for new directions in which to develop denim in a race to gain market share and brand recognition. The denim market has gone from strength to strength in recent years.

In 2001, LYCRA® set the scene for the future of leather with the launch of breakthrough technology: Leather with LYCRA®. Using proprietary techniques, the technology fuses layers of leather with layers of LYCRA®. This new structure gave the natural leather a 'memory' which enables it to stretch and recover without losing any of its original quality or natural appearance.

Leather with LYCRA® was launched to the fashion world by Randolph Duke in Los Angeles, Carlos Miele in São Paulo, and Lawrence Steele in Milan who all featured collections which showcased the versatility of LYCRA®.

INVISTA™ has also made important contributions to the hosiery sector in recent years. LYCRA® Curves are designed to flatten the stomach and lift the bottom comfortably. The LYCRA® LegCare range has been proved in tests to help prevent tired and swollen legs – a common symptom among busy women who spend their days standing and walking. LegCare hosiery has a 'massaging' effect, which allows the blood to flow more easily in the leg, reducing swelling and feelings of heaviness and fatigue.

INVISTA™ has continued to innovate to keep LYCRA® at the cutting edge of sports and fashion technology. LYCRA® POWER is specially designed to reduce muscle fatigue and increase endurance; Soft Comfort LYCRA® offers improved comfort for hosiery garments and LYCRA® 3D is a knitting technique that further improves appearance, comfort and fit.

Recent Developments

Throughout 2003 and 2004, INVISTA™ launched a completely new innovation that delivers specific well-being benefits in clothes: LYCRA® Body Care. The LYCRA® Body Care collection uses textile finishes and specially engineered yarns to deliver freshness, moisturising and massaging benefits to clothes. Freshness is delivered by technologies that inhibit the growth of odour-causing bacteria as well as trapping odour-causing molecules that are then released in the next wash. Micro-encapsulation means moisturising agents are stored in the fibre structure which break open and release their contents to continuously hydrate the skin. Compression technology and temperature management in high-tech hosiery yarns offers massaging action.

The launch of LYCRA® elastic fibre T-400 represents another significant development. This completely new fibre under the LYCRA® umbrella has a dimensional stability which gives it

superior dyeability and colourfastness. It is ideal for applications such as denim, shirts and other woven fabrics that require moderate stretch.

INVISTA has also introduced a revolutionary new scanning technology to safeguard the LYCRA® brand against fraud and ensure customers can have confidence in the integrity of the product. LYCRA® BrandScan™ is a sophisticated scanning system, which determines whether a fabric or garment labelled as containing LYCRA® really does contain the brand.

The ability of the LYCRA® brand to respond to consumer needs via innovation was reinforced in 2004 through strategic partnerships with other global brands such as Rimmel and Coca-Cola. In February, Rimmel LYCRA® Wear was launched in the UK following an exclusive licensing agreement with parent company Coty Inc, one of the world's leading manufacturers and marketers of personal fragrances and colour cosmetics. Rimmel LYCRA® Wear is an addition to the brand's nail product portfolio; a longer lasting shockproof nail varnish. The partnership is the first collaboration of the science between cosmetics and textiles, and for the first time introduced LYCRA® in liquid form. In April 2004, LYCRA® and Coca-Cola commissioned Colcci to design their first joint collection. Colcci is a major Brazilian casual and jeanswear company. The collection, named Coca-Cola by Colcci is now available throughout stores in Brazil.

INVISTA's commitment to innovation is evidenced in its prolific launch of new products over the last 12 months. Black LYCRA®, launched in September 2004, is the world's first truly black elastane. It offers reduced elastane 'grin through' in dark fabric shades and remains black even after repeated wash cycles. The colour integrity of Black LYCRA® helps reduce fabric returns, can achieve simplifications in fabric manufacturing and is suitable for wovens, circular knits and seamless constructions.

LYCRA® 275B was created to meet the needs of serious swimmers and pool lovers alike. Both have high expectations of their swimwear and LYCRA® 275B offers a longer lasting fit and shape retention. Using INVISTA proprietary technology, swimwear made with LYCRA® 275B keeps its fit and shape five to 10 times longer than those which contain unprotected elastane.

Promotion

The promotional strategy of LYCRA® is essentially two-pronged. Its most important audiences are retail and manufacturing partners who include the fibre in their garments and fabrics. But to do this, designers and retailers have to be convinced that there is strong consumer demand for clothes containing LYCRA®. Consequently, INVISTA™ invests US$1 million annually in research to understand consumer behaviour, to better target its audience and generate LYCRA® demand at retail.

INVISTA™ co-ordinates trade and consumer advertising to increase awareness of the brand among trade partners and end-users alike.

INVISTA™ has always invested heavily in marketing the LYCRA® brand, a fact which explains why it continues to enjoy such strong awareness among business and consumer customers. In 2002 INVISTA™ launched a US$40 million global advertising and promotion campaign, part of a US$200 million three-year investment in the brand. The 'Has It' campaign illustrates the benefits of LYCRA® by associating the brand with a confident and stylish lifestyle attitude – 'you either have it or you don't'. The aim of the campaign is to engage consumers with the LYCRA® brand in order to motivate them to actively look for garments with the LYCRA® label. INVISTA™ has also introduced new 'LYCRA® Has It' hang tags to further drive awareness in store.

LYCRA® ownership of 'style' continued with its innovative sponsorship of a unique TV experience in Asia. LYCRA® My Show was a nationwide talent competition.

Over 12 episodes, the programme was aired on the Oriental TV Channel as well as three other local TV channels in different parts of China. The show supported individualism, talent and hidden potential thus embodying some of the aspirational brand values that LYCRA® has become synonymous with. The investment in LYCRA® My Show recognises INVISTA™'s commitment to Asia both as a business partner and a market opportunity.

2004 saw LYCRA® continue its dedication to high-end fashion, teaming up with designers Zac Posen and Sebastien Pons. The highly anticipated LYCRA®-sponsored 'Western Gypsy Love Story' collection by Pons showcased denim with LYCRA®, whilst Zac Posen's Spring 2005 collection presented a number of garments using the latest LYCRA® technology to give traditionally rigid fabrics a sexy fit, stretch and comfort.

Brand Values

INVISTA's marketing for LYCRA® focuses on a key product promise – that LYCRA® equals comfort, fit, shape retention and freedom of movement.

Whilst this is the functional brand promise, recent marketing has aimed to establish the brand's lifestyle appeal. These include projects like the sponsorship of a 20-page pan-European supplement with Elle magazine.

www.lycra.com

Market

Britain is a nation of potato lovers, so despite all the fads and diets that come and go, potatoes remain a staple and much-loved food, which McCain Foods is synonymous with.

In the UK alone, the frozen potato market is worth £479 million. This splits into two categories: frozen chips and potato specialities. In 2004, 262 million packets of frozen chips were sold, with a market revenue of more than £303 million. Potato specialities sold 156 million packets, which delivered a market value of more than £176 million. McCain's value share of the frozen chips market is 56%, while its share of the potato specialities market is 27% (Source: ACNielsen).

The frozen snack market is still in its infancy, worth £50 million, with McCain's value share standing at 48%. Two of the major sectors are filled bread, worth £23 million, which has recently been boosted by the launch of the McCain Anytime range. The snack pizza market is worth £15 million (Source: ACNielsen).

Achievements

While the purveyors of Atkins, South Beach and similar slimming regimes fatten up on cookbook sales, it's been 'chin up' for the world's number one maker of branded chips. The company's bottom line remains firmly in good shape; turnover reached the US$6.4 billion (Source: Canadian) mark in 2003, up 4.9% over 2002.

McCain produces one-third of all frozen chips consumed in the UK. In addition to ranking as the world's largest manufacturer of frozen potato products, McCain is the nation's second largest producer of frozen foods.

McCain has been applauded many times for its creative product developments. In 2003 it received the prestigious Queen's Award for Innovation – a top honour for stellar business performance – for its Home Fries.

Launched in 1997, Home Fries were an instant success that quickly became the bestselling frozen potato item on the market. The chunky-cut chips are specially prepared so that they actually fry in the oven, the golden-crisp coating resulting in an authentic homemade taste.

It wasn't the first time that the company has been chosen for a Queen's award, which brings with it official permission to use the Queen's Award emblem on products, packaging and stationery for a five-year period. In 1980 McCain Foods was honoured for its Export Achievement.

History

McCain Foods was first established in January 1957 in Florenceville, New Brunswick. The Canadian headquartered frozen food producer has come a long way since then.

Today the company sells French fried potatoes and other frozen foods in more than 110 countries. It employs more than 20,000 people internationally and operates more than 55 production facilities on six continents.

McCain Foods established its first UK factory in Scarborough, Yorkshire back in 1968. In those days the company was extensively engaged in production of frozen potato products – mainly frozen chips for the catering market.

Business blossomed from the start, as a significant business and demand for the company's products had already been built on imports from Canada, which had begun in 1965.

In 1976 a second UK plant was constructed in Whittlesey, Cambridgeshire, to produce more frozen chips. In 1979 McCain Foods began making pizza products at its Scarborough facility.

Today, additional plants in Wombourne, Grantham and Hull help keep up with demand for potato-based products, while the Hull operation also produces appetisers. McCain now employs approximately 2,500 people and operates five plants in Britain alone.

Product

Along with the staple McCain Oven Chips, which contain less then 5% fat, McCain Foods constantly innovates and refreshes its range in order to maintain consumer interest. One such example is the Simply Mash line extension. McCain is always endeavouring to make life easier for families, so Simply Mash is designed to take away all the hassle and mess from making mashed potato.

Consumers can also have something different on the side, with McCain Wedges. New flavour extensions to the range include Sour Cream & Chives and Sea Salt & Cracked Black Pepper.

Other products in the range include McCain Potato Smiles, which are made from fresh mashed potatoes. McCain Home Roasts offer a time saving solution to serving roast potatoes, while McCain Hash Browns cross generations with this breakfast product made from shredded potatoes in the form of crispy golden wedges.

A recent addition to the shredded potato range is McCain Rosti, large potato cakes made from coarsely grated fresh potato.

The company ensures the freshness of its potato products by working with a network of 400 dedicated potato-growers, from whom it sources 600,000 tonnes of British-grown potatoes every year. With its own seed business and its model of vertical integration 'from plough to plate', McCain stands out from the rest of the potato processing industry.

But the company doesn't only make potato products. Its expansion into the light meals category has grown rapidly as it has geared up production of microwaveable products to supplement its Micro Chips and Micro Pizza lines. Grab-and-go, hand-held items such as Micro Chicken Nuggets and Micro Toastie are at the forefront, building momentum behind the Micro portfolio expansion, which now includes Micro Wings, Micro Garlic Bread, Micro Ribs, Micro Baguettes and the recent launch of the

Anytime Sandwich Range is a further move into the light meals category. The products target both families and single-person households who lead busy lifestyles.

Recent Developments

In March 2005, McCain sponsored Comic Relief for the first time, with its 'Raising Smiles for Comic Relief' Campaign. Limited edition packs helped towards a massive £500,000 donation to Comic Relief.

In 2004, McCain celebrated the 25th anniversary of Oven Chips, which were originally launched in October 1979. The anniversary of this occasion was too big an opportunity for the brand not to celebrate. It gave McCain the chance to further increase affection for the brand by celebrating the anniversary in an original way.

The first elements of the campaign were inauspicious, with an appeal from McCain in the small ads of the Scarborough Evening News for someone to come forward with a copy of a forgotten three and a half minute promotional film, shot in 1979 to commemorate the launch of McCain's revolutionary oven chips.

The story was picked up by the national press, after the discovery of the lost reel. The three and a half minute short film, which aired over an entire Coronation Street ad break on October 10th 2004, turned out to be vintage footage of Valerie Singleton heralding the launch of the oven chip. But as the film rolled, the viewer becomes aware that the film is in fact a modern-day hoax, as Valerie makes some suspiciously accurate predictions.

Promotion

In August 2003, Britain was introduced to the 'Chin Up' advertising campaign. Running on TV, posters and press, the campaign highlights the fact that life is full of everyday hiccups and annoying little incidents but McCain can put a smile on your face even after you've had 'one of those days'.

The £15 million campaign, running well into 2004, proved to be a flexible one. McCain showed how different products can give people Chin Up

moments in different ways, from the 'guilt-free' Chin Up of 5% fat oven chips, to the 'taste the chip from heaven' Chin Up of Home Fries, which one execution shows as providing the antidote to such a dramatic mishap as falling down a well. The message was that McCain may not change your life, but can bring a smile if you've had 'one of those days'.

In 2005 the campaign has evolved, adding product-led ads to the campaign. For oven chips, a young lady is seen in various scenarios that leave her feeling a little bit guilty. But the one thing she does not have to feel guilty about is indulging in McCain Oven Chips containing less than 5% fat.

The creative idea has also allowed for tactical executions around both seasonal and topical events, including a match between local McCain football team Scarborough and Chelsea. The event included free 'Chin Up' chips and caviar for Scarborough and Chelsea fans respectively.

In August 2004, McCain sponsored a fleet of 'Chin Up' branded cabs. These roamed city centres on Monday mornings offering free rides. Cabbies were given lessons in comedy patter to help keep

their customers entertained for the duration of the trip. This stunt generated further coverage in local press and radio.

McCain is also working in partnership with Delia Smith at Norwich City Football Club, and has developed a unique 'Fuel Time Plan' incorporating a high-carb and low-fat diet, which has been scientifically designed to increase stamina and energy – meaning the players can feel stronger for longer. McCain Oven Chips, Home Roasts, Simply Mash and Rosti will all feature within this plan and mean that players can have their favourite foods while being healthy at the same time.

McCain's marketing activity over the past 18 months has been richly layered, innovative and highly integrated. The results demonstrate the power of such a brave and disruptive approach. By focusing on building affection for McCain as a brand as well as at product level, and by carving out a distinct emotional territory for McCain, the marketing activity delivered significant market share gains and volume sales growth. McCain increased its share of the total frozen potato market from 30% in August 2003 to a record 35.4% in January 2005.

Brand Values

McCain aims to provide 'food that hits the spot', delivering reliable, filling, hassle-free, quality food for customers.

Its vision is to be not only known as potato experts, but also to provide light meal solutions that fit in with consumers' lifestyles. It endeavours to achieve this by being informal and humorous, conveying its warmth towards consumers with slogans such as 'with McCain, everyone comes up smiling.'

In essence, McCain strives to be known for its good mood food.

www.mccain.co.uk

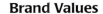

Market

McDonald's operates within an increasingly competitive marketplace, including hamburger and pizza chains, traditional fish and chips shops, Chinese and Indian restaurants and the burgeoning number of sandwich, salad and coffee outlets. But through a combination of quality, value, fast and friendly service, clean and pleasant surroundings, insightful marketing and high-street profile, McDonald's continues to have a strong presence in the market.

By the end of 2004, McDonald's had 1,248 restaurants and directly employed 44,229 restaurant staff in the UK, as well as another 25,000 employed by McDonald's franchisees. The chain provides food and drink to around 2.5 million Britons per day, and upwards of £400 million is spent annually in its supply chain, much of which is spent on British ingredients. Its UK turnover is in excess of £1.6 billion a year. Despite global economic challenges, the McDonald's brand continues to innovate and expand.

Achievements

McDonald's is the largest food-service company in the world, with more than 30,000 restaurants serving 46 million people each day in more than 110 countries and territories, from Andorra to The Virgin Islands.

The strength of the brand is recognised by journalists, marketers and analysts. Recently it was named one of the best global companies by Global Finance magazine, while Fortune ranked it number one in the social responsibility category of its Most Admired Companies listing.

The company is committed to customer satisfaction that competitors are unable to match and recognises that well-trained and motivated staff are key; the development of all employees at every level of the organisation is a high priority. Training is a continuous process and employees attend courses in the restaurants as well as at the company's six Management Training Centres. When they complete their initial training, all employees are eligible to receive an independently validated Basic Certificate in Food Hygiene, and McDonald's has been approved to deliver National Vocational Qualification Level 2 in Quick Service to staff, which is equivalent to five GCSEs graded A-C. Having gained centre status from City & Guilds, the company is also approved to deliver the

Vocational Assessor and Internal Verifier qualifications to management employees.

McDonald's commitment to the development of its employees was nationally recognised in 1998 when the company achieved the Investor in People accreditation, the company has subsequently been successful in maintaining this status. McDonald's has been named as one of the UK's leading employers in The Times Top 100 Graduate Employers for the past seven years, and has been in the top 50 for the past five years.

Alongside its successes as a business, McDonald's contributes to the communities it belongs to. In the US, it established its worldwide Ronald McDonald House Charities (RMHC) in 1984, in memory of company founder Ray Kroc. The organisation's main aims are to keep families together by providing accommodation to the parents and siblings of seriously ill children – through its Ronald McDonald Houses and Family Rooms at children's hospitals and hospices – and to provide grants to charities, schools and hospitals that will benefit children. To date, RMHC's has awarded US$300 million in grants worldwide and, in the UK, the independent charity Ronald McDonald Children's Charities has raised more than £20 million.

In addition to these activities, McDonald's in the UK has been involved in a range of good causes from fundraising work with local schools, youth groups and hospitals to supporting environmental and anti-littering campaigns.

Aside from all this, the real achievement of McDonald's is self-evident. No matter how unfamiliar the surroundings, there is always a McDonald's nearby.

History

Two brothers called Dick and Mac McDonald founded McDonald's. But the real driving force behind the chain's expansion was a visionary salesman called Ray Kroc, who started out supplying milkshake mixers to the brothers' restaurant in San Bernadino, California, in the 1950s. Kroc worked out that they were selling one 15 cent hamburger with fries and a shake every 15 seconds – which meant in excess of 2,000 milkshakes a month. The entrepreneur saw the potential of the business and decided to get involved, buying a franchise from the brothers and setting up his own McDonald's restaurant in Des Plaines, a Chicago suburb, in April 1955.

It was an instant hit and more branches of McDonald's rapidly followed.

The chain sold 100 million hamburgers in its first three years of trading and the 100th branch opened in 1959. Two years later, the ever-enterprising Kroc paid US$2.7 million to buy out the McDonald brothers' interests and, in 1963, the billionth McDonald's hamburger was served live on primetime television.

The McDonald's Corporation went public in 1965 and was listed on the New York stock exchange the following year. In 1967, the first restaurants outside the US were launched in Canada and Puerto Rico,

and the McDonald's formula travelled successfully. The first branch in the UK was opened in Woolwich, south east London, in 1974. Three years later the 5,000th restaurant opened in Kanagawa, Japan. Today, it is possible to buy a McDonald's hamburger in almost any city around the world.

In 2001, the business acquired a minority interest in the popular UK sandwich chain Pret A Manger – a brand that shares its enthusiasm for quality food and unmatched customer service.

Product

One of the company's strengths is its flexibility, especially in its ability to adapt to – and often predict – customer demand. The Filet-O-Fish, for example, was developed by Cincinnati-based franchisee Lou Groen, whose restaurant was based in a predominantly Catholic area. Groen had noticed that takings were considerably lower on Fridays and realised it was because many Catholics traditionally abstain from eating red meat on that day of the week. He gave them an alternative, which proved so popular that it appeared on international menus in 1963. In 1968 a franchisee from Pittsburgh – Jim Deligatti – created the Big Mac, it became the chain's most successful menu item ever.

McDonald's has also demonstrated an ability to adapt to local cultures, rather than taking a 'cookie cutter' approach to growth. A character from the film Pulp Fiction famously pointed out that beer is served in McDonald's in France – it is also worth noting that restaurants there serve a spin on the French 'croque monsieur' snack, as well as croissants and pain au chocolate.

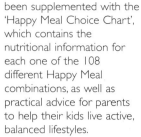

Happy Meal™ Choice Chart

108 Happy Meal combinations so you can make the right choice for your child

Perhaps the best example of local adaptation is to be found in India, where the cow is a sacred animal. So in 1996 McDonald's opened its first restaurant that did not sell beef. Instead, mutton is used and the Big Mac is known as the 'Maharaja Mac'.

Recent Developments

McDonald's is committed to providing its customers with food of the highest quality. This is achieved by using the best quality raw ingredients, sourced only from approved suppliers and ensuring that food is prepared to a consistently high standard. The menu is continually reviewed and enhanced to ensure that it meets – and wherever possible exceeds – expectations.

To help customers make informed decisions about their whole diet, McDonald's was the first quick service restaurant to provide a complete ingredient listing and detailed nutritional analysis of its menu. Recently this has

been supplemented with the 'Happy Meal Choice Chart', which contains the nutritional information for each one of the 108 different Happy Meal combinations, as well as practical advice for parents to help their kids live active, balanced lifestyles.

This evolution continues unabated, with 2004 seeing the launch of the new Salads Plus range across key markets around the world, a range of fresh salads, mineral water, yoghurt and fresh fruit. 2004 also saw the introduction of porridge, fruit toast and filled bagels as part of a wider breakfast menu. McDonald's also responded to consumer feedback by offering fruit bags that could be swapped for fries as part of a Happy Meal.

2004 also saw McDonald's distribute a series of 'Brand Books' with each one going to more than 23 million homes throughout the UK, in order to tell people about some of the new choices available, as well as bringing them up to speed with what McDonald's has been up to and giving them discount vouchers to encourage them to try the new items.

Promotion

The McDonald's brand is extremely high profile and its advertising expenditure corresponds. Ray Kroc once commented: "There is something just as basic to our success as the hamburger. That something is marketing the McDonald's style. It's bigger than any product or person bearing the McDonald's name."

2003 saw the launch of a worldwide marketing initiative; the 'i'm lovin' it' campaign. This is a global push that continues to connect the McDonald's brand with its customers around the world through engaging stories about their lives and how the McDonald's brand fits into it. New initiatives include a relationship with pop group Destiny's Child. This saw the group featuring in advertising and also involves them with McDonald's charitable initiatives.

Worldwide, McDonald's has demonstrated a strong commitment to sports sponsorship. Nowhere is this more evident than in the UK, where the brand has long been successfully linked with football – one of the nation's favourite sports.

In August 2002, the company announced a four-year community partnership with the English, Scottish, Welsh and Irish Football Associations to develop football at grass roots level. The scheme will create 10,000 new community-based coaches for young players and spearhead the drive to increase football volunteering.

Sponsorships have included the World Cup since 1994 and the Champions League between 1996 and 2000. 2004 saw McDonald's sponsor the Euro 2004 tournament and, as part of this involvement, gave 682 young children a day to remember as McDonald's recruited them to be one of the children that escorts the players onto the pitch before each match.

Of course, marketing is not all about big sponsorship deals. McDonald's actively encourages its restaurant managers to put time and resources back into the local community. Supporting local football teams has proved an effective way to do this. Hundreds of youth teams play in kit donated by McDonald's across the country, taking the brand into the heart of everyday British life. Throughout the UK, more than 300 youth teams and 500 restaurants are involved in McDonald's sponsored leagues.

Local restaurants also devote time to developing links with their customers. This can range from free coffee mornings for senior citizens, organising children's parties, or fund-raising work with local schools, youth groups and hospitals.

Brand Values

Ray Kroc developed his brand vision for McDonald's around a simple but effective consumer-driven premise: quality, service, cleanliness and value. These values remain the cornerstone of the company.

Around the world, the key to the company's success has been its capacity to touch universal human needs with such consistency that the essence of the brand has always been relevant to the local culture, no matter how different that culture is from the origins of McDonald's.

www.mcdonalds.co.uk

THINGS YOU DIDN'T KNOW ABOUT

McDonald's

> McDonald's is now the UK's biggest retailer of pre-prepared fruit.

> Worldwide locations include Beijing in China, Pushkin Square and Gorky Street in Moscow and a ski-thru in Sweden. There is also a McDonald's on a ferry that sails between Stockholm and Helsinki.

> In the UK, McDonald's uses 100% free-range eggs for its breakfast menu.

> McDonald's provides food and beverages to in excess of 46 million people per day worldwide.

> The first drive-thru McDonald's was created in 1975 to serve soldiers from an army base in Sierra Vista, Arizona, who were forbidden to leave their cars while in uniform.

we thought we'd come to you for a change

TASTY
SAVINGS – AT LEAST
£24
INSIDE

i'm lovin' it

Microsoft®

Market

Microsoft, the company whose software is widely held to power more than 90% of all the world's personal computers, has been a leader in the wave of personal computing innovation that has created new opportunity, convenience, and value over the past three decades. During that time, it has created many new products, added new lines of business, and expanded its operations worldwide.

Microsoft now does business almost everywhere in the world. It has offices in more than 90 countries, which are grouped into six corporate regions: North America (the US and Canada); Latin America (LATAM); Europe, the Middle East, and Africa (EMEA); Japan; Asia Pacific (APAC); and Greater China. It also has operational centres in Dublin, Ireland; Humacao, Puerto Rico; Reno, Nevada, USA; and Singapore. The operational centres are responsible for licensing, manufacturing, as well as operations and logistics.

Microsoft believes that over the past few years it has laid the foundations for long-term growth by making global citizenship an integral part of its

business, delivering innovative new products, creating opportunity for partners, improving customer satisfaction, putting some of its most significant legal challenges behind it, and improving its internal processes.

Achievements

Microsoft prides itself on providing software and services that help people communicate, do their work, be entertained, and manage their personal lives. Over the past 30 years, innovative technology has transformed how people access and share information, changed the way businesses and institutions operate, and made the world smaller by giving computer users instant access to people and resources everywhere. All of Microsoft's businesses grew in 2004, increasing its total revenue by US$4.65 billion, or 14% year-on-year, to US$36.84 billion.

However, Microsoft's mission extends beyond making and selling products for profit. Through its business activities and community support, it aims to leave a lasting and positive impression on the communities and society in which it works. Years ago, it was convinced that its original vision of 'a PC in every home' could change lives. It remains convinced of the broad and positive power of giving people better technology. It takes corporate responsibilities seriously, and in its interactions with its employees, customers, partners, suppliers and the communities where it works, it aims to reflect its broader awareness and ambitions.

Founded in 1983, Microsoft Community Affairs was one of the first corporate giving programmes in the high-tech industry. Today, Microsoft is the largest contributor in the high-tech industry and the third-largest among all businesses in the US. Last year,

Microsoft donated more than US$47 million in cash and US$363 million in software to non-profit organisations throughout the world. In the UK, Microsoft gives to a range of major charity projects both financially and through the donation of software. Charities including NSPCC, Childnet International, Leonard Cheshire, AbilityNet and Age Concern have all benefited from Microsoft's giving programme.

In March 2005, Microsoft's founder Bill Gates was granted an honorary knighthood by Queen Elizabeth II. As an American citizen he cannot use the title 'Sir' but will be entitled to put the letters KBE after his name. Now the world's wealthiest man, Bill Gates, 48, is worth an estimated £28 billion.

Bill Gates and his wife Melinda, who have three children, are also known for their charitable work. As well as investing millions in research for an AIDs vaccine, their foundation has established a scholarship scheme to enable the brightest students to go to Cambridge University. The Bill and Melinda Gates Foundation is currently working on a global health programme in the developing world.

History

Microsoft this year celebrates its 30th anniversary. The company that made Redmond, Washington, a household name was founded in 1975 in Seattle by two young men, one of whom was a college dropout.

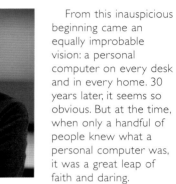

From this inauspicious beginning came an equally improbable vision: a personal computer on every desk and in every home. 30 years later, it seems so obvious. But at the time, when only a handful of people knew what a personal computer was, it was a great leap of faith and daring.

This revolutionary idea not only made technology a powerful tool for everyone, it also created a new industry that changed the world.

Today, Microsoft employs more than 57,000 people worldwide. It continues to expand the possibilities of personal computing by developing new ways to empower its customers anytime, anywhere and on any device.

Product

Microsoft is a worldwide leader in software, services and solutions designed to help people and businesses realise their full potential. It generates revenue by developing, manufacturing, licensing, and supporting a wide range of software products for many computing devices. Its software products include operating systems for servers, personal computers (PCs) and intelligent devices; server applications for distributed computing environments; information worker productivity applications; business solutions; and software development tools.

Microsoft provides consulting and product support services, and trains and certifies system integrators and developers. It sells the Xbox video game console and games, PC games, and peripherals. Online communication services and information services are delivered through its MSN portals and channels around the world. It also researches and develops advanced technologies for future software products. Microsoft believes that delivering breakthrough innovation and high-value solutions through its integrated platform is the key to meeting customer needs and to its future growth.

Just as Microsoft constantly strives to update and improve its products, it aims to continually evolve its company to be in the best position to accelerate new technologies as they emerge and to better serve its customers. In addition to research and development and corporate functions, Microsoft's operational structure includes seven business groups: 'Windows Client', including the Microsoft Windows XP desktop operating system, Windows 2000, and Windows Embedded operating system; 'Information Worker', including Microsoft Office, Microsoft Publisher, Microsoft Visio®, Microsoft Project, and other stand-alone desktop applications; 'Microsoft Business Solutions', encompassing Great Plains and Navision business process applications, and bCentral™ business services; 'Server and Tools', including the Microsoft Windows Server System™ integrated server software, software developer tools, and MSDN; 'Mobile and Embedded Devices', featuring mobile devices including the Windows Powered Pocket PC, the Mobile Explorer microbrowser, and the Windows Powered Smartphone software platform; 'MSN', including the MSN network, MSN Internet Access, MSNTV, MSN Hotmail and other Web-based services; and finally 'Home and Entertainment', including Microsoft Xbox®, consumer hardware and software, online games, and Microsoft's TV platform.

Recent Developments

Microsoft is deeply committed to the research and development that enables it to meet its customers' needs today and that ensures that it stays at the leading edge of innovation.

2004 saw Bill Gates deliver Microsoft's vision of digital entertainment anywhere, unveil Windows XP Media Center Edition 2005, and showcase a variety of sleek new computer designs, portable media devices, and digital content services.

In a step towards that vision, May 2005 saw the launch of Windows Mobile 5.0, the newest instalment of Microsoft's software for mobile devices, designed to power a new generation of phones, personal digital assistants and media players for people who want to stay connected while on the go. Based on feedback from partners and end users, Microsoft® Windows Mobile 5.0 is designed to deliver new productivity enhancements, offer a rich multimedia experience, provide mobile operators and device-maker partners with more opportunities to develop differentiated devices, and allow end users to better customise devices to fit their needs.

In the same month, Microsoft launched Xbox 360, its 'future-generation' video game and entertainment system designed to

place gamers at the centre of the experience. More than 200 new Xbox game titles launched in 2005, with hundreds more planned for 2006 and beyond. Xbox also enables gamers to link up and play against each other through Xbox Live. Now in its third generation of transforming and uniting Xbox gaming communities, with presence in 24 countries worldwide, Xbox Live is designed to take online game-play and entertainment to unprecedented heights. With a rapidly growing global community, Xbox Live offers best-in-class games, intelligent matchmaking, tournaments, unique programming and integration through Xbox.com.

During 2004, Microsoft resolved a number of legal disputes. Some of those involved legal issues such as the antitrust lawsuit brought by the US Department of Justice, a number of consumer class-action antitrust suits filed in various states, and private antitrust lawsuits brought by other companies. Resolving these legal issues clears the way for new collaboration with leading companies that were litigants. At the same time, a few new issues emerged in fiscal year 2004, most notably the European Commission's decision that Microsoft had infringed European competition law, and the lawsuit filed by RealNetworks, Inc.

Promotion

Microsoft's marketing has come along way since it kicked off its first television advertising campaign in 1992, designed to build on the success of Windows and Windows-based applications.

On October 25th 2001, the launch day for Windows XP, the Windows Team achieved a Guinness World Record. It produced the fastest-ever music video from

filming to broadcast, and the record still stands. Using Windows Movie Maker on Windows XP, it took just 3hrs 46 min 19sec from filming to actual broadcast on MSN. The music video featured a cameo appearance by Microsoft chief executive Steve Ballmer with the band Electric Soft Parade. 143 million people read about the record breaking attempt in 150 pieces of UK press coverage including three national TV and 12 national newspapers, while 20,000 people in the UK viewed the video in its first week on MSN.

No stranger to high-profile launches, most recently, Microsoft linked up with MTV Europe to launch its next generation Xbox 360 game system in May 2005. Elijah Wood, Scarlett Johansson, The Killers and Snow Patrol hosted a half-hour star studded European premier of the new product with performances from both bands airing exclusively on MTV channels across Europe on May 13th. Viewers got an exclusive look at the new Xbox 360 in the programme, which also featured MTV News specials and backstage action.

Brand Values

Microsoft's corporate mission is to enable people and businesses throughout the world to realise their full potential.

Its mission reflects its core values: integrity and honesty; passion for customers, for its partners, and for technology; openness and respectfulness; taking on big challenges and seeing them through; constructive self-criticism, self-improvement, and personal excellence and accountability to customers, shareholders, partners, and employees for commitments, results, and quality.

These values embody Microsoft's ethical approach to business and its role as a committed corporate citizen in each of the countries and communities where it operates. Its ability to deliver on its mission depends on intelligent, creative people who share these values.

www.microsoft.com

THINGS YOU DIDN'T KNOW ABOUT

Microsoft

> The Windows 95 launch was set for August 24th because it had never rained in Redmond, WA during that week in recorded history. It sold more than one million copies in the four days following its launch.

> In 1990, kicking off its 15th anniversary celebration, Microsoft became the first personal computer software company to exceed US$1 billion in sales in a single year, with revenues of US$1.18 billion.

> In December 2004, Microsoft announced a commitment of US$3.5 million in financial support for relief and recovery efforts in response to the Indian Ocean Tsunami.

> Bill Gates, Microsoft chairman, and Steve Ballmer, chief executive, first met at Harvard University.

> In 1975, inspired by an article in Popular Electronics Magazine, Bill Gates and Paul Allen developed their first BASIC programming language for the Altair 8800.

Miss Selfridge

Market

Britons spend around £30 billion every year on clothing (Source: KeyNote 2004), with womenswear accounting for around half all garment sales, women are now looking to keep up with the latest trends while also being more careful with their money.

All good news for value fashion retailers, who have steadily improved their image, style and quality, and made life a little harder for more expensive brands. The reach upmarket is not only coming from the established lower-cost chains, but also from supermarket groups like ASDA, Tesco and Sainsbury's – all of which are aggressively expanding into clothing.

The new style means that if a store wants to charge more than its competition, it has to offer ranges that are noticeably different or superior.

Miss Selfridge successfully distinguishes itself in this highly competitive sector. Although a few years ago Miss Selfridge was linked with the younger end of the market, the brand has now re-established its historically broad appeal, targeting confident, independent women whose age matters less than their attitude to life. There are few brands on the high street genuinely offering a specially edited range that appeals to fashion aware mothers and daughters alike.

Achievements

Over four decades, Miss Selfridge has proven itself to be one of the most tenacious and durable brands on the British high street. Despite numerous changes in ownership, some of which would have spelled the end for weaker brands, Miss Selfridge has proven that its name, reputation and brand power have stood the test of time.

Born in 1966 as the youth brand in Selfridges, Miss Selfridge played a big part in the fashion revolution of the 1960s. A pioneer of its time and has continued to go against the grain. Four decades of ground-breaking advertising campaigns have helped to 'discover' a host of famous models, photographed for the Miss Selfridge fashion collections. The brand's brochures have become collectors' items, featuring early shoots with now world-famous models such as Kate Moss, Naomi Campbell and Yasmin Le Bon.

Miss Selfridge is proud of its reputation for being an innovator. It was the first fashion retailer to advertise on London buses in the early 1970s, and the first to launch its own make up range, 'Kiss and Make Up' in 1978. It was also the first to use window installations and has won several awards for its revolutionary and bold work in this area, including the Retail Interiors Award for 'Visual Merchandising and Display Solution of the Year', in 2002.

Miss Selfridge has long been a high street favourite for finding something special and different, a reputation it first gained in the 1980s when it introduced its revolutionary 'Limited Edition' range.

More recently, Miss Selfridge is seeing success with its in-store 'destination boutique' driven by the brand Director, Sim Scavazza and her growing team of designers and buyers. The concept, launched in March 2004 and expanding to 147 stores by May 2006, including 38 international stores.

The strategy is working well for the business, with limited edition boutique items helping Miss Selfridge increase its average selling price by 10% year-on-year. The media has responded enthusiastically to the boutique initiative, with additional product placement and brand features helping boost overall press coverage to the advertising equivalent of over 1.1 million pounds per month.

Favourable media comment has come from the national press as well as a range of womens' magazines. For example, Pippa Holt of Vogue commented "The Miss Selfridge A/W 2005 collection hits all the right buttons – 2005 could be Miss Selfridge's year!" while Sara Buys of Harpers & Queen says Miss Selfridges' S/S 2005 collection has, "…gorgeous ethnic influences – hits the right note just in time for an ethnic revival". Vanessa Gillingham of Glamour states "The collections just get stronger and stronger." The broadsheets also have high regard for Miss Selfridge, with Simon Chilvers at The Guardian saying, "Miss Selfridge is clearly going to be the A/W high street winner," after viewing the catwalk collections in 2005.

The brand's high media profile has been helped by a celebrity following. Pixie Geldoff said, "We do love going to all the fashion shows and I love shopping. It's cool mixing high street with designer gear and my top is from Miss Selfridge."

oops
Miss Selfridge

History

On September 13th 1966, The Beatles topped the charts with 'Yellow Submarine', England had just won the World Cup, man had not yet walked on the moon and in the London department store Selfridges, a new concept, Miss Selfridge opened its doors. Selfridges' owner, Charles Clore, originally created the youth boutique Miss Selfridge for his daughter. The logo was penned by his secretary, Winifred Sainer.

The initial expansion for Miss Selfridge came through concessions in department stores, such as John Lewis, but independent branches soon opened on the high street and in shopping malls. The first standalone stores to open were in London's Regent Street and Brompton Road where Miss Selfridge created its own boutique style which remains its trademark today.

Even in those early days, the brand was never simply about buying clothes, but about lifestyle. Miss Selfridge boutiques catered for a mood of dressing, and offered the complete 'look', from lingerie to coats, and shoes to mascara. Mannequin styling and visual presentation inside the stores was always of utmost importance, and still is.

Not aimed at the mass market, Miss Selfridge never attempted to grow too large, limiting itself to a maximum of 100 stores. Despite not going for out and out growth, Miss Selfridge nevertheless became Britain's leading young fashion retailer.

By the early 1970s, Miss Selfridge became a limited company and was subsequently bought by the Sears Group – one of Europe's largest retail chains.

Another change in ownership came in 2000 when Miss Selfridge was acquired by The Arcadia Group, which was then bought by the retail billionaire Philip Green in 2002.

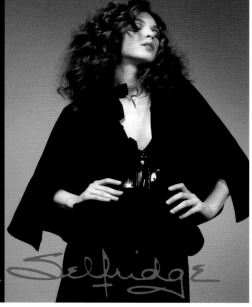

Product

Miss Selfridge is one of the smaller brands in the Arcadia Group, with a UK chain of 147 stores, 92 of which are standalone outlets.

The brand has a highly distinctive character and style, making it stand out from many retailers on the high street. Always paying attention to detail, with an individual, feminine and sassy style, Miss Selfridge nods to the trends of the day, but interprets them in its own unique way.

As a boutique brand, Miss Selfridge works hard for its customers, ensuring it is giving them something different. Whether it is using designs from vintage print collections, sourcing its cloth from Rhajastan and Russia, or using its own graphic design team to create unique prints, Miss Selfridge takes its inspiration from a variety of sources. The aim is to eliminate homogeneity, and create a distinctively feminine, confident and contemporary Miss Selfridge style.

The brand's individuality has been heightened by Miss Selfridge boosting its in-house design team, from two to nine designers over the last two years.

Miss Selfridge doesn't just want women to buy things that they might throw away when styles change next year. It wants them to find the kind of treasured pieces that you look for in a boutique, and never want to dispose of.

The shopping experience in Miss Selfridge is designed to be intimate. Unlike the vast retail sites of some fashion retailers, Miss Selfridge stays true to its boutique character.

Branching off from the main collections, Miss Selfridge is in collaboration with designers such as Bella Freud to reach particularly fashion-savvy consumers. In 2005 the non-conformist British designer Bella Freud launched an exclusive collection, 'Bella' at Miss Selfridge.

Miss Selfridge has always had a reputation for turning stock around quickly and never runs repeats on high fashion lines. This has built loyalty to the brand as customers can therefore rely on Miss Selfridge to give them something unique that not everyone will be wearing, while also freeing up space to introduce fresh product lines at least three times a week.

Miss Selfridge is gaining a reputation for its Petites range, which unlike the majority of the high street brands, is focussed on the newest looks and unique pieces rather than being basics driven.

Also featured in the flagship Oxford Circus store, is the Miss Vintage Concession, which comprises clothing, accessories and shoes from the 1970s. Other regional boutiques such as Birmingham and Edinburgh also boast local vintage concessions.

Miss Selfridge is planning to launch a new range of limited edition pieces in the main city centres in November 2005. This will be a capsule collection designed exclusively by a new in-house team, to appeal to the more designer-aware customer.

Miss Selfridge also offers its customers the chance to experience the brand on the internet with its online boutique, launched in 2003. Online sales have grown 400% year-on-year, with visitors numbering 50,000 every week.

Recent Developments

Miss Selfridge supports up and coming designers and, since 2002, has partnered with the Royal College of Art's School of Fashion. A competition conceived through this collaboration challenges young designers to create a collection for Miss Selfridge, with the winner not only receiving £1,500 towards the development of their own collection, but also the opportunity for a paid work placement, during which time they can be involved in their garment going from design to production. The winning collections open the RCA's Graduates Gala catwalk, elements of which can then be seen in Miss Selfridge stores nationwide.

In 2004, Miss Selfridge launched its new Autumn/Winter 2004 collection, staging a ground-breaking event, called 'Miss Me'. Inspired by the glamour of 1930s cinema, the event saw 20 models in brunette wigs, posing against the backdrops of film sets depicting a diamond heist. Well received by the press, the event was one of the most memorable high street happenings that year.

In 2005, Miss Selfridge followed up 'Miss Me' by staging its very first catwalk show in London's Wallace Collections. The event showcased the Autumn/Winter 2005 collection to London's 'It Girls' and key opinion formers.

Other big plans for 2005 include the launch of a new in-store concept and a new visual expression for the brand, being rolled out across all Miss Selfridge stores.

Miss Selfridge run lifestyle events that bring the brand to life, such as the 'Hot Summer Nights' shopping events, in association with ELLE magazine.

Miss Selfridge has collaborated with The Royal Institution, hosting lectures on fashion topics, such as 'Why we chose what we wear?' not only watched by fashion opinion formers, these Forums were opened up to a vast audience through web casting.

Promotion

Miss Selfridge has always been ahead of its time in terms of understanding the importance of being a brand and not just a retailer. It is not one of the biggest advertisers in fashion, but it is known as an innovator, with a strong marketing heritage stretching back to its ground-breaking ads on London buses in the 1970s.

True to its brand values, it has always had a witty marketing style, not afraid of mocking itself and echoing how it regards fashion as, above all, being fun.

From the first day of trade, Miss Selfridge knew that having a strong visual identity was crucial to its long term success. The brand has always led by example rather than following the pack, and many British women will have an emotional response to many of the memorable marketing campaigns over the decades.

As well as conventional marketing, Miss Selfridge also gets a lot of valuable promotion though public relations, using product placement in editorials in influential fashion media to showcase its products. Its links with the Royal College of Art are also good for its brand, allowing it to communicate how it is supporting and encouraging the next generation of top British designers.

Miss Selfridge is also a brand with a conscience, and the current charity that it supports is The Lavender Trust at Breast Cancer Care. The Lavender Trust was co-founded by Vogue contributing editor Justine Picardie, and raises money specifically to fund information and support for younger women with breast cancer. Miss Selfridge has helped to support the charity through various projects, including the sale of limited edition Lavender Trust T-shirts, exclusively designed by Bella Freud for Miss Selfridge.

Brand Values

Miss Selfridge has a proven track record for innovation, fashion authority and unique product. Boutique brands like Miss Selfridge behave differently and are not afraid to go against the grain. Its mantra is: think big, act small. Be intimate.

It is increasingly hard to be heard on the high street. But while many fashion brands deliver a fast, loud, quick fashion hit to their customers, Miss Selfridge prefers to confidently do its own thing and delivers a relaxed boutique playground where customers can make fashion discoveries and be inspired.

The intimacy of the brand is reflected in its people. Everyone at Miss Selfridge has a passion for fashion, putting the product that goes into the stores above all else. Its driving force and vision is to satisfy the customer with truly unique feminine fashion in an inspirational, vibrant environment that embodies sassy confidence.

www.missselfridge.co.uk

Market

Having a baby is full of surprises and one of the biggest shocks is the amount of items the new parent needs to clothe, feed and cosset their treasured new arrival. Mothercare is the UK's longest established and best-known one-stop-shop for all these needs and, as such, operates in several retail markets such as infant wear, nursery equipment and baby carriages, each with very different competitors.

Factors such as the rising number of older and, therefore, more affluent mothers and also a greater emphasis on children's fashion are helping to underpin market growth.

A further boost to Mothercare's fortunes is well underway, with the UK's birth rate increasing by 40% in 2003 – the first increase since 1990 (Source: ONS).

Indeed, retail analysts Verdict corroborate the mini-baby boom in the UK, with baby retailers benefiting if they can offer products to meet the needs of this new market. In 2004, the infant-wear market was estimated to be worth £1.26 billion, indicating a growth of 5.4% on the previous year, outperforming the overall clothing market (Source: Verdict).

Clothing is a major area where Mothercare competes for business, specialising in clothes for 0-8 year olds – a market valued in the year to January 2004 at 32,029 million (Source: Fashion Trak TNS). Mothercare is in the top three for infants' clothing aged 0-2 years.

Mothercare is the UK's dominant player in hardware with a 29% share and has 19.3% of the baby feeding category (Source: FSA July/August 2004).

Achievements

Despite the fact that it was founded back in 1961, Mothercare remains the only high street retailer dedicated solely to catering for parents-to-be and new parents. Its near unassailable position as the leader of the babycare market has seen it expand into a chain of 232 stores in the UK with 217 additional outlets around the world. Mothercare has become one of the most instantly recognisable consumer brands on the British high street, inspiring trust and promising value for generations of new parents. It prides itself on customer service, making its stores parent and child-friendly environments, staffed by people who can offer knowledgeable unbiased advice. This is especially important for new parents, unversed in the technicalities of things like baby feeding equipment, cotbeds, pushchairs and car seats.

The high regard for Mothercare has been reflected over the years by a string of accolades, including awards in no

fewer than eight of the categories in the 2004 Prima Baby Awards. The awards included six Best Buy awards for products including its Newbury Cot and the 'Going South' potty, along with two best value awards for the Miami highchair and the Tango stroller.

Mothercare also scooped two gold honours at the Mother & Baby magazine awards for its Mothercare Xtreme Sherpa 3-wheeler travel system and its Mothercare wipes. These awards saw the highest-ever number of products entered since the awards launched 12 years ago. More than 452 products were entered, with 200 products short listed for testing. Next, 103 mums spent eight weeks testing the products and eventually 140 actually made it onto the final shortlist. All entries were judged on quality, innovation, design, value for money, unique selling points, price and packaging.

History

The first Mothercare store, catering for mothers and mothers-to-be, opened its doors in Kingston, Surrey in 1961. Initially focused on maternity, Mothercare expanded its age range to include children up to five. By 1990, the age range had been adjusted to 0-8 year olds.

A key development in the company's history was setting up its mail order business in 1962. With its authoritative product range and strong brand positioning, the mail order arm soon helped Mothercare establish its reputation overseas. By 1968 the company had opened its first international store in St Gallen, Switzerland. This was followed by a store in Austria in 1970 and Belgium in 1977.

Initially all of these overseas stores were run by the Mothercare parent company in the UK but, in 1984, Mothercare International began a franchise operation. Carefully selecting partners in chosen countries has helped the overseas business to flourish even further.

In 1972 Mothercare became a public company, merging 10 years later with Terence Conran's Habitat chain to form Habitat Mothercare which, in 1986, merged with British Homes Stores to form Storehouse plc. In 1992, Storehouse rationalised by selling Habitat to IKANO, the retail group that also owns IKEA, leaving Storehouse to focus on its two core brands, Bhs and Mothercare.

In May 2000, Mothercare became an independent entity once again following its de-merger from Bhs.

Product

Whether it's for newly pregnant women, new parents or parents wanting to encourage their toddlers to explore the world around them, Mothercare has the answer. The company is well-known for its strength in product innovation, holding more than 24 patents for products it has developed.

Overall, Mothercare's sales can be divided into: clothing (38.5%), home and

travel (49.7%) and toys (11.7%). The range comprises five main product groups, each aimed at different stages of parenthood.

Mothercare is the dominant force in the maternity market, providing a comprehensive range of fashionable clothing and maternity essentials (such as bras and toiletries) as well as specialist products such as the Breastfeeding Chair, designed by Dr Lynn Jones, a Principal lecturer in Furniture Design and the culmination of months of research.

Mothercare's baby range offers function as well as fashion in its products, which are often designed in consultation with midwives, reinforcing the authority and expertise that is inherent in the Mothercare brand.

Clothing ranges for young children start at two years, also with a view to combining functionality with a flair for fashion.

Mothercare is renowned for its nursery equipment and is the market leader, especially in the areas of car safety, transport and bedding. Mothercare achieves consistent growth in these areas through ongoing product innovation and working closely with manufacturers and suppliers.

Toys are an increasingly important business opportunity for the company and the ranges have been recently restructured to target specific ages and stages to help stimulate and support children's development.

Mothercare sells its products via three main channels: high street shops; out-of-town superstores, called Mothercare World; and home shopping via a twice-yearly catalogue and its website.

Recent Developments

2004 saw Mothercare embark on a three-year turnaround programme with the objective of rebuilding Mothercare and progressing plans for longer-term growth. The company has now completed year one of the turnaround programme, with profit exceeding £23.9 million – a much stronger outcome than predicted

at the beginning of the period when compared with a loss of £24.8 million in 2002-03. As part of the turnaround, Mothercare stores are getting a new logo and fascia designed to appeal to today's customers.

The turnaround plan is focused on five key projects: store proposition, customer service, supply chain, internal infrastructure, product and sourcing.

Indeed, the company has stepped up product innovation and 2005 sees it introduce a range of co-ordinated bedroom furniture for children.

Co-ordinated ranges in a choice of styles means girls and boys will be spoilt for choice. There are elegant carved wood Provencal dressing tables with matching stools or pink-roofed doll's house storage units for girls. Boys will no doubt prefer the Nordic-style beds and the animal-print duvet and wall light. Fun for all comes in the form of blackboard easels in stylish pine.

From April 2005, Mothercare is launching its new Gift Service in 43 high street and out-of-town stores. The range of tastefully pre-packaged products provides ideal gift solutions whether it's a new arrival, christening, birthday or special occasion that's being celebrated.

With prices ranging from £5 to £100, the range is designed to be accessible to all purses, although the branding, products and presentation shout 'premium product' and the 'shop within shop' layouts further emphasise the top-quality aspect. Around 80% of the lines are bespoke gift packs and, to provide a complete polished package, The Gift Service, which is also available online and has its own catalogue, will offer cards and wrappings.

Promotion

Mothercare is proud of the service and advice it already offers parents-to-be but is now taking communication up a level, having launched its very own Pregnancy Magazine. The twice-yearly magazine, which launched in February 2005, is targeted at first-time mums-to-be.

The initial print-run is 350,000, with 78% of magazines distributed in-store, where free copies will be included in packs given to mums-to-be by the pregnancy direct marketing and sampling company, Bounty. The remainder will be mailed to the Mothercare customer database.

As part of this drive to get closer to new mums, Mothercare has also recently secured a new deal with Bounty, which means that toddler and mum-to-be packs are now exclusive to Mothercare and all Bounty guides within the packs will now carry Mothercare advertising. This strategy provides targeting that traditional above-the-line advertising could not.

However, Mothercare has not abandoned traditional advertising. In September 2004 it hit the airwaves with its first above-the-line campaign in more than two years. The radio ads, voiced by Davina McCall, ran for four weeks and covered areas around 75% of its stores. They were supported by direct mail to customers on the Bounty databases, as well as leaflets dropped through doors in some areas. Research is currently underway to look at the impact of the activity for future marketing plans.

Working with experts in special baby care units, Mothercare has developed a range of clothing specifically for premature and low birth-weight babies. For every £30 ten-piece gift set sold, Mothercare gives £3 to the Action Medical Research 'Touching Tiny Lives' campaign. The campaign aims to raise £3 million over the next three years.

In addition, Mothercare has launched its own charity to help families and children in need. The Mothercare Charitable Foundation aims to relieve poverty and sickness, to advance education and to preserve, promote and protect good health.

Brand Values

Mothercare remains one of the pillars of British retailing and was born out of an idea to provide parents and parents-to-be with a one-stop-shop where they could find all the best quality and innovative products for their children under one roof. That still remains a central tenet of the Mothercare business today. The business has been criticised in the past for losing its way and not keeping pace with its competitors. However, the recent initiatives put in place by management are restoring the brand to a position of strength again and new generations of parents appreciate the blend of good quality, value for money and strong product development delivered with knowledge, expertise and authority.

Overall, Mothercare understands what it means to be a parent – the highs and the lows – and strives to make every mum and dad be the best parent they can and give their little ones the best possible start in life.

www.mothercare.com

Market

The UK bread and morning goods market is worth over £3 billion and is one of the largest sectors in the food industry (Source: The Federation of Bakers).

Mother's Pride, valued at £40 million, is one of the key players within the UK standard bread sector. In Scotland it is bought by over one third of all Scottish households (Source: TNS).

Within the morning goods market, Mothers Pride constitutes the second-largest brand within bakery snacks.

It is the largest branded player in the scones market with more households buying Mothers Pride scones than any other scones brand. It also holds the highest share of crumpets, muffins and fruit buns in the London region, which is significant given that households in London, together with Lancashire, spend the most on bakery snacks (Source: TNS).

The success of Mothers Pride has extended beyond England to Scotland, where Mothers Pride holds the top position for sales of scones and fruit buns (Source: TNS).

Achievements

During the late 1970s and 1980s, Mothers Pride was the number one white bread brand and, although recent years have seen the rise in popularity of premium bread brands, today Mothers Pride is the fourth largest standard bread brand in the UK.

In Scotland, Mothers Pride is the number one standard bread brand. Its strength is driven by Mothers Pride Scottish Plain bread, which is the number one brand of Plain bread, widely available in Scottish retail outlets and the fourth largest selling white bread product in Scotland.

History

Now almost 70 years old, the Mothers Pride brand made its first appearance in the north in 1936 and became a national brand in 1956.

Originally, Mothers Pride was sold wrapped in wax paper, but as packaging technology progressed, the now-familiar plastic bread bag was introduced. However, as a nod to tradition, Mothers Pride Scottish Plain can still be bought in wax-wrapped bags.

Mothers Pride began baking 'Plain' bread in Scotland in 1958 and the product has since had a long and proud association with the nation. Indeed, until the 1970s, it was the only type of bread really available in Scotland.

The product itself is quite unique in both taste and appearance with tall, thin slices and a dark crust. It's a truly Scottish product, rarely found south of the border. Mothers Pride Scottish Plain is generally not distributed further south than Newcastle. However, it does make its way down in small quantities and can sometimes be found in the larger supermarkets' stores. Sales in the south tend to be concentrated where there is strong representation of Scottish Exiles, such as Corby. Yet Plain loaf devotees have been known to use the power of consumer demand to get retailers to stock it.

In addition to its 13 bakeries dotted around England, Mothers Pride has a bakery in Glasgow and a distribution depot in Mossend. The Mothers Pride bakery in Glasgow produces around a quarter of a million loaves per day, 80,000 of which are Plain bread.

Product

Bread is an important source of fibre in the diet. Indeed, it provides more than a quarter of our daily intake of fibre. Naturally low in fat, bread is a good source of carbohydrate, making it a nutritious snack. Mothers Pride recognises the nutritional importance of bread and therefore provides a varied range to appeal to most tastes, preferences and occasions.

Although white bread is the vanguard for the Mothers Pride brand, coming as standard or long-life loaves, Mothers Pride also offers a brown loaf and a 'Danish' white loaf (or 'diet' loaf).

In addition to being a household bread brand, Mothers Pride also makes a whole range of bakery snack products. From burger or finger rolls for summer BBQs, to white rolls for the lunch box, Mothers Pride strives to provide a roll for every occasion.

As well as the traditional favourites, such as Mothers Pride English muffins, crumpets, fruited teacakes and currant buns, there is an assortment of regional specialities, including Mothers Pride Derby scones, Devon scones and Scotch pancakes, along with the seasonal lines, such as Mothers Pride hot cross buns.

In Scotland, Mothers Pride has been baking a 'Plain' loaf since 1958. Until the 1970s plain bread was a bigger selling loaf than the standard 'pan' bread, so called because it is baked in a 'pan' or a tin. Scottish Plain is very much an integral part of the Scottish Culture and is particularly popular on the West Coast of Scotland. Ask any Scot what reminds them of Scotland and Plain bread – also sometimes called 'Square' bread – will frequently be one of their answers.

Scottish consumers associate Mothers Pride Scottish Plain with tradition and as something that was fed to them by their mothers. Scots are loyal to it for its taste, freshness, nutrition and texture. Some people think that white bread isn't as nourishing as brown but Mothers Pride Scottish Plain is naturally rich in protein, with 15% more than ordinary Mothers Pride white bread per 100g, so it is also a healthy option.

Scottish Plain is also considered by many as the best type of bread to make toast. Research conducted by Mothers Pride found that consumers felt Scottish Plain toast to be far superior to normal white breads. The research also found that Scottish Plain doesn't deteriorate in texture when spread with butter or served as beans on toast and remains firm when dunked in soup – what's more, it is said to make great 'soldiers' when dipped in boiled eggs.

Mothers Pride also makes other traditional Scottish fare, including potato scones, part of the great Scottish breakfast, often served fried with the traditional cooked breakfast of bacon, eggs, sausage, black pudding or haggis and soda scones, which are served either hot or cold with butter or jam.

Growing competition and wider demand for premium bread led to the launch of Mothers Pride Scottish Pan, a premium white sliced loaf, in October 1998. Milled and baked with the finest ingredients, Mothers Pride Scottish Pan premium white bread is traditional in shape, with tall slices and soft, round topped crusts.

Recent Developments

Mothers Pride was re-launched in late 2000 with a new look and increased shelf life after research demonstrated

that 20% of convenience shoppers who sought to purchase bread were unable to because of lack of bread on the shelf.

Mothers Pride invested in extending its product life across the range of bread and bakery snacks by an average of three days, with no loss of product quality and with no additional cost to the independent retailer.

As well as extended shelf life, Mothers Pride invested in new packaging that incorporates modern lively graphics and visuals designed to be eye catching and appealing to key target audiences. A new logo has also been designed that was voted unanimously by consumers as being 'warmer and friendlier'. The re-launch was supported by a consumer PR campaign themed 'A Slice of Family Life', which aimed to raise awareness of the brand's new qualities.

Mothers Pride Longlife, which comes in medium and thick slices, was launched in the late 1990s. With a shelf life of seven days from the date of purchase,

actress, Kirsty Graham, eating a 'jeely piece', Scotland's traditional jam sandwich made with plain bread familiar to generations of Scottish children. The well-known Jeely Piece song accompanied the advert, sung by St. Joseph's School Choir of Castlemilk. The famous lines go: "Oh ye cannae fling pieces oot a 20 storey flat, 700 hungry weans will testify tae that. If it's butter, cheese or jeely, if the breed be plain or pan, the odds against it reaching earth are 99 to wan."

Mothers Pride also sponsored the popular Scottish TV Soap, High Road, from August 1999 to September 2001 on Scottish and Grampian TV. The sponsorship credits revealed the adventures of one man and his dog, Doug, as they searched for the mythical village of Glendarroch, home of the High Road TV show. In their search, Doug and his master got up to all sorts of adventures in a bid to capture the hearts of viewers across Scotland.

Mothers Pride has used many different forms of sales promotion over its history. One of the most popular was the 'kids to go free' promotion, which started in October 2001 and ran for a year. By collecting coupons from special promotional packs, consumers enjoyed reduced prices or 'kids go free' at a number of leisure attractions around mainland UK and free children's places at Moat House hotels.

Brand Values

Mothers Pride has always appealed both to mums and children. As soft white-sliced bread, Mothers Pride makes the preparation of essential family foods easy for parents. To children, the enjoyable taste and texture of white-sliced bread is one of the staple nursery foods, ranking alongside fish fingers, baked beans and milk chocolate. For people who want a convenient branded product with consistent quality, Mothers Pride is still seen as the down-to-earth, unpretentious brand that is seen by many as, 'the soft white taste you never grow out of'.

North of the border, things are slightly different. Scots have a somewhat distinctive taste palate, interlinked with a proud cultural identity. This is reflected in the Mothers Pride range of locally inspired products, which in themselves are proudly distinctive, helping to maintain the enduring values and distinctiveness and character of Scotland in an ever-changing and more indistinct world.

its aim is to reassure the consumer that there is always something edible in the bread bin throughout the week.

This was followed by the re-launch of an improved Mothers Pride standard loaf. Mothers Pride now offers a whole family of white bread, offering different slice thicknesses to suit both sandwiches and the toaster, from thin, medium and thick, through to the jaw aching, extra thick 'Big T'.

Promotion

Mothers Pride was heavily advertised throughout the 1960s and 1970s. Several of its campaigns won awards, including some memorable press ads that appeared during the 1974 general election. The punning lines included 'Support your local MP', 'Meet your MP tonight' and 'The MP for any party'.

Other famous Mothers Pride adverts include 'I'm the Mother in Mothers Pride' featuring the voice over of Thora Hurd, 'Mother knows best' and Dusty Springfield as 'The Happy Knocker Upper'.

Perhaps the most famous Mothers Pride television advertisement – 'Jeely Piece' – was screened in Scotland in 1995. The advert featured a young

The Great Scottish Run is Scotland's largest sports participation event and one of the best-attended half marathons in the UK, attracting huge crowds despite the notoriously grey Scottish weather. Mothers Pride sponsored this event in August 2000, the first of the new Millennium which, for one year only, featured a full marathon together with the usual half marathon. The event was a resounding success attracting almost 12,000 runners and Mothers Pride continued its support with sponsorship of the 2001 event.

At the end of 2000, Mothers Pride and the Scottish paper, The Sunday Post, teamed up in a nationwide search to find the person who most deserves the title 'Mothers Pride'. It goes without saying that all parents are proud of their children, whoever they are or whatever they've done. But Mothers Pride wanted to hear all about those children who had achieved something extra special that makes them 'Mothers Pride'. The winner was awarded a top prize worth £2,500.

www.britishbakeries.co.uk

Mothers Pride

> Around one billion slices of Mothers Pride bread are produced every year.

> The familiar tartan wrapping of the much-loved Mothers Pride Plain loaf is an officially recognised tartan. Mothers Pride tartan was registered with the Tartan Society on June 1st 1996 and is used on the packaging of the range of Mothers Pride Scottish bread and bakery products.

> The 'Jeely Piece' song was written by Adam Tulloch McNaughton and is about life in the tenement blocks of Castlemilk, Glasgow.

> Kirsty Graham from the Mothers Pride 'Jeely Piece' commercial was the star of the film, Loch Ness, where she starred alongside Ted Danson.

Mr KIPLING
EXCEEDINGLY GOOD CAKES

Market

For many British people, cake is still synonymous with the traditional Sunday afternoon tea. Today, the cake market is buoyant with the majority of cake being consumed in the home, predominantly during the afternoons and evenings. Indeed, the total UK ambient packaged cake market is currently valued at more than £916 million, growing at 5% year-on-year (Source: IRI).

Yet the challenge for manufacturers within today's market is to maintain the place of cake on the nation's everyday menu, despite changing consumer needs and lifestyles. There are huge opportunities within the ambient cake market, from expanding product lines to driving value growth through high quality innovation.

Achievements

Mr Kipling launched in 1967 and since then has been a driving force in the development of ambient packaged cake in the UK. By 1970 the brand had risen to national status and by 1976 Mr Kipling was a brand leader, a position that has been retained for three decades.

Within a year of going national, there was 89% awareness of the brand and over the following 30 years, Mr Kipling became synonymous with cake. It has been the only consistent advertiser in the ambient cake market, contributing significantly to the creation of a brand with a powerful and longstanding reputation.

Today the Mr Kipling brand is worth more than £144.5 million in terms of retail sales (Source: IRI). This represents more than 130 million packets of cake being sold per year.

Mr Kipling's share of the cake market is 16%, making it the biggest brand within this market (Source: IRI).

History

In 1965, RHM began work on a brand new range of cake – completely different from existing product offerings. The company had conducted research among 6,000 housewives, which revealed a distinct lack of choice within the packaged cake market. Of the limited range available, the research indicated that most were seen as dull and unappetising, with packaging that did little to enhance this impression.

Having identified a gap in the market, RHM set about filling it. Several RHM bakeries were involved in the process of creating the unique new range. The programme was allied to the installation of modern plants in the bakeries.

The concept demanded not only expertise in the manufacture of cakes but also that these groundbreaking new products should be delivered in the best-designed packaging the market had ever seen.

By 1967, the total cake market was worth £150 million and average annual spend per head was £3. Although cake was as popular as ever, traditional corner shops and village bakeries were already in decline, with supermarkets and grocery stores accounting for an ever-increasing percentage of packaged-goods sales.

RHM decided that the market was ready for its new range of packaged cake products that carried the same stamp of quality, integrity and expertise that local bakers had provided but in a more modern and convenient format.

Meanwhile, advertising agency J Walter Thompson had been tasked with creating an identity for the products. The identity needed to both distinguish Mr Kipling products and familiarise the customer with them. It was felt that they should be perceived as being made by a person, a specialist, so in May 1967 the concept of Mr Kipling was born.

The initial range of 20 Mr Kipling products was based on products found in the traditional baker's shop but was packaged in colourful premium boxes with handles for carrying home. The range included Ginger Cake, Swiss Rolls, Lemon Meringue Tarts, Chocolate, Apricot and Florida Jam Sponges, which have all played an important role in the range over the past 30 years. Others that performed exceptionally in the initial research were Manor House Cake, French Fancies, Jam Tarts, Battenberg and Almond Slices and these remain firm favourites in the Mr Kipling range today.

Product

The Mr Kipling strategy is to produce quality cakes that are as good as homemade. Prior to the launch of Mr Kipling, small cakes, including Tarts, Iced Cakes, Cream Cakes and Slices, accounted for around a third of all cake sales, yet there was an almost complete absence of good packaged small cakes in the market.

The Mr Kipling concept of a master baker was reinforced by concentrating on small cake ranges. These had the dual advantage of being easier to use while being harder to replicate at home. This meant that Mr Kipling established a position traditionally held by the small local baker.

Despite the growth of the brand to a £144.5 million business, Mr Kipling cakes still come with the guarantee of boxed cakes that are as good as home-baked. The Mr Kipling range currently includes 38 different lines of cake. In addition to this, there are more than 15 seasonal products and limited edition launches every year, which bring variety and refreshment to the brand, reflecting the constant drive for innovation.

As well as TV advertising, investment has also been channelled into poster ads outside major supermarket chains and heavyweight PR and print campaigns targeting consumer women's and lifestyle press. The advertising is supported with strong in-store promotional activity, new point of sale material and merchandising.

Brand Values

The essence of the Mr Kipling brand has always been to produce high quality cakes that are crafted by traditional methods to create the closest thing to homemade.

This translates into a concept of a treat designed to generate a feeling of happiness from a brand that strives to be seen as warm, friendly and personable, rather than simply a food.

The brand values have evolved to reflect a product that can be eaten any time, any place, with modern convenient packaging to appeal to today's consumers.

www.mrkipling.co.uk

Recent Developments

Continuing its positioning of 'the closest thing to homemade in a box', January 2005 saw RHM subsidiary Manor Bakeries invest £8 million in the re-launch of the Mr Kipling cake brand. Comprising new packaging, new products and a new advertising campaign, this marked the biggest investment ever put behind the brand.

Four premium whole cakes joined the existing Manor House Cake. These were Carrot Cake, Coffee & Walnut, Victoria Sponge and Lemon Drizzle, all of which had been created to ensure a homemade appearance and taste.

By introducing innovative ranges of premium products and packaging, Mr Kipling can satisfy the growing consumer demand for quality and authenticity. Further new product developments in its other cake sectors include a Victoria Slice six-pack, five Sticky Toffee Cake Bars, Blackberry & Custard and Red Cherry Pies, while Millionaire's Shortcake, Apricot & Sultana Flapjacks and Chocolate & Pecan Brownies make up the new Mr Kipling Squares range.

In small cakes, new additions to the Mr Kipling Mini Classics range are Ginger and Carrot & Walnut.

As well as investment in new products, the company placed a significant spend behind the packaging, which focuses on high quality food and ingredient photography designed to demonstrate what's in the box and also the 'master baker' credentials of the Mr Kipling brand. The impact and premium positioning is very much in keeping with the brand heritage of 'exceedingly good cakes'.

Promotion

The original objective of expressing the personality of the Mr Kipling brand not only through the products themselves but also through the brand name, packaging, pricing, above and below-the-line promotional campaigns, display and merchandising still remain today.

Television was chosen as the primary launch medium, partly for its impact and immediacy and partly for its ability to express the intended warmth and friendliness of the Mr Kipling character. TV has continued as a major medium for the brand over the past 30 years and the phrase 'exceedingly good cakes' has become one of the best-known slogans in advertising. Although Mr Kipling himself is a fictitious character, RHM has cultivated his image among consumers as a kindly old gent, very British, respectable and proper, with a dry sense of humour and a twinkle in his eye. Most importantly, he is perceived as a master baker and craftsman.

Mr Kipling TV campaigns have evolved over the years, reflecting the changing nature of the brand and bringing it more up-to-date. This continues in 2005 with a new creative campaign to show Mr Kipling back in the kitchen doing what he does best: developing 'exceedingly good cakes'.

THINGS YOU DIDN'T KNOW ABOUT

Mr Kipling

> Every week the nation consumes 723,267 Mr Kipling Mini Battenbergs.

> Mr Kipling uses 60 million English Bramley apples in its individual apple pies every year.

> The voice in all advertising campaigns is not that of Mr Kipling but of his friend. Over the years the voice has been read by four different actors.

> Mr Kipling cakes are exported to America, New Zealand, Hong Kong, mainland Europe and the Middle East.

> The most popular Mr Kipling cake sold is the Cherry Bakewell, with more than 220,000 consumed every day.

> Mr Kipling produces 1,104,484 French fancies every week.

> Every year, Mr Kipling sells more than 791 million cakes.

Market

Over the past few years a combination of key factors, including a rise in the number of people living alone, increased interest in healthy eating and greater demand for convenience have all played a key role in the growth of chilled pot desserts. Yoghurts, fromage frais and yoghurt drinks – now referred to as short-life dairy products (SLDPs) – hit all the right buttons for today's busy consumer who seeks increasing variety and innovation.

SLDPs continue to be a key driver of grocery sales. Penetration rose to a record level of 96% in 2004 as consumers were given a variety of new reasons to buy into the category. Total sales are up 7.4% to £1.67 billion and continue to grow ahead of the overall grocery market.

With UK consumers last year spooning their way through 1.5 billion pots of Müller products alone – enough to fill more than 200 Olympic-size swimming pools – it's no surprise that yoghurt is the key driver of the SLDP market, holding the biggest share. Sales in the category leapt £35 million to £810 million in 2004, making it one of the fastest-growing food sectors (Source: ACNielsen).

However, it is drinking yoghurt that is the star performer at present. Although it holds only 12% share of the market, it is growing at an impressive 69% year-on-year, with Müller Vitality driving growth at 86% year-on-year. Just three years ago drinking yoghurts were viewed as a niche product area but with penetration now at 42% and growing, it is clear that these products are moving into the mainstream.

Chilled desserts is the second largest sector in the SLDP market, worth £459 million. It is also this category where consumers' preferences are most polarised; they are either seeking low-fat healthy options or indulgent products, both in a convenient format. Müller is the number one brand name in chilled desserts, particularly driven by Müllerice.

Müller, the third largest grocery brand in the UK (Source: ACNielsen) has played a key role in the development of the SLDP market. Its commitment to quality, value and innovation has driven the category and helped differentiate it from the competition, reinforcing its position as the UK's principal SLDP manufacturer.

Achievements

Müller currently holds more than a 38% share of the yoghurt market and more than 24% of the total SLDP market, with retail sales in excess of £407 million. Since its

introduction as an unknown brand to the UK in 1987, Müller has become the UK's sixth-largest grocery and the fourth-largest food brand with more than 70 product variants.

The key to Müller's success has been the launch of innovative high quality products, supported by strong brand building communication. Müller Corner, for instance, is now the UK's bestselling yoghurt, with more than 20% of the market. There are 21 varieties and 2004 saw Müller continue its strategy of high-profile partnerships, linking with the number-one biscuit manufacturer, McVitie's.

Müllerlight is the second bestselling yoghurt as well as the UK's favourite best selling virtually fat free yoghurt. Müllerice, which created a completely new sector when it was introduced to the UK, is now one of the country's top-selling pot desserts.

2004 was also a successful year for Müller Vitality, the UK's first probiotic yoghurt drink with added vitamins. The low fat drink showed the strongest brand growth among the Drinking Yoghurts sector, up 86% year-on-year.

In 2003, Müller extended its production capacity with a state-of-the-art bottling plant at its Market Drayton factory in Shropshire, which is capable of filling 100ml bottles at a speed of almost 50,000 per hour.

The amount that Müller now sells in one day is greater than the total first year's sales back in the launch year of 1987.

History

In 1896, Ludwig Müller founded a small village dairy in the Bavarian region of Germany. 74 years later, in 1970, his grandson Theo Müller took the helm and broadened the company's horizons. He recognised that the success of his dairy's products as popular regional brands could be transformed into national successes if he improved the recipes and gave the products some heavyweight marketing support.

The first product he launched was buttermilk. It proved to be a great success and from here the company began to grow rapidly. In 1980 an innovative product, which had both fruit sauce and dairy rice in the same container, was successfully brought onto the market. This led to the development of Müller's now-famous twin-pot concept.

In 1987, recognising the possibilities of taking the brand into the rest of Europe, Theo Müller started his British company by test marketing Fruit Corner and Crunch Corner in the Borders region. Due to the success of the trials, Müller products were launched nationwide the following year. The brand revolutionised the yoghurt sector with its modern fun image and continued to steadily increase its presence in each sector.

In 1990 the company launched the virtually fat-free yoghurt, Müllerlight and the rice-based snack Müllerice, with Müller Thick & Creamy following two years later.

Five years after its UK launch the brand had become the yoghurt market leader overtaking long-established British brands. Since then the company's philosophy has been one of continuous innovation, with the introduction of new products such as Müller's range of luxury yoghurts, Müller Amore.

'Pure and Sinful for Fruit Corners, 'So much pleasure, where's the pain?', for Müllerlight and 'Life would be duller without Müller' as part of a corporate campaign.

However, in 2001 the brand took a new approach to its marketing and promotion, launching 'Müllerlove' its first umbrella campaign to support the growing portfolio of Müller products. It tapped into consumers' 'love' for the product while capitalising on the fun and irreverent values of the brand itself.

At the start of 2005 Müller launched a new TV campaign. The 'Lead a Müller Life' campaign rejoices in the fact that Müller products have three key benefits: 'great taste', 'goodness' and 'convenience'. It aims to convey the idea that consumers can enjoy life to the full with Müller products. The campaign began with an overriding Müller master brand ad and then focused on individual brands and the positive attitude to life that they most epitomise.

The advertising helps ensure brand awareness, which remains at an enviable 99% of the core target audience.

Brand Values

Müller's mission is to provide innovative products for its diverse range of customers. The three cornerstones of the company's success are its commitment to quality, relentless innovation and robust market support for its product range. While engaged in the serious business of producing healthy snacks, it has extended the fun and irreverence exemplified in the innovative split pot through its marketing communications.

www.müller.co.uk

Product

One of Müller's key beliefs is that consumers respect quality – it therefore aims to set a new quality gold standard for the market. The company's commitment to quality extends from the products themselves back through its modern production facility to its relationships with its suppliers. Every step of the process is meticulously monitored to ensure that every pot leaving the dairy is in perfect condition.

Recent Developments

The Müller Vitality brand continued to outperform the market in 2004 with the expansion of both the drinks range, with the new Vanilla and fat-free Tropical

varieties plus new yoghurt multipacks. Each product in the Vitality range contains both good probiotic bacteria and probiotics; together these combine to maintain balance in the digestive system, which can positively contribute to overall health and well-being.

A highly successful move, which began in 2003, has been the introduction of the six-pack multipack across a number or ranges. Corners, Vitality and Müllerlight have all benefited from the introduction. The packs are designed to make consumers' lives easier by offering families a convenient good value selection.

The start of 2004 saw the flagship brand Müller Corner extend its successful partnership with key brands, by developing new products with McVitie's. The move offered an innovative extension to the Corners, range. Recognising the need to continually meet consumers' desires to try something new, Müller Corner introduced a new range featuring McVitie's leading brands Milk Chocolate Digestives, Penguin and Jaffa Cakes. The Corners brand alone is now worth £168 million and is one of the UK's top 20 grocery brands.

In keeping with the brand's innovation philosophy, Müller brought a number of new brands onto the market in 2003. It launched a new premium brand – Müller Amore Luxury Yoghurt – reinforcing Müller's longstanding reputation for quality, innovation and leadership in the market. The Müller Corners brand, when first launched, was perceived by consumers as a luxury yoghurt range but through consumers' familiarity with the product and pricing it has, over time, become more of an everyday family treat. Müller's Amore range targets women who are actively looking for a more luxurious product.

The Müllerlight brand is still growing, with new dessert-style flavours such as Apple Pie and Lemon Cheesecake driving growth by combining their virtually fat-free benefits with a creamy dessert taste.

Promotion

As a major advertiser, Müller's aggressive sales and marketing activity has allowed it to establish lines before other manufacturers have the chance to react. Consistent price promotions and ongoing product innovation have also helped drive the brand forward.

The brand has used several straplines in its advertising campaigns for individual products over the years including

Nikon
At the heart of the image

Market

Digital products now account for around 80% of the UK photographic market, where the influx of non-traditional camera brands has helped create a competitive and vibrant environment (Source: GfK).

In the UK, Nikon has ridden this wave of newcomers to repeatedly outgrow the market, doubling business in three years. In 2004, its most successful financial year to date, Nikon UK achieved a record-breaking £100,000,000 turnover and exceeded market growth by 14%.

Nikon's success stems from an ability to differentiate itself from the competition with products that excel in design and performance. Partnerships with acclaimed experts such as Identix, Fotonation and Apical Limited, enable Nikon to develop some of the best software technology available. This, together with Nikon's traditional excellence in hardware and camera design, has resulted in its strongest range to date.

Nikon's main target is the rapidly growing digital SLR market, expected to increase this year from sales of almost 100,000 to more than 180,000 units. Nikon UK's expectation is to achieve a 40% share of this sector.

Launched last year, Nikon's first consumer digital SLR, the D70 is already a multi-award winner. Over a million D70s were sold worldwide and the camera helped Nikon UK take a 30% share of the market (Source: GfK). This year's major launch, the D50, is expected to extend the digital SLR market beyond photo enthusiasts.

Achievements

Nikon has achieved iconic status through its design and build quality. It has a 'less is more' approach to camera design with well thought out features that address the needs of specific audiences rather than using technology for technology's sake.

This philosophy produced the world's first autofocus SLR – the F3AF; the first fish-eye lens and the D1: the first purpose-built digital SLR. The D1 revolutionised professional photography, paving the way for the D70 and D50.

The D70 was Nikon's first digital SLR aimed at non-professional photographers. It is the embodiment of Nikon's long history of SLR design and manufacture. As such, the D70 has won every major industry award, including the European Imaging and Sound Association (EISA) European Digital Camera of the Year 2004-2005; Technical Image Press Association (TIPA) Best Consumer Digital SLR in Europe 2004 and the prestigious Japanese Camera Grand Prix 2004.

In the UK, it was named Digital SLR and Product of the Year 2005 by Amateur Photographer magazine. Based on votes by the editorial team and reviews throughout

the year, these awards are the most prestigious in the UK photographic industry.

Nikon dominated Amateur Photographer's awards, notching up wins in several other categories: the F6 won '35mm SLR of the Year', the Coolscan V ED was named 'Scanner of the Year', and the Coolpix 5200 won 'Consumer Digital Compact of the Year'.

History

Nikon was founded as an optical company in 1917 and began by manufacturing binoculars. In 1920, the company set up a glass research laboratory to evolve new methods and techniques for developing and producing high quality optical glass.

By the 1930s, it was manufacturing camera lenses, although it didn't produce a camera of its own until the following decade. The company's first camera, launched in 1948, was the first product to feature the Nikon trademark.

Nikon entered the photographic market fully in the 1950s. Its first SLR camera, the Nikon F, was launched in 1959 and was the first to feature the bayonet mount still in use today on Nikon's digital SLRs.

Many groundbreaking products have followed. Nikons have been used by professional and amateur photographers worldwide to capture historic as well as ordinary day-to-day events. Nikon cameras have travelled into space as well as to the depths of the ocean.

Nikon positioned itself at the forefront of the digital revolution, beginning with the NT1000 film transmitter in the mid 1980s, and continuing with the latest generation of professional and consumer digital SLRs such as the D2X, the D2Hs with wireless capability, the D70 and the recently launched D50.

The same optical expertise on which the company was founded remains at the heart of the business. Nikon still produces its own glass, giving control over the manufacture of its lenses.

Today however, although photography is what Nikon is best known for, it is just one dimension of a multi-faceted business whose existence was born out of two simple elements: light and glass.

Product

More than 2,300 products carry the Nikon name, including cameras, binoculars, telescopes, microscopes, spectacles and sunglasses, ophthalmic equipment and

hearing aids. Nikon is also a leader in telemedicine.

The Nikon camera range is now almost entirely digital. In an intensely competitive environment, a new breed of Nikon camera has evolved incorporating pioneering developments in software technology that distinguish Nikon from the competition.

The Coolpix S1 digital compact is typical of this new generation. Although design-led, it is also a very functional camera, with features that make it easy for anyone to get good results.

The D70 is aimed at the photo enthusiast, for whom photography is a hobby. The smaller, lighter and more affordable D50 will extend the sector to non-enthusiasts, particularly families.

Like the S1, the D50 uses the best available technologies to ensure ease of use when capturing images. The help button is available throughout the menu system, guiding the user through each feature. The Vari Program menu gives the optimum settings for a range of typical photographic situations and includes a new Child Mode. In this mode, the D50 gives the ideal combination of shutter speed and exposure for natural looking images of children – who are notoriously difficult, constantly mobile subjects. PictBridge software has also been incorporated to allow direct printing from the camera: a handy tool for family use.

Two new lenses announced with the D50 are themselves examples of how Nikon is using technology to stay ahead.

The AFS DX 18-55mm and 55-200mm are suitable for a wide range of situations eliminating the need for a bagful of optics. Importantly, both incorporate Silent Wave Motors and ED glass elements, previously the reserve of Nikon's most expensive professional lenses.

Referred to by one reviewer as the 'finest film camera ever made', the F6 professional 35mm SLR continues the lineage of Nikon greats such as the F, F3 and F5. It shares some of the technology found in Nikon's top-end digital SLRs and ironically, it is unlikely that the F6 would exist were it not for advances in digital technology. The F6 is expected to

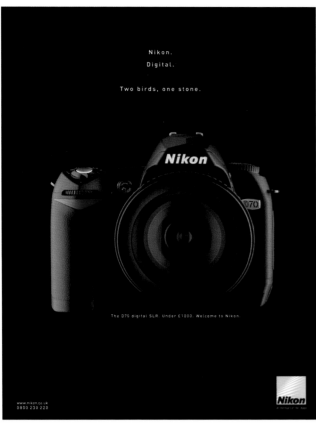

photo is taken; and D-Lighting by Apical Limited, which automatically adds light and detail to underexposed and backlit images, ensuring that photos are always bright, clear and perfectly contrasted.

In the professional sector, the D2X offers the best of both worlds: a resolution high enough for commercial studio work and an option of fast frame rate for sports or news photographers.

The D2Hs is a pure action and sports SLR that combines speed, image quality and workflow efficiency. Its fast wireless transmission rates are an important advantage for professional photographers.

Nikon was the first to launch an off-the-shelf Wi-Fi pack, originally comprising the D2H and the WT-1 transmitter. The technology, now in its second generation, enables photographers to get images online within seconds of capture, without the need for a laptop.

The system helped freelance photographer, John Cassidy, meet an important deadline for The Times newspaper at 2004's Wimbledon Tennis Championships. Cassidy was covering a Tim Henman match that stretched to 9pm and time was running out for the paper. There are 40 transmitters around Wimbledon's courts, so using the WT-1, Cassidy was able to transmit images direct to The Times from his D2H while continuing to shoot. His image of Henman's dive was with the picture desk within two minutes of capture.

Promotion

Nikon UK's advertising throughout 2004 focused on one product: the D70. But the company saw this as more than a product advertisement. It was also designed to elevate and position Nikon as a premium brand.

The advertisements each featured one of four beautifully shot images of the D70 supported by just a few lines of text. This minimalist approach was a statement of confidence from a company that aims to assure customers that its products are in a class of their own.

The flexibility of the campaign matched the creativity of its execution. Essentially comprising four advertisements, its reach was extended through 12 different headlines, each designed to appeal to a different target group. The same strapline: 'The D70 digital SLR. Under £1000. Welcome to Nikon.' was constant.

'Nikon. Digital. Two birds. One stone.' appeared in the Sunday supplements of broadsheet newspapers and 'The future of photography: An overview' was used with a top view of the camera and ran in titles such as iD.

Nikon UK's most successful promotion of 2004 was the £50 Cashback offer for the Coolpix 5200. It ran during the three month Christmas shopping period, supported by advertisements in quality newspapers. Sales increased fivefold over the promotional period, without undermining brand values.

Nikon UK's website, www.nikon.co.uk, is an important route to its customers. Those registering online receive regular updates such as a monthly e-newsletter with product news and exclusive offers.

Chris Packham, renowned wildlife photographer and TV presenter, endorses Nikon binoculars in the UK. Chris already used Nikon Sport Optics binoculars and agreed to trial the HG L series from launch.

Brand Values

The essence of the Nikon brand is passion and inspiration combined with quality and reliability.

The company wants people to 'experience' Nikon and to feel a confidence that only it can provide, through products and services that convey the assurance of premium quality that Nikon users have come to expect.

Empowering people to realise their creative potential through photography is Nikon's aim, reflected by the brand statement, 'At the Heart of the Image.' This statement is used globally in advertising, brand communications and exhibitions. In the UK it is supported by 'Welcome to Nikon' in advertising and post-purchase communications such as the £300 voucher booklet given to every D70 customer.

Nikon's focus on after-sales service has contributed to the enormous loyalty and pride of ownership shown towards the brand. The website enables the level and quality of customer service and communications to improve continuously.

Environmental responsibility is an important issue to Nikon and research is ongoing to develop non-harmful processes such as Eco-glass. Nikon's use of recyclable packaging materials has also been increased.

www.nikon.co.uk

ensure Nikon's number-one position for as long as the film market exists.

Recent Developments

The D70 has brought digital SLR technology, previously only available to professional photographers, to the enthusiast market. The D50 now brings it to an even wider audience.

Nikon's partnerships with software experts mark a new direction for the company and are a positive response to new competitors. The collaborations have produced some exciting new features such as: Face-Priority AF by Identix, which always insures that the face is in focus regardless of where the subject is positioned; In-camera Red-Eye-Fix by Fotonation, which automatically detects and corrects red eyes as the

THINGS YOU DIDN'T KNOW ABOUT

Nikon

> More than 300 different types of glass are the essential components in Nikon products as diverse as camera lenses, scanners and sunglasses.

> By December 2004, 35 million Nikon lenses had been produced since manufacturing first began in 1935.

> Nikon cameras have been used in temperatures of below minus 50 degrees centigrade during a parachute jump from in excess of 8,000m, and by professional divers at depths of more than 100m.

> Nikon digital products were used at sub-zero temperatures on the 2004 Invesco Perpetual Trans-Antarctic Challenge. A D2H was the main camera, supported by a range of lenses and Coolpix compacts. Images were downloaded to Nikon Coolwalker mobile storage devices.

NIVEA

Market

With more and more people – men and women alike – interested in looking and feeling youthful and healthy for as long as possible, it's easy to see why skincare is big business.

Skincare products now offer something for everyone, from basic cleansing to advanced anti-age moisturising for men and women from deodorising to offering protection from the sun.

As the leading skincare brand in Europe, NIVEA has a 13% share of the enormous £880 million UK market. The largest and fastest-growing segment in the market is facial skincare, where product sales total £321 million, increasing by 4.0% year-on-year. The next largest is deodorant at £291 million (Source: IRI) which NIVEA launched into in 2002.

The health and beauty market is being driven by innovation. Consumers are becoming ever savvier about what is achievable through a good skincare and beauty routine through TV shows such as '10 Years Younger'.

With this increased interest in mind, consumers are eager to try new advanced formulas while demand for the next great innovation places enormous pressure on those companies active in this sector. Manufacturers must maintain a frenetic pace of new product development in order to keep up with their competitors.

The increase in male grooming products has come in response to a massive consumer trend, which is opening up a multitude of new product opportunities and brand extensions. In addition to existing players, the market has witnessed numerous new brand entrants over the past few years. The

growing number of men taking better care of their skin has translated into huge growth in NIVEA For Men sales of shaving, aftershave, conditioning and male facial products in recent years, giving NIVEA a 25.5% share of a £97.3 million category (Source: IRI).

Achievements

Present in 170 countries, NIVEA has built an enviable worldwide reputation. The popularity of the brand is demonstrated through the many awards won each year, voted for by consumers.

For the fifth consecutive year, NIVEA has been ranked as Europe's Most Trusted Brand of skincare in the 2005 Reader's Digest Readers' Survey.

The brand has also received awards from many UK national press and consumer lifestyle titles, such as the Mirror, the Daily Mail, FHM, Company, Top Santé, New Woman, Harpers & Queen and Bliss.

These consumers are not only voting with their pens but also with their wallets. In value terms, NIVEA holds the number one position in lip care, general purpose, body care, and in the male facial products, dominating 64% of the category. NIVEA is also the number three brand in women's facial skincare and number two in the sun protection market.

Indeed, NIVEA can take credit not only for launching the first mass market skincare cream back in 1922, but for continuing to drive forward the brand through consistent innovation to keep it at the forefront of consumers' minds.

History

NIVEA traces its roots back to 1911, when Dr Oscar Troplowitz, a medical researcher and owner of the Beiersdorf Company in Hamburg, turned his experience of making medical ointments to developing a new kind of cosmetic cream. The key to his plan was a 'secret ingredient' called Eucerit, used to form a new water in oil emulsion, making it an ideal skin emollient. This formula was also remarkable for its stability, meaning that it could be stored for a long time without separating. This made it ideal for commercial use, as it could be packaged, shipped and marketed on a global scale without losing product quality.

Dr Troplowitz joined forces with Eucerit's creator, Dr Isaac Lifchütz, and dermatologist Professor Paul Gerson Unna to conceive, develop and market a new cream blending this formula with glycerine, citric acid, rose oil and lily of the valley.

The team was so impressed by the cream's brilliant pure whiteness that they decided to call it NIVEA, a name derived from the Latin expression 'Nix Nivis', meaning snow white.

The brand quickly took off on a global scale, reaching the UK and the US in 1922 and South America in 1926. Over the next 50 years NIVEA Creme's reputation as a soothing and effective skin moisturiser was cemented.

Then, in the 1970s, NIVEA began to spread its wings, driven by advances in technology and changes in consumer demand. This expansion of the portfolio set the brand on the road to where it is today; a trusted brand with a comprehensive range of skincare products.

Product

Through more than 90 years' experience in skincare, and extensive research, NIVEA has managed to gain a deep understanding of the natural ingredients and processes present in healthy skin. Wherever possible, NIVEA tries to replicate these processes and ingredients in its products, because the closer an ingredient is to the natural substance in the skin, the more effective it should be and the less likely to cause any reaction.

While NIVEA Creme, in its iconic blue tin, remains the brand's signature product, the range now encompasses a wide portfolio of products addressing specific skincare needs. These sub-brands include: NIVEA Visage, NIVEA Sun, NIVEA Body, NIVEA Hand and NIVEA for Men.

NIVEA Visage is a complete range of products specifically developed to care for the face and is the sub-brand that carries most of NIVEA's technical innovations. It offers cleansing and moisturising formulas for women of all ages and innovative anti-ageing formulas, including the highly successful Anti-Wrinkle Q10 Plus range, that provide older skin with accessible and effective products that challenge the prestige versus mass-market divide.

NIVEA Sun offers a complete range of caring products for the whole family, from sun sprays to children's protection, sunless tanning and added-benefit protection such as firming or skin shimmer products. The brand is committed to broadening consumers' knowledge of how to help protect skin from the sun's harmful rays and keep skin healthy.

The NIVEA Body range provides body moisturisers to meet the needs of all skin types below the neckline. The product range includes both essential products and more advanced formulations such as Firming Lotion Q10 Plus to meet the breadth of needs of the different body care consumers.

The NIVEA Hand range comprises caring nourishing formulations to help hands remain soft, supple and young-looking.

NIVEA For Men, offering shaving, aftershave, conditioning and male facial products, has proven to be particularly successful and is now the leading range of men's skincare in the UK and other parts of Europe.

Recent Developments
New product development and innovation is at the heart of long-term brand development. The sophisticated new Research Centre at NIVEA's headquarters in Hamburg, Germany, which opened in August 2004, is devoted to helping identify and develop the latest products.

One of the many significant UK developments in 2005 was the launch of NIVEA Visage Young, a sub-range within a sub-brand. This new skincare range is targeted at the important recruitment market where the younger consumer aged 14-19 has skincare needs that sit between medical spot remedies and skincare that is increasingly focused on an anti-age proposition.

This also means a chance to develop brand loyalty for a new generation of users whose first point of contact with the brand isn't necessarily through NIVEA Creme. The launch of NIVEA Visage Young has been supported by TV, print and online advertising as well as heavyweight sampling.

The past two years have also seen NIVEA launch several other new products, including a handbag sized hand cream Sculpting & Smoothing Cream Q10 Plus formulated to help lift and firm problem areas like thighs and buttocks, Pure Deodorant proven to offer 24 hour protection without the white marks, Rice & Lotus shower products, proven to invoke the spirit of the Orient in the shower and an SOS balm for the lips.

For men, NIVEA has launched Aqua Cool deodorant, while in suncare, NIVEA has launched a range of protection sprays and lotions proven to work as soon as they are applied so the general advice to wait 20-30 minutes before venturing into the sun is not necessary.

Promotion
NIVEA has a strong marketing heritage, with campaigns as far back as the 1920s focusing on many of the benefits and values that the brand still stands for today.

Nowadays, each section of the brand portfolio is supported by a fully integrated multimedia strategy, encompassing above- and below-the-line advertising, sampling, direct marketing, PR and ambient media such as ads on in store advertising.

Education goes hand in hand with many campaigns, as NIVEA sees it as its responsibility to promote skin protection and the association between healthy skin, general fitness and wellbeing. The strategy of educating the consumer through promotion has helped NIVEA build new markets such as the male skincare segment.

While this may prove costly in the short term, long-term investment in the skincare sector serves to consolidate NIVEA's position as a leading skincare manufacturer and a source of valuable advice that inspires consumer trust and loyalty.

Brand Values
The emotional values associated with the NIVEA brand have changed little in the past 94 years. 'NIVEA cares for your skin' encapsulates NIVEA's brand values.

These values are communicated via clean, fresh, healthy and positive imagery in all NIVEA's promotional material and advertisements. NIVEA is dedicated to protecting the skin of the entire family, therefore family values form a vital part of its brand character.

NIVEA's consistently strong brand imagery ensures that it remains stylish and fashion conscious, and by creating products that fit in with the latest cosmetic trends, it retains its contemporary appeal to each generation.

It is a tribute to the strength and years of experience of the NIVEA brand that it can appeal to consumers on so many levels.

www.nivea.com

Market

Almost 90% of the UK population currently has a mobile phone and the trend towards a society that is always in touch is forecast to grow by a further 11% between 2004 and 2008. This means over 62.8 million subscribers (Source: Euromonitor).

Some 20 years after conception, the mobile market is still intensely competitive, hugely challenging and full of surprises. In this market, O₂ UK is one of five licensed operators in the UK's mobile communications market competing principally against Vodafone, Orange, T-Mobile and 3.

For a number of years, UK mobile brands had recorded significant growth on the back of a growing market but by 2002, as penetration reached a plateau, revenue growth stalled. This mature market presented new challenges. Revenue growth had to be found either by enticing customers away from the competitors or increasing average revenue per user (ARPU) – primarily by stimulating the usage of non-voice services.

O₂ has recognised that while voice services remain a key driver in the use of mobile handsets, customers are increasingly comfortable with and interested in mobile data services. This began with simple text messages, but is now moving towards more innovative applications such as media messaging (MMS), mobile games and video services.

Achievements

In May 2004, illustrating the progress made by O₂ since its launch in spring 2002, the Financial Times wrote: "Not long ago mmO₂ was the ugly step-sister of Europe's mobile operators. Now it's increasingly looking like Cinderella. The main impetus behind the turnaround was mmO₂'s business in the UK, where, despite increasing competition from the likes of new entrant 3, the company recorded a 16% increase in revenues to £3.2 billion on the back of a 10% increase in new customers."

Today, O₂ is an entirely different animal to its predecessor, BT Cellnet. Towards the end of its seventh year of trading, top of mind awareness of BT Cellnet stood at 20% (Source: TNS). After two years, the level for O₂ was 28% (Source: Millward Brown), making O₂ the most salient brand in the market.

This has been confirmed by tracking that shows clear blue space between O₂ and its traditional rivals: 21% see O₂ as 'refreshingly different'. Only 3, with its unique 3G technology, is seen as more 'refreshingly different' (Source: Millward Brown). By January 2004, O₂ had achieved 68% spontaneous brand awareness among all mobile phone users in the UK (Source: NOP).

History

O₂'s story is one of a corporate transformation. In April 2002, BT Cellnet was a troubled business, losing ground consistently to competitors. A month later it was reborn as O₂: a vibrant, modern brand that generated a turnaround that would have been inconceivable only weeks before.

On November 19th 2001, mmO₂ plc (formerly BT wireless) was de-merged from BT plc in a one-for-one share offer, creating a wholly independent holding company. The UK brand, BT Cellnet, was re-launched as O₂ in April 2002.

The new brand faced significant challenges – challenges that BT Cellnet had manifestly failed to tackle. The market had matured, making revenue growth increasingly hard to come by. And competition for that growth was intensifying.

Of course, O₂ has made on-going improvements to its business structure, but the most significant change has been the re-engineering of the brand. O₂ is a case study of how brand engineering can transform not just the metrics of a business, but the morale of its staff, the esteem of its public, its ability to sustain competitive advantage and its potential to deliver future earnings.

Product

From the start, customers rather than products have been at the heart of O₂'s approach. Consumer research revealed that while consumers had moved on with mobile telephony, the brands operating in the sector had not.

Where existing brands tried to force-feed technical innovation, consumers had grown wise, able to identify those aspects of technology that were actually of relevance to them.

Other brands in the market seemed remote from their day-to-day product offering. They established an image and a personality through their brand and, almost in isolation of the brand, used their product offering (such as bonus airtime, new tariffs, etc) in a tactical way, to drive short term sales.

Instead of adopting this 'parallel' approach, presenting products as technical gizmos, or tariffs as tactical one-offs, O₂'s communications wrap them in the brand idea. This is intended not only to create consumer-focused propositions that are of genuine interest and relevance, but also to drive positive associations with the brand.

This 'brand-product-communications continuum' has generated new offers from O₂, such as 'Bolt Ons', 'Home', 'Friends' and 'Happy Hour'.

The 'brand-product-communications continuum' has also been adopted in O₂'s sponsorship of Big Brother, designed to stimulate actual usage of non-voice services (e.g. Big Brother games, text alerts, text chat-room) which, in turn, help build positive associations with the brand.

Recent Developments

In addition to the launch of new mobile services, O₂ is committed to brand development. Following the high of its award-winning Rugby World Cup campaign, O₂ showed its loyalty by signing contract extensions with the RFU, O₂ rugbyclass – a grassroots coaching scheme – and a new partnership with Premiership Rugby. After an eight-year association with the sport, O₂ was looking for new ways to make an impact for the brand.

It wanted to create a rugby event from its existing assets that O₂ could 'own', and that would be a platform for brand-marketing activities outside the England matches. Any activity had to support the brand's 'fresh and different' approach and its new rugby positioning – 'part of the game'.

It created O₂ Scrum in the Park at London's Regent's Park. Held on October 10th 2004, the event was a free public

rugby festival, featuring the Webb Ellis Trophy, kicking competitions, interactive games, England Sevens and Women's rugby demonstrations. In addition, Harlequins, Martin Johnson, England team autograph sessions, O₂ rugbyclass coaching, O₂ touch rugby tournament finals and as a finale – the first ever 'open' England training session with the England squad.

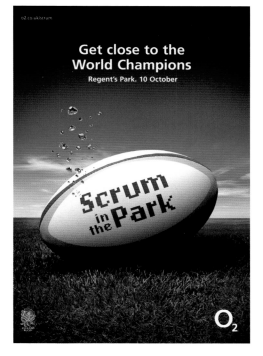

raising the profile of mobile services. O₂ looks in particular to support initiatives where mobile services can be used to tackle social needs and where its employees can become involved.

O₂ UK has launched a partnership with Weston Spirit, the charity co-founded by Simon Weston OBE, in order to help young people reach their full potential. Its partnership includes a ground-breaking peer-mentoring programme, bringing together O₂ employees and Weston Spirit to support personal development of young people. In the first six months of the programme, it recruited more than 70 O₂ mentors who have been trained to provide advice, support and encouragement to the young peer mentors assigned to them. In addition to monthly meetings, the O₂ mentors use text to ensure regular contact with the young people.

Brand Values

Branding involves more than simply projecting an image. For service businesses in particular, it means changing the inner world – how people on the inside of the business see the brand, how they think and how they behave. This was the challenge that faced O₂ when it parted company with BT – the need to reinvent the brand both internally and externally.

Three years on, O₂ possesses a new and optimistic sense of self – a fresh and distinctive personality, built on four core values that have been set out to define the brand.

Firstly, O₂ is bold, a company that is full of surprises, continually coming up with ideas that are practical and relevant, opening up a world of possibilities. Secondly, O₂ is clear and straightforward, with the knack of turning highly complex technology into products that are easy to understand and easy to use. Thirdly, it is open and candid – a brand that tells it as it is. Finally, O₂ is trusted by its customers, a responsive brand that listens to people, is accurate and truthful and does not over-claim.

Above all else, O₂ is a brand that makes things possible – a brand with a 'can-do' attitude to life. Today, three years into its new life, O₂ is on course to achieve what Cellnet was unable to achieve in two decades. It projects a modern attractive and internationally persuasive brand identity and is at last capitalising on its extensive networks, depth of experience and customer knowledge.

www.o2.co.uk

O₂ also used the event to showcase its product technology – the use of 'Prozone' by the England coaches and players on the Xda; and the delivery of news, data and pictures to rugby fans by phone. 3,000 attendees downloaded an England shirt on to their mobile. 4,000 O₂ customers were treated to a special added-value experience – the O₂ Snug – a purpose-built, luxury bolthole from the cold, exclusive to O₂ customers, with free hot drinks, sofas and papers.

The objectives were to create a high quality, fresh and different brand experience for around 15,000 attendees, who were treated as general sports fans; to create a memorable and exclusive experience for O₂ customers and staff encouraging loyalty and word of mouth promotion and to create a focal point for a brand advertising campaign that would communicate key brand messages to a broad audience of rugby fans and also 18-34 technology savvy mobile users.

A six-week brand campaign leading up to the event transformed a one-day brand experience into a marketing campaign. The ad message: 'Get close to the World Champions' featured in papers, websites, on tubes, buses, taxis, lampposts, outdoor posters (including two special builds) and in special Evening Standard 'wraps'.

The PR team used interviews with players to promote the event, ran promotions to meet the team and invited journalists to experience the event first hand. A week's breakfast show promotion on Capital FM promoted the event, the sport and the brand.

Promotion

O₂'s communications strategy has addressed one of the key challenges facing businesses operating in mature markets: how to build an attractive, long-term brand whilst at the same time delivering short-term revenue growth. More than 80% of O₂'s marketing funds have supported sales-driving initiatives. Yet because of its brand-centric approach to communicating these initiatives, they have been unusually

effective in securing long-term sales, akin to what might typically be expected of brand communications.

In fact, through econometric modeling, it became apparent that O₂'s investment in integrated communications is expected to pay for itself more than 60 times over. This extraordinary effect was recognised by the marketing industry when the brand won the IPA Grand Prix Award for Effectiveness in Advertising 2004.

Effectiveness Awards

O₂ invested heavily in Big Brother sponsorship and also sponsored the England team at the Rugby World Cup. By the end of the third series of Big Brother, more people associated O₂ with TV sponsorship than Coronation Street sponsor, Cadbury's (Source: NOP). By the end of series four, 78% of 16-34 year olds spontaneously cited O₂ as the sponsor of Big Brother. This level of awareness will have been augmented by the high levels of PR coverage that the sponsorship generated. Big Brother 4,

for example, triggered 126 pieces of free PR for O₂ (Source: Drum PHD).

In 2005 churn across the category increased dramatically and therefore O₂ introduced 'Loyalty Rewarded', a campaign to reward the loyalty of its existing customers. Based on the premise that customers usually have to be 'new' to get all the perks, it is highlighting the fact that O₂ is offering existing customers the same deals as new customers.

O₂ is committed to corporate responsibility. It believes that companies that respond to the needs of the communities in which they work are more likely to succeed. Its approach is to create mutual benefits, helping the people it supports while enhancing its reputation and

A world that revolves around you

Loyalty rewarded. O₂

THINGS YOU DIDN'T KNOW ABOUT

O₂

> Manx Telecom, part of the O₂ Group, piloted Europe's first live 3G network in December 2001.

> O₂ is title sponsor of the England Rugby team.

> In the six weeks leading up to O₂'s Scrum in the Park, 28,000 mini rugby balls were distributed by O₂ 'hit squads'.

> O₂ customers send the most text messages 2.83 billion in three months in the UK.

OasIs

Market

The UK market for clothing retailers has grown by 4.5% since 2002 to reach a value of £35 billion in the second half of 2004. The sector is dominated by womenswear retailers, which accounted for 38% of the market, at £13.3 billion in 2003 (Source: Euromonitor).

The UK clothing market is forecast to grow by 12% between 2003 and 2008 to reach a value of £39.2 billion. Womenswear is expected to continue to make up the majority of the clothing market, accounting for almost 38% of value sales by 2008 (Source: Euromonitor).

Leading retailers in the UK clothing sector include both department stores and multiple clothing chains. Large chain specialists are the largest clothing retailers, accounting for 35% of retail sales in 2003. Oasis is a well-established and mature brand within the market. It operates and differentiates itself from the mainstream middle market brands and competes with fashion brands such as Warehouse, River Island, Next, Zara and Mango, targeting the fashion-conscious female consumer. Its brand philosophy is to create a carefully considered range of clothing and accessories aimed at fashion-conscious 18-30 year olds. However, satisfying the needs of the fashion-conscious consumer is not as easy as it may sound. Indeed, some six out of ten people fall into the 'choosy' category, with the implication that these consumers do not slavishly follow fashion (Source: Euromonitor).

Achievements

Since a management buyout in 2001, the Oasis brand continues to grow from strength to strength within the fashion retail industry, achieving an annual average turnover of £200 million.

Oasis fashion stores operate from 107 outlets and 133 concessions across the UK & Ireland. The company already operates 90 international stores spanning more than 15 countries from Sweden to China and is planning continued store development for the future in both existing and new markets.

The success of Oasis as an affordable and aspirational fashion retailer has resulted in the achievement of numerous fashion awards and recognition from the

fashion industry and its customers, most recently claiming the Drapers Record award for Business Initiative in November 2004.

In addition to industry recognition, awards have been received from fashion magazines such as Company, Cosmopolitan, Marie Claire, More and Now.

The fashion credibility of Oasis is evidenced in the extensive PR coverage that is achieved season on season. More than £8 million of PR coverage was achieved in 2004 from product placement and features in leading consumer publications, including glossy magazines, national newspapers, supplements, regional and trade publications.

History

Oasis was founded by Michael and Maurice Bennett in 1991 and was floated on the London Stock Exchange in 1995. Following the acquisition of the womenswear retailer Coast, in 1998, a Management buyout took place in 2001.

In 2003 the Icelandic group Baugur supported a refinancing of the Group, with the intention of supporting a strategy to 'buy and build', leveraging the experience, skills and infrastructure of the Group.

In June 2004 Mosaic Fashions Ltd – the parent company of Oasis and Coast – bought Karen Millen and Whistles, to create a leading womenswear group of four strong brands, trading from over 650 outlets internationally with total sales of over £350 million. The acquisition has created a strong portfolio of women's fashion – the next step is to consolidate and integrate operations and infrastructure, while ensuring each of the brands retain their individual identities.

Oasis' management team is headed up by chief executive Derek Lovelock who, with more than 30 years of experience in women's fashion retailing, supports the commercial development of the Oasis brand to fulfil its full potential.

Product

The Oasis product range includes clothing, accessories, footwear, jewellery, lingerie and lifestyle products for women. Oasis has a reputation for colour and femininity

within its ranges and provides a strong breadth of products that span both the casual end of the market to the more formal. Occasion wear, knitwear and tailoring are three of the product categories renowned as being the heartland of Oasis and are highly competitive areas on the high street. Another area of strength within the product offer includes a differentiated accessories range that is growing season on season.

There are also limited edition ranges and exclusive buys that can be found at many of the Flagship stores, where the idea is that there is always something fresh and new available in store.

Recent Developments

Customer research carried out in December 2003 indicated a growing demand from the Oasis customer for more desirable and aspirational collections. It showed that a third of Oasis sales were coming from the 35-plus age group and that there was potential to provide for a new customer base that was looking for 'something different', as well as reaching an already loyal customer that extended beyond the core target market.

In response to meeting the demands of the new and existing customer, Oasis has broadened its product range further with the launch of three sub-brands: New Vintage, which launched in October 2003, Odille Lingerie, which first came out in spring 2004 and Love Rosa, which hit the streets in summer 2004.

Design and innovation are the lifeblood of the Oasis business, so each new sub-brand has its own identity. This is carried through from the initial concept and design of the garment to the branding, packaging and development of a new merchandising concept with bespoke fixtures for each brand.

The launch of these sub-brands alone achieved a combined PR value of £1.6 million in one year alone, in consumer press coverage. The PR coverage has been instrumental in driving the profile and credibility of the Oasis brand among key fashion press and opinion formers.

The launch of the Oasis store in the Birmingham Bullring in September 2003

All new Oasis store openings and refurbishments feature the 'secret garden' concept, combined with new additions to ensure each new store remains fresh, relevant and individual.

Promotion

The Oasis marketing strategy is fully integrated across the whole marketing mix and ranges from brand advertising through windows and visual merchandising to the company's corporate social responsibility strategy.

The Oasis brand advertising campaign runs across key fashion titles including; Glamour, Elle, Marie-Claire, Company, Cosmopolitan, and Image & U in the Republic of Ireland. The campaign is supported by advertorial promotions and promotional partnerships with key fashion titles.

PR is pivotal to the success of brand positioning, awareness and leveraging the brand. Product placement secures day-to-day coverage and is a major part of the on-going strategy – the launch of the newest addition to the Oasis product range, Oasis Premium Denim is reflective of the success of this strategy. Key pieces from the range have recently been requested by celebrities such as Jodi Kidd and photographed on Leah Wood.

Innovative product placement is also secured through sponsorship of events which raises the profile of the brand among trendsetters. On February 14th 2005 Oasis participated in London Fashion Week, for the first time, by hosting a joint first birthday party in association with ICM models. Attendees included Jodi Kidd, Lizzie Jagger and Isabella Blow.

Back in the realms of the consumer, the Oasis cardholder programme allows the retailer to talk directly to its most loyal and responsive customers. Monthly communication includes information on exclusive discounts, offers a programme of special flagship events, free gifts and new brand launch information. The website, www.oasis-stores.com acts as a key communication tool, with the number of unique visitors increasing 40% year-on-year.

The website provides a dynamic, online experience of the Oasis brand. Sections include a dedicated area for New Season collection updates, a micro-site for sub-brands (Love Rosa and Odille), a 'Dates for your Diary' section keeps customers informed of ongoing activity for in-store events and promotions, there is an online cardholder application service and, finally, the most popular part of the site is the 'Clothes Rail', where visitors can create outfits and email the pictures to their friends for approval or rejection. A Product Finder facility was introduced in late 2004 to track and locate products in-store. An email strategy to a database of registered users also forms a key part of the web and email campaigns, with communication sent out on average once a month.

In physical terms, windows and visual merchandising play a key part in the Oasis brand experience and promotion. With a reputation for its innovative window installations, updated at least six times a year, the window displays are a key differentiating factor on the High Street. While branding and packaging is considered an important part of the experience and promotion of the brand. This is reflected in the unique design of the current Oasis carrier bag, a range of product labels and garment tickets for special product ranges and point of sale material.

Oasis's corporate and social responsibility strategy includes support for the London children's hospice, the Richard House Trust and Fashion Targets Breast Cancer.

Brand Values

Oasis cultivates its reputation for femininity, colour, fun and in-house design. The brand philosophy is carried through into all aspects of the Oasis experience, from the considered selection of each store location and their bespoke interiors, to the development of all Oasis imagery packaging and labelling, all of which are designed to identify with the fun-loving spirit of the customer.

Oasis collections are fashionable, wearable and colourful; innovation, quality and differentiation are key Oasis brand values. More aspirational than other high street brands, price points are justified by quality of fabrics, production and attention to detail in design.

These aspects create the unique Oasis fingerprint, which separates the retailer from the rest of the high street and enables customers to identify with the brand.

Oasis has a loyal customer base which is on-trend, in fashion, independent and young. The typical Oasis customer is described as living life to the full and shopping is her favourite past time, she loves to shop with her friends.

LOVe
ROSa

www.oasis-stores.com

shows part of the evolution of Oasis and its vision for the future. All aspects of the store's design follow the ethos of creating an entire brand shopping experience and communicate Oasis' independent attitude to retailing on the high street. Working with interior design consultants, Oasis created interiors that aim to provide a haven of luxury guaranteed to delight any customer; the 'secret garden'.

The Birmingham store is designed to take the customer on a complete journey through a number of salon-style rooms, each with their own look and feel, delivering a boutique-style shopping experience in a larger space.

THINGS YOU DIDN'T KNOW ABOUT

Oasis

> In 2004 Oasis used 8.5 million carrier bags throughout its stores and expects to use 10 million in 2005.

> In 2004 Oasis sold more than 76,000 of its best-selling sequinned scarves over 32 weeks.

> The average Oasis garment passes through 18 people from conception to delivery.

> For Oasis Denim, Oasis uses 18,000 rivets per week – that's 72,000 per month and 864,000 per year.

ODEON
FANATICAL ABOUT FILM

Market

2004 was a great year for ODEON helped by impressive box office performances from films such as 'Shrek 2' and 'The Incredibles'. Cinema admissions rose 3% year-on-year in 2004, representing the second-highest level of cinema admissions in more than 30 years. According to the Cinema Advertising Association (CAA), admissions for the year totalled 171 million, averaging 3.29 million a week. The CAA also predicts continued growth with admissions rising to approximately 185 million in 2005.

Importantly, ODEON continues to be at the heart of the success of UK cinema. By the end of 2004 ODEON operated 94 sites, making it the largest cinema chain in the UK. Its 2004 UK market share was 22.3%, compared to its nearest competitor, which had a share of 16% (Source: Dodona).

In addition, ODEON's market leading position will potentially strengthen as a result of current changes in ownership in the UK market. There are plans for considerable consolidation, with the sector now being dominated by four key businesses: Terra Firma (which owns ODEON and UCI), Blackstone (which owns Cineworld and UGC), Vue Cinemas and National Amusements. Private equity firms now own all of the above cinema brands excluding National Amusements. As a result there is likely to be continued investment in UK

considered to be the number one venue for hosting a film premiere in the UK. Testament to this fact, ODEON has hosted more than 300 Worldwide, UK and Royal Film Premieres at the ODEON Leicester Square alone.

In addition, ODEON prides itself on its high standards of customer service. ODEON is very proud of its record as an employer and has achieved the 'Investors in People' standard – another first for a UK cinema chain. ODEON also leads the way in the use of customer insight to drive the business forward. The business focus is firmly on the needs of the customer, offering easy to use advance booking technologies, and a product range including the best of world film as well as new concession and bar concepts.

History

ODEON is a brand that has been a part of British culture for more than four generations and its story is one of the most remarkable in British Film. On August 4th 1930, the first ODEON cinema opened in Perry Barr, Birmingham as a joint venture between Oscar Deutsch and several other businessmen. This cinema bore the first angular ODEON logo that was to become the company's recognised trademark. The name was based on the Greek word 'Odeion', which was the name of an amphitheatre on the slopes of the Acropolis in Greece.

and film. In addition, the major exhibitors Rank and Thorn EMI announced 'British Film Year' and implemented a yearlong campaign designed to help reverse the downward trend of cinema admissions. In 1985, UK cinema admissions rose for the first time after many years of decline.

In 1998, ODEON implemented an extensive re-branding and refurbishment campaign to reinforce its position as market leader in the UK. The strap-line 'Fanatical About Film' was introduced to the UK cinemagoer and the campaign culminated in the £3 million upgrade of the ODEON Leicester Square.

The highly successful ODEON chain was later sold in February 2000 to Cinven, a venture capitalist company. Cinven then merged the newly re-branded ODEON chain with its existing ABC cinema chain, beginning the process of consolidation that we see in the market today. All ABC cinemas were rebranded ODEON and the resulting chain of cinemas enjoyed more than two years of continued positive growth.

cinema to ensure business growth. Also, there is likely to be less chance of cinema development in local markets that cannot viably sustain increased screen numbers. The net result being continued growth in UK cinema with ODEON continuing to lead where others follow.

Achievements

ODEON celebrates its 75th Anniversary in 2005. Since the opening of the first ODEON in 1930, ODEON has long been considered to be synonymous with film. 75 years on, the ODEON brand remains the most recognised cinema brand in the UK. At the end of 2004, ODEON was the largest cinema chain in the UK showing around one million performances a year and accounting for around one in four cinema tickets sold in the UK.

ODEON also has a pioneering history of optimising new technology. ODEON was the first cinema chain in the UK to sell cinema tickets online and Odeon.co.uk is now the biggest cinema exhibitor website in the UK, receiving more visits and taking more bookings than any other cinema website. ODEON was also the first cinema chain to launch WAP and SMS mobile phone booking systems, and the first cinema chain in the world to launch cinema ticketing through interactive TV.

ODEON is also the first choice venue for film premieres. ODEON's flagship site on Leicester Square is

However, ODEON later came to be known more popularly as an acronym for 'Oscar Deutsch Entertains Our Nation.'

By 1936, 56 new ODEON cinemas had opened across the UK and in 1937 the ODEON Leicester Square opened on the site of the old Alhambra Theatre. It was just one of 36 ODEON cinemas to open that year, but has since proved to be the British Film Industry's most glamorous cinema address.

In 1939, J. Arthur Rank injected capital into the rapidly expanding company and took a seat on the main board. Three years later, when Oscar Deutsch sadly passed away at the age of 48, Rank secured Oscar's shares in the business and ODEON continued to grow under the Rank Organisation.

However, in 1955, the arrival of ITV led to a sharp decline in cinema attendance, a decline that was to last some 30 years. All exhibitors felt the impact and many cinemas were converted by Rank into bingo halls and bowling alleys in an effort to maintain profitability. This heralded a UK trend of converting cinemas to other uses in the face of declining admissions. By 1961, a third of ODEON cinemas had closed and the industry continued to struggle for a further 20 years.

However, in 1985, the fortunes of UK cinema changed. The arrival of the multiplex cinema and VHS video served to re-stimulate interest in cinema

Following this success, Cinven sold ODEON to a consortium of investors early in 2003. The principal partners in the purchase were WestLB, The Entertainment Group and Robert Tchenguiz of Rotch.

Most recently, in September 2004, ODEON was acquired by private equity firm Terra Firma, which also acquired UCI cinemas. As a result, ODEON is looking forward to an exciting period of development during which it will continue to build on its unique position as the UK's number one cinema chain.

Product

From one-screen key city centre sites to state-of-the-art multiplex cinemas, ODEON has a cinema portfolio able to cater for all consumer tastes. Importantly ODEON has always been at the

forefront of cinema development – offering seating designed for comfort combined with leading screen and sound technology. Also, with over 600 screens, ODEON play everything from Hollywood blockbusters to foreign-language films. Showing a wide variety of films at performance times to suit the increasingly hectic lives of the UK population has helped ODEON remain ahead of its nearest competitors.

Naturally, watching a film on the silver screen wouldn't be the same without popcorn, but ODEON offers an ever increasing choice of food and beverage options. ODEON is constantly developing new concession concepts as well as continuing to integrate Häagen-Dazs café-bars in most cinemas. Also, new products such as 'Ice-Blast' appeal to ODEON's young customers, whereas popcorn and drink 'combo' deals prove popular with all cinemagoers.

Recent Developments

Developing technology has enabled ODEON to further enhance customer service during recent years. ODEON has pioneered advance ticketing in the cinema industry, offering its customers

the flexibility to book cinema tickets in advance using five different channels. During 1998, ODEON launched the first public-facing telephone speech recognition system in Europe. Subsequently, in 2004, ODEON made this 'Filmline' system totally speech recognition driven and now takes on average more than 300,000 calls per weekend.

Odeon.co.uk, was the first UK cinema website to offer online ticketing and is the most popular cinema exhibitor website in the UK. ODEON were also the first cinema chain in the world to launch cinema ticketing via interactive TV.

ODEON has also developed the largest 'registered customer' database of any UK cinema chain providing a much-enhanced understanding of consumer behaviour and demand. As a result, ODEON is able to communicate directly with customers, offering more targeted promotions and film information.

Finally, ODEON has always strived to remain at the forefront of cinema projection technology. The ODEON Leicester Square was the first cinema in the UK to use

Digital Projection in 2000 showing the first digital screening of 'Toy Story 2' in the UK. Digital Projection has also allowed ODEON to show alternative content such as music concerts, live sports and even interactive gaming. ODEON was the first cinema to broadcast the Football World Cup in screens across the country in 2002 and following this success; the Rugby World Cup was screened at ODEON in 2003. It's not just sporting events that have been a big success on the big screen, music concerts have also proved popular. Artists such as David Bowie and Robbie Williams have used Digital Projection at ODEON to beam exclusive events to fans across the UK. Importantly, this represents a potential new revenue stream for UK exhibitors.

Promotion

ODEON is very proactive when it comes to sales promotion, working closely with third-party brands and key suppliers to drive the business forward. In 2004 alone, ODEON implemented more than 50 promotions – the majority of which were exclusive to ODEON within the cinema sector. ODEON also conducts many film-specific promotions including ticket based and added value activity.

What's more, ODEON has also developed an online promotional database. Through the effective targeting of email messages, ODEON has been able to influence consumer purchase behaviour and increase customer value.

Such high profile promotional activity has proven to be both an excellent means to generate incremental

business, as well as a vehicle for the promotion of the ODEON brand. Importantly for promotional partners, ODEON can provide unrivalled access to key audience demographics, which is one of the reasons why so many brands choose to work with ODEON.

Brand Values

The ODEON brand remains young, cool, stylish and accessible. Its positioning statement: 'Fanatical About Film' communicates the brand's passion for film and everything related to it, and serves to differentiate ODEON in the competitive UK marketplace.

Through effective media planning, advertising, promotions and high profile PR campaigns ODEON has developed brand strength greater than any other cinema chain in the UK.

www.odeon.co.uk

Market

As a nation of dedicated dog lovers, the UK market for dog food is becoming increasingly premium. As the consumption of nutritionally enhanced, functional and organic foods increases among humans, pets too are being treated to the same lifestyle choices.

Over the past ten years the market has been evolving, with notable shifts into super-premium brands at the top end of the category and own label at the bottom. Super Premium brands are either positioned on their health-giving qualities or their a la carte recipes, whereas own label has been experiencing a surge in market share as supermarket brands begin to infiltrate our cupboards.

As a result, mainstream brands such as Pedigree have been suffering a squeeze in a highly competitive market. The key players vying for a share of dog's appetites are Pedigree, Bakers, Cesar, Winalot, Butchers, Iams and Hills Science Diet.

The market is product-format focused, being split into three categories: Wet, Dry and Snacks & Treats, all available in a number of different packaging formats and sizes. Today's trends within dog food point to a decline in canned wet food and dry mixer, an increase in single-serve pouches and trays and complete dry food and a continuing trend for treating. The key deciding factors within dog feeding are: dog enjoyment, health benefits, variety and convenience.

Achievements

As a global brand with the love of dogs at its core, Pedigree feeds dogs on six continents and in more than 50 countries. Worldwide, the brand is worth US$2.1 billion, which puts it in the top 20 of the biggest global consumer brands (Source: ACNielsen).

Pedigree is the UK market's number one dog food and has also been voted the number one trusted pet food in a recent survey (Readers Digest Trusted Brands 2004).

In addition to being the bestselling brand in the category, Pedigree is also one of the broadest with a wide portfolio in dog food, spanning cans, pouches, complete, mixer and snacks and treats.

Like the market itself, Pedigree has not stood still, contributing to advancing the science behind pet nutrition and pet care through its dedicated research centre The WALTHAM Centre for Pet Nutrition. WALTHAM is designed to provide a cumulative source of expertise and influence, which is pre-eminent in its field. WALTHAM is the scientific authority that unifies the research and development expertise of the Mars Pet Care Companies worldwide.

History

Chappel Brothers, the company from which Masterfoods originated, was acquired by the Mars family in 1935, when the name changed to Chappie Ltd. The Chappie dog food brand was then launched. 25 years later, Chum canned dog food launched, with the first varieties being chicken and liver.

1964 was a landmark year for the brand: it was re-launched as Pedigree Chum, had its first associations with the Crufts show, where Silbury Soames was the first dog fed on Pedigree Chum to win Best in Show, and the 'Top Breeders Recommend It' advertising campaign began. The Pedigree brand's roots are in the UK, where it contributed to the invention of mass-produced dog food, but during the 1960s and 1970s, the brand was extended into Europe, exporting the pattern of UK success.

In 1984 Pedigree entered the dry category in the UK with Pedigree Mixer to compete with Spillers and then in 1992 with Complete Dry.

Called Chum in the UK and Pal on the continent, the brand wasn't harmonised across Europe as Pedigree Chum or Pedigree Pal until the late 1980s. Today most markets have dropped 'Pal' and 'Chum' to make the brand simply Pedigree.

In 2005, Pedigree is present in virtually every market in the world with the exception of all African countries but South Africa, and has at least 500 individual product lines consisting of various sub-brands, product formats, varieties and sizes.

For more than 60 years, Pedigree has been the nations' most trusted and favourite, dog-loving brand, to feed our dogs. Pedigree is, and always has been, the number one dog food brand in the UK. It is trusted, revered and held in high regard as being committed to dogs and what's best for them.

Product

Pedigree strives to be a dog-centric company. Its employees are dog lovers and therefore share with consumers the appreciation of how much joy dogs bring to their owners' lives.

That's why regardless of shape, size or purity of breed, Pedigree is dedicated to providing owners food from the broadest portfolio of products that helps them bring out the best in their dogs everyday.

In addition to Pedigree's nutritious wet and dry foods, it also offers special large-breed, small-breed, light, sensitive, puppy, junior and senior recipes. As well as an assortment of functional snacks and treats designed to be delicious for dogs.

Recent Developments

Pedigree is continually looking for ways to help bring out the best in dogs and nourish the bond between them and their owners. This is what drives the brand's research and development and therefore new product launches.

Although 80% of dogs over the age of three suffer from gum problems, which can lead to further health complications, this is largely due to a lack of understanding that dogs need their teeth cleaned too. Pedigree DentaStix – a new product in the Snacks & Treats range that cleans the dogs' teeth as it chews – is designed to

provide an easy solution to the problem and help to reduce tartar build up by up to 60%.

Pedigree understands owners' desires to give treats to their dogs – after all they are one of the family – but this can lead to weight management problems for some dogs. So Pedigree has introduced a range of Snacks & Treats called 'Light & Tasty'. As the name suggests, this is a range of tasty treats that owners can give to their dog regularly because they are low in fat.

Promotion

Pedigree has been advertising since the early days of commercial television. The 1960s and 1970s were a time of exploration for the Pedigree brand, which was trying to find its own motivating positioning. Many approaches were tried in multiple markets.

Then, in 1964, the UK marketing team hit upon a powerful advertising technique: using credible authority figures, such as breeders of championship dogs and experts with practical expertise in dogs, to promote the Pedigree brand. For the next 25 years, Pedigree maintained one global positioning and one global campaign – 'Top breeders recommend it' – that ran in 80 countries.

This campaign was a very efficient route to global branding. The campaign worked by creating local brand authenticity through the local authenticity of the breeder.

The campaign established Pedigree as the best food owners can feed their dogs, proven by the fact that top breeders recommend it and champion dogs love it. The product support for the campaign rotated around 'Solid Meaty Nourishment', 'Five kinds of meat' and 'The Building Blocks of Good Nutrition'.

However, having enjoyed 30 years of success, the breeders campaign began to lose its relevance, the idea had become formulaic and the brand's image risked being aloof and superior due to its links with pure breeds only.

The brand needed to harness the emotional potency of what the breeder represented, but create a new campaign, and indeed positioning, that would drive a fundamental reappraisal of the brand. So, the most recent campaign started with the objective to communicate to consumers Pedigree's 'real' commitment to sharing their love of all dogs and being a company of dog lovers.

The campaign concept has been to invite dog owners to join Pedigree in spreading the message to other owners that it is a dog lover too. This idea is summed up in the new endline for the campaign 'It's a dog thing'.

Alongside communicating Pedigree's values, this new campaign also sees the redefinition of the brand away from being just about 'pedigree' dogs to being for all dogs, whether mongrels, pretty or scruffy, playful or lazy.

As well as TV advertising, Pedigree makes extensive use of print, direct mail and the internet to engage consumers. Pedigree welcomes new Puppy owners into its 'Dog Lover Community' with the Pedigree 'Puppy Pack', full of advice, information, products and money-off vouchers.

The re-branded website, launched in May 2005, invites Dog Lovers to come onto the site to share their stories about 'their dog's thing', be entertained by the adorable images of dogs, and to find out more about Pedigree products.

Brand Values

Pedigree loves dogs, and everything it does is for the love of dogs. The brand's values are all about sharing its passion for dogs with like-minded dog owners and celebrating them, warts and all. Pedigree is about being straightforward and approachable and about inviting fellow dog lovers to share with the brand a complicit relationship of dog love.

www.uk.pedigree.com

THINGS YOU DIDN'T KNOW ABOUT

Pedigree®

> 72% of all dogs in the UK – more than 4.7 million dogs – are fed a Pedigree product every year, including the Queen's Corgis.

> Five cans of Pedigree are opened every second of every day in the UK.

> The now-famous yellow Pedigree packaging was only introduced in the UK in 1992.

> In excess of 14 billion Pedigree Complete Kibbles are consumed by dogs in the UK each year.

> More than 3.5 million dogs in the UK enjoyed a Pedigree Snack or Treat in the past year.

♪ioneer
sound. vision. soul

Market

Technology has driven dramatic sales growth in certain sectors of the UK market for consumer electronics, causing relatively rapid development in some areas of the market. However, technological advances often result in a change in consumer purchasing from an established product type, as with the trend away from VCRs in favour of DVD players.

Rapid changes in technology have found a ready response with UK consumers, who have enjoyed a generally increasing level of disposable income. The low interest rates and easily available credit that have characterised the past few years have facilitated spending. Consumers are also becoming generally more confident in the selection of the right product to suit their requirements at the premium end of the market and increasingly treat bottom-of-the-range TVs, VCRs, DVD players or audio systems almost as disposable items.

Sales of consumer electronics have also been boosted by the fact that UK consumers are increasingly purchasing second or third units of some products for use in different locations within the home. In addition to the main TV and VCR in the living room, many households now have additional TVs and VCRs in the kitchen or in bedrooms. For a typical family of two adults and two children, this can result in ownership of three or four TVs in a single home. A similar pattern is evident for personal/portable audio and in-home hi-fi systems and is beginning to emerge for DVD players.

The UK consumer electronics market is dominated by leading global manufacturers – predominantly Japanese companies – which are able to hold a commanding lead in most market sectors by exploiting their technological expertise and strong brand equity.

Achievements

Founded in 1938 in Tokyo, Pioneer Corporation's shares are traded on the New York Stock Exchange.

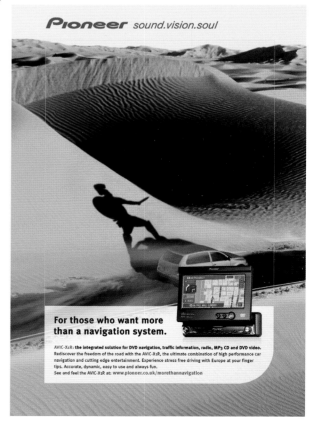

Pioneer has a comprehensive strategy focused on four core business objectives to be achieved by March 31st 2006. Firstly, to be number one in DVD worldwide: as a leading proponent of next-generation audio/video recording and playback, Pioneer seeks to build upon a heritage as a digital optical disc pioneer to become a leading global enterprise in the DVD industry.

Secondly, Pioneer aims to establish a strong business foundation for plasma and Organic Electroluminescent (OEL) displays, which were introduced to the world by Pioneer in 1999. Pioneer lives up to its name with high definition plasma and OEL displays, offering both thin and self-emitting light, flat panel screen designs for crystal clear pictures and wide-angle visibility.

Thirdly, Pioneer aims to encourage consumers to move from standalone to network environments. As the use of the internet and digital broadcasting spreads among households and the information society evolves, 'network' technologies become more important.

Finally, Pioneer is expanding its core business from manufacturing and marketing products of its own brand to supplying its key devices and key technologies to other companies, taking advantage of its leading development of DVD, plasma displays, OEL displays, speakers and car stereo equipment.

History

The Pioneer story began in 1937 when the company's founder, Nozomu Matsumoto, successfully developed the A-8 dynamic speaker. The company was established a year later in Tokyo under the name Fukuin Shokai Denki Seisakusho.

Almost a quarter of a century later, the company became Pioneer Electronic Corporation (now Pioneer Corporation) and its shares were listed on the Tokyo Stock Exchange Second Section. It was around this time that the company introduced the world's first separate stereo system.

In 1966, Pioneer established sales companies in Europe and the US before listing shares on the Tokyo Stock Exchange First Section and the Osaka Securities Exchange.

A decade later, the mid 1970s saw Pioneer introduce the world's first component car stereo and the Supertuner, a high-sensitivity tuner for the car stereo. This marked the first time a car-audio tuner offered the same high quality sound that was found in a home-audio tuner.

Pioneer's shares were listed on the New York Stock Exchange in 1976. A few years on, Pioneer introduced the CD player, followed by the world's first car CD player, which was released in 1984.

By the 1990s, Pioneer was busy introducing the world's first GPS car navigation system, the DVD/CD player and the world's first DVD/LD/CD compatible player for home use.

Today, Pioneer employs more than 36,000 people in its worldwide consumer electronics business.

Product

Pioneer operates as four main divisions: home electronics, car electronics, what the company describes as 'others' and patent licensing. Pioneer develops and manufactures innovative products for all hi-tech entertainment needs – home, car audio, multimedia and DJ equipment.

DJ / VJ用DVDプレーヤー
DVJ-X1

By combining cutting-edge technology with sophisticated design, its products transport the customer to a world of ultimate entertainment.

The Home Electronics division aims to make the home the ultimate in personal entertainment. Pioneer's stylish and technologically advanced products – from High-Definition ready plasma TVs, hard-disk drive DVD recorders and wireless home cinema systems – provide superior clarity of sound and breathtakingly clear images. And with High-Definition Television (HDTV) soon to launch in the UK, Pioneer is again at the forefront of the next television revolution. Pioneer's mobile entertainment products include GPS car navigation systems, which combine DVD, HDD and wireless communication technologies as well as car stereo products incorporating OEL displays. The enhanced, award-winning AVIC-X1R for example, incorporates pin-point positioning, turn-by-turn route guidance and state-of-the-art entertainment. In short, Pioneer's range of car stereo products ensures that the brand remains at the forefront of the growing mobile entertainment market.

Pioneer's 'Others' business deals with industrial systems and business solutions. It manufactures DVD authoring systems and plasma display panels for commerce, plus high-precision devices, OEL displays and factory-automation systems for clients who appreciate the value its equipment adds to their brands.

Pioneer has patents for DVD, CD, MD, and all other types of optical discs and related equipment. This is a measure of Pioneer's heritage of optical disc innovation that leads the industry to this day.

Recent Developments

For 2005, Pioneer has given new meaning to the phrase 'home cinema'. Pioneer plasmas are the only screens with an HDMI input (which always uses HDCP encryption) and are also the only screens that can do 720p or 1080i at both 50/60hz. In a nutshell, the Pioneer screens are high-definition TV compliant and are also fully EICTA compliant.

With its new digital home cinema packages and systems, Pioneer home entertainment has become extremely attractive and practical, with surround sound effect and razor sharp images with intense colours.

Pioneer's in-car products include new top-level navigation systems – so that customers can be entertained by the most extensive AV line-up ever. Breaking the sound barrier between multimedia and driving are Pioneer's MP3/WMA compatible head units. Pioneer is also a leader in amps, subwoofers and speakers.

At the start of 2005, the company launched the DJM-1000 professional DJ mixer – the result of extensive industry research and development with world-renowned DJs, club technicians and installation engineers. Early the same year, Pioneer launched the CDJ-200, a fully MP3 compatible CD turntable which allows DJs to include the very latest downloaded tracks in their sets, without having to convert the audio from other formats.

Promotion

The Pioneer brand is generally promoted via a number of routes – its sponsorship of the London Philharmonic Orchestra, product showcasing at London's Ideal Home Show, press, TV and online competitions. In addition, for the first time, in 2005 Pioneer became the headline sponsor of the British Academy Television Awards. The event saw the introduction of the Pioneer Award, which sets out to honour programme-makers whose novel and bold approach has brought both critical praise and commercial success. The Pioneer Award shortlist was reached by a committee of national television critics and the winner selected by the public.

Brand Values

Pioneer's slogan: 'sound. vision. soul' enables it to clearly communicate its group philosophy and group vision to its customers. 'Sound' defines the company's heritage as an audio industry pioneer, perceptions of the brand, healthy business activities, solid financial structure and resonance with customers.

'Vision' defines the company's foresight and reflects its approach toward DVD, plasma display, organic light-emitting diode (OLED) display and other video products. 'Soul' embraces Pioneer's unique spirit in taking entertainment to higher levels of sensation.

Pioneer's philosophy is to 'Move the Heart and Touch the Soul.' The realisation of this spirit is defined in Pioneer's group vision as an Entertainment-Creating Company.

www.pioneer.co.uk

High Definition is the future.

A future where 7 billion colours explode.

PURE VISION

Like you, we lead where others follow. Take a look at the latest Pioneer High Definition Plasma TV and you'll find out yourself. Thanks to cutting-edge technologies like Advanced Super Clear Drive and Direct Colour Filter, you'll receive a quantum leap in picture quality. Unique viewing pleasure with 7 billion colours, unmatched brightness and detail in high definition. Now available in 50-inch and 43-inch models whose timeless, slim design is as exciting as its performance...

Don't wait for the future, experience it now.

http://www.pioneer.co.uk

THINGS YOU DIDN'T KNOW ABOUT

Pioneer

> Pioneer GB is the headline sponsor of the British Academy Television Awards in the UK in 2005. Winners were announced at the Awards Ceremony on Sunday 17th April, at the Theatre Royal Drury Lane, London.

> As part of the BAFTA sponsorship, Pioneer launched a new award at the ceremony. The Pioneer Award was developed to honour programme-makers whose novel and bold approach has brought both critical praise and commercial success. The winner was voted for by members of the public.

> In 1962, Pioneer introduced the world's first separate stereo system.

> For the past 23 years, Pioneer has been providing sponsorship to the London Philharmonic Orchestra.

> Pioneer introduced the world's first high-definition, 50 inch plasma display for consumer use back in 1997.

PP PRETTY POLLY

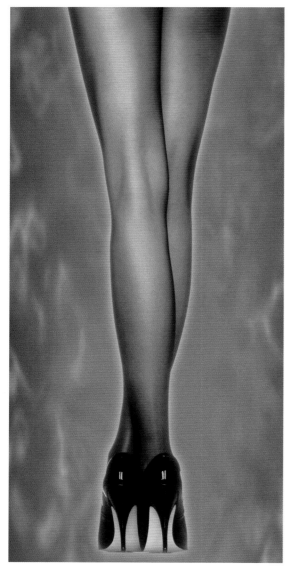

Market

Knitted hose have been worn for the past 1,000 years. Initially worn by men and not women, the first stocking knitted on a circular machine was created in 1589.

The market has come a long way since then. The first nylon stocking was invented in 1938 and the first tights were created in 1966.

Over the years stockings have become less popular and, most recently, knee-highs have become very popular due to more and more women opting to wear trousers rather than skirts. Today's hosiery market is split between sales of tights (84%), stockings (3%), hold-ups (4%) and knee-highs (9%).

In 2004 the fine hosiery market was worth in excess of £250 million, with more than half a million pairs of tights, stockings and hold ups being sold every day. Legwear is the most frequently bought item of clothing with women buying on average ten pairs a year.

The average price of a pair of tights in 2004 was £1.19, however, this covers a wide price range of between 35p a pair through to luxury tights at £20 a pair. Pretty Polly has the largest distribution of all the hosiery brands and commands over 50% market share of the branded market with average prices at almost twice the average (£2.30 per pair).

The industry is highly innovative and products have changed significantly over the years. Most tights now include Elastane or LYCRA® (by Invista), to give stretch and strength, although most are still made principally of nylon yarns which are much finer and stronger. Deniers are now much sheerer with the average denier being a 10 or a 15 denier worn everyday.

Achievements

Pretty Polly is well-renowned for its commitment to product innovation. It was the first brand to market with hold ups – a stocking held up without the use of a suspender belt – which were featured on Tomorrow's World in 1967 and launched by Pretty Polly later that year. Still at the forefront of innovation, Pretty Polly was the first UK hosiery company to link legwear to bodywear with the Link Up system, which has been lauded as the greatest legwear innovation since the hold up.

Pretty Polly has consistently worked with iconic women such as Sarah Cox, Jade Jagger, Jemma Kidd, Rachel Stevens and Jamelia and won the Creative Circle Gold, Silver & Bronze awards in 1997 for innovative advertising across three different categories.

Pretty Polly is one of the most recognised brands for women, remaining number one legwear brand in the UK. Despite operating in a consistently declining market, Pretty Polly achieved strong sales growth in 2004.

History

In 1919 two manufacturing technicians, Harry Hibbert and Oswald Buckland formed a hosiery company in Sutton in Ashfield, Nottinghamshire, to manufacture and sell ladies stockings.

In 1927, Hibbert and Buckland took over a hosiery wholesaling company originally set up by a bookmaker's daughter. The bookmaker had prospered greatly from the legendary racehorse, Pretty Polly, and so had insisted that his daughter's business bear the same name.

Having acquired the name Pretty Polly, Hibbert and Buckland quickly built up the brand name under the famous parrot trademark. During the period, silk and rayon seamless stockings were in vogue, with fully fashioned stockings first appearing in 1924.

Nylon, invented in 1937, revolutionised the hosiery industry. The first nylon stockings were knitted under top secret conditions in America before the invention was officially announced a year later. Nylons first went on sale in 1940 restricted to three pairs per customer. The initial US stock of four million pairs was sold out in four days.

Meanwhile, Hibbert and Buckland had achieved an excellent reputation for high quality. Between 1932 and 1938, annual overall sales of fine-gauge hosiery increased to more than 48 million pairs in the UK.

After World War II Hibbert and Buckland expanded, aided by the introduction of nylon. In 1959 Pretty Polly introduced the first ever non-run seam-free stockings.

In March 1967 Pretty Polly invented and launched Hold Ups. These were instantly successful, freeing women from suspender belts. The product was such an overnight success that Pretty Polly became the number-one selling brand in the UK. Also in 1967, Pretty Polly launched new one-size stockings. These were followed in 1968 by Pretty Polly tights – an overwhelming success with the advent of the mini skirt.

The birth of the maxi skirt and revival of denim jeans in the early 1970s dictated a need for a different hosiery product. Pretty Polly responded with the Sheer Knee High. Throughout the decade Pretty Polly remained the hosiery innovator introducing the first low-cost high quality Support Tights, the first tights with knitted-in contrasting polyester body and cotton gusset, the first lightweight control brief, the first tights with combined control top and sheer support leg and the first Super Lightweight Support Tights in 15 denier nylon.

In 1982 Pretty Polly introduced LYCRA® into its 15 denier range and was the first hosiery brand to successfully combine ultrafine bare LYCRA® with a fine denier textured yarn giving a much improved fit for fashion hosiery.

At the close of the 1980s Pretty Polly became the first company in the world to produce five-denier hosiery.

Product

With many different styles to choose from in the current range, Pretty Polly has a proven track record of innovation, consistently producing stylish products of the highest quality to meet consumer demand.

Backed by continuing investment in machinery and yarn

technology and supported by creative marketing campaigns, Pretty Polly is committed to producing the very best in hosiery.

Pretty Polly has always aimed to get to know women and how they feel about hosiery. By commissioning its own research and combining it with trade data, Pretty Polly has got to the bottom of what women really want from their hosiery and has acted on it.

Pretty Polly products range from the basic to the designer. Archetypal ranges include the Naturals range of sheers to match the wearer's skin tone, Italia for 'party-girl' sheers, stockings and hold-ups, fun opaques for fashion shades and patterns and contemporary, daywear fashion.

Breakthrough ranges, such as the new Link Up range, create a modern way to wear stockings and reinforce Pretty Polly's strength for innovation. Creating ranges for designers, such as Julien Macdonald, permits more extravagant product development and gives consumers access to catwalk designer styles.

Recent Developments

2003 heralded the major repositioning of Pretty Polly with a total overhaul of its branding and targeting. First to change was the iconic logo, which was freshened up and curved to look more modern, young and fresh.

Branding on packs is constantly being updated to reflect these brand values with lifestyle images, as opposed to static photography, giving Pretty Polly strong standout against competitor packs which often feature more static images.

Innovation is vital to the continued success of any hosiery brand and this year Pretty Polly launched its truly innovative new range: Link Up. This product is the only one of its kind on the UK market that truly connects legwear to bodywear, freeing women from the hassles of suspender belts and stockings and giving them a smooth, clean line under clothes.

Seamless briefs, in key shapes, connect to different leg looks by use of one simple hook and further developments will take the range further into fashion giving women a complete choice.

Recently Pretty Polly has begun to collaborate with key designers to develop cutting-edge designs that lead Pretty Polly into the high-fashion end of the hosiery market, giving the brand a licence to break new boundaries.

Promotion

Advertising and marketing have always played an important part in building the Pretty Polly brand. Press campaigns have been used regularly throughout Pretty Polly's history, together with famous poster campaigns. Pretty Polly is also notable for its innovative use of television advertising, beginning in 1980 with the first-ever hosiery campaign. Pretty Polly has, since, consistently backed its ranges with memorable TV ads including Nylons, Legacy and Legworks.

In 1996 Pretty Polly made headline news with the first-ever vertical poster advertisements. The 'Long Legs' campaign was instrumental in putting the image and glamour back into the Pretty Polly brand. In autumn 1997, Pretty Polly launched Secret Slimmer with the most traffic-stopping advertising ever seen. Shapely model Miriam's dress disappeared to reveal the tummy-shaping tights on billboards across the country. Miriam herself launched the campaign, producing massive PR coverage on TV and in newspapers and magazines.

The same year saw Pretty Polly expand into new categories with the launch of Miss Polly's: tights for 5-12 year olds. A competition to find the face of Miss Polly's 97 ensured strong PR coverage for the brand.

The following year, Eva Herzigova became the new face and legs of Pretty Polly. She appeared in a national advertising campaign, on point-of-sale and in shop windows wearing nothing but Pretty Polly tights. This heralded the start of a national tour of Leg Clinics, where Pretty Polly gave advice to women on every aspect of legs and how to make them drop-dead gorgeous.

Renowned for its high impact, award-winning ads

 featuring impossibly long legs with an

amusing tagline, Pretty Polly ads have become iconic and even today people request pictures of old ads.

Proving ever-innovative, Pretty Polly has moved with the times to concentrate its communications on iconic women who embody the brand values and have always been stars of the time. From Eva Herzigova (New York Legs) to Sara Cox (All Day Up) to Jemma Kidd (Perfectly Naturals). The current face of the brand is R&B singer Jamelia. Using such high-profile stars ensures vast media coverage, which allows the brand to communicate its core messages for each product.

Brand Values

Part of the national heritage, Pretty Polly is a UK brand that has dressed many generations of British women.

Today, it is aimed at 15-35 year old females and aims to be seen as spontaneous, friendly, fashionable, vibrant, young and trendy. In essence, Pretty Polly is a brand that fun-loving girls can relate to: it is all about sexy prettiness and boosting confidence.

www.prettypolly.co.uk

Pretty Polly

❯ Pretty Polly has the highest brand awareness of any female brand in the UK.

❯ Pretty Polly sells 30 pairs of tights a minute.

❯ The first product of their kind, Hold Ups appeared on Tomorrow's World in 1967.

❯ Known for daring, innovative campaigns, Pretty Polly 'longest legs' adverts were almost banned as they caused car accidents with drivers looking at the billboards instead of the road.

❯ Pretty Polly is synonymous with beautiful women, and in 2005 signed the first black face of Pretty Polly, R+B diva Jamelia.

PRUDENTIAL

Market

The financial services market has undergone rapid change over recent years. In the past decade there have been many new entrants to the market, from online banking operations to supermarkets and other businesses with large customer bases and wide-scale consolidation.

One of the greatest challenges to both providers and consumers is the 'savings gap'. With people now living longer and a smaller proportion of the population in full-time work, responsibility for funding a comfortable retirement is shifting from the state to individuals. But according to the Pensions' Commission, 12 million people are either not saving at all, or not saving enough for their old age.

It has been estimated by the Association of British Insurers that there is a £27 billion gap between what the public is saving and what they would need to put aside for an adequate retirement income.

Achievements

Prudential is one of the UK's leading life and pensions providers, with operations in the UK, Europe, the US and Asia.

In January 2005, Prudential earned accreditation under the Raising Standards quality mark scheme for the fourth consecutive year. In February, it was awarded Best TV Advertisement by MoneyMarketing magazine. This was followed by the Money£acts Innovation Award in March for its PruFund product.

2004 saw Prudential win a range of awards, including Best Pension Provider, as voted by the readers of What Investment magazine, Most Competitive Annuity Provider of the Year (for the second consecutive year) and Best With-Profits Bond, both awarded by Money£acts, and the Insurance Times Award for Best Call Centre (for Prudential's general insurance call centre, operated by UKI).

In 2003 Prudential also won a wide range of awards, most notably Gold and Silver Echo awards for its 'Plan from the Pru' campaigns.

History

Prudential has been in business for more than 150 years. It was established in 1848 as the Prudential Mutual Assurance

Investment and Loan Association in Hatton Garden, London, offering loans and life assurance to professional people.

Six years later, industrial life assurance was introduced to provide 'penny policies' for working people. Following this, in 1856, Prudential pioneered policies that allow parents to assure the lives of children under the age of 10.

The company took several innovative steps over the following years. In 1871 it became the first in the City of London to employ female clerks. In the same year, calculation machines were introduced to save time with processing an increasing volume of business.

By the end of the 1870s Prudential had moved into Holborn Bars, a purpose built office complex designed by Alfred Waterhouse. The building quickly became a popular architectural landmark and today remains an integral part of Prudential's property portfolio.

Prudential continued to grow after the move and, by 1900, a third of the UK population was insured with Prudential. Total assets exceeded £40 million, confirming the company's status as a 'national institution'.

Following the National Insurance Act in 1912, Prudential worked with the Government to run Approved Societies, providing sickness and unemployment benefits to five million people.

At the beginning of the 1920s, the first overseas life branch was established in India, with the first policy being sold to a tea planter in Assam. This period also saw Prudential's shares being floated on the London Stock Exchange and Group Pensions being established, which built on expertise gained from Prudential's own staff pension scheme.

Prudential continued to expand its horizons. Significantly, in 1997, Prudential acquired Scottish Amicable Life to strengthen its role in the IFA market. The following year Egg was created as a radical new internet-based financial services company that has grown to become a strong brand it its own right.

In 1999 Prudential acquired M&G, who had pioneered unit trusts in the UK and were the leading provider of investment products. In the following year Prudential plc was listed on the New York Stock Exchange.

In 2002 Prudential took stock of the public's views on financial services and launched 'The Plan from the Pru' in the UK, a major new advertising campaign illustrating the importance of undertaking financial planning at every stage of life.

Product

In the UK, Prudential specialises in providing pensions, savings and investments and protection products, distributed direct to customers (telephone, internet and mail), through financial advisers and employers and through partnerships (affinities and banks).

It offers a range of financial services and products to businesses and consumers, including life assurance, pensions, annuities, investments and lifetime mortgages.

It also provides general insurance, operated by UKI, and health insurance under the PruHealth brand through a joint venture between Prudential UK

and a leading South African healthcare provider, Discovery Holdings.

Recent Developments
Prudential's brand re-launch in autumn 2002, introducing 'The Plan from the Pru' (PFTP), is one of its most significant recent developments. The objective was to announce the launch of this new approach and raise awareness of the new proposition around the PFTP. The media strategy focused on building high levels of coverage and impact (heavyweight national TV, consecutive colour pages in newspapers, large formats on outdoor and Newslink and Classic FM radio stations).

Following the re-launch, the 2003 and 2004 strategy was designed to reach a much more tightly defined group of people (broadly those aged 45+, interested in reviewing their savings and investments).

Another significant recent development was the launch of PruHealth in October 2004, a joint venture combining Prudential's brand and distribution strength in the UK and Discovery's product, underwriting and management expertise for private medical care.

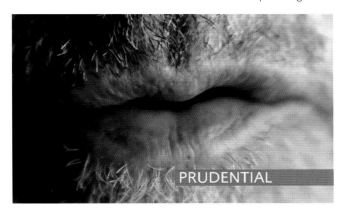

PruHealth's revolutionary philosophy is to reward people who make efforts to lead a healthy lifestyle with lower premiums. Members are able to reduce the cost of their health insurance in a variety of ways such as annual health assessments, joining a gym or giving up smoking.

Promotion
Historically, Prudential has high levels of awareness, coupled with a strong heritage. 'The Man from the Pru', which was first used as an advertising image in 1949, had been a household phrase since the turn of the century. Until recently he remained as the public face of Prudential. Over the years the image was gradually updated, the suit changed to match the fashion of the day and the

hat disappeared. This key symbol has been developed rather than replaced in recent years.

After almost a decade away from mainstream above-the-line communication, Prudential needed to restore some of the closeness and familiarity that people felt towards 'The Man from the Pru', making the brand more top-of-mind and increasing its relevance to a public now concerned about providing for their retirement for themselves.

This thinking led to the creation of 'The Plan from the Pru', which reinvented 'The Man from the Pru' and rebuilt the relationship he had previously established with consumers. It cut through financial jargon and communicated with both new and existing customers on their level, showing that Prudential understands the issues and fears that consumers face when considering their financial futures.

Poetry was used in a campaign which invited consumers to 'get themselves a Plan from the Pru'. It was designed to touch a nerve with consumers and help them associate themselves with the words of the particular poem. In addition, other media such as TV, radio, national press, poster ads and direct mail were used to provide more information about 'The Plan from the Pru'.

2004 and 2005 campaigns focused on promoting Prudential's financial strength and stability, to reinforce its standing as a major player in the financial arena. This was portrayed through solid facts that demonstrated the company's size, financial strength and investment expertise.

Educating people about the world of financial services by bringing it to life in an interesting and unusual way was also important. In 2004 and 2005 Prudential looked beyond conventional advertising to find a way of stimulating people's interest in financial services. 'Composer's Notes', Prudential and Classic FM's series looking at how money influenced the lives, loves and successes of our greatest classical composers, was one key strategy, while Prudential's 2004 and 2005 sponsorship of Michael Parkinson's TV show further stimulated public interest. Parkinson is known for his honest, approachable and warm personality and truly personifies Prudential's 'straightforward' tone of voice.

Brand Values
Prudential's aim is 'to make it possible for everyone to enjoy a secure future'.

To achieve this, the brand is working to deliver a set of values – 'trustworthy', 'helpful' and 'easy'. The brand also aims to hold these together with an internal as well as external atmosphere of 'honest dialogue'. This sentiment is captured in 'The Plan from the Pru', creating a very human brand which is unusual in the world of financial services.

Prudential is also considered sensible and secure, prudent and deliberate. It strives to be perceived as a risk-averse financial institution that has an obligation to provide a better future for its customers.

The PFTP is about simplification, being straightforward and optimistic; values that easily translate into more fruitful working practices and office environments.

www.pru.co.uk

THINGS YOU DIDN'T KNOW ABOUT

Prudential

> Prudential has seven million customers in the UK and 16 million worldwide.

> In 2004 alone, 250,000 Pru customers were invited to the company's monthly 'MeetPru' events, where they had the opportunity to speak face to face with chief executive Mark Wood and other members of the executive team.

> Prudential conducts an annual Retirement Index survey, examining the realities of financial life for the 10 million plus retired people in Britain.

> Prudential's AA+ financial strength rating from Standard and Poor's is unbeaten by any other UK life company.

> Prudential UK employs 6,200 full time staff.

Market

Throughout history, people have indulged in bathing for many different purposes – not just to get clean – but for religious reasons, health purposes and pleasure too. It isn't known exactly when bathing for pleasure first began but there is evidence to suggest it was as early as the times of prehistoric man.

Despite this legendary history, bathing certainly isn't stuck in the past. The UK washing and bathing market was worth a huge £523 million at the beginning of 2005 (Source: IRI) and has seen great developments in the use and variety of products, in the bath, shower, body wash, bar soap and liquid handwash segments.

These developments have been rewarded with continuing growth in the shower and liquid handwash segments, with shares up +4.1% and +7% respectively by January 2005 (Source: IRI).

Achievements

Sara Lee is the number one manufacturer in washing and bathing with a 19% share. Radox, the UK's favourite washing and bathing brand, accounts for 14.2% of this share, and has shown growth of almost 200% during the past 10 years.

The brand's core Radox Herbal Bath range is the market leader with a 21.8% share, while Radox Shower leads in its category with 15.2% (Source: IRI).

Radox has also achieved success internationally, holding leading positions in South Africa and Australia, with consistent year-on-year growth.

Yet it's not just in terms of market share that Radox is number one, but also with regard to innovation. Radox was the first in the market to develop both bubble bath and shower gel, the first to develop the Proven-To-Relax formulations in Radox Herbal Bath, as well as the first to introduce the hook-shaped bottle to its Radox Shower range in 1975 (which many other brands across the globe have adopted since, as a popular packaging choice for shower products), and the first to introduce the innovative non-drip valve to its Radox Shower packaging in 1993.

In recognition of Radox's commitment to innovation, the Radox GoodNight range was voted winner of its category in the 2004 Product of the Year awards.

Consumer and trade magazines have also recognised the brand. Pure Beauty magazine voted Radox Herbal Bath winner of the 'mass bathing category' in its 2004 awards, and the recently launched Radox Aromatic Bath Essences range was awarded Silver in the 'Best Aromatherapy range' category in the 2004 Pure Beauty magazine awards. In addition, Radox Spoil Me Aromatic Bath Essence was chosen by celebrity singer Javine for the bath/shower category in the 2004/05 Bliss magazine Beauty Awards.

History

Radox first appeared in the UK market early in the 20th century as a salts foot bath that 'RADiated OXygen' – hence the name. The white powder in a pink packet with a strong perfume was the brainchild of Harry Marland, who worked for the Griffiths Hughes Company. There is some belief that the salts were initially launched to help weary soldiers bathe their feet on returning from war.

By 1957 Radox was known as a relaxing bath – still in a salts format – to be enjoyed after sport, gardening or other physical activities. In 1960 the brand passed into the ownership of Aspro-Nicholas and in the following years underwent a period of product development where new fragrances, colours and herb extracts were added and Radox Salts rapidly became one of the leading products in the market. It was heavily advertised on national television, concentrating on hard water areas, with the slogan 'Relax in a Radox bath'.

By the end of the 1960s, the Radox brand was moving forward rapidly. The marketing team looked at the liquid market, which at the time consisted solely of luxury priced products such as Badedas and Fenjal, so liquid Radox was developed as an easier and better format to use in the bath. A radical frothing agent was also introduced to deliver a foaming bath. It was first marketed as a blue liquid version of Radox Salts, emphasising the herbal extracts and the relaxing effects of a Radox bath, still using the slogan 'Relax in a Radox Bath'. It was an immediate success. It was voted one of the ten most successful products to be launched in the grocery trade in its first year and created a totally new sector: the mainstream liquid bath additive market.

The range was developed to bring in different variants and Radox gained brand leadership, despite being imitated by every own-label supplier, and has remained brand leader ever since. The brand became a product for general bathroom use and between 1960 and 1975 Radox sales had expanded over thirteen-fold.

On the strength of this success, further areas of development were assessed. In the mid 1970s, there was a move towards showers, with the increasing number of showers being installed in the nation's homes. Radox Shower was launched as a product with its defining hook – specifically developed to hang in the shower. This brand extension really took off in the 1980s, by which time the use of showers was more widespread in the UK.

The basis for the success of the Radox brand was adding value. The therapeutic elements have always been key, along with the fragrances and the added power of water. The Radox brand has built on its heritage of being a trusted and efficacious brand with a background in herbs and minerals.

Product

Radox recognises that people bathe for many different reasons; to ease aches and pains, to help change their mood, to relax and de-stress, to aid sleep, to revive the senses or to indulge in some 'me time' pampering. As with bathing, Radox also appreciates that people have varying needs from a shower depending on who they are and what they are doing.

Radox has built on its herbal heritage to develop an expansive core product range to suit a wide range of everyday washing and bathing needs and mood states. Renowned for its ability to help change the way bathers feel both mentally and physically, Radox has developed its bath, shower and handwash ranges by

selecting, blending and testing the most mood enhancing and therapeutic combination of natural herbs and minerals. In addition to the core unisex shower range, there is also a sub range of three variants for men, called 'Refuel'.

For a more luxurious pampering experience, there's Solutions – Radox's premium range of four foaming bath essences that combine natural ingredients renowned for their therapeutic benefits with a specific blend of essential oils.

Radox also appreciates real-life issues, including the impact that the stresses and worries of modern life can cause, such as the increase in mild insomnia. In response to this problem and the growing number of people that need help getting to sleep, Radox launched GoodNight, a range of specially developed products designed to help prepare your body for a good night's sleep. Each product (Comforting Bath Soak, Body Wash, Body Moisturiser, and Pillow Spray) contains Lavender and Chamomile, renowned for their sleep inducing properties and is produced in association with the Sleep Council.

On top of continuing brand developments and expansions, Radox Salts – the original core of Radox – still have a fond place in the hearts of many consumers. The range consists of two variants, Muscle Soak and Vapour Therapy.

Recent Developments

In August 2004, the Radox bath range was re-launched comprising the six favourite Herbal Bath variants, each with a new formulation containing a blend of natural herbs and minerals and even more bubbles, in a new modern bottle shape. According to the botanist, biologist and author of 'All about Herbs' Roger Tabor: "The popularity of herbal products has massively increased over the last few years, and consequently many know and trust this type of product. However, not only has Radox used herbal extracts for a long time, but it has chosen its signature herbs wisely for their individual properties."

Radox also added four new Aromatic Bath Essences to the range, which, while still based on herbal materials, have turned to the more exotic spectrum of botanics such as Jasmine and Ylang Ylang to appeal to women looking for a more indulgent bathing experience. Luxurious Gentle Embrace was also added to the Solutions range in time for Christmas 2004.

April 2005 saw Radox Shower radically re-launched in a new modern translucent pack that still has its convenient hook for hanging in the shower, but that also tucks away to fit tidily in a wash bag or bathroom cabinet. There are eight shower variants in the core range, each with its own signature herb and new skin-friendly formulations in softer colours.

At the same time, the brand re-launched its handwash range also in a modern translucent pack, with improved graphics and clearer communication of benefits. There are six variants to choose from, based on different hand washing needs, and to suit different rooms in the home.

Promotion

TV advertising leads Radox's promotional activity with new campaigns aired every year to communicate the brand message. The latest 'Radox, that's better' campaign features separate adverts for Radox bath and shower ranges. The adverts show individuals transforming and 'feeling better' while taking their Radox bath/shower. The transformation includes reflection on all the events that have taken place during their 'less than brilliant day'. The bathroom in each case changes to look like a Broadway stage, with the day's events performed in the style of a musical. It is expected to be highly effective at delivering brand growth and represents the brand's highest-ever TV spend.

TV advertising is supported by a mix of below-the-line activities based on strategies for the year ahead. The strategy includes an ongoing public relations campaign to deliver a consistent, integrated and continual brand presence throughout the year, to support new product launches.

Brand Values

The strength of the Radox brand has been attributed to the importance placed on building a strong emotional engagement with consumers. Radox has a universal appeal, derived from its reliability, effectiveness and its image as a mainstream, everyday brand. In addition, the efficacious ingredients in the products are of a high quality. There is a real sense of the brand having been passed through the generations.

Radox is in the enviable position of being trusted to improve the way people feel, and some consumers even claim their doctors have recommended it as a remedy for tension.

Radox also prides itself on its ability to change with the times, first seen more than 30 years ago with the introduction of shower gel with the first hook pack, followed by the first non-drip valve. Since this point Radox has produced effective innovations such as the Solutions, GoodNight and Aromatic ranges.

www.radox.com

Market

More than 5.6 million people in the UK roll their own tobacco (Source: TGI) and, with more than three quarters of UK roll-your-own smokers choosing to use Rizla papers (Source: ACNielsen), the brand is truly synonymous with the rolling papers category.

Achievements

Rizla is a global brand, performing as the world's market leading paper and available in more than 120 countries worldwide. In the UK, four out of five rolling paper booklets sold are Rizla.

Total sales of Rizla papers are in excess of 330 million booklets per year, more than 15 billion leaves of papers.

To date, more than 300 varieties of papers have appeared under the Rizla marque.

History

Rizla is the original rolling paper, Pierre de Lacroix, founder of the family business that went on to define the roll-your-own papers market over the following four centuries, began making paper in 1532.

In 1660, the Lacroix family began producing rolling papers for tobacco in the Dordogne.

Surviving huge political and economic upheaval in France throughout the French Revolution and Napoleonic Wars, the brand survived and, by 1850, the manufacture of rolling papers as a mass-market product was finally perfected.

The Rizla brand name was first registered – as Riz-La+ – in 1866, and is derived from 'riz', referring to the rice paper used at the time and 'la+', an enigmatic abbreviation of the founding family's name: Lacroix. In 1954, the brand lost its gap and became 'Rizla+.' which it has been ever since.

During the late 1800s and early 1900s Rizla was honoured with a series of world trade awards. The first Rizla Blue was introduced in 1910 and the first rolling machine in 1928. With the introduction of gummed paper during the 1940s Rizla went from strength to strength, consolidating its position as the world's favourite rolling paper.

In 1928, Rizla embarked on a music strategy with the development of the 'Rizla Musical Van' and its 1,500 watts of broadcasting power. The van toured cities in the UK, broadcasting the biggest names of the time; Gracie Fields, Ernest Hastings and Robert Radford to name just a few. Music has been a core ingredient of Rizla's success ever since.

With the first King Size Rizla launched in 1977, the brand continued to innovate to meet the demands of the modern smoker, liquorice papers followed in 1981 to cater for a key consumer taste.

In 1999, more innovation based on consumers' preference for thinner, longer and slimmer papers meant Rizla King Size Slim hit the market with a key strategic launch in London, followed by roll out to the rest of the UK market six months later.

Four years later, Rizla Silver was launched, raising the standards of premium rolling papers to the next level, with its 'regular' version hitting the market in October 2004.

Product

The beauty of the roll-your-own category is the level of choice offered to the consumer. From the vast array of loose tobaccos available on the market and the choice of different weights, widths and lengths of paper, the consumer expresses his taste and personality through the choice he makes over tobacco and papers.

Choice is key and the Rizla range offers something for every type of smoker. From the ubiquitous Green papers through to Liquorice Regular, the varying weights, burn rates, cut, length and gum, ensures that Rizla is at the forefront of rolling paper development.

As of March 2005, the Rizla range included Rizla Regular papers in Green, Red, Blue, Silver, Liquorice & White, Rizla King Size Green, Red & Blue, Rizla King Size Slim Blue & Silver. Complementing the papers is a choice of rolling machines and filter tips.

Produced out of factories all over the world, Rizla is one of the most widely available products in the UK. Trading through varied channels from local corner shops to major multiple grocers, distribution of Rizla is key to the success of the brand. By offering customers a trusted product, through as many touch points as possible, Rizla is proud to be ubiquitous.

As technology has improved, Rizla has been able to push the boundaries of paper production to create some of the most advanced rolling papers in the world.

Recent Developments

The launch of Rizla King Size Slim Silver in 2003 illustrates the brand's leading edge position in the rolling papers category. Rizla King Size Slim Silver is an ultra-thin paper, so allowing the full flavour of the tobacco to be appreciated. This premium product has the brand logo and crest watermarked on to the papers and quality silver packaging.

The launch was supported through all channels including limited edition clothing designed by Mrs Jones, who designs clothes for celebrities such as Madonna and Kylie.

As well as outdoor and lifestyle press advertising, the Rizla-Suzuki Superbike Team deserted the established 'Rizla-Blue' identity and turned up in a new silver livery for the bikes, riders, leathers, garage, hospitality area and so on.

A direct mail campaign sent to smokers of papers and premium cigarette brands offered consumers this new pioneering product before it hit the market, giving consumers social currency and generating immediate word of mouth.

Promotion

The brand is endowed with such a rich heritage that the challenge is how to take it forward and continue to innovate through communications as well as new products.

As the consumer landscape changes, Rizla must constantly evolve its branding and promotional strategy to ensure it strikes the correct tone in the marketplace.

Print and outdoor advertising is a key awareness driver for the brand. The creation and subsequent launch of the 'What You Make of It' campaign by long-term Rizla agency Ladders has ensured that the irreverent tone of the brand has a share of voice in leading lifestyle media and key urban conurbations. The campaign features a well-known phrase or saying in

a colourful and incongruent setting for the iconic Rizla pack.

For a brand such as Rizla, ambient and PR activity will always be a key promotional tool. Ensuring that the brand fits and appears in the right arenas has been a constant challenge.

Rizla's involvement in music can be traced back to the early days of the Rizla Musical Van but undertaking a strategic involvement in the music scene began in earnest in the late 1990s with the development of the Rizla Café.

The Café formed a major part of the PR campaign for a number of years. Providing a warm, clean, comfortable haven in environments that are often cold and wet, such as the Glastonbury Festival, Rizla was pioneering in this imaginative form of communication.

A shift in direction came with the appointment of creative consultancy Exposure. By interrogating Rizla's positioning, the brand team and agency developed a new strategy for 2004 based on inspiration which saw the launch of Rizla's 'inspired-by' creative proposition.

'inspired-by' was developed to align the brand's values with a tangible offering to Rizla's core target audience. Inspiration provides such a rich vein of thought for so many; it was felt it would be the perfect positioning for a brand of Rizla's standing.

Inspiration runs true through music, film, art and the like, key touch points for Rizla consumers. The latent affection held by many for the brand ensures that Rizla is welcomed into these arenas, especially when the brand acts as an enabler and catalyst for experiences not normally available to the average consumer.

One such example is Rizla's 'inspired-by' Tour. Now in its second year, the tour champions new music. It is unique in that it is all about celebrating iconic inspirational figures from the past and present through the talent of today.

Events in 2004 included Ash at the Astoria in London playing Thin Lizzy's 'The Boys Are Back In Town' and the Undertones 'Teenage Kicks' as a tribute to the late Radio One DJ John Peel.

Already in 2005, the 'inspired-by' proposition has been developed further with a partnership with the world-renowned music magazine NME that saw the creation of the 'inspired-by Rizla Award' at the prestigious annual NME awards. It also led to the

co-production of the NME New Music 'inspired-by Rizla Tour' featuring seven hot new bands and 12 nights of new music.

The 'inspired-by' concept is a proposition that can develop and grow since it is not limited to one specific area and is set to continue into 2006 and beyond.

2005 sees the brand venture yet further into music with a comprehensive strategy that takes in the electronic scene.

The 'inspired-by' Rizla Silver tour is set to celebrate dance/electro/crossover technical pioneers and innovators, past and present, in sophisticated environments. Visiting five UK cities the tour will showcase some of the best DJs and producers in the UK.

The Silver proposition was brought about to celebrate the launch of Rizla Regular Silver. By continuing to push boundaries technologically in paper production, as well as creatively through promotional and brand activity, Rizla has been able to reinvent itself time and time again.

Rizla has a long history with music festivals and, during 2005, has been back outdoors during the summer season with some limited edition 'inspired-by festivals' Rizla packs. Aimed at creating mass awareness amongst a core target audience, the limited edition packs will draw on Rizla's tongue in cheek style with three looks for three different festivals.

A mud-splattered look will be hitting Glastonbury, the 'Legends' pack will debut on the Isle of Wight and in rock style the 'Gatecrash' look will be breaking into Download.

Rizla recognises the high penetration of paper users interested in motor sport, specifically motorbikes, through its successful sponsorship of the Rizla-Suzuki British Superbikes Team.

With the ongoing presence of Team Rizla-Suzuki in the British Superbike Championships 2005, Rizla continues to strengthen its position in this area. With British Superbikes being fast-paced, colourful and accessible, the sport matches with the Rizla brand and its commitment to two-wheel sport, music and arts.

Rizla was awarded the prestigious 'Best Brand Sponsorship' award by Hollis in 2004, a reflection of

rizla.co.uk

RIZLA+ It's what you make of it.

a champion brand that continues to lead the rolling papers category through innovation and communication.

Underpinning all of Rizla's promotional activity is an online strategy that has seen the development of rich content websites via Rizla's online agency Sense. The online strategy continues at www.rizla.co.uk and is supporting the 'inspired by' positioning with the www.inspired-by.co.uk site.

Brand Values
The Rizla brand's rich heritage provides it with strong foundations from which to evolve and innovate in order to retain loyal consumers and attract new ones. Its colourful, down-to-earth and irreverent brand values have been with it since its inception almost five centuries ago and they continue to serve the brand well to this day.

www.rizla.co.uk

Established in Switzerland 1895

Market

In 2004 the UK watch market was valued at £786 million, with 15.8 million watches being sold annually. This is according to GfK, the leading market research provider, which tracks the UK watch market via a consumer panel.

The majority of Rotary's product range spans the £100-£200 price bracket and, in this sector of the market, the mid-market, Rotary dominates with a 22% market share by value, almost twice that of its nearest competitor.

In this price band, key competitors are Seiko and Tissot as well as more recent fashion entrants such as Armani.

Achievements

In the annual UK Jewellery Awards administered by RJ Magazine, the leading trade title for the watch and jewellery industry, Rotary has been a consistent victor, winning the Volume Watch Brand of the Year title in 1998, the Watch Supplier of the Year award for two consecutive years in 2002 and 2003 and was a finalist for the Watch of the Year Award in 2004.

The coveted Supplier of the Year award reflects the immense level of investment that has been undertaken by Rotary to ensure that it sets standards of supply and service that surpass all expectations. In 2000 Rotary launched the trade's first and only B2B trade website, allowing retailers to order online with guaranteed delivery the following day for orders placed before 4pm.

Not only did this set new standards of customer service but it provided transparency in the form of online stock availability, which is updated in real-time via data links to the company's management information system, online statements and invoices, service and repair tracking as well as spare parts ordering.

The same trade title, RJ Magazine, runs a monthly retailers' poll by telephone of 200 retailers to ascertain the bestselling brands. Rotary has the distinction of topping this retailers' poll of bestselling watch brands for 24 months in succession.

In addition, Rotary Revelation™ was voted 'Watch of the Year' by the duty free title TFWA in 2004, while Rotary was runner up in the watch category of Maxim magazine's Style Awards in 2004.

History

It was in 1895 that Moise Dreyfuss began making timepieces in a small workshop in the Swiss town of La Chaux-de-Fonds. For more than a century Rotary Watches has preserved this heritage, crafting watches with the same quality materials and testing each watch to ensure it can withstand the rigours of everyday life.

Demand for good value, quality merchandise ensured the business grew quickly and within 12 years, Georges and Sylvain Dreyfuss, two of Moise Dreyfuss' three sons, opened an office in Britain to import the family watches.

The company continued to grow and, in 1925, they introduced the now famous Rotary logo, the 'winged wheel'. In the 1940s Rotary was appointed as official watch supplier to the British army.

Almost 50 years later, in 1985, the Swiss business and its trademarks, with the exception of the rights for the UK and Gibraltar, were sold. But in 1992 Rotary UK bought the trademarks back and now owns the right to use the trademark worldwide.

One watch, two unique looks

REVELATION™

LS02901/07/19 £299.00

ACHIEVE TWO VERY DIFFERENT LOOKS WITH ONE WATCH! SIMPLY ROTATE THE FACE TO TURN DAY INTO NIGHT. SWISS MADE, STAINLESS STEEL, STONE SET, LEATHER STRAP WATCH WITH SAPPHIRE GLASS, TWO MOVEMENTS AND TWO DIFFERENT FACES. ONE GLAMOROUS STONE SET LOOK FOR EVENINGS WITH A BLACK ARABIC DIAL AND THE OTHER A MOTHER OF PEARL ROMAN DIAL MORE SUITED FOR DAYTIME WEAR. THE TWO MOVEMENTS ALLOW THE WEARER TO MAINTAIN TWO DISTINCT TIME ZONES

ROTARY
Established in Switzerland 1895

FOR YOUR COPY OF OUR LATEST BROCHURE CALL 08705 100846 OR VISIT WWW.ROTARYWATCHES.COM. FOR STOCKISTS INFORMATION CALL +44 (0)207 434 7546

ROTARY
Established in Switzerland 1895

ROTARY REVELATION™ TWO FACES, TWO TIMES... ONE WATCH

GS02901/01/04 £299.00

SWISS MADE STAINLESS STEEL CASE, WITH LEATHER STRAP, TWO QUARTZ MOVEMENTS AND SCRATCH RESISTANT SAPPHIRE GLASS
FOR A COPY OF OUR LATEST BROCHURE CALL 08705 100846 OR VISIT WWW.ROTARYWATCHES.COM

Many of the world's most famous watchmakers started as family firms. Most have grown into vast conglomerates, losing touch with the traditions of their founders. Rotary has remained in the same family for four generations. In 1987 Robert Dreyfuss, now chairman, joined the company becoming the fourth generation of the Dreyfuss family to run the company.

Rotary continually invests heavily in new product development, staff training and leading information technology to ensure it stays one step ahead of the competition.

Product

Rotary's product range is specifically a dress watch range, offering ladies and gents contemporary classic styles at affordable prices. The core range is priced from £85-£329 with 9ct and 18ct gold ranges increasing to £1,600.

Unique to Rotary is the 'Rotary Revelation™', which offers two movements and two different dials in a rotating case. Ideal for globetrotters who can not only maintain two distinct time zones when travelling but can have the option of choosing from two different dial designs. In the UK this retails from £299.

The Rotary Revelation™ is also available in a ladies' version, in which one dial is a black stone-set design for glamorous evening wear and the other is a simple, white roman design, created with daywear in mind. The Rotary Revelation™ is stainless steel and, of course, Swiss made. In 2005, the range is expanding to include a new round shaped Rotary Revelation which is expected to be a huge success for the company.

In 2004, Rotary launched the ladies 'Sofia' watch. With a unique patented design, 'Sofia' morphs effortlessly from a stone-set watch to a non-stone-set watch courtesy of retractable side bars. A simple release button on the case back allows the wearer to pop the stones out and then simply push them back in again. This mechanism allows the total versatility of choosing either a daytime or an evening look – it acts as two watches in one.

In 2003, Rotary launched the first of four special Limited Edition models. Limited to just 500 worldwide, each piece is individually engraved on the case back with the series number and comes with a signed authenticity certificate. For a price tag of £300, the consumer is assured of a Swiss-made watch with an automatic movement, scratch resistant sapphire glass and stainless steel, complete with a beautiful oak-wood watch-winder box.

Recent Developments

In 2005 Rotary launched the Dolphin standard of waterproof watches. Unique for a number of reasons, not least because the standard marks a move away from the complex and confusing system of water resistance criteria to which the rest of industry subscribes. Dolphin delivers what consumers want; namely a simple promise 'Swim and dive all day'.

The other revolutionary feature of the Dolphin standard is that, unlike most competitor brands which reserve water-resistance features for a limited number of chunky sporty models, Rotary has applied the Dolphin standard to virtually its entire range – remarkable considering the range is purely a dress watch range.

SOFIA
'Day before night, business before pleasure'
One watch, with retractable stones; two unique looks

ROTARY
Established in Switzerland 1895

A NEW COLLECTION OF
LIMITED EDITION WATCHES
RESTRICTED TO 500 PIECES WORLDWIDE

A Limited Edition automatic watch exclusively for you from Rotary Watches
• Limited to 500 pieces worldwide
• Complimentary self winding, hand crafted, oak-wood presentation box
• Unique authenticity certificate • Each piece is engraved with a limited edition number
Swiss made, stainless steel watch with automatic movement, sapphire glass and water resistant to 30 metres.
LE00004/12 £300.00   www.rotarywatches.com

'Business Builder' is Rotary's trade programme that revolutionises the way the watch and jewellery industry works. Launched in 2003, 'Business Builder' is a new approach to managing stock and ordering and is recommended by Rotary's sales team to increase turnover and profit, improve cash flow and reduce levels of working capital.

The programme encourages independent retailers to carry a core range, viewable on Rotary's business to business website and order little and often so that sales follow demand. In return, Rotary guarantees stock availability the following day right up till Christmas Eve.

For Rotary this has meant working to halve the lead-time in its supply chain. The results have been very successful, with retailers on the 'Business Builder' programme enjoying growth of on average 10% points higher than retailers who have remained true to the industry norm of placing large orders just two or three times throughout the year.

Promotion

Rotary does not sell direct to consumers. Rather, the company supplies the trade and, as such, is committed to a major programme of trade marketing encompassing teams of field trainers who use state-of-the-art multi-media training CDs to make staff training fun and interactive.

In terms of above-the-line activity, Rotary uses a combination of press advertising and PR to communicate to its target audience, choosing to focus creative executions on anchor products such as 'Rotary Revelation' and 'Sofia'.

In 2003, Rotary reached its target of £100,000 raised for The Prince's Trust charity via a series of charity auctions. Celebrities from stage, screen and sport including Liz Hurley, Ewan McGregor,

Lennox Lewis, Tim Henman and Geri Halliwell, as well as players from Leeds United, Tottenham Hotspur, Manchester City and Glasgow Rangers, came together to paint plates that were turned into wall mounted clocks and auctioned at various high-profile venues including the Groucho Club and the Beaufort Polo Club.

Brand Values

While many of the world's most famous watchmakers started as small family firms, most have now grown into vast corporations, losing touch with the traditions of their founders. Rotary, however, has remained in the Dreyfuss family for four generations and prides itself on its tradition of family watchmaking using the strapline 'Where watchmaking is still a family affair'. Indeed, the essence of the brand is: heritage, know-how, value for money, quality, longevity and innovation.

www.rotarywatches.com

Market

Pottery and ceramics are a strong indicator of the art and lifestyle of a given age. Indeed, archaeologists rely on shards of pottery fragments to establish the level of sophistication of past civilisations.

Today's consumers are more demanding and discerning than ever before. The rise in home entertainment has been matched by the introduction of contemporary, functional tableware. At the other end of the spectrum, however, the decrease in traditional family meals and rise in solo eating, TV dinners and convenience foods has seen companies extend their casual tableware ranges.

Withstanding market fragmentation, ceramic giftware has enjoyed considerable growth – gift-giving, home decoration and investment being the main motivations. Despite the introduction of many alternative forms of gifts, the ceramic form is sought after as offering true qualities of heritage, craftsmanship and real, long lasting value for money.

The key markets worldwide for premium ceramic tableware and giftware are the UK and Continental Europe, North America, Asia Pacific and Australasia.

Achievements

The Royal Doulton Company is one of the world's largest manufacturers and distributors in the premium ceramic tableware and giftware market. Its illustrious brand names include Minton, Royal Albert and the core Royal Doulton brand.

With 200 years of heritage, The Royal Doulton Company is a thriving global organisation, with around £102 million annual turnover, employing around 2,800 people across its production sites and numerous distribution operations worldwide. Approximately half of all sales are generated overseas.

The Royal Doulton Company is a market leader within the ceramics and chinaware markets around the world.

The company's Hotel and Airline division is also one of the world's largest suppliers of bone china to the international airlines industry. Indicative of its continuing favour, the division holds major contracts to supply chinaware to British Airways Club World and Club Europe.

The company's Hotelware division supplies some of the most prestigious addresses in London, including 10 Downing Street, Buckingham Palace, The Savoy Hotel, The Ritz and Claridges.

In total, The Royal Doulton Company offers a range of 6,000 different items across a broad range of product groups.

History

The Royal Doulton Company has been producing ceramics and tableware for 200 years. As far back as 1815 the company founder, John Doulton, began producing practical and decorative stoneware from a small pottery in Lambeth, South London.

His son, Henry Doulton, built up the business, relocating it 60 years later to Stoke-on-Trent. By 1901 the quality of Doulton's tableware had caught the eye of King Edward VII, who permitted the company to prefix its name with 'Royal' and the company was awarded the Royal Warrant.

The Royal Doulton Company expanded its production facilities and by the 1930s was involved in the manufacture of figurines and giftware. The company was awarded the Queen's Award for Technical Achievement in 1966, for its contribution to china manufacturing – the first china manufacturer to be honoured with this award.

In 1972, Royal Doulton was bought by Pearson and merged with Allied English Potteries.

In 1993, The Royal Doulton Company was demerged from Pearson and became a publicly quoted company listed on the London Stock Exchange.

Today, Royal Doulton is part of the Waterford Wedgwood Group.

Product

Each of the company's principal brands – Royal Doulton, Minton and Royal Albert – enjoy a long association of royal patronage, and hold at least one Royal Warrant. They are also trademark registered.

When drawing up new product design, the designers study the market, analyse consumer research and often refer to their own museum and archives for inspiration.

The Royal Doulton Archives house a variety of material dating from 1815 to the present day. Contents include Royal Doulton Pattern Books containing over 10,000 hand-painted water-colours illustrating the talent of artists employed over the years.

Apart from providing an invaluable historical record of decorative ceramic styles – from the exquisitely gilded and delicately hand-painted cabinet and

tableware of the Victorian and Edwardian era, to the bright and bold angular design of the 1930s Art Deco – this collection is an inspirational source for Royal Doulton's current Design Studio.

Today, Royal Doulton provides a wide range of domestic tableware manufactured in bone china and fine china. The brand is also featured in an extensive range of crystal stemware and giftware.

Royal Doulton lists amongst its products an extensive giftware range, character jugs, china flowers and an array of collectable figurines often known as the Royal Doulton 'pretty ladies'.

For the junior members of the household, Royal Doulton also produces nurseryware and many of these ranges are of interest to adult collectors. Its most popular collection is 'Bunnykins', while 'Brambly Hedge' giftware, the Disney collections, such as 'Winnie the Pooh', have also excited and sustained much interest.

Royal Albert, which traces its origins back to 1896, has become an internationally recognised brand, offering domestic tableware and gift items. Equally famous, with an illustrious heritage dating back to its inception in 1793, is the Minton range, best known for its most popular pattern Haddon Hall, which is particularly favoured by the Japanese market. Minton is also renowned for its intricate gold patterns, where one plate can cost £5,000. These, however, are unique works of art, many of which are purchased as heirlooms. The artists in the Minton Studio also undertake special commissions.

The Royal Doulton Company is noted for its high standard of working practices and technology which is heralded as being amongst the most

offering through contemporary creations.

At grass roots level, The Royal Doulton Company continues to employ a variety of traditional promotional techniques ranging from in-store promotions, seasonal magazines and selected press advertising including supplements in bridal and lifestyle magazines.

There is also a strong and effective public relations campaign in place, which is reviewed annually.

As an acknowledged leader in china tableware, The Royal Doulton Company is working to maintain its position at the cutting edge of product development. Through building on its investments in areas such as a company owned factory in Indonesia, The Royal Doulton Company can maintain close control of its production and marketing throughout the world, making the most of its high brand awareness recognition.

Brand Values

Around the globe, The Royal Doulton Company is valued for its sense of heritage and quality. As one of the oldest and best-recognised chinaware brands in the world, The Royal Doulton Company has earned itself a reputation for excellence, quality and distinctiveness of design – values which it intends to build on in order to take the brand forward.

Prized by collectors the world over, The Royal Doulton Company has an international reach extending way beyond its English roots and product. To sustain its position, The Royal Doulton Company emphasis for future brand growth centres on its ability to focus on the consumer, to understand its buyers and then to produce products that suit individual tastes and needs.

The Royal Doulton Company identifies its core brand values as integrity, innovation, creativity, craftsmanship and decorative skills.

www.royaldoulton.com

Royal Doulton

> The largest and most expensive figure made by Royal Doulton takes more than 160 hours to hand paint and costs in excess of £14,000.

> Royal Doulton was the first china to enter space. China plates were carried on the inaugural flight of the space shuttle 'Discovery' in 1984.

> Royal Doulton ceramics are included in a time capsule inside the base of Cleopatra's Needle on the Thames Embankment in London.

> Royal Doulton's Royal Albert design 'Old Country Roses' has become the world's bestselling bone china tableware pattern, with more than 150 million pieces having been sold since its introduction in 1962.

professional and intensive in the entire international china industry.

As the corporate ambition is to generate 50% of its sales overseas, an extensive distribution chain is required to oversee global sales and marketing. The company currently operates in over 80 different markets and has distribution companies in the US, Canada, Australia and Japan.

Recent Developments

The Royal Doulton Company is undergoing an important period of change in its long history as it implements a three brand master strategy as a first step in developing the company's brands. New global merchandising systems, 'etail' internet site, product packaging, point of sale and designer endorsement have all been identified as key to the branded development. In early 2004 a license agreement was set up with the fashion icon Zandra Rhodes. She will not only be acting as a spokesperson for the Royal Albert brand but will also be endorsing her own range entitled 'My Favourite Things'. The range has been designed using classic Zandra fabric prints with her signature Butterfly and Wiggle as the common theme that runs across both giftware and tableware. Zandra is an ideal match for Royal Albert, with both brands being quintessentially English and colourful as well as both being children of the 1960s. The range launched in September 2004.

Following on from the successful launch of two glassware ranges in 2004, Royal Doulton is again working with the young fashion designer Julien Macdonald on the development of a new tabletop collection.

The Royal Doulton Company has continued to do what it does best – produce top quality chinaware collections. The new ranges of casual diningware are stylish, functional and user friendly, suited to all modern appliances including dishwashers, microwaves, ovens and freezers.

The Licensing Division, created in the mid 1990s to propel the three brands into new product sectors, has achieved considerable success, not least with the launch of Bunnykins clothing, silverware and children's furniture product ranges. Other categories inspired by the company's rich heritage and design include an extensive collection of fine art prints, teas, textiles, jewellery and ties in Japan.

In the UK, licensed products include home textiles, jewellery, candles, stationery, children/baby gifts and accessories.

Promotion

Central to The Royal Doulton Company, promotional and marketing activities have been the development and rationalisation of the brand and its communication. The introduction of everything from new logos to in-store promotional material and branded fixtures have demanded that the focus of activity be centred on the communication and effective introduction of the recent significant changes.

The Royal Doulton Company's immediate goal is to become more global, offering greater consumer relevance through a diversity of products and an extension of its

SCOTTISH WIDOWS

Market

The financial sector is in the middle of the greatest Government-led shake up in over half a century. Following a period of market and economic uncertainty, consumers in this sector are more knowledgeable, demanding and less trusting. In this context, the power of the Scottish Widow brand becomes more evident and infinitely more significant.

Being a well-known and respected brand is more important than ever before. Despite prevailing consumer perceptions of the financial services industry, Scottish Widows achieves one of the highest brand-recognitions

as a familiar and trusted brand. Mintel's research recorded a high recall rate (82%) for Scottish Widows' TV advertising. "The Scottish Widows brand is one of the most recognised in the UK financial services sector and serves to underline the company's core values: 'trust, security, reliability, quality and good returns'. Scottish Widows, therefore, represents a good

example of where advertising and promotion has played a key part in creating a familiar and trusted brand – which is quite an achievement given consumers' general perceptions of the investment and pensions industry at the present time." (Source: Mintel 'The Effectiveness of Promotion and Advertising in Financial Services, Finance Intelligence, April 2004)

The irony is that, perhaps, the name 'Scottish Widows' and a woman in a black cloak would not be the first image that a brand consultancy would suggest for a financial services' company. Yet it works exceptionally well as brand leverage.

It's now widely accepted that the state alone in the UK and elsewhere cannot guarantee people a comfortable retirement. The savings and investments market is well-placed to meet the opportunities presented by this 'savings gap'. And the UK life and pensions market is already the third largest in the world (after the US and Japan) and, in Europe, the market is expected to double in size over the next ten years (Source: Scottish Widows Investment Partnership 2004).

Achievements

Founded in 1815 as Scotland's first mutual life office, Scottish Widows has grown from strength to strength, becoming one of Britain's largest providers of life, pensions and investment products.

£82 billion of client funds are managed by the company's investment arm. Scottish Widows Investment Partnership, as at December 2004, making it one of the leading fund managers in Europe (Source: Scottish Widows Internal).

Equally importantly, Scottish Widows gained five stars for the quality of its customer service in the prestigious Financial Adviser/LIA Awards 2004 for life and pensions products.

The company was also reaccredited in 2004 for the third year running under the 'Raising Standards' quality mark scheme. Launched in 2001, the scheme provides rigorous and independent quality standards for customers, which brands must achieve each year in order to qualify.

Scottish Widows has won awards for Best Stakeholder Pension Provider and Best Personal Pension Provider (Source: Moneywise September 2004) and sales awards including Young Sales Person of the Year and Sales Leader of the Year (Source: National Sales Awards February 2004).

History

On March 25th 1812, at the height of the Napoleonic Wars, a number of eminent Scotsmen crunched their way through the snow down Edinburgh's High Street towards the warmth of the Royal Exchange Coffee Rooms. There, they discussed the prospectus for 'a general fund for securing provision to widows, sisters and other females'.

The women in question were relatives of deceased clergymen, schoolmasters and other professionals: the fund provided a safety net should they be left in poverty. It wasn't the only fund of its type, but it had one vital difference; it would extend its benefits throughout the UK.

The Scottish Widows' Fund and Equitable Assurance Society opened for business in 1815. From the start, Scottish Widows had the secret of profitable growth. In September 1821, the Society had funds of £20,000; by 1831, it stood at well over £250,000; and in 1845, it exceeded £1,700,000.

A continuous tradition of value for money, good returns and care for the customer transformed into a powerful brand with the 1986 launch of 'The Scottish Widow' – a landmark in advertising. The widow personifies and powerfully conveys the company's core qualities: strength, heritage, reliability, integrity and style.

In March 2000, Scottish Widows demutualised and relinquished its mutual status to become Scottish Widows plc. By joining forces with the Lloyds TSB Group of companies, it absorbed Lloyds TSB's previous life, pensions and investment businesses.

Product

Ultimately, Scottish Widows' product is always about providing long-term financial security. This is what customers seek at every stage of life, even though their specific needs change over time; the company meets their needs by packaging strong, dependable, investment performance into different flexible products.

Scottish Widows focuses on four main product areas – retirement, protection, savings and investments and corporate pensions.

Scottish Widows' Bank also offers a variety of deposit and mortgage products.

Recent Developments

The company has a well-established multi-channel sales capability. By becoming part of Lloyds TSB Group – the UK's largest bank branch network – Scottish Widows is well-placed to promote its brand and products to an even wider customer-base, as well as through independent financial advisers, direct marketing and online.

SCOTTISH WIDOWS

Open your eyes to a new investment opportunity

by 'Lights' in 1997, 'Boardroom' in 1998, 'In the Black' 2000, 'Brighter Future' 2002 and, more recently, 'Show of Confidence' in 2004.

The choice of directors and photographers is equally important: David Bailey, one of the world's best-known photographers, struck the ideal balance of style and humanity. This balance is an essential aspect of the branding and it is maintained by all subsequent advertising and promotion – in print, on posters, and online. Careful use of her expression and gestures, combined with effective headline and copywriting, has enabled this living icon to express even the most complex aspects of financial services in a way the public responds to – and remembers.

The widow imagery has been carefully guarded since her introduction in 1986. The brand guidelines, 'An Expression of our Brand' were entered in the 1999 New York Festival's Advertising and Design Awards, winning a prestigious bronze medal.

Brand Values

As a long-term savings and investment company, Scottish Widows is asking for people's trust, often over an entire lifetime. Trust is hard to obtain and easy to lose.

The brand values expressed in the company's advertising must be completely genuine; any conflict between expectation and experience loses customer confidence. Market research reveals that the values people associate with the brand are indeed those the company hopes to project: quality, expertise, trust, security and value for money (Source: Scottish Widows Brand Literature Research May 2002). The Widow embodies these values in an enduring and contemporary way, communicating a powerful proposition in the marketplace.

www.scottishwidows.co.uk

And, as part of the Lloyds TSB Group, the company is well-capitalised; its financial strength is among the greatest in the industry.

Promotion

The strength of the Scottish Widows' brand is based on one simple but radical marketing decision taken in 1986: to create a living logo.

Although the Scottish Widow was well known among professionals such as solicitors, bankers and accountants, the company was competing against over 30 other companies in the market. Six of these had the word 'Scottish' in their

name. What's more, widows, in general, do not generate positive associations in most people's minds.

How best could Scottish Widows build brand awareness while conveying the idea that it was 'good with your money' in every aspect of financial management?

The solution was simple: create an icon that countered all the negative values associated with the word 'widow' by presenting them as positives – young, confident, assured, professional and sophisticated.

The impact of the first television commercial, 'Looking Good', featuring this modern Widow was immediate. Name awareness, which had hovered around 30%, shot up to 86% within six weeks of the campaign launch – and stayed there.

A new corporate logo was also developed for the company. It was stylish, clean and instantly recognisable.

After two years, Millward Brown, declared Scottish Widows "the most successful insurance advertising ever monitored"; and a comparison of the advertising spend of top financial brands showed that Scottish Widows' awareness levels easily beat those of brands with much higher advertising budgets.

The first Widow, chosen after a long and careful selection process, was Debbie Barrymore, the daughter of actor Roger Moore. Debbie appeared in several television commercials. 'Birthday Party' in 1990 marked the 175th Anniversary of the company. 'Venture Out' in 1992 was set in a gentleman's club. In 1994, the model Amanda Lamb succeeded Debbie Barrymore. Her first commercial was 'The Maze', shot on location at Ross on Wye and Gloucestershire in 1994. This was followed

THINGS YOU DIDN'T KNOW ABOUT

Scottish Widows

> The company had a role in Scotland's literary history, issuing a £3,000 with-profits policy to Sir Walter Scott in 1824.

> Among the lives lost in the Titanic disaster, two were insured with Scottish Widows. A bandsman for £100 and a valet of one of the passengers for £200.

> The model who represents the Scottish Widow, Amanda Lamb also presents the television programme 'A Place in the Sun'.

Market

Adhesive tape is often associated with the home and office where products like Sellotape Original are commonplace. Demand for natural adhesives, including tape, continues to increase because of a growing environmental consciousness among manufacturers with a desire to conserve resources and to use renewable raw materials where this is economically viable.

The total European clear sticky tape market is worth an estimated US$335 million annually, with the Sellotape brand recognised in all sectors. The brand's competitors include 'own brand' tapes that have increased in numbers over recent years.

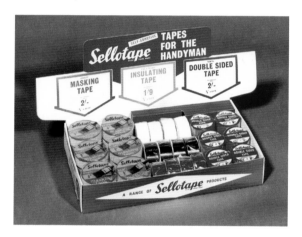

Achievements

Sellotape was launched in the stationery sector in the 1930s. Such is the brand's success that the word 'Sellotape' has been synonymous with clear adhesive tape for generations. Furthermore, the product even has its own entry in the Oxford English Dictionary.

Consumer awareness of the brand is very strong. In the UK where Sellotape enjoys 89% spontaneous recognition as a brand of clear tape, research has found that seven out of ten consumers claim that they would buy Sellotape in preference to other brands of sticky tape (Source: RSG Marketing Research 2003). Additionally, the brand is the favourite cellulose tape throughout Europe and is the clear brand leader in New Zealand and number two in South Africa.

Sellotape film is biodegradable and has received an environmental award from the British Office Systems and Stationery Federation (BOSSF) every year since 1996. The company's emphasis on performance measurement has earned it supplier accolades from ASDA Wal-Mart, Homebase and Kingfield Heath.

Sellotape also won the Research International/Superbrands 'Most Trustworthy Brand 2003' award. This was determined by original research gathered from over 1,000 managers throughout the UK by Research International on Superbrands' behalf. The research project identified drivers of exceptional brand performance and perception. Sellotape beat brands such as Rolls-Royce and Virgin Atlantic in the 'Most Trustworthy Brand' category.

History

The earliest reference to tape can be found in Thomas Mace's Musick's Monument published in 1676 where lute makers used 'little pieces of paper, so big as pence or two pences, wet with glew' to hold the thin strips of sycamore in place during construction of their musical instruments.

The first use of 'pressure sensitive' tape, which is how Sellotape Original is described can be found in 1845 in a US patent taken out by Shecut and Day where a natural rubber, pressure sensitive adhesive was used in the manufacture of sticking plasters.

In the midst of the American Civil War, it is known that sticky bandages were first used.

However, real progress was not made in this field until the mid 1920s when Henry Ford pioneered the industrial uses of adhesive tapes. Masking tapes were used in the spray-painting process, where different coloured cars – aside from the ubiquitous black of the time – were assembled.

The Sellotape brand dates back to 1937 when Colin Kininmonth and George Gray coated cellophane film with a natural rubber resin, creating a 'sticky tape' product which had been based on a French patent. They registered their product under the name 'Sellotape'. Manufacturing soon commenced in Acton, West London.

On the outbreak of hostilities in 1939 the company was put on war work and made cellulose tape for sealing ration and first aid packs and a cloth tape for sealing ammunition boxes. A product was also developed for covering windows as protection from shattering glass.

In the mid 1960s Sellotape became part of the British paper and packaging conglomerate, Dickinson Robinson Group (DRG). In the late 1990s DRG was broken up and the transformation of Sellotape began. Sellotape was restructured and investment in new plant and systems followed. In 1995 the brand was re-launched and the company started to expand and extend its product portfolio to new sectors with offerings such as the Sellotape Office.

Today, Sellotape products are highly popular and used widely in offices and homes worldwide. It is sold in a wide variety of retail outlets from corner shops and post offices to high street stationers and DIY stores as well as through mail order stationary company's which specifically target the office market.

Sellotape is a truly international brand and is a registered trademark in 119 countries with manufacturing sites in Europe and Asia Pacific. In 2002 the company was purchased by Henkel Consumer Adhesives, part of the Henkel Group which employs 50,000 people worldwide. Henkel brands and technologies are available in 126 countries and operates in three strategic business areas – Adhesives, Sealants & Surface Treatments, Home Care and Personal Care.

Product

Sellotape Original is Europe's biggest selling clear cellulose pressure sensitive tape. A pressure sensitive tape is defined as any adhesive tape that will stick to a variety of clean dry surfaces, with only a minimum amount of pressure being applied. Other properties are that it is ready to use and does not need to be activated by water, a solvent or heat.

This kind of tape consists of a relatively thin flexible backing or carrier, coated with an adhesive that is permanently sticky at room temperature. The tapes can be manufactured with adhesive coating on one or both sides of the carrier.

Sellotape Original contains the only completely biodegradable film in the European market. It is made from cellulose a natural wood pulp product. Its natural origins provide a number of intrinsic benefits over rival products which make it naturally static-free for no tangle handling as well as making it easy to tear by hand.

Constant innovation has resulted in extensive development of both the consumer and office product ranges beyond clear sticky tape with which the Sellotape brand is identified.

The Sellotape range has been expanded in recent years to include tapes for a variety of jobs. Products such as Invisible, Double Sided and Sticky Hook & Loop give consumers a wider range of solutions to their needs.

The company has carried out extensive research to design a range of more than 70 products to suit every 'sticky' need around the home, office, garage and garden with applications as diverse as binding books to repairing a broken hose.

Despite wide awareness, the brand has never been complacent and has kept abreast of the latest trends and technological developments. Now that it is part of the Henkel portfolio the brand can expect even more support and New Product Development (NPD). It is clear that the strength of the brand is fast becoming as significant for the business sector as it is for the domestic market.

The 'Sellotape Office' brand provides a range which targets the needs of the office market including the 'Small Office Home Office' (Soho) sector with new products packaged with upbeat graphics and a creative promotional programme.

Sellotape has expanded its product range beyond actual tape with a range of innovative tape dispensers the most popular of which is the elegant Chrome dispensers which provides a stylish and useful desk accessory. One of Sellotape's recent successes has been in fixing products, as this area has witnessed real growth. These include Sticky Fixer, double sided foam pads and strips which provide a swift and easy way to display and hang objects.

Recent Developments

Sellotape has investigated possible ways of achieving optimum co-operation from retailers to maximise stand out in stores. It therefore developed a 'pre-loaded POS' system which includes pre-loaded 'clip strips' and one piece 'Dbins' which require no assembly in store and make it easy for the retailer to display Sellotape products.

Promotion

In April 2003 the brand returned to television after a 25 year absence to reinforce its position as the UK's best known sticky tape brand. The campaign took advantage of Sellotape's generic status to remind consumers to look out for and choose the brand. In the commercial a mind reader tells viewers he is about to show them an object and then asks them to describe it with the first words that spring to mind. He holds up a roll of sticky tape for a few seconds before telling his audience: "I know what you're thinking." The ad closes with a pack shot and the endline 'There's only one Sellotape'.

Innovative and creative promotional concepts have become central to Sellotape's marketing strategy, with the aim of adding value to the brand and generating customer demand.

In the commercial stationery market the company often runs promotional campaigns to support its trade customers, encouraging office staff to specify Sellotape as their preferred office tape.

The brands biggest office promotion was launched in January 2005 – targeting Office Secretaries, Managers and PA's. The promotion ran on the biggest selling Sellotape sku – Original 25mm x 66m in boxes of 12. Sellotape teamed up with Nirvana Spa (winner of UK spa day of the year) who provided the prizes. From January 1st – March 31st 2005 any customer who bought two boxes of Sellotape Original 25mm x 66m has the choice of receiving either the Nirvana Spa Body Lotion, Body Scrub or Body Cleanser by completing the promotional flyer found in the box.

In addition, each completed and submitted flyer was entered into a Prize Draw giving customers the chance to win a special day for two at Nirvana Spa.

In the retail channel Sellotape focuses it promotional activity at two key times – 'Back to school' and Christmas. Back to school features items priced at pocket money levels that offer value for money and are often collectable items with Kids appeal, such as coloured glitzy dispensers or Sellotape 'Mini Rolls' a pack containing three small coloured dispensers containing high lighter tape, invisible tape and crystal clear tape.

At Christmas, the focus is on the Sellotape flagship product – 'Original' – which is the most widely used tape at this time of year. Offers such as '20% extra free' are put in place to encourage additional sales.

This kind of support activity enables Sellotape to sell at premium prices and generate strong sales for its trade customers. Indeed, EPOS data shows that Sellotape promotional packs achieve the highest stock turns of

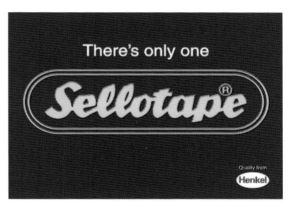

any supermarket stationery product and are among the highest of any non-food product during the Christmas period.

Brand Values

Sellotape products are high quality, reliable, efficient and very solution oriented. The brand's success attests to the fact that a distinct and honest proposition can enjoy long term popularity with the consumer and build itself a prestigious, highly valued brand name that produces high customer loyalty.

Sellotape's customer service is also taken very seriously. Delivery performance is measured weekly and monthly in several operating countries to ensure targets are met.

www.sellotape.co.uk

Market

With people in the UK working the longest hours in Europe and stress-related illnesses on the increase, consumer interest in and demand for simple and effective forms of preventative healthcare is growing.

Seven Seas has been at the vanguard of natural healthcare's progress from niche health-food store to pharmacy and supermarket shelf. The company's reward for building a vitamin, mineral and supplements (VMS) market worth approximately £313 million – the largest of all OTC categories – is outright market leadership, accounting for almost one in four of all sales in the UK (Source: IRI March 2005).

Central to this success is Seven Seas' dominance of the two top VMS sectors: multivitamins and cod liver oil.

The introduction of Seven Seas Advanced Formula Multibionta in 2000 created a unique sub-sector that revitalised an underperforming market. Achieving double-digit growth since launch, Multibionta has boosted growth of the sector and seized a market leading share of the complete multivitamins sector (Source: IRI March 2005).

Cod liver oil is the supplement on which Seven Seas built its fortunes. With two-thirds of the sector, Seven Seas still dominates cod liver oil.

Seven Seas has also taken control of two important emerging sectors: the Omega-3 market and the glucosamine market.

The market for Omega-3 supplements is showing a meteoric rise and the 'joint care' market as a whole continues to record rapid growth. Seven Seas are market leaders in both these sectors (Source: IRI March 2005).

Achievements

Seven Seas' defining achievement is the balance it has struck between progress and tradition. Despite being at the forefront of nutritional science and production technology, Seven Seas has never forsaken its heritage. The brand has been voted 'Most Trusted Brand in European VMS' by subscribers to Reader's Digest several times in recent years.

In 2005, Seven Seas celebrates its 70th anniversary. Since its beginnings, Seven Seas has grown from a small local co-operative to a major international healthcare company and its product portfolio has expanded from a single food supplement to a broad range of vitamin, mineral and health supplements, herbal and homoeopathically-prepared remedies and over-the-counter medicines.

Today, the company operates one of the most technologically advanced production facilities in the UK and its products, packaging and marketing expertise have been recognised by consumers and industry alike. Its products regularly receive consumer accolades, among them 'Best Multivitamin' for Seven Seas Multibionta (2004 and 2005) and 'Best Cod Liver Oil' for Seven Seas NeutraTaste (2004) in polls conducted among customers of Boots. In the same year, its SportFlex sports supplement brand was acclaimed 'OTC Marketing Innovation of the Year' by industry title, OTC Bulletin.

History

By the early 20th century, cod liver oil was established as a cure for the crippling bone disease, rickets, explained by the discovery that cod liver oil was a rich source of vitamin D as well as vitamin A and polyunsaturated fats. This was sufficient evidence for the trawler owners of Hull to invest in the commercial production of cod liver oil, a product that is essentially a by-product of the fishing industry. Seven Seas forerunner, British Cod Liver Oil Producers, was formed.

In these early days the company was a major supplier to the animal feed industry and it wasn't until 1938 that cod liver oil for human health was launched under the Seven Seas brand name. Not long afterwards, the first-ever easy-to-take cod liver oil capsules were introduced, originating the now widespread use of soft-gelatin capsules for healthcare products.

During World War II food rationing, cod liver oil liquid was distributed free to pregnant and nursing mothers and children up to five years old through the Ministry of Food's Welfare Food programme – a product endorsement that has never been surpassed in healthcare's history. After the war, the company diversified into supplying oils and fats for the margarine and bakery trades and sales of Seven Seas branded cod liver oil declined as a result.

Everything changed in the 1970s with the identification of the long-chain omega-3 fatty acids and the realisation that cod liver oil was a rich and rare source of these important nutrients. Suddenly, cod liver oil was at the forefront of nutritional science.

In 1981, a range of seven vitamin and mineral supplements was launched. At a time when Britons were becoming more willing to take charge of their own good health, the new range was well placed to capitalise on the new 'health consciousness'. Interest in cod liver oil also revived in the 1980s as a result both of accumulating scientific evidence for the health benefits of the omega-3 fatty acids it contains and television advertising featuring the Seven Seas Tin Man character, who recommended cod liver oil for 'oiling the joints'.

The 1980s also saw Seven Seas acquire New Era Laboratories, whose homoeopathically-prepared tissue salts offer a gentle, non-pharmaceutical option for the treatment of minor ailments; Höfels range of garlic and herbal supplements; and Minadex children's tonic.

In the 1990s it acquired Haliborange, the leading brand of children's vitamin and mineral supplements.

Growth accelerated in 1996 when Seven Seas changed ownership to come under the umbrella of German pharmaceutical giant, Merck KGaA. With the expertise and investment of its new parent company, Seven Seas has flourished, continuing to grow through a combination of innovation and acquisition.

Today, Seven Seas products are available in more than 100 countries across the globe and the Seven Seas company and its brands are market leaders in Ireland, the Middle East, Africa, the Caribbean and Far East.

Product

Over the years, supplementation has become an established routine for some 17 million people in the UK. Seven Seas brands are at the forefront of this trend, making the company one of the most successful in UK healthcare today. Its brand portfolio is impressive, fielding five brands that are brand leaders in their category: Seven Seas cod liver oil, Minadex, Haliborange, Multibionta and JointCare.

In addition to its range of cod liver oils in a choice of capsules or liquid, Seven Seas' supplements span most popular segments of the VMS market and include single vitamins and minerals from A to E, calcium to zinc and combination supplements that group nutrients to meet a life stage or life style need. Multivitamin and mineral formulations offer nutritional support for times when intake from diet is compromised; antioxidants help boost the immune system; evening primrose and starflower oil aid hormonal balance; and Seven Seas Tonic speeds convalescence. Sub-brands include Seven Seas Pulse Pure Fish Oils for heart health maintenance. Most products are available in easy-to-swallow One-A-Day capsules and four are available in chewable capsules.

Recent Developments

Launched recently in the UK, Multibionta has become the nation's best-selling multivitamin. A full spectrum multivitamin and mineral product with added probiotics, Multibionta is now the number one complete multivitamin in the largest of all VMS sectors. Seven Seas Advanced Formula Multibionta Probiotic Multivitamin is the only clinically-proven complete probiotic multivitamin supplement. This unique formula contains three probiotic strains as well as 100% of the Recommended Daily Allowance (RDA) of vitamins and selected minerals to help users stay fit, healthy and full of energy. Its performance lives up to its promise, which is why it has become the leading product in the market and remains the fastest-growing brand.

Recent Seven Seas research projects have highlighted the global potential for the development of products that target both the young and the ageing populations. The Jointcare range of glucosamine combination products for joint health and new Haliborange orange-flavoured Omega-3 Fish Oil for improved concentration in children, are two of

the latest examples of how Seven Seas continues to lead in all matters concerning nutrition and supplementation. Seven Seas JointCare is a range of five products specifically formulated to help adults in middle- and third-age maintain the health of their joints and is a unique player within the glucosamine market.

Haliborange, the expert in children's nutrition, has continued to extend its Omega-3 for Kids range following the great success of Haliborange Omega-3 for Kids Syrup and its Orange Chewy Fruit Bursts. Haliborange Omega-3 for Kids is now the best selling Omega-3 supplement in the market (Source: IRI March 2005). The Omega-3 market, in turn, is driving growth within the total VMS category.

In 2004 the cod liver oil revival was further boosted when scientists from Cardiff University revealed new clinical data showing that 86% of pre-operative knee replacement patients with arthritis, who took cod liver oil capsules daily, had absent or significantly reduced levels of the enzymes that cause cartilage damage compared to 26% of those given a placebo capsule.

The appeal of Seven Seas heartland cod liver oil has now spread to a younger generation. Seven Seas NeutraTaste Cod Liver Oil for Daily Flexibility features a process that micro-emulsifies the oil so that it is easily-absorbed and taste-free. Packaging, advertising and promotion spearhead the NeutraTaste marketing thrust to attract new users to the brand. The launch of Seven Seas NeutraTaste Sportflex, a multi-nutrient supplement for people who play sport, has extended the brand franchise among its target audience.

Promotion

To support its retail customers and inform and educate consumers, Seven Seas invests heavily in product and brand promotion across its ranges, consistently outspending its competition.

Recent and forthcoming support for its brands features a £3.5 million campaign for Multibionta using terrestrial and satellite TV backed by national press advertising and posters to increase visibility of the key message: 'Multibionta puts back what life takes out'.

The introduction of Multibionta 50+ takes the message 'Because in your head you're still 21' to the over-50s via print advertising in national newspapers and the third-age press.

The meteoric growth of Seven Seas JointCare has been driven by a heavyweight advertising and public relations campaign as well as a training initiative recognised by the National Pharmaceutical Association to help educate and inform pharmacists and pharmacy assistants.

Seven Seas Cod Liver Oil advertising consistently appears on television and in the national daily press and has been a major factor in the growth of Britain's best selling supplement brand.

Brand Values

Seven Seas is a trusted family oriented company with a long heritage of providing good health naturally. The company is committed to developing and marketing evidence-based, innovative health protection products that are clearly differentiated, providing innovative solutions for health protection and added value through trusted brands. Seven Seas strives to develop mutually profitable business in sustained partnership with customers, through quality brands that satisfy family needs to maintain good health.

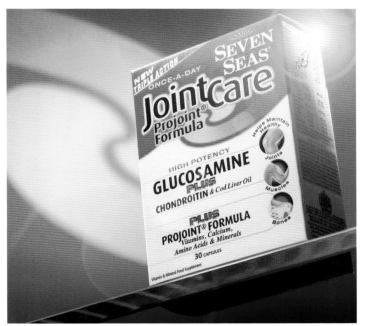

Market

Over recent decades British tastes have changed enormously. With more and more people cooking and eating Indian, Chinese and Thai food, stir-fries and curries are now part of our everyday lives.

In the past ten years the market for home-cooked Asian food has grown by 74% and is currently worth £282 million (Source: IRI).

In the past year, more than 18 million UK households bought ambient Indian and Chinese cooking sauces, ingredients and meal accompaniments (Source: IRI).

This growth has been fuelled by the rise of long-distance travel, increased popularity of TV cookery programmes and increasing demand for spicy, exotic flavours, tastes and textures; as a result, consumers' are increasingly willing to experiment with and enjoy more exotic food in their own homes.

These underlying consumer trends are forecast to continue which is excellent news for the future of the Asian food market in the UK. Other key consumer drivers that Sharwood's believe will influence future market growth include an increasing demand for healthier products, the growth in snacking and the gradual shift away from the traditional seated meals to lighter eating occasions. The broad range of different tastes and textures that Asian food offers makes the cuisine the perfect partner for exciting, quick and easy meals.

Achievements

Sharwood's has been at the forefront of developing the popularity of Indian and Oriental cuisine in the UK. First created in the 1880s, the brand now comprises an extensive range of products covering Indian, Chinese and Thai food. The range includes cooking sauces and pastes, ingredient sauces, dipping sauces, curry powders, noodles, naans, puppodums, prawn crackers and, of course, its famous 'Green Label' mango chutney; Sharwood's also sells a range of frozen ready meals.

Sharwood's has a history of firsts under its belt. It was the first brand to introduce tikka masala to Britain in the early 1980s and was also the first on the market with cook-to-eat puppodums. In its quest to bring the best food from Asia to Britain, Sharwood's travelled to Chennai (formerly Madras) in India in the late 1980s to track down the perfect ingredients. Bought as small,

uncooked discs, the puppodums are fried at home and expand to the size and freshness of those in Indian restaurants. The success of theses cook-to-eat products led to Sharwood's subsequent launch of a selection of ready-to-eat puppodums in 1985. More than 1,000 ready-to-eat puppodums are eaten every hour in the UK alongside a curry or simply as a tasty snack and Sharwood's sells more than 65% of the ready-to-eat puppodums sold through supermarkets. It's a similar story with naan bread, which Sharwood's was the first to develop for the UK eat at home market ten years ago. A traditional accompaniment for an Indian meal, naans are soft, lightly baked breads made from wheat flour blended with natural yoghurt. Alongside puppodums, naans can complete a Sharwood's curry, especially when eaten with a healthy dollop of mango chutney.

Today, Sharwood's 29% market share makes it the biggest brand in the Asian market. With its broad portfolio of products, the brand is able to cater for people with a range of tastes as well as for people with a variety of different cooking skills.

History

The origins of Sharwood's lie in the 1800s. In 1864 James Allen Sharwood, a city broker turned speciality food purveyor, travelled to India and the Orient in search of new spices to bring back to the West.

In 1889 he founded JA Sharwood & Co as 'importers and exporters of foreign produce' in London. He was an avid traveller and was fluent in French, German, Spanish and Italian. Above all, he was a gourmet who turned food and travel into a business.

The early Sharwood's price lists covered an extensive range of 'specialities, sweetmeats and delicacies' that James had discovered on his travels. Indian foods such as curry powders, pickles and chutneys from Bombay and Madras were first introduced to the UK under Mr Sharwood's expert guidance.

By 1927, James had hung up his exploring gear but his reputation for introducing Britain to some of the finest food from around the world lives on today in the brand that bears his name.

Since then, Sharwood's has twice been awarded the Royal Warrant. In 1947, the brand won the privilege as Manufacturers of Chutney and Purveyors of Indian Curry Powder and, in 1994, as 'Manufacturers of Oriental sauces'.

In 1963 RHM acquired Sharwood's. Since then, it has further developed the popularity of Indian and Oriental cuisine and built up Sharwood's in the UK and overseas,

particularly in Australia. It has helped to transform the original pioneering import and export business into one of the country's biggest brand names.

Product

At the heart of Sharwood's success is its team of chefs and product designers who are experts in Indian, Thai and Chinese cuisine. As Asian food experts and regular travellers across Asia, all are dedicated to turning inspiration from delicious authentic dishes into food that

can be prepared and enjoyed by British consumers. This team ensures that Sharwood's is continually pioneering the introduction of new Asian flavours to the UK. Whatever your cooking ability and whatever the occasion, be it a quick meal or one with all the extras to bring the full restaurant experience into your home, the Sharwood's range provides everything you need.

As an extension to this expertise, Sharwood's offers a 'Kitchen Direct' service. This phone line allows consumers to get advice from a team of trained chefs in the Sharwood's kitchen on how to create their meal. The service

answers a wide range of customer queries, from what to do with a curry that is too hot to suggestions for vegetarian meals. The Sharwood's website also offers this service at www.sharwoods.com.

Recent Developments

In summer 2004, Sharwood's re-launched the brand and invested in sales and marketing support. The re-launch, comprised a packaging redesign, new product launches and advertising and promotional support. Through stronger branding, the re-design reinforced Sharwood's premium and ethnic values and increased the brand's impact at point of purchase.

The new products included new recipes across the Sharwood's range of Indian and Chinese cooking sauces, a range of three new Noodle Recipe Kits and quick-cook Stir-Fry Egg Noodles, crispier puppodums and a new Cracked Black Pepper flavour variant.

With around one third of adults claiming to be trying to eat better at any one time (Source: TGI), in Spring 2005 Sharwood's launched a range of healthier Indian cooking sauces. The sauces offer reduced fat, salt and sugar and are designed to complement the core range of everyday Indian cooking sauces.

In Spring 2005, Sharwood's also launched a selection of grill, barbeque and bake coating sauces for chicken, pork or fish in four varieties: Thai Sweet Chilli & Herbs, Chinese BBQ & Sesame, Tandoori and Spicy Mango; these new sauces are specifically designed to extend Asian flavour into lighter eating meal occasions.

Promotion

All Sharwood's products got a new design in 2004 and the new products were supported with TV and poster advertising, PR and in-store promotions.

Sharwood's was boosted early in 2005 with the Chinese New Year on February 9th heralding the Year of the Rooster. This was Sharwood's biggest Chinese New Year campaign to date, with promotions featuring sauces, crackers and noodles and marketing carried out through press, radio, posters, PR and events.

Brand Values

Sharwood's has always prided itself on its passion for and expertise in Indian and Oriental food.

The brand's strengths lie in the breadth of its range and in the accessibility of the products that it creates for British consumers – all inspired by authentic dishes from Asia.

This combination encourages consumers to trust the brand and feel safe enough to have the confidence to be more experimental in their cooking.

www.sharwoods.com

THINGS YOU DIDN'T KNOW ABOUT

Sharwood's

> Sharwood's products are eaten in more than 50 countries worldwide.

> Sharwood's chutney has been sold in Sweden since World War II; Swedish consumption of chutney is a staggering 200 tonnes per year.

> The British eat their way through 2,100 tonnes of Sharwood's curry sauces each year.

> All Sharwood's puppodums are made in India using an authentic Indian recipe and method. They are made by hand and dried in the Indian sun.

> Sharwood's noodles are based on the traditional method and recipes used in China and are hung to dry.

> Sharwood's most popular products are Plain Puppodums, Green Label Mango Chutney, Medium Egg Noodles and Hoi Sin sauce.

> Sharwood's Bundh range of premium Indian sauces is based on a unique slow oven cooking method used by the ancient Mugals, who arrived in India from the North. The Mugals held incredibly lavish feasts and were renowned for their extravagance, which included crushing pearls into their food purely for the luxuriousness of it.

Market

Shell is one of the most enduring brands amongst service stations. It competes on a global basis with names such as BP, Esso, Mobil and Texaco.

The retail fuel market is dominated by petrol and diesel sales which, in 2003, accounted for 98.7% of total sales of £27.7 billion (Source: IP/Mintel). Motor oil and antifreeze products make up the rest.

Unleaded petrol accounts for the majority of volume sales in the fuel-retail sector and, although sales as a whole have been declining since 2000 due to the economic slowdown, fewer two-car homes and environmental concerns, the super-unleaded and diesel sectors are growing due to their environmental and economic efficiencies, respectively. Low-sulphur fuel, which has a sulphur content of 50 parts per million or less, is another growth area.

But while many consumers might only connect the name Shell to the fuel they put in their car or the service stations they see by the roadside, it is a brand that touches their lives in many more ways. Shell is not just an oil company; it operates across the broader energy business, exploring for, producing and marketing natural gas – a business in which it is a leader. This clean-burning, environmentally friendly fuel has become a major energy source in homes and businesses throughout the world and demand is growing rapidly – up 75% in the last decade. In this field, Shell already stretches across 35 countries and, as the world searches for greener forms of energy, Shell expects demand for natural gas – the cleanest hydrocarbon – to double over the next two decades.

In the area of new and renewable energy, Shell is developing businesses in solar, wind and hydrogen to meet customer needs around the world.

Achievements

Over its long history and thanks to continued marketing investment, Shell has one of the most recognisable brands in the world. According to Interbrand's annual analysis, Shell's brand, represented by the globally recognised red and yellow Pecten (scallop shell), is one of the world's 100 most valuable brands, worth nearly US$3 billion.

Shell has been a leader in North Sea oil and gas since production began in the 1960s, investing more than £50 billion in the area and bringing a quarter of total North Sea oil production to the surface. Shell's development of the Brent oil field, the biggest discovery in the UK sector of the North Sea, is recognised to be one of the greatest technical feats of British enterprise.

The company has a commitment to ensure that environmental and social issues are taken into account in any activity, alongside the financial objectives. Since 1997, it has produced the annual 'Shell Report', in which it reviews the Group's performance against environmental, ethical and social criteria. The 'Tell Shell' initiative, which enables stakeholders and concerned groups to communicate directly with the company, was one of the first websites of its kind and is notable for its open dialogue on all topics.

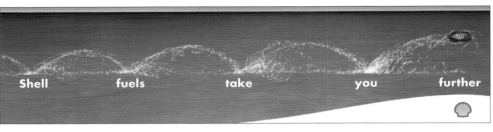

Shell fuels take you further

Only recently, the ethics management-rating firm Management & Excellence issued their 'Ethics in the Oil Industry 2005' report, which selected Shell as the most ethical oil company, followed by Exxon/Mobil and BP. The report was issued after examining the areas of ethics, corporate social responsibility, transparency, environment and corporate governance.

History

Shell's origins can be traced back to 1833, when Marcus Samuel opened a small shop in London dealing in antiques, curios and oriental seashells. His trade in shells became so profitable that he set up regular shipments from the Far East. Before long this had turned into a general import-export business.

The connection with oil was not established until early 1890 when Marcus Samuel Junior visited the Black Sea coast where Russian oil was exported into Asia. Samuel started exporting Kerosene to the Far East, sending the world's first oil tanker through the Suez Canal. Samuel remembered his father's original business when he branded the kerosene 'Shell'.

In 1897, Samuel elevated the status of the Shell name, calling his enterprise The Shell Transport and Trading Company. A seashell emblem was chosen to give the name visual emphasis.

Release your engine's potential.

Shell V-Power is specially designed to clean your engine as you drive. And the cleaner your engine, the better it responds. But then, what else would you expect from a fuel developed with Ferrari?

V-Power

Ten years later, Shell formed a close alliance with a Dutch oil company also active in the Far East: Royal Dutch Petroleum. Rapid growth followed, leading to the development of an international network of oil exploration and production facilities. As with many other petroleum companies, the new motorcar age literally fuelled their growth for decades to come.

By the late 1950s, oil had become the world's major energy resource. Supply and demand both boomed and, during this period, Shell supplied almost one seventh of the world's oil products. During the 1960s, there was a similar boom in the market for natural gas, leading to the exploration for and production of natural gas in the North Sea. Shell was a major player in these early years of North Sea operations, especially when major oil fields were also discovered there in the early 1970s.

At this time, Shell also started diversifying into a new growth area – producing chemicals from petroleum products. Over the next 20 years its chemical product range grew enormously and was manufactured in 30 locations around the world.

Product

Through its global network of some 40,000 retail outlets, Shell delivers the essential ingredients for personal mobility – vehicle fuels, motor oils, car-care products, food and drinks, groceries, travel-related and other items, all available at the same point in a single purchase.

The range of innovative products and services on offer is constantly expanding, supported by extensive research and development activities. Products such as low-sulphur diesel, lead replacement fuel and, more recently, differentiated fuels including Shell Pura, Shell Optimax, Shell V-Power, Shell V-Power Racing and Shell V-Power Diesel are tailored to meet growing customer requirements for more environmentally friendly fuels and improved engine performance.

Shell is a global leader in finished lubricants and operates an extensive network of base oil and lubricant blending plants in more than 120 countries. Shell lubricants companies manufacture and market some of the most recognised lubricants brands including Shell Helix, Shell Rimula, Pennzoil and Quaker State.

Products range from passenger car motor oils and light, food-quality formulations used in soft-drink canning plants, to thick industrial greases that protect the massive roller bearings in steel mills.

Although Shell is best known for keeping people on the move, it is also present in homes with Liquified Petroleum Gas, which can be used throughout the home to fuel all kinds of appliances including heating, hot water and cooking systems.

Recent Developments

Shell is successfully pioneering synthetic fuels such as GTL fuel from its proprietary Gas to Liquids technology. GTL fuel is a clean transport fuel derived from natural gas rather than conventional crude oil. It can be used in conventional diesel engines without the need for modification and can be supplied through existing infrastructure, which makes it a practical, cost effective option.

GTL fuel, currently produced from the only commercial plant of its kind in Bintulu, Malaysia, provides the fuel for a series of global trials to demonstrate a reduction in emissions without affecting performance. Following on from trials held in Berlin with Volkswagen Golfs, in London with Daimler Chrysler buses and in Tokyo with Mitsubishi trucks in 2003, Shell GTL fuel has successfully completed trials with heavy-duty trucks in California and in London with Toyota cars in 2004. It was also used to power one of the winning Audi cars at the Michelin Bibendum Challenge.

Blends of synthetic GTL fuel with conventional diesel are currently being sold. Shell Pura Diesel is on sale at Shell retail stations in Thailand, helping motorists meet local emissions' regulations. Shell Diesel 2004 was launched in Greece during the Olympic Games to contribute to a cleaner environment and Shell V-Power Diesel has been introduced in Germany and The Netherlands.

Shell Hydrogen recently opened the first hydrogen dispenser at a retail gasoline station to service a fleet of six fuel-cell vehicles from General Motors. Located in Washington, the station is part of a collaboration between Shell and GM to demonstrate hydrogen fuel cell

vehicles and refuelling infrastructure technology, an important contribution in making fuel cell vehicles an everyday reality. Shell offers both compressed and liquid hydrogen at the station.

Bio-fuels are non-fossil and are often considered as a more environmentally friendly and sustainable transport fuel. These fuels can be derived from all kinds of biomass such as crops (ethanol) and vegetable oils (bio-diesel) and can be blended with traditional fuels. In 2002, Shell bought a stake in Iogen Energy, a Canadian company with a technology that could narrow the cost gap between bio-fuels and gasoline.

Shell is working on a range of sustainable mobility initiatives, including cleaner fuels and local air quality. It is a core member of 'Mobility 2030', a cross-industry project led by the World Business Council for Sustainable Development.

Promotion

Shell's promotional activity takes place on many fronts, regularly targeting motorists, as well as opinion formers, businesses and the public at large.

Shell's relationship with Ferrari began in the 1930s with the sponsorship of Enzo Ferrari and later the first contract with Ferrari for Formula One in 1950. Ferrari has won Drivers and Constructors awards in 2001, 2002, 2003 and 2004. Shell and Ferrari have won more than 100 Formula One World Championship races together.

Today, Shell's role within Ferrari's Formula One operation is not only to provide the high performance fuels and lubricants but also to ensure a team of specialised Shell engineers provide Ferrari with state-of-the-art fuel and lubricant analysis at each Grand Prix. Technology in fuels and lubricants developed and proven in Formula One has been made available in Shell service stations, providing millions of motorists with high quality fuels that are cleaner and more efficient and offer the utmost protection for their engines with lubricating oils tested under extreme conditions.

Another major aspect of Shell's marketing activity is its global corporate communication programme. This has played a crucial part in encouraging a debate on Shell's position on important issues facing society and closing the knowledge gap with stakeholders on the company's environmental and social activity. The programme uses a combination of PR and advertising, part of which includes 'Living the Values' TV commercials, featuring Shell staff who tell their story to illustrate the way in which Shell does business. The campaign is now evolving to cover Shell business activity in general and build relationships with stakeholders across the financial, environmental and social activity.

Brand Values

Shell is committed to carrying out its business operations efficiently, responsibly, profitably and ethically. In order to achieve this, Shell will search for innovative energy solutions with the intent of improving the well-being of the planet and its people.

The 'Waves of Change' theme is used to convey these values in all communications, relating Shell with the sea. As the company's origins are linked to the sea, this provides a useful metaphor to convey the values of the Shell brand – honesty, integrity and respect for people – using a wide range of emotions and visual ideas.

www.shell.com

THINGS YOU DIDN'T KNOW ABOUT

Shell

> Shell is the world's largest single-branded retailer.

> Shell's retail network serves around 20 million customers per day, from more than 40,000 service stations, in more than 140 countries and territories.

> Every four seconds, 1,200 cars visit a Shell service station.

> Approximately 3% of the world's oil and approximately 3.5% of the world's gas is produced by Shell companies.

Market

Consumers today have a wide range of beds to choose from, with prices starting from about £100 to more than £10,000. In 2004, almost six million beds were sold in the UK, with a total market value of £1.5 billion (Source: GfK).

Traditional divan set mattresses, which accounted for 39% of bed sales in 2004 (Source: GfK), have been improved through the use of better spring systems and modern materials, such as latex and foams that mould to the body, offering greater comfort.

However, the growing trend in the bed market is towards bedsteads, which have become increasingly popular, accounting for 37% of bed sales in 2004 compared to 30% in 2000 (Source: GfK). This is an increasingly important area for Silentnight Beds, as consumers, particularly younger ones, choose bedsteads with mattresses over traditional divan products. In 2004, following extensive research and in response to this high level of consumer demand, Silentnight Beds, one of the UK's top bed manufacturers, launched 'imagine with Silentnight Beds'™, a range of bedsteads crafted from a variety of woods, metal and upholstery.

Achievements

The Silentnight Beds range for children, My First Bed™, won the Marketing Society's Award for Best Brand Development in 2004. But this was not the first accolade the product had received since its launch at the Furniture Show in January 2003. It made an immediate impression by scooping the 'Bed of the Year' accolade at The Furniture Awards. Furthermore, the judges called the product a 'clear winner'.

In 2004, Silentnight scooped this prestigious award for a second consecutive year for 'hibernate with Silentnight Beds'™, which gives adults the opportunity to design their own bed by choosing from a range of bases, headboards, feet and luxurious fabrics and adding either a Miracoil™ mattress or the deluxe Miracoil™ Latex mattress. The concept allows customers to create a comfortable piece of furniture that will fit the style of their bedroom and also reflect their personality.

hibernate™ has also received acclaim from the consumer press, winning the House Beautiful award for Best Furniture Range in March 2004. This is a huge achievement in a category that included all furniture for the home.

History

Tom and Joan Clarke formed Clarke's Mattresses Limited in 1946 in Skipton, North Yorkshire. In 1951 the name was changed to Silentnight Limited, and by the late 1950s the company was producing more than 4,000 divan sets each month and the workforce had grown from 25 to 150.

In 1961 the company relocated to Moss Shed, its current manufacturing site. The 1980s were a hugely exciting time for the company. In 1986, Silentnight Beds

'Ultimate Sleep System' became the first new spring system in the UK for three decades. The launch was supported with a successful TV advertising campaign, featuring the product demonstrators, Hippo and Duck.

The campaign focused on the unique construction of the 'Ultimate Spring System', which meant that partners of different weights would not roll together. In the late 1990s the spring system was improved and renamed the 'Miracoil™ Spring System'.

Silentnight continued to grow through expansion and the acquisition of other bed brands. Today, it is the UK's largest bed manufacturer and is part of the Silentnight Group, which is the market leader in the UK bed market – one in four beds sold in the UK is a Silentnight Group bed brand.

Product

Silentnight Beds signature spring system, Miracoil™, has three main benefits. Firstly, No Roll-Together: the springs run from head-to-toe instead of running across the bed, providing individual sleep zones for each partner. Secondly, No Roll-Off: the springs run right to the very edge of the bed, providing edge-to-edge support, and finally, a Posture Zone: more springs are concentrated in the centre third of the mattress, providing greater

support where it is needed most. These unique-selling points are at the heart of every product in the Silentnight range.

To remain brand leader, Silentnight Beds recognises the importance of innovation. In 2003 extensive research was carried out among children and parents, leading to the development of My First Bed™, the only full-sized single divan to be designed especially for children.

The distinctive blue-and-white striped My First Bed™ mattress has the same Miracoil™ spring system as all Silentnight Beds, providing a superior level of support for the child. The product range consists of eight headboard and divan base colours, six 'play pals', five styles of bed feet and two base types (storage or sleepover). Using Silentnight Beds' exclusive 'Create Your Beds Personality'™ concept, the parent and child can choose from these components to design their favourite bed from 3,840 possible combinations.

Launched in 2004, 'hibernate with Silentnight™' also uses the 'Create Your Bed's Personality'™ concept to allow the consumer to create their own bed from a range of bases, headboards, feet and luxurious fabrics. This bespoke range of fashion-led and design-focused beds represents the first time that an adult's bed can be customised in this way.

The range, which was officially launched in February 2004, enjoyed a high-profile PR campaign throughout 2004 and a creative advertising campaign in glossy women's and home interest

magazines. The launch of www.hibernatewithsilentnight.co.uk, allows the consumer to create their bed online with the 'Create Your Bed's Personality'™ tool. Other features include details of the innovative new range and lifestyle photography of hibernate beds in themed rooms.

Recent Developments
The new range of bedsteads from Silentnight Beds, branded under the name 'imagine with Silentnight Beds'™ and launched to retailers in June 2004, is a range of innovative bedsteads crafted in a variety of different woods, metal and upholstery. The range was designed to have broad appeal to all consumers – while at the same time attracting those with a specific style in mind. Following extensive research among consumers about the styles of bedrooms they prefer, the imagine™ range has been divided into five moods: 'pure', inspired by the beauty of nature; 'essence', inspired by the far-flung corners of the world; 'love', homely beds designed for the whole family; 'alive', designed to be vibrant and stylish for a loft-style surrounding; and 'serene', designed as timeless, modern classics. These five broad 'moods' mean that whatever style the consumer wants to create, there should be a bedstead in the range to help them achieve it.

To complement the range and to ensure the bedsteads offer the best possible comfort, Silentnight Beds has created the first ever non-slip mattress system. An anti-slip treatment is applied to the slats and the underside of the mattress, ensuring that the mattress does not slide around on the slats, providing a more secure sleeping surface and a more comfortable night's sleep. The consumer can choose their preferred mattress from a choice of four – Miracoil™, Miracoil™ Supreme, Miracoil™ Latex and Miracoil™ Memory.

The new imagine™ bedstead collection was launched to more than 120 retailers at Shepperton Studios in the biggest bed launch for more than a decade. The launch event proved to be successful, with 95% of guests signing up to stock imagine™.

Promotion
The Silentnight Beds brand was refreshed in 2000, when it became apparent that although the brand's demonstrators – Hippo and Duck – were still highly recognisable to consumers, awareness of the brand had been significantly eroded since the 1987 television campaign. A brand building exercise began to increase awareness and create a stronger, more coherent brand identity. It included in-depth research into the target consumer (primarily females, aged 25-55, BC1C2) and their understanding of the Silentnight Beds brand. The image of the Silentnight Beds corporate identity was strengthened at this point by tying the Hippo and Duck characters into the corporate logo. The duo was redrawn in a 'softer' animated format and the brand undertook an overhaul of all point-of-sale material with brighter branded imagery and innovative mechanisms.

January 2001 saw a brand new Silentnight Beds commercial, which was designed to reach and appeal to as many of the target consumers as possible. Actress Jane Horrocks was selected to be the voice of the sassy, quick-witted Duck, while Clive Rowe was the voice of the larger-than-life Hippo. The Hot Chocolate song 'You Sexy Thing (I believe in Miracles)' is an essential feature, with Hippo singing it to his wife and, quite possibly, his second love – his Silentnight bed. In 2003, to support the launch of My First Bed™, the nation was introduced to Hippo and Duck's 'family' (Hippo & Duck children and a baby Hippo) in a brand new advertisement. The ad was designed to reach the parent, with Hippo and Duck demonstrating the features of the product as they tuck the children up in their new beds.

Silentnight Beds claimed a furniture industry first when the My First Bed™ advertisement went into cinemas nationwide in 2003 and 2004. In 2005 the My First Bed™ advertisement returned to the big screen for a 12-month cinema advertising campaign that will include the biggest family movies of the year such as Harry Potter and the Goblet of Fire and Magic Roundabout. It is expected that 25 million cinemagoers will have seen the ad by the end of the campaign.

The hibernate™ range, developed by Silentnight Beds in response to consumer demand for a bed that doesn't sacrifice comfort for style, benefited from the attention of Gharani Štrok, the leading London fashion design duo, at London Fashion Week when they created their very own bespoke hibernate™ bed. Designers Nargess Gharani and Vanya Štrok, created an exclusive bed using fabric from their Spring/Summer 2005 collection. The bed – a one-off that will be given away for charity – was the first time that furniture and high fashion have been brought together in this way.

Brand Values
Silentnight Beds is committed to offering the consumer choice, quality, comfort and support, whilst constantly innovating to produce the ultimate bed selection. The core Silentnight Beds brand is strongly associated with Hippo and Duck, the well-loved characters who add warmth and friendliness to the brand's other qualities.

The three sub-brands, My First Bed™, hibernate™ and imagine™, have successfully extended the Silentnight Beds brand into new areas. While the My First Bed™ brand extends the warmth and trust of the core Silentnight Beds brand into the children's market, the hibernate™ and imagine™ ranges have taken the brand into a new style-led market, proving that while comfort and support are still key, Silentnight Beds is also capable of design-led products.

www.silentnight.co.uk

Market

Smirnoff® vodka is the number one selling spirit in the UK, accounting for six out of every 10 vodka-mixed drinks consumed in British pubs and bars. In that sector, its popularity makes the brand worth in excess of £600 million – more than the entire blended whisky category. It is twice the size of its nearest competitor, Bacardi (Source: ACNielsen).

More than 7.5 million people in the UK drink Smirnoff® vodka, versus four million Bacardi drinkers and one million Absolut drinkers (Source: TGI).

Globally, Smirnoff® vodka is now the number one spirit by retail value (Source: Impact International). In the year ending June 2004, the brand's top five markets were the US, Great Britain, Canada, South Africa and Brazil (Source: Diageo).

Achievements

In 2004 24.2 million nine-litre cases of Smirnoff® vodka were sold across the world. This was a 5% year-on-year increase in volume terms and a 4% net sales increase (Source: Diageo).

An established innovator, the launch of ready-to-drink variant Smirnoff Ice®, an opaque, citrus-flavoured drink was the most successful new alcoholic product launch ever. It became a billion-dollar business within three years and is now the clear leader in the global ready-to-drink category (Source: Impact).

Smirnoff has consistently been named in the Business Week/Interbrand annual Most Valuable Brands Survey as a Top 100 global brand. Most recently, in April 2005, in a blind taste test of the world's leading premium vodkas, experts for the New York Times voted Smirnoff No. 21 Red their "hands-down favourite".

History

The SMIRNOFF brand traces its origins to late 19th century Russia where Piotr Arseneevich Smirnov – known by his initials, P.A. – founded a distillery in Moscow and began selling vodkas under his name.

With the abolition of serfdom, P.A. set out in the early 1860s to trade high quality vodka and other alcoholic drinks. In 1864, he founded his vodka distillery and three years later began selling his vodkas at 1 Piatnitskaya Street, known as 'his house by the Iron Bridge', in Moscow.

Although experts disagree as to whether Poles, Russians, or others invented vodka, its origins can be traced to the early 15th century. For much of its early history, vodka was plagued with off-tasting impurities. Distillers consequently experimented with a variety of purification techniques, such as freezing, or infused their vodka with fruit, spices, herbs or other flavours to mask the bad taste.

In the late 18th century, it was discovered that many impurities could be removed by filtering vodka through charcoal made from charred hardwoods. P.A. filtered his vodkas through more charcoal than his competitors. He routinely passed his vodkas through a battery of charcoal-filled columns as many as five times. The Russian Government later credited P.A. with contributing in large measure to the development of the method of charcoal filtration known as the 'St. Petersburg model'. This tradition lives on today. Smirnoff® vodka is filtered through seven tonnes of hardwood charcoal for a full eight hours, resulting in a characteristically pure, smooth taste.

In 1886 P.A. was awarded the title 'Official Purveyor to the Imperial Russian Court'. The firm was also awarded the honour of using the Russian state coats of arms four times between 1877 and 1896. During that time Smirnov's products won numerous awards at international exhibitions in Vienna, Paris, Barcelona and Stockholm.

The Russian Revolution meant that all private industries in Moscow were confiscated by the Bolsheviks. One of P.A.'s three sons, Vladimir – who, as well as learning the family business, had once been one of the most successful horse breeders in the country and socialised with Moscow's literary elite including Maxim Gorky and Anton Chekov – joined the anti-Bolshevik White Army. In 1919 he was arrested and sentenced to death but escaped Russia.

Ending up in Paris, Vladimir was without the enormous wealth he had always known but had still his expertise in making vodka. He adopted the French spelling of his family name, Smirnoff, and battled to make a success of his new company 'Pierre Smirnoff Sons', touting his vodka as made from the finest spirit and filtered through charcoal.

Following an end to prohibition, Smirnoff vodka was made in the US for the first time. Later, in the 1940s, it was marketed as 'White Whisky'. The brand found real success, however, as the ultimate mixable spirit. Smirnoff® began to replace gin in cocktails such as the Martini, the Collins and the Gimlet, becoming more famous than the spirit it had replaced. James Bond immortalised the Vodkatini with his "shaken, not stirred" line in the film Dr. No in 1962.

With a spend of £7 million for 2005 being invested in areas such as the sponsorship of high profile TV shows including Derren Brown's 'Trick of the Mind' on Channel 4, the dominance of the Smirnoff brand in the UK vodka market looks set to continue.

The brand is continuing to invest in Smirnoff Experience®, its flagship experiential marketing campaign designed to bring Smirnoff to life for 21-29 year-olds through music activities and events. Now in its seventh year, Smirnoff Experience began as a club night in Glasgow and soon became a global programme of events, with one million consumers attending events internationally each year. The campaign in the UK includes a groundbreaking advertiser funded TV series, The Joy of Decks, which was shown on ITV in 2004 and a short film for cinema launched in 2005.

Today, Smirnoff Experience brings together Smirnoff products and the best in music talent from around the world to deliver original events in 28 markets including South America, West and East Europe, Africa, the Caribbean and Australia, as well as six TV shows, eight radio shows, a Smirnoff Experience bar in Ibiza and three exclusive CDs.

Brand Values
Smirnoff brand values include versatility, purity, inventiveness and originality. These values are summed up in the brand's core guiding principle: to 'be clearly original'.

www.smirnoff.com

The Smirnoff and Smirnoff Experience words and associated logos are trademarks.

In the early 1950s Smirnoff®, now owned by American drinks company Heublin, arrived in the UK courtesy of an agreement with W&A Gibley of England, which was licensed to manufacture and sell Smirnoff in England, Canada, Australia, New Zealand and South Africa.

Today, Smirnoff® vodka, owned by Diageo, is sold in 130 countries on six continents. A bottle of Smirnoff vodka is sold every six seconds.

Product
Smirnoff® vodka is created by a process steeped in century old traditions and involving three distillations and ten stages of filtration. It is this filtration process that is unique and gives the product its point of difference and characteristically pure, smooth palate.

Like many premium spirits, Smirnoff vodka is first triple-distilled in high-column plate stills. Then it is ten-times filtered through Polish hardwood charcoal for a full eight hours – in what could be described as an almost obsessive dedication to purity. Indeed, its purity is designed to make it an ideal blank canvas for mixing.

As a New York Times review of an expert panel's blind tasting of 21 vodkas in January 2005 put it: "Vodka is measured by purity, by an almost Platonic neutrality that makes tasting it more akin to tasting bottled waters or snowflakes... As the 21 vodkas were sipped and the results compiled, the Smirnoff was our hands-down favourite."

This is the vodka used to make the Smirnoff ready-to-drink variant, Smirnoff Ice, an opaque, citrus-flavoured beverage.

The most recent addition to the Smirnoff family is Smirnoff Norsk, 'the vodka that hates mixing', which is blended with a distillate of real Nordic berries for an extra smooth taste and is designed to be served neat over ice.

Smirnoff Blue (Recipe No. 57) is 'the ultimate cocktail vodka'. Like original Smirnoff® vodka, it is triple-distilled in high-column plate stills and ten-times filtered through charcoal, but made to export strength – it is vodka distilled to a higher ABV/Proof.

Smirnoff 'Black' (Recipe No. 40), is slowly distilled in small batches in a copper pot using only select quality ingredients. This traditional method captures the mellow and smooth character that defines Smirnoff Black.

Smirnoff Penka, described as 'the finest cut', is the super-premium variant that displays the full extent of Smirnoff vodka-making expertise. Quadruple distilled in small batches and made in Poland from top-quality rye-grain, the master distiller takes only the 'finest cut' of the batch to be bottled by hand. It is a luxury vodka designed to be sipped and savoured.

Recent Developments
Smirnoff has always been known for premium quality vodka. In 2004, the brand's look became sharper and more contemporary than ever as the brand launched distinctive new packaging designed to reinforce its premium status and quality. The new look includes an eagle icon that is inspired by the brand's authentic Russian heritage and marks its premium quality.

As part of its re-launch marketing campaign, Smirnoff hosted the 'Smirnoff Rocketman' event in London in April 2004. At this unique publicity event to celebrate the re-launch of Smirnoff® vodka's new eagle icon, the world's one and only Rocketman, whose past appearances include the 1984 LA Olympics, set a new world record for the highest-ever human elevation aided only by a rocket belt. By reaching the height of a 13-storey building – equivalent to a tower of 142 bottles of Smirnoff® vodka – Rocketman set a Guinness World Record. His flight was measured using a high-tech device called an Altimeter, which was strapped to him during the flight.

Promotion
Over the past three years, Diageo has invested more than £17 million in Smirnoff® vodka advertising. During that time, 80% of all vodka advertising was from Smirnoff, which has attracted in excess of two million new customers to the brand since 1999 (Source: TGI).

An epic-style new campaign, 'Not the usual', with executions including 'Russian' and 'Diamonds' was launched in April 2004 in cinemas and on TV. Consumer research carried out by Millward Brown shows that consumers believe the 'Not the usual' campaign to be among the best ads they have seen. Indeed, 3% of off-trade sales from April to July 2004 were attributed to the campaign (Source: Carat Econometric model).

SONY®

Market

Technology has driven dramatic sales growth in the UK market for consumer electronics, causing relatively rapid development in some areas of the market (Source: Euromonitor).

Changes in technology, such as the move away from VCRs in favour of DVD players, have found a ready response with UK consumers, who have enjoyed a generally increasing level of disposable income. The low interest rates and easily available credit of the past few years have facilitated spending. Consumers are also becoming generally

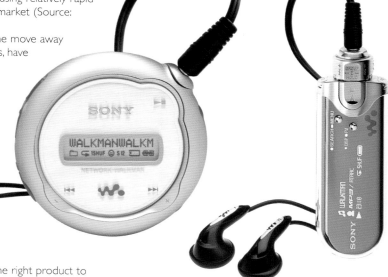

more confident in the selection of the right product to suit their requirements at the premium end of the market, and increasingly treat bottom-of-the-range TVs, VCRs, DVD players or audio systems as almost disposable items.

According to Euromonitor, sales of consumer electronics have also been boosted by the fact that UK consumers are increasingly purchasing second or third units of some products for use in different locations within the home. For example, in addition to the main TV and VCR in the living room, many households now have additional TVs and VCRs in the kitchen or in bedrooms. A similar pattern is evident for personal/portable audio and in-home hi-fi systems, and is beginning to emerge for DVD players.

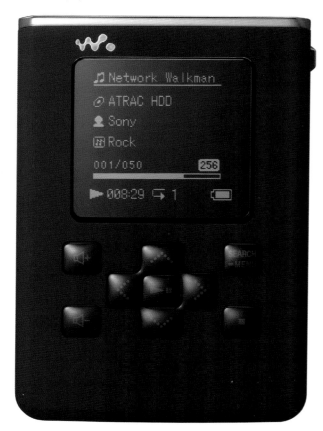

The UK consumer electronics market is dominated by leading global manufacturers – predominantly Japanese companies – which are able to hold a commanding lead in most market sectors by exploiting their technological expertise and strong brand equity.

One such company is leading market player Sony, which manufactures audio, video, communications and information technology products for the global consumer and professional markets. With its music, pictures, game and online businesses, Sony is poised to become a leading personal broadband entertainment company in the 21st century, currently employing more than 160,000 people worldwide. Sony Europe, which handles manufacturing, R&D, design, sales and marketing of consumer and business products in Europe from its corporate headquarters at the Sony Center in Berlin, is a subsidiary of Sony Corporation, Tokyo.

Achievements

Sony is a leading global audio-visual electronics and information technology company. A publicly held company, its shares are listed on 16 stock exchanges worldwide, including Tokyo, New York, and London.

It is currently the second-largest music company in the world, a leading motion picture and television production company and the co-developer of the CD, DVD, and Super Audio CD.

In its history, which spans almost 60 years, Sony has invented, developed, manufactured and marketed a wide range of consumer audio-visual products that have changed the way many people live today. These include the Walkman personal stereo, the Digital8 Handycam camcorder, the FD Trinitron WEGA television, the Mavica digital camera, VAIO personal computers, the MiniDisc player/recorder, the Memory Stick IC flash media; and the PlayStation, PlayStation2 and soon PlayStation3 games consoles.

In Europe, Sony recorded consolidated annual sales, including electronics, music, pictures and games of €13.47 billion for the year ending March 2004. Sony Europe, headquartered at the Sony Center in Berlin, is responsible for the company's European electronics business and registered consolidated sales of €8.71 billion for the year ending March 2004.

History

In 1946, Masaru Ibuka, an engineer, and Akio Morita, a physicist, invested the equivalent of £845 to start a company located in the basements of a bombed-out Tokyo department store.

With 20 employees repairing electrical equipment and attempting to build their own products, the company was initially called Tokyo Tsuchin Kogyo. Its fortunes began to change in 1954, when it obtained a licence to make transistors. The transistor had been invented in America but it had not been applied to radios, which were value-driven appliances. Sony made Japan's first transistor in May 1954 and the first all-transistor radio.

Akio Morita recognised from the beginning that his company needed to have global ambitions and not restrict its activities to Japan alone. He was also a brand visionary, insisting that the Sony name be prominent on all the company's products. Guided by these principles, Sony quickly became an international force, with Sony Corporation of America formed in 1960 and Sony UK founded in 1968.

As Sony grew, Akio Morita was determined to maintain its spirit of enterprise and innovation. His philosophy can be described as 'global localisation'. Operations were centred in small business groups that acted as self-sufficient companies designing and developing products that are sold by the larger group. The corporate functions of research and strategic planning, as well as the advertising and marketing activities, bound the companies together.

In line with its development in consumer electronics products, Sony has in recent years turned its attention to establishing a leading position in the content market as well. In 1988 Sony acquired CBS Records Inc. to form Sony Music Entertainment, and in 1989 it purchased Columbia Pictures to form Sony Pictures Entertainment. The launch of the Sony PlayStation in 1995 saw Sony take a leading position in the video games market.

Product

Sony's most famous product, the Walkman, was launched in 1979. First described as a 'small stereo headphone cassette player', the Walkman introduced the concept of mobile entertainment. At first, retailers reacted badly to the Walkman, arguing that there was no future for a cassette player without a recording mechanism. The public thought differently and Sony sold 1.5 million Walkmans in its first two years on the market.

Today, Sony's product portfolio includes more than 5,000 products. This vast range includes DVD players, cameras, PCs, televisions, hi-fi equipments and semiconductors. These are organised around a brand portfolio that includes Walkman personal audio, Trinitron televisions, VAIO computers, WEGA wide-screen TVs, HandyCam camcorders, Cybershot digital cameras and the PlayStation games console.

Recent Developments

12 years after the introduction of the original PlayStation and six years after the launch of PlayStation2, Sony Computer Entertainment announced at a press conference in Los Angeles, California in May 2005 that it is to launch the PlayStation3, the newest platform with the most advanced next generation Sony computer entertainment technology in May 2006. The entertainment system will incorporate state-of-the-art technologies featuring Cell, a processor jointly developed by IBM, Sony Group and Toshiba Corporation, graphics processor (RSX) co-developed by NVIDIA Corporation and Sony Computer Entertainment, and XDR memory developed by Rambus Inc.

In terms of more traditional Sony products, Qualia is a new exclusive range of digital Sony products, including cameras and projectors, some of which will be launched in the UK in the summer. The first product to launch in the UK will be the 004 projector.

Tipped to be the big selling point in TV for the next few years, High Definition is picking up speed in the UK. From a professional video point of view Sony is currently supplying High Definition video equipment to Sky, the

BBC and other large broadcasters. On the consumer side, the company is getting ready for a big push to get High Definition TV equipment into customers' homes.

As a showcase of Sony's capabilities in the areas of information technology and artificial intelligence, it has produced the QRIO robot. The resulting technologies will be applied to a wide range of Sony products and services, beyond robots.

Promotion

For Sony, marketing is not simply a department; it is a cornerstone of the company's business philosophy. Almost as much attention is paid to innovation in marketing as it is in the development of Sony's new products. This commitment has helped keep Sony at the top of its markets for more almost 60 years.

In the UK, Sony invests more than £40 million per year in the marketing support of its brands, using a mixture of television, cinema, specialist and consumer magazine press advertising, PR and sponsorship. Most recently, it has announced that it is to become an official partner of the FIFA World Cup. The US$305 million contract will run from 2007 to 2014 and will allow Sony to exercise various rights as an official sponsor of more than 40 FIFA events. These include the FIFA World Cup, due to be held in South Africa in 2010 and South America in 2014, as well as the FIFA Women's World Cup, the FIFA Confederations Cup and the FIFA Interactive World Cup.

The agreement makes Sony a 'FIFA Partner', the highest level of sponsorship status, which is accorded to only six companies. Only one FIFA Partner is chosen for a number of defined industry or business categories. Sony has been chosen for the 'Digital Life' category, which will be established in 2007. 'Digital Life' covers a wide variety of business activities from entertainment to electronics and as a FIFA Partner in this category, Sony will be able to exercise certain exclusive rights.

Through this partnership contract, Sony has been given a broad array of rights at FIFA events. Sony will be able to use the partner logo at the FIFA World Cup and other FIFA events as well as having rights to the use of certain FIFA images and archive materials. Other rights will include advertising boards in stadia, TV sponsor credits, on-screen IDs and preferential negotiation rights for TV Commercial spots.

The key sectors of the Sony group (including electronics, movies, music and game) will be involved in its partnership with the word's most popular sport: football. As a FIFA Partner, Sony will mobilise its personnel, material and intellectual property resources and develop new marketing methods to create new value for customers. Sony also hopes to make a real contribution to the sport of football around the world through this long-term partnership with FIFA.

Brand Values

Research by Millward Brown shows that Sony is one of the world's most respected brands, with 65% of people

saying Sony makes products they like to be seen with and 57% of customers saying they would buy more Sony products in the future. In order to maintain Sony's leading position in virtually all of its markets, the company works hard to ensure its marketing supports the Sony brand image of originality, uniqueness, high performance, ease of operation and cutting edge design.

To this end, 2005 saw Sony implement a major new brand positioning as part of its continued drive to engage with its core markets and maximise growth in an increasingly competitive consumer electronics market. The new positioning will see the introduction of the new advertising line 'like.no.other' which will replace the existing line 'You make it a Sony'. The like.no.other campaign is designed to build on Sony's strategy and guiding principle to innovate and offer technological insight into the consumer electronics market. Sony sees the campaign as a major opportunity to build on its past and create a new future for the business.

www.sony.co.uk

Market

Two thirds of the adult population wear glasses or contact lenses – a proportion of society that has been growing gradually along with increased life expectancy.

The optical market is, therefore, driven by an ageing population, in particular the over 45s, because the older we get the more likely we are to need glasses. By the time we are in our 60s, nearly 90% of us will require corrective vision.

Contact lens wearers, which account for only 6% of the population, tend to be in the younger age range, the under 40s.

The current market for eyecare products and services is estimated at more than £2 billion with less than 40% still being provided by small independent opticians (Source: GfK Marketing Services).

For many years now Specsavers Optical Group has been recognised as the market leader in optics – today, one in three people who wear glasses buy them from Specsavers (Source: GfK Marketing Services).

The brand's value market share is more than twice that of its nearest high street competitors. New brands in the market include Optical Express and supermarket retailers ASDA Wal-Mart and Tesco.

With more than 650 stores across the UK, Ireland, the Netherlands and Sweden, Specsavers is one of the most successful brands in retail optics and is the largest privately owned opticians in the world.

Achievements

With sales in 2004 of £620 million, Specsavers' main achievement has been one of almost entirely organic, continuous and sustained growth, despite a slowing down of the retail economy.

Specsavers' advertising campaigns, which are produced by an in-house creative team, regularly appear in Marketing magazine's Adwatch column and the brand's TV commercials have been much acclaimed, with 2004 seeing the highly successful 'Should've gone to Specsavers' campaign win

many awards, including the prestigious Retail Week Marketing Campaign of the Year for the second year running – an unprecedented achievement.

Specsavers' customer magazine View, which is also produced in-house, has won several awards, including the British Association of Communicators in Business Award of Excellence for three years running. Its annual Drive Safe campaign has, over the past four years, been hugely successful in highlighting the need for drivers to have regular sight tests. So much so, that more than 5,000 people signed a petition lobbying the Government to introduce a series of measures aimed at making UK roads safer.

Specsavers' annual modelling competition, which aims to find the sexiest glasses wearer in the UK, is in its ninth year and attracts thousands of entrants, emphasising the fact that glasses are a fashion accessory as well as an optical necessity.

Above all, since its first store opened in 1984, Specsavers greatest achievement has been that it has revolutionised the optical market through its joint venture philosophy and transparent approach to pricing.

The abiding tenet of the Group is that professional and retail optics should be led by the opticians themselves, who own and run their own stores and are responsible for the day-to-day running of their business.

A full range of support services, expertise, experience and information is provided to stores by Specsavers Optical Group (SOG), based in Guernsey, ensuring partners receive help in all aspects of their business, tailored to their specific requirements.

Because the opticians own their own stores and retain profits, paying a management fee to SOG for their support services and marketing activity, they have a vested interest in serving the community and making their business a success.

Specsavers was the first optician to advertise its products and services on television and still spends more on TV than any other optician. Furthermore, it was the first to introduce Complete Price, whereby the cost of glasses includes single vision lenses. It was also the first to promote Two for One offers and free eyecare for children.

Always a trend setter, Specsavers was also the first to offer a full range of contact lenses that could be paid for by monthly direct debit – more than half a million

customers pay for their lenses this way – making what was once seen as an expensive product more widely available.

Specsavers is forging ahead with its European expansion programme and is already the third largest optical group in Holland, having grown from just three stores in 2000 to nearly 70 stores today. In addition, Specsavers has strengthened its position in Europe with the acquisition of Swedish optical groups Blic and Två Blå as well as furthering expansion into Scandinavia. Somewhere in the UK or Europe, a new Specsavers store opens nearly every week.

History

Specsavers was founded in 1984 by Doug and Mary Perkins, who started the business in their spare bedroom on a table-tennis table.

The Perkins had moved to Guernsey after selling a small chain of opticians in the West Country but, in the early 1980s, they saw a gap in the optical market when the UK Government deregulated professionals, including opticians, freeing them to advertise their products and services for the first time.

Seizing this opportunity, Doug and Mary opened their first Specsavers' opticians in Guernsey and Bristol, followed shortly by stores in Plymouth, Swansea and Bath.

From the outset, the Perkins wanted to offer a wide range of stylish, fashionable glasses at affordable prices for everyone.

Specsavers' first logo reflected its value for money approach with two '£' signs replacing the lenses in a pair of glasses. The strapline that went with this – Local Eyecare Nationwide – also demonstrated Specsavers' desire to be seen as trustworthy an optician as a local independent but with the buying power of a national company that meant savings could be passed on to the customer.

Having quickly established the brand in the marketplace as a provider of affordable eyecare, Specsavers changed its logo in 1996 to further reflect the quality of its products and services.

The new logo – two green overlapping ellipses – was coupled with a new strapline, Now You Can Believe Your Eyes, reflecting the customer's expectations that at last they could buy top quality glasses and contact lenses at affordable prices.

With the onset of an ageing population, Specsavers commissioned research that revealed that people over 40 were least attracted to Specsavers and would typically go to an independent, who they perceived as offering a more professional service.

To enhance the credibility of the brand among older people a new campaign began and a new strapline was introduced – Your Eyesight Matters.

TV commercials featuring artist David Shepherd and wheelchair-bound physicist Stephen Hawking, who depend a great deal on their eyesight, successfully illustrated that Specsavers is not just about special offers and promotions but also about professionalism.

The public's perception of the brand has changed significantly over recent years and the brand's current straplines – Number One Choice For Eye Tests and Number One Choice For Contact Lenses – reflect its position as market leader.

Product

Specsavers has always been known for its wide choice of glasses and now offers more than 2,000 styles and colours made from the latest high-tech materials, including titanium and stainless steel.

Its glasses are sourced from all over the world and many are made by the same manufacturers that are responsible for some of the top name designer brands.

Specsavers is also market leader in contact lenses with its own brand of easyvision monthly and daily disposable lenses. It has also pioneered the use of continuous wear lenses that can be worn for up to 24 hours a day for 30 days and is estimated to have at least 40% of the UK market. It is also leading the market with a new group of consumers who require multifocal contact lenses.

Specsavers is also the largest provider of home delivery contact lenses in Europe through its Lensmail service and Specsavers Direct, whereby customers can order their lenses by phone, post or online at www.specsaversdirect.co.uk, as well as more conventionally in store.

Recent Developments

To satisfy younger customers, Specsavers has added glasses by STORM, fcuk®, Boss, Red or Dead, Monsoon and most recently Quiksilver, to complement its own designer ranges Osiris and Ultralight. New styles are introduced continually to keep apace with changes in fashion and technology.

Thanks largely to popular characters such as Peter Parker (Spiderman) and Harry Potter, children are now more confident about wearing glasses from an early age, so in 2004 Specsavers launched its kids' designer range, with Beano, Barbie and Action Man branded glasses now available.

Specsavers' own lens manufacturing laboratories – three of the largest in Europe – mean that it can supply the latest high-tech lenses at high volume and low cost using efficient Robotics.

Specsavers' contact lens department is always on the look out for new lenses, such as varifocal contact lenses for older customers or lenses that help correct colour blindness.

Specsavers website has been developed and refined so that customers can now view the latest frames, order contact lenses online and review the current offers and promotions available at their local store.

As well as rapid expansion in Europe, Specsavers branched out into the hearing aid industry in 2003, with the acquisition of the HearCare franchise and currently has more than 26 Specsavers HearCare stores in the UK. The deal, which is creating 400 new jobs over three years, is seeing the roll out of 100 new private hearing aid centres retaining the HearCare brand and mirroring Specsavers hugely successful joint venture business model.

Promotion

Although most people should have a thorough eye examination at least every two years, many choose to leave it much longer and are either oblivious of their declining vision or mistakenly think that an eye test is only about a prescription. The reality is that the eyes can also be an indication of poor health.

As well as highlighting visual problems, an eye examination can also help detect diabetes, glaucoma, high blood pressure, even the presence of a brain tumour. Through the eye test, many opticians at Specsavers have saved lives.

Convincing people that they must have their eyes tested for the sake of their health as well as their sight is therefore of primary importance to Specsavers.

There is no fixed period for selling glasses or contact lenses – it is not a seasonal product – which is why the brand advertises year-round special offers and promotions.

Specsavers therefore aims to reach as many people as possible throughout the year via carefully targeted promotions aimed at young people, contact lens wearers, fashion-conscious customers and older people who may need different types of lenses, such as varifocals and bifocals.

Specsavers' in-house marketing and media buying departments make full use of the media mix, including television, radio, press and public relations, nationally and on a regional and local level to emphasise that Specsavers is a professional optician serving the local community with quality products.

It also has a duty of care to inform people when their next eye examination is due, which is done through

direct mail. Specsavers sends out 280,000 letters a week reminding people that they are due a sight test, or that their contact lenses are ready for collection or delivery and of current and forthcoming offers.

Its in-store magazine View, which is published twice a year, is available free of charge in all stores and is mailed out to 600,000 customers.

Brand Values

Specsavers' brand values have remained consistent throughout its 20-year history – it aims to be the best value optician, satisfying personal eyecare needs at affordable prices in a simple and clear manner that everyone can understand.

Throughout its history, Specsavers has continued to focus on what Doug and Mary strived to achieve since the beginning; an optician that passionately provides high quality and affordable eyecare for everyone.

The brand is now the most well known of all the opticians – of those surveyed, 96% recognise the Specsavers logo (Source: TNS) – something of which the brand is immensely proud considering the age of some of the brands with which it competes.

www.specsavers.com

Market

The hand tools sector has a degree of dependence on the strength of some key industries such as the construction and engineering markets. In addition, a further major end use market for hand tools is that of the DIY sector. This market has become a well-established element of consumer spending which has been growing over a prolonged period. Householders' enthusiasm for undertaking work in their homes has been spurred on by numerous related TV programmes and magazine articles that relay the positive affects of home improvements.

Stanley's total hand tools market value share continues to grow year-on-year, with the 12 month period ending April 2004 showing an increase of 3.5% from £35.3 million to £36.6 million (Source: GfK). In terms of market value, Stanley now controls 27.3% of the market and 20.5% in terms of market volume (Source: GfK). Out of the top 20 best selling products during that period 16 were from Stanley, including the number one product, the retractable trim knife.

Achievements

Stanley is one of the world's oldest tool manufacturers and largest hard goods manufacturers. It is renowned for its classic Stanley knife, which has earned its place in the vernacular, becoming frequently used as a generic term. The Stanley 99E knife is the best selling branded line in the entire UK DIY hand tools market.

The Stanley brand has a near perfect (99%) prompted awareness level in the consumer market and is stronger in Europe than anywhere else in the world. Indeed, a total of 30% of the brand's revenue is driven by European sales.

Stanley received what may have been the very first patent issued for ergonomic tools and since then have had numerous firsts, be it patents on new product designs or design improvements on existing products. In addition, the brand won three prestigious 'Good Design' awards from The Chicago Athenaeum Museum of Architecture for products in its storage range and has also won a clutch of medals in The Business Week/IDSA Awards. The brand has also won the praise of numerous industry leaders for advertising creativity, product innovation and design.

Furthermore, many of Stanley's tools have become status symbols among professional tradesmen. In addition, some Stanley tools have become valuable antiques and collectors' items – giving credit to the brand's strong heritage.

History

Sheffield has traditionally been the home of steel production and is often associated with Stanley despite it being an American who founded the company. Frederick T Stanley,

with his brother William, first conceived Stanley Bolt Manufactory in New Britain, Connecticut in 1843 – little did they know that the company would eventually grow to employ 16,000 people. They began by manufacturing door bolts and hinges in a humble workshop but quickly gained a reputation for quality and value – a reputation that still exists to this day.

With expansion, the Stanley brothers pooled their funds with other investors, nervous of risking all their resources in one concern, to create a corporation. Stanley was established on July 1st 1852 and was officially titled The Stanley Works – which remains as the company's official name today.

In 1920 Stanley Works acquired the Stanley Rule & Level Company founded by Henry Stanley, who was a distant cousin of the brothers, that sold levels, planes, rules, hammers, carpenters' squares and various hand tools. This went on to become the famous tools division of Stanley, producing innovative and practical equipment such as the Bailey plane, the Powerlock rule and the Surform shaper.

In 1937 Stanley purchased the Sheffield-based steel and fine tools maker J A Chapman and began manufacturing in the UK – based at Woolside, where tools are still manufactured today.

The brand continued to work with its core values in mind and built on the strong heritage that had been established by the Stanley brothers to steer the brand towards the 21st century.

Following a £1.4 million investment, Stanley announced that its Hellaby plant in Rotherham would become a 'Centre of Excellence'. It is now the worldwide producer and supplier of knives, blades, chisels, screwdrivers and the Surform shaping tool to all Stanley's global markets.

Product

In the UK, Stanley is most recognised for its hand tools in the consumer sector.

Indeed, a recent survey showed 87% of consumers and 97% of professionals owned at least one Stanley tool.

Stanley understands that the key to winning a strong retail position is to have innovative products merchandised effectively. This strategy is complemented with a single look and feel achieved through consistent product colours and packaging design. Stanley's distinctive yellow and black branding makes products clearly stand out on the shelves of the nation's DIY stores. Indeed, the range is so extensive that in many stores a rash of yellow can been seen running down a whole isle.

The Stanley range is divided into six main product areas; hand tools – including knives, screwdrivers, saws, hammers etc; decorators products – incorporating paint brushes,

rollers, stripping knives etc; home solutions – namely sliding wardrobe doors; fastening systems; mechanics' tools and storage units – including toolboxes and workbenches. All these products carry the brand's 160 year-old hallmark of quality and design.

Recent Developments

Although in a very strong position in the marketplace, Stanley has not become complacent about the need for innovation. Following the success of its Discovery Team programme in the US, Stanley began rolling out the programme in Europe. The teams, known as the eyes and ears of the business, have worked with US professionals on site since 1997, enabling Stanley to evaluate the development potential of tools.

Globally, it has taken a strong acquisition approach to expand its consumer offering over the last 12 months. Recent purchases include CST Berger, a leading designer and manufacturer of laser and optical levelling and measuring equipment, for US$62 million cash, and Blick, a market leader in the design, installation and maintenance of a complete range of security, communication and time management solutions to businesses. The Blick acquisition denotes a new direction for Stanley as they enter the service sector for the first time and this corporate initiative, seen in 2004, is likely to be an ever-increasing trend for the company in future years.

Stanley does, however, exist far beyond this, producing over 50,000 different tools, hardware, decorating and door products for professional, industrial and consumer use. Additionally, Stanley continues to cement the brand's position in the storage sector making it synonymous with excellence in tool and household storage. With the re-launch of the company's Home Solutions division, following its sale to Wellspring Capital Management in October 2004, the brand will continue to support a product range that offers homeowners the opportunity to transform their living space with an exciting range of products ranging from mirrors to interior storage systems and sliding doors.

Promotion

Since 1998, more than 325 products have been introduced and over 26 licensing agreements have been signed for ancillary products (e.g. work gloves, torches and power tool accessories).

Stanley continues to promote the message that encourages interaction with their products with the strapline 'Feel the Stanley Difference' featuring some of the best selling products and the strapline that Stanley is the 'number one brand for tools – demanded for their performance by professionals, enthusiasts and DIY'ers alike.'

Feel
the STANLEY difference

From the timeless Classic 199 "Stanley Knife", a design icon of the 20th century, to the new range of FatMax™ hand tools, innovation and quality are synonymous with the Stanley name. Stanley is the number one brand for tools – demanded for their performance by professionals, enthusiasts and DIYers alike.

Stanley in the 21st century is much more than just knives. In addition to the world famous hand tools the Stanley range now includes paint brushes and rollers, sliding doors, pneumatic fastening solutions and mechanics tools.

Stanley UK Sales Ltd, Beighton Road East, Drakehouse, Sheffield S20 7JZ
Tel: 0114 276 8888   Fax: 0114 276 4078

The brand aims to inspire and motivate consumers to realise their skills fully. It also hopes to be visionary and creative and, as a result, remain in the position of brand leader in the hard goods industry. Furthermore, commitment to continuous innovation has created a steady stream of new products and business opportunities worldwide.

Stanley believes that key enablers to its growth are competitiveness and exceptional customer service, both of which depend on simplicity, standardisation and systemisation.

Brand Values

The Stanley brand has four key strengths – namely quality, innovation, knowledge and integrity. This is backed up by the way in which Stanley tools are designed and built for professionals and for those that think like professionals.

www.stanleyworks.com

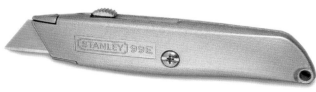

Market

Not a brand in the traditional sense of the word, the FAIRTRADE Mark is an independent certification label, licensed in the UK by the Fairtrade Foundation. It harnesses the purchasing power of consumers to address inequalities in trading relationships, guaranteeing a fair deal for farmers in some of the world's poorest countries. The FAIRTRADE Mark is available on products sourced from the developing world that meet internationally agreed Fairtrade standards.

Key sectors for Fairtrade are currently hot beverages (coffee, tea, chocolate drinks), fruits and juices (including bananas, pineapples, mangoes and grapes) and cakes, biscuits and confectionery (using ingredients such as cocoa, sugar, honey, dried fruit or nuts).

UK sales of products with the FAIRTRADE Mark grew by 51% in 2004, fuelled by growing consumer awareness of the guarantees behind Fairtrade, the wider availability and expanded range of Fairtrade products. Repeat purchasing by consumers was another reason, driven by recognition of the high quality of Fairtrade products and consumers buying into the positive impact that their choice has for the producers.

While the £140 million spent by UK shoppers in 2004 is a tiny part of the nation's total food market, Fairtrade products have achieved a market share of more than 3.5% in coffee (with 18% in the premium roast & ground sector) and 5% in bananas. Consumer panel research suggests that more than one in five UK households have purchased a Fairtrade product in the past 12 months. There are now more than 900 products in the UK carrying the FAIRTRADE Mark – a huge rise from around 150 in 2003.

Fairtrade products are now stocked by all the major national supermarket chains and are well established in independent outlets, mainly in the specialist health and whole-food sectors. The Co-op supermarket has consistently blazed a trail for Fairtrade products in its stores. The Co-op's own-label Fairtrade offering now boasts 100 products and the FAIRTRADE Mark appears on all Co-op own-label coffee and chocolate. Sainsbury's and Waitrose have also been strong players for many years while the ongoing mainstreaming of Fairtrade is both reflected and encouraged by increased availability in Tesco and ASDA.

Achievements

In 2004, its 10th anniversary year, the Fairtrade Foundation was named Charity of the Year. In addition, the Fairtrade Fortnight media campaign for 2004 was declared PRWeek's Campaign of the Week.

Awareness of the FAIRTRADE Mark has grown predominantly by word of mouth. Despite a negligible advertising budget for generic promotions, growth in

sales and awareness has unfailingly been impressive. Sales grow by around 40% year-on-year, while recognition among consumers was 50% in 2005, up from 39% in 2004 and 25% in 2003 – and the percentage of people able to correctly associate the FAIRTRADE symbol with the definition 'Guarantees a better deal for Third World producers' increased from 33% in 2003, to 42% a year later, reaching 51% in 2005 (Source: MORI).

In its early days the Fairtrade Foundation was run by a staff of two and a half, plus a small team of dedicated volunteers. From such tiny beginnings growth was only possible by reaching the supporter bases of the Fairtrade Foundation's founding organisations such as Oxfam, Christian Aid and the World Development Movement and inspiring them to spread the message about Fairtrade to their friends and colleagues.

In Britain, the FAIRTRADE Mark now appears on products from 150 companies while, across the world, Fairtrade is working with more than 450 producer organisations in 50 countries, with benefits from the global market reaching around five million people – farmers, workers and their families.

And it is in developing countries that Fairtrade's greatest achievements lie. Farmers, once marginalised in the trading chain, now earn a fair deal under the Fairtrade system. Sales across the 20 countries where Fairtrade labelling operates were estimated to have reached US$500 million in 2004, delivering US$50 million more to producer groups than they would have received on the conventional market.

History

Fairtrade labelling first appeared in the Netherlands in the late 1980s when world market prices for coffee had plummeted to an all-time low. A group of Mexican farmers turned to Solidaridad, a Dutch development agency, and asked for 'trade not aid'. Their coffee was bought at a price that covered the cost of production and the first coffee appeared on the shelves in the Netherlands in 1986 with the 'Max Havelaar' Fairtrade logo, named after a fictional Dutch character who opposed the exploitation of coffee pickers in Dutch colonies.

Labelling initiatives quickly grew in other European countries, under the names of Max Havelaar, Transfair and, in 1992, the Fairtrade Foundation was established in the UK. It was funded by a consortium of development agencies including CAFOD, Christian Aid, New Consumer, Oxfam, Traidcraft and the World Development Movement. These founding organisations were later

joined by Britain's largest women's organisation, the National Federation of Women's Institutes, and a further seven organisations.

With its international partners, the Fairtrade Foundation established Fairtrade Labelling Organisations International in 1997 to co-ordinate the setting of standards and monitoring of the supply chain. Fairtrade extended its range into other sectors, based on where it could have an impact on the problems faced by farmers and workers in developing countries together with consumer demand for a Fairtrade alternative.

Today, 20 organisations license the FAIRTRADE Mark across Europe, North America, Japan and Australasia, with labels also being established in developing countries such as Mexico.

Product

1994 saw the launch of the first Fairtrade-labelled product in the UK: Green & Black's Maya Gold Chocolate, which used organic cocoa sourced from Belize. This was followed by Cafédirect Coffee and Clipper Tea. All three remain highly popular Fairtrade products. In 2005, over 900 Fairtrade-certified products are on sale in the UK.

Cafédirect has consistently been the best-known brand within Fairtrade, for both its total commitment to the scheme (all of its products carry the FAIRTRADE Mark) and for its partnership with the Foundation over 11 years. The success of this partnership is demonstrated in Cafédirect's achievement as the sixth-largest coffee brand in the UK and, with its associated brand, Teadirect, the fastest-growing tea brand. Other brands that incorporate the FAIRTRADE Mark as an integral part of their marketing include Traidcraft and the Divine and Dubble ranges from The Day Chocolate Company. However, the FAIRTRADE Mark certifies specific products rather than generic brands or companies and most of the Foundation's partners offer Fairtrade products as an element in their portfolio – the best-known and longest-established of these are Percol and Green & Blacks.

Anyone buying a product that bears the FAIRTRADE Mark – from coffee, tea, chocolate and fresh fruit to roses, honey, footballs or wine – can be sure they are helping to make a difference to the lives of the farmers and workers who've helped produce them. The FAIRTRADE Mark demonstrates that products have been independently verified as complying with Fairtrade standards.

Recent Developments

The Fairtrade Foundation is constantly working to bring new products under the Fairtrade umbrella. Recent additions

CHECK OUT THE GROWING RANGE OF FAIRTRADE PRODUCTS

Guarantees a **better deal** for Third World Producers

CHECK OUT FAIRTRADE
www.fairtrade.org.uk

consistent messaging across a wide range of media. An estimated 7,500 local events and more than 1,500 media mentions were achieved during the period of the promotion. Representatives of Fairtrade farmers from across the world travel to the UK every year to play a major part in Fairtrade Fortnight. They meet at first-hand those at the other end of the supply chain – the people who buy their produce.

Local campaigns have been key to the growing take-up of Fairtrade in the out-of-home sector as part of public sustainability policy, local business social responsibility practices and developments in restaurants and catering. There are now more than 100 Fairtrade Towns in the UK, together with Fairtrade Churches, Universities and Schools.

Brand Values

Fairtrade's brand values emphasise vision and partnership. The brand is encapsulated in the following words from Arturo Gomez, a Costa Rican banana farmer: "Before I was someone who took a box and loaded it onto a train. That was my only responsibility. I was just a farmer. In this new Fairtrade system, I have become an international businessman."

www.fairtrade.org.uk

THINGS YOU DIDN'T KNOW ABOUT

The FAIRTRADE Mark

> Fairtrade products can be found in the Houses of Parliament, in Salvation Army hostels, in Virgin Airlines' Upper Class Lounges – and at the exclusive Sanderson Hotel in central London where patrons can enjoy one of six Fairtrade chocolate Martini cocktails, made with Fairtrade Divine chocolate.

> More than three million Fairtrade hot drinks and almost half a million Fairtrade bananas are consumed every day in the UK.

> Many Fairtrade products have organic accreditation and are marketed as double certified, that is organic and Fairtrade. Some Fairtrade products are described as 'practically organic' by the farmers, because herbicides are not used and use of pesticides has been cut dramatically.

> The FAIRTRADE Mark on a product increases interest and sales. When Ehrmanns wine obtained the FAIRTRADE Mark for its Los Robles wine in September 2004, sales doubled at Sainsbury's.

> Many new Fairtrade products are composite items – everything that can be Fairtrade certified in their ingredients is Fairtrade. So Fairtrade chocolate swiss rolls, Fairtrade coffee beer, muesli and many other items are now available.

> Glastonbury Festival has committed to Fairtrade certification for all coffee and hot chocolate sold at the festival.

include roses, footballs, wines and beers. Major projects for 2005 include the development of cotton and cotton products carrying the FAIRTRADE Mark, as well as rice. Fairtrade seafood is also being explored.

Out-of-home is the fastest growing sector of sales of products carrying the FAIRTRADE Mark – sales increased by more than 70% in 2004. This includes Fairtrade products being consumed in workplace canteens, boardrooms, schools, universities, restaurants, cafés, pubs and clubs. 100% Fairtrade vending machines are also on the rise.

Fairtrade coffee (and increasingly a wider range of beverages and foods) has been adopted as standard by high street café chains such as AMT Coffee, which operates hot beverage kiosks in train stations and airports, and Marks & Spencer's Café Revive chain, while other chains such as Costa Coffee, Pret A

Manger and Starbucks include Fairtrade products either on particular lines or as an option on request.

The Government's Department for International Development awarded the Fairtrade Foundation a grant of £750,000 in 2005. This will be used for expanding the range and distribution of Fairtrade products and extending the benefits of Fairtrade to more producers, building the reputation of the FAIRTRADE Mark as a guarantee of the highest standards.

Promotion

A new international FAIRTRADE Mark was launched in 2002, and although the Mark bore few similarities to its predecessor, there was no loss in recognition by the public. This is one indicator of the success of the Foundation's promotional work, which has been largely based on below-the-line activity, complementing the direct promotion of its licensees' brands. The Foundation works with a wide range of commercial and not-for-profit networks to achieve maximum impact. Campaigns reflect the core Fairtrade values of community and social development, enabling local innovation and broad participation to drive forward a dynamic, people-centred brand.

LUIS WANTS A FAIR PRICE FOR HIS CROP. THE FAIRTRADE MARK GUARANTEES IT.

Guarantees a **better deal** for Third World Producers

CHECK OUT FAIRTRADE
www.fairtrade.org.uk

Fairtrade Fortnight, held annually at the beginning of March, provides concentrated promotional opportunity generating a significant level of media impact. The strategy combines community activity and a strong retail element, so that local debates, open-air events or tasting stands in workplaces, churches, town halls and schools are complemented with in-store promotion. Annual themes have focused on the quality of Fairtrade products (such as Trust Your Taste in 2003, and A Taste for Life in 2004), as well as the guarantees of the FAIRTRADE Mark.

In 2005, the Check Out Fairtrade theme covered both the core guarantees provided by the FAIRTRADE Mark and the incentive to take Fairtrade products to the checkout. The Fairtrade Foundation worked with companies and retailers to deliver in-store promotional offers, point-of-sale, tastings, magazine features and staff communications which enabled

THE ✦ TIMES

Market

The UK newspaper market is the most competitive market in the world, with 37 million people reading a national paper each week and one in two adults reading a paper every day.

Over the past five years, the pace of change in information provision has continued to move at a breakneck speed due to the proliferation of satellite TV channels, radio stations and the internet. In spite of the crowded marketplace, quality newspapers have continued to build their reputation as credible sources of information. This reputation has been nurtured and nourished over hundreds of years and the editorial integrity of the newspaper is entwined with the brand.

Presented with so much choice, consumers often don't know who to trust for information and they turn to brands that they trust. This means that quality newspapers hold a valued position in the media market today as 'the' leading credible source of news.

But with opportunities come challenges and – for one of the oldest media – newspapers have been very adept at moving with the times. The aim of The Times is to be the best newspaper in the world. The goal is to deliver accurate, intelligent and engaging information to an ever-larger, ever more discerning audience. The Times has had a traditional role as a journal of record since its establishment in the 18th century. As the delivery of information has changed, so the role of the journal of record has evolved.

The role of The Times has evolved not only in response to increased media channels but also in tune with reader attitudes and behaviour.

Historically a quality newspaper was seen as a serious informer, commentator, advertiser and campaigner and consumer demand now asks that they also entertain, by providing lifestyle opinions and by fuelling the passions of their readers, be they sport, entertainment, or health and well-being. A paper must also reflect the changing pace of life and the fact that more and more people are on the move. It is this understanding of people's lives today that led The Times and The Independent to revolutionise the newspaper industry by launching compact versions of their papers in 2003.

Achievements

2004 was a landmark year in the history of The Times. From November, The Times broadsheet was consigned to the archives, as the paper became fully compact from Monday to Saturday.

The compact revolution has driven the newspaper industry forward into the 21st century; it has deconstructed the old 'broadsheet/tabloid' paradigm and demonstrated that quality writing is not determined by format. It has also rejuvenated the broadsheet market after years of declining sales. The Times has enjoyed substantial circulation growth since the compact was first introduced in November 2003. It has benefited from 14 months of consecutive growth in real sales, while The Daily Telegraph has endured 14 months of consecutive decline.

Since changing its format, The Times has retained its core audience but has also attracted readers from other titles. Among these switchers are an enviable number of upmarket and affluent young readers. Of all the national quality dailies, The Times has the highest number of ABC1 and AB readers under 45.

The success of the compact has not only been restricted to sales and readership: The Times has recently been voted the most trusted newspaper in Britain by an independent survey and according to research, brand perceptions of The Times as a dynamic, contemporary and progressive newspaper have also increased.

In addition to pioneering change in the newspaper industry, The Times and its journalists have continued to collect numerous awards, most recently Giles Coren was named Food and Drink writer of the year, Richard Cannon Feature Photographer of the year, Gill Morgan Magazine Editor of the Year, Anne Spackman Property Writer of the Year, Robert Crampton Interviewer of the Year, Carol Midgely Feature Writer of the Year, Matthew Parris Writer of the Year, Simon Barnes best Olympic Writer, The Times sports section was named Team of the Year, The Times was named as the UK's best financial newspaper by the prestigious Wincott Awards and won best paper for sport in The Sports Industry Awards.

The Times also continues to collect accolades for its communications. 'Director', The Times' London Film Festival advertisement, won Silver at Creative Circle, an Epica award and was shortlisted for the Institute of Practitioners In Advertising's Best of the Best. 'Bottle' and 'Banana' both won Silver Lions at Cannes. 'Biggest for Sport' posters won silver at the Campaign Poster awards and The Times won the Hollis award for the most effective use of sponsorship for Channel 4 cricket activity.

History

The Times has been at the forefront of journalism since it was founded in 1785. One of the world's oldest surviving daily newspapers, The Times quickly gained the reputation as a hard-hitting newspaper and, after an article in 1830, acquired the nickname 'The Thunderer', by which it is still known today.

Yet between 1908 and 1926 its position was under threat due to spiralling costs and strike action during the General Strike. Lord Thomson first brought the two different titles, The Times and The Sunday Times, together in 1966. By 1981, both The Times and The Sunday Times were sold to News International. It was in 1986, with a new state-of-the-art printing works built in Wapping, that News International took the significant steps that would change the newspaper industry forever.

JONNY WILKINSON
WRITES EXCLUSIVELY FOR THE TIMES.

THE ✦ TIMES
JOIN THE DEBATE

Other newspaper companies soon followed News International by moving out of Fleet Street. Continuous change and production innovation have been at the heart of The Times since it was first founded and right up to the present day.

Product

The Times newspaper has always been regarded as the quality 'quality'. It is one of the world's most recognisable, trusted and respected newspapers.

The Times breaks more news stories than any other newspaper, is the number-one paper for business, enjoying 49% more business readers than the FT and has more sports coverage than any other daily newspaper.

Over the past two years, The Times' commitment to sport has developed significantly, with an all star line-up of writers from across the sporting spectrum including Jonny Wilkinson, Michael Owen and Matthew Pinsent. The Times was the first paper to launch the sports handbook, which it continues to produce covering football, rugby, cricket, golf, tennis and athletics.

In 2002 it launched The Game on Mondays, the only dedicated football supplement in the quality market and in 2004 it launched The Euro Game, a bespoke Champions' League supplement featuring Gabby Logan and Mark Pougatch.

Furthermore, The Times has embarked on a series of sponsorship activities to support its commitment to sport. As the Official Newspaper of English Rugby, The Times supported England's autumn internationals and Six Nations campaign with bespoke publishing activity and a wealth of in-paper content, including exclusive extracts from Jonny Wilkinson's autobiography My World. The Times also sponsors the drive-time show on Talksport, which has been re-branded The Game. Other sponsorship activity includes The Times British Film Institute London Film Festival for which the newspaper is the lead sponsor.

The Times also has a strong portfolio of dedicated sections throughout the week. 2003 saw the launch of Public Agenda on Tuesdays, a section dedicated to reporting the highlights from the public sector. Screen on Thursdays, a standalone film section which carries the latest film reviews, industry news and gossip. On Friday, Bricks and Mortar presents the latest facts, figures and fantasies from the world of property. Also new in 2003 was the re-launched Saturday Times which included four new sections, The Knowledge, a weekly insider's guide to life in London, The Eye, a guide to what's on the big and small screens, Weekend Review, the intelligent read for high- and low-brow culture and Body & Soul, a supplement dedicated to health and well-being. Body & Soul is the only section of its kind in the UK newspaper market. 2004 saw the launch of Career, a weekly supplement targeting graduates to middle managers with advice on how to get jobs and where to find them.

As well as outstanding editorial content, the paper is committed to dynamic design – The Times now has the most ambitiously designed sections of any newspaper in the world and it has a strength in design, graphics and photography that is unmatched by any of its competitors.

As a paper of record, The Times is famous for the Obituaries, Court and Social, Birthdays and Anniversaries and the Debate section – all of which are under the title of The Register. Furthermore, The Times would not be The Times without its challenging crossword, the Letters to the Editor and the Comment section.

Recent Developments

The most significant recent development at The Times has been the switch to become a fully compact newspaper. Reader response has been overwhelmingly positive and the new format has introduced many new readers to The Times.

New readers are attracted by the format and captivated by the content. However, the compact is just the start in the next phase of the ongoing evolution of The Times as it continues to deliver an exciting, engaging, accessible and confident product for its readers.

Promotion

Communication for The Times reflects the changes in the paper and the changing attitudes towards the paper through the new brand campaign, 'Join the Debate'.

As a concept, 'Join the Debate' goes to the heart of why people read newspapers, principally to acquire knowledge enabling them to participate in the conversations and debates of the day. In advertising, this is expressed through two personalities debating a particular issue, which acts as a metaphor for the balance of opinion, wit and stimulating content in the paper. Personalities in the television commercials include Gabby Logan and Jonny Wilkinson discussing the merits of rugby versus football and comedians Sanjeev Bhaskar and Harry Hill debating what is the greatest film of all time. 'Join the Debate' is not just an advertising idea but a brand concept that The Times aims to bring to life on every page of the paper.

The Times' promotional strategy is to work closely with branding activity to reinforce the values of the paper. As the brand campaign continues to focus on re-appraisal through key editorial areas such as sport, entertainment and health and well-being so, too, will the promotions.

The Times has continued its hugely successful 'Eat out for £5', which moves into its 10th year, while its partnership with WH Smith has evolved from free books in travel stores to free DVDs in high street stores.

The alliance with Starbucks has continued to grow; The Times is now sold in over 250 stores and it has recently teamed up with Air Miles for an unprecedented three-month, seven-day token collect scheme.

Brand Values

The Times has long enjoyed a reputation as one of the world's leading newspaper brands. At the heart of the brand lies the paper's objectivity and integrity. The Times is renowned for delivering coverage of the issues of the day that is fair, honest and objective. Its commitment to providing readers with a breadth of opinions and perspectives ensures the newspaper maintains the reader's trust and respect.

Furthermore, the provision of this breadth of opinion and analysis is driven by the brand's aim to equip the reader with essential, engaging and enjoyable news, comment and analysis. This goal is fundamental to the paper's values and one of the principal reasons why The Times today continues to command the reputation as 'the definitive quality.'

Alongside these guiding values, the paper's passion for each subject matter is ever evident. This promises not only an informed read but one that also absorbs, entertains and stimulates readers.

As the newspaper market continues to evolve, these values will continue to shape The Times' celebrated reputation and will help to ensure that the paper remains the powerful brand it is today.

www.timesonline.co.uk

THINGS YOU DIDN'T KNOW ABOUT

The Times

❯ The Times was the first newspaper ever to use the title 'The Times' when it changed its name from the 'Daily Universal Register' to 'The Times' on January 1st 1788.

❯ On October 3rd 1932, the first typeface (Times New Roman) specifically designed for use by a newspaper was launched and became the most successful in history.

❯ Over one year, The Times prints 2.2 million miles of newspaper – enough to go to the moon and back more than four times – and of which more than two-thirds is recycled paper.

❯ In 1971, The Times was the first newspaper ever to show a nude photograph – a naked lady, in full colour for an advert – which caused some controversy.

Timberland Make it better.™

Market

We all know the power of a global Superbrand but nowhere is that influence felt more keenly than in the fashion industry. The trend towards more casual dressing has particularly favoured the sports and leisure orientated Superbrands that are the true engines of growth in the market.

The market for sports clothing continues to grow in value terms, with a market value of £3.25 billion at retail selling price in 2004 – an estimated 8.6% share of the entire £38 billion clothing market (Source: Key Note).

The fashion industry is in constant flux, with brands constantly extending from traditional areas of speciality. For example, many fashion brands have extended into eyewear, including Timberland, hailing from areas as diverse as outdoor boots and childrenswear. In such a brand-conscious market, the power of the brand can carry manufacturers across numerous category boundaries.

The strategy has proven very successful, with Timberland now known not only for its rugged outdoor gear, but also as a trail-blazer of inner city urban cool.

Achievements

In just over 30 years, Timberland has turned itself from a small bootmaker into a US$1.2 billion global lifestyle brand.

It all began with Timberland's wheat-coloured Classic Boot which defined a new footwear category and inspired a host of imitators. This kudos of being the genuine article has inevitably boosted the reputation of Timberland as an outdoor classic and helped it establish credibility across its wider clothing and footwear range.

Like all true classics, Timberland's reputation is built on a legacy of innovation and outstanding quality. In 1965, in a footwear industry first, brothers Sidney and Herman Swartz tackled the problem of leaky work boots by using injection moulding technology to fuse rubber lug outsoles to waterproof leather uppers, resulting in guaranteed waterproof leather workboats. This revolutionary new boot was branded Timberland and a legacy was born.

Other trail-blazing product innovations by the company include the 1978 creation of the rugged casual footwear category. Timberland combined a boat shoe upper with a rugged lug boot sole to create a new style of shoe that has become another modern classic.

In 1988, Timberland created a lightweight leather hiker boot called the Euro Hiker. In its first year the Euro Hiker flew off the shelves and a new outdoor footwear category called 'day hiking' was established.

Timberland has also brought creative solutions to clothing, with innovations like premium leather jackets made from Timberland's exclusive, silicon-impregnated waterproof leathers. These products continue to be icons in the industry today.

Timberland has applied its innovation ethos to the way it conducts business. In addition to making quality products, Timberland believes that it also has a responsibility to help effect positive change in the communities where its employees and consumers work and live. All around the world, Timberland demonstrates a deep commitment to 'doing well and doing good' through its Path of Service programme. Encouraged to pull on their own boots and make a difference, Timberland employees are granted 40 hours of paid time off to do community service every year. Over the past eleven years, this has yielded more than 230,000 hours of service around the globe.

The company also stages a global annual community service event, called 'Serv-a-palooza', in which employees, consumers and the company's partners take part in a host of projects all over the world. For one day in 2003, 4,500 Timberland employees, business partners and consumers participated in the company's sixth annual Serv-a-palooza. This one-of-a-kind community service event generated more than 31,000 hours of community service at 150 service events in 21 countries – all in one day.

History

Timberland can trace its origins back to 1952, to New England, USA, when Nathan Swartz bought a 50% interest in the Abingdon Shoe Company, a Massachusetts-based outfit manufacturing 'own label' shoes for leading US footwear brands.

By 1955, Swartz had bought the remaining interest in the business and was joined by his two sons. Swartz and sons made their first boots under the Timberland name in 1973. Thanks to the revolutionary injection-moulding technique they had introduced eight years earlier, they were guaranteed to be waterproof and were an instant hit. As its leather boots and shoes appeared on the market, the brand became well-known and in 1978 the business changed its name to The Timberland Company.

In 1980 Timberland footwear was launched in Italy, its first foray into the international market. In 1986, the first Timberland store opened in Newport, Rhode Island, USA. Two years later, Timberland introduced the HydroTech boat shoe as well as its first men's sportswear collection. Timberland came to the UK in the 1980s through distributor partnerships but a subsidiary of the business was set up in 1989.

In 1991, Jeffery Swartz, the grandson of founder Nathan, was named as Chief Operating Officer. Timberland began trading on the New York stock exchange under the symbol TBL and in the following year became the founding national sponsor of City Year, making its first US$1 million investment.

In 1996 a new line of women's casual footwear was introduced, as was a multi-purpose outdoor line of performance footwear. Kids' footwear was also launched and new licensing agreements were signed for gloves, travel gear, eyewear, socks and legwear. In 1998 Jeffery Swartz became Timberland's president and, in the same year, revenues hit US$862.2 million.

Today, Timberland operates more than 180 stores throughout Europe and more than 150 stores in markets including Chile, Israel, Poland and South Africa.

Product

The Timberland Company designs, engineers and markets premium quality footwear, clothing and accessories under the Timberland brand name and the Timberland PRO series sub-brand.

Timberland products for men, women and children include premium boots, casual shoes, hiking boots and boat shoes, as well as outdoor-inspired clothing and accessories built to withstand the elements. The Timberland PRO series is engineered to meet the demands of the professional worker.

Timberland's products are sold primarily through Timberland stores, other specialty stores, high end department stores, concept shops and shoe stores throughout the world. Consolidated revenue in 2002 totalled US$1.2 billion.

As Timberland grows into a total lifestyle brand, it increasingly licenses its brand name out to reputable manufacturers of accessories. This range has increased over the years, with the introduction of watches, luggage and back packs, children's clothing and eyewear.

Recent Developments

As it looks towards growing and refining its womenswear business in Europe, Timberland recently opened a London-based International Design Centre (IDC). It handles women's and men's clothing design for Europe and will soon expand into footwear.

The IDC is home to a dedicated team of designers with the aim of bringing European styling and fit to the Timberland range of men's and women's clothing.

Timberland has also appointed a specialist as its women's wear director. Up until now, the US has been responsible for the design of men's clothing and men's and women's footwear. The aim is to make women's wear more feminine and to create a more fully integrated collection.

In the UK, Timberland's footwear range has been enhanced with the innovative technology of the Smart Comfort System, designed to work with the foot as it moves. At the foundation of the Smart Comfort System is a revolutionary sole that contracts and expands with every step, which helps feet feel comfortable all day long.

In Autumn 2003, Timberland began developing the Smart Comfort system beyond its casual shoes incorporating it, where possible, into its footwear.

2005 sees the re-invigoration of Timberland's Outdoor Performance product range, with the introduction of new technologies such as Agile IQ™ and the continued development of the women's apparel market.

This year also sees the introduction of Comforia™ technology to women's footwear. This technology embeds various components within the footbed of the shoe designed to deliver constant comfort.

As it expands its range of branded accessories, Timberland has developed a new range of eyewear, signing a contract with Marcolin, S.p.A of Italy to develop, manufacture and distribute Timberland eyewear around the world. Marcolin launched the new Timberland sunglasses and ophthalmic frames in March 2004, coinciding with Vision Expo East in New York. Working closely with Timberland, Marcolin will be responsible for strategy, design, manufacturing, and worldwide distribution.

Timberland also recently launched a new collection of packs and travel gear, representing the first line created by another new licensing partner TRG Accessories. The range comprises daypacks, duffels, travel bags, briefcases and travel accessories for outdoor adventures as well as everyday use.

In 2004, Timberland doubled the impact of its Serv-a-palooza annual event through increased support from business partners, community organisations and consumers. Service events will take place in 21 countries, benefiting local schools, parks, camps, community centres and social service organisations.

Promotion

Timberland promotes its brand through an integrated product offering, based on 30 years of innovating rugged outdoor-inspired products. Advertising is centralised through Timberland's US Head Office, while subsidiaries and distributors worldwide ensure that it reaches each individual market's target consumer.

With the 2005 launch of The Timberland Scholarship, the company is striving to equip people to make a difference. The Timberland Scholarship is a UK-only sponsorship fund set aside by Timberland to sponsor great ideas, initiatives, challenges or adventures. As part of the programme, Timberland is looking for interesting, unique, adventurous or community-focused projects to sponsor.

The Scholarship is open to everyone in the UK above 18 years of age. It could be an individual, team, commercial organisation or charity. It could be an existing project that is already running or a new idea that people are trying to get off the ground.

2005 also marks Timberland's 10th anniversary as 'Official Footwear Sponsor' to Skandia Cowes Week, the largest and most prestigious international sailing regatta in the world. The event lasts for eight days and takes place each August in the Solent waters off Cowes on the Isle of Wight.

Brand Values

The Timberland brand is infused with an ethos of healthy living. It harnesses the power of the outdoors and helps make it accessible to consumers by developing a full range of premium footwear, clothing and accessories. This passion for the outdoors and the knowledge that the outdoors has a transformational power to challenge and give people a new perspective on the world, has helped Timberland grow from a mere bootmaker into a global lifestyle brand.

Ever since Timberland developed the first guaranteed waterproof boot, the company has been committed to quality, durability, authenticity, value and performance and to delivering the experience of the great outdoors to its customers. The central pillar of Timberland's long-term strategy is to provide value and innovation to consumers throughout its entire product offering.

A commitment to 'good business' is another vital part of the Timberland brand. The company's core belief is that business can and should be a force for positive change. It sees this 'business of business' being about responsibility, engagement, partnership and positive change. While many companies call it corporate social responsibility, Timberland talks about 'doing well and doing good', and is committed to strengthening communities through service and sustaining the environment by minimising the company's impact on it.

www.timberland.com

THINGS YOU DIDN'T KNOW ABOUT

Timberland

> A pair of Timberland Classic Boots is sold every minute somewhere around the world.

> In 2004 more than 5,000 employees, business and civic partners performed 40,000 hours of service for 150 non-profit organisations in 21 countries.

> Timberland was listed on Fortune magazine's Hall of Fame, which means it is one of 22 companies that has appeared on the Fortune 100 Best list every year since its 1998 inception.

> Timberland was named as one of the '100 Best Companies for Working Mothers' by Working Mother magazine. The list rewards companies that offer benefits such as flexible scheduling, time off for new parents and child-care options.

TONI&GUY

Market

In the 40 years since the birth of TONI&GUY, hairdressing has grown from the downmarket little sister of mainstream fashion, to become a huge and sophisticated industry commanding acres of press coverage, making its major players millions of pounds and spawning some of the most influential and creative artists in the beauty sector. In 2004 the UK hairdressing industry (including beauty services within a salon) was valued at almost £4 billion with an ongoing annual increase expected of 5% year-on-year (Source: Office of National Statistics).

While there are some renowned names in hairdressing including Vidal Sassoon, Charles Worthington and Trevor Sorbie, TONI&GUY has long been considered a pioneer and innovator within the hair industry, changing the face of the British high street, not just hairdressing. The TONI&GUY franchise model, which has maintained the company's education and creative standards, protected the brand and made successes of hundreds of TONI&GUY hairdressing entrepreneurs worldwide, has also been the inspiration for many companies since.

Achievements

A supporter of the industry for more than 40 years, TONI&GUY has helped to change the face of the industry on an international scale. With TONI&GUY dominating the UK high street and represented in 35 countries worldwide, it today achieves an annual turnover of more than £175 million. There are 217 UK TONI&GUY salons and 139 international plus 70 essensuals salons worldwide.

None of its competitors can lay claim to the worldwide brand identity that TONI&GUY enjoys, nor boast the combination of brand presence and creative excellence supported by a strong business model and education network. TONI&GUY currently operates 21 teaching academies globally – five in the UK and 16 internationally with more than 4,500 employees in the UK and a further 2,500 worldwide.

The success of the company is based on a total commitment to continuous education and training. The unique ongoing educational system that is the backbone of TONI&GUY is based on the philosophy of motivation and inspiration through teamwork and has been successfully developed into the comprehensive educational formula that is practiced at TONI&GUY academies worldwide.

As testament to this, TONI&GUY has won in excess of 45 British Hairdressing regional and UK awards including 'Best Artistic Team' a record 11 times and British Hairdresser of the Year three times. Co-founder and chief executive Toni Mascolo is a former winner of London Entrepreneur of the Year, while his daughter, international group creative director Sacha Mascolo-

Tarbuck was the youngest ever winner of Newcomer of the Year at just 19, has won London Hairdresser of the Year and has been nominated for British Hairdresser of the Year. The company currently holds the titles of both London Hairdresser of the Year and Newcomer of the Year.

TONI&GUY haircare products have won numerous awards from magazines including FHM, Hair Magazine and New Woman. Most recently it was commended at the 2005 New Woman Awards for Best New Styling Product for TONI&GUY Iron-It Heat Defence Spray. In addition, the company currently holds the Hair Magazine Readers' Choice Award for Best UK Salon. 2005 also sees the launch of the new TONI&GUY salon brand, label.m. Developed with the creativity, professionalism and expertise of the TONI&GUY art team, the brand is sure to have prestigious awards dedicated to it in the near future.

History

TONI&GUY was founded in 1963 and has since grown from a single unit in Clapham, South London to a multinational company comprising of salons and academies worldwide, a wide range of products, plus a growing portfolio of associated companies.

Founded by the Mascolo brothers Toni and Guy, who arrived in the UK in the early 1960s, and were later joined by Bruno and Anthony, the company's creative destiny now lies in the capable hands of Toni's

eldest child, Sacha Mascolo - Tarbuck, with the commercial side of the business masterminded – as ever – by Toni Mascolo.

In a family long associated with the hairdressing profession – Toni's wife Pauline is also heavily involved in the running of the business – tradition lives on with the next generation of Mascolos following in their father's footsteps. Toni's eldest son Christian co-launched sister-brand essensuals and sits on the main board, while Sacha's husband James Tarbuck masterminded the newly formed TONI&GUY Media Department incorporating TONI&GUY's own TV channel, TONI&GUY.TV, award-winning magazine, PR and design – the

first communications model of its type in the UK.

The company currently comprises two global, franchised hair salon groups – 217 in the UK and 139 international, a professional product range, two retail hair product ranges, an Italian-style deli-café chain, opticians and companies specialising in IT support, salon design, salon supplies and financial services. In 2002, Toni Mascolo also founded the TONI&GUY Charitable Trust, which is currently raising money for a TONI&GUY ward at Kings College children's hospital.

Product

TONI&GUY salons are set up to offer a consistent level of service, guaranteed quality, a fantastic image and affordable hairdressing throughout the world. The simple but well-designed salons offer a centre of excellence for great customer care, exceptional cutting and innovative colour. All the techniques practiced by the stylists are taught by highly experienced educators in academies around the world. From 'catwalk to client' sums up the TONI&GUY salon philosophy, as fashion trends are adapted to suit individuals and looks are tailor-made for suitability and maximum impact.

TONI&GUY offers a lifestyle choice, not just a hairdressing appointment. Within the salons, clients don't just experience a great hair cut, they can also watch TONI&GUY.TV, read the TONI&GUY Magazine, enjoy extended consultation time and take away samples of luxury brands exclusive to the TONI&GUY experience.

Salon design is constantly evolving and responding to the client's needs without resorting to gimmicks, and with its instantly recognisable branding is a feature of every high street. A strong image, great atmosphere and a guarantee of up-to-the-minute professional hairdressing has made TONI&GUY the market leader for more than 40 years.

In addition to the salon experience, TONI&GUY offers three distinct ranges of haircare products: label.m, Red&White and Insights.

Launched in 2005, label.m is an exclusive salon range created by the International Artistic Team at TONI&GUY. Comprising 30 products, the philosophy behind the range is simplicity, performance and quality. Specifically designed as a fashion label for hair, it helps TONI&GUY professionals interpret catwalk trends into wearable high-street style.

TONI&GUY 'Red&White' Signature range, available on the high street, is a

distinctly fashion-inspired styling range designed to appeal to a younger market who like to add 'attitude' to their individual style. Comprising 22 products, the range was updated in 2004 to include products aimed at a more male-oriented purchaser, plus miniature-sized products for those requiring on-the-go styling in a hurry.

Also available on the high street nationwide and designed to bridge the gap between aesthetic appeal and professional results, Insights exemplifies luxury hair care for today's modern woman wanting a range that is

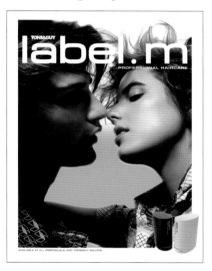

'Beautiful', 'Feminine', 'Elegant' and 'Aspirational'. The range is split into four distinct categories – Shine, Moisture, Volume and Colour, targeting every requirement for healthy looking hair.

Recent Developments

There are clear targets for the future of TONI&GUY. Toni Mascolo's goal is for the group to be the biggest, most respected and stylish hairdressing brand in the world with a representation in every country.

His plan is for label.m to be the most desirable global haircare label on the high street and to be as popular with his teams as it is with his clientele. He is aiming for it to be worth US$1 billion in five years' time.

Toni Mascolo is also looking forward to the continuing development of the TONI&GUY Media Department, which he expects will find new ways of achieving ultimate communication throughout the industry and across the globe. "Every initiative we've launched – from education techniques to window collections – has been copied, so we make sure we never stand still." says Toni Mascolo. Indeed, 2006 will see the launch of essensuals salons in the US & Canada.

Promotion

TONI&GUY has been at the forefront of high street hair styling for more than 40 years. As a brand it has managed to walk the sometimes precarious line between establishing a reputation for quality and reliability and maintaining its cutting-edge credentials. Juggling the need for consistency and the desire to be fashionable, the reassurance of solid service values and the excitement of the avant-garde is an ongoing focus for all within the TONI&GUY team. It becomes particularly crucial with the potential loss of control and identity that could arise as the TONI&GUY brand spreads across the globe.

In this context, the delicate job of strengthening and evolving the brand is pivotal to its continued success, which has been lead by International Group Creative Director, Sacha Mascolo-Tarbuck, alongside her husband, Head of Media, James Tarbuck. TONI&GUY Media has tackled this complex task in the past 18 months via several channels, which interlink to form a cohesive brand-enhancing strategy and build upon the sophisticated and innovative above-the-line campaigns of the past three decades. The core areas have been: the creation of TONI&GUY.TV, the launch of TONI&GUY Magazine, the sampling of luxury products, the extension of the TONI&GUY product range and the development of the PR strategy.

TONI&GUY Magazine, launched in October 2003, is the lynchpin of the strategy. Focusing on key trends in fashion, the arts, beauty, grooming and travel, this is a key development of the TONI&GUY brand. Distributed in salons across Europe and globally as far afield as Australasia, the magazine promotes an exciting, inspirational and yet accessible face of the company to both customers and employees/franchisees alike. A vindication of the magazine came in November 2004 when it won the APA's Launch of the Year.

Adding yet another facet to the media department, TONI&GUY.TV launched in March 2003 to enhance clients' in-salon experience. Containing original content, from music and fashion to travel and interviews with the TONI&GUY artistic team, it adds an extra dimension to a client visit that can last anything from 45mins to two hours. With more than 1,000 screens in

the UK it has also become a unique way for associated brands to advertise to this sought-after audience of 18-45, ABC1 men/women.

Integrated into both the magazine and TV channel is TONI&GUY's sampling initiative, which has seen it form mutually beneficial relationships with key brands such as Mars, Bailey's and Peugeot. Sampling is a means of rewarding loyal clients through in-salon giveaways, and by carefully selecting partners who are totally on-brand, TONI&GUY can strengthen and grow the image of what it is and what it represents – both to clients and to its salon staff.

Finally, TONI&GUY remains committed to its involvement in, and support of, the fashion industry with its sponsorship of London Fashion Week and London Fashion Weekend, which began in the 2004/05 season. This commitment to the fashion industry is bolstered by the company's in-house annual awards ceremony and support of entrants to external competitions such as the British Hairdressing Awards and the L'Oréal Colour Trophy.

Brand Values

TONI&GUY's reputation has been built on an impeccable pedigree, fashion nous, and friendly, professional service. TONI&GUY aims to acknowledge the importance of local, customer-led service while avoiding the pitfalls of parochialism and fragmentation by promoting an authoritative, cohesive and – most importantly – inspiring voice. TONI&GUY strives to be seen as the most powerful hairdressing brand in the world, offering the best education and guaranteeing superlative cutting and innovative colour. Aiming to be perceived as über-cool but friendly and welcoming, the brand's objective is to provide the ultimate link between fashion and hair – from catwalk to client.

www.toniandguy.com

TOPSHOP

Market

Responding quickly to emerging trends has been a key success factor for retailers such as Topshop, which has carved out a reputation for its ability to pre-empt the latest catwalk styles at affordable prices and with the shortest possible lead times.

The UK market for women's clothing is forecast to grow by almost 10% between 2003 and 2008 to reach a value of nearly £12.8 billion. Tops will remain the largest sector contributing a value of £2.9 billion by the year 2008, accounting for almost 23% of value sector share (Source: Euromonitor).

Achievements

Topshop has undergone a transformation since the mid 1990s, blossoming from a 'cheap and cheerful' store for the nation's teenagers to a seriously cool, trendsetting brand.

It has become a high street retail phenomenon, enjoying a huge growth in sales and creating a distinctive personality with an individual brand mix. It continues to headline in nearly every fashion title and broadsheet, establishing a reputation for bringing innovation and style to the high street.

While many other retailers belatedly copy the latest look, Topshop frequently sets trends of its own. Topshop has received numerous accolades in recent years – fashion bible Vogue wrote: "Topshop has become the favourite label of the moment among the fashion pack and the entire staff of Vogue checks in almost daily for new deliveries", while The Times declared: "it's now a fashion faux-pas not to go there."

Topshop has become a multi-award-winning brand, carrying off numerous industry gongs. Most recently, it won Customer Service Initiative of the Year for its new Topshop To Go service at the Retail Week Awards 2005. The past year has also seen it win awards from magazines including Company, In Style and Time Out.

The driving force behind the transformation of Topshop is the team led by brand director Jane Shepherdson, who has been rated as one of the fashion industry's most influential figures. As well as the expertise of buyers and designers, the team relies on gut instinct to introduce elements they feel are right for the brand.
With 300 UK stores and a further 67 international stores, this is a philosophy that seems to be paying dividends.

History

Although Topshop itself was launched in 1964, its parent company, The Arcadia Group, dates back to 1900 when it was launched by Montague Burton with an investment of £100. Initially the menswear chain Burton was the company's principal brand, but the launch of Topshop in the 1960s took the group into the women's fashion market.

It was a small start, with Topshop initially only having space in a Sheffield department store called Peter Robinson. A year later, the same store allocated Topshop space in the basement of its Oxford Circus store in London.

In 1974, Topshop was taken out of Peter Robinson and set up as a standalone retailer, catering for 13-25 year-olds. In 1978, a boys' and young men's version, Topman, was introduced and in 1982, Top Girl, for 9-14 year-olds, arrived.

In 1992 Topman and Topshop combined forces at 214 Oxford Circus to create the world's largest fashion store. Six years later, the flagship store was reopened as a stunningly refurbished flagship store, welcoming in excess of 200,000 shoppers every week.

Product

Topshop Boutique was created as a destination area in store to appeal to its more design-aware customers, celebrities and industry insiders. Boutique houses Topshop design, UNIQUE and also the latest capsule collections from selected designers such as Zandra Rhodes, Jonathan Saunders and Emma Cook. There are now dedicated Boutique spaces at Oxford Circus, Kensington High Street, Manchester, Glasgow, Birmingham, and in the Topshop concessions in Selfridges London and Manchester.

Topshop's design-led collection UNIQUE is created a fresh each season by Topshop's in-house design team. Topshop UNIQUE prides itself on thinking big, doing the unexpected and striving to do it first. UNIQUE was

originally created in 2001 to dispel the myth that Topshop's sole aim was to copy the catwalk. The launch of Topshop UNIQUE has established Topshop's reputation in design, ultimately positioning the brand as an authority in fashion. Topshop UNIQUE has been hugely successful for the brand, keeping it ahead of the game and stretching it not only in terms of personality but also in terms of design and credibility.

Topshop has been trading vintage clothing in its flagship store at Oxford Circus for more than 15 years. The section has a great following from regular Topshop customers and celebrity and industry shoppers, and continues to evolve with current fashion trends.

There are currently three vintage clothing brands stocked at Oxford Circus, each providing a different category of product: Peek a Boo – a high-fashion collection offering everything from 1950s prom-style to cotton day dresses; Vintage Princess – quirky dresses and skirts; and finally Vintage clothing – traditional casual products from college T-shirts to cord blazers. There are also four vintage accessory concessions; Peek a Boo, Styled Generation for vintage shoes and trainers, Jeepers Peepers for vintage sunglasses and Affinity for fashion-led printed scarves and belts. Vintage is now also available from Topshop High Street Kensington, Topshop Birmingham, Topshop Glasgow and on the website www.topshop.co.uk.

Recent Developments

Spring 2004 saw Topshop launch its first maternity line, 'b' by Topshop'. Designed to be stylish, reflective of the seasonal trends and easy to wear, the collection aims to reinvent the traditional notion of maternity dressing. 'b' by Topshop' aims to

updated daily and limited edition pieces available from flagship stores. The site is updated every week with more than 100 new products.

To maximise the popularity of the site, Topshop communicates every week with its loyal customer database of 150,000 subscribers through a newsletter informing them of everything new on the site. Response rates are up to 25%, showing that the newsletter is an eagerly awaited weekly event for online shoppers. Up to 300,000 people now browse Topshop online during peak trading times.

In its drive to give something back, Topshop supports a number of charities relevant to its shoppers, holding the Jumbo Thrift Sale in December 2004 in aid of the Terence Higgins Trust, supporting Refuge and Women's Aid on International Women's Day and also linking with Fashion Targets Breast Cancer.

Brand Values

Topshop is a fashion emporium that blends cutting-edge style with affordability. Loved by fashionistas, models and celebrities alike, Topshop has evolved into a fashion label that epitomises up-to-the-minute affordable fashion.

Topshop has earned celebrity endorsement, reflecting its reputation as a high street fashion Mecca.

At the core of the brand is a respect for creativity and innovation in every form. Creativity is the engine that fuels the success of Topshop.

www.topshop.co.uk

provide mothers-to-be with a fashionable range of clothes to see them through their pregnancy in style. All garments have been designed to sit comfortably under the bump rather than featuring the traditional elasticated waistbands found in many other maternity lines – pieces instead have discreet expandable waistbands neatly positioned on each hip. 'b' is available at 44 stores nationwide and from the Topshop website www.topshop.co.uk/maternity.

Inspired by the huge success of Topshop footwear introduced two years ago, the brand launched its first standalone shoe store, Shoes by Topshop, on Manchester's King Street in August 2004, where the best of Topshop footwear, limited edition collections, imported brands and vintage shoes are available in an inspired shopping environment alongside a luxury foot spa with bespoke treatments. Shoes by Topshop presents focused products and service in an innovatively designed space, with a vision to expand the format in the coming years.

Since the launch of Topshop's Style Advisors in 2001, the service has gone from strength to strength. Now available in 35 stores nationwide, it offers a personal styling service to customers by appointment or on an ad-hoc basis. Following its success, Topshop launched a mobile style service in May 2004 entitled 'Topshop To Go'. The service is designed to provide the ultimate in home shopping as the Style Advisor team visits homes or work places in the Topshop To Go car – complete with clothes, shoes and accessories for any occasion. As with the in-store Style Advisor service, there is no fee for the service and no obligation to purchase. The service is currently available in London within the M25 area.

The latest service to launch in store is Topshop Atelier, a made-to-measure dress service. The service is available by appointment only at Oxford Circus and already has a number of celebrity customers and a massive waiting list.

This summer sees the launch of Topshop's latest product offering, Moto Surf, complete with wetsuits, board shorts, rash vests and bikinis – it fuses fashionability with high specification technology.

March 2005 saw the re-launch of the Topshop/Topman flagship store on Argyle Street, Glasgow making it Topshop's first flagship store in Scotland. The newly refurbished 13,653 sq m space, designed by retail specialist Zebra, has a contemporary feel with clean lines and simple lighting. Lines include Topshop Shoes, Boutique, Designers for Topshop, selected Topshop Unique, Vintage and Vintage shoes, Lingerie, Topshop Maternity and Homeware. The store also offers the Topshop To Go service, launched alongside the existing Style Advisor service. Topshop will continue to relaunch stores in key markets.

Promotion

Topshop's marketing mix consists of authoritative advertising, constant innovation and the sponsorship of young design talent.

Topshop is the biggest supporter of London Fashion Week with its sponsorship of the prestigious New Generation Award now in its sixth season. Known for launching the careers of 'fashion royalty', the New Generation Award has previously been won by now-established names such as Alexander McQueen, Matthew Williamson and Clements Riberio.

Committed to the cultivation of a reputation for cutting edge design, Topshop runs a popular student initiative known as 'Lock-ins'. Twice a year it holds a round of 'Lock-ins' around the country in student-populated towns. The after-hours shopping events take part in local stores and students receive a 20% discount when they shop on the evening, free drinks and a free gift, as well as a DJ playing to entertain the shoppers.

The Topshop website is also a key element of the brand's marketing strategy. Having started from a back room in Topshop's flagship store at Oxford Circus with just one person picking and dispatching orders from the store's stock room, this all turned around. April 2005 saw www.topshop.co.uk launch its new look, with must-have products on the home page, a most-wanted item

Topshop

> Topshop's celebrity customers include Gwyneth Paltrow, Kate Moss, Liv Tyler and Lizzie Jagger.

> A white trouser suit owned by Cherie Blair and worn at a photo call after her husband's 2001 election victory was one of the main attractions at Topshop's Jumbo Thrift Sale in December 2004.

> Topshop customers spend an average of 44 minutes in-store.

> Topshop sells 30 pairs of knickers every minute and more than 33,000 pairs of jeans every week.

> Topshop's flagship Oxford Circus store is open 73 hours per week, with 1,000 staff working there at any one time. It covers 90,000sq ft and has 200 changing rooms, as well as a VIP changing area.

TRAILFINDERS

THE TRAVEL EXPERTS

Market

The nature of travel has changed a great deal since Trailfinders' inception in 1970, with more and more people travelling further and further afield.

Where once only the affluent Brit holidayed abroad, usually in the Mediterranean or France, nowadays travel to many exotic destinations is not only feasible and fashionable, but also affordable.

From long weekends in New York to safaris in Africa, beach retreats in Asia to skiing in North America or even dream holidays in Australia, the possibilities are limited only by the imagination.

Although increasingly seeking independence from the traditional package, travellers today still seek the reassurance of a reliable, confident and experienced travel professional to put together what could be a complex itinerary.

Achievements

Despite several difficult years for the travel industry following September 11th, SARS and the Asian tsunami

to name but a few, Trailfinders has weathered the storm. As a thriving business, it has adhered to its expansion plans and continued to recruit. The result is that by August 2005 it will have opened seven new UK travel centres since 2001, taking the total number to 22 across the UK, Ireland and Australia.

Most of Trailfinders' 600 travel consultants are graduates and all have travelled extensively and independently before embarking on their career at the company.

Trailfinders was the first 'bucket shop' to be granted IATA and ATOL licenses back in 1979 and the first travel agent to advertise cheap flights in the National Press.

It can boast numerous awards, not only from within the trade but more importantly from the public. Readers of the Observer voted it Best Travel Agent on six occasions while Telegraph readers have awarded it 'Best Specialist – Independent Travel' every year since the inception of their awards.

For luxury travel, Trailfinders' dedicated First & Business Class team, staffed by its most experienced travel consultants, provides premium levels of customer service and product knowledge. With access to a range of special rates in the premium cabins of the world's best airlines and at the world's most luxurious hotels, Business Traveller magazine listed Trailfinders' First and Business Class team the 12th largest business travel agency in the UK in 2003.

History

In 1970, former SAS Officer Mike Gooley founded Trailfinders as an overland tour company with a staff of four, of whom three were unpaid.

Two years later, Trailfinders had become the first independent flight consolidator, offering exceptional value airfares worldwide. Bucking the trend for package holidays, Trailfinders also pioneered the concept of tailormade travel, where each holiday and each client is treated as unique.

In 1989, Trailfinders opened its flagship London Kensington Travel Centre, the 'one-stop travel shop' incorporating a Travel Clinic, retail space for books and travel essentials, Visa & Passport Service, a dedicated First and Business Class department and a unique Information Centre.

Today, Trailfinders sends in excess of 690,000 clients abroad each year and employs more than 1,000 staff across 22 travel centres in the UK, Ireland and Australia. Despite its growth, the company remains privately owned and The Trailfinders Group now includes an airline, sports club, luxury rainforest lodge in Far North Queensland and a catering company.

Product

Always seeking to broaden the scope of what it can provide for its clients, Trailfinders offers a complete range of travel services from hotels, tours, cruises and vehicle hire, all ranging from budget to luxury standards, to visas and passports and even a wedding and gift list service.

Trailfinders offers competitively priced discounted flights with hundreds of airlines to destinations worldwide, but as the pioneers of tailormade travel, it offers far more than just flights alone. It has access to discounted rates at 4,000 hotels with more than 1.5 million rooms allocated for Trailfinders clients. It also offers competitively priced car and motorhome hire, along with tours and cruises to destinations around the globe.

Dedicated departments within the company now include: Worldwide; European; First and Business Class; Islands, dealing specifically with island and resort holidays in Asia, the Indian Ocean and the Caribbean; Skiing in the USA & Canada; and a dedicated Weddings and Honeymoon team. Trailfinders' speciality is customising individual itineraries, be it a round-the-world trip for a gap year student, a family motorhome holiday in the USA, a comprehensive tour of Australia or an ultra-luxurious holiday of a lifetime.

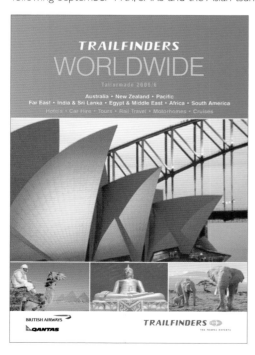

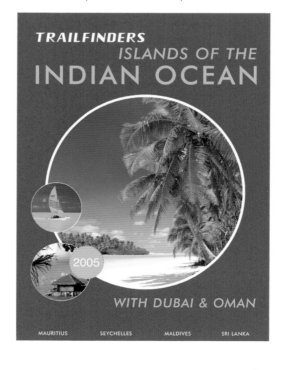

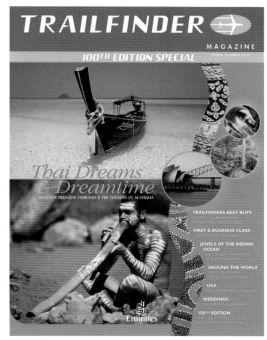

Trailfinders produces a range of brochures to inspire and inform clients about the kind of trips they might like to consider, yet each booking is individual and pieced together by a skilled consultant. The company's website is a useful way to keep abreast of all Trailfinders' services, however there is a deep-seated belief that there is no substitute for the value of the human touch provided by their highly skilled and knowledgeable consultants, which is why no online booking facility exists as yet.

Customers instead benefit from the convenience of seven-days-a-week opening at Trailfinders Travel Centres, and a multitude of additional services, all provided with a high level of expertise and attention to detail.

Indeed, customer service is a top priority, with word of mouth having always been Trailfinders' strongest marketing tool. Indeed, 80% of clients have either booked with Trailfinders previously or been referred by friends. Throughout every level of the company there is an aim to understand what the customer wants and how to deliver it.

Recent Developments
Consistently positioning itself at the cutting edge of all things travel, Trailfinders constantly strives to improve its service and the facilities available to its clients. It has recently developed ViewTrail, an online facility allowing clients instant real time access to details of their personal travel booking, providing the ability to book express trains to the airport, view destination guides and Trailfinders' Top Tips and review detailed flight itineraries that can be shared with family or business associates.

Trailfinders also operates a caller line identification system, which enables its consultants to instantly recognise a client who has booked with the company before, thereby avoiding the need to repeat personal details every time the customer calls.

Trailfinders' most recently opened travel centre was in Nottingham in 2004 and in 2005 it will open centres in Norwich and Cardiff.

Adapting to the constantly changing needs of its clients, Trailfinders has

recently launched an 'Exclusive Touring' programme, offering a choice of five small group luxury tours exclusive to Trailfinders clients in Egypt and Jordan, South Africa, China, Australia and New Zealand, while the 'Wedding Service' is proving very popular with discerning couples seeking a unique wedding and honeymoon.

Promotion
Whilst most of Trailfinders' custom is achieved through word of mouth, regular newspaper advertising of current best-buy deals is important in maintaining the brand's competitive profile in a crowded marketplace.

'Trailfinders – The Travel Experts' has been the company's most frequently used strapline, supporting clients' view that their consultants are much more than simply booking clerks.

The Trailfinder magazine, published three times a year and written and designed entirely in-house, is the brand's chief direct marketing tool. It offers a wide range of holiday ideas, information and special offers, with destination features and independently-written travel articles. The magazine is mailed out to a database in excess of 800,000 previous clients and enquirers, with a further 400,000 copies distributed through the travel centres and various distribution sites around London including the Royal Geographical Society. Spring/Summer 2005 saw the publication of the 100th edition, which included the results of one of the foremost consumer travel surveys detailing Trailfinders' clients' favourite destinations, hotels and airlines in which over 15,000 households participated.

Brand Values
Customer feedback tells Trailfinders that it is the company's consistently professional yet friendly consultants, who make even a potentially complex itinerary a pleasure to book, that keeps them coming back to the company. The ability to offer first-hand knowledge and experience of almost every destination means that clients can feel confident in entrusting their valuable travel plans to Trailfinders.

As an independent, privately owned company, Trailfinders has always insisted on transparent pricing and fairness, being one of the few in the industry not to impose surcharges on credit card payments or make a charge for consumer protection against airline collapse. In addition, it operates no premium cost telephone numbers, so its clients are assured that they are receiving exceptional value for money with no hidden extras added on at the end of a booking.

The backpackers who used Trailfinders' low-cost flights service in the 1970s are often the same people who now use the company to travel in style on business or with

their families. Over the years their travel needs have changed and Trailfinders has changed with them. The fact that Trailfinders' First and Business Class Department is one of the fastest-growing sectors of the company reflects the trust that clients have in the quality of service, regardless of their budget.

www.trailfinders.com

Market

Bangers and mash, sausage sarnies, devilled, barbecued, or even cold out of the fridge from the night before; however you prefer them, there is no denying sausages are a much loved staple in the British diet and have been for many years.

Such is the British obsession with sausages that half of all households serve sausages for at least one meal every week. And that obsession is now worth £416 million in a market that is growing at more than 5% year-on-year (Source: ACNielsen 2005). It is estimated that each year we eat 321 million packs of sausages (Source: ACNielsen 2005). Nearly 80% of the population buy sausages, and do so at least eight times a year on average (Source: ACNielsen 2005). In addition to casseroles and sandwiches, sausages feature at countless summer BBQs, and increasingly the British public is getting more sophisticated with sausages at mealtimes with concoctions as adventurous as sausages stuffed with mozzarella, basil pesto and Mediterranean vegetables to name just one recipe.

Achievements

Wall's has been making sausages for more than 200 years so it's not surprising that it is the best known sausage brand in the UK. Familiarity apart, consumers know that Wall's is a trustworthy brand offering a range of products that meet their various needs, not only in sausages but in bacon too. As a brand, Wall's is worth £88 million and commands a 10% share of the sausage market. The brand enjoys 91% awareness amongst the British public, thanks not only to its strong heritage, but also to its memorable marketing and advertising campaigns throughout the years.

Wall's was swift to respond to consumer demands for convenience products with the introduction of Wall's Micros. This demand for convenience is still the key driver for Micros, and subsequently the sub-brand has enjoyed massive growth year-on-year of more than 16% from a £4.2 million base. This growth has been driven by increased awareness due to successful TV campaigns since 2003 and with the latest campaign in 2005.

History

Sausages have been around for centuries. The Greeks ate them and they were also a standard item on the menu of the Romans, who introduced them to Britain. Indeed, the word sausage comes from the Latin 'salsicius' or 'salted' which was a general term for preserved meats. The original 'salsicius' was probably a dried sausage, not dissimilar from products such as salami, which would keep in the hot Italian climate. The British developed their own version and each county created its own particular method of producing and flavouring their local sausage, from Cumberland sausages in the Lake District to the taste of sage associated with Lincoln sausages.

Wall's sausages made their debut when the father of Thomas Wall, Richard, opened a sausage and pie business in St James's Market, London in 1786. Wall's reputation as

a superb pork butcher and sausage producer par excellence quickly spread and by 1812 the company received its first Royal Warrant as Pork Butcher to the Prince of Wales. Successive generations of Royals have remained loyal to the sausage. Queen Victoria was specific about how her sausages should be made, while more recently Prince William revealed he had a great fondness for sausages and chips.

The business continued to flourish under Wall's son Thomas and gained more royal appointments. Wall's continued to thrive, even during World War II, because sausages were one of the few foods to escape rationing. It was during this period that sausages earned their affectionate nickname 'bangers' because wartime production methods meant they would often spit and explode in the frying pan.

In the 1950s Wall's was quick to spot the potential of television advertising and has used the medium ever since to maintain brand presence. Throughout the 1980s and 1990s the brand grew its market share through TV advertising featuring 'Charlie and Sniff the dog'. Kerry Foods bought the brand in 1994 and continued with this advertising until 2000.

In the past four years, the brand has continued to grow through new product development, with the introduction of innovative BBQ products, Wall's Micro-Sausages and Wall's Balls range and in autumn 2003 Wall's introduced a new look for its sausage and bacon range. These launches have benefited from strong marketing support, which has included press, TV, cinema, outdoor and the highly successful 'We want Wall's' campaign. The campaign was backed by a consumer press advertising push using the endline 'Why eggs want to be laid'. The new look builds on Wall's heritage of 'Best quality for 200 years'.

In 2004 the brand reintroduced its much-loved icon, the Wall's dog, which conjures affectionate memories with consumers.

Product

The uncompromising quality standards that are used in making Wall's products, first adopted by Thomas Wall more than 200 years ago, are still maintained. Wall's expertise offers the consumers a wide range of both fresh and frozen products that are designed to appeal to everyone.

Wall's standard sausages follow a traditional pork sausage recipe, and are suitable for everyday use and at any meal time. They are available in Thick, Thin and Skinless variants.

Wall's Lean Recipe sausages deliver all the flavour off a standard Wall's sausage, but at less than 5% fat, this lean recipe is the perfect substitute for the health conscious. Furthermore, as part of its ongoing commitment to producing healthier products, Wall's has undertaken to reduce salt and fat levels across its entire portfolio.

Answering the consumer demand for convenience products, Wall's developed its first Micros product; a microwavable sausage, ready in just one minute.

Wall's Balls are crumb-coated sausage meatballs that can be cooked from freezer to dinner-plate in fifteen minutes. The product was created to give busy mothers another choice at children's tea-time, which had previously been dominated by frozen chicken and fish-based products.

Thanks to its unique cure, Wall's believes its bacon is arguably the best-tasting on the market. As a result of this curing process, Wall's bacon has less water, and produces less 'exudate' (the white frothy stuff produced when cooking bacon) than any other brand on the market. Wall's bacon is available in smoked, un-smoked and streaky varieties.

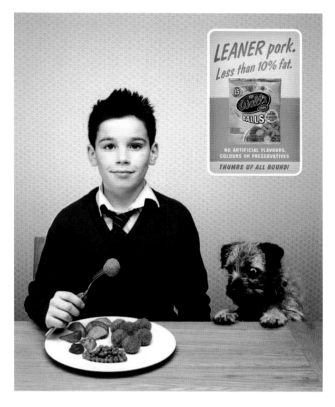

advertising from May to September 2005.

The success of the loveable Wall's Dog character can be attributed to the humorous way in which a cute, normally docile family pet can turn very jealous and self serving when Wall's sausages are up for grabs. So popular is the Wall's dog, that in 2005, for the first time ever, consumers will be given the opportunity to own their very own Wall's dog soft toy as featured in the commercials.

Brand Values

Wall's endeavours to maintain the same high standards insisted upon by Thomas Wall when he started making his famous sausages more than 200 years ago.

Additionally the brand offers consumers a wide range of products and a depth of choice – all attributable to one thing – Wall's expertise.

The brand has a warm, fun personality and is regarded as unpretentious and approachable, while maintaining contemporary appeal. Wall's stands for the satisfaction of good, honest grub, providing sausages and bacon for everyone.

www.wewantwalls.co.uk

Recent Developments

The Favourite Recipe range, introduced in June 2004, is the latest addition to the Wall's family and has been a huge success for the brand. The range, which consists of sausages which use the best pork cuts and are delicately seasoned for a subtle but distinctive taste, is already worth nearly £12 million, and growing by 16.6%.

Aimed at families, the Favourite Recipe range is a premium range of succulent sausages in three traditional flavours – Lincolnshire, Cumberland and Classic Pork.

The products are foil wrapped to preserve flavour, which marks a first for the sector, and with continuing growth in penetration and awareness, Favourites is set to be a jewel in the Wall's crown.

With more than 75 million BBQs held in the UK in 2004 (Source: National BBQ Association), and ever-mindful of the consumer demand for convenient, tasty products to BBQ, Wall's has expanded its BBQ offerings in 2005. The Frozen BBQ Jumbo sausage remains a firm favourite, but in addition, Wall's has introduced a 'Summer Twin Pack' in 2005. This consists of eight standard pork sausages and eight BBQ flavour pork sausages in a convenient pack for occasions such as a spontaneous family BBQs.

Promotion

Television has always been an important medium for Wall's when communicating with the British public, but a variety of other media is used by the brand to reach people from all walks of life.

Wall's advertising has for many years featured a loveable border terrier in communicating with the British public. In 2004 'The Wall's Dog' was resurrected (after a few years' retirement) in a thoroughly modern way. The modern Wall's dog made his debut in January 2004 with the TV commercial for Wall's Favourite Recipe and was an immediate hit.

This success was translated across other Wall's brands later in 2004, including Wall's Balls, and more recently in 2005 Wall's Micros has starred the Wall's dog, in a £1 million TV campaign that aired in March and April 2005. The spots, which aired on all major TV channels, targeted eleven million young adults.

Wall's Balls, again starring 'The Wall's Dog' is in press throughout 2005, with a further run of the TV commercial on terrestrial and satellite stations.

Wall's Lean Recipe press advertising featuring the Wall's Border Terrier runs annually during the key dieting period from January through to April, while Wall's Bacon is also heavily supported with press

THINGS YOU DIDN'T KNOW ABOUT

Wall's

> In the past year, on average, one Wall's product was sold every second of every day (Source: ACNielsen 2005).

> Wall's sausage meat was originally ground by a donkey working a treadmill in the cellar of Thomas Wall's prestigious butcher's shop at 113 Jermyn Street in 1834.

> In 2004, Wall's produced 17,388 tonnes of sausages – the equivalent of 31 Airbus A380s – the world's largest-ever passenger jet.

> In 1840 Thomas Wall was awarded the Coronation Medal by Queen Victoria's half-brother, Prince Karl von Leiningen.

Sizzle without the shrivel.

Wickes

Market

The nation's obsession with home-improvement and DIY shows no sign of abating. Wickes services the trade, DIY and home-improvement market, which has been growing steadily over the past few years, above the level of general retailers. Indeed, the repair, maintenance and improvement market is worth approximately £28.5 billion, excluding high street furniture sales (Source: Verdict Research).

The landscape of this market has changed over the years with the merger and acquisition of Texas, Do it All and Great Mills. Wickes has changed hands a number of times in the past five years, most recently being purchased by the Travis Perkins Group.

Wickes offers its customers a proposition of convenience, low prices, easy shopping, product availability and helpful staff. This has proven a highly successful formula in a highly competitive market.

Wickes appeals to a variety of customers not only within the DIY market, but across the whole of the repair, maintenance and improvement market and is seen as appealing to the smaller builder and the DIY enthusiast. Wickes also attracts people who undertake any home improvement projects themselves, by offering a high quality selection of kitchens, bedrooms, bathrooms and conservatories.

Wickes not only competes in a variety of markets but has a unique appeal by offering a highly specified own-brand product range.

Achievements

In its 30 year history, Wickes has established an envied market position – it is one of only a handful of retailers in its sector that have created a brand of their own. Based upon the brand endorsement of its trade heritage, it has built up a level of trust that allows it to sell almost exclusively own-brand products.

Its market position – between a DIY retailer and builders' merchant – is also unique, allowing it to draw on the custom of both trade and DIY market sectors and to service both well.

Wickes enjoys the highest sales per square foot of any retailer in its sector. At £191 this compares favourably with those achieved at key rivals Homebase (£125) and B&Q (£175) (Source: Verdict Research).

Wickes has perhaps the best-known and best-differentiated marketing tool in the business: its booklet, which is distributed to targeted UK postcode sectors eight times per year.

History

Wickes opened its first store in the UK in 1972 at Whitefield in Manchester.

The concept was launched as a joint venture between the US group, Wickes Corporation, and the UK builders merchant, Sankeys.

In 1987, Wickes was floated on the London Stock Exchange. At that time the company was trading from 41 units in the UK.

Almost a decade later, Wickes underwent a change of management followed by a rights issue and the sale of its European stores in 1997. Six years after that, Wickes was acquired by Focus, although the majority of Wickes key operational management was retained. Within the Focus Wickes Group, Wickes grew significantly, with an increase in store numbers from 131 at October 29th 2000 to 172.

In March 2003, the first new larger-format store – Wickes Extra – was opened at Barking with a further four Extra stores within the estate at Taunton, Maidstone, Hedge End and Glasgow.

In December 2004 the Focus Group sold Wickes to Travis Perkins for £980 million. Wickes now has a portfolio of 168 standard and five Extra stores. These stores are situated in large population centres where there are concentrations of tradesmen and serious DIY enthusiasts.

Product

Wickes aims to be the principal destination for the small tradesman and serious DIY-er, by offering high quality own-brand products at unbeatable prices. It sells a range of builders' merchants and core DIY products, the majority of which are its own-brand products.

The own-brand strategy enables Wickes to set the right specification for its products at the right quality. As the majority of Wickes' products are own-brand, the entire reputation of the brand is at risk if a product is not good enough.

Working closely with suppliers, with an uncompromised focus on quality, every Wickes product is specified to be as good as, if not better than the brand leader in its given category. This commitment, when combined with low prices, offers outstanding value for money.

All stores offer a targeted range of competitively priced home improvement products, with particular emphasis on both building products – such as timber, bricks, cement, doors, flooring – and on its 'showroom range' – home-delivered kitchens, conservatories, bathrooms and bedrooms. The stores also stock a wide constructional-gardening range.

Wickes has a relatively small number of suppliers, many of which it has developed long-term strategic relationships with. This relationship, combined with a concentrated range of own-brand products, has resulted in Wickes achieving a market-leading position in terms of product availability.

The Wickes format is kept relatively simple, and varies little from store to store. Consumer research has shown that Wickes has a large loyal customer base that visits on a regular basis, and in the case of the tradesman, uses more than one store. The whole design and layout is focused on making the shopping experience fast, simple and easy for both trade and DIY customers.

If you want cheaper sand, you could go to Blackpool.

Wickes
just the job

**Building Sand
900kg* Jumbo Bag
£28**

*Minimum packed weight 900kg

Recent Developments

Wickes has recently developed the 'Extra' format. These stores, introduced in March 2003, are significantly larger than the Standard stores, averaging approximately 51,000 sq ft of net selling space per Extra store versus approximately 25,000 sq ft of net selling space per Standard store. From a visual perspective, Extra stores are different in terms of presentation, layout and assortment. They are clearly divided into two halves, one of which incorporates the decorative and aesthetic ranges and the other the construction and building material ranges. The former section is open-plan, has clear signage, no high racking and is easier to browse for female customers. The latter section has a similar layout to a Standard store but incorporates a broader range of products.

The Extra stores also have wider aisles to make bulk buying easier and quicker, as well as a loading bay for bulk purchases. Trade customers have their own entry and exit to ensure that they are able to get in and out as quickly as in a Standard store. Also included are an upgraded trade desk, an extended paint-mixing facility, larger and more aspirational showroom displays, 'shops within shops' for a range of categories such as flooring, lighting and power tools, and a small range of plants to complement the Garden Project Centre.

Wickes has had an information website for the past four years. It has been used to promote new initiatives and products, as well as giving the customer useful tips and techniques on products. Work is now underway to construct a transaction website by early 2006.

Promotion

The Wickes marketing strategy for its core products is based on Every Day Low Prices, value for money project-driven pricing, supplemented by short, sharp, tactical promotions designed to drive volumes through its stores. On the showroom side, the strategy is one of sale and discount offers.

The overall strategy is delivered predominantly through door-to-door distribution of its booklet. The booklet has been hugely successful in raising awareness levels of the Wickes brand and product offering and subsequently driving sales, as well as providing clear differentiation in an increasingly cluttered market place.

The booklet is supplemented by additional above- and below-the-line activity targeted at its core customers. The Wickes' no nonsense, down to earth approach is reflected in the style of the booklet and in the creative approach employed in all advertising materials.

A more recent initiative has been the successful development of 'Sports Affinity' advertising in specific sections of national newspapers. This successful linkage to football has been consolidated, with Wickes becoming the official home-improvement partner of the Football League Championship, signing a three-year deal that began in August 2005.

As part of an ongoing strategy to raise awareness of its unique proposition, Wickes has recently invested in stands at the Ideal Home Show, National Homebuilders Show and BBC Gardeners' World. The shows have been successful both from a brand-building and sales perspective, with Wickes winning the award for best stand at the Ideal Home Show in 2004.

Brand Values

Wickes is designed to offer everything needed to complete a job. It serves three specific kinds of customer. Firstly, the small tradesman or 'jobbing builder', the 'man with a van', skilled in various trades who prefers to deal in cash rather than on account and visits a Wickes store on average three times per week, spending on average only ten minutes in store per visit. Convenient locations, quality products, low prices, availability and ease of shop layout makes Wickes first choice for the trade customer. In turn, loyalty to Wickes from the trade adds credibility to the brand. Products that are the right quality and right price for the trade encourages their domestic customers to 'trade where the trade trades'.

The second core customer group is the serious, enthusiastic home improver who has the confidence and capability to undertake big home-improvement projects. Typically this customer is a male, family orientated homeowner, to whom quality, low prices and helpful service are important when completing projects. This is a serial home improver.

The third core customer group is the 'female specifier', who sees the decorative and showroom areas as important. For this customer, aspirational matters of style and considered choice relating to kitchens, bathrooms, conservatories and decoration have high importance.

These three key customer types make up more than 85% of Wickes' business. Each group has a unique expectation of the brand, which strives to be seen as 'The trusted brand for home improvement'. Its brand values are built upon a long-established reputation for market-leading product quality, value for money, helpful service and ease of shopping.

www.wickes.co.uk

THINGS YOU DIDN'T KNOW ABOUT

Wickes

❯ More than 98% of the products sold by Wickes are Wickes own-branded products.

❯ Today, Wickes enjoys a total net selling space of approximately 4.36 million sq ft.

❯ Wickes' top 20 suppliers contribute the products that account for more than half of total purchases from Wickes.

❯ Wickes has printed and distributed more than one billion of its booklets, making it one of Europe's top publishers.

❯ Wickes sells enough paint each year to fill more than a third of a million family baths.

❯ Wickes invented the DIY conservatory and now sells more per year than anyone else in Britain.

Yakult

Market

The past decade has seen a quantum leap regarding attitudes to health in the UK. When it comes to exercising or eating a healthy balanced diet, awareness and involvement of the population has reached a record high.

Much of this increased health-consciousness stems from initiatives such as the Government's five-a-day scheme, which encourages consumers to eat at least five portions of fruit and vegetables on a daily basis. At the same time, key food and drink manufacturers have played a vital role in educating consumers and offering healthy products.

The probiotic alternative has been greatly received by the UK population since 1996, when Yakult UK created the market. Since then, the company has invested more than £38 million on educating consumers about the benefits of a healthy lifestyle, a balanced diet and probiotics.

With more than three million people suffering from constipation every month and two million people hit by food poisoning every year in the UK, it's not surprising that the investment has paid off. While in 2001, 11.7% of the UK population were buying probiotic drinks, by 2004 this had risen to almost 30%, with each buyer purchasing around 86 bottles per year (Source: TNS).

As a result, the total sales of probiotic milk drinks have shown consistent growth, with value sales growing from around £40 million in 2000 to reach £150 million by 2004 (Source: ACNielsen).

Achievements

Despite stiff competition from relatively new entrants to the daily probiotic drinks market, Yakult has maintained second position in the top ten yoghurts and drinking yoghurts brands with sales of more than £30 million in the year to October 2004. Yakult's sales grew by over 15%, the eighth year of consistent growth since Yakult's launch in 1996 (Source: ACNielsen).

Yakult's pioneering spirit means it has dominated the probiotic yoghurt drinks sector for many years until its rivals were brave enough to dip their toes in the water. The brand remains a force to be reckoned with and is fighting back with innovations such as the launch of Yakult Light, which reportedly added around £6 million to the brand's value (Source: The Grocer).

In addition to its position in the dairy drinks top ten, Yakult is also the 25th

best-selling soft drink in the UK – a position it has held for the past two years.

Although Yakult was first manufactured commercially some 70 years ago, it only arrived in the UK in 1996 and the Republic of Ireland in 2005. Yet, within a few short years, it has become a household name. It was sold nationwide after shoppers voted it one of the top 100 products in Sainsbury's stores.

Today in the UK 300,000 bottles of Yakult are now sold every day by all supermarket chains and through a variety of other distribution channels.

History

It all started more than 70 years ago, when Dr Minoru Shirota, a researcher at the Faculty of Medicine at Kyoto University began investigating Lactic Acid Bacteria (LAB). The role of these bacteria in human health had been noted by the Nobel Prize winning scientist Dr Elie Metchnikoff at the turn of the 20th century.

As he studied Metchnikoff's work and continued his own research, Dr Shirota became convinced that a positive balance of beneficial bacteria in the gut was the basis of a long and healthy life. He realised that making the benefits of LAB available to all might raise the general standard of health. This was to become his life's work.

His breakthrough came in 1930, when he succeeded in isolating particular LAB, which had the unique ability to survive the harsh conditions of the stomach, where most bacteria are destroyed by gastric juices. This enabled it to reach the intestines alive and make a positive contribution to the balance of the gut flora. The bacteria was named 'Lactobacillus casei Shirota' in his honour.

Dr Shirota developed the Yakult milk drink as an easy and pleasant way to get his bacteria to the masses. He wanted to make the drink available to everyone in the world. In common with many around this time, Dr Shirota believed that Esperanto would become the international language, so he chose 'Yakult', derived from the word 'Jahurto', meaning 'yoghurt' in Esperanto as the name of the drink.

Originally, Dr Shirota made Yakult in his clinic and dispensed it from there, later setting up a door-to-door delivery service, which made Yakult accessible to all in Japan. By 1955 demand had grown to such a point that he established the Yakult Honsha Company in Tokyo.

Today, some 25 million people drink Yakult every day and the company now operates in 26 countries, across South America, Asia, Australasia and Europe. The Japanese-based operation, which generates an annual turnover of 156 billion yen, has expanded to five main divisions of activity including food & beverages, cosmetics, pharmaceuticals, research & development & chemical analysis – all of which have evolved from the company's expertise in microbiological research and Dr Shirota's concern for a healthy society.

EVERY BODY NEEDS DIGESTIVE HEALTH.

Rushing, travelling, working, stressing. How you live can upset your digestive health. By staying fit, eating healthily and including friendly bacteria in your daily diet, you're stacking the cards in your favour.

Yakult was developed 70 years ago in Japan by a scientist called Dr Shirota. His invention of the first one-a-day friendly bacteria drink showed the importance of caring daily for your digestive health.

Yakult's little bottle isn't big enough to quench your thirst but big enough for all those friendly bacteria. (Only a scientist would stop there.) It contains 50kcal and virtually no fat. For a free information pack, call 0845 769 7069 or visit www.yakult.co.uk.

Digestive health matters

Product

Yakult is a fermented milk probiotic drink. Each bottle contains 6.5 billion 'friendly' Lactobacillus casei Shirota bacteria – the original strain cultivated by Dr Shirota after many years of research. This strain is unique to Yakult and has many positive characteristics. Most crucially, it's resistant to stomach acid so it can reach the intestines alive.

Drinking Yakult everyday is a convenient way to top up the beneficial bacteria in the gut. When in the gut the friendly LAB supports the work of other beneficial bacteria, keeps the harmful micro-organisms in check and encourages growth of beneficial bacteria.

Today there are two versions of Yakult: the original and Yakult Light. Both contain Lactobacillus casei Shirota but have differences in calorie count, taste and ingredients.

All decisions about Yakult's size, name and odd colour become clear when you realise they were made by Dr Shirota – a bacteriologist, not a marketing man. It is pinky-brown because it contains no artificial colours. Its name is derived from 'Esperanto' – which he believed would become the universal language. It comes in a little bottle because it is designed only to deliver a specific amount of friendly bacteria – not to quench thirst.

Recent Developments

Early in 2004, Yakult Honsha and France-based Groupe Danone entered into a beneficial and supportive partnership alliance. Leveraging upon both companies' unique strengths, cultures and business models, the purpose of this alliance is to strengthen global leadership in the food and beverage markets and to further accelerate the growth of both companies. Using the technological strength in probiotics and unique distribution channel of Yakult Honsha, and the established global presence and marketing expertise of Groupe Danone, both companies will develop a relationship through various synergistic collaborations – focusing initially in the area of probiotic products outside of Japan.

Yakult, made from Irish milk powder, went on sale in December 2004 in all major multiples in Ireland. Further cementing

its links to the country from which it purchases several hundred tonnes of milk powder every year, the company hosted a one-day conference in Dublin in March, entitled Bacteria in Food and Health – attended by hundreds of food industry, research and medical professionals.

In February 2005, Yakult announced that it is to set up a research institute in Ghent, Belgium. As a worldwide pioneer and innovator in the field of preventative health solutions and probiotics, Yakult will use the new base to further research intestinal flora and digestive function in Europe.

At the start of 2005, Yakult launched new Trial Packs of existing products Yakult Original and Yakult Light. The new pack sizes were initially made available throughout various UK supermarket chains, with a seven-figure sum being spent on their introduction. Fresh product packaging has been specially designed to attract people new to Yakult. Each Trial Pack exterior features unique male and female characters – demonstrating that Yakult is for everybody, male or female, young or old.

Promotion

Yakult practices its philosophy of 'Working on a Healthy Society' by actively supporting social and cultural activities in the community. In Holland it sponsors the Dutch Philharmonic Orchestra and in Germany it supports the Kinder Opera.

Since Yakult UK was established in 1996, it has sponsored organisations and projects in Great Britain. In 1997 it joined forces with the Royal Academy of Arts, with thousands of pupils in schools across the country benefiting from interactive life drawing classes run by the Royal Academy of Arts and Yakult Outreach Programme.

However, Yakult's responsibility to the community is perhaps best illustrated by the unique distribution system that operates in Japan. Some 50,000 women, known as the 'Yakult Ladies', regularly call on the community, bringing not only a supply of Yakult drinks but also a friendly face and a source of health information. It is this personal contact with the individual that has informed and inspired Yakult's communication strategies in other parts of the world.

Yakult also works closely with the medical and scientific world, regularly holding symposia for health professionals. These conferences bring the world's top researchers together to discuss health matters relating to intestinal flora and have won recognition for their contribution to the promotion of scientific research.

Indeed, in 2002, Yakult was listed by the NHS, with over one hundred UK hospitals now ordering in regular supplies for both patients and visitors.

Yakult employs a wide and varied range of programmes and initiatives to support its trade partners. With an advertising spend of around £4.6 million per year in the UK (Source: ALF), Yakult is no stranger to British TV screens. Its 'friendly bacteria' campaign by cdp-travissully, centred on the unlikely friendship of a bacteria-obsessed boffin and an attractive woman, has consistently performed well in consumer recall tables, with the highest recall rates in the probiotic category.

The start of 2005 saw the third TV ad featuring 'the Geek and the Girl', which was aired until the end of February and during key periods in 2005, with more than £2 million spent on its initial burst. Additional advertising activity during the year will include a comprehensive consumer print and internet campaign.

Yakult also strives to educate consumers. All communications seek to highlight the benefits of Yakult's friendly bacteria and help consumers look after their digestive health. Consumers can contact its acclaimed Consumer Information Service or surf its award-winning new website. They can also order a range of endorsed booklets and newsletters; containing news and information about the digestive system, probiotics and Yakult, plus useful healthy eating and lifestyle tips.

Brand Values

A powerful advocate of preventative medicine, Dr Shirota believed firmly that physical health, mental health and social well-being were all important for a healthy life. He also believed that good health should be available to everyone. These beliefs were distilled into the philosophy 'Working on a Healthy Society', which remains Yakult's motto and core belief.

www.yakult.co.uk

Yakult

> Yakult's founder, Dr Shirota, was a powerful advocate of preventative medicine; believing prevention was better than cure.

> Yakult is the global leader in probiotics and the pioneer of Lactic Acid Bacteria (LAB) in health, with 70 years of dedicated scientific research. The company is the expert in LAB technology; innovating 250 food, drink, pharmaceutical and cosmetic products for better health.

> 25 million people in 26 countries drink Yakult every day.

> Yakult Ladies began to deliver product to homes all over Japan in 1963. Today, there are 50,000 Yakult Ladies across Japan and 34,000 Yakult Ladies active in countries including Mexico, Indonesia, the Philippines and China.

> The name Yakult is inspired by the Esperanto word for 'yoghurt'.

> Yakult contains the original strain of probiotic bacteria Lactobacillus casei Shirota. This is unique to Yakult and resistant to stomach acid so it can reach the intestines alive. Every bottle contains 6.5 billion bacteria – an amount more than sufficient to contribute positively to the good bacteria in the intestines.

> 2005 is the 70th anniversary of Dr Shirota's discovery.

Market

Yellow Pages is part of Yell, a leading international directories business and the biggest player in the £4.2 billion UK classified advertising market (Source: The Advertising Association 2003).

The market consists of a range of media, including other printed directories, local and national newspapers and online directories. In 2004, Yell published 90 regional editions of Yellow Pages in the UK, containing more than one million advertisements, and distributed almost 28 million copies.

Yellow Pages is a key part of Yell's integrated portfolio of products, comprising printed, online and telephone-based media: Yellow Pages, Yell.com and Yellow Pages 118 24 7. The portfolio supports Yell's overall business proposition to put buyers in touch with sellers through a range of simple-to-use, cost-effective advertising solutions.

Achievements

Since Yell's first Yellow Pages was published almost 40 years ago, the directory has become a part of everyday life and both consumers and advertisers trust Yellow Pages to deliver the results they require year after year. Consequently, Yellow Pages is used 1.2 billion times a year, helping to generate more than £240 million a day for businesses that appear in the directory, or £88 billion a year (Source: Saville Rossiter-Base 2004).

Yellow Pages is well known for its award-winning and memorable advertising campaigns, which have contributed to keeping the directory at the forefront of people's minds for many years.

Yell is very aware of environmental and social issues and its impact on the wider community and this affects the way all parts of its business and operations are managed. For instance, Yellow Pages works with local councils to encourage the recycling of old directories; 94% of UK councils have the facilities to recycle Yellow Pages directories and 51% of people say that they recycle their directories (Source: FDS International 2004). In addition, all of its new directories are made from 48% recycled fibres. The remaining part comes from sustainable forests in Finland.

Yell has an overall commitment to excellence and has achieved and maintained registration to ISO9001, ISO4001 and ISO18001, the international management, environmental and health and safety standards.

Both in 1999 and, again, in 2004 Yell won the prestigious European Quality Award, the coveted pan-European business excellence award created and managed by the European Foundation for Quality Management (EFQM). Yell is the first company ever to win the award twice.

Yell also won a Queen's Award for Enterprise for its integrated approach to sustainable development in 2002. It was acknowledged for demonstrating outstanding commercial success, whilst at the same time ensuring work practices that benefit society, the environment and the economy.

In the same year, Yell won a Green Apple Environmental Award for its directory recycling scheme and, in 2003, won a further Green Apple Award for environmental best practice.

Yell was also, in 2003, awarded a BIG TICK by Business in the Community, the independent organisation that helps businesses to improve their positive impact on society. The BIG TICK recognises companies that have reached a measurable standard of excellence in the field of corporate responsibility.

Yell was also a finalist in the 'Business in the Environment' category of the Business in the Community Awards for Excellence.

History

The first directories date as far back as Elizabethan times, when street directories were published detailing the names and addresses of local residences and businesses. But the forerunner of modern day directories did not properly emerge until the 1840s, with the publication of Kelly's London Post Office directories. These contained information on local gentry and traders, listed by county.

The growth of the telecommunications industry offered further potential to publishers of directories. Yell's first Yellow Pages directory appeared in 1966, bound into the standard Brighton telephone directory. From 1973, Yellow Pages was rolled out across the UK and existed as a product in its own right, becoming a registered trademark in 1979.

Over the years, Yellow Pages has continued to improve and enhance its product, as well as extending into new areas to keep up with the developing directories' industry. Aside from Yellow Pages, Yell's products in the UK also include the following:

Business Pages, a specialist directory covering business to business suppliers, introduced in 1985; Yell.com, a leading site for finding businesses, shops and services in the UK that was launched in 1996 and Yellow Pages 118 24 7, a telephone-based information service providing in-depth classified business information and business and residential listings. It was launched in 2003 following the deregulation of 192 directory enquiries

and replaced the Talking Pages service that had been introduced in 1988.

In 1999 Yell expanded into the US with the purchase of Yellow Book USA, the largest independent publisher in the US. Since then there has been further expansion in the US. The most significant development was the purchase of the McLeod directories business in April 2002, which doubled Yell's geographic US footprint. With the additional purchase in December that year of National Directory Company, Yell consolidated its position as the largest independent publisher of yellow pages directories in the US. In March 2004, the acquisition of Feist took Yell's US presence to 42 states and Washington DC.

In July 2003, having been sold by BT to a private equity consortium in 2001, a new milestone in Yell's development

was heralded with the company's listing on the London Stock Exchange – the biggest flotation in the London market for two years.

Product

Yell is committed to supporting the growth and development of businesses in the UK. It aims to understand, anticipate and meet the changing demands of advertisers and users and to take advantage of new technologies and communication methods in the development of world class products and services.

New customers are shown the value of Yellow Pages advertising packages with attractive pricing schemes. Customers are retained year after year through the provision of excellent service and products. Over the past four years, Yellow Pages has won more than 100,000 new advertisers a year in the UK and has a high customer retention rate, reflecting

by business type, name and location. In January 2005 the site generated 65 million page impressions. The information that Yell.com provides can now be accessed through the website and via mobile telephone, including mobile internet and text message.

Yellow Pages 118 24 7 offers callers a classified business directory service, including additional details such as opening hours and store locations, as well as residential directory listings. In the financial year 2004, 3.9 million enquiries were received and Yellow Pages carried advertisements for nearly 64,000 paying advertisers.

Recent Developments

Yellow Pages is constantly looking at new and innovative ways of attracting new advertisers and retaining existing ones, as well as ensuring the directory is easy to use and relevant to local needs.

In March 2005, Yellow Pages launched for the first time in Hull, completing Yellow Pages' delivery coverage of the entire UK.

A significant and striking redesign of the Yellow Pages directory was launched in June 2004 to highlight to users the 'added value' content within the directories. The design uses a new colour coding system flagged on a new-look

In 2004 the 'Haircut' TV advert won a Silver Lion at the Cannes Advertising Festival and a Diploma at the British Television Advertising Awards.

Brand Values

The Yellow Pages brand is built on its reputation for accessibility, trustworthiness, reliability and warmth.

Yellow Pages is ubiquitous, with 97% of adults having a copy at home and 64% of workers having a copy in the workplace (Source: Saville Rossiter-Base 2004).

Research shows that Yellow Pages is well ahead of the classified advertising competition on value, with the vast majority of advertisers saying they feel it offers good value for money (Source: Saville Rossiter-Base 2004).

Similarly, research carried out over a number of years has shown that users are more satisfied with Yellow Pages directories than any other information source such as local newspapers, TV text services, local libraries, classified magazines and even friends and neighbours (Source: Consensus Record 2002).

In keeping with the brand's friendly and helpful personality, Yellow Pages' involvement with charity and environmental projects reflects its concern with issues that affect individuals and communities throughout the UK.

strong satisfaction. By proving the value of its advertising and building on its relationships with customers, Yellow Pages also encourages existing advertisers to expand their advertising programmes.

Today there are more than 2,200 classifications in the Yellow Pages directory and these are reviewed on a regular basis to ensure that it is as easy as possible for Yellow Pages' users to find the products and services they need. By classifying businesses under the most relevant and up-to-date headings, Yellow Pages makes life simple for its users. Alongside more traditional classifications such as Builders and Plumbers, recent additions include Insurance – Pet (2004) and Graffiti Removal (2005), reflecting current social and market trends.

Yell.com now features approximately two million UK business listings, searchable

front cover and incorporates iconography supported by vibrant colour imagery. The design creates a more contemporary look and feel to increase the appeal of the directory to users.

The 'added value' content has been refreshed and features expanded information sources such as a 'Your Area Guide' that highlights community, leisure, travel, sports and shopping information and 'Consumer Information'.

In October 2001 full-colour advertisements were published in Yellow Pages for the first time. It is an innovation that has proved popular with advertisers, allowing them more flexibility in the style of their advertisements.

Other developments across the Yell portfolio include the launch of Yell.com mobile in 2004. It is the first mobile business information service of its kind in the UK, enabling users to access Yell.com's business information from a mobile handset. Yell.com mobile also helps users to get where they want to go by offering full colour street maps and walking and driving directions.

Promotion

Yell has launched a new strategic marketing approach for 2005, promoting the full Yell 'family' of products in an integrated campaign.

Four new TV adverts have been produced featuring actor James Nesbitt and using the strapline 'Whatever you want – just Yell'. The adverts show the 'James' character in a variety of humorous situations, demonstrating each product's versatility for finding businesses and services when and where you need them.

The TV adverts form the basis of a through-the-line marketing approach, including outdoor campaigns, radio advertising, direct mail and public relations activity.

Yellow Pages has consistently used strong advertising campaigns to build and reinforce awareness of the brand. The famous JR Hartley TV advertisement 'Fly Fishing' won a British Television Silver Award in 1983 and, in 2000, came 13th in a Channel 4 poll of the '100 Greatest TV Ads of all Time'.

Yellow Pages has worked with Marie Curie Cancer Care since 1999, supporting the annual 'Great Daffodil Appeal', which has raised more than £11 million for the charity to date.

Yellow Pages' support of the Directory Recycling Scheme (DRS) forms part of the company's ongoing commitment to the environment. A major schools recycling initiative – The Yellow Woods Challenge – was launched in October 2002 with Kirk, a woodland creature, as its mascot. Its aims are to educate children about recycling and conservation and to encourage them to recycle old Yellow Pages' directories.

www.yellgroup.com

THINGS YOU DIDN'T KNOW ABOUT

Yellow Pages

> New classifications include Allergists & Allergy Testing (2005), Fair Trade Goods (2004) and Quad Bikes & All Terrain Vehicles (2005). Recently deleted classifications include Shoulder Pads, Pot Pourri, and Hairpiece Manufacturers & Importers (2004).

> The most popular classifications for users are Restaurants, Insurance (all), Garage Services, Plumbers, Builders and Car Dealers & Distributors (Source: Saville Rossiter-Base 2004).

> Yellow Pages is used 3.3 million times per day in the UK and 100 million times a month (Source: Saville Rossiter-Base 2004).

> Almost 28 million Yellow Pages' directories were distributed in 2004 to households and businesses in the UK.

> In 1991, following popular demand, the book 'Fly Fishing' was written – eight years after the commercial featuring the JR Hartley character first aired. It became a Christmas bestseller.

> Yellow Pages can be recycled into animal bedding, fake snow, stuffing for jiffy bags, egg boxes and cardboard.

Market

In the UK consumption of seafood is rising faster than beef, lamb and poultry (Source: TNS Frozen and Chilled Protein Trend, 12 weeks to March 2005).

Young's Bluecrest is the UK's largest seafood company. It was created in July 1999 with the merger of Bluecrest, the former seafood division of Booker plc, and Young's, the seafood division of United Biscuits. The business has an estimated 36% share of the UK retail seafood market, which is worth £1.8 billion.

The Young's brand has been at the forefront of driving growth in this market, growing from £100 million to £190 million in the last four years. By focusing on making fish easier for consumers, Young's is helping to remove many of the barriers which have historically prevented consumers from eating fish, such as dislike of skin and bones; and a lack of confidence regarding how to prepare fresh fish.

Young's is the clear market leader in frozen seafood, with a 21% share, well ahead of second-placed Birds Eye. Young's is the leading brand in most categories, including scampi, prawns, coated fish, natural fish and seafood ready meals. It is also the number one brand in battered fish with its Chip Shop range, which in itself generates sales in excess of £50 million.

In the last couple of years, the brand has launched 'Young'uns', bringing much needed innovation into the children's market. This range is now worth over £5 million.

In chilled seafood, a category historically dominated by retailer brands, Young's has also built a strong position since entering the market in 2000. It now has a £38 million presence in this area and has more than doubled its sales in the last year. The Young's chilled range offers both fresh fish and pre-prepared recipes, including fresh prawns, mussels, salmon fillets and complete meals such as Young's Fishermans Pie and traditional Haddock Mornay.

Achievements

A testament to the strength of the Young's brand is that since its re-launch in 2000, it has reinvigorated the whole seafood market, using its experience and expertise to fire consumer enthusiasm for eating fish.

The strength of the Young's brand is reflected in its leadership of all of the major seafood categories. Young's

Admirals Pie is the UK's best selling ready meal (by volume), selling over 10 million pies a year, while the success of The Young's Chip Shop brand has encouraged consumers to buy frozen battered fish. This brand extension has helped overcome perceptions that battered fish is unhealthy, promoting an 'oven healthy' message to help Young's Chip Shop increase its share of category from 29% in 2000 to 43% in 2005.

The successful re-launch of the brand saw Young's scoop a prestigious Marketing Society award for brand development in 2002, and also a major accolade from Food Manufacture magazine. In addition, Young's has recently had three products shortlisted for the 2005 Seafood Awards. The company was also shortlisted in the 'Technical Innovation' category for a pioneering environmental protection project in the Hebrides.

History

The story of Young's began in 1805, when Elizabeth Young started trading in prawns and whitebait in Greenwich. Joined soon afterwards by her sons, William and George, the family business became famous for the quality of its fish – even supplying whitebait (which was then considered a delicacy) to cabinet ministers in the Government.

In the next century, Young's became famous for its potted shrimp, which were sold in distinctive blue pottery jars – now considered to be collectors' items. The company was also responsible for a number of notable 'seafood firsts' such as the introduction of the very first frozen peeled prawns, importing the first frozen salmon and the 'invention' of scampi in the 1940s.

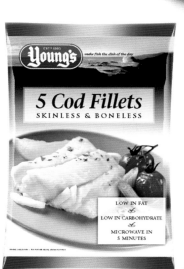

In the 1980s, the company became famous for its 'golden' coated seafood products, and then introduced its Ocean Pie and Chip Shop brands, which remain flagship products in the Young's range today.

When Young's Bluecrest was formed in 1999, it was the start of a new era of seafood growth and development. Demand for salmon and ready meals grew rapidly, and Young's embarked on the next stage of its development, starting to create seafood dishes to suit every occasion and taste.

Product

Young's is the UK's leading specialist fish brand. With 200 years experience, it enjoys an unrivalled reputation for fish expertise, providing reassurance to its consumers. Young's aim is to inspire people to eat more seafood by making fish easier to use and also to offer excellent product quality, whether frozen or chilled.

new product areas. For example, in 2004, the acquisition of The Macrae Food Group – the largest processor of delicatessen seafood products in the UK – opened up new opportunities in speciality products and smoked salmon.

In 2000, a new brand architecture was devised to represent the Young's brand and its established icons (the red and blue logo, seascapes and black) in a powerful but distinctive way.

The new architecture defined the optimum balance between consistent brand communication and uniqueness of individual product ranges and was intended to re-establish and emphasise Young's territory as the specialists in fish.

Additionally, the brand has rapidly expanded its product range. For example, in 2004, Young's launched a range of natural fillets and steaks in frozen – historically, a commodity product area. To build on the food credentials of the brand, all of the pack designs show the fish in the context of a meal and also include a simple, step by step guide to show consumers how to prepare and cook the fish.

Promotion

The re-launch of the Young's brand in 2000 was backed by the distinctive 'Have a Fishy' marketing campaign. This advertising idea was based on a fusion of a traditional folk song with scenes of contemporary Young's chefs preparing fish recipes. Designed to inspire people to put Young's on their shopping lists by building awareness of the Young's brand for fish dishes, the campaign also aimed to 'normalise' fish in the minds of consumers. In addition, the advertising reinforced the perception of Young's as having unrivalled expertise in both fish and its preparation.

With research by the company showing that although people love to eat fish, they are put off preparing it at home, the campaign set out to quell consumers' worries with the message that Young's takes the trouble away by 'doing the work for you'.

Market tests have proven that the advertising has had a significant effect on increasing prompted awareness of the brand, which now stands at an impressive 95%. It has also boosted sales, by up to 15% for core products like Chip Shop, and by 45% for new launches like Salmon En Croute.

Although TV based, the campaign idea has developed naturally into print, radio and an extensive consumer website. A key part of the marketing strategy has been to

With access to fish species from around the world, Young's produces a vast range of products, both chilled and frozen, from traditional favourites such as Prawns and Scampi to Chip Shop Battered Fish and Ocean Pie. It also produces a wide range of ready-to-eat seafood, such as smoked salmon, canapés and terrines.

Recent Developments

Since 1999, the business has seen significant growth, fuelled by a rapid period of acquisition. This has enabled the Young's brand to expand into many

concentrate TV ads at the end of the week, traditionally a time to eat fish and also a time when most shopping is done. Young's calls this strategy 'Fishy Friday'.

The campaign is continually developing and being refreshed so that people continue to 'make fish the dish of the day'.

Brand Values

Young's mission is to 'own fish' in the consumer's mind because they are the Fish Specialists. It pursues an ambition to be famous by making it accessible for consumers, inspiring them with ideas and by being the brand people trust, above all others, for fish.

www.youngsbluecrest.co.uk

Unravelling Brand Value

A paper prepared by Jane Piper of Jane Piper Brand Strategy Consultancy on behalf of The Superbrands organisation

JANE PIPER

Independent Consultant
www.janepiperbrandstrategy.co.uk

Jane Piper is an independent consultant with specialist expertise in creating, managing and developing brand value for large, medium and small organisations.

She has 20 years consultancy experience gained both in-house and independently, focusing on the strategic development and management of brands, for clients across key market sectors such as travel and leisure, financial services, the public sector, energy, food and drink.

Her clients are wide and diverse, and have included both market leaders as well as medium-sized business, all of whom have an interest in understanding and maximising the value and return on investment in their brands.

Since RHM first placed a balance sheet value on their key brands in 1988 and the London Stock Exchange endorsed the concept in 1989 (allowing the inclusion of intangible assets in class tests for shareholder approvals during takeovers), the door has opened for companies to value their brands and include them as intangible assets on their balance sheet.

However, the issue of exactly how to value brands has been the subject of much debate ever since.

Despite subsequent recognition in the finance department that brands are valuable assets with many useful attractions, often making a significant contribution to the total value of a company, the lack of consistency and clarity in approach to valuing them has contributed towards confusion particularly in the marketing community.

As brand guardians, it is no longer good enough to understand what constitutes a brand, we need to know how to calculate their worth, and to adopt branding strategies to develop and maximise their value potential.

The purpose of this paper is to provide an independent and introductory overview to valuing brands for the benefit of the marketing community, as well as to provide some clarity on the differing methodologies that are used to calculate their value.

It has been compiled independently in conjunction with the co-operation of a number of leading brand valuation practitioners, to whom we are grateful for their time and contribution in furthering the cause of branding.

Brands - Valuable Assets

As brands are often a company's most important and valuable intangible asset, particularly in certain market sectors, the subject regularly fills column inches in the business pages of the national press and other journals as the debate rumbles on about how to value them.

Intangibles are now accounting for an ever-increasing % of market value, approximately 60% across the FTSE All Share Index – up from only 10% some 50 years ago (PricewaterhouseCoopers (PwC) Research, Intellectual Asset Management 2003).

Later research shows that in the US merger and acquisition market in 2003, some 48% of corporate value was placed on brands and intangibles (PwC Research US 2004).

Historically, it is those businesses with strong brands that commanded a higher share price, as demonstrated by the following chart:

Businesses with strong brands command higher share prices

In addition, the current rise in trademark applications in the US & UK (following the blip in numbers as the dot.com bubble burst post 2000) demonstrates the continuing trend in launching new brands – and the creation of whole new brand-led markets.

For example, US lawyers Decherts quote almost four new 'carb' related brands being posted daily in the US for trademark status at the height of the Atkins publicity in 2004.

With new brands in new sectors and new delivery technologies, it is not surprising that there is increased interest in realising the power and value of the brand outside of the traditional consumer arena in sectors such as banking, energy and transport.

> *"A powerful brand adds value to all the assets a company has – product and package features and benefits, manufacturing plants, employees, customer relationships, marketing, promotions. With a powerful brand every relevant econometric can be, and should be, more productive."*
>
> *AT Kearney*

Along with the rise in importance of brand value since its conception there has been much focus on determining more precise, rigorous and robust methods to calculate value:

> *"The valuation debate has moved on considerably since the advent of Interbrand's methodology and its focus on the capital base of a company when determining brand value.*
>
> *Brand valuation may be an art but it is becoming a more sophisticated art."*
>
> *Gravitas*

But whilst the brand valuation debate continues there is at least wide recognition that the value of a brand can be a significant proportion of total business value.

The damage to a company's brand by the adverse actions of one particular group of stakeholders has the ability to inflict serious harm to its reputation, and wipe millions off its market value as was demonstrated most vividly with Arthur Anderson.

Today's business environment places Corporate Governance as the number one boardroom issue. The links between governance, trust and reputation are becoming ever closer since Alan Greenspan's famous comments:

> *"Corporate Reputation is rising out of the ashes of the debacle as a significant economic value."*
>
> *Chicago, May 2003*

To all intents and purposes, a company's corporate brand and reputation is one and the same thing, if anything a brand is seen as something more 'tangible'.

Place a value on your brand – place a value on your reputation has never been more relevant. In addition it is even more important to give greater clarity on the subject of brand value with the introduction of new international accounting standards this year.

Exactly What Is The Brand Asset?

Even the valuation industry itself acknowledges the confusion:

"PwC recognises that there is confusion in the marketplace related to:

● the terminology that is used eg. brand equity/brand value
● the purposes and benefits of brand valuation
● the brand valuation methodologies

Delving deeper, there is even confusion as to what exactly a brand means, particularly in valuation terms. Different people interpret the term differently in different environments.

Establishing clear definitions should be considered fundamental before undertaking a brand valuation exercise.

Brands have been interpreted at its most simple level as the heart of an organisation's visual identity i.e. its name and logo. This is usually protected as a trademark.

At the next level, it includes both trademarks and all forms of intellectual property that go with the brand, including product design, patents and rights, domain names and any other associated visual or verbal communication of the brand.

The widest and fairest assessment of brand for valuation purposes, includes identifying the role of brand within the value chain of the organisation as a whole.

This interpretation has been simplified as:

"the first we refer to as the trademark, the second we refer to as the brand, and the third we refer to as the branded business"

Brand Finance

Whilst there is still confusion and lack of understanding as to what constitutes a brand for valuation purposes, the above definition is largely supported by the practising industry.

For example, Ernst & Young would take a commercial assessment of a business and believe that a brand is created and supported by other functions.

"Taking a typical example, a retail brand is reliant on the quality of its product (from materials to manufacturing, source and supply), its retail design and merchandising, its design team and quality of customer service as well as the strength of its property outsourcing contracts.

All of these interlink to drive value in the brand – if one element fails such as distribution, it will have a negative knock-on effect on the value of the brand."

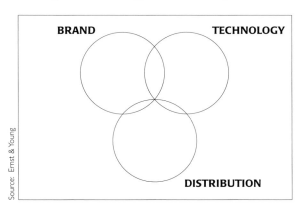

The Requirement To Value
Things are changing ...
2005 sees the introduction of International Financial Reporting Standards (IFRS), designed to bring some uniformity in accounting standards and interpretations around the world.

What does this mean for brands and valuing brands?

Around the world international accounting standards for brands have varied according to the different regulatory standards that are in place in each country.

IFRS will bring some consistency in the overall requirement to value listed-company brands. This includes valuing all brands bought and sold and a requirement for an ongoing annual re-assessment of the value of acquired brands known as an impairment review where the brand does not have a specified useful economic life.

A software brand may for example have a useful economic life applied to it, by the very nature of the rapidly changing technology marketplace, in which case there would not be a need for an annual impairment review. It would, however, need to be depreciated or amortised over the period of its specified economic life.

Corporate brands may or may not have a useful economic life specified and therefore if corporate change has taken place, may be liable for an annual impairment review.

A recent example would be in the acquisition by Spain's Banco Santander of abbey.

Some of these new standards are already in place in certain countries, for example in the US, but what it does mean is consistent international standards on how, why and when brands need to be valued for accounting purposes.

In reality, this will mean that when a company acquires a business, a value will have to be placed on the brand it is acquiring. Surely it makes sense for this information to be used as a basis and benchmark for more targeted and focused brand and marketing strategies to drive greater value out of the brand it is acquiring?

And in addition, if there is a requirement to annually re-assess and monitor value in the form of an impairment review, this provides the ideal opportunity to assess the success or otherwise of marketing strategies and their return on investment. The Board can then use a gain in brand value as an important point in its investor communications on delivering greater shareholder value (although it cannot be revised upwards on the balance sheet).

"For many businesses, the strength of their brands is a key driver of profitability and cash flows. Recognising these assets will reinforce this message to investors and help them judge whether brands are in good health. The accounting requirement to regularly review the value of acquired brands means there will be an ongoing judgement of the success of marketing strategy for investing in brands"

KPMG

What Is In It For Marketing?

" Brand Value is a hot topic for accounting and finance professionals, but an even hotter topic for marketing professionals"

FutureBrand

The big advantage to the Marketing Department is that brand valuation can provide a strong and viable basis to relate the success of its strategy and return on investment to enhanced business performance, which is what the CEO is primarily concerned about. This is particularly relevant where there is big-ticket advertising or significant retail investment.

"The irony is that often a brand is being valued anyway, its just that the marketing department often doesn't know about it, as the finance team may think its not relevant to them - despite the extensive levels of

consumer and market-based research that is undertaken, and the strategic insights and options that are identified."

PwC

The issue is how often the finance department and the marketing department realise the potential of the link between statutory financial information being used to shape marketing strategies that deliver superior results.

In reality, there is little crossover between marketing and finance at a strategic level, with the exception of the annual budget rounds, despite the increasing pressure to demonstrate marketing effectiveness.

FutureBrand quote figures from the Marketing Leadership Council that "66% or 2/3rds of its members need to demonstrate financial results of marketing or to show its worth". Superbrands research in 2001 showed that 79% of its members felt that they had adequate metrics/procedures in place to measure marketing effectiveness, 69% brand health and only 44% brand value.

Surely by qualifying and quantifying brand values and demonstrating return on marketing investment marketeers would provide the ultimate evidence of their success?

Why Do Companies Get Brands Valued?

There is common agreement that there are two main reasons why brands get valued:

- Financial Transactions
- Strategic Purposes

The use of brand valuation in **Financial Transactions** is wide and varied and may include:

Tax planning: Transfer of ownership of brands to a more cost-effective tax haven i.e. Switzerland or the Cayman Islands, whereby operating companies are then charged a royalty for the use of the brand. The brand has to be transferred at a market rate requiring commercial validation.

Transfer Pricing: Tax-related or otherwise, where the use of a brand is an integral part of a deal, for example the injection of fresh capital.

Mergers and Acquisitions: Brands have to be valued on merger, acquisition or divestment by listed companies; the premium value placed on intangible assets in particular the brand, often form the heart of the commercial basis of a deal.

In a hostile takeover situation, the value of a brand can often play a key part of a defence to secure a higher valuation.

Security/Securitisation: The value of the brand asset is increasingly being used to provide security particularly in private equity deals, and sometimes in securitisation.

Refinancing/restructuring: Using the value of the brand asset to raise finance, whether for corporate restructuring or for expansion purposes.

Licensing: In either a straightforward financial transaction where licensing is involved, or a situation where a strategic decision may have been taken to license a brand to a third party, its value is fundamental to the deal. This is particular prevalent in the pharmaceutical sector, as well as hotels and entertainment businesses.

Joint Ventures: In setting up and branding a joint venture, particularly between two brand-led businesses possibly in a new market place.

Litigation: In any number of disputes ranging from infringed intellectual property rights and trademark disputes, through to the damage to brand value from the failure of a third-party distribution network.

Investor Relations: To demonstrate the increased worth of the brand and other intangible assets, or the benefits of a brand rationalisation programme and subsequent direct contribution towards improving shareholder value.

There are many **Strategic Reasons** why a brand may need to be valued, including:

Strategic assessment: A changing competitive environment may require re-assessment and the possible re-positioning of a brand.

Corporate restructuring: As an aid to corporate restructuring, particularly in large, diverse international conglomerates.

Brand portfolio management: To review the value in a brand portfolio and to restructure or rationalise brand architecture, based on qualified and quantified consideration of the potential growth, opportunities and risks that exist.

Co-branding: In positioning co-branded ventures, or joint ventures.

New market entry: To understand the brand contribution to the success of a new market entry.

Brand stretch: To explore the 'stretch' potential of a brand.

Global brand management: To assess the performance of localised marketing strategies. This is particularly relevant in international organisations with devolved geographic marketing management structures.

Performance Management: To optimise the effectiveness of marketing and brand strategies through evaluation.

Return on Investment: Analysing the return on brand investment for a variety of reasons, including assessing marketing expenditure and effectiveness.

Brand strategy should today be directly geared towards realising and increasing real value and price premium from brands and as such, be a top-level management issue.

"The goal is to increase the value-added potential of the brand towards customers, employees and capital markets"

"Branding is not just about advertising and creativity – it is the discipline of creating value by orchestrating the whole business system towards the brand."

The Boston Consulting Group

Not unsurprisingly, it is the Finance Department that drives brand valuation in financial transactions, and either an enlightened CEO or Marketing Director in a strategic situation.

They understand that brands create value in the market and the importance of having a strategy that makes the brand accessible and visible to the customer.

Rarely do the two crossover. **The issue is what is happening in your company?**

"The finance director may be after a figure to create greater value in the business, but it is very rare that this is used as a benchmark to guide the strategic development of both brands and marketing strategies to deliver a greater return and enhance value."

Gravitas

Who Is In The Business Of Valuing Brands?

The companies tend to fall into four main categories:

- The accountancy firms
- Specialist valuation businesses
- Branding businesses with a recognised model in place
- Leading management consultancies

These businesses tend to use methodologies that are recognised by the US Internal Revenue Service and the UK's Inland Revenue, as well as US GAP and International Accounting Standards.

Many other brand-focused and marketing services businesses will offer 'brand value' consulting and may have their own models in place to monitor brand equity or 'value'. It is wise to take independent advice as to whether they are recognised or use robust financial modelling methodologies to realise the value of the brand for dual financial and marketing purposes.

Who Did We Talk To?

For the purposes of this overview we reviewed a range of methodologies and spoke to leading players in this market including:

- Accountancy and professional service firms Ernst & Young, KPMG and PricewaterhouseCoopers.
- Valuation businesses Gravitas and Brand Finance.
- A branding business with a recognised model in place, FutureBrand.
- Management consultancies AT Kearney and The Boston Consulting Group.

The above were happy to contribute as part of a **collective effort** to improve the understanding of brand valuation within the marketing community, and for which we are most grateful for their time and contribution.

This paper is not intended to be an endorsement or otherwise of any one approach to valuing brands, rather an informative overview of the different approaches, contexts and methodologies that are used to calculate brand value.

It is designed to be a practical and helpful initial reference guide to the marketing community on understanding the requirement for and the merits of brand valuation, the different approaches to valuing brands, and the strategic options and practical advantages that arise as a result of understanding the financial value in brands.

Different Types Of Businesses – Different Approaches

The first thing that is apparent is that there is no one common approach to valuing brands, which is why the subject causes such confusion.

Some practitioners advocate a single formulaic approach to valuing brands, whilst others use a variety of valuation methodologies, dependent on the situation or purpose for which they are providing an opinion of value, for example:

Market Value: What someone else is willing to pay for the brand? (Acquisition, Licensing, IFRS)

Value in Current Use: What is the value of the brand asset to the business in its current use? (Tax, Litigation)

Strategic Value: What could the asset be worth going forward – what strategic options are open to maximise value? (Corporate restructuring, Performance Management, Private Equity)

Who Does What

The management consultancies and the branding businesses advocate a single approach to valuing a brand for all situations.

The accounting and valuation businesses may use a number of different methodologies to compare outcomes and determine a broader opinion of value, dependent on the reasons and context for the valuation.

Their logic for this is that it is feasible that the market value of a brand in a transaction situation may be higher than its value-in-use to its existing owner. Clearly it is therefore important to identify the context of the valuation.

"No single methodology is better than any other, and as a valuer we use as many of the methodologies as possible on any brand.

As with many methodologies, however, it is in their application that the skill lies to ensure that the real economic value of the brands is identified."

Ernst &Young

Broadly-speaking, all the practitioners valued brands for both financial transactions as well as strategic reasons, with the main exception of the management consultancies Boston Consulting Group and AT Kearney, who are primarily concerned with brand valuation as part of a broader strategy review:

"Brand Valuation is primarily a Management Tool ... but also a

systematic analytical indication for financial purposes

The primary objective is ...
- To provide a customised tool for the client to evaluate the strength of their brand portfolio
- To provide a pragmatic framework for continuous usage
- To provide a common language for discussions between different management levels and functions
- To develop a proxy planning tool for making brand investment decisions"

The Boston Consulting Group

More surprisingly, the accounting businesses also undertake brand valuations for strategic purposes, by understanding how brand strategy translates into value and share price, in addition to straightforward financial transactions.

"Changing brand strategy – implications including internal and external management, change management and communication are integral to the success of improved brand and shareholder value."

KPMG

What Is On Offer?

Despite the varying approaches that exist which we will review in this paper, they do fall into a number of categories and there are some consistencies in valuation techniques offered from the differing practitioners.

Whilst there are similarities in valuation approach, there are also undoubtedly great differences in the context in which brand valuation is offered from the range of practitioners.

Some practitioners are straight valuation experts; some are very flexible in the range of services they provide from an initial valuation through to detailed value-based strategy, and some use brand valuation as primarily a management tool within a specific strategic context.

Companies considering whether or not to undertake an assessment of brand value are well advised to seek independent guidance as to which type of approach would best suit their own individual situations, particularly when requiring comparable situations from differing practitioners.

For clarity and to avoid repetition, the technical approaches to brand valuation in the market have been grouped into the following categories, as reflected by the majority of practitioners.

• **Economic-based approach:** the value of the brand based on how much the business benefits from owning and using the brand.
• **Income approach:** the value of the brand based on the net value of earnings attributable to the brand. There are individual financial methodologies based on the income approach, that are sometimes referred to individually as separate categories, such as **Royalty Relief and Premium Profits** (referred to as direct methodologies) and **Residual Earnings** (referred to as an indirect methodology).

Whilst different techniques, they are all based on the theme of identifying future earnings attributable to the brand over a particular period of time, and then discounting these back to present day values. This constituent element is common to both an Economic Use and an Income Approach, and has sometimes been

referred to as an **Earnings Split**.

• **Market-based approach:** the value of the brand estimated using prices from market transactions involving the sale of comparable assets.
• **Cost-based approach:** the value of the brand based on the historical costs of creating the brand and the estimated costs of replacing or recreating the brand.
• **The asset-based or elimination approach:** the value of the brand based on subtracting the net tangible assets from the business' full market value.

It should be noted that some practitioners would use a particular technique (for example **Royalty Relief**) to identify the value of a brand for a number of differing situations – ranging from what it is worth in economic use to the business, as well as to form a market valuation.

As previously stated, the accounting and valuation practitioners tend to use a variety or combination of methodologies, depending on which is more appropriate to the individual situation, as well as to cross-check their findings and form an opinion of value.

They may also use some of their own valuation techniques such as **Real Options Valuation™** a probability analysis technique at PwC.

The management consultancies use a single model based on an income approach, and again may have developed their own valuation methodologies/techniques for certain situations.

For example at The Boston Consulting Group, **Brand Option Value®** identifies the future potential value of the brand based on strength and exploitation opportunities, and **Brand Flagship Value®** measures the attractiveness of a brand towards employees, other customers and potential investors.

A Deep Understanding Of The Consumer

Regardless of the technical methodology used to calculate the worth of a brand, in the majority of situations the one underlying and common approach to all, is the extensive and detailed qualitative and quantitative analysis of the brand internally and externally, prior to its assessment in financial terms.

The extent and structure of this research will depend on the nature of the valuation, the degree of information that exists already and the context in which the valuation is required, as well as the individual model used by the practitioner.

Usually this involves a comprehensive assessment and qualification of the brand through primary and secondary, internal and external research including:

• Financials and trading history (including margins and sales trends)
• The components of the brand within the value chain
• Detailed market segmentation
• History, heritage and longevity
• Competitive positioning and benchmarking
• Brand environment, positioning and profile
• Global reach
• Levels and effectiveness of marketing support for the brand

As well as looking to the future at:

• Trading potential
• Levels of market innovation

• Brand life cycles
• Levels of brand risk

The above is required in order to qualify (in particular with consumers), and quantify the market drivers, the brand value drivers and the brand equity.

Whilst the research obviously addresses the revenue generation of the brand, it also addresses the cost of support, which varies from business to business. For example BMW support its brand with substantial advertising, but its brand is also based on superior technology for which there is a cost. Similarly in retail there is a substantial property cost associated with flagship stores.

The research may often take a view on the strength of management, recognising the potential of 'fads', the lack of any true USP's in me-too brands, as well as shifts in consumer spending patterns.

The strength and quality of consumer data provides invaluable input to key valuation assumptions, including customer behaviour models. The real key in valuation is the interpretation of this information as a financial model.

All practitioners have their own individual ways of identifying, interpreting and assessing this information as a basis for their valuation methodology(s).

This may involve working with external specialist or research models that exist in-house.

The Individual Approaches
Economic Use Approach
This assesses the economic use of the brand based on what the brand is worth to the business.

For the purposes of clarifying this approach, an Economic-Use model is based on identifying the value of a brand as part of the intangible earnings returns of a business, specified as returns above the cost of capital.

"It seeks to value the asset as part of the ongoing business concern– i.e. its current use to its current owner, being a common reference"

Brand Finance

Economic-Use is a widely used term, but practitioners may use a variety of methodologies under this heading, which can cause confusion.

This model for calculating brand value is widely accepted by tax authorities worldwide.

It is based on identifying the incremental returns and earnings attributable to all intangible assets, through:

• Identifying the sales revenues from the brand

• Subtracting from this all the operating costs (including depreciation)

To identify:

• Earnings Before Interest, Tax and Amortisation
• And Net Operating Profit after Tax (NOPAT)
• Charges for capital employed are then subtracted from NOPAT
• Which then identifies intangible earnings overall

To then identify the specific earnings attributable to the brand, detailed research is undertaken to identify how the brand drives customer demand and what income and cash flow it generates for the business(s) in each individual market/customer segment.

Brand Strength analysis then identifies its strength and weaknesses and subsequent risk profiles in order to identify an appropriate brand discount rate.

Brand Value is calculated by taking a brand earnings forecast for a future period of time and using the brand discount rate to track it back to today's value.

The advantages to this methodology are that it focuses on future earnings or cash flow, facilitates comparisons and is widely accepted and understood. The disadvantages are a degree of subjectivity on cost allocation and assumptions and extensive information requirements.

Income-Based Approach

The value of a brand is estimated using the present value of earnings (profits) attributable to the brand asset.

Similar to an economic use approach but with greater emphasis placed on income i.e. earnings attributable to the brand with a cost for capital factored in, rather than earnings specified as returns above the cost of capital.

For the purposes of clarifying this approach, we have defined an income-based approach as one that identifies the value of a brand based on specifying the future forecast level of earnings that is attributable to the brand (after allowing for depreciation).

This is achieved by looking at past performance, as well as future performance on actual levels by:

• Identifying the net annual cash-flow from a business.
• Establishing which proportion of net margin is directly related to the brand (price premium or volume premium).
• Looking at the lifetime of a brand and determining future brand earnings and cash flows over a specific forecasting period.
• Identifying the right discount rate (in accordance to industry and incorporating a charge for capital), to apply to cash flow over this specific forecasting period.
• To use this discount rate to track back to the present time and to calculate the net present value of the brand.

As with an economic-use approach the aim is to identify the specific margin and earnings attributable to the brand. Detailed research is undertaken to identify how the brand drives customer demand and what income and cash flow it generates for the business(s) in each individual market/customer segment.

The income approach is very similar to the economic use approach, but with subtle differences such as how earnings attributable to intangibles are calculated and where costs for capital are factored in.

Sometimes an Income Approach to formulating brand value may use the following technical methodologies whose fundamentals remain broadly as above.

Direct Methods

Royalty Relief based approach: This provides the value of the brand based on a royalty from the revenue attributable to the brand being calculated.

The principle behind this method is identifying what royalty rate would need to be paid by a company for the use of a brand that it does not own.

This is by far the most commonly used single technique and methodology for calculating brand value. It is widely used to give an opinion of both market value and sometimes the economic use of a brand. In certain industries for example pharmaceuticals, hotels and garment manufacturing it is commonplace to license the use of the brand.

This methodology is again based on estimating the revenue attributable to the brand over its economic life.

Many practitioners have either their own, or access to, extensive databases of existing licensing agreements, whereby it is possible to identify the royalty rate paid for the use of comparable brands, which is usually expressed as a % of sales.

With existing brand revenue (sales) figures and an identified royalty rate, it is possible to calculate the difference between owning a brand rather than licensing it in.

This is calculated from identifying the future projected sales of a brand, estimating the royalty savings (after tax), and applying an appropriate discount rate back to present day value.

It has the advantage of being better for industries where the granting of licenses in exchange for a royalty payment is relatively simple and common, and is likely to be most appropriate for trademarks, patents and technologies. It is universally recognised by Revenue authorities worldwide.

It does, however, rely on some subjective information i.e. future forecasts of brand revenue allocations and the information being available on comparable royalty rates.

Premium Price (Profits)

Is conceptually very simple and based on identifying a 'base case comparison'.

For example, if a branded tin of baked beans retails for 50p and an unbranded tin of identical beans retails for 30p, then the annual premium profit is 20p, multiplied by the number of tins produced annually. The annual profit then needs to be capitalised, and a value based upon a view as to how long the brand maintains its market position, how the market will develop and the cost of keeping the brand up there.

This methodology is most useful for food and fmcg brands and relies upon being able to identify a generic product for base case comparison, which is not always possible.

The advantage of this procedure is that it is relatively simple to calculate. However, with the current retailing environment seeing increasing price pressures placed on manufacturers by the enormous buying power of the major multiples such as Tesco and Wal-Mart, profit margins are continually being eroded. This can have an adverse and inaccurate impact on the value of the brand.

The disadvantages are that it is very rarely that there are two direct comparables and that it maybe unfair to assume the entire price premium is due to the brand. Other factors such as quality of product and distribution may play a role.

Indirect methods

Maybe referred to as Residual Value or Residual Earnings Method, or Return on Assets.

This method is less robust than direct methods and can sometimes lead to anomalous results. It assumes normal returns for fixed assets and working capital of a business, and that brand value is the rest – the residual value.

It requires less assessment than other methods and therefore is less precise as to the contribution of the brand.

It is, however, widely used for US accounting purposes although more commonly used for non-brand intangibles with less readily identifiable cash flows.

It would not be a recommended approach individually, rather as a package of measures to crosscheck.

Market-Based Approach

A brand is valued by reference to prices of comparable assets in recent transactions, using multiples of revenue, gross margin, brand contribution and profit after tax, adjusted to reflect brands' differences.

If comparables exist, it is a relatively easy methodology and has the advantage of reflecting an actual similar market value. But it is rare that actual comparable transactions exist.

Overall, it may be an important indicator of value, but is mostly used as a crosscheck on other methodologies as sufficient information on recent transactions involving comparable brands is rarely disclosed.

"The principle advantage is that it is a practical approach which allows values to be based on real transactions and market evidence. This results in values that best reflect the price that would be negotiated between a third party buyer and seller.

The disadvantage is that there are relatively few third party arms' length transactions involving brand names that are directly comparable. There are more frequent transactions involving shares of companies owning brand names but it is usually difficult to allocate out value between business and brand name.

As a result historically, many values have tended to use income-based approaches as the principal valuation method. The requirement of IFRS 3 to allocate value to material intangible assets including brands in a company acquisition, should improve the availability of market data on brand values."

KPMG

Cost-Based Approach

The value of the brand is calculated based on two cost options:

- Historical cost measuring the actual cost incurred in creating the brand.
- Replacement cost quantifying the estimated cost of replacing the brand or recreating an equivalent asset.

The advantages are that it is objective and can be consistent, if the information is readily available, which is not always the case. Historic cost data is reliable.

On the negative side, there is no correlation between expenditure on the asset and its value, it is also difficult to distinguish between brand maintenance and brand investment expenditure and replacement costs are subjective, particularly when looking at this approach in relation to entering a new market i.e. China. It may also not accurately reflect a fair market value for a brand.

It has limited range and appeal as a true measure of brand value, but can be a useful tool.

Asset-Based Approach Or Elimination Method

This approach values a business in its entirety as a market capitalisation, but then deducts the tangible assets to calculate the value of the intangible assets which will include patents, copyright, brands, customer lists, workforce, know how and goodwill.

Certain of these intangible assets can then be valued with reasonable levels of certainty; it is also possible to rank the most valuable to the least valuable of the identified intangible assets. It becomes possible to allocate the intangible asset value into each class and derive a value for the brand.

The advantages are that it is a simple and quick approach, which can then be used to benchmark the aggregate value of brands.

The disadvantages are that there is no guidance on how value should be allocated between a group of brand names. It also assumes that the market price is a fair price.

Again this is not a primary method due to its limitations, but can be a useful benchmark on the aggregate value of a company's brands.

What This Report Tells Us

❯ There needs to be greater clarity in the definition of what constitutes a brand for valuation purposes

Establishing common terminology in the market place for valuation purposes would significantly aid understanding and clarity in valuing brands.

❯ There is no single 'correct' way to measure brand value

Despite the obvious attractions and benefits of there being a single recommended approach to valuing brands, there is no 'one size fits all' that stands out head and shoulders above the rest.

Some approaches, for example Economic Use and Income-based which have some close similarities, are also more holistic than others. They are therefore much more useful in certain situations particularly for strategic purposes.

The use of a range of techniques to calculate the value of a brand is well established with some practitioners, who state that the circumstances drive the use of

techniques and that relying on a single approach can throw up an anomalous result.

Greater clarity and consistency in the communication, description and relevance of approach from practitioners, would greatly assist in reducing confusion and drive forward a greater understanding in the marketing community.

Independent advice should always be sought on which direction is the best for the particular circumstances.

❯ Brand valuation ... more than another financial calculation it can be a strategic value enhancing model

A value credited to a brand is not just a black-box figure.

Despite the appearance of the methodologies as detailed financial calculations, the basis of identifying a qualified and quantified set of Brand Value Drivers and potential opportunities for growing Future Brand Value, is a fundamental for commercial success.

Detailed knowledge of the market, the company's position in that market in relation to competitors, and detailed consumer perceptions of a brand are all well established marketing principles. Qualifying and quantifying this information internally and externally within a model to derive a financial value on a brand, is a natural extension of performance management.

❯ Greater collective co-operation between finance and marketing

A value may already have been placed on a brand as an intangible asset on the balance sheet and the marketing department is either unaware of it or unaware of its potential relevance to brand and marketing strategies.

Relating brand and marketing strategy to value-growth and return on investment is the language of the Chief Executive and Finance Director, and will increase the strength of the relationship right across the Board.

Marketing people need to become more financially literate and equally, finance needs to become more marketing aware.

❯ The brand asset as security – use it

The value of the brand asset is increasingly being used as security in a wide range of situations, particularly in the private equity market.

This may include a company looking to raise finance for any number of reasons such as a management buy-out/buy-in or for future securitisation.

❯ Every business should conduct an overview of value in its brands

This might not necessarily involve a precise valuation, rather an understanding of what creates value in a brand or a portfolio of brands and how to make it work harder.

The value of the brand asset has often been over-looked in many businesses ranging from small to medium-sized companies, right through to larger conglomerates operating in less consumer-driven markets.

However, industrial and manufacturing companies across Europe are now waking-up to realising the value in their brands.

A recent article in the Financial Times 'Industry Plays The Name Game' (February 8th 2005) highlighted the extent that some engineering and industrial companies have gone to build the value of their brands, and the subsequent benefits this has brought.

"Having a good brand means you can compete in ways other than by having a lower price"

FT February 8th 2005

This same article also highlighted an example of what happened when not enough consideration was given to the value of brands:

"At Invensys, the UK engineering group established in 1998 after a merger of Siebe and BTR, pressure to integrate the businesses meant senior managers failed to devote enough attention to linking the different brands and divisions within the original companies.

... A casualty of this was Foxboro, a well-regarded US-based maker of control equipment that had formerly been part of Siebe. It was discouraged from using its well-known brand name – one factor behind a subsequent slide in Foxboro's fortunes. Such setbacks exacerbated Invensys' problems and in 2001 the company suffered a series of financial disasters that brought it close to collapse."

FT February 8th 2005

Clearly understanding where the value lay in the portfolio of brands in this instance was a tool that could have aided both corporate restructuring and the creation of a new brand architecture.

❯ "The techniques used to value brands are merely a set of tools – the real skill is in the way the information is used to create growth and enhance value."

Jane Piper

A paper prepared by Jane Piper of Jane Piper Brand Strategy Consultancy on behalf of The Superbrands organisation

118118

CATHERINE BOYD
Marketing Manager

Catherine's career in brand communications began at Freeserve in the early days of its launch, up until the time it re-branded as Wanadoo. Prior to joining The Number she worked as a communications consultant in Australia for a number of different companies including AAPT, a leading telecommunications company.

ALEXANDRA LEWIS
Marketing Director

Alexandra's career has spanned both agency and client side. Before The Number she co-founded an agency, Myrtle, working with Orange, The Big Issue and Audi. Previous to Myrtle she worked at RMG on Mercedes and Sainsbury's, at Orange, and she launched The GM Card from Vauxhall.

American Express®

THIERRY CAMPET
Head of Advertising & Customer Experience

Thierry joined American Express® in 2000 as Marketing Head of Interactive for Europe.
In 2004 he became Head of Advertising and Customer Experience for American Express UK. Prior to joining American Express®, Thierry held various positions both in France and in the UK, at boo.com, Ogilvy and Mather and Sony Pictures.

LAUREL POWERS-FREELING
UK Country Manager

Laurel joined American Express® as UK Country Manager and Head of Consumer and Small Business Cards in 2005. She is a Non-Executive Director of the Bank of England. Previously, she was CEO of Marks & Spencer's financial services business, M&S Money. She has also held senior positions with Lloyds TSB Group and Prudential.

Andrex®

The Andrex® team works across five different variants of the UK's largest non-food grocery brand: Andrex® mainstream, Andrex® Moistened, Andrex® enriched with Aloe Vera, Andrex® Puppies on a roll and, the newest variant, Andrex® Quilts. Each team member is integral to driving brand and category growth through innovation, creativity and a single-minded brand vision.

® Registered Trademark of Kimberly-Clark Worldwide, Inc. or its affiliates

Ann Summers

JACQUELINE GOLD
Chief Executive

Jacqueline, Chief Executive of Ann Summers and Knickerbox, is one of Britain's most successful business women and an inspiration to thousands of women. She has been voted the second 'Most Powerful Woman in Retail' by Retail Week, one of Britain's top 10 'Most Powerful Women' by Cosmopolitan, top 12 women by Good Housekeeping Magazine, one of Britain's 100 Most Influential Women by the Daily Mail, Business Communicator of the Year 2004, and was made a new entry in Debrett's 'People of Today' 2005 for her contribution to British Society. Jacqueline has been the subject of several documentaries including 'Back To The Floor' (BBC2, 2001), 'Ann Summers Uncovered' (ITV1, 2003), and 'So What Do You Do All Day' (BBC2, 2004), and co-presented the daytime business series 'Mind Your Own Business' (BBC1, 2005). Her autobiography 'Good Vibrations' was published in 1995 (Pavilion Books). She is a regular columnist for 'Retail Week'.

ASDA

All 140,000 colleagues employed by the company, from the head office in Leeds to all of ASDA's nationwide stores and distribution centres are responsible for the continuing success of the ASDA brand.

Ask Jeeves

RACHEL JOHNSON
VP Marketing Europe

Rachel is responsible for the strategic development of the European Marketing Plan, supporting the global brand strategy for Ask Jeeves in the UK and Europe. She is accountable for managing the implementation of all TTL activity and is a member of the European Executive Committee for Ask Jeeves. She joins Ask Jeeves from Levi Strauss & Co where she held the role of Marketing Director Northern Europe. Previous roles that she held during her time at the company included Acting UK Country Managing Director and Marketing Manager North Europe.

Rachel's extensive marketing experience has also included roles for Whitbread Beer Co. as Marketing Manager for the Heineken brand where she drove the strategic re-positioning of the brand in the UK and with SmithKline Beecham as a Group Product Manager.

Avon

ANDREA SLATER
Vice President, Marketing

Andrea is responsible for Category and Brand Management, Creative and Brochure Development, Campaign Planning and Marketing Support, Public Relations, New Business Development, internet and Direct and Product Supply.

Andrea has held previous roles at Avon including: General Manager of Overseas Business Development where she was responsible for managing Avon's joint venture and distributor businesses in Turkey, Egypt,

Greece, Saudi Arabia and the Baltics, as well as developing and implementing the new market opening strategy for Europe, Middle East and Africa: General Manager for a new subsidiary business which she set up for Avon European Holdings Ltd, which designed, manufactured and sold costume jewellery and fashion accessories and also held the position of Head of Strategic Planning and Research.

BlackBerry

CHARMAINE EGGBERRY
Vice President – Enterprise Business Unit, EMEA, Research In Motion

Charmaine has overall responsibility for RIM's European enterprise business, including its growth targets and all sales and marketing activities. This includes managing the Company's expansion into new European markets and establishing strategic partnerships across the region.

Charmaine has extensive senior level experience in the telecommunications and technology sectors. Before joining RIM in 2002 as Marketing Director for Europe she worked for Lucent Technologies.

SARAH WEST
Head of Corporate Marketing – EMEA, Research In Motion

With 10 years experience in B2B and consumer marketing communications Sarah is head of corporate marketing EMEA for Research In Motion (RIM). Responsible for the brand and communications strategy for BlackBerry, Sarah has overseen a programme that has significantly increased brand awareness and media coverage of BlackBerry across Europe. Sarah has also supervised the launch of BlackBerry in new markets, with new carriers and new products.

Bratz

NICK AUSTIN
CEO, Vivid Imaginations

Nick, a business graduate, worked in sales/marketing for Procter & Gamble and Matchbox Toys before embarking on an entrepreneurial career by starting Vivid Imaginations, now the UK's largest toys/games company. A joint venture with MGA Inc relaunched the Bratz brand in 2004, toppling Barbie off the top spot in less than 12 months by more than doubling sales and market share.

ISAAC LARIAN
Founder, Chairman & Chief Executive Office, MGA

Issac founded MGA Entertainment under the name Surprise Gift Wagon, an importer and distributor of brand name consumer electronics products in 1979. In 1993, under its new name, MGA Entertainment, Inc., he formally transitioned MGA from a consumer electronics company to a consumer entertainment products company and has transformed MGA into one of the leading family entertainment companies in the United States. Issac oversees all divisions of the Company, and is a major contributor to the development of new products and the vision behind MGA.

Center Parcs

MARTIN DALBY
Chief Executive

Martin joined Scottish and Newcastle in 1978 and held various accounting positions before joining Center Parcs UK in January 1995, as Financial Controller. In 1997, Martin became Finance Director of Center Parcs UK and in July 2000 he was promoted to the position of CEO. Since then he has restructured the UK senior management team to suit the future direction and objectives of the business and has significantly improved financial performance.

MARTIN ROBINSON
Executive Chairman

Martin started his career in brand management with Reckitt & Coleman and then moved to the Sara Lee Corporation. From there, he spent four years with McKinsey & Co and then joined Scottish and Newcastle Retail as Marketing Director in 1994. He became Managing Director of Center Parcs Belgium, Netherlands and Germany in October 1997. In November 1999, he was appointed as Chairman of the Board of Management of the whole Center Parcs group. He is now Chairman of Center Parcs UK and CEO/Chairman of the European joint venture of Center Parcs and Gran Dorado (Center Parcs Europe).

Classic FM

DARREN HENLEY
Station Manager

Darren is the Station Manager of Classic FM. Since 1992, his roles at Classic FM have included newsreader, producer, news manager, programme manager and managing editor. Prior to joining Classic FM, he was a journalist for ITN and Invicta Radio in Kent. He is the author of eight books about classical music and musicians.

GILES PEARMAN
Marketing Director

Giles started his marketing career in 1989 with Unilever plc joining their ice cream business Wall's. His last role before leaving Unilever was as Senior Brand Manager for the UK ice cream marketing department responsible for brands such as Magnum, Feast and Solero. Giles joined GWR Group plc in 1999 as Brand Controller and was promoted to Marketing Director in July 2004.

Cosmopolitan

JAN ADCOCK
Group Publishing Director

Jan started her career in media when she joined Ulster TV as a Sales Executive. Her first magazine appointment was with Carlton Magazines on Options. She then worked on the Murdoch magazine launch, Mirabella, as Advertisement Manager.

Jan joined Hachette Magazines in 1991 as the Advertisement Director on British ELLE and after two years moved to the National Magazine Company. Within a year she had been promoted to Publisher on Company, before

moving to the parenting titles, M and Having A Baby as Group Publisher in April 1999.

In 1998 Jan was short-listed for PPA Publisher of the Year, and Company magazine was shortlisted for Magazine of the Year. Jan was made Publishing Director of the Cosmopolitan group in September 2000.

She joined the National Magazine Company Exectuve Committee in June 2002 and became a company director in April 2003.

Duracell®

GEORGE ALLAN
Business Unit Director

George joined Duracell® in 1985 and has worked in a combination of sales, marketing and finance roles for Duracell and Gillette®. George moved to The Netherlands in 2001 to look after Duracell® Benelux before returning to the UK to manage the Duracell® UK Ireland and The Netherlands business. George is currently Business Unit Director responsible for Gillette's Blades and Razors business and Duracell.

early learning centre

TIM PATTEN
Director of Marketing

Tim Patten joined Chelsea Stores Holding Ltd as part of the management team involved in the buyout of The Early Learning Centre in 2004. Prior to this, he had an extensive career in Advertising and Direct Marketing working at Abbott Mead Vickers and latterly as Managing Partner of Proximity London. He was also the Founding Partner and MD of Harrison Patten Trouton Brand Response and a former Head of Communications for BT.

NIGEL ROBERTSON
CEO

Nigel is CEO of Chelsea Stores Holdings Ltd, the owners of Early Learning Centre and Daisy & Tom. His previous positions include Managing Director of Ocado the online grocery retailer in partnership with Waitrose, Divisional Director at Marks and Spencer, and Vice President of Kings Supermarkets USA based in New York. Previous to this, Nigel was an officer in the RAF.

George

All 140,000 ASDA employees, from the head office in Leicestershire, to colleagues in ASDA stores, George standalone stores, George departments worldwide and distribution centres are responsible for the continuing success and growth of the George at ASDA brand.

Gillette®

GEORGE ALLAN
Business Unit Director

George joined Duracell® in 1985 and has worked in a combination of sales, marketing and finance roles for Duracell and Gillette®. George moved to The Netherlands in 2001 to look after Duracell® Benelux before returning to the UK to manage the Duracell® UK Ireland and The Netherlands business. George is currently Business Unit Director responsible for Gillette's Blades and Razors business and Duracell.

Good Housekeeping

LIZ KERSHAW
Executive Group Publishing Director

Liz currently has responsibility for the Good Housekeeping and Country Living brands. This includes the magazines plus their extended businesses. She was previously Executive Group Publishing Director of the Luxury Group and was appointed to the board of the National Magazine Company in 1993. In 1995 she was awarded PPA Publisher of the Year, Highly Commended in 2004 and 2005 and was Media Week's Publisher's Publisher in 1997.

LINDSAY NICHOLSON
Editor-in-Chief

Lindsay's first editorship was of Prima magazine where she also launched Prima Baby and Your Home and was named Editor of the year in 1999. She was appointed Editor-in-Chief of Good Housekeeping six years ago. Lindsay currently chairs the PPA's Editorial Training Consultants Committee and is a Fellow of the Royal Astronomical Society.

HUGGIES®

SHIV GOPALAN
Brand Manager

Shiv joined Kimberly-Clark in 1994 after completing his Masters from Louisiana State University, USA. He has worked with K-C across multiple developing markets in a variety of business development and marketing roles. Shiv is now Brand Manager for HUGGIES® Super-Flex, responsible for the day to day running of the brand.

JOHN WATERS
Marketing Director

John joined Kimberly-Clark in 1977 after graduating from Nottingham University. He has held various roles including 13 years in Sales and National Accounts. For most of the last 10 years he has worked in marketing and is now responsible for the HUGGIES® brand in the UK and Eire.

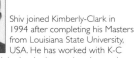

innocent

RICHARD REED
*Marketing Director
& Co-Founder*

Richard began his business career at the tender age of 16 with a lawn mowing business called 'two men went to mow'. Since then he has had a few other jobs, most notably as an account man for four years at BMP. In 1999 he left advertising to set up innocent with his friends Adam and Jon and has been marketing director and brand guardian ever since.

Intel

SIMON SHIPLEY
UK & Ireland Brand Manager

Simon joined Intel in 2000 and has held several Sales and Marketing positions. Simon has recently moved from the position of Retail Marketing Manager, taking on the challenge of leading Brand Marketing in the UK. His new role entails responsibility for all Intel's brand activities including advertising and marketing.

Jaeger

BELINDA EARL
Group Chief Executive

Belinda started her career at Harrods as a graduate trainee. In 1985 she joined Debenhams in Buying and Merchandising. As Trading Director in 1998 she was responsible for Designers at Debenhams, homewares, cosmetics and accessories. In 2000 she became Chief Executive of Debenhams PLC. She joined Jaeger in September 2004 as Group Chief Executive.

Belinda is a graduate and a Fellow of the University of Wales, Aberystwyth and is a Patron of Skillsmart, the retail sector skills council.

HAROLD TILLMAN
Chairman

Harold studied at London College of Fashion and has had extensive experience within the textile and clothing industry. He has been involved in the public flotation of several companies within the textile sector since 1969. He has experience in both retail and wholesale distribution in Europe, the Far East and the US. He acquired Jaeger in 2003.

Kiss 100

ANDY ROBERTS
Group Programme Director

Andy is responsible for the output of all of Emaps 26 radio stations including Kiss100/The Big City Network, Kerrang! 105.2 and d.a.b/freeview digital services.

Andy initiated the Kiss positioning as 'the station for young fun London' and tripled the Kiss audience. He was responsible for hiring some of the most famous Kiss presenters including Bam Bam, Ugly Phil and Robin Banks.

The Financial Times voted him one of the 30 most creative people in business.

MARK STORY
*Emap's Managing Director of
Radio Programming*

Mark was Managing Director of Kiss from 1998-2004. During this time Kiss won 'Sony radio station of the year.' Mark also took the station to market leader for 15-24 year olds and then its current position of market leader for all adults under the age of 35.

Mark has worked in Radio for over 30 years working for Capital Radio, Radio One, Virgin Radio and launched Magic 105.4. Most recently he acted as organiser and Chairman of RadioAid which registered the highest recorded audience for a single radio broadcast.

KLEENEX®

CATHERINE BAUDINETTE
Marketing Manager

Catherine joined Kimberly-Clark in 2001 and has worked on the HUGGIES® brand on Central & Eastern Europe and the UK prior to managing KLEENEX®. Before joining Kimberly-Clark she worked for seven years with Mars, initially managing a number of pet food brands in Australia, and then subsequently managing the entire Mars pet food and snack food portfolio in South Africa.

EMMA LEECH
Brand Manager

Emma Leech graduated from Nottingham University in 1998 with a degree in Management Studies with French. She joined Kimberly-Clark in 2003 to work as the Brand Manager for KLEENEX® within the UK. Prior to this she spent five years working in various marketing roles within The Boots Company.

Kwik-Fit

DOUG MCKENZIE
Marketing Director

With 18 years multi-site brand marketing experience, Doug McKenzie started his marketing career with Next plc. He joined Kwik-Fit in 1993 as Marketing Manager and following experience with subsidiaries in Poland and Spain, Doug was appointed Marketing Director in 2002. He directs all UK marketing operations across a network of 672 centres, 192 mobile tyre-fitting vehicles and 15 different local brands.

lastminute.com

MATHEW HART
Marketing Director

Mathew spent six years at Thomson Holidays in various product, marketing and commercial roles before moving to Holiday Autos in 1999 where he held the positions of overseas director and group ecommerce director. Following acquisition by lastminute.com in 2003 he became managing director. His current role is Marketing Director for all direct and trade brands in lastminute.com's UK portfolio.

BRENT HOBERMAN
Chief Executive Officer

Brent co-founded lastminute.com in April 1998. Previous roles include business development at LineOne, five years consulting at Mars & Co and Spectrum Strategy Consultants. Brent was also Head of Business Development and founding member of QXL.

Brent is instrumental in maintaining and developing the Group's relationship with all the key stakeholders in the business including the financial community, lastminute.com's other shareholders and our customers.

McCain

SIMON EYLES
Head of Communications

Simon is responsible for all aspects of brand strategy and communications at McCain Foods. Simon has been instrumental in the creation of the current brand 'Chin Up' campaign, designed to increase brand affection, warmth and personality.

Simon joined McCain Foods four years ago, having previously worked at Arla Foods, where he was responsible for growing and extending the Lurpak brand, overseeing the launch of both Lurpak Spreadable and Lurpak Lighter, resulting in the brand becoming brand leader for the first time in its history.

SUE JEFFERSON
Marketing Director

Sue's marketing career began at Danone with International Sales & Marketing for the Lea & Perrins sauces portfolio. After four years she moved to the Jeyes Group where she became Head of Marketing before joining McCain Foods (GB) in 1997 as Marketing Manager. Sue then spent three years as Customer Marketing Controller in Retail Sales, before being promoted to Marketing Director in December 2003 and today is focused on delivering ambitious growth through Marketing, Innovations and Customer Relations.

Nikon

SIMON COLEMAN
General Manager,
Imaging Division

Having joined Nikon UK in 1987, Simon became General Manager of Nikon UK, Consumer Products and Electronic Imaging divisions in 1996. Over the following two years, these merged to form the Imaging Division. His career highlights include steering Nikon from niche to mass market player in the digital sector, and growing the Imaging business fourfold in eight years.

JEREMY GILBERT
Group Marketing Manager

Jeremy joined the company in 1986 and now looks after above- and below-the-line marketing, plus product planning and the UK website. He has an enviable technical knowledge of all things photographic and a genuine love of the company's products. His career highlights include leading the campaign to refocus the brand and establish Nikon's position as market leader in the digital sector.

ODEON

The Marketing team at ODEON is responsible for the continued success of the ODEON brand. Driving the business forward through understanding customers' needs, whilst planning and implementing the company's marketing strategy ensures ODEON remains the UK cinema market leader with the highest brand awareness.

Pretty Polly

We recognise as the current custodians of the Pretty Polly brand we have a huge responsibility in keeping this 80 year old as fresh and relevant today as she has always been. She is famous for great products, daring campaigns and associations with glamour and beauty. We hope we are succeeding. The recent successes of the Pretty Polly brand are directly attributable to this talented team of marketing professionals.

Prudential

ANGUS MACIVER
Director of Brand & Insights

Angus joined Prudential in 2003 after 10 years at PepsiCo in Marketing, Sales, Franchise Management and Insights, including four years on their Central European Management Committee and three years on their Walkers board. Before that he spent six years at Procter and Gamble in Brand Management.

ROGER RAMSDEN
Director of PruLab & Marketing

Roger joined Prudential in 2001, having previously spent six years at Safeway where he started as Brand Marketing Director, moving on to become Marketing Director and then Retail Format Director. Before Safeway he was at Boston Consulting Group for seven years. He started his career at Unilever as a brand manager.

Radox

JULIE BAKER
Marketing Director

Julie Baker is Marketing Director for Sara Lee H&BC, responsible for brands such as Radox, Sanex, Ambi-Pur, Brylcreem and Kiwi. Julie has been with Sara Lee for 11 years, previously she worked for Unilever.

KERRY OWENS
Marketing Manager

Kerry has been with Sara Lee for four years and is currently Marketing Manager on Radox. Prior to this she held a number of marketing positions within Sara Lee including working on Sanex and Brylcreem.

Rizla

GARY KEOGH
Brand Group Manager

Gary joined Imperial Tobacco in 1998 in the UK Sales Force in London. Having completed time in UK Sales and International Cigarette Marketing Management he was appointed Brand Manager for Rizla in January 2003. In the last two years Rizla brand share and value have increased by 13% & 12% respectively from an already strong position. Having created clear direction for Rizla to retain its number one position in the UK market, Gary has shaped the sponsorship and PR landscape for the brand via the Award winning Rizla-Suzuki Superbike property and 'inspired-by...' live music platform.

Scottish Widows

ALAN WHITING
Brand Development

Alan began his career at Scottish Equitable in 1984, helping to form their Marketing Division. He joined Scottish Widows in April 2001 to help create a new IFA strategy and has recently taken up responsibility for Brand Development.

Shell

VENETIA HOWES
Vice President Global Brands

Venetia has responsibility for the strategic development of the Shell brand. Her experience includes business to business marketing in chemicals, shipping, and lubricants, and she was previously the Marketing Manager for Shell's global aviation business. She took the CIM post-graduate Diploma mid-career and is an active member of the Worshipful company of Marketors.

RAOUL PINNELL
Chairman, Shell Brands International AG

Raoul developed an early interest in business whilst at school, Bradfield College, leaving to pursue Business Studies, subsequently followed by a post graduate Diploma in Marketing. Following 17 years with Nestlé, five years at Prudential and three years at NatWest, Shell International appointed him to head its Global Brands and Communications division in 1997.

Silentnight Beds

NEAL MERNOCK
Managing Director

Neal began his career in Product Development at Unilever, followed by Brand Management at Fisons. He then became Account Director and MD of the biggest ad agency in the North, with FMCG accounts like Fox's Biscuits and McCain. After joining United Biscuits as Marketing Director of KP Nuts he was next appointed MD of Phileas Fogg. Neal became MD of Silentnight Beds in 2002.

Specsavers Opticians

ANDREW MOLLE
Marketing Director

Andrew has been instrumental in establishing the brand as a market leader and was responsible for changing and developing the logo so that it is now recognised by 95% of the population. He has also led the team that keeps the face of the brand fresh and up to date on the high street.

DOUG & MARY PERKINS
Founders

Doug and Mary founded the Specsavers Optical Group in 1984. The couple, who met at Cardiff University where they were both studying Ophthalmics, still have a pivotal role in the success of the company and take a hands-on approach to ensuring the long-term security of the joint venture partnership.

The FAIRTRADE Mark

Many thousands of Fairtrade supporters are also Brand Guardians as they promote The FAIRTRADE Mark in workplaces, schools, universities and other locations and devise creative stunts to gain increased awareness for the Mark. In the UK much of this takes place during the annual Fairtrade Fortnight in March.

IAN BRETMAN
Deputy Director

Ian Bretman has worked with the Fairtrade Foundation since 1997 and has been Deputy Director since 2001. During this time he has overseen the growth in annual sales from £6 million to £140 million. Ian was central to the development of the international FAIRTRADE Mark in 2002, creating a Fairtrade emblem that crossed national boundaries.

The Times

RICHARD LARCOMBE
Senior Brand Manager

Richard's career began at Grey Advertising working on Lee jeans, Mars and SmithKline Beecham. After 18 months he moved to Abbott Mead Vickers where he spent six years as an Account Director working on BT, Norwich Union, Cancer Research UK, Wrigley and New Business. He joined News International as Senior Brand Manager for The Times and Sunday Times in February 2004.

ANDREW MULLINS
Marketing Director

Andrew's marketing career began at Lever Brothers. After nine years he moved to Diageo as Global Brand Director for the UDV Gin Portfolio. In June 2001, Andrew joined NI as Marketing Director for The Times and Sunday Times where he has overseen the rollout of The Times compact and the launch of The Month on the Sunday Times.

TONI&GUY

TONI MASCOLO
Chairman & Chief Executive

Toni Mascolo, co-founder of the TONI&GUY empire and winner of London Entrepreneur of the Year, has enjoyed a career that spans more than 40 years and has been directly responsible for changing the face of modern hairdressing. His company spans a global hairdressing franchise, award-winning product ranges, an international education programme and a successful portfolio of related companies.

SACHA MASCOLO-TARBUCK
International Group Creative Director

Creative direction for the TONI&GUY group is provided by Sacha Mascolo-Tarbuck, daughter of co-founder and chief executive Toni Mascolo. At just 19, Sacha was the youngest-ever winner of Newcomer of the Year at the British Hairdressing Awards. Sacha works closely with her international art team to interpret future seasonal trends, develop product ranges and create the strong, yet commercially aware image that shape the TONI&GUY brands.

Trailfinders

Trailfinders team of over 1,000 staff are responsible for building and maintaining the strength of the Trailfinders brand. Their passion for travel, enjoyment of their work and desire to provide a consistently high standard of customer service is integral to the success of the company.

MIKE GOOLEY
Chairman

Former SAS officer, Mike Gooley founded Trailfinders in 1970. As the driving force behind building the UK's largest independent travel company he maintains an active role in the organisation, overseeing its' continued growth and brand development.

Yellow Pages

PHILIPPA BUTTERS
Head of Design

Since joining Yell in 1997, Philippa has worked on the creation and implementation of all the product brand identities, including the transformation of the Yellow Pages and Business Pages directories, the Yell group corporate identity and most recently the design implementation for the new Yellow Pages 118 24 7 service.

Young's

JIM CANE
Group Commercial Director

Jim joined Young's Bluecrest in 2000 as Group Commercial Director. Prior to that, he held various general management positions within United Biscuits, latterly as Managing Director of UB Frozen and Chilled Foods. Prior to general management, Jim was Marketing Director of Ross Young's frozen foods group.

JAMES TURTON
Marketing Director

James joined Young's Bluecrest in 2001 as Head of Marketing. He has since been promoted to Marketing Director. Prior to that, he spent 10 years within United Biscuits where he held various senior marketing roles, including Head of Marketing at the McVities Cake Company. Immediately prior to his appointment at Young's, he held a Marketing Director role within the Sara Lee group.

118118
The Number UK Ltd
Liberty House
222 Regent Street
London
W1B 5TR

American Express®
American Express Services Europe Ltd
Portland House
Stag Place
London
SW1E 5BZ

Andrex®
Kimberly-Clark Ltd
1 Tower View
Kings Hill
West Malling
Kent
ME19 4HA

Ann Summers
Ann Summers Ltd
Gold Group House
Godstone Road
Whyteleafe
Surrey
CR3 0GG

AOL
AOL (UK) Ltd
80 Hammersmith Road
London
W14 8UD

ASDA
ASDA Stores Ltd
ASDA House
Great Wilson Street
Leeds
LS11 5AD

Ask Jeeves
Ask Jeeves Internet Ltd
53 Parker Street
London
WC2B 5PT

Audi
Audi UK
Yeomans Drive
Blakelands
Milton Keynes
MK14 5AN

Avis
Avis Rent A Car Ltd
Trident House
Station Road
Hayes
Middlesex
UB3 4DJ

Avon
Avon Cosmetics Ltd
Nunn Mills Road
Northampton
NN1 5PA

Bisto
Centura Foods Ltd
Bourne Business Park
6 Dashwood Lang Road
Addlestone
Surrey
KT15 2HJ

BlackBerry
BlackBerry/Research In Motion
Centrum House
36 Station Road
Egham
TW20 9LF

Bratz
Vivid Imaginations
Ashbourne House
The Guildway
Old Portsmouth Road
Guildford
Surrey
GU3 1LS

BT
BT
BT Centre
81 Newgate Street
London
EC1A 7AJ

BUPA
BUPA
BUPA House
15-19 Bloomsbury Way
London
WC1A 2BA

Center Parcs
Center Parcs Ltd
One Edison Rise
New Ollerton
Newark
Notts
NG22 9DP

Classic FM
GCap Media plc
7 Swallow Place
Oxford Circus
London
W1B 2AG

Coca-Cola
Coca-Cola Great Britain
1 Queen Caroline Street
Hammersmith
London
W6 9HQ

Cosmopolitan
The National Magazine Company Ltd
National Magazine House
72 Broadwick Street
London
W1F 9EP

DHL
DHL International (UK) Ltd
Orbital Park
Great South West Road
Hounslow
TW4 6JS

Direct Line
Direct Line Group Ltd
Direct Line House
3 Edridge Road
Croydon
Surrey
CR9 1AG

Dockers®
Dockers® UK Ltd
Levi Strauss & Co
1 Little Marlborough Street
London
W1F 7BH

Duracell®
Gillette Group UK Ltd
Great West Road
Isleworth
Middlesex
TW7 5NP

Dyson
Dyson Ltd
Tetbury Hill
Malmesbury
Wiltshire
SN16 0RP

early learning centre
early learning centre
Burdett House
15-16 Buckingham Street
London
WC2N 6DU

Elastoplast
Beiersdorf UK Ltd
2010 Solihull Parkway
Birmingham Business Park
Birmingham
B37 7YS

Emirates
Emirates
95 Cromwell Road
London
SW7 4DL

Ferrero Rocher
Ferrero
Awberry Court
Hatters Lane
Croxley Business Park
Watford
WD18 8YJ

Ford
Ford Motor Company Ltd
Eagle Way
Warley
Brentwood
Essex
CM13 3BW

George
George
George House
Magna Park
Lutterworth
Leicestershire
LE17 4XN

Gillette®
Gillette Group UK Ltd
Great West Road
Isleworth
Middlesex
TW7 5NP

Good Housekeeping
The National Magazine Company Ltd
National Magazine House
72 Broadwick Street
London
W1F 9EP

Gossard
Gossard
Units 1-4 Ridgeway Court
Grovebury Road
Leighton Buzzard
Bedfordshire
LU7 4SF

Horlicks
GlaxoSmithKline
GSK House
980 Great West Road
Brentford
Middlesex
TW8 9GS

Hovis
British Bakeries Ltd
Hovis Court
PO Box 527
69 Alma Road
Windsor
Berkshire
SL4 3HD

HUGGIES®
Kimberly-Clark Ltd
1 Tower View
Kings Hill
West Malling
Kent
ME19 4HA

Hush Puppies
Hush Puppies (UK) Ltd
3 The Osiers Office Park
Braunstone
Leicester
LE19 1DY

innocent
innocent Ltd
Fruit Towers
3 The Goldhawk Estate
Brackenbury Road
London
W6 0BA

Intel
Intel Corporation (UK) Ltd
Pipers Way
Swindon
Wiltshire
SN3 1RJ

Jaeger
Jaeger
57 Broadwick Street
London
W1F 9QS

KFC
Yum! Brands Inc
32 Goldsworth Road
Woking
Surrey
GU21 6JT

Kinder
Ferrero
Awberry Court
Hatters Lane
Croxley Business Park
Watford
WD18 8YJ

Kiss 100
Emap
Mappin House
4 Winsley Street
London
W1W 8HF

KLEENEX®
Kimberly-Clark Ltd
1 Tower View
Kings Hill
West Malling
Kent
ME19 4HA

Kwik-Fit
Kwik-Fit
216 East Main Street
Broxburn
West Lothian
EH52 5AS

lastminute.com
lastminute.com
39 Victoria Street
London
SW1 0EE

L'Oréal Paris
L'Oréal (UK) Ltd
255 Hammersmith Road
London
W6 8AZ

Lucozade
GlaxoSmithKline
GSK House
980 Great West Road
Brentford
Middlesex
TW8 9GS

LYCRA®
INVISTA (International) S.à.r.l.
2, Chemin du Pavillon
1218 Le Grand-Saconnex
Geneva
Switzerland

McCain
McCain Foods (GB) Ltd
Havers House
Havers Hill
Scarborough
YO11 3BS

McDonald's
McDonald's Restaurants Ltd
11-59 High Road
East Finchley
London
N2 8AW

Microsoft
Microsoft UK Ltd
84 Microsoft Campus
Thames Valley Park
Reading
Berkshire
RG6 1WG

Miss Selfridge
Arcadia Group Ltd
3rd Floor
70 Berners Street
Colegrave House
London
W1T 3NL

Mothercare
Mothercare
Cherry Tree Road
Watford
Hertfordshire
WD24 6SH

Mothers Pride
British Bakeries Ltd
Hovis Court
PO Box 527
69 Alma Road
Windsor
Berkshire
SL4 3HD

Mr Kipling
Manor Bakeries Ltd
Third Floor
Minton Place
Victoria Street
Windsor
Berkshire
SL4 1EG

Müller
Müller Dairy (UK) Ltd
Shrewsbury Road
Market Drayton
Shropshire
TF9 3SQ

Nikon
Nikon UK Ltd
380 Richmond Road
Kingston Upon Thames
Surrey
KT2 5PR

NIVEA
Beiersdorf UK Ltd
2010 Solihull Parkway
Birmingham Business Park
Birmingham
B37 7YS

O₂
O₂ UK Ltd
260 Bath Road
Slough
Berkshire
SL1 4DX

Oasis
Oasis Stores Ltd
69-77 Paul Street
London
EC2A 4PN

ODEON
ODEON
54 Whitcomb Street
London
WC2H 7DN

Pedigree®
Masterfoods
National Office
Waltham on the Wolds
Melton Mowbray
Leicestershire
LE14 4RS

Pioneer
Pioneer GB Ltd
Pioneer House
Hollybush Hill
Stoke Poges
Slough
SL2 4QP

Pretty Polly
Sara Lee Courtaulds Legwear
PO Box 54
Haydn Road
Nottingham
NG5 1DH

Prudential
Prudential
8th Floor
3 Sheldon Square
London
W2 6PR

Radox
Sara Lee Household & Body Care UK
225 Bath Road
Slough
SL1 4AU

Rizla
Imperial Tobacco UK Ltd - Rizla+
PO Box 525
South Ville
Bristol
BS99 1LQ

Rotary Watches
Rotary Watches
84-86 Regent Street
London
W1B 5RR

Royal Doulton
The Royal Doulton Company
Sir Henry Doulton House
Forge Lane
Etruria
ST1 5NN

Scottish Widows
Scottish Widows plc
69 Morrison Street
Edinburgh
EH3 8YF

Sellotape
Henkel Consumer Adhesives
Apollo Court
2 Bishops Square Business Park
Hatfield
Hertfordshire
AL10 9EY

Seven Seas®
Seven Seas Limited
Hedon Road
Kingston Upon Hull
HU9 5NJ

Sharwood's
Centura Foods Ltd
Bourne Business Park
6 Dashwood Lang Road
Addlestone
Surrey
KT15 2HJ

Shell
Shell Brands International AG
Baarermatte
CH-6340 Baar
Switzerland

Silentnight Beds
Silentnight Beds
PO Box 9
Barnoldswick
Lancashire
BB18 6BL

SMIRNOFF® vodka
The Smirnoff Co.
8 Henrietta Place
London
W1G 0NB

Sony
Sony United Kingdom Ltd
The Heights
Brooklands
Weybridge
Surrey
KT13 0FW

Specsavers Opticians
Specsavers Optical Group
La Villiaze
St Andrew's
Guernsey
GY6 8YP

Stanley
Stanley UK
Europa View
Sheffield Business Park
Europa Link
Sheffield
S9 1XH

The FAIRTRADE Mark
The Fairtrade Foundation
Room 204
16 Baldwins Gardens
London
EC1N 7RJ

The Times
Times Newspapers Ltd
1 Virginia Street
Wapping
London
E98 1GE

Timberland
Timberland
Wexham Springs
Framewood Road
Wexham
Slough
SL3 6PJ

TONI&GUY
TONI&GUY
58-60 Stamford Street
London
SE1 9LX

Topshop
Topshop
Colegrave House
70 Berners Street
London
W1T 3NL

Trailfinders
Trailfinders Ltd
9 Abingdon Road
London
W8 6AH

Wall's
Kerry Foods Ltd
Thorpe Lea Manor
Thorpe Lea Road
Egham
Surrey
TW20 8HY

Wickes
Wickes Building Supplies
120 Station Road
Harrow
Middlesex
HA1 2QB

Yakult
Yakult UK Ltd
12-16 Telford Way
Westway Estate
Acton
London
W3 7XS

Yellow Pages
Yell
Queens Walk
Oxford Road
Reading
RG1 7PT

Young's
Young's Bluecrest Seafood Ltd
Ross House
Wickham Road
Grimsby
North East Lincolnshire
DN31 3SW